A NEW DICTIONARY OF SAINTS

A NEW DICTIONARY OF
SAINTS

Compiled by
DONALD ATTWATER

Edited and revised by
JOHN CUMMING

A Liturgical Press Book

THE LITURGICAL PRESS
Collegeville, Minnesota

A *New Dictionary of Saints*
first published in the United States of America 1994
by The Liturgical Press, St John's Abbey, Collegeville,
Minnesota 56321

and in Great Britain 1993
by Burns & Oates, Wellwood, North Farm Road,
Tunbridge Wells, Kent TN2 3DR

First published as A *Dictionary of Saints*, 1938
Second impression 1942
Third impression 1948
New edition, revised by Donald Attwater, 1958
Further revised by John Cumming, 1993

ISBN (U.S.) 0-8146-2324-7

Typeset by Search Press Ltd and Genesis Typesetting, Rochester
Printed in Finland by Werner Soderstrom Oy

PREFACE

This book is a catalogue with brief particulars of the principal saints, *beati* and *beatae* venerated through the ages in the Catholic Church and retained after, or not specifically suppressed by, the reforms of 1969.

Saints have this in common with hymns: that they are exceedingly numerous, but only a few are well known to everybody. Nobody knows, or can know, how many holy men and women have received a *cultus*, veneration, official or "popular", in the Church during the course of nineteen centuries. There is no single list or "canon" of them. Their names have to be sought in many martyrologies, synaxaries, menologies, calendars, service-books, relic-lists, and the like. The Roman Martyrology alone contains some 4,500 entries; of these, sixty-seven are of saints called Felix, to mention only one name. (Among the beatified martyrs of England and Wales, forty-seven are called John; there are seventy-two Colmans in the Martyrology of Gorman.) The world total then must be huge. And among all the known names, nothing more whatever is known of many; of many more, only the place of veneration and the saint's description (martyr, etc.) have survived, to which perhaps an approximate date can be added.

This book lists almost all those holy ones, over 2,500 in number, who figure in Alban Butler's *Lives of the Saints*, as revised by the late Father Herbert Thurston, S.J., and Donald Attwater, and published in a second edition, in four volumes, in 1956. With each entry herein, an index reference is given to the fuller treatment in "Butler". Saints and *beati* or *beatae* officially recognized after 1956 are not included in that edition of "Butler", which explains why some of the entries have no index reference (they will appear in a new edition now in preparation). Where there is question of large groups of martyrs, such as those of the Far East, most of them are dealt with under the names of certain representative individuals; but all the beatified English, Scottish and Welsh martyrs have separate references.

It will be noticed that many entries do not give the date of canonization or beatification or confirmation of *cultus* of the person concerned. It is perhaps well to remind the reader that the complex and thorough process of beatification and canonization as we now know it has been in force in the Church only since the pontificate of Pope Urban VIII (1623–44), the right of canonization having been gradually reserved to the Holy See during the previous five centuries. Before then, the public honouring of a holy man or woman was sanctioned, in various ways, by the local bishop or by a council or by the pope himself; or, in the case of the earliest saints, such as the Lord's apostles, by the universal agreement of the Church. It follows that many of the greatest saints have never been canonized at all, in the sense that the word is understood today. It also means that some few people are called Saint whose cause of canonization, were it to be introduced now, would probably not reach a successful conclusion. Saints removed from the reformed Calendar of 1969, usually because they did not exist, being pious or anti-Semitic fabrications, or were doubtful, are not included in this edition. Some other merely quaint or doubtful saints not in Butler, but included in the 1958 edition, have been removed to make space for the many *beati* and *beatae* created since then. Nevertheless, some very odd and probably fictitious characters await official condemnation. In some cases, names and cults not officially suppressed have been retained for the sake of local or national affiliations, or even to stand as warnings against anti-Semitic and other reprehensible interests. In all such cases the origin and quality of the cult are indicated as clearly as possible within the scope of an average entry.

The marking of a name with an asterisk (*) in the pages that follow indicates that the saint referred to figures in the Roman Martyrology. This martyrology is an official book of the Roman rite; in churches where the Divine Office was celebrated in choir, the pertinent passages from it were read daily after Prime. It was first issued in 1583–84, the work principally of Cardinal Baronius. It is universal in scope, but is not, of course, intended to be a complete, all-inclusive record of saints whose names are known; and, with a few exceptions, it does not include *beati*. The Roman Martyrology has not yet been subjected to thorough revision; with small modifications, and the additions made necessary by new canonizations, it is in substance still the work of the great and learned Baronius, as authorized by Pope Benedict XIV in 1749. From the point of view of historical scholarship, therefore, it labours under the disadvantage of being almost untouched by the research and learning of the past three and a half centuries.

It is perhaps not out of place here to refer to another relevant matter, of more general concern, and to do so in the terms in which it is written of in the fourth volume of Butler's *Lives*, under the feast of All Saints. It is sometimes objected against the ideal of holiness held up by the Church before all indiscriminately that it is incompatible with that secular life in which the overwhelming majority of men and women are, and are meant to be, engaged. And in support of this objection it is alleged that more clergy and members of religious orders of both sexes become saints than do lay people, more relatively and perhaps absolutely. This is not known to be so, and is impossible of proof. If, however, it be a question of *canonized* and *beatified* saints, then it is true that there are far more clergy and religious than lay people, and also far more bishops than priests and men than women. But canonization and beatification are exterior marks, "certificates", if the expression may be allowed, with which the Church honours certain individuals, a selection from among those many holy ones who contribute to its holiness. And in the making of that selection some purely natural factors necessarily come into play. A religious order has the means and the motive for forwarding the "cause" of an individual who in other circumstances would have never been heard of outside his or her own circle; the episcopal office brings its holder into greater prominence, lends of itself a weight to his name, and carries with it the means and influence to prosecute his cause; and men, as opposed to women, have by their very gender greater opportunities of notable achievement and of the fame of their virtues becoming widespread in the world.

But even so a modification is taking place. Among those saints or candidates for canonization in our own day whose cause was or is the interest of so many diverse people that it could almost be said to be proposed by the Church itself, and not by a particular country, order or diocese, a greater variety of "states of life" is exhibited: a pope, St Pius X, and a country parson, St John Vianney; St Teresa of Lisieux, a simple nun; Bd Contardo Ferrini, Ludovic Necchi, Matt Talbot, Frederick Ozanam, Camille Feron and Philibert Vrau, laymen; Bd Anne Mary Taigi was the wife of an obscure manservant. As Alban Butler reminds his readers so often, there is but one Gospel, one Sacrifice, one Redeemer, one Heaven, and one way to Heaven: it has been traced out by Jesus Christ, and the rule of salvation laid down by him is invariable and the same for all.

In this dictionary the heading of each entry consists of the name of the saint and description; date of commemoration (when ascertainable), and volume and page reference to Butler's *Lives* (four-volume edition) (if relevant) come in italics at the end.

Name. The names are indexed so far as possible in the form most usual in English; failing that, generally in the Latin form. The Latin form of a name is also often given in italics at the end of the notice, and has usually been taken from the Roman Martyrology. The original names of many more recent saints are to be found in the entries. A few groups of martyrs are indexed under the name of the place where they suffered, or otherwise; see the entry MARTYRS herein. When names are commonly coupled (*e.g.* Cosmas and Damian, Cyril and Methodius), the persons concerned are generally dealt with together.

Description. This is given as *apostle, pope, martyr, bishop, doctor, abbot, virgin,* usually according to the liturgical office of the saint or the Roman Martyrology. This description does not necessarily agree with historical fact or probability. When there is no description, the saint was either a *confessor* or *holy woman,* according to gender.

Date of commemoration. This is, according to circumstances, the date (or principal date) on which the saint's feast is or was observed, or the date given in the Roman Martyrology or other calendar, or the day of death. The dates of individual martyrs among collected groups are generally the day of death, and the dates of some Franciscans have been altered to bring them into line with the calendar of Friars Minor. Known changes in dates of commemoration have been included.

Order of names. When there are several saints of the same name the order is as follows: the name alone; the name alone with a partner; the name followed by surname, in alphabetical order of the surnames; the name followed by an epithet of place, and then the name followed by any other epithet, both in alphabetical order of epithets. For example:

John
John I
John and Paul
John Colombini

PREFACE

John Fisher
John of Beverley
John of Parma
John the Almsgiver
John the Baptist

When a name may also be found under another form, or referred to in connection with another saint, cross-references are given separately after the entry, or series of entries, of the name.

Abbreviations

    b. = born
    d. = died
    c. = *circa,* about
   cd = canonized
   bd = beatified
   c.c. = ancient *cultus* confirmed by the Holy See
 h.d.q. = hanged, drawn and quartered

The editor of the new revised edition is grateful to the Vice-Principal and Librarian of Gillis College, Edinburgh, to the staff of the National Catholic Library, and to the Librarian of Heythrop College, London, without whose help the work could not have been completed. He would be pleased to receive diocesan and national reports on the inclusion of individual names in, or their removal from, local calendars. These and any other pertinent corrections will be incorporated in future editions of this Dictionary.

D.A., London, 1958; J.C., Edinburgh, 1993

A

The last line of each entry gives the date of commemoration or death, and the volume and page reference for a fuller account in Alban Butler's Lives of the Saints, *four-volume edition of 1956, edited by Father Herbert Thurston, S.J., and Donald Attwater. The abbreviations and order are explained in the preface.*

AARON, ST

A sixth-century hermit venerated in Brittany. He is said to have lived on the island where Saint-Malo now stands, which was called after Aaron until the twelfth century. *July 3. See also under* Julius.

ABACHUM. *See under* Marius.

ABBO, ST, ABBOT

Before becoming abbot of Fleury Abbo was for two years director of the monastery school at Ramsey in Huntingdonshire. He was among the most conspicuous monks of his time, and he wrote a Life of St Edmund, king and martyr. While trying to restore discipline in a Gascon monastery he was killed in a brawl between two parties whom he sought to reconcile, in 1004. *November 13, iv, 333.*

ABBO. *See also* Goericus.

*ABDON AND SENNEN, SS, MARTYRS

They were Persians who were martyred at Rome, probably in the persecution of Diocletian. Their feast was already known in 354. *July 30, iii, 213.*

*ABERCIUS, ST, BISHOP

He was bishop of Hieropolis during the second half of the second century and knowledge of his existence and of his visit to Rome at the age of seventy-two is due to the epitaph written by himself; the authenticity of this epitaph was confirmed archaeologically by Sir W. M. Ramsay in 1882. *October 22, iv, 174.*

ABIBUS. *See under* Gurias.

*ABIBUS, ST, MARTYR

He was a deacon at Edessa, martyred by burning, and buried with his friends, SS Gurias and Samonas. Fourth century. *November 15, iv, 348.*

*ABRAHAM KIDUNAIA, ST

A hermit in the desert near Edessa, who had fled from his wealthy home and the marriage arranged for him. He was much sought after for spiritual guidance. Eventually he was ordained priest and converted the heathen town of Beth-Kiduna after he had received much ill-treatment at the hands of its inhabitants. The story of his niece Mary, which is associated with the life of St Abraham, is probably spurious. Sixth century. *March 16, i, 605.*

ABRAHAM OF CARRHAE, ST, BISHOP

A hermit in Syria who forwarded the conversion of a village in the Lebanon by borrowing money to pay its taxes. He was made bishop of Carrhae in Mesopotamia. d. *c.* 422. *February 14, i, 334.*

ABRAHAM OF KRATIA, ST, BISHOP

He was b. at Emesa in Syria in 474, and while very young became abbot of a monastery at Kratia in Bithynia; later he was made bishop in the same place. Twice he ran away from his offices in search of quiet; the second time he found a refuge in a Palestinian monastery, where he d. *c.* 558. *December 6, iv, 507.*

ABRAHAM OF ROSTOV, ST, ABBOT

A rather uncertain figure in Russian church history. He seems to have been a missionary monk during the twelfth century, who founded the monastery of the Epiphany at Rostov. *October 29, iv, 218.*

ABRAHAM OF SMOLENSK, ST, ABBOT

An outstanding figure among the holy men of pre-Mongol Russia. He was an ikon-painter, preacher and biblical exegete, and his scriptural interpretations gave his enemies occasion to stir up trouble for him. Abraham was a man of stern and uncompromising character, but under his guidance "many passed from sin to repentance". He became abbot of the monastery of the Mother of God at Smolensk and d. there in 1221. *August 21, iii, 377.*

*ABUNDIUS, ST, BISHOP

A Greek priest who became bishop of Como; he was an able theologian and preacher, and was Pope St Leo's legate to the Council of Constantinople in 450. d. *c.* 468. *April 2.*

*ABUNDIUS AND ABUNDANTIUS, SS, MARTYRS

Their legendary *acta* state that Abundius was a Roman priest, Abundantius a deacon, and Marcian a senator whose son, John, was raised from the dead by Abundius. They were all martyred *c.* 303. *September 16, iii, 568.*

ACACIUS, ST, MARTYR

Or *Agathus.* He was a Cappadocian centurion, stationed in Thrace, who was beheaded for the faith of Christ at Byzantium in 303 or 305. *May 8, ii, 250.*

ACCA, ST, BISHOP

Acca was a disciple of St Wilfrid and suc-
ceeded him in the see of Hexham, where his activity was very varied. St Bede refers to him as being "great in the sight of God and man". d. 740. *October 20, iv, 156.*

ACHARD. *See* Aichardus.

ACHATIUS, ST, BISHOP

Or *Acacius.* A bishop in hither Asia who is said so to have impressed the emperor Decius by his defence of Christianity that he was suffered to profess his religion in peace. d. *c.* 251. *March 31, i, 708.*

ACHILLEUS. *See under* Felix *and* Nereus.

*ACISCLUS AND VICTORIA, SS, MARTYRS

These martyrs were put to death, probably at Cordova, in the imperial persecutions, but even the approximate year is not known. *November 17, iv, 367.*

ADALBALD OF OSTREVANT, ST, MARTYR

A grandson of St Gertrude of Hamage, and attached to the court of Dagobert I. He married a Gascon girl called Rictrudis, with whom he lived in great holiness and happiness. But some of her relatives did not approve of the match, and as long as sixteen years after, in 652, ambushed Adalbald and killed him. Rictrudis is also venerated as a saint (May 12). *Adelbaldus.* *February 2, i, 36.*

*ADALBERT OF EGMOND, ST

He was a Northumbrian who was a monk in Ireland and then one of the deacons of St Willibrord in Friesland. His gentleness, patience, and humility made a deep impression around Egmond, where he laboured and died. Eighth century. *Adelbertus, June 25, ii, 641.*

ADALBERT OF MAGDENBURG, ST, BISHOP

Adalbert was sent from Trier as a missionary to Russia in 961, but all his companions were slain, and he returned to become abbot of Weissenberg, where he did much to encourage learning. In 962 he was nominated first archbishop of Magdeburg; in this office he laboured unceasingly for the conversion of the Wends. d. 981. *June 20, ii, 590.*

*ADALBERT OF PRAGUE, ST,
BISHOP AND MARTYR

Born in Bohemia in 956 and educated by St Adalbert of Magdeburg. He was elected bishop of Prague in 983, but his holiness seemed to make no impression on his flock and he retired for five years to Rome, where he became a Benedictine. Twice he attempted to return to his diocese, but each time was unable to do anything with the turbulent people there. He went to preach the gospel with more success among the heathen of Prussia; but he met with opposition there as well, and was martyred in 997. *April 23, ii, 152.*

ADAM OF LOCCUM, BD

This Cistercian monk of Loccum in Saxony lived early in the thirteenth century: nothing is known of him except that he said he had been twice miraculously cured of sickness. *December 22, iv, 598.*

ADAMNAN, ST, ABBOT

Adamnan (Eunan, "Adam"), fifth abbot of Iona, is best remembered for his Life of St Columba, one of the most important ancient hagiographical documents in existence. He spent a good many years propagating the celebration of Easter on its right date in Ireland and other Celtic centres, but he was not successful in imposing it in his own monastery. d. 704. The feast of St Adamnan is observed in the diocese of Argyll and the Isles, and a commemoration is made of him throughout Ireland (he was b. at Drumhome in county Donegal), but the Eunan of Rephoe was probably a different person. *Adamnanus. September 23, iii, 625.*

ADAMNAN OF COLDINGHAM, ST

He was an Irish monk at Coldingham, near Berwick, who lived a life of great austerity. He foretold the destruction of his monastery because of its irregularities. d. c. 680. *January 31, i, 214.*

ADAUCTUS. *See under* Felix.

*ADAUCUS, ST, MARTYR

Adaucus was a distinguished Roman, a magistrate and imperial finance minister, who was put to death for the faith in 303 while still holding the latter office. With him are connected a number of Phrygian Christians whose town was burnt over their heads and them with it. *February 7, i, 268.*

ADDAI AND MARI, SS, BISHOPS

They are venerated as the evangelizers of East Syria and Persia, where they are known as the Holy Apostles. St Addai (Thaddeus) was probably a missionary in Edessa, before the end of the second century; of St Mari nothing certain is known. *August 5, iii, 265.*

ADELA, ST

She was the sister of St Irmina. When she became a widow she established and ruled a convent at Pfalzel, near Trier. She is probably the Adula who was St Gregory of Utrecht's grandmother. d. c. 734. *December 24, iv, 605.*

ADELAIDE OF BELLICH, ST, VIRGIN

Abbess of Bellich, near Bonn, and then of a convent at Cologne. d. 1015. *Adelheidis. February 5, i, 258.*

ADELAIDE OF BURGUNDY, ST

On the death of her husband, Lothair of Italy, she was treated with great brutality by Berengarius of Ivrea, but was rescued by the emperor Otto the Great, who married her. After his death in 973 she was badly treated by her son Otto II, and later by her daughter-in-law, who was regent for Otto III. Adelaide herself succeeded to this position, but she was then too old to cope with it. She was peace-loving and generous, and took as her counsellors St Adalbert of Magdeburg and SS Majolus and Odilo of Cluny. d. 999. *December 16, iv, 572.*

ADELARD, ST, ABBOT

Otherwise *Adalhard*, b. 753. Grandson of Charles Martel. Became a monk and abbot of Corbie. Forced by Charlemagne to take part in public life, and persecuted for political reasons. Founded the abbey of New Corbie. d. 827. *Adelardus. January 30, i, 205.*

ADELELMUS, ST, ABBOT

In French, *Aleaume*. Benedictine abbot of

Chaise-Dieu and then of Burgos. d. *c.* 1100. *January 30, i, 205.*

ADEODATUS. See Deusdedit.

*ABO, BD, BISHOP

He became archbishop of Vienne in 859 and was an altogether admirable prelate, but he is best remembered as the compiler of a martyrology which bears his name; this and other writings of his were responsible for the perpetuation of a number of baseless and misleading statements. d. 875. *December 16, iv, 571.*

ADOLF, ST, BISHOP

Little is known of him except that he was bishop of Osnabrück and d. June 30, 1224. *Adolphus. February 14, i, 338.*

ADOLF KOLPING, BD

Adolf Kolping was born on November 8, 1813. He was known as the "German Don Bosco". He was a priest and an eminent organizer of social work and social schemes, especially of widespread clerical–lay enterprises. The present-day "Kolping movement" extends to forty countries and some 4,000 local bodies and 420,000 members. The Kolping house or centre is a welcome and familiar sight in many towns and cities. Bd Adolf awakened Catholics to their socio-political responsibilities. John Paul II called him the "precursor of the great social encyclicals". d. 1865. bd October 27, 1991. *December 4.*

ADRIAN, ST, MARTYR

During one of their numerous descents upon the coast of Scotland, the Danes murdered St Adrian and his fellow missionary monks on the isle of May in the Firth of Forth, *c.* 875. His identity and earlier history are uncertain. *Hadrianus. March 4, i, 480.*

*ADRIAN III, ST, POPE

He became pope in 884 but there is nothing in the little that is known of his brief pontificate (he d. 885) to account for his ancient *cultus* in the diocese of Modena, which was confirmed in 1892. *July 8, iii, 41.*

*ADRIAN AND **EUBULUS, SS,**
MARTYRS

Martyred at Caesarea in Palestine when they came to visit the Christians in prison there in 309. *March 5, i, 484.*

*ADRIAN AND **NATALIA, SS,**
MARTYRS

Adrian is said to have been a pagan officer at the imperial court at Nicomedia. He was imprisoned for identifying himself with the persecuted Christians, and his wife Natalia tended him and his fellow prisoners. After the execution of Adrian in *c.* 304 Natalia gathered up his relics and fled to Argyropolis, where she died in peace but is reckoned amongst the martyrs. There was formerly a very considerable *cultus* of this St Adrian, who was reckoned a patron of soldiers and butchers. *September 8, iii, 507.*

ADRIAN FORTESCUE, BD, MARTYR

Sir Adrian Fortescue, knight of the Bath and of St John, tertiary of the Order of Preachers, was b. in 1476. He married (1) Anne Stonor of Stonor, (2) Anne Rede of Boarstall, and had five children. He led the life of a gentleman of his time. In 1539 he was attainted by Parliament, with Cardinal Pole and others, for "treasons and sedition" against King Henry VIII, and was beheaded on Tower Hill. His feast is kept by the knights of the order of Malta and in the archdiocese of Birmingham. bd 1895. *July 11, iii, 72.*

ADRIAN OF CANTERBURY, ST,
ABBOT

An African, abbot of Nerida near Naples. Sent by Pope St Vitalian to England with St Theodore of Tarsus. Became abbot of SS Peter and Paul's at Canterbury where he d. 710. *January 9, i, 58.*

ADULF, ST, BISHOP

The brother of St Botulf. He is said to have become a missionary bishop in what is now The Netherlands. Seventh century. *Adulphus. June 17, ii, 567.*

AEDESIUS OF TYRE, ST

The companion of St Frumentius at the beginning of the evangelization of Ethiopia. Aedesius afterwards returned to his home in

Tyre, and supplied the information about their adventures given by Rufinus in his *Ecclesiastical History*. d. c. 375.
October 27, iv, 208.

AEDH MAC BRICC, ST, BISHOP
He was a disciple of St Illathan at Rathlihen in Offaly, and is said to have founded churches at Cill-air and other places in his native Meath. Many miracles are recorded of St Aedh. Sixth century. *Aidus.*
November 10, iv, 308.

AEGIDIUS. *See* Giles.

AELRED, ST, ABBOT
or *Ailred*. Born in north of England in 1110. Master of the household of King St David of Scotland. Became a Cistercian monk at Rievaulx in 1133; abbot of Revesby in Lincolnshire, then of Rievaulx. Author of several treatises, *e.g.* "On Spiritual Friendship", "The Mirror of Charity", and biographies of saints. Sternly austere, yet notably gentle with his monks, of whom he dismissed not one in seventeen years. In spite of ill health made several long journeys, including one to Cîteaux. d. January 12, 1167. cd 1191. His feast is kept on March 3 in the dioceses of Hexham, Liverpool, and Middlesbrough, and by the Cistercians. *Aelredus. March 3, i, 473.*

AEMILIANA. *See under* Tharsilla.

AEMILIUS. *See under* Castus.

AENGUS, ST, BISHOP
Aengus or Oengus is generally distinguished as "the Culdee"; he was a very famous holy man but no early account of him is extant and he is not commemorated liturgically in any Irish diocese. He is said to have been first a monk at Clonenagh and then at Tallaght, where he composed the famous metrical hymn to the saints called the *Félire* or *Festilogium*. He returned to Clonenagh, where he was made abbot and bishop, and d. c. 824. *March 11, i, 559.*

AENGUS. *See also* Macanisius.

AFAN, ST, BISHOP
A bishop, perhaps in the sixth century, whose tombstone is preserved at Llanafan Fawr in

Breconshire. Nothing is known of his life. *Avanus. November 16, iv, 354.*

*AFRA, ST, MARTYR
Afra was a martyr who suffered at Augsburg and was venerated there from early times. She was probably a victim of the persecution of Diocletian, c. 304, but the story of her being a converted harlot from Cyprus is worthless. *August 5, iii, 267.*

*AGAPE, ST, VIRGIN AND MARTYR
She is specifically honoured at Terni in Umbria as a martyr and contemporary of the bishop St Valentine. Nothing certain is known about her and she has probably been confused with other martyrs of the same name. *February 15, i, 341.*

*AGAPE, CHIONIA AND **IRENE, SS,** VIRGINS AND MARTYRS.
Agape, Chionia, and Irene were three sisters at Salonika during the persecution of Diocletian. With three other women and a man they were charged with refusing to eat meat sacrificed to false gods; Agape and Chionia were sentenced to be burnt alive; Irene, who had been detected also in concealing Christian sacred books, was exposed in a brothel and put to death later; 304. *April 3, ii, 19.*

*AGAPITUS, ST, MARTYR
A martyr of unknown date, buried at Palestrina. His *acta* are spurious. *August 18, iii, 345.*

*AGAPITUS I, ST, POPE
Agapitus was pope for only eleven months, dying in 536. This short time was spent in contending with various heresies. His memory was honoured by St Gregory the Great. *April 22, ii, 145.*

AGAPITUS. *See also under* Felicissimus.

AGAPIUS. *See under* Timothy.

*AGATHA, ST, VIRGIN AND MARTYR
There is good evidence for the early veneration of St Agatha, but nothing can be confidently affirmed about her history except that

she was martyred in Sicily. She is named in the canon of the Roman Mass.
February 5, i, 255.

AGATHA KIM, BD, MARTYR
One of the numerous Koreans killed for the faith between 1839 and 1846. Before being beheaded, she was suspended by her hair and wrists from a pole, which was fixed to a cart and the cart driven about over rough ground. bd 1925. *September 21, iii, 612.*

AGATHA LIN, BD,
VIRGIN AND MARTYR
A Chinese schoolteacher put to death for the faith at Maoken in 1858. bd 1909.
January 28, i, 365.

AGATHANGELO AND **CASSIAN, BB,**
MARTYRS
Agathangelo (Noury) of Vendôme and Cassian (Vaz López-Neto) of Nantes were Capuchin friars who were sent to Egypt in 1633 to work for the reconciliation of the dissident Coptic Christians. Their mission was so handicapped by the ill-behaviour of the European Catholics there that they went on into Ethiopia, where there were many more Christians outside Catholic unity. Here King Fasilidas had them arrested and hanged by the cords of their Franciscan habits, in 1638. bd. 1905. *August 7, iii, 277.*

*AGATHANGELUS, ST, MARTYR
St Agathangelus is honoured together with St Clement of Ancyra in some oriental churches and appears in the Roman Martyrology, but the accounts are unreliable. He was converted and made deacon by St Clement. It is said that he was arrested with his master, shared his sufferings for many years, and was put to the sword with him *c.* 308.
January 23, i, 153.

AGATHO, ST, POPE
A Sicilian Greek who became pope in 678. Sent legates to the sixth ecumenical council (Constantinople III), with a letter condemning the monothelite heresy. He restored St Wilfrid to the see of York. d. 681.
January 10, i, 64.

*AGATHONICE, ST, MARTYR
A matron who is commemorated with SS

Carpus and Papylas. When she came up for execution, the crowd admired her beauty and besought her to have pity on her children: but she replied that God would care for them, and she was burned alive. *c.* 170 or 250. *April 13, ii, 84.*

*AGATHOPUS AND **THEODULUS, SS,**
MARTYRS
Martyred by drowning at Salonika for refusing to give up the sacred books, in 303.
April 4, ii, 27.

AGAUNUM, THE MARTYRS OF. *See* Theban Legion.

*AGERICUS, ST, BISHOP
In French, *Airy.* He was bishop of Verdun and enjoyed the friendship of St Gregory of Tours and St Venantius Fortunatus. d. 588.
December 1, iv, 454.

AGILBERT, ST, BISHOP
He was a Frank who studied in Ireland and came as a missionary to England, where he was made bishop of the West Saxons and was a leader of the "Roman party" at the Synod of Whitby. When King Coenwalh got tired of having a French bishop, and divided the Wessex diocese, St Agilbert resigned and went home, where he became bishop of Paris in 668. d. *c.* 685. *Agilbertus.*
October 11, iv, 87.

AGNELLO OF PISA, BD
He was appointed by Francis himself to establish the Friars Minor in England and landed at Dover in 1224 with companions, three of whom were English. Agnello himself founded the Canterbury friary and then went to London to take charge of the house founded on Cornhill by Friar Richard of Ingworth. He then established the friary at Oxford, with a school which became very famous. Agnello gained the friendship of King Henry III and in 1233 negotiated with the insurgent Earl Marshall. d. at Oxford 1236, c.c. 1892. Bd Agnello's feast is kept in the archdiocese of Birmingham, as well as by the Friars Minor. *March 13, i, 589.*

*AGNES, ST, VIRGIN AND MARTYR
A Roman maiden who was martyred and

buried beside the Via Nomentana, where a basilica was built in her honour before 354; Pope St Damasus wrote an epitaph for her. Her name occurs in the canon of the Mass and as a special patroness of chastity she is one of the most popular of saints. But little reliance can be placed on the details of the story of her martyrdom as it has come down to us: it alleges that she was unharmed in a brothel whither she was sent to break down her constancy to Christ, and put to death (by stabbing?) at a tender age. *January 21, i, 133.*

AGNES SAO KUY, BD, MARTYR

A young Chinese widow, tortured to death for her religion at Kwangsi in 1856. bd 1900. *February 25, i, 365.*

AGNES OF ASSISI, ST, VIRGIN

She was the sister of St Clare and was first abbess of the Poor Clare convent of Monticelli at Florence, which became only less famous than San Damiano itself. d. 1253. *November 16, iv, 358.*

AGNES OF BENIGAMIN, BD, VIRGIN

A nun of the barefooted Augustinians at Benigamin in Spain. d. 1696. bd 1888. *January 22.*

AGNES OF BOHEMIA, ST, VIRGIN

Also known as Agnes of Prague, she was the daughter of King Ottokar I of Bohemia and niece of Andreas II of Hungary, and until she was twenty-eight or so her life was a series of sojourns in convents and betrothals to various royal suitors. She accepted none of them, but with the help of Pope Gregory IX became a Poor Clare, founding a convent at Prague to which St Clare sent five of her nuns. Agnes was a religious here for forty-six years, and there are extant four affectionate letters written to her from Assisi by St Clare. d. 1282, c.c. by Pope Pius IX; cd by John Paul II, 1989. *June 8, i, 462.*

*AGNES OF MONTEPULCIANO, ST, VIRGIN

Born 1268. At a very youthful age she was abbess of a convent at Procena and afterwards returned to Montepulciano to take charge of a new house of Preacheresses. A number of very remarkable visions and other supernatural manifestations are narrated of St Agnes, who also had gifts of healing and prophecy. d. 1317, cd 1726. *April 20, ii, 135.*

*AGRECIUS, ST, BISHOP

A bishop of Trier, who was at the Council of Arles in 314 and died *c.* 330. According to a quite unreliable document he had been patriarch of Antioch and brought our Lord's seamless robe ("the Holy Coat") to Trier, together with other unlikely relics. *January 13, i, 74.*

*AGRICOLA, ST, BISHOP

In French, *Arègle.* Bishop of Chalon-sur-Saône and a contemporary of St Gregory of Tours, who knew him well. d. 580. *March 17, i, 619.*

AGRICOLA. *See also under* Vitalis.

AGRICOLUS, ST, BISHOP.

He is said to have succeeded his father as bishop of Avignon and to have d. in 700. He has been venerated as patron saint of that city since 1647 only and information about him is very unreliable. *September 2, iii, 469.*

*AGRIPPINA, ST, VIRGIN AND MARTYR

She is said to have been a girl of good position who was executed for her faith in Rome in 262 (?). She is specially revered in Sicily, whither her relics are supposed to have been translated (the Greeks say they were later taken to Constantinople). *June 23, ii, 620.*

*AICHARDUS, ST, ABBOT

Or *Achard.* He was for many years a monk at Ansion in Poitou and eventually became abbot of Jumièges. St Aichardus was specially scrupulous in his observance of the Lord's Day. d. *c.* 687. *September 15, iii, 556.*

*AIDAN, ST, BISHOP

St Aidan was sent from Iona to help the king St Oswald to spread the faith among the people of Northumbria. He established his see at Lindisfarne (Holy Island), where he founded a monastery under the Celtic rule observed at Iona, and St Bede writes of the fruitfulness of his character and apostleship.

St Aidan d. at Bamburgh in 651, surviving St Oswald by only eleven days. He was an important figure in the conversion of the northern English, and his feast is kept in several English dioceses and in Argyll and the Isles. *Edanus. August 31, iii, 451.*

AIDAN OF FERNS, ST, BISHOP

Aidan (*Maedoc*) is venerated in Ireland as the first bishop at Ferns in county Wexford, where he founded a monastery. When young, we are told, he visited St David in Wales, and is alleged to have worked many strange miracles. d. 626. *January 31, i, 214.*

AIGNAN. *See* Anianus.

AIGULF OF BOURGES, ST, BISHOP

In French, *Ayoul.* He was bishop of Bourges and d. in 836; a church was built over his tomb, so much was he honoured. *May 22, ii, 367.*

*AIGULF OF LÉRINS, ST, ABBOT AND MARTYR

Aigulf was elected abbot of Lérins *c.* 670. There is considerable uncertainty about the circumstances of his death. With four monks he is said to have been forcibly removed to an island near Corsica, where they were killed, perhaps by Moorish pirates, *c.* 676. *September, 3, iii, 480.*

AILBHE, ST, BISHOP

A commemoration of the feast of St Ailbhe (*Albeus*) is made throughout Ireland but his recorded life is a confusion of legends and contradictory traditions. He is venerated as the first bishop at Emly, in the early sixth century, and is the reputed author of a monastic rule. *September 12, iii, 544.*

AILRED. *See* Aelred.

AIRY. *See* Agericus.

ALAN DE SOLMINIHAC, BD

He was b. 1593 and entered the abbey of Chancelade in 1613 when aged 20. He was bishop of Cahors, France, from 1636 until his death in 1659. He was committed to the spirit of Trent. bd October 4, 1981. *January 3.*

*ALBAN, ST, MARTYR

St Alban is venerated as the protomartyr of Britain and his feast is observed throughout England and Wales. He is said to have been a citizen of Verulamium (now Saint Albans) who was executed on Holmhurst Hill at that place for having sheltered a persecuted priest and declared his own Christianity. The date is uncertain, and the details of the story are much discussed. *Albanus. June 21, ii ,612.*

ALBAN ROE, BD, MARTYR

A monk of St Benedict, called Bartholomew in baptism, who underwent long imprisonment for his priesthood under King Charles I. He was a man of very lively disposition, and laughed and joked on the scaffold at Tyburn. h.d.q. 1642. bd 1929. *January 21, i, 140.*

ALBERIC, ST, ABBOT

One of the three founders of the Cistercians. Alberic was prior at Molesmes when St Robert was abbot and St Stephen Harding a monk there. They found it impossible to restore discipline in this monastery, so in 1098 they took up their abode at Cîteaux, where Alberic soon became abbot, and no doubt had considerable influence on the development of Cistercian life, though he lived but a short time. The black and white Cistercian habit is said to have been revealed to Alberic in a vision by our Lady. d. 1109. *Albericus. January 26, i, 173.*

ALBERIC CRESCITELLI, BD, MARTYR

A Neapolitan missionary who went to China in 1888 and was tortured and killed by the Boxers in 1900. bd 1951. *July 22, iii, 62.*

ALBERT OF BERGAMO, BD

Albert was a peasant farmer who suffered much from a shrewish wife and jealous relatives. Late in life he lived at Cremona where he was credited with miracles. d. 1279. Bd Albert is venerated by the Dominicans as a tertiary of their order. c.c. 1748. *Albertus. May 11, ii, 274.*

ALBERT OF CASHEL, ST, BISHOP

Patron saint of the archdiocese of Cashel, where he is said to have laboured when he came from England. Afterwards, it is related that he went with St Erhard to lead a wandering life on the continent and that Albert died at Ratisbon upon returning from Jerusalem. He probably lived and died in the seventh century but his true history is extremely obscure. *January 19, i, 119.*

ALBERT CHMIELKOWSKI, ST

Albert (Adam) Chmielkowski, b. 1845 near Cracow, Poland, took part and lost a leg in the Polish uprising against Russian oppression in 1863. He escaped from prison and was sent to France by his parents. He studied art and engineering and returned to Poland as a painter after the 1874 amnesty. He became a Franciscan tertiary in 1888 and made his studio a refuge for tramps and poor people. He founded two congregations of Franciscan tertiaries for the service of the poor and outcasts, living as a tramp and dying in the Cracow hospice for the poor on Christmas Day 1916, after establishing 21 refuges. His life was a combination of Polish patriotism and loving self-sacrifice for the marginalized of his time. d. 1916. He was beatified by John Paul II during a visit to Cracow on June 22, 1983. cd 1989. *December 25.*

ALBERT OF JERUSALEM, ST, BISHOP

Albert was an Italian canon regular who was called from the see of Vercelli to be Latin patriarch of Jerusalem in 1204. He was also papal legate and for nine years had to deal with a variety of matters that exercised his prudence and patience to the utmost, for the Latin kingdom in Palestine was already in dissolution. It was St Albert who gave their first written rule to the Frankish hermits on Mount Carmel, at the request of St Brocard. He was murdered at Acre in 1214 by a Hospitaller whom he had deposed from office. *September 25, iii, 638.*

*ALBERT OF LOUVAIN, ST,
BISHOP AND MARTYR

He was born *c.* 1166 at Mont César, Louvain, and in 1191 was elected bishop of Liège. The appointment was challenged on behalf of another Albert, and in the politico-ecclesiastical dispute that followed (Pope *versus* Emperor) St Albert was murdered at Rheims

by German knights, in 1192. *November 21, iv, 400.*

ALBERT OF MONTECORVINO, ST,
BISHOP

He was bishop of Montecorvino. In old age, when he was blind, he was treated with the most amazing indignity and cruelty by his vicar and the man's friends. d. 1127. *April 5, ii, 36.*

*ALBERT OF TRAPANI, ST

This Albert was b. at Trapani in Sicily *c.* 1240. He became a Carmelite friar and was famous for successful preaching, for his missionary journeys, and for his miracles. d. 1306. c.c. 1476. *August 7, iii, 276.*

*ALBERT THE GREAT, ST,
BISHOP AND DOCTOR

Albert was a Swabian by descent, joined the Dominicans, was a master of St Thomas Aquinas, and in 1248 was appointed regent of the house of studies in Cologne. He became provincial of his order in Germany, went to Rome to defend the mendicant friars against the attacks of the secular clergy, and in 1260 was made bishop of Regensburg. He resigned two years later, and spent most of the rest of his life at the Cologne *studium*, though he played an active part in the Council of Lyons and went to Paris to defend some of the writings of St Thomas when they were attacked. Albert was called "the Great" and "the Universal Doctor" in his lifetime and his printed works fill thirty-eight quarto volumes, including treatises on logic, metaphysics, mathematics, ethics, and physical science, as well as biblical and theological works and sermons. But his principal fame is due to his application of Aristotelian methods and principles to the study of theology; he was the chief pioneer and forerunner of the scholastic system that was brought to perfection by his pupil St Thomas. Albert d. at Cologne in 1280 and was bd in 1622. He was equivalently canonized by being declared a doctor of the Church in 1931. *November 15, iv, 345.*

*ALBINUS OF ANGERS, ST, BISHOP

In French *Aubin*. He was bishop of Angers in the first half of the sixth century and his widespread *cultus* appears to be due to the large number of miracles attributed to his intercession. d. *c*. 550. *March 1, i, 452.*

ALBINUS OF MAINZ, ST, MARTYR

According to tradition Albinus (or Albanus) was a Greek priest from Naxos who travelled across Europe and became a missionary among the Arian heretics around Mainz: here he was killed, either by heretics or barbarians, before 451. There is doubt if there be any historical foundation for this story. *June 21, ii, 608.*

ALCMUND, ST, MARTYR

He was son or nephew of King Alfred of Northumbria, but it is not certain in what circumstances he was slain or why he was venerated as a martyr, first at Lilleshall and then at Derby. d. *c*. 800. *Alcumundus. March 19, i, 635.*

ALCMUND OF HEXHAM, ST, BISHOP

He was the seventh bishop of Hexham and d. in 781. No details are known of his life. *September 7, iii, 504.*

ALCUIN, BD, ABBOT

Alcuin was b. in England, probably at York, *c*. 735. He was head of the cathedral school at York, visited Rome thrice, and in 781 became ecclesiastical adviser at the court of Charlemagne and head of the palace school at Aachen and elsewhere. Alcuin was a theologian and an exegete, and he left his mark on the liturgy of worship in the West. But his greatest fame is as an educator; he was "the schoolmaster of his age", and his contemporaries (with little critical acumen) looked on him as a second Horace. His best-known surviving works are his letters. d. at Tours, 804. *Albinus. May 19, ii, 348.*

ALDA, BD

Or *Aldobrandesca*. Upon the death of her husband leaving her childless Bd Alda undertook a life of almsdeeds and mortification at Siena. d. 1309. *April 26, ii, 166.*

*ALDEGUND, ST, VIRGIN

An abbess of Maubeuge; d. 684 from cancer of the breast. *Aldegundis. January 30, i, 205.*

ALDEMAR, ST, ABBOT

A monk of Monte Cassino who after a rather disturbed career founded a monastery at Bocchignano and other religious houses in the Abruzzi; these he ruled with much success. d. *c*. 1080. *Aldemarus. March 24, i, 669.*

*ALDHELM, ST, BISHOP

Born in Wessex in 639 and educated at the monastery of Malmesbury and under St Adrian at Canterbury. He was given charge of the school and abbey at Malmesbury in middle life and was counsellor to King Ine. Aldhelm was the first English scholar of distinction, his vernacular hymns were treasured by King Alfred, and he did much for religion and education in Wessex, where he founded monasteries at Frome and Bradford-on-Avon. In 705 he became the first bishop of Sherborne. d. 709. A treatise on virginity and other works of St Aldhelm have come down to us. His feast is observed in the dioceses of Clifton and Plymouth, and in Southwark on May 28. *Aldelmus. May 23, ii, 391.*

ALDRIC, ST, BISHOP

Chaplain to the Emperor Louis the Pious, and bishop of Le Mans in 832. He was noted alike for his public activities and private virtues. Some of his regulations for his cathedral and his three testaments are still extant. d. 856. *Aldericus. January 7, i, 48.*

ALEAUME. *See* Adelelmus.

ALED, ST, VIRGIN AND MARTYR

A hermitess at Brecon in Wales, perhaps during the sixth century, whose legendary story bears a suspicious likeness to that of St Winifred. According to Giraldus Cambrensis, her shrine was the scene of remarkable occurrences in his time (twelfth century). The name takes various forms: Eiluned, Almedha, Elevetha. *August 1, iii, 239.*

*ALEXANDER, EVENTIUS AND THEODULUS, SS, MARTYRS

These were three Roman martyrs, buried on the Via Nomentana, but nothing else is known of them. This Alexander has been erroneously identified with Pope Alexander I (early second century), of whose life also nothing certain is known. *May 3, ii, 223.*

ALEXANDER AKIMETES, ST

A somewhat turbulent archimandrite, best known for his institution of the "sleepless" monks (*akoimetoi*) who sang the Divine Office in relays without intermission day and night. d. c. 430. *February 23, i, 402.*

ALEXANDER BLAKE, BD, MARTYR

An ostler who was hanged in Gray's Inn Lane, London 1590, for assisting a priest (Fr Christopher Bales). bd November 22, 1987. *March 4.*

ALEXANDER BRIANT, BD, MARTYR

He was a secular priest, arrested on the English mission and cruelly tortured to make him disclose the whereabouts of Father Persons, S.J. He was h.d.q. with Bd Ralph Sherwin and Bd Edmund Campion at Tyburn in 1581 and on the same charge. bd 1886. *December 1, iv, 469.*

ALEXANDER CROW, BD, MARTYR

A secular priest b. at Howden, Yorkshire. He followed a trade for some years, then studied and was ordained priest at Rheims. He went on the English mission in 1584, was arrested on his way to a christening, and h.d.q. at York in 1586 when thirty-six years of age. bd November 22, 1987. *November 30.*

ALEXANDER RAWLINS, BD, MARTYR

A secular priest, h.d.q. for his priesthood at York, 1595. bd. 1929. *April 7, ii, 50.*

*ALEXANDER SAULI, ST, BISHOP

Born at Milan in 1534. He joined the Barnabite clerks regular, was for many years the director of St Charles Borromeo, and was appointed bishop to reform the Corsican diocese of Aleria in 1570. He carried on this very difficult task for twenty years, and with such success that he was translated to Pavia, where he d. in the following year, 1592. cd 1904. *October 11, iv, 90.*

*ALEXANDER OF ALEXANDRIA, ST, BISHOP

As archbishop of Alexandria he was a deter-mined opponent of the heresy of Arius, against whom he wrote two encyclical letters. With his deacon St Athanasius he was the principal champion of orthodoxy at the first ecumenical council at Nicaea. d. 328. *February 26, i, 423.*

*ALEXANDER OF COMANA, ST, BISHOP AND MARTYR

Alexander, a charcoal-burner, was promoted from that trade to be bishop of Comana in Pontus; he gave his life for Christ in 275 (?). *August 11, iii, 303.*

*ALEXANDER OF CONSTANTINO-PLE, ST, BISHOP

Alexander of Byzantium became archbishop of Constantinople in his seventy-fourth year, filled the office for twenty-three years, and d. in 340. He was a strong opponent of Arianism. In a common feast with him the Catholic Byzantines join two other patriarchs of Constantinople, John III (d. 577) and Paul IV (d. 784). *August 28, iii, 434.*

*ALEXANDER OF JERUSALEM, ST, BISHOP AND MARTYR

He was bishop of his native city in Cappadocia and suffered imprisonment during the persecution of Severus. Some time after his release he was made coadjutor to the bishop of Jerusalem — the first recorded example of an episcopal translation and coadjutorship. In the persecution under Decius he was again imprisoned and died in chains at Caesarea in 251. *March 18, i, 626.*

ALEXANDER. *See also under* Epimachus, Epipodius *and* Sisinnius.

*ALEXIS FALCONIERI, ST

One of the Seven Founders of the Servite Order (*q.v.*). *February 17, i, 311.*

ALEYDIS, ST, VIRGIN

Or *Alice*. A young Cistercian nun of Brussels whose simple life, written down by a contemporary, has survived. In early life she contracted leprosy and had to be segregated from her community; she bore her affliction with ever-increasing patience, and was strengthened by ecstasies and visions. d. 1250. c.c. 1907. *June 15, ii, 549.*

ALFERIUS, ST, ABBOT

Alferius was founder of the great abbey of La Cava, which within a few years of his death in 1050 had over thirty other establishments dependent on it in southern Italy and Sicily. The *cultus* of eleven other abbots of La Cava was confirmed in 1893 and 1928. *April 12, ii, 80.*

ALFWOLD, ST, BISHOP

Last bishop of the see of Sherborne in Dorset; he was noted for his simple life and his devotion to the memory of St Cuthbert. d. *c.* 1058. *Alfwoldus. March 25, i, 678.*

ALICE. *See* Aleydis.

*ALIPIUS, ST, BISHOP

He was a close friend of St Augustine, under whom he studied in Africa, and after a severe struggle shared his master's conversion. He became bishop of Thagaste *c.* 393 and was Augustine's chief assistant in all his public work. d. *c.* 430. *August 18, iii, 348.*

ALIX LE CLERCQ, BD, VIRGIN

Bd Alix was b. of good family in Lorraine in 1576. In consequence of certain dreams and visions she associated herself with St Peter Fourier, then parish priest at Mattaincourt, and together they founded the congregation of Augustinian Canonesses Regular of our Lady, for the education of girls, in 1598. In those days such an enterprise called for quite unusual faith, courage and determination; those qualities Bd Alix had, and they were tried to the utmost. The formation and development of the congregation were full of difficulties and trials, and eventually the co-foundress had to relinquish her leadership. But "she had only one ambition; and that was again to be a simple sister, teaching their letters to the four- and five-year-olds in the lowest class". Mother Alix was on all hands acclaimed as a saint at once after her death at Nancy on January 9, 1622, but it was not till 1885 that her cause was properly undertaken; she was beatified in 1947. *Alexia. October 22, i, 59.*

ALLOWIN. *See* Bavo.

ALLUCIO, ST

He began life as a herdsman in Tuscany and was appointed master of an almshouse at Val di Nievole, near Pescia, being in effect a second founder of the charity; he was responsible for the undertaking of several other public works. d. 1134. c.c. by Pope Pius IX. *October 23, iv, 185.*

*ALMACHIUS, ST, MARTYR

Otherwise *Telemachus.* Put to death by the people at Rome for protesting against gladiatorial sports, in consequence of which the Emperor Honorius is said to have abolished such spectacles, *c.* 400. *January 1, i, 3.*

ALMEDHA. *See* Aled.

ALNOTH, ST

He was first a cowman on the land of St Werburga's monastery at Weedon and then a solitary in the woods of Stowe, near Bugbrooke in Northamptonshire. He was murdered by robbers *c.* 700 and for long was venerated in the neighbourhood, a feast being kept in his honour. *Alnothus. February 27, i, 434.*

ALODIA. *See under* Nunilo.

ALONSO. *See* Alphonsus.

*ALOYSIUS GONZAGA, ST

Luigi Gonzaga was b. in 1568 in the castle of Castiglione in Lombardy. He is the classical example of a saint whose popular estimation has been seriously damaged by the inadequate presentation of biographers and the weak sloppiness of his pictorial representations: some later writers have done their best to repair these mistakes. He was a lively boy of high birth, who refused to give in to the wickedness and mere worldliness of court life, and whom neither cajolery nor force could stop from serving God as a Jesuit. In 1585 he joined the Society at Rome; within six years he sickened from nursing the plague-stricken, and d. 1591. cd 1726. St Aloysius is the patron saint of youth. *June 21, ii, 603.*

ALOYSIUS GUANELLA, BD

Luigi Guanella was b. into a peasant family with thirteen children in northern Italy in 1842. He was ordained priest in 1866 when twenty-four. A disciple of St John Bosco, he founded homes and refuges and the Servites of Charity and of the Daughters of St Mary of Providence for the care of the aged and disadvantaged. Church authorities and anti-clericals alike opposed his "unorthodox" approach. d. 1915. bd for his humanitarianism in 1964. *October 25.*

ALOYSIUS ORIONE, BD

Luigi Orione dedicated his life as a priest to the unfortunate and marginalized in Italy and Latin America, Poland and England. He worked for the victims of the Messina and Marsica earthquakes. He founded the Little Work of Divine Providence, the Little Missionary Sisters of Charity, and the Blind Sacramentines and Hermits of St Albert. d. 1940. bd October 26, 1980. *March 8.*

ALOYSIUS PALAZZOLO, BD

Luigi Maria Palazzolo was b. at Bergamo on December 10, 1827, entered Bergamo seminary in 1844 and was ordained priest on June 23, 1850. He cared for the poor, marginalized and children at La Foppa oratory, which he directed from 1855. He founded an order of nuns to care for poor and orphan girls, and later an orphanage for boys and an order of men, the Brothers of Holy Family. d. June 15, 1886. His Sisters of the Poor of Bergamo have 233 houses in Italy, France and elsewhere. bd by Pope John XXIII March 19, 1963. *June 15.*

ALOYSIUS RABATA, BD

A young Sicilian Carmelite of whom little is known. He d. in 1490 from the effects of a blow on the head from an assailant whom he refused to bring to justice. c.c. by Pope Gregory XVI. *May 11, ii, 275.*

ALOYSIUS SCROSOPPI, BD

An Italian ordained priest in 1827, Luigi Scrosoppi was b. 1804 and founded the Sisters of Divine Providence for the Christian education of young girls. He was noted for his exceptional charity and prayer-life. d. 1884. bd October 4, 1981. *October 5.*

ALPAIS, BD, VIRGIN

She was a bed-ridden peasant girl at Cudot in France whose patience and goodness made a very great impression on her contemporar-

ies. d. 1211. c.c. 1874. *November 3, iv, 253.*

*ALPHAEUS AND ZACHAEUS, SS,
MARTYRS

Zachaeus was deacon at Gadara beyond the Jordan and his cousin Alphaeus was a reader. They were beheaded at Caesarea in 303. *November 17, iv, 366.*

*ALPHEGE OF CANTERBURY, ST,
BISHOP AND MARTYR

A monk of Deerhurst, raised to the bishopric of Winchester in 984 and translated to Canterbury in 1006. He was deeply beloved, and when the Danes raided Kent in 1011 he was urged to take refuge. Alphege refused and appealed to the invaders to moderate their savagery; they replied by imprisoning him and demanding a huge ransom. Alphege retorted that the country was too poor to pay such a sum and the Danes accordingly killed him, at Greenwich in 1012. In St Anselm's opinion St Alphege was a martyr in that he died rather than connive at injustice, and he has always been venerated as such. His feast is kept in the dioceses of Westminster, Clifton, Portsmouth and Southwark. *Elphegus. April 19, ii, 129.*

ALPHEGE OF WINCHESTER, ST,
BISHOP

Also called "the Elder" or "the Bald", to distinguish him from St Alphege the martyr. He became bishop of Winchester in 935 and helped on the religious vocation of his young kinsman St Dunstan, whom he ordained and whose future greatness he prophesied. d. 951. *March 12, i, 577.*

*ALPHIUS, ST MARTYR

With his companions Philadelphus and Cyrinus, St Alphius is venerated as a martyr, in southern Italy and Sicily, in 251, but the extant accounts of them are quite unreliable. *May 10, ii, 265.*

ALPHONSA MATTAHUPADATHUS,
BD, VIRGIN

Sr Alphonsa of the Immaculate Conception of the Syro-Malabar rite was the first Indian *beata*. b. 1910, she became a tertiary Claretian of Malabar in 1927, made her final profession in 1936 and died of prolonged illness in

1946 at age thirty-six. Her order now has 4,000 sisters. bd February 8, 1986 in Kerala. *February 8.*

*ALPHONSUS DE' LIGUORI, ST,
BISHOP AND DOCTOR

Born of a distinguished family near Naples in 1696. He became a very successful advocate but gave up the law and received holy orders in 1726; four years later he played a prominent part in the reorganization of the convent of Scala, near Amalfi, into the first house of Redemptoristine nuns. In 1732 St Alphonsus founded at Scala a new congregation of missioners to work among the peasants of the country districts, now known as the Redemptorists; this establishment was made in the face of huge difficulties, in the course of which Alphonsus was condemned, under a misapprehension, by Pope Pius VI and removed from its control; the congregation was still riven by schism and opposition at the time of the founder's death. He had been appointed bishop of Sant'Agata dei Goti in 1762 and governed the small diocese with great wisdom and industry until 1775, when ill-health forced him to resign; it was after this that the difficulties of the Redemptorists became even more distressing but while dealing with them St Alphonsus found time to devote himself anew to ascetical and moral theology. His experience in a lay profession combined with natural common sense and sweetness of disposition helped much to make him a very famous moral theologian. During the last eighteen months of his life he was tormented with the most fierce spiritual trials, but he died in peace in 1787, within two months of his ninety-first birthday. cd 1839 and declared Doctor of the Church in 1871.
August 1, iii, 242.

ALPHONSUS NAVARETTE, BD,
MARTYR

Bd Alphonsus was a Spanish Dominican who became a missionary in the Philippines and in 1611 was sent on to Japan. He was executed for his faith at Omura in 1617. bd 1867. *June 1, ii, 446.*

ALPHONSUS DE OROZCO, BD

He was an Augustinian friar and was ap-

pointed preacher at the court of Philip II of Spain. Here he exercised a very beneficient influence for many years and wrote a number of mystical and other works. d. 1591. bd 1881. *September 19, iii, 602.*

*ALPHONSUS RODRIGUEZ, ST

He was the son of a wealthy merchant of Segovia. After his business had failed and death had taken his wife and children, Alphonsus, in 1571 at the age of forty-four, was accepted as a temporal coadjutor (laybrother) of the Society of Jesus and sent to Majorca. For the rest of his life he was porter at the Montesione college there; he was held in the deepest respect by the many and various people who got to know him at the door, one of the most famous who came to him for advice being St Peter Claver. St Alphonsus d. after years of physical and spiritual suffering in 1617. cd 1888. He must be distinguished from the other but uncanonized Jesuit Alphonsus Rodríguez, a writer on spirituality, and *see also* the next entry.
October 30, iv, 225.

ALPHONSUS RODRIGUEZ, BD,
MARTYR

One of the three Jesuit martyrs of Paraguay. He was killed at the same time and place as Bd Roque González in 1628. bd 1934. *November 17, iv, 377.*

ALTMAN, ST, BISHOP

He became bishop of Passau in 1065 and was one of the four south German bishops who opposed the emperor Henry IV on behalf of Pope St Gregory VII. He was driven from his see, but continued to exercise great influence from the borders of the diocese. d. 1091. c.c. by Pope Leo XIII.
August 8, iii, 282.

ALTO, ST, ABBOT

Alto probably was an Irishman, who founded and governed a monastery at the place in Bavaria now known as Altomünster. d. *c.* 760. *February 9, i, 290.*

ALVAREZ OF CORDOVA, BD

He entered the Dominican house at Cordova in 1368 and worked with great success in Andalusia and Italy. He became adviser to the Queen-mother of Spain, Catherine (daughter of John of Gaunt), and tutor to her son Juan II. He was a follower of Bd Raymund of Capua and founded a strictly observant Dominican priory near Cordova; this was soon a centre of learning and religion, and of opposition to the Avignon pope Peter de Luna. Alvarez used himself to go questing for his house, and he set up stations of the cross that attracted many pilgrims. d. *c*. 1430. c.c. 1741. *February 19, i, 378.*

AMADEUS AMIDEI, ST

One of the Seven Founders of the Servite Order (*q.v.*) *February 12, i, 311.*

AMADEUS OF LAUSANNE, ST,
BISHOP

In 1139 St Bernard appointed this Amadeus to be abbot of the Cistercian house of Hautecombe in Savoy, and soon afterwards he was promoted to the see of Lausanne; four years before his death he was made chancellor of the kingdom of Burgundy. d. 1159. c.c. 1910. *January 28, i, 189.*

AMADEUS OF SAVOY, BD

Born at Thonon in 1435 and succeeded to the dukedom of Savoy in 1455. Amadeus suffered from epilepsy, and eventually resigned his office in favour of his wife. In spite of his malady he led a very austere life and was revered as a saint after his death in 1472. bd 1677. Bd Amadeus is patron of the royal house of Savoy, of which he was an ancestor. *March 30, i, 706.*

AMADOUR, ST

He is honoured in Quercy and the Limousin as the first hermit of Gaul and founder of the shrine of our Lady known as Rocamadour, but nothing whatever is known about him. *Amator. August 20, iii, 366.*

AMALBURGA, ST

Amalburga, or Amelia, was the wife of Count Witger and mother of St Gudula and others. When Witger became a monk she joined the convent of Maubeuge. d. *c*. 690. *July 10, iii, 64.*

*AMALBURGA, ST, VIRGIN

Often confused with the above. She was a nun at Munsterbilsen in Limburg. d. *c*. 770. *July 10, iii, 65.*

*AMAND, ST, BISHOP

A great missionary figure in the Merovingian epoch. After living as a solitary in Bourges for fifteen years he was consecrated bishop with no fixed see. He preached in Flanders and Carinthia, reproved King Dagobert for his crimes, and founded several monasteries in Flanders. d. *c*. 679. *Amandus.* *February 6, i, 263.*

*AMANDUS, ST, BISHOP

He was a bishop of Bordeaux whose wisdom and virtue is spoken of by St Paulinus of Nola, whom Amandus had prepared for baptism. d. *c*. 430. *June 18, ii, 578.*

AMATA, BD, VIRGIN

One of the three beatified nuns who began the first convent of Preacheresses at Bologna, with Bd Diana d'Andolo; she had formerly been at San Sisto in Rome d. *c*. 1270. c.c. 1891. *June 9, ii, 512.*

*AMATOR OF AUXERRE, ST, BISHOP

In French, *Amatre*. He was a bishop of Auxerre who during a long episcopate converted the remaining heathen in the diocese, built two churches, and was the instrument of many miracles. d. 418. *May 1, ii, 207.*

*AMATUS, ST, ABBOT

While a monk of Luxeuil St Amatus (*Amé*) turned the heart of St Romaric to God, and when this nobleman founded the monastery of Remiremont *c*. 620 Amatus was appointed the first abbot. d. *c*. 630. *September 13, iii, 549.*

*AMATUS, ST, BISHOP

This Amatus was bishop of Sion in the Valais (not of Sens), but he was driven from his see by the enmity of King Theoderic III and was confined in monasteries for the rest of his days. d. *c*. 690. *September 13, iii, 550.*

AMATUS. *See also under* Romaric.

*AMBROSE, ST, BISHOP AND DOCTOR

He was b. *c*. 340 in Gaul, where his father was prefect, and became a barrister at Rome.

Before he was thirty-five Ambrose was appointed governor of Liguria and Aemilia, with his headquarters at Milan, and he was called to be bishop by acclamation there in 374, although still only a catechumen. He proved to be one of the greatest and most beloved bishops of all time. He distributed his worldly wealth to the poor and set to work to administer his diocese, preaching and writing against the rampant Arianism with tremendous energy. He censured the Eastern emperor for his cruelty and defied the Western empress for her heresy; he was at home to all comers; and he wrote many homilies and treatises. So persuasive was Ambrose on the excellence of virginity that the civil authorities accused him of "antisocial" activities, to which he retorted that it is war, not maidenhood, that destroys peoples. While the Empire was declining in the West, St Ambrose inaugurated a new lease of life for the Latin language, in the service of Christianity. One of his last treatises was "On the Goodness of Death", and he died soon after, on Good Friday, April 4, 397, being hardly fifty years of age: December 7 is the anniversary of his episcopal consecration. He is named in the canon of the Milanese Mass. *Ambrosius. December 7, iv, 509.*

AMBROSE AUTPERT, ST, ABBOT

When he left the court of King Pepin the Short he became a monk at St Vincent's in the duchy of Benevento, where he spent the rest of his uneventful life. The writings of St Ambrose were very highly valued in the Middle Ages, and his learning was considerable. d. *c.* 782. *July 19, iii, 149.*

AMBROSE BARLOW, BD, MARTYR

He was professed a monk of St Gregory's at Douay in 1615 and worked on the English mission in his native Lancashire for twenty-four years. After being in prison and released four times he was h.d.q. for his priesthood at Lancaster in 1641. bd 1929. Bd Ambrose was named titular cathedral-prior of Coventry a week before his execution. *September 10, iii, 535.*

AMBROSE OF CAMALDOLI, BD, ABBOT

During thirty years as a Camaldolese monk at Florence Ambrose Traversari became a conspicuous religious and literary figure, a characteristic "all-round" man of the Renaissance: he read (especially in Greek), wrote, translated, and collected a good library. From 1431, when he was appointed abbot general of the Camaldolese, he was engaged in public affairs of church and state, in which he was as effective as he was as a scholar. d. 1439. *November 20, iv, 397.*

AMBROSE OF SIENA, BD

Ambrose Sansedoni was a Dominican student with St Thomas under St Albert the Great and became a renowned preacher in Germany, France, and Italy. He fulfilled various missions for the Holy See and was Master of the Sacred Palace. His death in 1286 was hastened by the vehemence with which he preached against usury. c.c. 1622. *March 20, i, 644.*

AMÉ. *See* Amatus.

AMELBERGA. *See* Amalburga.

AMICUS, ST

He was a hermit and monk at Cameriono, Torano dell' Aquila, and Fonteavellana. d. *c.* 1045. *November 3, iv, 249.*

*AMMON, ST, MARTYR

Ammon, Zeno, Ptolemy and Ingenes, soldiers, with one Theophilus, were beheaded at Alexandria in 249 for encouraging a Christian confessor who showed signs of wavering at his trial. There have been several other martyrs named Ammon.
December 20, iv, 578.

AMMON, ST

Ammon was one of the earliest and greatest of the hermit monks of the Nitrian desert, a life that he entered on after having lived for eighteen years with his wife as brother and sister. On the advice of St Antony, he assembled the cells of his followers more or less together, under a general overseer. In his later years Ammon ate only once every three or four days. d. *c.* 350.
October 4, iv, 32.

*AMPHILOCHIUS, ST, BISHOP

Amphilochius, a close friend of St Basil the

Great, was bishop of Iconium and showed great activity against the Macedonian heresy, in the course of which he wrote a work on the Holy Ghost which was approved by St Jerome. d. c. 400. *November 23, iv, 408.*

*ANASTASIA, ST, MARTYR

Anastasia was martyred at Sirmium in Dalmatia, probably under Diocletian, but only worthless legends have survived concerning her. She was venerated in Rome in the fifth century and, under the influence of Byzantine officials there (Anastasia's relics had been translated to Constantinople), her memory became associated with the second Mass of Christmas; she is still commemorated at that Mass in the Roman Missal, though the Byzantines keep her feast on December 22. She is named in Eucharistic Prayer I (the Roman canon).
December 25, iv, 613.

*ANASTASIA AND CYRIL, SS, MARTYRS

The *passio* of this maiden and the boy who brought her water during her sufferings is a fictitious composition; it is not certain that they ever existed. *October 28, iv, 214.*

ANASTASIA PATRICIA, ST, VIRGIN

Hers is one of the several stories of women who lived disguised as monks or hermits, in her case to escape marriage with the emperor Justinian. The tale is in all probability nothing more than a pious romance.
March 10, i, 546.

ANASTASIA. *See also under* Basilissa.

*ANASTASIUS I, ST, POPE

Anastasius I, a Roman, is chiefly remembered for his condemnation of the errors attributed to Origen. d. 401.
December 19, iv, 584.

*ANASTASIUS I OF ANTIOCH, ST, BISHOP

This Anastasius, patriarch of Antioch, was banished from his see for many years by the Emperor Justin II for opposing the imperial politico-theological opinions. He was a man

of very great learning and piety. d. 599. *April 21, ii, 142.*

*ANASTASIUS II OF ANTIOCH, ST, BISHOP AND MARTYR

A monk who became patriach of Antioch in 599. During the rising of the Syrian Jews against the oppression of the emperor Phocus in 609, Anastasius was murdered by the mob and was looked on as a martyr.
December 21, iv, 592.

ANASTASIUS OF CLUNY, ST

He was a monk first of Mont-Saint-Michel and then of Cluny, and d. as a hermit near Toulouse in 1085. *October 16, iv, 130.*

*ANASTASIUS THE FULLER, ST, MARTYR

He plied his trade at Salona in Dalmatia, where in 304 he was put to death by drowning for his confession of Christ. The date of his feast is August 26. *September 7, iii, 502.*

*ANASTASIUS THE PERSIAN, ST, MARTYR

A Persian convert at Jerusalem who became a monk in 621. He was arrested and tortured at Caesarea and then taken to the Persian king in Mesopotamia, by whose orders he was eventually slain in 628. A miraculous picture of St Anastasius was put in as evidence at the seventh ecumenical council at Nicaea in 787, which was held against Iconoclasm. This picture, with the martyr's head, is said still to be at the monastery of SS Vincent and Anastasius at Rome.
January 22, i, 144.

ANASTASIUS. *See also* Astrik.

ANATOLIA. *See under* Victoria.

ANATOLIUS OF CONSTANTINO-PLE, ST, BISHOP

Nothing is known of the private life of this patriarch of Constantinople and his public life is somewhat equivocal for one who is acclaimed as a saint; but the Bollandists have vindicated him and his feast is kept by Byzantine Catholics in the East. He was appointed to the see of Constantinople in 449 and d. 458. *July 3, iii, 12.*

*ANATOLIUS OF LAODICEA, ST, BISHOP

He was a bishop of Laodicea, eminent as a philosopher and mathematician, and at one time in charge of a school at Alexandria, his native city. d. 283. *July 3, iii, 10.*

*ANDREW, ST, APOSTLE

Andrew, brother of St Peter, was the first of Christ's apostles in the order of time; all that is certain about him is found in the Gospels. He is said to have preached the gospel in Asia Minor and Greece and to have suffered martyrdom by crucifixion at Patras in Achaia. His alleged relics were stolen from Constantinople in 1210 and now rest in the cathedral of Amalfi in Italy. St Andrew is the patron saint of Scotland, Russia, and Greece. *Andreas. November 30, iv, 450.*

ANDREW ABELLON, BD

A confessor of the Order of Preachers, who was prior of the royal friary of St Mary Magdalene at Saint-Maximin. d. 1450. c.c. 1902. *May 17, ii, 340.*

*ANDREW AVELLINO, ST

Born near Naples in 1521. He was at first an ecclesiastical lawyer, and then, after being nearly killed by those who were interested in maintaining the disorder of a convent which he had been commissioned to reform, joined the Theatine clerks regular. He founded houses of this order in several parts of Italy, and his success as a preacher was confirmed by gifts of prophecy and miracle. St Andrew (christened Lancelot) was a personal friend and adviser of St Charles Borromeo. d. 1608. cd 1712. *November 10, iv, 305.*

ANDREW BESSETTE, BD

André Bessette, b. 1845, was a Canadian Holy Cross brother who built St Joseph's Oratory, Montreal. He was a man of prayer and a humble friend of the poor. A manual worker until the age of twenty-five, he served the Brothers as a porter for forty years and as guardian of the oratory for thirty more. d. 1937. bd May 23, 1982. *January 6.*

*ANDREW BOBOLA, ST, MARTYR

A Jesuit of Vilna who was specially successful in reconciling dissident Orthodox with the Holy See. His missionary labours met with a great deal of opposition and in 1657 he was tortured and murdered by a gang of Cossacks at Janow, near Pinsk. cd 1938. *May 21, ii, 363.*

*ANDREW CORSINI, ST, BISHOP

Born in Florence in 1302 of the great Corsini family. His early adolescence was dissipated and vicious, but the reproaches of his mother brought him round and he became a Carmelite friar. He studied in Paris and Avignon, was made prior at Florence, and then bishop of Fiesole. He was devoted to the causes of the poor and of peace in the quarrelsome Italian states, and was sent by Pope Urban V to pacify Bologna. St Andrew set the example of a prelate of a most noble house living according to the austerity of the religious rule he had professed. d. January 6, 1373. cd 1629. *February 4, i, 246.*

ANDREW DOTTI, BD

A confessor of the Servite Order, wherein he was a disciple of St Philip Benizi and accompanied him on his preaching journeys. Bd Andrew was a figure of importance in the early days of the Servites, and ended his days as a solitary. d. 1315. c.c. 1806. *September 3, iii, 483.*

ANDREW FERRARI, BD, BISHOP

Cardinal Andrea Carlo Ferrari was b. in 1850, ordained priest in 1873, consecrated in 1890, then appointed archbishop of Milan in 1894 after becoming a cardinal. He d. of cancer of the throat on February 2, 1921. bd May 10, 1987. *February 2.*

*ANDREW FOURNET, ST

Andrew Hubert Fournet was b. in 1752 at Maillé, near Poitiers. After several false starts, he was ordained and made parish priest of his native town. After the revolution he worked untiringly as a missioner, preacher, and confessor, and with St Elizabeth Bichier founded the congregation of Daughters of the Cross, in whose favour St Andrew's prayers several times miraculously increased food. d. 1834. cd 1933. *May 13, ii, 303.*

ANDREW HIBERNON, BD

A Spanish Franciscan lay-brother who converted many by his frankness and simplicity. d. 1602. bd 1791. *April 18, ii, 124.*

ANDREW KAGWA, ST, MARTYR

One of the martyrs of Uganda (*q.v.*). He was the chief of Kigowa and the instrument of several conversions, including his own wife and two sons of the chief counsellor of the persecuting Mwanga. He was executed just before the final holocaust in 1886. bd 1920. cd 1964. *June 3, ii, 469.*

ANDREW KIM, ST, MARTYR

Andrew Kim Taegon was the first Korean priest to be put to death for Christ. b. 1821, he was sent when fifteen to Macao to prepare for the priesthood as a missionary to Korea. He returned to Korea on January 2, 1845 and contacted the Christian communities. He was ordained in Shanghai in the same year and was in Korea again in October. He was imprisoned in 1846 and executed when the French fleet off Seoul demanded an explanation for the execution of missionaries in 1839. He was beatified in 1925 and canonized by John Paul II at Seoul on May 6, 1984. d. September 16, 1846. *September 21, iii, 613.*

ANDREW KIM, PAUL CHONG AND THEIR 101 MARTYR COMPANIONS, SS. *See also under* Korea, the 103 Martyrs of, and separate entries.

ANDREW OF ANAGNI, BD

Andrew dei Conti di Segni was a nephew of Pope Alexander IV but was himself a Franciscan lay-brother, held in great veneration both in life and after death. d. February 1, 1302, c.c. 1724. *February 17, i, 360.*

ANDREW OF ANTIOCH, BD

This Andrew was b. at Antioch c. 1268 of Norman parents, a descendant of Robert Guiscard. He was a canon regular of St Augustine, and near the end of his life was sent into Europe to collect funds for the eastern houses of his order. He d. at Annecy in Savoy c. 1348, having earned a great reputation for holiness during the course of his travels. *November 30, iv, 452.*

ANDREW OF CRETE, ST, BISHOP

Or "of Jerusalem". He was b. at Damascus, became a monk of Mar Saba and then at the Holy Sepulchre, and a deacon of the Great Church at Constantinople. From thence he was promoted to the archbishopric of Gortyna in Crete, where he distinguished himself as a preacher and a writer of hymns. He is said to have introduced the *kanon* into the Byzantine office. d. 740 (?). *July 4, iii, 15.*

*ANDREW OF CRETE, ST, MARTYR

Otherwise "the Calybite". He was a monk of Crete who went to Constantinople to take part in the Iconoclast controversy. He accused the emperor of heresy and was stabbed to death by a fanatical iconoclast while being led through the streets in derision, in 766. *October 20, iv, 157.*

ANDREW OF FIESOLE, ST

He is said to have been an Irishman and archdeacon to St Donatus at Fiesole at the end of the ninth century. His alleged relics are preserved there, but the story is probably fictitious: it includes the miraculous transportation of Andrew's sister Brigid to Fiesole. *August 22, iii, 382.*

ANDREW OF MONTEREALE, BD

For fifty years Bd Andrew, an Augustinian friar, preached the gospel in Italy and France and was remarkable for his holiness and learning. d. 1480. c.c. 1764. *April 12, ii, 80.*

ANDREW OF PESCHIERA, BD

A Dominican friar who evangelized a part of southern Switzerland for forty-five years. d. 1485. c.c. 1820. *January 19, i, 123.*

ANDREW OF PISTOIA, BD, BISHOP

Andrew Franchi was a Dominican who became bishop of Pistoia in 1378 and for twenty-three years was revered by his flock for his simplicity and justness. d. 1401. c.c. 1921. *May 30, ii, 426.*

ANDREW OF RINN, BD, MARTYR

A boy alleged to have been murdered by Jews out of hatred of the faith at Rinn, near Innsbruck, in 1462. This is an anti-Semitic myth. Pope Benedict XIV allowed the continuation of the local *cultus,* but refused a request for Andrew's canonization. *July 12, iii, 86.*

ANDREW OF SIENA, BD

Andrew de' Gallerani was a distinguished Sienese soldier who, having murdered a man, gave up the rest of his life to prayer and charity. d. 1251. *March 19, i, 635.*

ANDREW OF SPELLO, BD

Andrew Caccioli was a well-to-do secular priest who gave all his riches to charity and became one of the first seventy-two followers of St Francis of Assisi. He was subjected to persecution and imprisonment for his active opposition to innovations introduced among the Franciscans. d. 1254. c.c. by Pope Clement XII. *June 9, ii, 466.*

ANDREW OF STRUMI, BD, ABBOT

Andrew, called "the Ligurian", was a chief supporter of the deacon Bd Arialdo and the church-reform party in the Milanese strife of the mid-eleventh century. After the murder of Arialdo. Andrew retired from the world to join the Vallombrosan monks. He became abbot of San Fedele at Strumi and divided his time between writing, governing his house, and public affairs; he negotiated a peace between Florence and Arezzo, in consequence of which the prestige of his order was greatly increased. d. 1097. *March 10, i, 549.*

*ANDREW THE TRIBUNE, ST, MARTYR

Authentic *acta* of this famous martyr have not survived, but he is said to have been an officer in the army of Maximian Galerius who became a Christian with a number of his comrades. They took refuge in the Taurus mountains in Turkey but were tracked and put to death, c. 300. *August 19, iii, 354.*

*ANDRONICUS AND ATHANASIA, SS

A man and wife of Antioch who, after the death of their two children, went their ways to lead a solitary life in the Egyptian deserts. Years later they met and occupied adjoining cells, Andronicus not recognizing his wife until after she was dead. Such is the story. These saints are particularly venerated in Ethiopia. *October 9, iv, 69.*

ANDRONICUS. *See also under* Tarachus.

ANGADRISMA, ST, VIRGIN

In French *Angadrême.* She was abbess of Oroër-des-Vierges, near Beauvais. d. *c.* 695. *October 14, iv, 109.*

*ANGELA MERICI, ST, VIRGIN

She was b. near Brescia in 1470 or 1474, and for some years devoted herself to the education of young girls, the care of sick women, and similar work, in which she was joined by several companions. These she formed into a congregation under the patronage and title of St Ursula (then in the calendar, now suppressed) in 1535, the first specifically teaching order of women to be established in the Church; it is now spread throughout the world. d. 1540. cd 1807. *January 27, ii, 432.*

ANGELA OF FOLIGNO, BD

One of the great mystics and contemplatives of the Middle Ages. She was b. of a good family at Foligno about the middle of the thirteenth century. She married and had several sons, but led a self-indulgent and perhaps sinful life until, as the result of a sudden conversion, she became a Franciscan tertiary. After the death of her husband and children she gradually stripped herself of all her possessions and became the leader of a large family of tertiaries, both men and women. At the request of her confessor, Friar Arnold, she dictated to him an account of her visions and ecstasies, from which we learn most that is known of her life. Her very remarkable visions are narrated in a restrained and convincing way, and she reveals clearly the spiritual heights and depths to which she was led. She died peacefully in 1309. c.c. 1693. *February 28, i, 440.*

ANGELA OF THE CROSS, BD, VIRGIN

The Spanish foundress in the late nineteenth century of the Sisters of the Cross recruited from peasant families for service in rural areas. A heroic practitioner of service to others, and especially the "poorest of the poor", and of a spirituality of the Cross in a life of poverty, detachment and humility. bd by John Paul II at Seville during a visit on November 5, 1982. *March 2.*

ANGELINA OF MARSCIANO, BD

Her husband died when she was seventeen and she was inspired to establish a convent of regular tertiaries of St Francis at Foligno, the first of its kind, which was completed in 1397. Other such houses were established before her death in 1435. c.c. 1825. *July 21, ii, 160.*

*ANGELO, ST, MARTYR

This Angelo was an early member of the Carmelite Order who was killed at Leocata in Sicily in 1220 by a man whose wickedness he had denounced; he is venerated as a martyr. *Angelus. May 5, ii, 239.*

ANGELO OF ACRI, BD

After two unsuccessful efforts and then a stormy novitiate this Angelo was professed among the Capuchin friars. He began his public preaching in 1702, but it was not till 1711 at Naples that he overcame initial difficulties; from then onwards he was famous all over southern Italy, and his preaching was supported by miracles. d. 1739. bd 1825. *October 30, iv, 228.*

ANGELO OF BORGO SAN SEPOLCRO, BD

This Augustinian friar was a contemporary of St Nicholas of Tolentino and is said to have established houses of his order in England, but reliable particulars of his career are lacking. d. *c.* 1306. c.c. 1921. *February 15, i, 345.*

ANGELO OF CHIVASSO, BD

Angelo was a senator of Piedmont who joined the Observant Friars Minor at Genoa. His merits and abilities were recognized both by promotion to offices in the order and by his popularity among people of all ranks and kinds, and he was tireless in his efforts to save poor people from the clutches of usurious money-lenders. When over eighty Angelo preached among the Waldensians with considerable success. d. 1495. c.c. 1753. *April 19, ii, 81.*

ANGELO OF FLORENCE, BD

Angelo Augustine Mazzinghi was b. in Florence in 1377 and was a model religious of the Carmelite Order. d. 1438. c.c. 1761. *August 18, iii, 350.*

ANGELO OF FOLIGNO, BD

A confessor of the Augustinian friars who founded three houses of his order in Umbria. d. 1312. c.c. 1891. *August 27, iii, 422.*

ANGELO OF FURCIO, BD

A confessor of the order of Hermits of St Augustine who d. in 1327, his *cultus* being approved in 1888. *February 6, i, 266.*

ANGELO OF GUALDO, BD

Born at Gualdo in Umbria *c.* 1265, and was distinguished all his life for his extreme simplicity, innocence, and gentleness. After making several pilgrimages he became a Camaldolese hermit. d. January 25, 1325. c.c. 1825. *February 6, i, 266.*

ANGILBERT, ST, ABBOT

As a young man Angilbert was nicknamed "Homer" but his life at the court of Charlemagne was worthy neither of that name nor of his own better self. He mended his ways and became abbot of Saint-Riquier, near Amiens, where he is said to have introduced continual choir service in relays. He continued to take part in public affairs and was one of the executors of Charlemagne's will. d. 814. *Angilbertus. February 18, i, 371.*

*ANIANUS, ST, BISHOP

He is said to have been the helper and successor of St Mark as bishop of Alexandria and "a man well pleasing to God". First century. *April 25, ii, 162.*

*ANIANUS, ST, BISHOP

In French, *Aignan.* He was a bishop of Orleans, and d. 453. *November 17, iv, 367.*

ANNE, ST, VIRGIN

She was a maiden of Constantinople (also called Susanna), who lived for over twenty years as a solitary on the Leucadian promontory in Epirus. d. *c.* 918. *Anna. July 23, iii, 171.*

*ANNE, ST

Anne (Hannah = "Grace") is the name traditionally given to the mother of the Blessed Virgin Mary. Her *cultus* was known in the sixth century in the East and early in the eighth in the West, but it did not become widespread till the middle of the fourteenth. Nothing certain is known about her.
July 26, iii, 189.

ANNE JAVOUHEY, BD, VIRGIN

Foundress of the Congregation of St Joseph of Cluny. She was b. in Burgundy in 1779, the daughter of a farmer, who in 1812 bought a former friary at Cluny for the headquarters of his child's educational and charitable work. Bd Anne's success as an educator led to her being asked to establish schools for indigenous children in various French colonies, where she also undertook other and less usual works. These included the training of hundreds of Negro slaves, men, women, and children, in Guiana in preparation for emancipation, and the settling of them in their own homes. From time to time Mother Javouhey had to meet, and overcome, opposition from the authorities, ecclesiastical and civil, and from French colonists who resented her activities; she was deprived of the sacraments for two years through the extraordinary behaviour of a prefect apostolic. Among her defenders were King Louis-Philippe, Lamartine and Chateaubriand. She was a woman of truly remarkable faith, courage and strength of character. d. 1851. bd 1950. *July 15, iii, 114.*

ANNE LINE, BD, MARTYR

A widow (*née* Heigham, of Dunmow) who had charge of Father John Gerard's secret clergy house in London. She was arrested for harbouring priests, and was hanged at Tyburn in 1601. bd 1929.
February 27, i, 436.

ANNE MICHELOTTI, BD, VIRGIN

Anna Michelotti was born at Annecy, France, on August 22, 1843. Her father was Piedmontese. She founded the Congregation of the Little Servants of the Sacred Heart at Turin in 1874. The sisters were especially active as home helps to the indigent sick. Bd Anna died at Turin in 1888. bd November 1, 1975. *February 1.*

ANNE MONTEAGUDO, BD, VIRGIN

Sr Ana de los Angeles Monteagudo, Sister Anne of the Angels, was b. at Arequipa, Peru, in 1602. At nineteen she entered a Dominican convent, became prioress and d. there 1686. bd February 2, 1985.
February 2.

ANNE TAIGI, BD

Born at Siena in 1769, daughter of a druggist whose business failed; in 1790 she married Dominic Taigi, a servant of the Chigi palace in Rome. He was a good man but narrow, rather cantankerous and not very understanding, so that his tributes to his wife are the more valuable. Bd Anna Maria achieved holiness in the discharge of domestic duties and the bringing up of her children, but her light could not be hid and her counsel was sought by the great ones of Church and state. She read the minds of men and had the supernatural gift of foretelling the future. d. 1837. bd 1920. *June 9, ii, 513.*

ANNE WANG, BD, MARTYR

One of the fifty-two Chinese lay people in the second group of martyrs under the Boxers. bd 1955. *July 20, iv, 672.*

ANNE OF ST BARTHOLOMEW, BD, VIRGIN

This Anne, ex-shepherdess, was a Carmelite lay-sister and the special companion of St Teresa of Avila, who died in her arms. She was sent to France with other reformed Carmelites in 1696, was promoted to the choir, and became prioress at Pontoise and Tours. In 1612 Bd Anne founded a Carmel at Antwerp, one of whose nuns started the English Carmel there (now at Lanherne). d.1626. bd 1917. In making her foundations St Teresa declared that Sister Anne was more useful to her than anyone else.
June 7, ii, 499.

ANNEMUND, ST. BISHOP

Annemund, archbishop of Lyons, was friend and patron of the young St Wilfrid of York, who was present when Annemund was murdered at Chalon-sur-Saône in 658. Bede and others call St Annemund *Dalfinus*.
September 28, iii, 667.

*ANNO, ST, BISHOP

Anno was made archbishop of Cologne in 1056, but never succeeded in fully overcoming the prejudice against himself of his flock, which thought he was insufficiently well born to rule over them. Most of the events of his life belong to the troubled political history of the age, and they are not uniformly edifying; Anno was canonized (c. 1186) rather for the virtue of his private life and for his reforming energy in his diocese. d. 1075 *December 4, iv, 490.*

ANNUNCIATA COCCHETTI, BD, VIRGIN

Bd Annunziata Cocchetti was an Italian nun, and founded the Sisters of St Dorothy of Cemmo. She was born on May 9, 1880 in the province of Brescia. bd April 21, 1991. *March 23.*

*ANSANUS, ST MARTYR

St Ansanus was martyred at Siena in 304 (?) and is venerated as the apostle of that city. He is said to have made so many converts that he was called "the Baptizer". *December 1, iv, 454.*

*ANSBERT, ST BISHOP

Abbot of St Wandrille and then archbishop of Rouen. He was banished on a false accusation and d. in exile in Hainault c. 695. *Ansbertus. February 9, i, 290.*

ANSEGISUS, ST ABBOT

He was abbot of Saint-Germer, of Luxeuil, and finally of Fontenelle and a characteristic example of the Benedictines working for Christianity and civilization during the dark ages of Europe. Under his rule Fontenelle became famous for its library and *scriptorium.* d. 833. *July 20, iii, 155.*

*ANSELM OF CANTERBURY, ST, BISHOP AND DOCTOR

Born at Aosta c. 1033, abbot of Bec in Normandy in 1078, and nominated archbishop of Canterbury by King William Rufus in 1093. Almost at once he angered William by opposing his spoliation of sees and abbeys and his extortions from the clergy; Anselm went to lay his case before the Holy See in 1097 and had to remain abroad until William's death. He was at the Council of Bari in 1098, where he resolved the theological doubts of the Italo-Greek bishops. Difficulties arose with King Henry I because Anselm refused to allow lay investiture of spiritual offices and he had to spend a second period in exile. St Anselm was one of the first to oppose the selling of men as chattels, and is regarded as the "father of scholasticism"; his most famous written work is on the Incarnation, *Cur Deus Homo?* d. 1109. Like St Albert the Great in our time, he was declared a doctor of the Church (in 1720) without having been formally canonized. *Anselmus. April 21, ii, 138.*

*ANSELM OF LUCCA, ST, BISHOP

After his nomination to the see of Lucca he for long refused to accept investiture at lay hands—the emperor Henry IV—and he even withdrew from his diocese for a time on this account. He naturally strongly supported Pope Gregory VII in his campaign against lay investiture. Anselm was a man of great learning, especially as a canonist and in scriptural matters. He became papal legate in Lombardy, and worked hard to establish stricter observance among monks and canons, though he had no success with the canons of his own chapter. d. 1086. *March 18, i, 628.*

ANSELM OF NONANTOLA, ST, ABBOT

Anselm, duke of Friuli, founded monasteries at Fanano and Nonantola, the second of which he entered himself and governed as abbot until his death in 803. To each of his monasteries he attached a hospital for the sick. *March 3, i, 470.*

ANSFRID, ST, BISHOP

As a count of Brabant Ansfrid distinguished himself by the suppression of brigands and pirates, but in 994 was made bishop of Utrecht, where he was greatly beloved by the citizens. d. 1010. *May 11, ii, 273.*

*ANSKAR, ST. BISHOP

Born 801 near Amiens and was a monk first of Old and then of New Corbie, whence he was taken by King Harold of Denmark to work among the heathen Danes. He was appointed first archbishop of Hamburg and legate of the Holy See, and for thirteen years preached and organized missions in Scandinavia and northern Germany. In 845 the Northmen destroyed Hamburg, and Sweden and Denmark relapsed; the see of Bremen was united to that of Hamburg and St Anskar returned to Denmark and set to work to restore his damaged missions. But Sweden reverted completely to paganism after his death in 865. *Anscharius. February 3, i, 242.*

*ANSOVINUS, ST, BISHOP

A hermit at Castel-Raimondo, near Torcello, who was raised to the bishopric of Camerino; he accepted the office only on condition that he should be exempt from the feudal duty of providing soldiers for the imperial army, which he considered unbecoming in a bishop. Many miracles are recorded of him. d. 840. *March 13, i, 586.*

ANSTRUDIS, ST, VIRGIN

In French *Austrude.* She was probably the daughter of St Salaberga and abbess of a convent at Laon, where she underwent some persecution from the tyrant Ebroin. d. *c.* 700. *October 17, iv, 140.*

*ANTHELM, ST, BISHOP

Born in 1107, the son of a Savoyard nobleman, and became a secular priest. A visit to the charterhouse of Portes caused him to resign his offices and join the Carthusians, and in 1139 he was elected seventh prior of the Grande Chartreuse. He was responsible for the summoning of the first general Carthusian chapter at which the monks were organized into an order under a minister general, St Anthelm being the first. He resigned in 1152 but seven years later emerged from his retirement to intervene on behalf of Alexander III against the antipope Victor; much against his will he had to accept the bishopric of Belley in 1163. The diocese was in a disorderly state and after gentler methods had failed Anthelm proceeded to deprivation and excommunication —including the count of Maurienne, the sentence against whom he would not relax even at the bidding of the Holy See. He spent all his leisure at Carthusian monasteries and

took a very active interest in certain women solitaries and in a leper hospital he had founded. On one occasion he was sent to England to try and bring about a reconciliation of King Henry II with St Thomas Becket. d. 1178. *Anthelmus. June 26, ii, 650.*

*ANTHERUS, ST, POPE AND MARTYR

Put to death after about six weeks' pontificate in 236, and buried in the cemetery of St Callistus. *January 3, i, 26.*

ANTHIA. *See under* Eleutherius, April 18.

*ANTHIMUS, ST BISHOP

Bishop of Nicomedia, beheaded for confessing Christ in 303. *April 27, ii, 171.*

ANTHONY. *See* Antony.

ANTONIA MESINA, BD,
VIRGIN AND MARTYR

She was b. on June 21, 1919 at Orgoloso, Sardinia. She joined the young girls' Catholic Action group in 1934. In 1935, when gathering wood, she was attacked by a young man who killed her when she defended her virtue. bd October 4, 1987. *May 17.*

ANTONIA OF FLORENCE, BD

A young widow who was one of the first in Florence to become a regular tertiary of St Francis when Bd Angelina of Marsciano founded a convent there in 1429. Later she was made superioress at Aquila, and there with the help of St John of Capistrano she founded a community under the original rule of the Poor Clares. Her son and other relatives used to come and worry her with their disputes, for fifteen years she suffered from a painful disease, and she had numerous other difficulties, all of which she overcame with quiet perseverance. d. 1472. c.c. 1847. *February 28, i, 446.*

*ANTONINA, ST, MARTYR

Or *Antonia.* There is nothing but uncertainty about this martyr. She seems to be duplicated in the Roman Martyrology on March 1 and May 4 and is claimed by three different places called Cea; actually she may have suffered at Nicomedia (in 304?). *June 12, ii, 528.*

*ANTONINUS, ST, MARTYR

The Antoninus, a martyr at Pamiers, mentioned by the Roman Martyrology on September 2, is probably a mistake for the Antoninus, a stonemason, martyred at Apamaea in Syria, who is commemorated by the Byzantines on November 9.
September 2, iii, 469.

*ANTONINUS OF FLORENCE, ST, BISHOP

Antoninus Pierozzi was b. in 1389 at Florence and received into the Dominican Order by Bd John Dominici at Fiesole. While still young he was elected prior of the Minerva at Rome and in 1436 founded the friary of San Marco at Florence. In 1446 St Antoninus was made archbishop of that city and, though delicate in health, he ruled with skill and vigour at a time of political crisis; he was a people's prelate, too, loving and caring for the poor and oppressed and beloved in return. Antoninus was a moral theologian of some importance and a writer on local and international law. d. 1459. cd 1523.
May 10, ii, 263.

*ANTONINUS OF SORRENTO, ST, ABBOT

With the bishop of St Catellus he went to live on the mountain now called Monte Angelo, near Ancona, on account of the vision of St Michael that they had there. Later he became abbot of the monastery of St Agrippinus at Sorrento. d. 830. He is said to have been buried within the city wall and to have proved a powerful defence against attack.
February 14, i, 337.

*ANTONY, ST, ABBOT

The patriarch of all monks, called "the Abbot". He was b. in Upper Egypt in 251 and when he was about twenty he gave away all his goods and lived in solitary places in the neighbourhood of his birthplace. When thirty-five he went into the desert and about 305 established a community of hermits in the Fayum and another soon after at Pispir. About 355 he was invited to Alexandria to preach against the Arians, and died in 356 in his hermitage on Mount Kolzim, near the Red Sea. He was 105 years old but in spite of the extraordinary austerity of his life all his faculties were unimpaired and he had suffered no sickness. St Athanasius wrote a biography of St Antony and gives many details of his life and miracles. He was famous throughout Egypt and beyond, and secular rulers and bishops as well as crowds of lesser folk sought him out to consult with him. Though St Antony was not by any means the first Christian recluse, none before him had gathered them together into loose communities, and from the earliest times he was looked on as the father of Christian monasticism. *Antonius.*
January 17, i, 104.

ANTONY BALDINUCCI, BD

He was b. at Florence, and joined the Society of Jesus in 1681. He worked for twenty years among the poor and distressed of Viterbo and Frascati, and his somewhat startling missionary methods bore good fruit. He rarely slept more than three hours and worked without ceasing for the rest of the twenty-four, so that he wore himself out when just over fifty. d. 1717. bd 1893.
November 7, iv, 292.

ANTONY BONFADINI, BD

A confessor of the Friars Minor of the Observance who laboured in the Holy Land. d. 1482. c.c. 1901. *December 1, iv, 460.*

ANTONY CHEVRIER, BD

Fr Antoine-Marie Chevrier was b. in 1826 in Lyons. He served the poor as a priest in the suburbs of the city. Inspired by the Curé d'Ars, he cared for and inspired others to serve poor children. d. 1879. bd October 4, 1986 at the Eurexpo in Lyons. *October 2.*

*ANTONY CLARET, ST, BISHOP

Antony Mary Claret was brought up to the trade of weaving in Spain, but became a secular priest in 1835. Fourteen years later he was mainly instrumental in founding the congregation of Missionary Sons of the Immaculate Heart of Mary ("Claretians"), which spread from Spain to America and elsewhere. Antony was appointed archbishop of Santiago de Cuba, where several attempts were made on his life because of his drastic reforms; in 1857 he was made confessor to

Queen Isabella II and was exiled with her from Spain at the revolution of 1868. He had the gift of prophecy and of the healing of bodies. d. 1870. cd 1950.
October 24, iv, 195.

*ANTONY DANIEL, ST, MARTYR

One of the martyrs of North America (*q.v.*), slain at Teanaustaye on July 4, 1648. He had just finished celebrating Mass when the Iroquois set fire to the wooden church and threw him into the flames. cd 1930.
October 19, iii, 645.

ANTONY DAVELUY, ST,
BISHOP AND MARTYR

Antoine Daveluy was born at Amiens on March 16, 1818. He became a priest of that diocese in 1841, joined the Paris Foreign Missions in 1843, was sent to Korea in 1845 with St Andrew Kim, was consecrated at Seoul on March 25, 1857, and was beheaded on March 30 after his arrest on March 11, 1866. bd. 1968. cd by John Paul II at Seoul in 1984. *March 11.*

ANTONY DELLA CHIESA, BD

Bd Antony was b. in 1395, a collateral ancestor of Pope Benedict XV. He was a Dominican friar and a popular and effective preacher, especially against usury. He had the gift of discernment of spirits. d. 1459. c.c. 1819. *July 28, iii, 204.*

*ANTONY GIANELLI, ST, BISHOP

Born 1789 at Cerreto, near Pavia. As a secular priest he organized a congregation of missioners and another of teaching sisters, "of St Mary of the Garden", and in 1838 was appointed bishop of Bobbio, in which office he gave an example of heroic virtue. d. 1846. cd 1951. *June 7, ii, 500.*

ANTONY GRASSI, BD

He was a priest of the Oratory of Fermo in the Italian Marches, and its superior from 1635 until his death in 1671. An event that had a strong effect on his interior life was being struck by lightning in 1621, but in spite of this nerve-racking experience he was always noted for his unperturbable serenity. Bd Antony had the gift of reading consciences, and he had a way of dealing with people so gentle but effective that his influence extended far beyond his house and parish. Many miracles were attributed to his intercession and he was bd in 1900.
December 13, iv, 554.

ANTONY IXIDA, BD, MARTYR

A Japanese Jesuit who with five Franciscan and Austin friars was tortured for thirty-three days in a vain effort to make him apostatize. They were burned to death in 1632, and bd in 1867. *September 3, ii, 451.*

*ANTONY KAULEAS, ST, BISHOP

He was chosen patriarch of Constantinople in 893, and proved a vigorous and holy hierach in very difficult times. d. *c.* 901. *February 12, i, 317.*

ANTONY LUCCI, BD, BISHOP

Antonio Lucci, b. 1682, was an Italian Franciscan who became bishop of Bovino. He showed exemplary pastoral zeal, was a firm defender of the rights of the poor and defenceless, and led a life of evangelical simplicity and poverty. d. 1752. bd June 18, 1989. *July 25.*

ANTONY MIDDLETON, BD, MARTYR

A secular priest, b. at Middleton Tyas in Yorkshire; h.d.q. at Clerkenwell for his priesthood in 1590. bd 1929. *May 6, ii, 243.*

ANTONY NEYROT, BD, MARTYR

This Antony, Dominican friar, was carried off to Tunis by corsairs; there he apostatized to Islam and took a wife. Within a few months he repented, resumed his preacher's habit, and witnessed to Christ before the Bey of Tunis. He was accordingly put to death, in 1460. c.c. in 1767. *April 10, ii, 64.*

ANTONY PAGE, BD, MARTYR

A secular priest b. Harrow-on-the-Hill, Middlesex. He studied at the English Colleges at Rheims and Rome, was ordained priest in 1591, sent on the English mission and immediately arrested and h.d.q. for high treason at York in 1593 while not yet thirty years of age. bd November 22, 1987. *April 20.*

ANTONY PAVONI, BD, MARTYR

A Dominican friar and inquisitor general for

Liguria and Piedmont. After a vigorous sermon against heresy he was set upon and killed outside the church at Bricherasio, in 1374. c.c. 1856. He was, before his namesake of Padua, invoked for the finding of things lost. *April 9, ii, 61.*

ANTONY PECHERSKY, ST, ABBOT

This Antony was b. near Chernigov in Russia in 983. After living as a hermit on Mount Athos and elsewhere, he settled in a cave by the river Dnieper at Kiev, and was soon joined by others. This was the beginning of the monastery of the Caves (Pecherskaya Lavra) that still exists. Antony was a faithful follower and teacher of the very austere life of the early Egyptian monks. He lived to be ninety years old, and died at Kiev in 1073. *July 10, iii, 65.*

ANTONY PRIMALDI, BD, MARTYR

He was the leader of eight hundred citizens of Otranto, all men, who in a raid by the Turks in 1480 refused to apostatize to Islam in return for safety and were beheaded. Bd Antony was an aged artisan. c.c. 1771. *August 14, iii, 330.*

ANTONY PUCCI, BD

He was b. near Pistoia in 1819 and joined the order of Servites. In 1847 he was made parish priest of Viareggio and spent the rest of his life there, a model pastor. He was one of the pioneers in Italy of the Association for the Propagation of the Faith and of the Association of the Holy Childhood. d. 1892. bd 1952. *January 14, i, 90.*

ANTONY TURNER, BD, MARTYR

One of the Jesuit victims of the Oates "plot". He was the son of a Protestant clergyman, and became a Catholic *c.* 1650. He ministered for seventeen years in Worcestershire, and was h.d.q. at Tyburn in 1679. bd 1929. *June 20, ii, 598.*

*ANTONY ZACCARIA, ST

Antony Mary Zaccaria was b. at Cremona in 1502 and became a secular priest, having originally intended to be a physician. In 1530 he founded a congregation of clerks regular, which in 1522 was approved by Pope Clement VII under the name of Clerks Regular of St Paul, but from their headquarters at the church of St Barnabas at Milan they are commonly called Barnabites. St Antony d., worn out by his unceasing apostolic work, in 1539. cd. 1897. *July 5, iii, 19.*

ANTONY OF AMANDOLA, BD

A friar of the Augustinian order, who d. 1350. His feast is kept by the order and at Ancona. *January 28, i, 191.*

*ANTONY OF LÉRINS, ST

Antony was b. in Lower Pannonia and led an eremitical life in several places north of the Alps; unable to find complete solitude he went into Gaul and became a monk at Lérins, where he d. *c.* 520. *December 28, iv, 628.*

*ANTONY OF PADUA, ST, DOCTOR

This great saint of Italy was by birth a Portuguese, b. at Lisbon in 1195; in 1221 he left the Augustinian canons regular in order to become a Friar Minor. He is one of the most "popular" saints of the Church, with a reputation for retrieving the lost belongings of careless people (*cf.* "...the Lord ... shall place him over all his goods", in the communion verse of the saint's Mass), and he has always been famous as a wonderworker. Whether he was the instrument of miracles during his lifetime has been much discussed; to his contemporaries he was known, as well as for the holiness of his life, as a relentless and eloquent preacher against error and wickedness: he was indeed called the "hammer of heretics". A vision which, according to a late story, he received of the child Jesus is commemorated in all modern images of St Antony. He preached and taught in France as well as in Italy, and we are told that men closed their workshops and offices to go and hear him. He was declared a doctor of the Church in 1947. d. 1231. cd 1232. *June 13, ii, 534.*

ANTONY OF SIENA, BD

Antony de' Patrizi was a holy confessor of the order of Hermit Friars of St Augustine. d. 1311. c.c. 1804. *April 27, ii, 175.*

ANTONY OF STRONCONE, BD

Antony Vici became a Friar Minor of the Observance while very young and for more than ten years was engaged in combating the heretical Fraticelli. The rest of his life was spent in the solitude of the Carceri, near Assisi, where his reputation for virtue was very great. He d. at San Damiano in 1461. c.c. 1687. *February 7, i, 272.*

ANTONY OF TUY, BD, MARTYR

For ten years in the seventeenth century this Spanish Franciscan was a missionary of remarkable zeal in Japan. He was burned alive at Nagasaki on September 8, 1628, after many months of cruel imprisonment. bd 1867. *September 10, ii, 450.*

ANTONY THE PILGRIM, BD

Antony Manzi, or Manzoni, was a member of a good family of Padua who spent most of his life wandering over Europe as a simple pilgrim. On account of this vagabondish behaviour he was not well looked on by his relatives, especially by two sisters who were nuns. d. 1267. *February 1, i, 230.*

ANTONY. *See also under* John of Vilna.

ANUARITE NENGAPETA, BD, VIRGIN AND MARTYR

Sr Anuarite Nengapeta was a Zairian nun who suffered martyrdom in 1964 in defence of her virginity. She was beatified in Kinshasa on August 16, 1985. *December 1.*

*ANYSIA, ST, MARTYR

She is said to have been a young woman of Salonika who was killed by a soldier when she resisted his attempt to drag her to a pagan sacrifice. *December 30, iv, 642.*

*ANYSIUS, ST, BISHOP

He was an early bishop of Salonika, whose virtues were praised by Popes Innocent I and St Leo the Great. d. c. 410. *December 30, iv, 642.*

*APHRAATES, ST

On April 7 the Roman Martyrology mentions a St Aphraates, a hermit in Syria, who opposed Arianism during the reign of the emperor Valens. Efforts have been made to identify him with the Aphraates of whom Theodoret writes. d. c. 345. *April 7, ii, 45.*

*APOLLINARIS, ST, VIRGIN

The heroine of a religious romance who put on boy's clothes and lived undetected as the disciple of one of the saints Macarius in the Egyptian desert. *January 5, i, 33.*

APOLLINARIS FRANCO, BD, MARTYR

He was a Friar Minor, commissary general of his order's mission in Japan, and leader of the Franciscans in the Great Martyrdom of 1622. He was burned at Omura on September 12. bd 1867. *September 10, iii, 533.*

*APOLLINARIS OF RAVENNA, ST, BISHOP AND MARTYR

He was the first bishop and a famous early martyr, but it is not known in what persecution. *July 23, iii, 167.*

*APOLLINARIS OF VALENCE, ST, BISHOP

He was the elder brother of St Avitus of Vienne and became bishop of Valence, of which diocese he is the principal patron under the popular form of his name, "Aplonay". d. c. 520. *October 5, iv, 36.*

*APOLLINARIS THE APOLOGIST, ST, BISHOP

Claudius Apollinaris, bishop of Hierapolis in Phrygia, was a teacher of the second century who was formerly greatly valued, but little is now known of his life and writings. He is called "the Apologist" from the *apologia* for the Christian faith which he addressed to Marcus Aurelius soon after the victory the emperor had gained over the Quadi, at the intercession of the Christians, as is alleged ("The Thundering Legion"). d. c. 179. *January 8, i, 50.*

APOLLO, ST, ABBOT

After being a hermit in the Thebaïd for many years he became at a great age abbot over numerous monks at Hermopolis; many astonishing miracles are recorded of him. d. c. 395. *January 25, i, 165.*

*APOLLONIA, ST, VIRGIN AND MARTYR

This aged deaconess of Alexandria died by

fire in the year 249. She is invoked against toothache, presumably because her teeth were knocked out by the heathen mob. *February 7, i, 286.*

*APOLLONIUS THE APOLOGIST, ST, MARTYR

Apollonius, a Roman senator, was denounced as a Christian by one of his own slaves; an authentic account of his examination by the magistrate was discovered in an Armenian text in 1874: it includes the *apologia* for Christianity from which the martyr gets his name. He was beheaded, *c.* 185. *April 18, ii, 119.*

APOLLONIUS. *See also under* Philemon.

APPHIA. *See under* Philemon.

*APPHIAN AND THEODOSIA, SS, MARTYRS

He was martyred at Caesarea in 306 for trying to prevent the magistrate from offering public sacrifice to the heathen gods. Theodosia was a Tyrian girl cruelly put to death at the same place and about the same time. *April 2, ii, 13.*

APULEIUS. *See under* Marcellus.

*AQUILA AND PRISCA, SS, MARTYRS

Aquila and his wife Prisca were disciples of St Paul who are mentioned in the *Acts of the Apostles* and elsewhere in the New Testament. There is a tradition that they were eventually martyred in Rome. *July 8, iii, 38.*

AQUILINA, ST, MARTYR

A young girl of Byblus in Syria who was martyred at the end of the third century; she was formerly greatly venerated in the East but the account of her passion cannot be relied on. *June 13, ii, 538.*

*AQUILINUS, ST, BISHOP

After forty years in the service of Clovis II he retired with his wife to Evreux and became bishop there; it is said that he sought to live rather as a hermit than a bishop. d. *c.* 695. *October 19, iv, 150.*

ARAGHT. *See* Attracta.

*ARBOGAST, ST, BISHOP

Great uncertainty surrounds the life of St Arbogast, who was a bishop of Strasburg in the sixth century. *Arbogastus. July 21, iii, 158.*

*ARCADIUS, ST, MARTYR

A martyr in some city of Mauritania in Africa, perhaps under Diocletian. The extant account of his passion is not reliable. *January 12, i, 70.*

*ARCADIUS, ST, MARTYR

Arcadius and four other Spaniards (one of them a boy, Paulillus) were martyrs of the Arian Vandal persecution, suffering death in North Africa in 437. *November 13, iv, 328.*

ARCHANGELA GIRLANI, BD, VIRGIN

Born in Trino in Italy in 1460 and became a Carmelite at Parma. She was a model of every religious virtue, and was sent at the wish of the Gonzagas to found a Carmel at Mantua, where she d. in 1494. c.c. 1864. *February 13, i, 327.*

ARCHANGELO OF BOLOGNA, BD

Archangelo Canetuli was an Augustinian canon regular at Gubbio who was conspicuous for his holy life, prophetical gifts, and spirit of brotherly love. d. 1513. *April 16, ii, 106.*

ARCHANGELO OF CALATAFIMI, BD

He was a hermit in Sicily and afterwards a promoter of the Observant branch of the Franciscan Order in that island. d. 1460. c.c. 1836. *July 30, iii, 214.*

*ARCHELAUS, ST, BISHOP

He was said to be bishop of Kashkar in Mesopotamia in the third century, but was probably a literary fiction in a writing against Manicheism. *December 26, iv, 618.*

*ARDALION, ST, MARTYR

One of several martyrs at different times who are said to have been converted while ridiculing Christianity on the stage; *c.* 300. *April 14, ii, 91.*

ARDO, ST, ABBOT

He followed St Benedict of Aniane in the abbacy of that monastery, and wrote a biography of his predecessor. He was venerated at Aniane and an office sung in his honour. d. 843. *March 7, i, 516.*

ARÈGLE. *See* Agricola.

ARETAS. *See* Najran, Martyrs of.

ARIALDO, BD, MARTYR

A Milanese deacon who led a reform party against simony and other abuses during the eleventh century, and fell victim to the violence of his enemies in 1066. c.c. 1094. *June 27, ii, 549.*

ARMEL, ABBOT

Armel (also *Ermel, Arthmael, Ermin,* etc) was said to be a Welshman who went over into Brittany and founded the monasteries of Saint-Armel-des-Bochaux and Ploërmel. d. c. 570. *August 16, iii, 337.*

*ARMOGASTES, ST, MARTYR

Armogastes was an official under the Vandal Genseric who, at the same time as SS Archinimus and Saturus, suffered greatly at the hands of the Arians. They all died soon after, *c.* 455, and are accounted martyrs. *March 29, i, 698.*

ARNOLD, BD, ABBOT

He was abbot of St Justina's at Padua and was persecuted by the tyrant Ezzelino da Romano, who kept him in prison eight years until his death in 1254 at the age of seventy. *Arnoldus. March 14.*

ARNOLD JANSSEN, BD

Arnold Janssen was born at Gogh, in the diocese of Münster, Germany, on November 5, 1837. He was ordained priest in 1861. In 1875 he started a missionary magazine: "The Little Messenger of the Heart of Jesus". In 1875 he founded in the Netherlands the first German house for training members of what became, in 1886, the missionary Society of the Divine Word. He was elected superior-general in 1885 and d. on January 15, 1909. bd October 19, 1975. *January 15.*

*ARNULF OF METZ, ST. BISHOP

In French, *Arnoul.* He was a high official at the Austrasian court and his son married a daughter of Bd Pepin of Landen. About 610 Arnulf became bishop of Metz and chief counsellor of Clotaire of Neustria. His last years were spent in a hermitage in the Vosges with St Romaric. d. *c.* 643. *Arnulphus. July 18, iii, 139.*

*ARNULF OF SOISSONS, ST, BISHOP

He was abbot of Saint-Médard and then bishop of Soissons. He founded the abbey of Aldenburg in Flanders, where he d. in 1087. *August 15, iii, 335.*

ARNULF OF VILLERS, BD

A confessor of the Cistercian Order, who was a lay brother of very mortified and charitable life at Villers in Belgium. d. 1228. *June 30, ii, 679.*

ARRAS, MARTYRS OF. *See* Madeleine Fontaine.

*ARSACIUS, ST

He was a soldier in the Roman army who was persecuted for the Faith and became a hermit at Nicomedia. He d. during the great earthquake in 358, which he had foretold. *August 16, iii, 336.*

*ARSENIUS, ST

Called "the Great", "the Roman", or "the Deacon". As these names suggest, he was a deacon of the city of Rome, and he was made tutor to Arcadius and Honorius, the sons of the Emperor Theodosius I. From Constantinople in 393 he retired to the desert of Skete, and spent the rest of his life as a solitary in various places in Egypt; early writers about him all emphasize his gift of tears ("weeping over the feebleness of Arcadius and the foolishness of Honorius"). Arsenius d. at the Rock of Troë near Memphis, *c.* 449. *July 19, iii, 146.*

ARTALDUS, ST. BISHOP

He was a Carthusian monk, first at Portes and then at Valromey, in Savoy; when over eighty he was called to be bishop of Belley. Here he was visited by St Hugh of Lincoln.

d. 1206. c.c. 1834. In France he is called *Arthaud*. *October 7, iv, 52.*

ARTEMAS, ST, MARTYR

This martyr is supposed to have suffered at Pozzuoli, near Capua, where he was venerated in former times. Date unknown. *January 25, i, 164.*

*ARTEMIUS, ST, MARTYR

He seems to have been a veteran of the Roman army at Constantinople who was sent as prefect to Egypt; here he took strong measures against the pagans and accordingly when Julian the Apostate came to the throne he was beheaded, in 363. Artemius was an Arian and a persecutor of the orthodox, nor is there any record of his adjuring the heresy, but his identity with the martyr of that name is not certain. *October 20, iv, 155.*

ARTHELAIS, ST, VIRGIN

She is alleged to have been a young girl who fled from Constantinople to Benevento to avoid the attentions of the Emperor Justinian, but the extant record of her life is not trustworthy. *March 3, i, 467.*

*ASAPH, ST, BISHOP

Asaph was said to be the first bishop at Llanelwy, North Wales, where the cathedral city of Saint Asaph now stands. Seventh century. His feast is kept in the diocese of Menevia. *Asaphus. May 11, ii, 271.*

*ASCLAS, ST, MARTYR

A martyr in Egypt, in the third (?) century, formerly very famous. *January 23, i, 152.*

ASICUS, ST, BISHOP

Asicus (Tassach), a coppersmith, was one of the earliest followers of St Patrick. d. *c.* 470. His feast is kept throughout Ireland as having been the first bishop at Elphin. *April 27, ii, 171.*

ASTERIUS, ST, BISHOP

He was bishop of Amasea in Asia Minor and was a preacher of considerable power; twenty-one of his sermons are still in existence. d. *c.* 410. *October 30, i, 221.*

ASTERIUS. *See also under* Claudius.

ASTRIK, ST, BISHOP

Or *Anastasius*. He was probably a monk from Brevnov in Bohemia and first abbot of Pannonhalma in Hungary, being associated with King St Stephen in his work of evangelization. He became first archbishop of the Hungarians. d. *c.* 1040. *November 12, iv, 325.*

ASTYRIUS. *See under* Marinus.

*ATHANASIA, ST

She was widowed a few days after her marriage but married again. After a time her second husband wished to become a monk and Athanasia turned her own house into a convent and ruled it as abbess. The last seven years of her life were passed in a cell at Constantinople as adviser to the empress Theodora. d. 860. *August 14, iii, 329.*

ATHANASIA. *See also under* Andronicus.

*ATHANASIUS, ST,
BISHOP AND DOCTOR

Born at Alexandria *c.* 297. The title St Athanasius earned for himself, "Father of Orthodoxy", and the common saying "Athanasius against the world" indicate his life: he was the champion of Christian orthodoxy against Arianism from the day that, while still a deacon, he defended the deity of Jesus Christ at the Council of Nicaea. He was elected bishop of Alexandria in 328 and during an episcopate of over forty years he was five times driven into exile by heretics and politicians, spending a total of seventeen years away from his see, but never flagged in using all his powers—one of which was a humorous wit that was not always gentle—in support of the Catholic faith. d. 373. Athanasius is one of the four great Greek Doctors of the Universal Church. *May 2, ii, 212.*

*ATHANASIUS OF NAPLES, ST,
BISHOP

He was appointed to the see of Naples at the age of eighteen in 850 and after he had ruled it for twenty years he was driven into exile by his nephew Sergius, duke of Naples. During the troubles that followed Athanasius d. at Veroli in 872. *July 15, iii, 109.*

ATHANASIUS THE ATHONITE, ST,
ABBOT

Or "of Trebizond", from the place of his birth c. 920. He was a monk in Bithynia but migrated to Mount Athos and there in 961 founded the first monastery proper ("Laura") in what has ever since been a wholly monastic republic. Athanasius was opposed by the solitaries already living there, but he had the support of the emperors, and at his death through an accident c. 1000 was the superior-general of nearly sixty communities of hermits and monks on the Holy Mountain. St Athanasius is named in the preparatory part of the Byzantine eucharistic Liturgy. *July 5, iii, 20.*

*ATHENOGENES, ST,
BISHOP AND MARTYR

An Armenian bishop whom St Basil praises for his writings. He was martyred c. 305. *July 16, iii, 116.*

ARTHUR BELL, BD, MARTYR

Arthur (Francis) Bell OFM was a secular priest b. at Temple Broughton near Worcester in 1590. He studied at St Omer and the English College, Valladolid. He was ordained, became a Franciscan, and returned to England in 1632 and again in 1634. He was arrested at Stevenage on November 6, 1643 and h.d.q. at Tyburn aged fifty-four. bd November 22, 1987. *December 11.*

*ATTALAS, ST, ABBOT

A Burgundian monk who accompanied St Columban from Luxeuil to Bobbio. Attalas played a principal part in the founding of Bobbio and was its second abbot; he had great trouble with the monks, many of whom found the rule too severe and left, spreading false stories about the abbot. d. 627. *March 10, i, 547.*

*ATTALUS, ST, MARTYR

A Roman citizen and man of distinction, one of the martyrs of Lyons (q.v.). When he was being roasted alive he remarked, "This is indeed a consuming of flesh, and it is *you* who do it"—a reference to the charge of cannibalism so often brought against the early Christians. *June 2, ii, 456.*

*ATTICUS, ST, BISHOP

He was intruded as bishop of Constantinople during the second banishment of St John Chrysostom, but repented of his opposition to that saint and lived a holy life till his death in 425. He occurs in the *Acta Sanctorum* on January 8. *October 10.*

*ATTILANUS, ST, BISHOP

He was a disciple of St Froilan and became bishop of Zamora in Spain. Tenth century. *October 3, iv, 18.*

ATTRACTA, ST, VIRGIN

Attracta (*Araght*) was a solitary, first at Killaraght, on Lough Gara, and then at Drum, near Boyle, during the sixth (?) century. Her feast is kept throughout Ireland. *August 11, iii, 304.*

AUBERT OF AVRANCHES, ST,
BISHOP

He was made bishop of Cambrai in 633 and was notable for his encouragement of monasticism. d. c. 669. *December 13, iv, 551.*

*AUBIERGE. *See* Ethelburga.

AUBIN. *See* Albinus of Angers.

AUDIFAX. *See under* Marius.

*AUDOENUS, ST, BISHOP

In French *Ouen*. While a layman and chancellor at the court of King Dagobert I he founded the abbey of Rebais; later he was ordained, and in 641 was made archbishop of Rouen. For forty-three years he played an active part in ecclesiastical and civil affairs, and was very zealous against simony and other abuses. d. 684. *August 24, iii, 393.*

AUDOMARUS. *See* Omer *and* Othmar.

AUDREY. *See* Etheldreda.

AUGUSTINA PIETRANTONI, BD,
VIRGIN AND MARTYR

Livia Pietrantoni was b. at Pozzaglia Sabina, Italy, into a poor peasant family on March 27, 1864. She joined the Sisters of Charity of St Joan Antida Thouret in 1886 as Sr Agostina. On November 13, 1894 she was murdered in the Holy Spirit Hospital in Rome (where she had worked for seven years) by a TB patient in her care who had been expelled from the hospital for misbehaviour and improper advances to her. bd November 12, 1972. *November 13.*

*AUGUSTINE, ST, BISHOP AND DOCTOR

Born at Thagaste in North Africa in 354. In spite of the influence of his mother St Monica he lived until the age of thirty-two a life defiled morally by licence and intellectually by Manicheism. After a great inward struggle he was converted at Milan, baptized by St Ambrose, and returned to Africa, where he established a sort of monastery. In 396 he became bishop of Hippo. Augustine was the greatest of the Latin Fathers and his teaching is profoundly influential still; he refuted the heresy he had formerly held; and by his establishment of communities of priests and of women he became the father of countless canons, friars, and other religious. He preached almost every day and his sermons are frequently read in the Divine Office. During his thirty-five years as bishop Augustine had always to be opposing one heresy or another: Manicheism, the Priscillianists, the Donatists, Pelagianism, the Arian Vandals; he was one of the most outstanding intellects of history and one of the best-regarded men, for he is known by his own "Confessions". This and the *De Civitate Dei* are the most famous of his written works. d. 430. *Augustinus.*
August 28, iii, 426.

AUGUSTINE NOVELLO, BD

As Matthew of Taormina in Sicily he was chancellor to King Manfred and was left for dead on the battlefield of Benevento. He recovered from his wounds and became an Augustinian friar under the name of Augustine Novello; he helped to draft new constitutions for the order, became its prior general, and was appointed papal penitentiary and legate. The last nine years of his life he spent as a solitary. d. 1309. bd 1759. *May 19, ii, 353.*

AUGUSTINE WEBSTER, ST, MARTYR

One of the five protomartyrs of the Reformation in England and one of the three first Carthusian martyrs (*q.v.*), all of whom were priors of houses, Webster of Axholme in Lincolnshire. He was h.d.q. at Tyburn on May 4, 1535. *May 4, ii, 277.*

AUGUSTINE OF BIELLA, BD

He was a confessor of the Dominican Order, who d. 1493. c.c. 1872. *July 24, iii, 180.*

*AUGUSTINE, OR AUSTIN, OF CANTERBURY, ST, BISHOP

With other monks of St Andrew's on the Coelian Hill Augustine was sent by Pope St Gregory the Great to evangelize the English and strengthen what remained of the British church. They landed at Ebbsfleet in 597, and Augustine eventually established his episcopal see at Canterbury. He made considerable progress in converting the southern English, but failed entirely with the British Christians, whom he seems to have handled clumsily and overbearingly. d. *c.* 605. As the apostle of the English his feast is kept in England on May 26 (in the general calendar, May 28); he was formerly generally called *Austin* in English. *May 27, ii, 407.*

AUGUSTINE OF LUCERA, BD, BISHOP

Augustine Gazotich was a Dominican from Dalmatia who preached among the southern Slavs and Magyars and in 1303 became bishop of Zagreb in Croatia. Later he was translated to the see of Lucera in Italy. Bd Augustine had the gift of healing to a marked degree. d. 1323. c.c. 1702. *August 3, iii, 255.*

AUGUSTINE. *See also* Eystein.

AUGUSTUS CHAPDELAINE, BD, MARTYR

Born in France in 1814, ninth child of a peasant. After being a country curate he went as a missionary to China. After some years of devoted work he was tortured and put to death most barbarously in 1856, the required ransom of 300 taels not being forthcoming. bd 1900. *February 27, i, 364.*

AUGUSTUS SCHÖFFLER, ST, MARTYR

A priest of the Paris Society of Foreign Missions who was martyred by beheading in Vietnam in 1851. bd 1900. cd June 19, 1988. *May 1, iv, 282.*

AUNACHARIUS, ST, BISHOP

In French, *Aunaire*. He became bishop of Auxerre in 561 and was one of the most influential and respected bishops of his time in France. He enacted some very interesting disciplinary canons, throwing light on current popular abuses. d. 605. *September 25, iii, 634.*

AUREA, ST, VIRGIN

A solitary at the convent of San Millán, above the Upper Ebro in the diocese of Calahorra, Spain. d. *c.* 1100. *March 11, i, 563.*

*AURELIAN, ST, BISHOP

He became bishop of Arles in 546, and founded two religious houses there. He wrote to Pope Vigilius asking for an explanation of his qualified condemnation of the "Three Chapters". d. 551. *Aurelianus. June 16, ii, 554.*

AURELIUS, ST, BISHOP

He became bishop of Carthage in about 392 and had to oppose both the Donatists and the Pelagian heresy, in which he was notably mild and conciliatory; he was a close friend of St Augustine. d. 429. *July 20, iii, 153.*

*AURELIUS AND NATALIA, SS, MARTYRS

They were a Hispano-Moorish couple of good family at Toledo, who at the time of Moorish persecution openly professed the Christian faith; together with other martyrs they were beheaded *c.* 852. *July 27, iii, 196.*

AUSTIN. *See* Augustine.

*AUSTREBERTA, ST, VIRGIN

Daughter of St Framechildis and the count palatine Badefrid. She became abbess of Port (Abbeville) and had then to undertake the reform of the abbey of Pavilly, in the course of which she was denounced to its founder, Amalbert, who threatened her life. But she continued her work unafraid and remained abbess of Pavilly until her death in 704. *February 10, i, 294.*

*AUSTREGISILUS, ST, BISHOP

Abbot of Saint-Nizier at Lyons and then bishop of Bourges. d. 624. In France he is called *Outril. May 20, ii, 358.*

*AUSTREMONIUS, ST, BISHOP

Nothing certain is known of this saint except that he was a missionary in Auvergne (perhaps in the fourth century) where, as "St Stremoine", he is venerated as the first bishop of Clermont. *November 1, iv, 236.*

AUSTRUDE. *See* Anstrudis.

*AUXENTIUS, ST

A Persian soldier in the guards of the emperor Theodosius the Younger; he became a hermit in Bithynia. Sozomen writes of his purity of life and steadfast faith. d. 473. *February 14, i, 335.*

AVERTINUS, ST

In the diocese of Tours Avertinus is venerated as a Gilbertine canon who was deacon to St Thomas Becket during his exile; afterwards he was a solitary in Touraine. There is no reason to suppose that the hermit Avertinus had anything to do with the Gilbertine Order or with St Thomas. d. 1180 (?). *May 5, ii, 239.*

AVITUS, ST, ABBOT

An abbot in the French province of Perche of whom no certain information is forthcoming. d. 530 (?). *June 17, ii, 564.*

*AVITUS OF VIENNE, ST, BISHOP

Avitus succeeded his father Isychius as bishop of Vienne in 490 and lived respected by both Christians and heathen. He left a number of written works, most of which are lost. His contemporaries refer to his learning and love of the poor. d. *c.* 525. *February 5, i, 256.*

AYBERT, ST

He was a monk and hermit in the diocese of Tournai, one of whose devotional practices is of significance in the debate concerning the origins of the rosary. d. 1140. *April 7, ii, 47.*

B

*BABYLAS, ST, BISHOP AND MARTYR

The most celebrated of the early bishops of Antioch after St Ignatius. St John Chrysostom praised him and St Aldhelm of Sherborne wrote an account of him in prose and verse. He was martyred *c.* 250. *January 24, i, 160.*

BADEMUS, ST, ABBOT

Bademus was founder and abbot of a monastery near Bethlapat in Persia; during the persecution by Sapor II he was killed by an apostate by order of the king, 376. *April 10, ii, 61.*

BAGNUS, ST, BISHOP

In French, *Bain.* A monk of Fontenelle who became bishop of Thérouanne, whence he evangelized the Pas de Calais. He is the patron of the town of Calais. d. *c.* 710. *June 20, ii, 589.*

BAIRRE. *See* Finbar.

*BALBINA, ST, VIRGIN

A Roman maiden of early days about whom nothing is known. *March 31, i, 707.*

*BALDOMERUS, ST

Otherwise *Galmier.* A locksmith who in the seventh century was famous at Lyons for his goodness, and was at length persuaded to enter a monastery. d. *c.* 660. *February 27, i, 433.*

BALRED, ST

Or *Balther.* An anchorite who lived on the Bass Rock and elsewhere in ancient Northumbria. He was venerated at Durham together with another anchorite, St Bilfrid. Eighth century. *March 6, i, 502.*

BALTHASAR OF CHIAVARI, BD

He was a Friar Minor and a fellow preacher with Bd Bernardino of Feltre, venerated in the diocese of Pavia. d. 1492. c.c. 1930. *October 25, iv, 201.*

BAPTIST SPAGNUOLO, BD

This Carmelite possessed the gift of counsel to such a degree that he was six successive times elected vicar general of the friars at Mantua. Eventually he was made prior general of the order, an office he discharged with the same tact and success as the lesser one. Bd Baptist wrote over 50,000 lines of Latin verse, mostly with a specifically religious intention. d. 1516. bd 1885. *Baptista. March 20, i, 649.*

BAPTISTA VARANI, BD, VIRGIN

She was daughter of a lord of Camerino and, after leading the ordinary life of the world at her father's court, became a Poor Clare at Urbino in 1481. At once she had mystical revelations concerning the Passion which she embodied in a book called *I Dolori mentali di Gesù,* which contributed to the evolution of devotion to the Sacred Heart. After being transferred to the convent at Camerino she received other extraordinary graces, which she wrote down in obedience to her confessor. Her "instructions" on the spiritual life are marked by humour and common sense. d. 1527. c.c. 1843. *June 8, ii, 497.*

BARACHISIUS. *See* Jonas.

BARBASYMAS, ST,
BISHOP AND MARTYR

A metropolitan of Seleucia-Ctesiphon who in the persecution by the Persians under Sapor II was imprisoned and tortured, and eventually put to death with a number of companions in 346. *January 14, i, 82.*

*BARBATUS, ST, BISHOP

Bishop of Benevento, which diocese was sunk in paganism and indifference. He laboured in it for nineteen years to complete the work of reclamation he had begun there as a priest. d. 682. *February 19, i, 375.*

BARDO, ST, BISHOP

Abbot of Kaiserswerth and of Horsfeld and then, in 1031, archbishop of Mainz. At a time when great prelates were far too much concerned with temporal affairs St Bardo's interests were always primarily spiritual, and he was loved and trusted by his flock accordingly. His recreation was an aviary of rare birds. d. 1053. *June 15, ii, 549.*

BARHADBESABA, ST, MARTYR

He was deacon of the town of Arbela in Persia and was beheaded during the persecution of Sapor II, in 355. *July 15, iii, 107.*

*BARLAAM, ST, MARTYR

He was a martyr at Antioch, almost certainly identical with the "Barula" associated with St Romanus (November 18); his *acta* are spurious. *November 19, iv, 392.*

*BARLAAM AND JOSAPHAT, SS

"SS Barlaam and Josaphat" (Joseph) never existed. Their legend is a Christianized version of that of Siddartha Buddha; there has come down to us, embedded in it, the text of the apology for Christianity of Aristidea the Athenian. *November 27, iv, 432.*

BARLAAM OF KHUTYN, ST, ABBOT

A Russian (Varlaam) of Novgorod who became a hermit at Kutyn on the Volga and there founded the monastery of the Transfiguration. d. 1193. *November 6, iv, 277.*

*BARNABAS, ST, APOSTLE

"He was a good man, full of the Holy Ghost and of faith" (Acts xi, 24) and, following the example of St Paul, the Church has always numbered him among the Apostles because, although he was not one of the Twelve, he was divinely set apart to accompany St Paul on his missionary journeys. He is said to have been martyred in Cyprus, and is named in the Roman canon. *June 11, ii, 522.*

*BARONTIUS, ST

In middle age he retired with his son to the abbey of Lonrey and afterwards became a hermit near Pistoia. d. *c.* 695 (?). *March 25, i, 677.*

*BARSABAS, ST, MARTYR

It is said that Barsabas was a martyr in Persia under Sapor II, that he was an abbot, and that his monks suffered at the same time. But he is probably the same person as St Simeon Barsabae. *December 11, iv, 538.*

*BARSANUPHIUS, ST

He was an anchorite at Gaza, greatly revered in the East. d. *c.* 550. *April 11, ii, 70.*

*BARSIMAEUS, ST, BISHOP

Possibly a bishop of Edessa in the middle of the third century; the story of his martyrdom under Trajan has been exploded. *January 30, i, 203.*

*BARTHOLOMEA CAPITANIO, ST,
VIRGIN

Before her death at the age of 26, St Bartholomea had founded the congregation of the Sisters of Charity of Lovere, with St Vincentia Gerosa; she also left a considerable body of spiritual writings. d. 1833. cd 1950. *July 26, iii, 191.*

*BARTHOLOMEW, ST, APOSTLE

Beyond his existence as one of the Twelve, nothing is certainly known of this apostle: many scholars identify him with Nathaniel. The stories of his missionary activity in India and martyrdom in Armenia are not reliable. *Bartholomaeus. August 24, iii, 391.*

BARTHOLOMEW LONGO, BD

Bartolo Longo was a Dominican tertiary and founded the Daughters of St Rosario of Pompei. He was noted for his devotion to our Lady and his charitable work. d. 1905. bd October 26, 1980. *March 11.*

BARTHOLOMEW ROE. *See* Alban Roe.

BARTHOLOMEW OF CERVERE, BD, MARTYR

He was killed by heretics at Cervere while performing the duties of inquisitor in Piedmont in 1466. c.c. by Pius IX.
April 22, ii, 148.

BARTHOLOMEW OF FARNE, ST

A native of Whitby in Yorkshire who was ordained priest in Norway, became a monk of Durham, and spent forty-two years as a hermit on Farne Island; here he occupied St Cuthbert's old cell and his peaceful life was interrupted only by an unfortunate incident with a fellow hermit who implied a doubt about the genuineness of Bartholomew's abstemiousness. d. 1193. *June 24, ii, 634.*

*BARTHOLOMEW OF GROTTAFERRATA, ST, ABBOT

He was the fourth abbot of the Greek monastery of Grottaferrata, near Rome; he was its lesser founder, carrying through the work begun by St Nilus. d. 1055.
November 11, iv, 318.

BARTHOLOMEW OF MANTUA, BD

Bartholomew Fanti was a confessor of the Carmelite Order who lived and d. at Mantua, where he was famed for miracles of healing. d. 1495. c.c. 1909. *December 5, iv, 502.*

BARTHOLOMEW OF MONTEPULCIANO, BD

After many years of married life, Bartholomew Pucci-Franceschi became a Franciscan friar at Montepulciano and a "fool for Christ's sake". d. 1330. c.c. 1880.
May 23, ii, 379.

BARTHOLOMEW OF SAN GIMIGNANO, BD

Bartolo Buonpedoni, after being a lay servant in a Benedictine monastery, became a secular priest and Franciscan tertiary; he was appointed to the parish of Peccioli, near Volterra, where he contracted leprosy or a similar disease in 1280. He thereupon went to a leper hospital, of which he was made master, and spent twenty years ministering to his fellow sufferers with infinite patience. d. 1200. c.c. 1910. *December 14, iv, 560.*

BARTHOLOMEW OF VICENZA, BD, BISHOP

Bartholomew Breganza received the Preachers' habit from St Dominic and in 1233 founded at Bologna an association for the preservation of peace and public order (the "Fratres Gaudentes") which spread throughout Italy. He was made a bishop in Cyprus and in 1256 translated to Vicenza, where he was greatly venerated by the people. d. 1271. c.c. 1793. *October 23, iv, 186.*

BARULA. *See under* Romanus.

*BASIL OF ANCYRA, ST, MARTYR

After an unwearying confession of the true faith against the Arians, the priest Basil was put to death in 362 for opposing the emperor Julian the Apostate. *March 22, i, 658.*

*BASIL THE GREAT, ST, BISHOP AND DOCTOR

Born at Caesarea in Cappadocia in 329, son of saints and grandson of a martyr. Basil studied at Constantinople and Athens, visited the monasteries of the Near East and established the first monastery in Asia Minor, on the River Iris in Pontus. In 370 he was appointed to the see of Caesarea and proved to be one of the greatest of all bishops. He defended his huge province against the Arian heresy and defied the emperor in the process, wrote doctrinal works, numerous letters and homilies used in the Divine Office, and founded a hospital for the sick poor. St Basil's influence as a monk ranks in importance with that of St Benedict: he is regarded as the father of all Eastern monks, though his "rule" is ascetical rather than legislative. He was one of the greatest of preachers and the Council of Chalcedon referred to him as "the minister of grace who has expounded truth to the whole earth": in the East he is the first of the Three Holy Hierarchs, in the West one of the Four Greek Doctors. d. January 1, 349. *Basilius.*
January 2, ii, 539.

BASIL THE YOUNGER, ST

A hermit near Constantinople, who was tortured by the imperial officers on suspicion of being a spy. He was a hundred years old at his death in 952. *March 26, i, 688.*

*BASILISSA AND ANASTASIA, SS, MARTYRS

They are popularly supposed to be two Roman women who removed the bodies of SS Peter and Paul and had them buried, later suffering martyrdom themselves. But their existence is very doubtful. *April 15, ii, 98.*

BASILISSA. *See also under* Julian (January 9).

*BASILLA, ST, VIRGIN AND MARTYR

A maiden who suffered martyrdom for Christ in Rome in 304. She is said to have broken off her engagement to the patrician Pompeius at her baptism. *May 20, ii, 537.*

*BASOLUS, ST

Basolus (Basle) was a monk and hermit at Verzy in Champagne to whom many miracles were attributed. d. *c.* 620. His disciple St Sindulf is also named in the Roman Martyrology. *November 26, iv, 425.*

*BATHILDIS, ST

Bathildis was an English slave girl who became the wife of King Clovis II and mother of three kings, Clotaire III, Childeric II and Thierry III. For eight years she was regent of France, taking St Eligius as her adviser, putting down slavery, and restoring monasteries. When Clotaire came of age she entered the convent of Chelles as a simple nun and d. there in 680. Her biography was written by a contemporary. *January 30, i, 204.*

*BAUDELIUS, ST, MARTYR

Little is known of St Baudelius except that he suffered for Christ at Nîmes in the early centuries. *May 20, ii, 357.*

*BAVO, ST

Bavo, or Allowin, patron of the dioceses of Ghent and of Haarlem, was a famous hermit in Brabant. He was a nobleman who, after having led a very irregular life, became a widower, was converted by St Amand, and eventually led a solitary life in various places near Ghent and Liège. d. *c.* 655. *October 1, iv, 5.*

*BEAN, ST, BISHOP

The Roman Martyrology makes mention on December 16 of a St Bean, bishop in Ireland. The diocese of Aberdeen keeps the feast of St Bean, bishop of Mortlach at the beginning of the eleventh century, on October 26. *Beanus. October 26, iv, 206.*

BEATRICE D'ESTE, BD

This Beatrice was a niece of the following. She was a Benedictine nun at Ferrara, probably after having been married and widowed. d. 1262. c.c. 1774. *Beatrix. January 18, i, 116.*

BEATRICE D'ESTE, BD, VIRGIN

She was left an orphan at the age of six and her relatives tried to use her for the aggrandizement of the family by arranging a marriage; Beatrice fled secretly and became a Benedictine nun, dying at the age of twenty in 1226. Her shrine is at Padua. c.c. 1763. *May 10, ii, 267.*

BEATRICE DA SILVA, BD, VIRGIN

Beatrice ("Brites") da Silva was b. in Portugal in 1424 and left the court of Isabel of Castile to found the Congregation of the Immaculate Conception ("Conceptionists") at Toledo; the institute still exists in Spain, Italy, and elsewhere. d. 1490. c.c. 1926. *August 18, iii, 350.*

BEATRICE OF ORNACIEU, BD, VIRGIN

Bd Beatrice was a Carthusian nun of Parménie, of very austere life, who had numerous supernatural visions and manifestations. She was one of the earliest to practise prayer before the Blessed Sacrament. Late in life she was sent with other nuns to make a new foundation at the house called Eymeu and there she d. November 25, 1309. c.c. 1869. *February 13, i, 323.*

BEATRICE. *See also under* Simplicius.

BEATUS OF LIEBANA, ST

A priest from Asturias who opposed the

adoptionist errors of Elipandus of Toledo and was denounced as "a vagabond mountaineer who dared to set himself up against the archbishop of Toledo and the Church". He wrote a book against Elipandus in reply. Beatus also wrote a commentary on the Apocalypse, which still exists. d. c. 798. *February 19, i, 376.*

*BEATUS OF LUNGERN, ST

A hermit, supposedly early but of uncertain date, of Beatenberg above the lake of Thun, who is venerated as the apostle of Switzerland. On May 9 another St Beatus, who has better claims to historical authenticity, is honoured at Vendôme. *May 9, ii, 259.*

*BEDE THE VENERABLE, ST,
DOCTOR

The Venerable Bede, the only doctor of the Church of English birth, was b. at Wearmouth in 673. From an early age he was brought up at, and all his life lived in, the monastery of that town and the adjoining abbey of Jarrow. Bede was trained under St Benedict Biscop, ordained by St John of Beverley, and was always a simple and busy monk, a model of stability and detachment. He is best known as the author of the *Ecclesiastical History of the English People*, but the Bible was his principal study and he wrote on many and varied subjects; extracts from his homilies are read in the Divine Office of the Western church. d. 735. *Beda. May 25, ii, 401.*

BEGA, ST, VIRGIN

Bega or Bee, is said to have been a seventh-century Irish maiden who established a nunnery on the promontory in Northumberland now called after her, St Bee's Head. She seems not to be the same as either the Begu or the Heiu mentioned by Bede, but the whole matter is very confused and uncertain. The feast of St Bega is kept in the diocese of Lancaster. *September 6, ii, 498.*

*BEGGA, ST

She was a sister of St Gertrude of Nivelles and spent most of her long life as a nobleman's wife "in the world". On becoming a widow in 691 she established and ruled over a convent at Andenne on the Meuse. d. 693. *December 17, iv, 579.*

*BENEDICT, ST, ABBOT

Born at Nurcia in Umbria c. 480. While a young man he fled from the licence of Rome and lived as a hermit at Subiaco; disciples gathered round, and about 530 he founded the monastery of Monte Cassino, for whose monks he wrote the rule that bears his name. That rule spread throughout Europe and became the norm for all Western monks; its followers taught the barbarians to work with hands and head, and to pray: but Benedict himself lived and legislated for those things immediately at hand—the formation of communities for the glory of God and the salvation of souls called to the cenobitical life. The little that is known about St Benedict personally mostly comes from the second book of St Gregory's *Dialogues,* where he appears as a man who was as lovable as he was great. As St Basil is Patriarch of the Monks of the East, so is St Benedict of those of the West—and the father of western Europe as well. He was never a priest. d. c. 547. *Benedictus. July 11, i, 650.*

*BENEDICT II, ST, POPE

This Benedict, a Roman, was elected to the apostolic throne in 684 but d. in the following year. During his pontificate of eleven months he upheld the cause of St Wilfrid of York. *May 8, ii, 252.*

*BENEDICT, XI, BD, POPE

Benedict was the ninth master general of the Dominicans, being then known as Nicholas Boccasini, and as cardinal bishop of Ostia and papal legate he played a conspicuous part in the troubles between Pope Boniface VIII and King Philip IV of France. He was himself elected pope in 1303 but d. in the following year. In his private life he continued the austerity and simplicity of a friar. bd. 1736. *July 7, iii, 35.*

*BENEDICT BISCOP, ST, ABBOT

Biscop Baducing, a Northumbrian by birth, after two journeys to Rome, received the monastic habit at Lérins. After another stay in Rome he returned to Northumbria and founded a monastery, St Peter's at Wearmouth, where St Bede was his pupil. He went again to Rome for books, relics, and other matters, and then founded a twin monastery, St Paul's at Jarrow. There was an abbot for each, but Benedict himself was in general control. Among his achievements was to bring from Rome the precentor of St Peter's to teach the English monks chant and ceremonial *more Romano*; the constitutions of Wearmouth and Jarrow were drawn from those of seventeen monasteries that Benedict himself had visited. For the last three years of his life he was mostly confined to his bed, where he used to sing the Divine Office with monks who came to his cell for the purpose. d. 690. St Benedict Biscop is one of the patrons of the English congregation of Benedictines. His feast is also kept in the dioceses of Southwark, Hexham and Liverpool. *January 12, i, 72.*

*BENEDICT JOSEPH LABRE, ST

Labre is a representative example of those who, at all times in Christian history, have refused in the name of Christ to be "respectable". He was b. 1748, son of a prosperous French shopkeeper, and offered himself to several austere religious orders but proved unsuitable. He then began a series of pilgrimages on foot to the chief shrines of western Europe, living almost literally on what he could pick up. From 1774 Labre lived in Rome, spending his days in the churches and his nights in the ruins of the Colosseum, and he was revered as a saint throughout the city. He was found dying on the steps of Santa Maria dei Monti, and was taken to the house of a friendly butcher, where he d. 1783. His fame spread remarkably quickly, though the popular biographies of him (and not of him only) are apt to emphasize some of his less-important characteristics. cd 1883. *April 16, ii, 106.*

BENEDICT MENNI, BD

He was b. at Milan on March 11, 1841, revived his order in Spain and in 1880 founded the Sisters of the Sacred Heart of Jesus for the care of the sick. d. 1914. bd June 23, 1985. *April 24.*

BENEDICT OF ANIANE, ST, ABBOT

The part played by Benedict of Aniane in the revival of monastic discipline in the eighth/ninth centuries was considerable. He was brought up at the court of Pepin and after taking part in several campaigns became a monk at Saint-Seine, near Dijon. Later he founded the monastery of St Saviour on the banks of the river Aniane in Languedoc and Gascony. Louis the Debonair entrusted him with the reform of all the monastic houses of France and Germany and the bringing of monks and canons under uniform rules. The uniformity of discipline and central control was never carried to the lengths that St Benedict of Aniane seems to have desired, but the Synod of Aachen over which he presided in 817 was an important event in the history of Western monasticism. d. 821. *February 11, i, 309.*

*BENEDICT OF BENEVENTO, ST, MARTYR

This Benedict and his four companions were Benedictine monks, missionaries among the Slavs, who were massacred at their monastery near Gniezno in 1003. The group is sometimes called, rather misleadingly, the Five Polish Brothers. *November 12, iv, 324.*

BENEDICT OF COLTIBONI, BD

Benedict Ricasoli left the Vallombrosan abbey Coltiboni to live in a hermit's cell nearby, from whence he would come at great feasts to exhort his brethren to perseverance. d. c. 1107. c.c. 1907. *January 20, i, 132.*

*BENEDICT OF MILAN, ST, BISHOP

Benedict Crispus was archbishop of Milan for forty-five years in the seventh/eighth century. He wrote the epitaph for the tomb of the Anglo-Saxon prince Caedwalla in St Peter's at Rome. d. 725. *March 11, i, 559.*

BENEDICT OF URBINO, BD

A lawyer of Urbino who became a Capuchin at Fano in 1584. He was an effective preacher and accompanied St Laurence of Brindisi on his visitations in Austria and Bohemia. d. 1625. bd 1867. *May 14, ii, 201.*

*BENEDICT THE BLACK, ST

Benedict "the Black" was black. His parents were serfs near Messina in Sicily. He was invited to join some hermits, and on the death of their superior was elected in his place. The community was absorbed into the Friars Minor of the Observance and Benedict became a lay brother at Palermo, and in 1578, although he was illiterate and not a priest, was appointed guardian of the friary. He proved to be an ideal superior and showed many evidences of the direct supernatural help he received in the discharge of this and other offices. In his old age he returned to the kitchen, but was still sought there by his admirers. d. 1589. cd 1807. *April 4, ii, 30.*

*BENEDICT THE HERMIT, ST

A hermit in the Campagna who was marvellously preserved from a cruel death at the hands of the Goths. d. *c.* 550. *March 23, i, 664.*

BENEDICTA FRASSINELLO, BD, WIDOW

Benedetta Cambiagio was b. in 1791 and married Giovanni Frassinello in 1816. They both chose the religious life in 1825, and decided to help abandoned girls. In 1833 she founded the educational Institute of Benedictines of Providence in her village; it is still effective in Italy and Peru. d. 1858. bd May 10, 1987. *May 10.*

BENEN, ST, BISHOP

Benen, or Benignus, was an early disciple of St Patrick and succeeded him as the chief bishop of the Irish church. He is said to have evangelized Clare and Kerry and to have had a monastery at Drumlease. There is no reason to suppose that Benen died near Glastonbury. d. 467. *November 9, iv, 303.*

BÉNÉZET, ST

"Little Benedict the Bridge-builder" was a shepherd boy who was much concerned by the difficulties of people wanting to cross the Rhône. In consequence of a vision he went to the bishop of Avignon, who eventually agreed to help him build a bridge there. The work was done between 1177 and Bénézet's death in 1184, and is said to have been accompanied by many wonders. *Benedictus. April 14, ii, 93.*

*BENIGNUS, ST, MARTYR

Benignus is a third-century (?) martyr vener-ated at Dijon from early times. The account of him that came into the hands of St Gregory of Tours, connecting the martyr with St Polycarp of Smyrna, is spurious: it is the first link in a chain of religious romances describing the alleged beginnings of the Church in parts of eastern France. *November 1, iv, 236.*

BENILDUS, ST

Peter Romançon was b. at Thuret in Auvergne in 1805. He joined the Brothers of the Christian Schools, and worked faithfully for forty-two years in that congregation. Brother Benildus was a first-rate teacher, never sparing himself, and with a gift for reaching boys' hearts. A *curé* said that the visits of Benildus to his parish were as good as a mission for his flock. d. at Sauges, 1862. cd 1967. *August 13, iii, 325.*

BENINCASA, BD

A Servite friar of Florence who lived as a solitary near Siena. d. 1426. c.c. 1829. *May 11, ii, 275.*

*BENJAMIN, ST, MARTYR

A deacon martyred in Persia under Yezdigerd *c.* 421 for refusing to promise to keep silence about the Christian religion. *March 31, i, 709.*

*BENNO OF MEISSEN, ST, BISHOP

He was made bishop of Meissen in 1066 and played a somewhat equivocal part in secular and ecclesiastical politics, being at one time imprisoned and at another deposed from his see. Later biographers speak very highly of him as a man and a bishop. d. 1106. His canonization in 1523 greatly annoyed Martin Luther. *June 16, ii, 555.*

BENNO OF OSNABRÜCK, BD, BISHOP

He was a monk and master builder to the emperor Henry III. In 1068 he was appointed bishop of Osnabrück and for a time was active in the struggle between Henry IV and Pope St Gregory VII. He founded the abbey of Iburg, and d. there in 1088. *July 22, iii, 165.*

BENTIVOGLIA BE BONIS, BD

A native of San Severion in the Marches of Italy and one of the early but more obscure

Friars Minor. d. 1232. c.c. by Pope Pius IX. *Bentivolius. December 1, iv, 458.*

BENVENUTA OF CIVIDALE, BD,
VIRGIN

Benvenuta Bojani was a Dominican tertiary who lived in her own home at Cividale in northern Italy; she is said to have been miraculously cured of a serious illness of five years' standing. d. 1292. c.c. 1765. *October 30, iv, 223.*

BENVENUTO OF GUBBIO, BD

He was a native of Gubbio and an unlettered soldier; he joined the Franciscans in 1222 and at his own request was set to care for lepers, whom he tended most lovingly. d. 1232. c.c. 1765. *October 30, iv, 223.*

*BENVENUTO OF OSIMO, ST, BISHOP

Benvenuto Scotivoli was a Friar Minor of Ancona who was bishop of Osimo from 1264 till his death in 1282. He is said to have been canonized less than four years after his death. *March 22, i, 659.*

BENVENUTO OF RECANATI, BD

A lay brother of the Conventual Friars Minor. d. 1289. c.c. by Pope Pius VII. *May 23, ii, 362.*

BEOCCA. *See* Danes, Martyrs under the.

*BERARD, ST, MARTYR

Berard with four other Friars Minor (Peter, Accursio, Adjutus, Odo) was sent by St Francis to preach to the Mohammedans of the West. They passed from Seville into Morocco, where they were put to death in 1220, the protomartyrs of the Franciscan Order. cd 1481. *January 16, i, 103.*

*BERCHARIUS, ST, ABBOT

He was abbot of Hautvillers and in 685 or 696 was stabbed by a monk whom he had reproved; Bercharius d. from the wound and was mistakenly venerated as a martyr. *October 16, iv, 128.*

BERHTWALD OF CANTERBURY,
ST, BISHOP

Otherwise *Brithwald*. He was abbot of Reculver in Kent and became archbishop of Canterbury in 692. d. 731. *Britwaldus. January 9, i, 59.*

BERHTWALD OF RAMSBURY, ST,
BISHOP

A monk of Glastonbury and the last bishop of Ramsbury before that see was removed to Old Sarum. He was venerated by his contemporaries on account of his visions and prophecies. d. 1045. *January 22, i, 147.*

*BERNADETTE, ST, VIRGIN

Bernadette Soubirous, daughter of a miller, was the child who, in 1858 at the age of fourteen, was chosen by God for the revelation to the world of the healing shrine of our Lady at Lourdes. For some years following she was the victim of much publicity, in which some Catholic ecclesiastics showed themselves extraordinarily lacking in sensibility at her expense. In 1866 Bernadette joined the Sisters of Notre Dame at Nevers, where she continued to do all she could to keep out of the public eye; she suffered much from ill health and d. at the age of thirty-five in 1879. cd 1933. *Bernadetta, Bernarda. April 16, ii, 108.*

*BERNARD, ST, ABBOT AND DOCTOR

Born in 1090 near Dijon. When he was twenty-two Bernard joined the monastery and order of Cîteaux, in company with thirty other young noblemen, fifteen years after its foundation, and he formed and became abbot of the fourth house of the congregation, Clairvaux. His achievements were amazing: during his lifetime he established sixty-eight Cistercian monasteries, assisted at ecumenical and other councils, opposed and confuted Abelard, preached a crusade in France and Germany, wrote many treatises and sermons, particularly on the love of God and the *Song of Songs*, and engaged in complicated politics to preserve the peace of the Church—"he carried the twelfth century on his shoulders, and he did not carry it without suffering". Bernard defied princes and counselled popes, especially Bd Eugenius III, who had been one of his monks, and went on missions against the Albigensians in Cologne and Languedoc. d. 1153. cd 1174. Declared a Doctor of the Church ("The

Honeysweet Doctor") in 1830. *Bernardus. August 20, iii, 360.*

BERNARD SCAMMACCA, BD

He lived at Catania in Sicily and after an unruly youth became a Dominican friar. Details of his life are lacking, but marvels were reported of him both before and after his death. d. 1486. c.c. 1825.
February 16, i, 354.

BERNARD SILVESTRELLI, BD

Bernardo-Maria Silvestrelli was b. at Rome on November 7, 1831. He entered the Passionist novitiate in 1854, but was ordained priest in 1855 without entering the order; he took his first vows in 1857. He was elected superior general in 1878 and remained in the office for twenty-five years. d. 1911. bd October 2, 1988. *December 9.*

*BERNARD TOLOMEI, BD, ABBOT

Born in 1272 at Siena, where he was a man of public affairs till 1312 when, with other gentlemen, he retired to the desolate country near Mont' Amiata. They were given the Benedictine rule and white habit (instead of the usual black) by the bishop of Arezzo, and thus began the monastic congregation called "of Monte Oliveto", of which several more houses were established almost immediately. In a great plague at Siena in 1348 the monks all nursed the sick, and their founder, Bd Bernard, was among those who were infected and died. c.c. 1644.
August 21, iii, 379.

BERNARD OF BADEN, BD

In 1453 he handed over the rights of the margravate of Baden to his brother and went from court to court trying to organize a crusade against the Turks. He had no success, and d. in 1458. bd 1479. Bd Bernard was patron of the former duchy of Baden.
July 15, iii, 111.

*BERNARD OF CAPUA, ST, BISHOP

Bishop of Foro-Claudio, which see he transferred to Caleno hard by, where he was venerated as principal patron. d. 1109.
March 12, i, 577.

BERNARD OF CORLEONE, BD

While in sanctuary after an assault on the police, Philip Latini underwent conversion and joined the Capuchins as a lay-brother. He austerities were equalled only by his graces, and he had the unusual gift of healing animals by prayer. He d. at the friary of Palermo in 1667. bd 1768.
January 19, i, 124.

*BERNARD OF MONTJOUX, ST

Also called "of Menthon". He was for forty-two years vicar general to the bishop of Aosta, tirelessly visiting the most remote Alpine valleys of the diocese and being especially solicitous for the welfare of travellers. It was due to this that St Bernard established the two hospices on the great and little passes that bear his name, putting them in the charge of clerics who eventually became Augustinian canons regular. He d. probably in 1081, and in 1923 was named by Pope Pius XI patron saint of all mountaineers. *May 28, ii, 411.*

BERNARD OF OFFIDA, BD

He was a lay-brother of the Capuchins at Fermo, famous for his wisdom and miracles. d. 1694. bd 1795. *August 26, iii, 410.*

*BERNARD OF PARMA, ST, BISHOP

While abbot general of the Vallombrosan Benedictines this Bernard was created cardinal by Bd Urban II and entrusted with various legatine duties. He became bishop of Parma and was twice exiled for his opposition to usurped authority. He relinquished the temporal power his predecessors in the see had obtained. d. 1133.
December 4, iv, 493.

BERNARD OF TIRON, ST, ABBOT

Also called "of Abbeville"; he was founder of the abbey of Tiron, from which the Benedictine Tironian congregation sprang. d. 1117. c.c. 1861. *April 14, ii, 92.*

BERNARD OF VIENNE, ST, BISHOP

Also called *Barnard*. He was b. *c.* 777, and was founder of the abbeys of Ambronay and Romans; appointed archbishop of Vienne in

810. Though somewhat imprudent in his political activities, he was one of the most influential as well as one of the most saintly prelates of his age. d. 842. *January 23, i, 156.*

*BERNARDINO REALINO, ST

Born in 1530 near Modena. He joined the Society of Jesus and after working for ten years among the poor of Naples he was made rector of the college at Lecce, where he remained for the rest of his life. d. 1616. Some curious phenomena are recorded concerning certain relics of his blood. cd 1947. *Bernardinus. July 3, iii, 13.*

BERNARDINO OF FELTRE, BD

He was a Friar Minor of the Observance, clothed in 1456, and one of the outstanding Franciscans of his time in Italy. He preached almost extempore and with tremendous effect: "When he attacks wickedness he does not speak—he thunders and lightens"; he had great influence with the civil authorities; he was also the terror of evil-doers, who more than once tried to take his life. A famous acitivity of Bd Bernardino was the establishment of *montes pietatis,* charitable pawnshops that made loans on pledged objects at a very low interest to pay expenses: in this work he was an inveterate adversary of all usurers. d. 1494. bd 1728. *September 28, iii, 672.*

BERNARDINO OF FOSSA, BD

He was a Friar Minor of the Observance, well known in Italy, Bosnia and Dalmatia as a preacher and missioner. d. 1503. c.c. 1828. *November 27, iv, 437.*

*BERNARDINO OF SIENA, ST

Born in Siena in 1380. Bernardino was a great preacher throughout Italy and a restorer of strict observance in the Franciscan order, especially in the matter of poverty. His vernacular sermons were written down and are as fresh and lively and applicable today as when they were first spoken; his amusing pictures of such familiar things as a bachelor household, women's fashions, men's exactingness, "pious" superstitions, etc., have a bite in them—not for nothing is he called "the people's preacher". With St John of Capistrano he spread devotion to the

Holy Name, displaying the monogram IHS for veneration and having it painted on houses. d. 1444. cd 1450. *May 20, ii, 354.*

BERNO, ST, ABBOT

He was abbot of Gigny (which he founded), of Baumes-les-Messieurs, and finally of Cluny, of which house he was the first ruler, from 910 to 917. In view of the importance of the Cluniac Benedictine congregation strangely little is known of its first abbot general. d. 927. *January 13, i, 75.*

*BERNWARD, ST, BISHOP

The name of Bernward is associated with the encouragement of ecclesiastical art in general and with metal-working in particular; he was himself a good painter and metalsmith. He became bishop of Hildesheim in 993; his long episcopate was disturbed by a protracted dispute with St Willigis of Mainz, in which the conduct of Bernward was irreproachable. d. 1022. cd 1193. *Bernwardus. November 20, iv, 396.*

BERTHA, ST

There are no very reliable particulars extant about this French widow and abbess; she is said to have founded the convent of Blangy in Artois. d. *c.* 725. *July 4, iiii, 14.*

BERTHA DE ALBERTI, BD, VIRGIN

Sometimes erroneously called "de Bardi". She was abbess of a Vallombrosan convent which she was sent to reform at Cavriglia. d. 1163. *March 24.*

BERTHA. *See also under* Rupert.

BERTHOLD, ST

Berthold is often called the founder of the Carmelite Order; he seems to have been appointed the first general superior of the hermits on Mount Carmel by his kinsman Aymeric, Latin patriarch of Antioch, *c.* 1150. He rebuilt the monastery church and dedicated it in honour of Elijah the Prophet. d. *c.* 1195. *Bertholdus. March 29, i, 701.*

BERTHOLD OF GARSTEN, BD, ABBOT

He entered a monastery after the death of his

wife and was commissioned to introduce the rule of St Benedict in the collegiate house of Steyer-Garsten. He enjoyed a great reputation as a confessor. d. 1142. *July 27, iii, 197.*

BERTILIA, ST, VIRGIN

She led an uneventful life in the neighbourhood of Arras. She was married to a young nobleman, after whose death she became a solitary at Mareuil. Early eighth century. *January 3, i, 30.*

BERTILLA, ST, VIRGIN

When St Bathildis refounded the abbey of Chelles, St Bertilla was made its abbess and her rule attracted subjects even from foreign lands; her community eventually included two queens, Hereswitha of the East Angles, and Bathildis herself. d. *c.* 705. *November 5, iv, 268.*

BERTILLA BOSCARDIN, BD, VIRGIN

Annette Boscardin was b. into a poor peasant family near Verona in 1885. She was a simple sort of girl, and she knew it; but she was accepted as a postulant by the Sisters of St Dorothy of Vicenza, and duly professed. Sister Bertilla's duties were always of a very modest kind, but she distinguished herself in the hospital at Treviso during the air-raids of 1917. She was a characteristic example of "the little way". After years of ill health she d. at Treviso in 1922. bd 1952. *October 20, iv, 161.*

*BERTINUS, ST, ABBOT

He was a monk of Luxeuil sent as a missionary to help St Omer among the Morini in Artois. With St Mommolinus he founded two monasteries, of one of which, Sithiu, he became abbot; from there he evangelized and civilized the heathen of the surrounding wet and marshy country. His community grew so large that he had to establish a daughter house, the church of which became the first cathedral of the diocese of Saint-Omer. St Bertinus was a characteristic example of the monk missionary who civilized western Europe during the Dark Ages. d. *c.* 700. *September 5, iii, 493.*

BERTOUL. *See* Bertulf.

BERTRAND, ST, BISHOP AND MARTYR

Or *Bertram.* In 1334 he was appointed patriarch of Aquileia; in 1348 he transferred his residence to Udine, where he was a great benefactor of the town and patron of learning. He was set upon and murdered while on a journey in 1350, at the age of ninety, because he had resisted the simoniacal practices of the counts of Gorizia. c.c. by Pope Benedict XIV. *Bertrandus, Bertichramnus. June 6.*

BERTRAND OF COMMINGES, ST, BISHOP

St Bertrand was bishop of Comminges (now included in Toulouse) for fifty years, during which he showed himself a vigorous, enlightened, and fearless pastor and consequently encountered opposition, sometimes violent. Several miracles are related of him, one of which gave rise to the "great pardon" of Comminges. d. 1123. cd *c.* 1225. *October 16, iv, 130.*

BERTRAND OF GARRIGUES, BD

This Bertrand, a secular priest, was one of St Dominic's original group of preachers and helped in the first Dominican foundation at Paris. Later he rejoined his master and was the constant companion of his preaching, until Bertrand was made prior provincial of Provence where he spent the rest of his very active life. d. *c.* 1230. c.c. by Pope Leo XIII. *September 6, iii, 498.*

BERTRAND OF LE MANS, ST, BISHOP

He was appointed bishop of Le Mans in 587 and had a troubled pontificate owing to political factions. He was a great benefactor of the poor, being specially interested in good agriculture and vine-growing, but his benefactions did not prevent him from having wide lands to dispose of in his will, which is extant. d. 623. *June 30, ii, 676.*

BERTULF, ST

Otherwise *Bertoul.* He came from Germany into Flanders where he became a Christian and was for years steward to Count Wambert, whom he served with distinguished fidelity. After the count's death Bertulf founded a small monastery at Renty and governed it till his death in 705(?). *Bertulphus. February 5, i, 257.*

BERTULF OF BOBBIO, ST, ABBOT

He was abbot of Bobbio and obtained from Pope Honorius I the exemption of his monastery from episcopal control—the first recorded exemption of its kind. d. 640. *August 19, iii, 356.*

BESAS. *See under* Julian.

BESSARION, ST

An Egyptian who became a disciple of St Antony in the desert, where he wandered from place to place and lived to a great age, achieving a great reputation for holiness and wonders. He has always been much revered in the East. Fourth century. *June 17, ii, 563.*

BETTELIN, ST

Practically nothing is known about St Bettelin (Beccelin, Berthelm), except that he was a hermit at Croyland in the eighth century, succeeding St Guthlac there. This saint (or another of the same name) was patron of the town of Stafford. *Bertelmus. September 9, iii, 517.*

BEUNO, ST, ABBOT

St Beuno's principal establishment seems to have been at Clynnog in North Wales, where he is supposed to have been buried. In modern times he is best remembered for his alleged restoration to life of St Winifred, and as the titular saint of the well-known retreat house. d. *c.* 640. He is commemorated in the diocese of Menevia. *April 21, ii, 142.*

BILFRID, ST

An eighth-century hermit in Northumbria. He worked as a goldsmith and adorned St Cuthbert's gospel-book, now in the Cottonian Library of the British Museum. *March 6, i, 502.*

BIRGITTA. *See* Bridget.

*BIRINUS, ST, BISHOP

Birinus was a missionary bishop from Rome who came to England and converted Cynegils, king of the West Saxons. He was given Dorchester in Oxfordshire for his see and from thence he converted many people and built churches for them, earning the title of Apostle of Wessex. d. *c.* 650. The feast of St Birinus is celebrated in the dioceses of Birmingham and Portsmouth. *December 5, iv, 500.*

BLAAN, ST, BISHOP

Blaan (Blane) was a sixth-century (?) Scottish bishop, said to be trained by St Comgall and St Canice in Ireland; he was buried at the place now called Dunblane. His feast is kept in the dioceses of Saint Andrew, Dunkeld, and Argyll. *Blaanus. August 11, iii, 304.*

*BLAISE, ST, BISHOP AND MARTYR

It is supposed that St Blaise was bishop of Sebastea in Armenia and was martyred *c.* 316. There is no evidence for his *cultus* earlier than the eighth century, and credence cannot be given to his "acts". The Blessing of St Blaise against infections of the throat has reference to the statement that he saved the life of a boy who had got a fish-bone stuck in his throat. *Blasius. February 3, ii, 239.*

*BLANDINA, ST, MARTYR

Blandina is perhaps the best known of the martyrs of Lyons (*q.v.*). She was a slave girl, "in whom Christ made manifest that things which men esteem mean and of little worth are glorious in God's sight because of that love of him which is shown in truth rather than appearances". Her constancy under torture was an inspiration to her fellows. She was suspended from a stake in the arena, but the wild beasts would not touch her. Eventually she died, last of them all, with the boy Ponticus, being tossed and gored by a bull. *June 2, ii, 454.*

BLANDINA MERTEN, BD, VIRGIN

Blandine Merten was b. on July 10, 1883 at Duppenweiler, Trier, Germany, into a peasant family. She became an Ursuline at twenty-five and made her final profession in 1913. She wanted to dedicate herself to the religious instruction of children. She caught TB in 1914 and d. in 1918 when thirty-four. bd November 2, 1987. *May 18.*

BLESILLA, ST

St Jerome refers to this daughter of St Paula.

She d. at Rome in 383, a very young widow. *January 22, i, 144.*

BODO, ST, BISHOP

Bodo was the brother of St Salsberga, and was persuaded by his sister to become a monk, his wife entering a convent. He was made bishop of Toul and founded three monasteries. d. c. 670. *September 22, iii, 622.*

BOETHIUS. *See* Severinus Boethius.

BOGUMILUS, ST, BISHOP

He was elected archbishop of Gniezno in 1167 but, refusing to countenance abuses that he found himself powerless to remedy, he resigned five years later and became a Camaldolese hermit at Uniow. d. 1182. c.c. 1925. *June 10, ii, 519.*

BOISIL. *See* Boswell.

*BONAVENTURE, ST,
BISHOP AND DOCTOR

Born near Viterbo in 1221. At thirty-six years of age Bonaventure was elected minister general of the Franciscans, and he was nominated to, but refused, the archbishopric of York; in 1273 he was created cardinal-bishop of Albano. He was the greatest mystical theologian and among the greatest scholastics of the Middle Ages; he wrote sermons and commentaries on the holy scriptures, and laboured for unity among the friars of his order, of whose founder he wrote a biography. Bonaventure was the outstanding figure at the second general council of Lyons in 1274 and played a big part in the reunion of the Orthodox Greeks thereat; he was spared the sorrow of the speedy collapse of this work, for he died during the course of the council. cd 1482. Declared a Doctor of the Church in 1588. *Bonaventura.* *July 15, iii, 96.*

BONAVENTURE BADUARIO, BD

A friar of St Augustine, the first member of that order to be made a cardinal. He was killed in Rome by an arrow in 1386—perhaps murdered because of his defence of the rights of the Church. *June 10, ii, 521.*

BONAVENTURE BUONACCORSI, BD

When nearing middle age he was converted by the preaching of St Philip Benizi and joined the Servite friars. He had been a violent partisan of the Ghibellines and now gave himself up to preaching brotherly love, civic unity and peace. He made so great an impression that he was known as "il Beato" even during his lifetime. d. 1315. c.c. 1822. *December 14, iv, 561.*

BONAVENTURE OF BARCELONA, BD

A shepherd who, on the death of his wife, became a Franciscan lay-brother. In Rome two cardinals enabled him to establish several houses of retreat for his order. d. 1684. bd 1906. *September 11, iii, 542.*

BONAVENTURE OF FORLI, BD

Bonaventure Tornielli became a Servite friar in 1448 and was specially commissioned by Sixtus IV to preach throughout the papal states; this work he continued even after he had been elected vicar general of his order. d. 1491. c.c. 1911. *March 31, i, 711.*

BONAVENTURE OF POTENZA, BD

He was a confessor of the Conventual Friars Minor in the kingdom of Naples. d. 1711. bd 1775. *October 26, iv, 207.*

BONAVITA, BD

He was a blacksmith who lived and died in the little town of Lugo, near Ravenna, and was a devoted follower of St Francis, of whose order he was a tertiary. d. 1375. *March 1, i, 456.*

BONET. *See* Bonitus.

*BONFILIUS, ST

One of the Seven Founders of the Servite Order (q.v.). *February 12, i, 311.*

*BONIFACE, ST, BISHOP AND MARTYR

The Apostle of Germany, who was b. probably at Crediton in Devon. c. 680 and was christened Winfrid. He went to school at a monastery at Exeter and became a monk at Nursling in Hampshire. In 716 he left England to preach the gospel to the Germans and was a characteristic missionary monk of the early ages. He was consecrated bishop in Rome in 722 and laboured in Hesse,

Thuringia, Westphalia and elsewhere, establishing dioceses (he was made metropolitan in 731) and monasteries from which the political, social and economic as well as the religious life of the people was formed and cared for. He placed these foundations in charge of other Englishmen and from 743 to 747 he could be spared to play a leading part in ecclesiastical reform in Gaul. His metropolitan see was fixed at Mainz, and Pope St Zachary created him primate of Germany and apostolic delegate for Gaul as well. When over seventy St Boniface resigned his see and went to evangelize the Frieslanders; he was murdered by the heathen in 754 while about to confirm some of his converts at Dokkum. *June 5, ii, 477.*

*BONIFACE I, ST, POPE

He became pope in difficult circumstances in 418, being opposed by one Eulalius. Boniface was a mild and peaceful man, but energetically upheld the rights of the Roman See against Constantinople and others. d. 422. *September 4, iii, 485.*

*BONIFACE IV, ST, POPE

Very little is known of this pope who ruled the Church from 608 till his death in 615. He consecrated the Pantheon in Rome as a Christian church in 698, and was the recipient of a famous letter from St Columban. *May 8, ii, 252.*

BONIFACE OF LAUSANNE, ST, BISHOP

A native of Brussels who was made bishop of Lausanne c. 1230. His previous life as a university professor seems to have unfitted him for the episcopal office and he resigned in 1239. The last eighteen years of his life were spent as chaplain to the Cistercian nuns of La Cambre, near Brussels, and in pastoral work around his native city. d. 1260. c.c. 1702. *February 19, i, 376.*

*BONIFACE OF QUERFURT, ST, BISHOP AND MARTYR

He was b. at Querfurt, baptized Bruno, and became an ecclesiastic at the court of the emperor Otto III. In 998 he became a monk in Italy, changing his name to Boniface, and later went as a missionary to Prussia, being consecrated as a regionary bishop. He was slain by those whom he had gone to save in 1009. *June 19, ii, 585.*

BONIFACE OF SAVOY, BD, BISHOP

A member of the ducal house of Savoy and a Carthusian monk who first became bishop of Valence and then, in 1241, archbishop of Canterbury. He was a favourite with King Henry III (whose wife's uncle he was) but not with the bishops of England, with whom he entered on a dispute that was carried to Rome. He died in Savoy in 1270 and was buried at Hautecombe. Boniface was a man of great personal virtue and generosity to the poor and needy, and after his death he was a subject of a *cultus* in Savoy which was confirmed in 1838; but it never obtained in England. *July 14, iii, 102.*

*BONITUS, ST, BISHOP

In French, *Bonet.* A bishop of Clermont, who resigned his see owing to a scruple of conscience. d. 706. *January 15, i, 97.*

BONIZELLA, BD

On the death of her husband, Bonizella Piccolomini left Siena and devoted herself and her wealth to the service of the poor in the district of Belsedere. d. 1300. *May 6.*

*BONOSUS AND MAXIMIAN, SS, MARTYRS

According to their *acta,* they were officers of the Herculean cohort at Antioch, who under Julian the Apostate refused to recognize the pagan military standard, and were tortured and beheaded in 363. *August 21, iii, 374.*

BORIS AND GLEB, SS, MARTYRS

Boris and Gleb (called Romanus and David at baptism) were sons of St Vladimir by Anne of Constantinople. Both of them were murdered for dynastic reasons in 1015, by order of their half-brother Svyatopolk. Because they accepted an unjust death patiently and without resistance, the Christian people revered them as martyrs, and their *cultus* as such was approved by Pope Benedict XIII in 1724. In Russian terminology they are called "passion-bearers". *July 24, iii, 175.*

BOSA, ST, BISHOP

When St Wilfrid of York was exiled and his diocese divided, Bosa, a monk of Whitby, was chosen bishop of the southern part, Deira, with the see at York. St Bede describes him as "beloved by God ... a man of most unusual merit and holiness". d. 705. *March 9, i, 536.*

BOSWELL, ST, ABBOT

Otherwise *Boisil*. An abbot of Melrose who numbered St Cuthbert among his subjects. Cuthbert had a great admiration for him. St Boswell seems to have had the gift of knowledge of the future, and took a special delight in the Gospel of St John. d. 664. Apparently his feast was kept in Durham on July 7 or 8. *February 23, i, 404.*

BOTULF, ST, ABBOT

St Botulf (Botolph, Botwulf), greatly venerated in pre-Norman England, was founder of a monastery at Icanhoh, generally identified as Boston (Botulf's stone) in Lincolnshire, in 654. He appears to have led a peaceful life and to have died *c.* 680. His feast is still observed in the dioceses of Brentwood, Nottingham and Northampton. *Botulphus. June 17, ii, 567.*

BOTVID, ST

Botvid was a Swede, converted to Christ in England, who preached in his own country; he was basely murdered by a Finnish slave whom he had freed, in 1100. *July 28, iii, 204.*

*BRAULIO, ST, BISHOP

He was bishop of Saragossa, a friend of St Isidore, a scholar, and devoted to the poor; some of his letters and other writings have some down to us. d. 651. *March 26, i, 685.*

*BRENDAN, ST, ABBOT

Brendan the Voyager is one of the three most famous saints of Ireland. He was b. probably near Tralee and for five years was in the charge of St Ita; in 559 (?) he founded the monastery of Clonfert, and d. in 577 or 583 at Enach Duin. The voyages of St Brendan are now admitted to be fictitious, but he probably visited Scotland and perhaps Wales; his journey to discover the isles of the blessed

was known in most European languages in the Middle Ages. His feast is kept throughout Ireland. *Brendanus. May 16, ii, 328.*

BRIAN LACEY, BD, MARTYR

Lacey, a Yorkshire gentleman, was hanged at Tyburn in 1591 for aiding and abetting a priest, Bd Montford Scott, who was his cousin. bd. 1929. *December 10, iv, 533.*

*BRICE, ST, BISHOP

Although he was a troublesome character, this cleric was raised to the see of Tours in succession to St Martin. He was an unsatisfactory bishop and after twenty years was driven from his diocese. He went to Rome, reformed his life completely, and after seven years of exile was restored to his bishopric. So strong was the impression made on his flock by his new manner of life that after his death in 444 Brice was revered as a saint. *Britius. November 13, iv, 328.*

BRIDE. *See* Brigid.

*BRIDGET, ST

She was b. in 1304 and before she was fifteen married Ulf Gudmarsson, with whom she lived happily for twenty-eight years, having eight children, of whom one, Catherine, is also recognized as a saint. Bridget was a busy and accomplished housekeeper, giving much to the poor, and *c.*1335 became chief lady-in-waiting to the queen of Magnus II, king of Sweden, whose court she unsuccessfully tried to induce him to purge. After her husband's death numerous and remarkable visions and revelations came to her; she became the adviser of popes and kings, and the devoted servant of the poor of Rome, where she went to live. She d. there on July 23, 1373, and her body was taken home to the monastery of Vadstena of the order of nuns and monks (called after her "Bridgettines") that she had founded there. The book of St Bridget's revelations has been translated into numerous languages. She was cd in 1391 and is the patron saint of Sweden. *Birgitta. July 23, iv, 54.*

BRIEUC, ST, ABBOT

Born probably in Cardiganshire. He migrated to Brittany and founded two monasteries, one near Tréguier and the other where the town of Saint Brieuc now stands. The saint is also known in Cornwall. Sixth century. *Briocus. May 1, ii, 208.*

*BRIGID, ST, VIRGIN

Also *Bridget, Bride, Ffraid.* Brigid is among the greatest and most venerated of those many saints who gave glory to Ireland, but the numerous "lives" do not enable a connected account of her to be put together. She was probably b. *c.* 450 at Faughart, near Dundalk, became a nun at an early age, and founded the monastery of Kildare, thereby becoming the spiritual mother of Irish nuns for many centuries. d. *c.* 525. Her memory in the hearts of the people was identified with a great spirit of charity, and the greater part of the numerous miracles attributed to her represent her responding to some appeal to her pity or her zeal for justice. "Everything that Brigid would ask of the Lord was granted at once", says the *Book of Lismore*, "for this was her desire: to satisfy the poor, to drive out every hardship, to spare every miserable man... She is the Mary of the Gael". Her feast is kept throughout Ireland, Wales, Australia and New Zealand. *Brigida.*
February 1, i, 225.

BRITIUS. *See* Brice.

BROCARD, ST

He was superior of the Frankish hermits on Mount Carmel and in *c.* 1210 gave them a rule drawn up by St Albert of Jerusalem. He guided the Carmelite Order during difficult times, and was greatly respected by the Mohammedans. d. 1231 (?). *Brocardus.*
September 2, iii, 471.

BRONISLAVA, BD, VIRGIN

She was a cousin of St Hyacinth and joined the Premonstratensian nuns in Poland; later she became a solitary. d. 1259. c.c. 1839.
August 30, iii, 449.

*BRUNO, ST

He was b. in Cologne *c.* 1030, and from being chancellor of the diocese of Rheims retired with six companions in 1084 to the solitude of La Chartreuse in the mountains near Grenoble. Thus was founded the Carthusian Order, the most austere monastic organization in the Church, whose monks are semi-hermits. After only six years of this life Bruno was called to help the pope, Bd Urban II, in his reforms and his struggles with the antipope and emperor, and, though he was allowed to live at last with a community which he founded at La Torre in Calabria, he was never fully released from this service: so did St Bruno display in himself the extremes of the contemplative and active ways of life. d. 1101. St Bruno has never been formally canonized but his feast was extended to the whole Western church in 1674; in Calabria he enjoys all the veneration of a "popular" saint: the contrast of contemplative and active in his life is thus mirrored in the circumstances of his *cultus*.
October 6, iv, 40.

BRUNO OF QUERFURT. *See* Boniface of Querfurt.

*BRUNO OF SEGNI, ST, BISHOP

He defended the doctrine of the Real Presence against Berengarius of Tours and was made bishop of Segni in 1080. Bruno was an extremely vigorous fighter against simony, and firmly rebuked Pope Paschal II for trying to enforce ecclesiastical privileges by force of arms. For a time he was abbot of Monte Cassino, but d. in his see in 1123. cd 1183. *July 18, iii, 140.*

*BRUNO OF WÜRZBURG, ST, BISHOP

This Bruno was bishop of Würzburg, and spent his private fortune on building the cathedral of St Kilian and other churches. He was killed by the collapse of a gallery while dining with the emperor Henry III at Bosenburg on the Danube in 1045.
May 17, ii, 339.

BRUNO THE GREAT, ST, BISHOP

Though the epithet "the Great" would seem rather to belong to the founder of the Carthusians, it was commonly given to his namesake and predecessor who became archbishop of Cologne in 953. This Bruno was brother of the emperor Otto I and actively co-operated with him in the religious and social building-up of Germany and the Empire. He was as capable a statesman as he was good a man, and was made co-regent of the Empire during Otto's absence in Italy in 961. Bruno was only forty when he d. in 965. c.c. 1870. *October 11, iv, 88.*

BUDOC, ST, BISHOP
St Budoc gives his name to several places in Devon and Cornwall, and according to a local story he was a hermit from Ireland, but Wales is more likely. He may be the same as a Beuzec venerated in Brittany. Sixth century (?). *December 9, iv, 525.*

BULGARIA. See Seven Apostles of Bulgaria.

*BUONAGIUNTA, ST
One of the Seven Founders of the Servite Order (*q.v.*). *February 12, i, 311.*

*BURCHARD, ST, BISHOP
He was sent from Wessex to be a missionary in Germany and was appointed first bishop of Würzburg by St Boniface; here he founded an abbey which afterwards bore his name. d. 754. *Burchardus. October 14, iv, 110.*

BURGUNDOFARA. *See* Fare.

C

CADFAN, ST, ABBOT

He founded the monastery of Towyn in North Wales, which persisted into the Middle Ages as a college of priests, and was the first abbot of Ynys Enlli (Bardsey). Sixth century. *November 1, iv, 239.*

CADOC, ST, ABBOT

St Cadoc was the founder of the great Welsh monastery of Llancarfan or Nantcarfan, not far from Cardiff. He is said to have founded other monasteries in Wales and Scotland. He d. in the sixth century and, through reliance on a more than doubtful *vita*, is venerated as a bishop and martyr in the dioceses of Cardiff and Menevia. *Cadocus. September 23, iii, 633.*

CADROË, ST, ABBOT

Or *Cadroel*. He was said to be the son of a Scottish chieftain, and educated at Armagh. He is alleged to have saved London by his prayers from destruction by fire. He journeyed from shrine to shrine in England and continental Europe, and became abbot of Waulsort on the Meuse. d. 976. *March 6, i, 501.*

CAEDMON, ST

"The father of English sacred poetry". He was a herdsman of the monastery at Whitby, and after he was endowed with the gift of poetry (as narrated by Bede) he was admitted among the monks there. Bede gives a moving account of Caedmon's death, *c.* 680, when, holding the Eucharist in his hands, he declared himself at peace with all his brethren. "That tongue which had uttered so many wholesome words in praise of the Creator spake its last words also in his praise." *February 11, i, 305.*

CAEDWALLA, ST

He was the king of the West Saxons who died while on a visit to Rome, a few days after having been baptized by Pope St Sergius I, in 689; he was buried in the crypt of St Peter's. There is no evidence for any ancient *cultus. April 20, ii, 134.*

CAESAR DE BUS, BD

César de Bus was b. at Cavaillon, France on February 3, 1544. In 1565 he went to the court of Charles IX and witnessed the St Bartholomew massacre. He renounced his secular life and was ordained priest in 1582. He was influenced by Charles Borromeo and founded the Fathers of Christian Doctrine in 1592, for religious instruction. By the Revolution the order had sixty-four colleges or houses in France. He d. in Avignon in 1607. bd April 27, 1975. *April 15.*

CAESARIA, ST, VIRGIN

Sister of St Caesarius of Arles and abbess of the great monastery which her brother established in that city. Both Gregory of Tours and Venantius Fortunatus speak of her with admiration. d. *c.* 529. *January 12, i, 72.*

*CAESARIUS AND **JULIAN, SS,** MARTYRS

These martyrs at Terracina in Italy are mentioned in early martyrologies, but the particulars and date of their passion are not known. Their extant *acta* are not authentic. *November 1, iv, 235.*

*CAESARIUS OF ARLES, ST, BISHOP

Caesarius, a monk of Lérins, was made archbishop of Arles at the age of thirty in 500. He was the first "popular" preacher whose words have come down to us, in the form of short and homely homilies, and he took great pains for the fitting observance of public worship. He founded a famous monastery for women (which afterwards bore his name), putting it under the rule of his sister St Caesaria. Side by side with his ecclesiastical labours as metropolitan of a large province, St Caesarius had his share in the public upheavals of his time, and he sold the treasures of his churches to relieve the distress caused by the siege of Arles in 508. He is said to have been the first archbishop in western Europe to receive the *pallium* from the Holy See. d. 543. *August 27, iii, 418.*

*CAESARIUS OF NAZIANZUS, ST

Caesarius, brother of St Gregory Nazianzen, was a distinguished physician and public man, patronized by several of the Roman emperors. He elected to remain (so it seems) a catechumen nearly all his life, and was baptized only after a narrow escape in an earthquake, a few months before his death in 369. His name was inserted in the Roman Martyrology in virtue of his brother's panegyric. *February 25, i, 413.*

CAGNOALD. *See* Chainoaldus.

CAINNECH. *See* Canice.

*CAIUS, ST, POPE AND MARTYR

Nothing is known of the life of this pope nor of his death in 296. *April 22, ii, 144.*

*CAJETAN, ST

Cajetan (Gaetano) belonged to the nobility of Vicenza, where he was b. in 1480. He renounced his wealth and ecclesiastical dignities to devote himself to the poor and the suffering of his native town, and afterwards to the welfare of the pastoral office at large by founding in 1524 the first congregation of clerks regular: they were called "Theatines". St Cajetan was one of the most outstanding figures among the pre-Tridentine Catholic reformers, and his institution of pastoral clergy bound by vows and living in community was a very great force in the "Counter-Reformation", most notably through the Jesuits. Cajetan was active with Bd John Marinoni in establishing those charitable pawn-shops sanctioned some time before by the Fifth Lateran Council. d. 1547. cd 1671. *Cajetanus. August 7, iii, 272.*

CALAIS. *See* Carilefus.

*CALEPODIUS, ST, MARTYR

Calepodius, who gives his name to a Roman catacomb, is said to have been a priest who was martyred in 222. *May 10, ii, 265.*

*CALLISTUS, I, ST, POPE AND MARTYR

Callistus (Calixtus) was a Christian slave who had an eventful youth in what may have been rather discreditable circumstances. Later he was made superintendent of the Christian cemetery on the Appian Way, which still is known by his name, San Callisto, and *c.* 217 he was elected bishop of Rome. By his gentleness toward sinners he incurred the wrath of St Hippolytus and the rigorists *c.* 222, but the extant account of his passion is worthless. *October 14, iv, 107.*

CALLISTUS CARAVARIO, BD, MARTYR

Callisto Caravario was born at Cuorgne, Turin, on June 8, 1903. He became a Salesian in 1918 and followed Bd Louis Versiglia to China as a missionary in 1925. He worked on the island of Timor for two years and was ordained priest by Bd Louis in Shanghai in 1929 for the Lin-Chow mission. He was on his way there when he was killed by pirates at the same time as his bishop. d. 1930. bd May 15, 1983. *February 25.*

*CALOCERUS AND PARTHENIUS, SS, MARTYRS

These brothers, martyred in 304, are alleged to have been eunuchs in the household of Tryphonia, wife of the emperor Decius. *May 19, ii, 348.*

CAMERINUS. *See* Luxorius.

CAMILLUS COSTANZO, BD, MARTYR

An Italian Jesuit who was burned to death at

a slow fire in Japan in 1622. He had returned to the country after being banished from it as a Christian. bd. 1867. *September 25, iii, 535.*

*CAMILLUS DE LELLIS, ST

Camillus was b. in the Abruzzi in 1550 and for years was a soldier and an inveterate gambler. After his reformation of life he tried to join the Capuchins, but was prevented by a disease of the feet which afflicted him for the rest of his life; instead he became director of a hospital, and established at many places in Italy houses of the Ministers of the Sick, a nursing congregation which he had founded and which still flourishes. His own sufferings of body seemed only to encourage him to greater efforts for others. St Camillus was ordained by the last English bishop of the old hierarchy, Goldwell. d. 1614. cd 1746. With St John-of-God he is the patron of the sick and of their nurses. *July 14, iii, 134.*

CANDIDA. *See* Wite.

*CANICE, ST, ABBOT

Canice (Cainnech, Kenny) was b. at Glengiven in Derry, and perhaps was a monk under St Cadoc in Wales. He founded the monastery of Aghaboe and probably of Kilkenny, and was a zealous missionary in Scotland under St Columba. d. *c.* 599. St Canice's feast is kept throughout Ireland, and in the dioceses of St Andrews and Argyll. *Canicus. October 11, iv, 86.*

*CANTIUS, ST, MARTYR

Cantius and Cantianus with their sister Cantianella are said to have belonged to the Roman family of the Anicii; they were put to death for not sacrificing to the gods in 304 (?). *May 31, ii, 434.*

*CANUTE, ST, MARTYR

Canute IV, king of Denmark, was a natural son of Sweyn III, whose uncle, Canute, had reigned in England. Having defended his country against aggressors, he enacted severe laws to control his own *jarls*, and advanced the Church in Denmark. Canute was killed by rebels in 1086, and as this rebellion was concerned with the payment of tithes, which he had tried to enforce, he was accounted a martyr. *Canutus. January 19, i, 121.*

*CANUTE LAVARD, ST, MARTYR

Knud Lavard was duke of Schleswig and spent a good deal of his life coping with Viking pirates. He was slain by a conspiracy of his fellow Danes in 1131. cd. 1169. *January 7, i, 49.*

*CAPRASIUS, ST

In French, *Caprais.* A hermit on the island of Lérins who was the spiritual master and guide of St Honoratus who founded the great monastery there. d. 430. *June 1, ii, 440.*

*CAPRASIUS, ST, MARTYR

According to a worthless legend he was the first bishop of Agen and, seeing the martyrdom of St Faith (October 6) from his hiding-place, he gave himself up and was executed. *October 20, iv, 155.*

CARADOC, ST

He was a harper by profession, but became a hermit in South Wales, where he suffered from the depredations both of sea-rovers and of the Normans. At his death in 1124 he was buried with great honour in the cathedral of St Davids. *Caractacus. April 14, ii, 93.*

CARANTOC, ST, ABBOT

This sixth-century Welsh abbot founded the church of Llangrannog in Cardiganshire, and was associated with Crantock in Cornwall. There is also a widespread *cultus* of him in Brittany. *Carantocus. May 16, ii, 329.*

CARILEFUS, ST, ABBOT

In French, *Calais.* He founded and governed the abbey of Anisole in Maine. d. *c.* 540 (?). *July 1, iii, 3.*

CARMES, MARTYRS DES. *See* September, Martyrs of.

CAROLINE KOZKA, BD, VIRGIN AND MARTYR

Karolina Kozka was b. into a pious farming family at Wal-Ruda, Poland, on August 2,

1898. In 1914 she was murdered by a Russian soldier. bd by John Paul II at Tarnow, Poland, on June 11, 1987. *November 18.*

*CARPUS AND **PAPYLUS, SS,** MARTYRS
A bishop and deacon of Pergamos who were tortured and burnt alive either in the time of Marcus Aurelius or of Decius. Their extant *passio* is genuine. *April 13, ii, 83.*

CARTHAGE, ST, BISHOP
St Carthage (Carthach, Mochuda) was a Kerry man and *c.* 595 founded a monastery at Rahan in Offaly, for which he wrote a rule of life in verse; he seems to have had episcopal charge of the neighbourhood. In 635 the community was expelled and Carthage led the monks to the banks of the Blackwater where they laid the foundation of the great monastery and school at Lismore. d. 637. His feast is observed throughout Ireland. *Carthagus. May 14, ii, 306.*

CARTHUSIAN MARTYRS, THE ENGLISH
The first martyrs of the English Reformation were three Carthusian priors, John Houghton, Robert Lawrence and Augustine Webster, who, with Richard Reynolds and John Haile (*qq.v.*), were h.d.q. at Tyburn on May 4, 1535. Three more Carthusians, Humphrey Middlemore, William Exmew and Sebastian Newdigate (*qq.v.*) suffered a like fate on June 19. Two years later two more suffered at York, John Rochester and James Walworth (*qq.v.*), and nine were starved to death in London (John Davy, Thomas Green, Richard Bere and Thomas Johnson, priests, with William Greenwood, Robert Salt, Walter Pierson (*q.v.*), Thomas Scryven, Thomas Reding, lay-brothers). Brother William Horn (*q.v.*) suffered in 1540. The offence of these monks was their refusal to recognize King Henry VIII as supreme head of the Church in England. Their *cultus* was recognized by Pope Leo XIII in 1886, and their collective feast is kept in the archdiocese of Westminster and by the Carthusian Order. *May 11, ii, 277.*

*CASIMIR, ST
Casimir, patron saint of Poland and Lithua-

nia, is often referred to as king of Poland and Hungary, though he never occupied the throne of either country. He was the second son of Casimir IV of Poland, and in 1471 was sent by his father to seize the crown of Hungary; but he withdrew his troops without fighting, whereupon his father imprisoned him for three months. The remainder of Casimir's short life was spent in study and religious retirement. d. of consumption in 1484. cd 1521. The Latin original of the hymn "Daily, daily sing to Mary", often attributed to St Casimir because of his fondness for it, was written three centuries before his time. *Casimirus. March 4, i, 478.*

CASPAR BERTONI, BD
Gaspare Bertoni was born on October 9, 1777 at Verona, Italy. He founded the Congregation of the Holy Stigmatics of Our Lord Jesus Christ, concerned with schools, education and parochial care. It now has 440 members in seventy-eight houses and was a forerunner of Catholic Action. He died at Verona in 1853. bd November 1, 1975. *June 12.*

CASPAR DE BONO, BD
Born at Valencia in 1530. He was in the silk trade, a soldier, and finally a Minim friar, being twice corrector provincial of the Spanish province. d. 1604. bd. 1786. *Gasparus. July 14, iii, 104.*

*CASPAR DEL BUFALO, ST
Born in Rome in 1786, ordained 1808, and exiled with many other clergy by Napoleon. In 1814 he founded at Giano in the diocese of Spoleto the first house of the congregation of Missioners of the Most Precious Blood for mission work at home. It met with endless difficulties at first, but before long the dramatic and tireless methods of the missioners had spread them all over Italy. St Caspar also founded works of charity in Rome to engage the activities of all sorts and conditions of people, and opened a chapel for night-long prayer and confession. His last mission was preached in Rome during the cholera outbreak of 1836, and he d. in the following year at Albano. cd 1954. *January 2, i, 25.*

CASPAR STANGGASSINGER, BD

Kasper Stanggassinger was b. on January 12, 1871 at Unterkälberstein, Bavaria, Germany. He took a personal vow of chastity when sixteen. He became a Redemptorist in 1892 and was ordained priest in 1895. He taught at the missionary school at Dürnnberg but wished to be a missionary in Brazil. d. 1899. bd April 24, 1988. *September 26.*

CASPAR. *See also under* Three Wise Men.

*CASSIAN OF IMOLA, ST, MARTYR

He was a schoolmaster at Imola. The Roman Martyrology states that, having refused to sacrifice to the gods, he was exposed naked among two hundred boys "by whom he had made himself disliked by teaching them", and these put him to death by stabbing him with their iron pens. Date unknown. *Cassianus. August 13, iii, 316.*

*CASSIAN OF TANGIER, ST, MARTYR

When the centurion St Marcellus (October 30) was sentenced to death at Tangier in 298 the official shorthand-writer to the court, Cassian, threw down his pen and notebook in indignation at the injustice. He was at once arrested and a few weeks later executed. The story seems to be a fictitious addition to the genuine *acta* of Marcellus. *December 3, iv, 484.*

CASSIAN. *See also* John Cassian *and under* Agathangelo.

*CASSIUS, ST, BISHOP

He was a bishop of Narni, of whose virtues St Gregory speaks in his *Dialogues*. d. 538. *June 29, ii, 672.*

CASTOR, ST, BISHOP

He was a bishop of Apt and at his request St John Cassian wrote the *De institutis coenobiorum*. d. *c.* 425. *Castorius. September 2, iii, 469.*

CASTORA GABRIELLI, BD

She was wife and widow of a lawyer at Sant' Angel in Vado in Umbria, where she was greatly revered for her goodness and charity. d. 1391. *June 14, ii, 544.*

*CASTULUS, ST, MARTYR

A martyr in Rome under Diocletian in 286; a cemetery was named after his burial place on the Via Labicana. *March 26, i, 684.*

*CASTUS AND AEMILIUS, SS, MARTYRS

Martyrs in Africa *c.* 250, who had given way for a brief period under torture. *May 22, ii, 365.*

*CATALD, ST, BISHOP

St Catald (Cathal) presided over the monastic school of Lismore, but on his way back from a pilgrimage to Jerusalem was chosen bishop of Taranto, where he d. towards the end of the seventh century. His feast is kept throughout Ireland, with St Conleth. *May 10, ii, 266.*

CATHERINE DREXEL, BD, VIRGIN

Mother Catherine Drexel was born into a rich family at Philadelphia, U.S.A., on November 26, 1858. In 1891 she established the Sisters of the Most Holy Sacrament to assist indigent black and native Americans (Indians). She was superior general until 1937. She founded many catechetical centres and some sixty schools and colleges, including Xavier University in New Orleans, to ensure that some of those suffering from discrimination in the South received an education. She also set up a number of medical dispensaries. She died in Pennsylvania in1955. bd November 20, 1988. *March 3.*

*CATHERINE LABOURÉ, ST, VIRGIN

Born in the Côte-d'Or in 1806, daughter of a yeoman farmer. She joined the Sisters of Charity of St Vincent de Paul in 1830 and there soon began the series of visions that has made her name famous: in consequence of them the first "miraculous medal" was struck, so called because of the circumstances in which its design became known. Little is recorded of Catherine's personal life; she was an unemotional and matter-of-fact religious. d. 1876 at the Enghien-Reuilly convent, where she was portress. cd 1947. *November 28, iv, 443.*

*CATHERINE DEI RICCI, ST, VIRGIN

Born at Florence in 1522, and in 1535 be-

came a regular tertiary of St Dominic. She
filled the offices of novice-mistress and prioress, and her ecstasies and gift of miracles
brought her to the notice of St Philip Neri.
She had an extraordinary series of ecstasies
in which she beheld and enacted the scenes
of our Lord's passion; she is asserted to have
had the *stigmata*, and we are told that on
Easter Day, 1542, she received the spiritual
espousals. d. 1590. cd 1747. *Catharina.
February 13, i, 328.*

CATHERINE TROIANI, BD, VIRGIN
She was b. at Giuliano di Roma on January
19, 1813. In 1866 she founded the Sisters of
the Immaculate Heart of Mary. d. Cairo,
May 5, 1887. bd April 14, 1985. *May 6.*

*CATHERINE OF BOLOGNA, ST,
VIRGIN
She was maid of honour to Margaret d'Este,
and on Margaret's marriage joined a community of nuns at Ferrara who later became
Poor Clares. Catherine was baker, novice
mistress, and then superioress of the daughter house at Bologna in 1457. From an early
age she was subject to visions, both divine
and diabolical, of which one of the child
Jesus is particularly notable. Her religious
life was one long intercession for the conversion of sinners, and she had unusual powers
of healing the body as well. d. 1463. cd 1712.
March 9, i, 536.

*CATHERINE OF GENOA, ST
Caterinetta Fieschi was b. in 1447 and at the
age of 16 was married to Julian Adorno,
whose weak character was a cause of much
unhappiness to her. In 1473 Catherine underwent a sudden conversion, gave herself
to the care of the sick in a Genoese hospital,
and recruited two friends and her husband to
the same work. From this time on St
Catherine led a most intense spiritual life,
combined with unwearying and efficient
activity in the hospital, and is a remarkable
example of the Christian type of complete
"other-worldliness" united with the most
capable "practicality". She continued the
same life after the death of her husband, and
never became a religious or even a tertiary.
St Catherine wrote a treatise on Purgatory

and a *Dialogue* of the soul and the body,
which the Holy Office declared were alone
enough to prove her holiness: they are among
the more important documents of mysticism. d. 1510. cd 1737.
September 15, iii, 557.

CATHERINE OF PALLANZA, BD
VIRGIN
She was the first woman hermit in the mountain district above Varese, near Milan, where
she lived a life of very great austerity and
was soon joined by others. These she gathered into a community under the Augustinian rule. d. 1478. c.c. 1769. *April 6, ii, 44.*

*CATHERINE OF PALMA, ST, VIRGIN
Catarina Tomás was b. in 1533 on the island
of Majorca, where she spent her whole life.
She had a hard and unhappy childhood, but
eventually became a canoness of St Augustine at Palma. Here she was subject to many
strange phenomena, both consoling and
alarming, and she had the gift of prophecy.
She tried never to allow her experiences to
interfere with the discharge of her duties. d.
1574. cd 1930. *April 1, ii, 6.*

**CATHERINE OF PARC-AUX-
DAMES, BD,** VIRGIN
She was the daughter of Jewish parents at
Louvain and in the early thirteenth century
ran away from home and became a Cistercian
nun at Parc-aux-Dames. *May 4, ii, 232.*

CATHERINE OF RACCONIGI, BD,
VIRGIN
She was a Dominican tertiary living in the
world, who seems to have been favoured
with remarkable mystical experiences from
a very early age. She offered herself as a
victim for the disorders of war, and many
miracles are related of her. d. 1547. c.c.
1810. *September 4, iii, 488.*

*CATHERINE OF SIENA, ST, VIRGIN
Catherine, one of the greatest women of
Christendom, was b. at Siena in 1347 of
middle-class parents. When sixteen she
joined the third order of St Dominic, continuing to live at home, where her goodness
attracted a circle of *Caterinati*, men and
women, lay and clerical, who formed a sort

of informal college and helped and hindered her in her work. From looking after the poor and sick she was drawn into politics, and helped to persuade Pope Gregory XI to abandon Avignon for Rome (she used to write to him in terms curiously compounded of deference and familiarity). Then she was involved in the turmoil of the so-called great schism of the West, and in 1380 she d. Catherine left over 400 letters and a great mystical work, her *Dialogue*. "It is Catherine's devotion to the cause of Christ's Church that makes her such a noble figure." cd 1461. *April 29, ii, 192.*

*CATHERINE OF VADSTENA, ST

She was the fourth child of St Bridget of Sweden and married Eggard von Kürnen, a long-suffering man. He died while Catherine was in Italy with St Bridget, and henceforward for twenty-five years the lives of the two women were practically identified in charitable works, pilgrimages, and the welfare of the Bridgettine Order. After the death of her mother Catherine retired to the abbey of Vadstena, earning there a reputation for holiness and miracles. d. 1381. *March 24, i, 669.*

CEADDA. *See* Chad.

CEALLACH. *See* Celsus of Armagh.

*CECILIA, ST, VIRGIN AND MARTYR

The maiden marriage of St Cecilia, the conversion of her husband St Valerian, his martyrdom with his brother St Tiburtius, and the attempted suffocation and the beheading of Cecilia in her own house make up one of the best-known stories of the early martyrs, but it has no historical value. Cecilia (who is named in the Roman canon) perhaps owes her original *cultus* to her being the foundress of a church in Rome; there is no early record of a virgin martyr named Cecilia. Her being patron saint of musicians is unexplained except on the hypothesis of an inference unwarrantably drawn from a phrase occurring in her *acta* and, somewhat altered, in her office. *November 22, iv, 402.*

CECILIA CESARINI, BD, VIRGIN

This Cecilia was the first prioress of the Dominicanesses at Bologna, when Bd Diana d'Andolo's father helped to found their house there in 1222. She d. at a great age in 1282. c.c. 1891. *June 9, ii, 511.*

*CECILIUS, ST

He was, in the words of the Roman Martyrology, "a priest of Carthage who brought St Cyprian to the faith of Christ". His name was probably really Cecilianus. d. *c.* 248 (?). *June 3, ii, 460.*

CECILY. *See* Cecilia.

CEDD, ST, BISHOP

A brother of St Chad of Lichfield. He was one of four monks sent from Lindisfarne to preach the gospel in the midlands of England, and afterwards was ordained bishop for the East Saxons, among whom he founded two monasteries, of which one was at Tilbury. He also, in 658, established the monastery of Lastingham in Yorkshire. He was present at the synod of Whitby, where he was among those who abandoned the Celtic usages for the Roman ones. He d. at Lastingham in the same year, 664. *October 26, iv, 205.*

*CELESTINE I, ST, POPE

Celestine, b. in Campania, became pope in 422. Of his private life nothing is known; he encouraged the campaign of St Germanus of Auxerre against Pelagianism and commissioned Palladius to preach in Ireland a year or so before St Patrick began his work there. His feast is accordingly kept in Ireland, on April 6. d. 432. *Caelestinus. April 6, ii, 40.*

*CELESTINE V, ST, POPE

Peter Morone was b. *c.* 1210 of peasant parents. After his ordination he received the Benedictine habit and lived as a hermit on Monte Morone, near Sulmona, where he formed the beginning of a small congregation of hermit-monks, later called "Celestines". In 1294, when he was over eighty years old, he was elected pope by acclamation; he was utterly unequal to the task of ruling the Church and resigned the office five months later. He returned to his hermitage, but was seized by his successor Boniface VIII (lest he should be used to create a schism) and d. after ten months'

imprisonment in a castle near Anagni, in 1296. Dante in his *Inferno* appears to condemn Peter Celestine as a coward; the Church reveres him as a saint. cd 1313.
May 19, ii, 345.

*CELSUS, ST, BISHOP

Celsus (Ceallach) was archbishop of Armagh and inaugurated the reform movement carried on there by St Malachy. d. 1129. Feast kept throughout Ireland. *April 7, ii, 47.*

CELSUS. See also under Nazarius.

CEOLFRID, ST, ABBOT

After being a monk at Gilling and Ripon in Yorkshire he became abbot of Wearmouth and Jarrow, Bede being among his monks. St Ceolfrid resigned his charge in 716 and set out on a pilgrimage to Rome, dying on the way at Langres in the same year; he was carrying with him the manuscript of the Bible now famous as "Codex Amiatinus". The feast of this English abbot is still observed at Langres, under the name of "St Ceufroy". *Ceolfridus. September 25, iii, 635.*

CEOLWULF, ST

Ceolwulf was king of the Northumbrians and ended his days as a monk at Lindisfarne. St Bede dedicated his *Ecclesiastical History* to him, and there was some *cultus* of him in the north after his death in 764.
January 15, i, 98.

CERATIUS, ST, BISHOP

In French, *Cérase*. He was a bishop of Grenoble who d. *c.* 455. c.c. 1903.
June 6, ii, 488.

*CERBONIUS, ST, BISHOP

He is said to have become bishop of Piombino in Tuscany on being driven from his native Africa by the Vandals. He d. *c.* 575 in exile on Alba, where he had been driven by the Lombards. *October 10, iv, 80.*

CESLAUS, BD

He was admitted to the Order of Preachers at the same time as St Hyacinth. He was a great preacher in Poland and neighbouring countries. d. 1242. c.c. 1713. *July 17, iii, 131.*

CETHEUS. See Peregrine of Amiternum.

*CHAD, ST, BISHOP

Chad, or Ceadda, brother of St Cedd, was trained with him at Lindisfarne under St Aidan, and became abbot of Cedd's monastery at Lastingham. King Oswy appointed Chad to the see of York but he was removed by St Theodore in favour of St Wilfrid; Chad took this so well that Theodore arranged for him to be bishop in Mercia. St Chad removed the episcopal seat from Repton to Lichfield but ruled there only a couple of years, dying in 672. Part of his relics are preserved in St Chad's cathedral, Birmingham, and his feast is observed in that and other English dioceses. *Ceadda. March 2, i, 457.*

*CHAEREMON, ST, BISHOP AND MARTYR

While bishop of Nilopolis this old man was driven by the persecution of Decius into the mountains of Arabia with one companion in 250: they were never seen or heard of again.
December 22, iv, 597.

CHAINOALDUS, ST, BISHOP

In French, *Cagnoald* or *Cagnou*. When St Columban was exiled from Luxeuil, Chainoaldus accompanied him and helped in the foundation of Bobbio. He became bishop of Laon, and d. *c.* 633.
September 6, iii, 497.

CHARITY. See under Faith.

CHARLEMAGNE, BD

The life of Charlemagne (b. 742; king of the Franks, 768; first Holy Roman emperor, 800; d. 814) belongs to general history and his is a somewhat surprising name to find in a catalogue of saints. There does not seem to have been any noticeable *cultus* of him until 1166 when it developed under the unfortunate influence of Frederick Barbarossa and the antipope Paschal III. However, Benedict XIV, before he became pope, concluded that the title Blessed might not improperly be accorded to so great a protector of the Church, and a feast of Charlemagne has been observed in Aachen. *Carolus Magnus. January 28, i, 188.*

*CHARLES BORROMEO, ST, BISHOP

Charles was born in 1538, son of count Gilbert Borromeo by a Medici mother. While still a child he received a rich abbey *in commendam*, he was a cardinal at twenty-two, although he was not ordained priest and bishop till 1563. Though the successful reassembling of the Council of Trent and a great deal of its work was due to him, his chief fame is as a bishop; his large and important diocese was in a scandalous state and his life's work was the reordering of it, which be began in 1566. Among his works was the establishment of the Confraternity of Christian Doctrine for instructing children, thus anticipating the Sunday schools of Robert Raikes by two hundred years, and he particuarly provided for the proper carrying out of the sacred liturgy. His reforms were not carried through without an attempt on his life, but his selflessness during the plague of 1576 put the seal on his great influence. St Charles was the first great prelate of the Counter-Reformation, incredibly hard-working, personally austere, devoted to anything that would forward the cause of true religion. d. 1584. cd 1610. *Carolus. November 4, iv, 255.*

*CHARLES GARNIER, ST, MARTYR

He came to North America from France with St Isaac Jogues, and was killed by Iroquois in 1649, while ministering to his flock during a massacre. *See* North America. cd 1930. *October 19, iii, 645.*

CHARLES HOUBEN, BD

He was b. at Munstergeleen in the Netherlands, on April 11, 1821. He entered the Passionist novitiate in 1845, took his vows in 1846 and was ordained priest in 1850. He worked among the poor and humble in England and Ireland and d. in 1893. bd October 2, 1988. *January 5.*

CHARLES LWANGA, ST, MARTYR

Master of the "pages" of King Mwanga in Uganda, and their leader during the persecution of 1886. He was burned with special cruelty at Namugongo. cd 1964. *June 3, ii, 468.*

CHARLES DE MAZENOD, BD, BISHOP

Charles-Joseph-Eugène de Mazenod was born at Aix-en-Provence, France, on August 1, 1782. He became a prison administrator but entered a seminary in 1808 and was ordained priest on December 21, 1811. On January 2, 1816 he founded the Missionary Society of Provence, which in 1826 was renamed the Congregation of Oblate Missionaries of Mary the Immaculate. He became a titular bishop in 1832 and Bishop of Marseilles in 1837. d. 1861. bd October 19, 1975. *May 21.*

CHARLES MEEHAN, BD, MARTYR

Charles Meehan, OFM, was b. in Ireland. He was about thirty-nine when he d. at Ruthin, North Wales, 1679. bd November 22, 1987. *February 12.*

CHARLES SPINOLA, BD, MARTYR

Charles Spinola and other Jesuits and lay people were martyred at Nagasaki in 1622, in the Great Martyrdom of Japan. They were bd in 1867. *September 10, iii, 533.*

CHARLES STEEB, BD

Karl Steeb was b. into a Lutheran family at Tübingen, Germany, on December 18, 1773. He studied in Verona and became a Catholic on September 14, 1792. His parents disinherited him and he was ordained priest on September 8, 1796, served for eighteen years among the impoverished, wounded and diseased, and in 1840 founded the Sisters of Mercy of Verona, who now number 2,300 in 230 communities across the world. d. 1856. bd July 6, 1975. *December 18.*

CHARLES OF BLOIS, BD

He was b. in 1320. On his marriage to Joan of Brittany in 1341 he claimed the dukedom of Brittany, and was at once involved in warfare with John de Montfort that lasted for the rest of his life, for nine years of which Charles was a prisoner in the Tower of London. He was killed in battle in 1364; many miracles were alleged at his tomb, and his ancient *cultus* among the Bretons was confirmed in 1904. *September 29, iii, 685.*

CHARLES OF SEZZE, ST

A lay-brother of the Observant branch of the Franciscans, who was well known in Rome in the seventeenth century. d. 1670. bd 1882. cd 1959. *January 19, i, 125.*

CHARLES THE GOOD, BD, MARTYR

He was the son of the murdered king of Denmark, St Canute, and was brought up by his relatives, the counts of Flanders. On returning from the Second Crusade he succeeded Baldwin as count of Flanders, but had to fight against other claimants. Charles was so determined a defender of the poor that he was accused of an unfair prejudice against the rich, and during a famine in 1125 he was merciless to food-hoarders and "cornerers". This led directly to his death, for he was murdered by a conspiracy of clerical and secular profiteers in 1127. c.c. 1883. *March 2, i, 460.*

CHEF. *See* Theuderius.

CHELIDONIUS. *See* Emeterius.

CHIARA BOSATTA, BD, VIRGIN

Chiara Dina Rosatta, an Italian nun, was born in the province of Como on May 27, 1858, and became a member of the Daughters of St Mary of Divine Providence. d. 1887. bd May 21, 1991. *April 20.*

CHIARITO. *See* Claritus.

CHIONIA. *See* Agape.

CHRISTIAN, BD, ABBOT

He was abbot of the first Cistercian monastery in Ireland, at Melifont, to which he was sent from Clairvaux by St Bernard in 1142, at the request of St Malachy of Armagh. He is said also to have become papal legate and bishop of Lismore. d. 1186. *Christianus. March 18, i, 630.*

CHRISTIANA. *See* Nino.

CHRISTINA OF AQUILA, BD, VIRGIN

Christina Ciccarelli was an Augustinian nun at Aquila, remarkable for her humility and love of the poor. d. 1543. c.c. 1841. *January 18, i, 117.*

*CHRISTINA OF BOLSENA, ST, VIRGIN AND MARTYR

The Christina mentioned in the Roman Martyrology on July 24 seems to have been a maiden martyred at Bolsena in Italy at an unknown date. But she has been confused with another virgin-martyr, Christina of Tyre, whose very existence is doubtful. *July 24, iii, 173.*

CHRISTINA OF SPOLETO, BD

She was a daughter of a physician named Camozzi who lived near Lake Lugano, and after a very lively and rather disorderly youth she became a penitent about the age of twenty. After a few years of undisciplined austerity she d. at Spoleto in 1458. c.c. 1834. The common story that this Christina was a Visconti who ran away from home and wandered about the shrines of Europe is discredited. *February 13, ii, 324.*

CHRISTINA OF STOMMELN, BD, VIRGIN

Christina Bruso was b. in 1242 at Stommeln, near Cologne, where she lived for nearly the whole of her seventy years. Her life is one long record of astonishing phenomena. Were it not for contemporary personal testimony she would have to be dismissed as a devout but mentally diseased sufferer from hallucinations, and even so it must be supposed that she was not normally responsible for some of her statements; but her personal virtues are undoubted. d. 1312. c.c. 1908. *November 6, iv, 277.*

CHRISTINA THE ASTONISHING, ST, VIRGIN

This Christina was b. near Liège in 1150 and from the age of thirty-two was the subject of most extraordinary physical phenomena, which were written down by a contemporary, Cardinal James de Vitry. The evidence points to her having been a pathological case, and her local *cultus* seems never to have received official confirmation. d. 1224 *July 24, iii, 176.*

*CHRISTOPHER, ST, MARTYR

St Christopher was a martyr in an early

century; otherwise nothing is known of him. The famous legend connected with his name grew up in the East during the sixth century and was unknown in the West before the ninth: even then it had not attained its final form. According to it, he lived beside a river and carried travellers over the ford; and among his passengers one day was the child Jesus. *Christophorus* means one who carried Christ (in his heart). *July 25, iii, 184.*

CHRISTOPHER BALES, BD, MARTYR

Born at Coniscliffe in co. Durham. Trained at the English College, Rome, ordained at Douay, and sent on the English mission in 1588. Condemned for his priesthood and h.d.q. in Fleet Street, London, 1590. bd 1929. *March 4, i, 482.*

CHRISTOPHER BUXTON, BD, MARTYR

A secular priest from Derbyshire, who in 1588 was h.d.q. for his priesthood at Canterbury, less than two years after his ordination abroad. While imprisoned in the Marshalsea he wrote out a *Rituale* that still exists. bd 1929. *October 1, iv, 7.*

CHRISTOPHER MACASSOLI, BD

A priest of the order of Friars Minor, whose shrine is at Vigevano in the province of Milan. d. 1485. c.c. 1890. *March 11, i, 563.*

CHRISTOPHER ROBINSON, BD, MARTYR

A secular priest b. at Woodside, Carlisle. He studied and was ordained at Rheims. He was sent on the English mission in 1592. After his arrest Bishop Robinson of Carlisle engaged him in several disputations. He d. at Carlisle in 1598. bd November 22, 1987. *August 19.*

CHRISTOPHER WHARTON, BD, MARTYR

A secular priest b. at Middleton, Yorkshire. He studied at Trinity College, Oxford but went to Rheims where he was ordained by Cardinal de Guise on March 31, 1584 and sent on the English mission in 1586. He was celebrated for his humility and charity. He was arrested in a widow's house, refused to conform and d. at York in 1600 when sixty years of age. bd November 22, 1987. *November 28.*

CHRISTOPHER OF MILAN, BD

A Dominican preacher who exercised a very great influence in Liguria during the fifteenth century; at Taggia the people built a friary as a result of his preaching, and he was made the first prior. d. 1484. c.c. 1875. *March 1, i, 456.*

CHRISTOPHER OF ROMAGNOLA, BD

He was a parish priest in the diocese of Cesena who resigned his benefice and joined St Francis of Assisi; he established the Friars Minor in Gascony, and is sometimes called "of Cahors". d. 1272. c.c. 1905. *October 25, iv, 200.*

CHRODEGANG, ST, BISHOP

Chief minister to Charles Martel and then bishop of Metz. St Chrodegang is chiefly famous for his regulations for the life of secular clerics, whom he gathered together in chapters of canons with common life under a rule. He applied this first to his cathedral clergy and then to other churches, and this institution of secular and regular canons spread all over western Christendom. He also gave to his cathedral the pure Roman liturgy with the appropriate chant, Metz being probably the first church in the north to adopt them. The choir school that he established was for centuries the best known in Europe. d. 766. *March 6, i, 501.*

*CHROMATIUS, ST, BISHOP

He became bishop of Aquileia in 388 and was one of the most distinguished prelates of his time. He was a friend both of St Jerome and Rufinus, and a strong supporter of St John Chrysostom. Several of his scriptural treatises still exist. d. *c.* 407. *December 2, iv, 471.*

*CHRYSANTHUS AND DARIA, SS, MARTYRS

This husband and wife were early martyrs in Rome; they are said to have been stoned and buried in a sandpit. The legend concerning them is fanciful, and nothing else is known of them. *October 25, iv, 196.*

*CHRYSOGONUS, ST, MARTYR

This martyr is named in the canon of the Mass but nothing is known of him except that he probably suffered at Aquileia; a martyred Chrysogonus is associated with St Anastasia (December 25). *November 24, iv, 418.*

CIARAN. *See* Kieran.

CIRILO BERTRAN AND SEVEN COMPANIONS, BB, MARTYRS

Brothers of the Christian Schools, executed during the Spanish Civil War. Cirilo Bertran, FSC, b. March 20, 1880 at Lemna, Burgo, became head of Our Lady of Covadonga School at Turón after the governmental decree on the secularization of education. He was arrested during Mass on October 5, 1934, together with his companions: Marciano José (b. November 15, 1900 at El Pedregal), Julián Alfredo (b. December 24, 1902 at Cifuentes de Rueda), Victoriano Pio (b. July 5, 1905 at St Millán de Lara), Benjamín Julián (b. October 24, 1908 at Jaramillo de la Fuente), Augusto Andras (b. Mary 6, 1910 at Santander), Benito de Jesús (b. October 31 at Buenos Aires), Ancieto Adolfo (b. October 4, 1912 at Celada Marlantes). They were shot by firing-squad, together with the spiritual director of the community, Inocencio de la Inmaculada (*q.v.*), on October 9, 1934. bd April 29, 1990. *October 9.*

*CLARE OF ASSISI, ST, VIRGIN

She was b. at Assisi *c.* 1193 and at the age of eighteen ran away from home to join St Francis: her sister Agnes followed, and at San Damiano was established the first convent of Franciscan nuns, now called after her "Poor Clares"; she never left it again, except once, it is said, to sup with St Francis and talk with him of God. From San Damiano St Clare wielded a great influence: many came to consult her, and the sick were brought to be tended by the nuns and sometimes to be cured by her intercession. Similar convents were founded in other places and, Pope Gregory IX having imposed a rule on them which forbade communal poverty, Clare had the bitterness for many years of struggling for the restoration of the true Franciscan rule for all. She was successful two days before her death in 1253. cd. 1255. *Clara.* *August 11, iii, 309.*

*CLARE OF MONTEFALCO, ST, VIRGIN

She was abbess of a convent at Montefalco which during her lifetime exchanged the rule of the Franciscan tertiaries for that of the Augustinian nuns. She was noted for the faithfulness of her observance and the austerity of her penances, and for three physical phenomena of unusual interest: the incorruption of her body after death, the formation of a cross upon her heart, and the liquefaction of her blood. d. 1308. cd 1881. *August 17, iii, 341.*

CLARE OF PISA, BD

Clare was the daughter of Peter Gambacorta, who was at one time virtually the head of the state of Pisa. She was left a widow at fifteen and tried to join the Poor Clares, whereupon her father shut her up for five months. Then he relented and built a convent for Bd Clare and Bd Mary Mancini, who adopted the rule of the enclosed Dominicans. Clare had great financial difficulties to contend with in the conduct of the convent, and ill health that was brought on by seeing her brother cut down by a mob. d. 1419. c.c. 1830. *April 17, ii, 117.*

CLARE OF RIMINI, BD

Clara Agolanti was twice married; after her second widowhood she became a Franciscan tertiary and led a life of penance and alms-deeds. She founded a convent but never became a member of it herself. Some of her physical austerities were most extravagant and were so regarded even by her contemporaries of the fourteenth century. d. 1346. c.c. 1784. *February 10, i, 287.*

CLARITO, BD

Or *Chiarito.* He is venerated by the Augustinian friars as the founder of a convent of nuns of their order, wherein his own wife became a religious. d. 1348. *May 25, ii, 393.*

CLARUS, ST, ABBOT

Believed to have been abbot of the monastery of St Mercellus at Vienne in Dauphiny. d. *c.* 660. c.c. 1903. *January 1, i, 10.*

CLARUS, ST, MARTYR

He is said to have been a native of Rochester who became a hermit in France, and was murdered at the instigation of a woman whose advances he had refused. Eighth century (?). He gave his name to Saint-Clair-sur-Epte. *November 4, iv, 264.*

*CLAUD, ST, BISHOP

He was chosen bishop of Besançon in 685 after having been, it is said, abbot of Condate in the Jura mountains. He was already old, and resigned his see seven years later. d. *c.* 699. *Claudius. June 6, ii, 490.*

CLAUD LA COLOMBIÈRE, BD

Born near Lyons in 1641 and entered the Society of Jesus at Avignon. He was tutor to the sons of the minister Colbert and then professor of rhetoric at Avignon, where his preaching attracted much attention. At the age of thirty-three he was made superior of the college at Paray-le-Monial, where he met St Margaret Mary and was "her 'coadjutor' in propagating devotion to the Sacred Heart, and as one chosen by God to direct her in the time of her trouble and vexation of spirit". His next mission was as court preacher to Mary Beatrice d'Este, Duchess of York, and he made many converts in England. At the time of the Oates "plot" Bd Claud was in danger of death; but he was banished, and returned to France. For the rest of his life he was an invalid, due partly to his imprisonment in England. d. 1682. bd 1929. *February 15, i, 346.*

CLAUDIA, ST

A woman mentioned by St Paul in his second letter to Timothy (iv, 21); that she was a Briton and the wife of Martial's Aulus Pudens has been asserted but is most improbable. *August 7, iii, 274.*

CLAUDIA THÉVENET, ST, VIRGIN

Sr Claudine Thévenet, b. 1774, spent her life at Lyons. She dedicated her life to the education of the young and underprivileged. She founded the Congregation of Religious of Jesus-Mary which now numbers 200 sisters. d. 1837. bd October 4, 1981. cd 21 March, 1993. *February 3.*

*CLAUDIUS, ASTERIUS AND NEON, SS, MARTYRS

Claudius, Asterius and Neon were three brothers who were charged as Christians before the magistrate of Aegea in Cilicia by their step-mother, who hoped to inherit their estates; two women, Domnina and Theonilla, were on trial as Christians at the same time. The men were crucified and the women scourged to death, 303 (?). *August 23, iii, 388.*

*CLAUDIUS AND HILARIA, SS, MARTYRS

Claudius, a Roman tribune, Hilaria his wife, their two sons and seventy soldiers; this Claudius is a character in the legend of SS Chrysanthus and Daria. Others are mentioned in the Roman Martyrology on December 1. *December 3, iv, 483.*

CLAUDIUS. *See also* Four Crowned Martyrs.

CLELIA BARBIERI, ST, VIRGIN

Clelia Barbieri, the youngest founder of an order in the history of the Church, was born on February 13, 1847 into a working-class family in the Bologna diocese. She became a diocesan catechist at fourteen. She thought her extreme poverty barred her from joining an existing order. In 1868 she and some companions founded the community of Our Lady of Dolours for the service of the poor in joy, simplicity and contemplation. She died on July 31, 1870, when twenty-three. bd October 2, 1968. cd April 9, 1989. *July 13.*

*CLEMENT I, ST, POPE AND MARTYR

Clement was apparently the third successor of St Peter, and the first after him about whom any information survives. A letter he wrote to the church of Corinth is extant and is one of the most important documents of sub-apostolic times. He is venerated as a martyr, *c.* 99, but the fact of his martyrdom

is not certain. St Clement is named in the Roman canon. *Clemens.*
November 23, iv, 405.

CLEMENT MARCHISIO, BD

Clemente Marchisio, b. 1833, was an Italian priest who founded the Institute of Daughters of St Joseph. He was noted for his spirituality. d. 1903. bd September 30, 1984. *September 20.*

*CLEMENT MARY HOFBAUER, ST

He was the first to establish the Redemptorist congregation north of the Alps. He was a Slav, born in Moravia (real name, John Dvorak), and son of a grazier; after being a baker, and then a hermit, he joined the Redemptorists at Rome in 1783, at the age of thirty-two. Four years later St Clement established a house of the congregation at Warsaw, primarily for the benefit of the Germans in that city. From 1789 till 1808 they preached five times a day, in Polish and German, and made numerous conversions of Protestants, Jews and the lapsed. St Clement established an orphanage and schools and settled his congregation in several places, but much of his work was undone by Napoleon's suppression of the religious orders. He then retired to Vienna, where for twelve years he was the most respected and influential priest in the city; he founded a college for boys and prepared the ground for the ultimate firm planting of the Redemptorists in the German lands. d. 1820. cd 1909. *March 15, i, 601.*

*CLEMENT OF ANCYRA, ST, BISHOP AND MARTYR

We have no reliable knowledge of this saint or of his companion in martyrdom, St Agathangelus. d. 308 (?) *January 23, i, 153.*

CLEMENT OF OKHRIDA, ST. *See* Seven Apostles of Bulgaria.

CLEMENT OF ST ELPIDIO, BD

Or "of Osimo". As prior general he drew up and revised the constitutions of the order of Hermit Friars of St Augustine in 1270 and 1284, and so is regarded as their second founder. d. 1291. c.c. 1572. *April 8, ii, 54.*

CLEOPATRA, ST

She is said to have been a widow who secured the body of St Varus and enshrined it at her home at Dera'a in Syria. After the sudden death of her son, Varus appeared in a vision to comfort her. Fourth century (?). *October 19, iv, 149.*

*CLODOALD, ST

In French, *Cloud.* He was a grandson of King Clovis. At the time of the murder of his two brothers he was taken to safety in Provence. Later he became a solitary at the place near Versailles now called Saint-Cloud. There he d. at the age of thirty-six, *c.* 560. *September 7, iii, 503.*

*CLODULF, ST, BISHOP

Clodulf (Clou) was the son of St Arnulf, bishop of Metz, and himself was appointed to that see, which he ruled for forty years. d. *c.* 692. *June 8, ii, 503.*

*CLOTILDA, ST

Clotilda, b. at Lyons *c.* 474, married Clovis, king of the Salian Franks, and helped to bring about her heathen husband's conversion. After his death in 511 her life was saddened by family feuds and the quarrels of her three sons and by the misfortunes of her unhappily married daughter. In old age Clotilda went to live at Tours, where she spent the rest of her life in the service of God and the poor and suffering. d. 545. *Clotildis. June 3, ii, 462.*

CLOUD. See Clodoald.

*CODRATUS, ST, MARTYR

Codratus, with four companions, was martyred at Corinth in 258 (?), but the details of their passion are not reliable. *March 10, i, 544.*

CODRATUS. *See also* Quadratus.

COEMGEN. *See* Kevin.

*COLETTE, ST, VIRGIN

Nicolette Boylet was b. 1381, the daughter of a carpenter at Corbie in Picardy. She was first a Franciscan tertiary who lived as an anchoress beside her parish church, but in

1406 she set out to walk to Nice to lay before Peter de Luna (who was acknowledged as pope in France) her scheme for the reform of the Poor Clares. He was so impressed that he made Colette superioress of the whole order with full powers to carry out the reform. This she proceeded to do by visiting all the convents in France, Savoy and Flanders; some adopted her suggestions, others received her with contumely. In addition she founded new convents, and herself lived a life of sustained prayer. Colette exercised a notable influence by her simple goodness over people of high rank, such as James of Bourbon and Philip the Good of Burgundy. She d. at Ghent in 1447. cd 1807. *Coleta. March 6, i, 506.*

COLMAN OF CLOYNE, ST, BISHOP

He was a poet, royal bard at the court of Cashel, and was a heathen until middle age; he is said to have been baptized by St Brendan. After he was ordained Colman preached in Limerick and the eastern parts of Cork, and founded the church of Cloyne, of which he is venerated as the first bishop. Sixth century. His feast is observed throughout Ireland. The name of Colman was extraordinarily common in the early Irish church. *Colmanus. November 24, iv, 419.*

COLMAN OF DROMORE, ST, BISHOP

The founder of the monastery of Dromore in County Down during the sixth century and first bishop there. According to tradition he came to Ireland from Argyll. Feast kept throughout Ireland. *October 29, iv, 218.*

COLMAN OF KILMACDUAGH, ST, BISHOP

He founded the monastery at Kilmacduagh and is venerated as the first bishop in those parts. He had previously been a hermit on Aranmore and at Burren in county Clare. d. *c.* 632. The feast is observed throughout Ireland. *October 29, iv, 218.*

COLMAN OF LANN ELO, ST, ABBOT

This Colman is a nephew of St Columba, whom he visited on Iona. He founded a famous monastery at Lynally (Lann Elo), and the authorship of the *Alphabet of Devo-*

tion is attributed to him. d. 611. *September 26, iii, 654.*

COLMAN OF LINDISFARNE, ST, BISHOP

An Irish monk from Iona and the third bishop of Lindisfarne. During his short pontificate he took part in the Synod of Whitby in 664 and, rather than abandon Celtic in favour of Roman usages, he resigned his see and withdrew with his monks to Ireland. Here he established himself on Inishbofin, and later founded a separate monastery on the mainland for his English monks, as they did not get on with their Irish brethren. d. 676. The feast is kept in Argyll and the Isles. *February 18, i, 369.*

COLMAN. *see also under* Kilian (martyr).

*COLOMAN, ST, MARTYR

Coloman, an Irish or Scottish pilgrim, was put to death in 1012 at Sockerau on the Danube on the unjust suspicion of being a spy. A popular *cultus* sprang up and his body was enshrined at the abbey of Melk. *Colomannus. October 13, iv, 105.*

*COLUMBA OR COLMCILLE, ST, ABBOT

The most famous of the saints of Scotland, b. at Gartan in County Donegal *c.* 521. He studied at Moville and Clonard and left the monastery of Glasnevin to spend fifteen years preaching and founding churches and monasteries in various parts of Ireland. Then, in circumstances that have caused much discussion, he determined to leave his country. On Whitsun eve 563 he landed with twelve companions on the island of Iona and there founded the monastery that was to be famous throughout western Christendom, and from which he preached the gospel in Scotland, to the Picts and to the Scots: he is said to have penetrated even so far as Aberdeenshire. He revisited Ireland from time to time and folk of all kinds from all parts came to consult him at Iona; his influence dominated the church of Scotland, Ireland and Northumbria, and his monastic rule influenced western Europe for long after his death, which took place in 597. "He had the face of an angel; he was of an excellent nature, polished in speech, holy in deed, great in counsel ... loving unto all", is the verdict of his biographer Adamnan. St Columba's feast is kept throughout Scotland, Ireland, Australia and New Zealand. *June 9, ii, 506.*

*COLUMBA, ST, VIRGIN AND MARTYR

With other nuns of Tabanos she was driven from her convent by the Moors. Having gone before the magistrate and denied Mohammed as a false prophet, she was beheaded at Cordova in 853. *September 17, iii, 580.*

COLUMBA OF RIETI, BD, VIRGIN

She was a Dominican religious of the third order at Perugia, whose holiness and spiritual gifts caused her to be regarded in some sort as the city's patroness even in her lifetime. She was often consulted by the Perugian rulers, but is said to have been grievously persecuted by Lucrezia Borgia. d. 1501. c.c. 1627. *May 20, ii, 359.*

*COLUMBA OF SENS, ST,
VIRGIN AND MARTYR

She is said to have been a Spanish girl of Sens, put to death with other Christian Spaniards near Meaux. She had an extensive *cultus* in south-west Europe during the Middle Ages, but her story is quite unreliable. *December 31, iv, 645.*

*COLUMBAN, ST, ABBOT

Columban was b. in Leinster. He left Bangor with a dozen monks and founded the great monastery of Luxeuil in the Vosges. When in 610 he was exiled, at the instigation of Queen Brunhilda and other enemies, he went into Italy and there established the no less famous abbey of Bobbio. He was a somewhat intemperate upholder of Celtic customs, but the austere rule which he gave to his monks was exceedingly influential in western Europe during the sixth/seventh centuries, and his monasteries continued to exercise a great influence after they had become Benedictine. d. 615. The feast of St Columban is kept throughout Ireland; the Roman Martyrology and the Benedictines commemorate him. *November 23, iv, 409.*

COMGALL, ST, ABBOT

The feast of St Comgall is kept throughout Ireland as one of the founders of monasticism in that country. He was b. in Ulster *c.* 516 and founded the great abbey of Bennchor (Bangor), where he trained St Columban, giving to the monks a rule of his own composition. St Comgall seems to have made missionary journeys into Scotland. d. 603. *Comgallus. May 11, ii, 270.*

COMGAN, ST, ABBOT

An eighth-century Irish abbot in Scotland, whose feast is kept in the diocese of Aberdeen. *October 13, iv, 104.*

COMPIÈGNE, THE MARTYRS OF

Sixteen Carmelite nuns of Compiègne, together with a layman who befriended them, were guillotined in Paris in 1794 for being "enemies of the people" by reason of their religious belief and profession. They were bd in 1906, the first victims of the French revolution to be so honoured. *July 17, iii, 132.*

CONAN, ST, BISHOP

This Conan is believed to have been a bishop in the Isle of Man, but nothing is known for certain about him. Seventh century (?). *January 26, i, 172.*

*CONCORDIUS, ST, MARTYR

A subdeacon martyred at Spoleto under Marcus Aurelius, *c.* 178. *January 1, i, 3.*

CONDEDUS, ST

Condedus, said to have been an Englishman, was a solitary in France and for a time a monk of Fontenelle; he d. at a hermitage on an islet in the Seine, *c.* 685. *October 21, iv, 170.*

CONLETH, ST, BISHOP

He was a priest and metal-worker at Old Connell on the Liffey and became a friend of St Brigid. He is venerated as the first bishop at Kildare, and his feast is kept throughout Ireland with that of St Catald. d. *c.* 519. *Conlethus. May 10, ii, 266.*

CONRAD OF ASCOLI, BD

Conrad de' Miliani was a successful

Franciscan missionary in Libya and later a counsellor of Cardinal Jerome Masci, whose election to the papacy, as Nicholas IV, Bd Conrad had perhaps foretold when a boy. d. 1289. c.c. by Pope Pius VI. *April 19, ii, 132.*

CONRAD OF BAVARIA, BD
Born *c.* 1105, son of Henry the Black Duke of Bavaria. He became a Cistercian monk at Clairvaux, and d. in Apulia on his way back from a pilgrimage to the Holy Land in 1154. c.c. 1832, *February 14, i, 337.*

*CONRAD OF CONSTANCE, ST,
BISHOP
He became bishop of Constance in 934 and d. in 975. cd 1823. Considering the age in which he lived he seems to have kept remarkably aloof from secular politics. *November 26, iv, 425.*

CONRAD OF OFFIDA, BD
Conrad was an early Friar Minor whose sympathies were with the "Spiritual" and eremitical movements in the order. He was accompanied in his preaching journeys by Bd Peter of Treja, who shared his enthusiasm for evangelical poverty. Our Lady is said to have appeared to Bd Conrad one Candlemas day and to have laid the Holy Child in his arms. d. 1306. c.c. 1817. *December 14, iv, 560.*

*CONRAD OF PARZHAM, ST
No life could be more simple and unsensational than that of St Conrad. He was b. at Parzham in Bavaria, became a Capuchin lay-brother when he was thirty-one, and lived for forty years at the friary of Altötting. d. 1894. cd 1934. *April 21, ii, 143.*

CONRAD OF PIACENZA, ST
He was a nobleman who was nearly ruined materially by restitution he made in consequence of an act of injustice. His wife became a Poor Clare and Conrad joined some hermits who lived under the rule of the third order of St Francis. To avoid publicity he removed to Sicily, where he lived for over thirty years and d. there in 135. Many marvels are recounted of him. c.c. by three popes. *February 19, i, 377.*

CONRAD OF SELDENBÜREN, BD
He founded and endowed the abbey of Engelberg in 1082–1120, and became a lay-brother there. He was murdered at Zurich in 1126, having been sent there on business of the abbey. *May 2, ii, 219.*

CONRAN, ST, BISHOP
Nothing whatever is known about this alleged bishop in the Orkney Islands. *February 14, i, 336.*

CONSTANTINE, ST, MARTYR
There is very great uncertainty about this saint. He is said to have been a prince from Cornwall who was first a penitent in Ireland and then a missionary in Scotland, where he was murdered by pirates in Kintyre. Sixth century (?). His feast is still kept in the diocese of Argyll and the Isles. *Constantinus. March 11, i, 556.*

CONSTANTINE. *See also under* Theodore of Yaroslavl.

CONSTANTIUS OF FABRIANO, BD
Constantius Bernocchi was concerned in the reform of the Dominican friary of San Marco at Florence, and while a preacher in that city received the gift of prophecy. d. 1481. c.c. 1811. *February 25, i, 420.*

CONTARDO, ST
St Contardo the Pilgrim belonged to the Este family of Ferrara and d. while on a pilgrimage to Compostela in 1249; his tomb was honoured by miracles. *Contardus. April 16, ii, 104.*

CONTARDO FERRINI, BD
The man who "removed the primacy in Roman legal studies from Germany to Italy" (Mommsen) was b. in Milan in 1859. He studied at Pavia and Berlin, worked in many European libraries, and held professorial chairs in the universities of Messina and Pavia: his work, he used to say, was as a wife to him (he never married), and he made his scholarship and teaching "a hymn of praise to the Lord of all learning". Ferrini was active in public affairs, and his recreation was mountaineering. He was, declared Pope Pius XII, a man who "gave an emphatic Yes

to the possibility of holiness in these days". d. 1902. bd 1947. *October 27, iv, 210.*

CONVOYON, ST, ABBOT

Founder of the monastery of Saint Saviour near Redon in Brittany in 831, a foundation which was carried out under great difficulties. d. 868. c.c. 1866. *January 5, i, 37.*

*CORBINIAN, ST, BISHOP

He was a Frankish hermit, and was sent by the Holy See to preach the gospel in Bavaria, where he founded the see of Freising. The later years of his life were spent in semi-exile owing to the enmity of Duke Grimoald, whose irregular marriage he had opposed. d. 725. *Corbinianus. September 8, iii, 511.*

CORENTIN, ST, BISHOP

He is venerated as the first bishop of Cornouaille (Quimper) in Brittany, where he was a hermit at Plomodiern during the sixth (?) century. Corentin was known in the west and south of England, being called "St Cury" in Cornwall. *December 12, iv, 545.*

*CORNELIUS, ST, POPE AND MARTYR

The pontificate of Cornelius is important in ecclesiastical history because of the appearance of the first formal antipope, Novatian, and the controversy about this man's rigorism in dealing with Christians who had weakened under persecution. Pope St Cornelius was the first to suffer in the persecution of Gallus, in 253: he probably d. of ill treatment in exile at Centumcellae, though later accounts say that he was beheaded. This pope is named, with his supporter St Cyprian, in Eucharistic prayer I. *September 16, iii, 50.*

COSIMO DI CARBOGNANO. *See* Gomidas.

*COSMAS AND DAMIAN, SS, MARTYRS

They are the principal and best known of those saints venerated in the East as *anargyroi*, "moneyless ones", because they practised medicine without taking payment from their patients. They are said, with many legendary accretions, to have been twin Arab brothers, martyred in Cilicia under Diocletian, but their origin and true his-

tory are unknown. They are named in the Roman canon and the preparation of the Byzantine Mass. *September 27, iii, 659.*

CRESCENTIA HÖSS, BD, VIRGIN

This daughter of a weaver was admitted to a house of Franciscan regular tertiaries at Kaufbeuren at the request of the Protestant mayor, and was then neglected by the prioress and older nuns because she had not brought a dowry. After a time they discovered that she had brought the dowry of holiness, and had the grace to make her novice-mistress and then superioress. d. 174. bd 1900. *April 6, ii, 38.*

CRESCENTIA. *See also under* Vitus.

*CRETE, THE MARTYRS OF

The group known as the Ten Martyrs of Crete (SS Theodulus and his companions) suffered death by beheading near Gortyna during the persecution under Decius in 250. *December 23, iv, 599.*

*CRISPIN AND CRISPINIAN, SS, MARTYRS

These famous martyrs, patron saints of shoe-makers, were put to death at Soissons (or at Rome), but the extant account of them cannot be relied on. They have a local traditional association with the town of Faversham in Kent. *Crispinus, Crispinianus. October 25, iv, 197.*

CRISPIN OF VITERBO, BD

A Capuchin lay-brother at various houses of his order in Italy, in all of which he was revered for his holy life and miracles. d. 1750. bd 1806. *May 19, ii, 365.*

*CRISPINA, ST, MARTYR

St Augustine frequently mentions St Crispina, who was an African woman of rank, married, with several children. In 304 she was charged with ignoring the imperial commands to sacrifice to the gods; she was resolute in her disobedience, and was beheaded at Theveste. *December 5, iv, 497.*

CRONAN OF ROSCREA, ST, ABBOT

There are no reliable accounts of the life of

St Cronan, who founded several monasteries in Ireland. d. *c.* 626. *April 28, ii, 182.*

CRONION. *See under* Julian.

CROWNED MARTYRS. *See* Four Crowned Martyrs.

CUBY. *See* Cybi.

*CUCUFAS, ST, MARTYR
One of the most celebrated of the Spanish martyrs, b. of Punic descent in Africa; he was tortured and beheaded at Barcelona in 304. *July 25.*

CUMIAN, ST, ABBOT
This Cuimine, called Fota, had charge of the monastic school at Clonfert, and is said to be the Cumian who founded the monastery at Kilcummin, where he was an active defender of the Roman computation of Easter against the Celtic usage. d. *c.* 665. *November 12, iv, 323.*

*CUNEGUND, ST
Cunegund was the wife of the Holy Roman emperor St Henry II. A year after her husband's death she became a nun in the convent she had founded at Kaufungen, near Cassel. d. 1033 or 1039. cd 1200. St Cunegund had no children and she is commemorated liturgically as a virgin, but this seems to be an error. *Cunegundis. March 3, i, 470.*

CUNEGUND, BD, VIRGIN
In Magyar *Kinga.* She was the daughter of Bela IV of Hungary and niece of St Elizabeth. She married Boleslaus V of Poland and together they took a vow of perpetual continency; after his death she became a Poor Clare. d. 1292. c.c. 1690. *July 24, iii, 178.*

CUNGAR, ST, ABBOT
Cungar (Cyngar, Congar) founded several churches in Wales and a monastery at Congresbury in Somerset, for which reason his feast is observed in the diocese of Clifton. There may have been more than one Cungar, but particulars are very confused. Sixth century. *Cungarus. November 27, iv, 435.*

*CUNIBERT, ST, BISHOP
He was bishop of Cologne and a chief minister during the minority of Sigebert of Austrasia; but he did not live long to fulfil this office, dying with a great reputation of holiness. *c.* 663. *Cunibertus. November 12, iv, 322.*

CUNO. *See* Conrad (June 1).

CURY. *See* Corentin.

*CUTHBERT, ST, BISHOP
While a monk at Melrose and Lindisfarne he made missionary journeys far and wide in Northumbria, and was then a solitary for ten years until 685, when he was consecrated bishop of Lindisfarne. He "continued to be the same man that he was before", but only ruled his see for two years, dying on Farne Island in 687. St Cuthbert is one of the most famous of Scottish saints (the claim that he was Irish is not established): without intermission he preached, taught, distributed alms, and wrought so many miracles of healing that he was known during his lifetime as the "Wonder-worker of Britain". He travelled into the remoter parts of the north, visiting from cottage to cottage from Berwick to Solway Firth with the good news of Christ, and everywhere he was a welcome and honoured guest. His shrine at Durham was one of the most frequented in the Middle Ages; his feast is kept today in several northern English dioceses, and in Meath and Saint Andrew's. *Cuthbertus. March 20, i, 637.*

CUTHBERT MAYNE, ST, MARTYR
Cuthbert Mayne, b. near Barnstaple in 1544, was the first seminary priest to suffer martyrdom. He was a convert minister, ordained at Douay, and in 1576 was sent on the mission in England. He was stationed at Mr Francis Tregian's mansion at Golden in Cornwall, where he was soon arrested. At Launceston assizes he was found guilty of various offences under the Acts of Parliament 1 and 13 Elizabeth in such circumstances that a majority of the judges of the country thought the conviction could not stand. But the Privy Council directed that the sentence be carried out; Bd Cuthbert was

accordingly h.d.q. at Launceston in 1577. cd 1970. His feast is kept in Plymouth and several other English dioceses. *November 30, iv, 447.*

CUTHBURGA, ST

She was the wife of King Aldfrid of Northumbria, and became a nun at Barking in Essex under St Hildelitha. Later she founded the abbey of Wimborne, with her sister St Quenburga, and ruled it as abbess till her death *c.* 725. SS Cuthburga and Hildelitha are celebrated in a common feast in the diocese of Brentwood. *September 3, iii, 481.*

CUTHMAN, ST,

He lived with his mother at Steyning in Sussex, where he appears to have built the first church. d. *c.* 900. *February 8, i, 280.*

CYBARD. *See* Eparchius.

CYBI, ST, ABBOT

He is said to have been born in Cornwall, and migrated to Wales where he was a missionary monk in Anglesey. His chief centre was at Holyhead, called in Welsh Caergybi "Cybi's Town". Sixth century. *November 8, iv, 295.*

CYNEBURGA AND CYNESWIDE, SS

Cyneburga was a daughter of Penda of Mercia, and was married to Alcfrid, son of Oswy of Northumbria. In later life she founded and governed the abbey of Cyneburgecester, now Castor in Northamptonshire. Here she was joined by her sister Cyneswide and her kinswoman Tibba. These three holy women were all buried in Peterborough minster, which the two princesses had helped to endow. Seventh century. *March 6, i, 500.*

*CYPRIAN, ST, BISHOP AND MARTYR

St Cyprian, bishop of Carthage, played an important part in the history of the Western Church and the development of Christian thought in the third century, particularly in Africa; his works include many letters and a famous treatise on the unity of the Church. Caecilius Cyprianus was b. in proconsular Africa *c.* 200, became a lawyer, in due course was converted to Christianity and was con-secrated bishop *c.* 249. He went into hiding during the persecution under Decius, supported Pope St Cornelius against the anti-pope Novatian, and was prominent in the controversy about the treatment of Christians who had lapsed or weakened under persecution. In the plague of 252–54 St Cyprian organized his flock in Carthage for the relief of the sufferers. He was arrested under the first edict of Valerian and beheaded in 258: the record of his trial and death is a document of great interest. St Cyprian is named in the intercession of the Roman canon, which is the more notable because he had a serious disagreement with Pope St Stephen I concerning the validity of baptism given by heretics. *Cyprianus. September 16, iii, 561.*

CYPRIAN. *See* Felix and Cyprian.

CYRAN. *See* Sigiramnus.

CYRIACA. *See* Dominica.

*CYRIACUS, ST, BISHOP AND MARTYR

Judas Cyriacus, patron of Ancona, may have been a local bishop who was killed during a pilgrimage to Jerusalem, or possibly the Judas, bishop of Jerusalem, who lost his life in a riot in 133. The local legend makes him a bishop of Jerusalem martyred under Julian the Apostate. *May 4, ii, 229.*

*CYRIACUS, LARGUS AND SMARAGDUS, SS, MARTYRS

St Cyriacus was a deacon, martyred at Rome. With him are associated SS Largus, Smaragdus, and twenty others, but their story as told is simply a romance. *August 8, iii, 280.*

CYRICUS. *See* Quiricus.

*CYRIL AND METHODIUS, SS

These brothers are venerated with much enthusiasm as the apostles of the southern Slavs, but there is much in their story as it has come down to us that is doubtful. Cyril (Constantine) was a priest and Methodius a monk in Greece, who in 863 were sent as missionaries into Moravia. Cyril d. at Rome in 869, but his brother was consecrated bishop and sent back to Moravia and Pannonia with the permission of the Holy See to celebrate the liturgy in Slavonic. For this and other reasons Methodius incurred the opposition of the neighbouring German bishops, who for a time put him in prison; later he continued his mission, with the support of Pope John VIII but under great difficulties. He is said to have translated the Bible into Slavonic, as well as the *Nomokanon*. d. 885, *Cyrillus. February 14, iii, 29.*

*CYRIL OF ALEXANDRIA, ST,
BISHOP AND DOCTOR

Born at Alexandria *c.* 376; archbishop of that city 412. His name is bound up with the history of the early days of the Nestorian heresy, which he denounced to Pope St Celestine I. At the ecumenical council of Ephesus in 432, at which the heresy was solemnly condemned, St Cyril presided as representative of the Holy See, and the rest of his life was given over to the defence of the truth that in Jesus Christ there is but one divine person. He was a man of much vigour and determination, tending to the use of severe and hasty methods that were productive of trouble. d. 444. Declared a Doctor of the Church, 1882. *June 27, ii, 283.*

CYRIL OF CAESAREA, ST, MARTYR

A martyr at Caesarea in Cappadocia. According to the story, he was a boy who became a Christian without his father's knowledge; when he was turned out of his home he was arrested by the authorities and put to death. d. 251 (?). *May 29, ii, 419.*

CYRIL OF CONSTANTINOPLE, ST

He was prior general of the Carmelites in Palestine from *c.* 1232 to his death in *c.* 1235 (?). There has been some very peculiar confusion between him and two other SS Cyril, of Alexandria and Jerusalem. *March 6, i, 504.*

*CYRIL OF HELIOPOLIS, ST, MARTYR

A deacon of Heliopolis in the Lebanon, martyred under Julius the Apostate, *c.* 362. *March 29, i, 697.*

*CYRIL OF JERUSALEM, ST,
BISHOP AND DOCTOR

He was b. about 315 and succeeded St Maximus as bishop of Jerusalem, but not a great deal is known of his life beyond that he had a stormy episcopate. The works for which he is famous are chiefly two series of instructions, one for catechumens in Lent before baptism and the other on the effects of baptism, confirmation, holy communion, and the offering for the living and the dead, with details of the customs of the Eastern Church. These writings are said to be "the earliest example extant of anything in the shape of a formal system of theology". St Cyril, a man of gentle and conciliatory disposition, d. in 386. Sixteen of his thirty-five years of episcopate had been spent in exile. Pope Leo XIII named him a Doctor of the Church. *March 18, i, 623.*

CYRIL OF TUROV, ST, BISHOP

An outstanding hierarch and preacher in pre-Mongol Russia, but practically no particulars of his life have survived. He was "an exponent of the Greek tradition on the Russian soil", and "a unique example of theological devotion in ancient Russia". d. 1182. *April 28, ii, 182.*

CYRIL. *See also under* Anastasia.

CYRINUS. *See under* Basilides *and* Quirinus.

*CYRUS AND JOHN, SS, MARTYRS

Physicians of Alexandria who went to Canopus to succour a woman and her three young daughters who were being persecuted for Christ's sake. They were all put to death, *c.* 303. SS Cyrus and John were greatly venerated in Egypt and the East generally. *January 31, i, 212.*

D

DAGOBERT II, ST
Two French dioceses keep the feast of Dagobert II, king of Austrasia, but there seems no reason apart from popular tradition why he should be regarded as a saint. While in exile as a young man he became friendly with St Wilfrid of York, and he married an Englishwoman. His murder in 679 was popularly construed as martyrdom. *Dagobertus. December 23, iv, 601.*

DALMATIUS MONER, BD
The life of this Spanish confessor of the order of Friars Preachers was passed in the obscurity of his cell and the quiet discharge of his ordinary duties. d. 1341. c.c. 1721. *September 26, iii, 657.*

DAMASCUS, THE MARTYRS OF
These were among the victims of the Druse rising against the Christians in the Lebanon in 1860. They were Emmanuel Ruiz (*q.v.*), guardian of the Friars Minor at Damascus, and seven of his community with three Maronite laymen, the brothers Masabki, all slain within the walls of the friary where they had been betrayed. They were offered the alternative of accepting Islam or death. bd 1926. *July 10, iii, 68.*

*DAMASCUS I, ST, POPE
Damasus came to the papal chair in 366. He vigorously opposed Apollinarianism and other heresies and much increased the prestige of the Roman see; he encouraged St Jerome's biblical studies; and himself wrote inscriptions for buildings and for the tombs of the martyrs, many of which have survived. d. 384. *December 11, iv, 536.*

DAMIAN OF FINARIO, BD
Damiano Furcheri was a Dominican friar known for his preaching throughout Lombardy and Liguria. d. 1484. c.c. 1848. *Damianus. October 26, iv, 207.*

DAMIAN. See also Cosmas.

DANES, MARTYRS UNDER THE
During the ninth century the Danes raiding England showed special ferocity against representative Christians. Among their victims regarded as martyrs were the monks of Chertsey Beocca and Hethor, Abbot Hedda at Peterborough, Torthred and his companions at Thorney, and Abbot Theodore and other monks at Croyland. The best-known victim was the king of the East Angles, Edmund (*q.v.*). *April 10, ii, 62.*

*DANIEL, ST, MARTYR
Seven Friars Minor, led by Brother Daniel, arrived in Morocco in 1227 to preach the gospel to the Moors. Within three weeks they were all beheaded at Ceuta for refusing to apostatize to Islam. cd 1516. *October 10, iv, 81.*

DANIEL BROTTIER, BD
He was b. in 1876 and was a priest of the Congregation of the Holy Spirit and of the Immaculate Heart of Mary. He became a missionary in Senegal, Africa, with a special concern for orphans. d. 1936. bd November 25, 1984. *February 28.*

*DANIEL STYLITES, ST
He was the greatest and best known of the

pillar-saints after St Simeon the Elder, who was Daniel's inspiration. After being a hermit for some years near Constantinople he became a stylite, the emperor Leo I providing an arrangement of pillars which included a small shelter at the top. Here he was ordained priest by St Gennadius, and was as it were the oracle of Constantinople for many years; on one occasion he came down to earth, *c.* 476, to rebuke the usurping emperor Basiliscus for supporting the Monophysite heresy. d. 493. *December 11, iv, 539.*

DARERCA, ST, VIRGIN

Or *Moninne.* She is said to have been the first abbess of Killeavy, near Newry. d. 517(?). *July 6, iii, 26.*

DARIA. *See* Chrysanthus.

*DASIUS, ST, MARTYR

He was a Roman soldier put to death at Durostorum (Silistria) in 303(?) for refusing to take part in heathen observances at the Saturnalia. *November 20, iv, 393.*

*DATIUS, ST, BISHOP

He became bishop of Milan about 530 and was much troubled by both Goths and heretics. He was driven away to Constantinople, where he lived for the rest of his life and d. in 552, after supporting Pope Vigilius against Justinian in the "Three Chapters" controversy. *January 14, i, 83.*

DATIVA. *See under* Dionysia.

DATIVUS. *See under* Saturninus.

DAVID, ST, BISHOP

In Welsh, *Dewi Sant.* The patron saint of Wales lived in the sixth century. He founded a monastery Mynyw (Menevia) in the far west of Dyfed, South Wales, and is venerated as the first bishop in those parts, now called St Davids after him. The monks followed an extremely austere rule which included total abstinence from wine, whence they were called "the Watermen"; this led to controversy between St David and St Gildas, who said that the Menevian monks were more ascetic than Christian. The story that David was acclaimed "primate of Wales" at the Synod of Brefi and that he was conse-

crated at Jerusalem is fictitious. d. 589(?). His feast is kept in Wales and in the English dioceses of Westminster and Portsmouth. *March 1, i, 449.*

DAVID GONSON, BD, MARTYR

Knight of St John, condemned by attainder for denying the king's ecclesiastical supremacy; he was h.d.q. at Southwark, 1541. bd 1929. *July 12, iii, 73.*

DAVID LEWIS, ST, MARTYR

David Lewis (*alias* Charles Baker) was the last in order of time of the Welsh martyrs. He was b. in 1616 at Abergavenny, became a Jesuit, and was stationed at the Society's residence at the Cwm, near Monmouth. After the Titus Oates scare he was betrayed by an apostate and h.d.q. for his priesthood at Usk in 1679. cd 1970. *August 27, iii, 424.*

DAVID OF MUNKTORP, ST, BISHOP

This David was, it is said, an English monk, who joined the mission of St Sigfrid in Sweden and founded a monastery at Munktorp. He is also said to have been the first bishop of Västeras. d. *c.* 1080. *July 15, iii, 111.*

DAVID OF SCOTLAND, ST

King of the Scots, 1124–53. He founded bishoprics, monasteries and royal burghs and his friend St Aelred bore witness to the virtue of his life and the justness of his rule. d. 1153. *May 24, ii, 383.*

DAVID *See also under* Boris and Gleb.

DAVID. *See also under* Theodore of Yaroslavl.

DECLAN, ST, BISHOP

A missionary in Ireland who was bishop in the district of Ardmore. His feast is kept throughout Ireland. *Declanus.* *July 24, iii, 175.*

*DEICOLUS, ST, BISHOP

In French, *Desle.* He left Ireland with St Columban, but when his master left France he stayed behind and founded the abbey of Lure. d. *c.* 624. *January 18, i, 116.*

DEINIOL, ST, BISHOP

Deiniol founded the monastery of Bangor Fawr on the Menai Straits, where eventually the medieval see of Bangor was located, and was probably the founder of Bangor Iscoed on the Dee also. d. *c.* 584 (?). Deiniol's feast is kept in the diocese of Menevia. *September 11, iii, 540.*

DELPHINA, BD

Delphina of Glandèves was the wife of St Elzear and is said to have been a member of the third order of St Francis. She survived her husband for some thirty-five years, first in attendance on Queen Sanchia of Naples and then in retirement in her native Provence. d. 1360. c.c. by Pope Urban VIII. *September 27, iii, 661.*

DEMETRIAN, ST, BISHOP

He was abbot of the monastery of St Antony in Cyprus and then bishop of Khytri for many years. He is one of the most venerated of Cypriot saints. d. *c.* 912. *Demetrianus. November 6, iv, 276.*

*DEMETRIUS, ST, MARTYR

He was probably a deacon martyred at Sirmium in Dalmatia, but the centre of his *cultus* was at Salonika. Later fictitious legends made Demetrius a proconsul and a great warrior saint, in which capacity he was highly venerated all over the East: he is even named in the preparation of the Byzantine Liturgy. *October 8, iv, 63.*

DEMETRIUS OF ALEXANDRIA, ST,
BISHOP

He is reputed the twelfth bishop of Alexandria and was a close friend of Origen, whom later he disciplined for being irregularly ordained. Demetrius had the gift of reading secret sins and thoughts. d. 231. *October 9, iv, 67.*

DENIS. *See* Dionysius.

DENIS SEBUGWAWO. *See* Dionysius Sebugwawo.

DEODATUS OF AQUITAINE, ST,
MARTYR

Déodat de Rodez, from Aquitaine, a Franciscan companion of St Nicholas of Sibenik (Nicholas Tavelic), was martyred by Muslims at Jerusalem in 1393 and canon-

ized by Pope Paul VI on June 21, 1970. *December 5.*

DEODATUS OF NEVERS, ST, BISHOP

In French, *Dié, Didier.* He became bishop of Nevers in 655 but after some years retired to the Vosges mountains as a solitary. Later he was abbot of a community at Ebersheim, near Strasbourg, and then returned to the Vosges, where Saint-Dié is now on the site of his cell. d. 679 (?). *June 19, ii, 584.*

*DEOGRATIAS, ST, BISHOP

While bishop of Carthage he ransomed numerous captives who had been brought from Italy by Genseric and given to the Vandals and Moors as slaves. d. 457. *March 22, i, 658.*

DERFEL GADARN, ST

A local holy man venerated in Merioneth, part of whose wooden image was used at Smithfield to burn Bd John Forest. Folklore and superstition seem to have had a part in this *cultus.* Sixth century (?). *April 5, ii, 34.*

DESIDERATUS, ST, BISHOP

A bishop of Bourges during the sixth century, of whom little is known for certain. Called in French *Désiré. May 8, ii, 251.*

DESIDERIUS OF CAHORS, ST,
BISHOP

Desiderius followed his brother St Rusticus as bishop of Cahors in 630, and worked most zealously for the spiritual and temporal betterment of his diocese. d. 655. *November 15, iv, 348.*

DESIDERIUS OF THÉROUANNE, BD,
BISHOP

In French, *Didier.* A bishop of Thérouanne who founded the Cistercian abbey of Blandecques, "Blandyke", a word having special significance for the *alumni* of English Jesuit schools. d. 1194. *January 20, i, 133.*

*DESIDERIUS OF VIENNE, ST,
BISHOP AND MARTYR

He was bishop of Vienne, and his zeal for clerical discipline and against simony and profligacy at the court brought down on him the anger of Queen Brunhildis. In 607 he was murdered for rebuking the wickedness of King Theodoric, at the place now called Saint-Didier-sur-Chalaronne. *May 23, ii, 374.*

DESLE. *See* Deicolus.

*DEUSDEDIT, ST, POPE

Deusdedit, also called Adeodatus I, was pope from 615 till his death in 618. He worked nobly for the stricken during a plague, but otherwise little is known of him. *November 8, iv, 296.*

DEUSDEDIT OF CANTERBURY, ST,
BISHOP

Or *Frithona*. The sixth archbishop of Canterbury and the first Englishman to occupy the see. Nothing is known of his episcopate. d. 664. *July 14, iii, 100.*

DEWI. *See* David.

DIANA D'ANDALO, BD, VIRGIN

An original member of the first house of Dominican nuns at Bologna in 1222. Diana was a Bolognese whose family at first violently tried to prevent her becoming a religious. d. 1236. c.c. 1891. *June 9, ii, 511.*

*DIDACUS, ST

This Didacus (Diego) was born of lowly parents in Spain *c.* 1400, and became a Friar Minor of the Observance at Arrizafa. He was simply a lay-brother, but his ability and goodness were so remarkable that he was appointed guardian of the chief friary in the Canary Islands, at Fuerteventura, in 1445. Later he was recalled to Spain, where he d. at Alcalá in 1463. cd 1588. *November 13, iv, 327.*

DIDACUS OF CADIZ, BD

A Capuchin of Cadiz, famous for his sermons about the Holy Trinity, who ministered throughout Spain, but especially in Andalusia. d. 1801. bd 1894. *March 24, i, 672.*

DIDIER. *See* Deodatus, Desiderius.

DIDYMUS. *See under* Theodora.

DIÉ. *See* Deodatus.

DIEGO DE SAN VITORES, BD,
MARTYR

Fr Diego Luis de San Vitores, b. 1627, was a Spanish Jesuit who spent five years in the Philippines, then founded the first permanent mission to Guam and was its first martyr. d. 1672. bd October 6, 1985. *April 2.*

DIEMUT, BD, VIRGIN

Diemut or Diemoda was a solitary at Wessobrunn in Bavaria. She employed her time in copying manuscripts, some of which still exist. d. *c.* 1120. *March 29, i, 701.*

*DIONYSIA AND **MAJORICUS, SS,**
MARTYRS

On December 6 and 7 are commemorated certain martyrs in Africa at the hands of the Arian king Huneric in 484. Principal among them are St Dionysia, her young son Majoricus, and her sister Dativa. *December 6, iv, 507.*

*DIONYSIUS, ST, POPE

He was a Roman priest who came to the chair of Peter in 259 and restored the Roman church after Gallienus stopped persecution. St Dionysius was not the first pope to die in peace, but he is the earliest to whom the title "martyr" is not accorded liturgically. d. 269. *December 26, iv, 618.*

DIONYSIUS AND **REDEMPTUS, BB,**
MARTYRS

Dionysius (Peter Barthelot) was a French ship-master and trader, who became a Carmelite at Goa in 1635. When an embassy was sent thence to Sumatra in 1638 Dionysius went with it in the combined capacities of pilot and chaplain. The embassy was not welcome and among those put to death by the Sumatrans were the chaplain and his *socius*, Brother Redemptus. bd 1900. *November 29, iv, 448.*

DIONYSIUS SEBUGWAWO, ST,
MARTYR

A "page" at the "court" of Mwanga of Uganda (*q.v.*), murdered for teaching Christianity to another page. His death was the signal for the great persecution of 1886. bd 1920, cd 1964. *May 25, ii, 469.*

*DIONYSIUS OF ALEXANDRIA, ST,
BISHOP

This Dionysius became bishop of Alexandria in 247, after being head of the catechetical school there, and governed his diocese from Libya during the persecution of Decius; he was again exiled for a time under Valerian. He was very active in the controversies that troubled the church at that time (*e.g.* Novatianism), and was called by St Athanasius "the teacher of the whole Church". d. 265. *November 17, iv, 364.*

*DIONYSIUS OF CORINTH, ST,
BISHOP

A great leader of the church in the second century, who from his see at Corinth wrote letters to other churches, some of which have come down to us. In the East he is venerated as a martyr because he suffered much for the Faith. d. *c.* 180. *April 8, ii, 52.*

*DIONYSIUS OF MILAN, ST, BISHOP

He was made bishop of Milan in 351 and four years later was banished for upholding the cause of St Athanasius against the Arian emperor Constantius. d. *c.* 359.
May 25, ii, 389.

*DIONYSIUS OF PARIS, ST,
BISHOP AND MARTYR

This saint figures in the liturgical books as a composite of Dionysius the Areopagite, a disciple of St Paul (Acts xvii, 34), Dionysius, bishop of Paris ("St Denis of France"), who with Rusticus and Eleutherius is said to have been martyred at Paris *c.* 258, and pseudo-Dionysius, a famous early mystical writer of unknown date. *October 9, iv, 66, 67.*

*DIONYSIUS THE AREOPAGITE, ST

The Athenian who, with the woman Damaris and others, believed and followed St Paul (Acts xvii, 34); his feast is observed in the Byzantine and other eastern rites. In the Middle Ages certain much later mystical writings were attributed to him; *cf.* Dionysius of Paris, above. *October 9, iv, 66.*

*DIOSCORUS OF ALEXANDRIA, ST

A boy confessor who, remaining firm under cajolery and blows, was discharged because of his youth, and departed free "for the consolation of the faithful". Third century. *December 14, iv, 584.*

DISIBOD, ST, BISHOP

He is said to have been an Irish bishop who was forced by his stiff-necked flock to migrate to Germany, where he founded the monastery of Disibodenberg, near Bingen. d. *c.* 674. *September 8, iii, 509.*

DISMAS. See the Good Thief.

DODA. See Bova.

DODO, BD

He was a hermit at various places in Friesland and was reputed to have received the stigmata—possibly a case of older date than that of St Francis. d. 1231. *March 30, i, 706.*

DOGMAEL, ST

A Welsh monk who founded churches in Dyfed, Brittany, and elsewhere. Sixth century (?). *June 14, ii, 542.*

*DOMETIUS THE PERSIAN, ST,
MARTYR

A Persian monk who was stoned to death for the faith at Nisibis, *c.* 362(?).
August 7, iii, 275.

*DOMINIC, ST

He was born at Calaruega in Spain *c.* 1170 and became an Augustinian canon regular at Osma. At that time the Albigensian heresy was going from strength to strength in the face of slack orthodoxy in south-western Europe, and in 1206 Dominic founded a convent at Prouille whose first nuns were converts from this heresy; this was the germ of the Dominican Order. After a further ten years' preaching he established the Friars Preachers, first to combat Albigensianism and then to preach and teach throughout Europe, to hand on to others the fruits of contemplation. This new order was as successful as that of the contemporary Franciscans, and together they left an ineffaceable mark on the later Middle Ages; the Order of Preachers within a few years had spread all over Europe: it is now world-wide. Both during his life and since his death few saints have excited such personal affection as St Dominic, and few been so reviled by the ignorant: "Nothing disturbed the even temper of his soul," said one who knew him, "except his quick sympathy with every sort of suffering"; the beauty of holiness is remarkably apparent in him. d. 1221 (in another friar's bed and another's habit—because he had none of his own). cd 1234. *Dominicus. August 8, iii, 258.*

DOMINIC AND GREGORY, BB

Two Spanish Dominicans who preached in the villages of the Pyrenees; they were killed by a fall of rock near Besiano in 1300, and have been venerated there ever since. c.c. 1854. *April 26, ii, 166.*

DOMINIC HENAREZ, ST,
BISHOP AND MARTYR

He was a Spanish Dominican, auxiliary bishop of St Ignatius Delgado (*q.v.*) in Eastern Tongking, who was beheaded with his catechist Bd Francis Chien in 1838. bd 1900. cd June 19, 1988. *July 11, iii, 77.*

*DOMINIC LORICATUS, ST

When Dominic discovered that his ordination had been obtained by a simoniacal gift by his father he refused to exercise his priesthood, and became a hermit monk under St Peter Damian at Fonte Avellana. His physical mortifications were altogether extraordinary, and he was called *Loricatus*, "the Mailed", because he wore a rough coat of mail next to his skin. d. 1060. *October 14, iv, 110.*

*DOMINIC SAVIO, ST

This boy was born in Piedmont in 1842, son of a peasant. He became a student aspiring to the priesthood under St John Bosco, who wrote his biography, to which knowledge of the details of Dominic's life is mostly due. This schoolboy is said to have died at the age of fifteen, in 1857: his brief life had been one of doing even the smallest things in the light of love for God. cd 1954. *March 9, i, 539.*

DOMINIC SPADAFORA, BD

A confessor of the Order of Preachers in Sicily and Italy. d. 1521. c.c. 1921. *October 3, iv, 21.*

DOMINIC ZUBERO, BD

Iturrate Zubero, or Dominic of the Most Holy Sacrament, b. 1901 in the Basque country of Spain, was a Trinitarian noted for his spirituality and obedience. d. 1927. bd October 16, 1983. *April 7.*

DOMINIC OF PISA, BD

Dominic Vernagalli was a Camaldolese monk, founder of a hospital in Pisa. d. 1218. c.c. 1854. *April 20.*

*DOMINIC OF SILOS, ST, ABBOT

He was a monastic reformer in Navarre until the enmity of King Garcia III forced him to migrate to Castile, where he restored, and became abbot of, Silos. d. 1073. It was after Dominic of Silos that the founder of the Order of Preachers was named in consequence of Bd Joan of Aza's vision at the saint's shrine. *December 20, iv, 588.*

*DOMINIC OF SORA, ST, ABBOT

The founder of several Benedictine monasteries in Italy. d. 1031. *January 22, i, 147.*

*DOMINIC OF THE CAUSEWAY, ST

St Dominic of the Causeway is so called from the road which he made for pilgrims on their way to Compostela. He was a hermit in the wooded wilderness of Bureba in northeastern Spain, and it was there that he made his road. d. *c.* 1109. *May 12, ii, 289.*

DOMINIC OF THE MOTHER OF GOD, BD

Fr Domenico della Madre di Dio was b. into a peasant family near Viterbo, Italy, in 1792, the last of eleven children. He taught himself to read and write, entered the Passionists and was ordained priest at Rome in 1818. He became the provincial of the order and founded a province in England in 1840. He was an early ecumenist who thought that a more Christian life among Catholics was the best inducement to unity. He received John Henry Newman into the Church in 1845. d. at Reading, August 27, 1849. bd October 27, 1963. *August 27.*

*DOMINICA, ST, VIRGIN AND MARTYR

This saint, the best known of several of the

name, is said on very little authority to have been martyred in Campania under Diocletian. She may be the same as St Cyriaca (= Dominica) venerated in the East on the same date as a martyr at Nicomedia. *July 6, iii, 23.*

DOMINICA AND INDRACT, SS, MARTYRS

According to the legend, Dominica (or Drusa) was an Irishwoman, slain in England by the heathen Saxons, together with her brother Indract and others, *c.* 710. The bodies were said to be buried at Glastonbury. She gives her name to the parish of Saint Dominic in Cornwall. *February 5, i, 258.*

DOMITIAN, ST, BISHOP

He was bishop of Maastricht and evangelized the Meuse valley, where his relics are still venerated at Huy. d. *c.* 560. *Domitianus. May 7, ii, 246.*

*DOMNOLUS, ST, BISHOP

He was bishop of Le Mans, praised by St Gregory of Tours, d. 581. *May 16, ii, 329.*

DONALD, ST

He lived at Ogilvy in Forfarshire during the eighth century, and after the death of his wife led a sort of community life with his nine daughters (the "Nine Maidens"). *Donaldus. July 15, iii, 107.*

*DONATIAN, ST, BISHOP AND MARTYR

This Donatian, with four other bishops from the African province of Byzacena, was driven by the Vandals into the desert, where they died from hunger and thirst, *c.* 484. *September 6, iii, 496.*

*DONATIAN AND ROGATIAN, SS, MARTYRS

Gallo-Roman brothers who refused to sacrifice to the gods and so were beheaded at Nantes, probably in 289 or 304. *May 24, ii, 381.*

*DONATUS OF AREZZO, ST, BISHOP AND MARTYR

Donatus was the second bishop of Arezzo in Tuscany, but seems certainly not to have been a martyr. d. 362. *August 7, iii, 275.*

*DONATUS OF FIESOLE, ST, BISHOP

According to the tradition of Fiesole, Donatus was an Irish pilgrim who was miraculously indicated as their bishop and was accordingly elected. d. *c.* 876. The feast of St Donatus is observed throughout Ireland. *October 22, iv, 178.*

DONNAN, ST, MARTYR

Donnan was a monk of Iona under St Columba. He established a monastery on the island of Eigg in the Inner Hebrides, and with his monks was massacred by Danish raiders in 618. Their feast is kept in the diocese of Argyll and the Isles. *Donnanus. April 17, ii, 113.*

DOROTHEUS OF TYRE, ST, MARTYR

He was a priest of Tyre, driven into exile under Diocletian. He attended the Council of Nicaea, but under Julian the Apostate was arrested at Varna on the Black Sea and beaten to death, *c.* 362. That is the story, but it seems to be apocryphal. There has been much confusion of the holy men named Dorotheus. *June 5, ii, 481.*

DOROTHEUS THE YOUNGER, ST, ABBOT

Born at Trebizond, he became first a monk at Samsun on the Black Sea and then founder of a monastery at Khiliokomos nearby. He had the gifts of prophecy and miracles. Eleventh century. *January 5, i, 38.*

DOROTHEUS. *See also under* Gorgonius.

DOROTHY OF MONTAU, BD

She was a peasant girl of Montau in Prussia, and married a swordsmith named Albert: by her sweetness of character she modified his surly disposition and, when eight of their nine children had died, they used to go on pilgrimages together to various shrines. After the death of Albert, Dorothy became a recluse at Marienwerder and during the few months of life left to her acquired a reputation for holiness and supernatural enlightenment. d. 1394. This mystic still has a *cultus* in north-central Europe, but her canonization, though begun, was never carried through. *October 30, iv, 224.*

DOSITHEUS, ST

A rich young man who was converted to Christianity at Jerusalem and became a monk at Gaza, where he lost his health and scandalized his fellows by being unable to fast and work miracles. But, as his abbot pointed out, he had completely surrendered his own will. d. *c.* 530. *February 23, i, 403.*

DOUAY, THE MARTYRS OF

More than 160 "seminary priests" from the English College at Douay were put to death in England and Wales during the century following its foundation in 1568. Over eighty of them have been beatified or canonized as martyrs, and a collective feast is kept in their honour in the dioceses of Westminster and Hexham. *October 29, iv, 219.*

DRAUSIUS, ST, BISHOP

In French, *Drausin*. Bishop of Soissons in the seventh century. After his death *c.* 674 he was specially invoked against the machinations of enemies, and St Thomas Becket is said to have visited his shrine before returning to martyrdom in England. *March 7, i, 515.*

DRITHELM, ST

He was a Northumbrian who, in consequence of a vision of heaven and hell, divided his goods between his wife, his children, and the poor, and was admitted a monk of Melrose. Here he lived a life of great austerity in a cell near the monastery. d. *c.* 700. *September 1, iii, 462.*

*DROCTOVEUS, ST, ABBOT

In French, *Drotté*. He was abbot of the monastery of St Vincent and the Holy Cross at Paris, and d. *c.* 580. *March 10, i, 547.*

*DROGO, ST

Drogo, or Druon, a Fleming, left his home and inheritance to be a shepherd in France, an occupation which he varied by pilgrimages to Rome, until they were ended by a bodily affliction that made him a most unpleasant sight; he then shut himself up in a cell adjoining the church at Sebourg. d. 1189. St Drogo is a patron of shepherds and is invoked against hernia and the stone. *April 16, ii, 104.*

DROSTAN, ST, ABBOT

An abbot of Deer whose feast is kept in the dioceses of Aberdeen and Argyll. d. *c.* 610. *Drostanus. July 11, iii, 71.*

DUBRICIUS, ST, BISHOP

In Welsh, *Dyfrig*. His principal monasteries were at Henllan and Moccas from whence he made many religious settlements in what are now the borders of England and Wales. He is said to have made St Samson abbot at Caldey, later consecrating him bishop. In medieval legend St Dubricius was "archbishop of Caerleon" and crowned King Arthur at Colchester. Sixth century. His feast is observed on Caldey Island and in the archdiocese of Cardiff. *November 14, iv, 340.*

*DUNSTAN ST, BISHOP

Dunstan, the most famous of the Anglo-Saxon saints, was b. near Glastonbury and was appointed abbot of that monastery in 943. He gradually superseded its occupants by Benedictine monks and made it a centre of learning and religious observance. Dunstan was chief adviser to King Edred and initiated a vigorous policy of national unification and moral reform. For a time he was banished by King Edwy, but returned under Edgar and was successively bishop of Worcester and London and primate at Canterbury. He was appointed papal legate in 961 and, with St Ethelwold of Winchester and St Oswald of York, carried on his far-reaching reforms with increased zeal. With all this, Dunstan was active in pastoral work, recreating himself with smithing, painting and music, in all of which he was skilled. d. 988. His feast is kept by the English Benedictines and in several English dioceses. *Dunstanus. May 19, ii, 349.*

DUTHAC, ST, BISHOP

A bishop of Ross in Scotland, where his memory is preserved in several place-names, *e.g.* Kilduthie. d. *c.* 1065. His feast is kept in the diocese of Aberdeen. *Duthacus. March 8, i, 526.*

DYFRIG. *See* Dubricius.

*DYMPNA, ST, VIRGIN

The relics of St Dympna and of St Gerebernus

were discovered at Gheel, near Antwerp, in the thirteenth century and so many miracles of curing insanity, epilepsy, etc., were reported at their new tomb that St Dympna has ever since been venerated as a patroness of lunatics; there is a large and well-equipped sanatorium for the mentally sick at Gheel today, which had its origin soon after the finding of relics. The feast of St Dympna is kept throughout Ireland because of the popular story that she was an Irish princess and Gerebernus her chaplain, but the true story of these saints is not known. Dympna is not to be identified with the Irish St Damhnait. *May 15, ii, 320.*

E

EANSWIDA, ST, VIRGIN

She was the granddaughter of St Ethelbert of Kent, and founded a convent near Folkestone of which she was the first abbess. d. *c.* 640. *September 12, iii, 545.*

EATA, ST, BISHOP

He was an English disciple of Aidan and became abbot of Melrose; in 678 he was made bishop of part of St Wilfrid's diocese of York, and later exchanged with his pupil St Cuthbert for the see of Hexham. St Bede calls him "a most venerable man, meek and simple". d. 686. St Eata's feast is kept in the diocese of Lancaster. *October 26, iv, 206.*

EBBA THE ELDER, ST, VIRGIN

She was a sister of St Oswald of Northumbria and founded the monastery of Coldingham (*cf.* St Abb's Head), over which she ruled as abbess; but she seems to have been a not very successful superioress. d. 683. *August 25, iii, 402.*

EBERHARD, BD, ABBOT

He joined his friend Beeno in his hermitage at Einsiedeln in 934 and built at his own expense a monastery and church there; he is venerated as the first abbot of Einsiedeln. d. 958. *August 14, iii, 330.*

EBERHARD OF MARCHTHAL, BD, ABBOT

He was appointed abbot of the monastery of Marchthal in Swabia when it was handed over to the Premonstratensians in 1166. d. 1178. *April 17, ii, 116.*

EBERHARD OF SALZBURG, ST, BISHOP

Born at Nuremberg *c.* 1087. He gave up a canonry at Bamberg to take the Benedictine habit, was made abbot of Biburg, and in 1146 archbishop of Salzburg. He was a successful reformer of both clergy and laity in his diocese, and was one of the few German bishops who refused to support the antipope Victor on the orders of the emperor Frederick Barbarossa. d. 1164. *June 22, ii, 617.*

*EBRULF, ST, ABBOT

In French, *Evroult.* From being in the service of King Clotaire I he became a hermit in the forest of Ouche in Normandy; here a community grew up of which he was elected abbot. d. 596. *December 29, iv, 639.*

EBSDORF, THE MARTYRS OF

The army of King Louis III under Duke Bruno was caught in ice and snow in the winter of 880 by the Northmen and overwhelmed. Bruno, with two bishops, eleven noblemen and others were among the slain and were venerated as martyrs. This took place on the marshy heath of Lüneburg at Ebsdorf in Saxony. *February 2, i, 237.*

*EDBERT, ST, BISHOP

Edbert succeeded St Cuthbert in the see of Lindisfarne; he was remarkable for his knowledge of Holy Scripture and for his generosity to the poor. d. 698. Edbert is commemorated in the diocese of Hexham. *Eadbertus. May 6, ii, 242.*

EDBURGA OF MINSTER, ST, VIRGIN

This Edburga succeeded St Mildred as abbess of Minster-in-Thanet; she is chiefly known as a friend and correspondent of St Boniface. d. 751. *December 12, iv, 546.*

EDBURGA OF WINCHESTER, ST, VIRGIN

This Edburga, granddaughter of Alfred the Great, daughter of Edward the Elder, and abbess at Winchester, was venerated principally at Pershore in Worcestershire, where her relics were enshrined; the miracles alleged here were chiefly responsible for her fame. d. 960. There was a third Edburga, venerated in Oxfordshire. Seventh century. *June 15, ii, 548.*

EDITH STEIN, BD, VIRGIN AND MARTYR

Sr Teresa Benedicta of the Cross was b. at Breslau, then Germany (now Wroclaw, Poland), on October 12, 1891 as the eleventh child of a Jewish family. She studied philosophy. After reading the life of St Teresa she was baptized on January 1, 1922. A university professor at Münster and elsewhere and a profound thinker and mystic, she became a Carmelite at Cologne on October 12, 1933, and made her final profession in 1938. She left Cologne to protect her sisters from Nazi persecution and went to the Carmelite house in Echt, the Netherlands, determined to share the suffering of Christ. There she wrote "The Knowledge of the Cross". Her Jewish ancestry subjected her to the barbaric anti-Semitic laws applied during the German occupation. She was arrested on August 2, 1942. After the usual unspeakable experience of transport in a cattle-truck she was murdered on August 9, 1942 in the gas chambers of the German extermination camp at Auschwitz (Oswiecim), Poland. A model of virtue, self-denial and heroism, she was beatified by Pope John Paul II at Cologne on May 1, 1987. *August 9.*

EDITH OF POLESWORTH, ST

She was probably the widow of Sihtric, the Viking leader at York, whose name was Edith and who was buried at Tamworth, near Polesworth, probably before 950. *Editha. July 15, iii, 109.*

*EDITH OF WILTON, ST, VIRGIN

She was the daughter of King Edgar and Wulfrida, and while still a baby was taken to the convent of Wilton, which she never left. She chose to be professed at the age of fifteen, and refused the government of three abbeys, remaining a simple nun at Wilton. She d. at the age of twenty-two in 984. St Edith is commemorated in the diocese of Clifton. *September 16, iii, 571.*

*EDMUND, ST, MARTYR

When the Danes invaded East Anglia in 870 they slew St Edmund, who had become king of the East Angles when a youth in 855. According to tradition he was shot to death with arrows at Hoxne in Norfolk, having refused proposals from the Danes that were inconsistent with religion and justice. His shrine gave his name to the town and abbey of Bury St Edmund's. His feast is kept in the dioceses of Westminster and Northampton, and by the English Benedictine congregation. *Edmundus. November 20, iv, 394.*

EDMUND ARROWSMITH, ST, MARTYR

He came of a recusant yeoman family in Lancashire, was ordained in 1612 and worked on the English mission for fifteen years, during which he was received into the Society of Jesus. He was indicted in 1628 for being a priest and for reconciling converts, and was h.d.q at Lancaster. bd 1929. cd October 25, 1970. Cures of ill health are attributed to prayer at the shrine of St Edmund's hand, preserved in the church of St Oswald at Ashton-in-Makerfield. *August 28, iii, 439.*

EDMUND CAMPION, ST, MARTYR

St Edmund, b. in London *c.* 1540, was a "bluecoat boy"; he had a brilliant career at Oxford, was reconciled with the Catholic Church, and joined the Society of Jesus at Rome. After working in Bohemia he was sent on the English mission in 1580. After labouring most successfully for over a year, Campion was betrayed in Berkshire and taken to the Tower of London; he was accused of complicity in a bogus plot, racked in the hope of making him betray his associates, and h.d.q. at Tyburn in 1581. The feast of St Edmund is observed by the Society of Jesus and in the dioceses of Northampton, Portsmouth, Prague and Brno. bd 1886. cd October 25, 1970. *December 1, iv, 466.*

EDMUND CATHERICK, BD, MARTYR

Born in Yorkshire *c.* 1605. He was a secular priest on the English mission for seven years and was h.d.q. for his priesthood at York in 1642. bd 1929. *April 13, ii, 87.*

EDMUND DUKE, BD, MARTYR

A secular priest b. in Kent who studied at Rheims and at Rome, where he was ordained priest and sent on the English mission in 1590 but was soon arrested and confined in Durham jail. He was h.d.q. at Durham in 1590. bd November 22, 1987. *May 27.*

EDMUND GENINGS, ST, MARTYR

Genings was born at Lichfield in 1567. He was arrested after celebrating Mass at the house of St Swithin Wells, and was h.d.q. for his priesthood in Gray's Inn Fields, in 1591. bd 1929. cd October 25, 1970. *December 10, iv, 532.*

EDMUND SYKES, BD, MARTYR

A secular priest b. at Leeds, Yorkshire. He studied at Rheims, was ordained priest on February 21, 1581, and sent on the English mission on June 5. He was arrested *c.* 1585 and banished but soon returned to England, and was seized again. He was h.d.q. at York in 1587. bd November 22, 1987. *March 23.*

*EDMUND OF ABINGDON, ST, BISHOP

Edmund Rich was b. at Abingdon in 1180. He taught theology at Oxford, was a canon of Salisbury and apostolic delegate to preach the crusade in England, and was elected archbishop of Canterbury in 1233. Edmund's zeal for good discipline and monastic observance, and his resistance against the encroachment of royal powers, involved him in trouble with his chapter, with the monasteries, and with King Henry III, and his difficul-

ties were much increased by the opposition he encountered from the papal legate in England. In 1240 he retired to the Cistercian abbey at Pontigny in France, and d. in the same year. cd 1246. St Edmund's feast is kept in most English and two French dioceses and by the Cistercians. *November 16, iv, 355.*

EDWARD BAMBER, BD, MARTYR

A secular priest also known as Reding, b. at Carlton, Blackpool, or Poulton-le-Fylde. He studied at the English College at Valladolid or at Douay, was ordained priest and sent on the English mission, banished and returned. He was noted for his zeal and courage in pastoral work, instruction and disputation. He was arrested and escaped imprisonment twice. He was h.d.q. at Lancaster on August 7, 1646, aged forty-six. bd November 22, 1987. *August 7.*

EDWARD BURDEN, BD, MARTYR

A secular priest b. at Durham and educated at Trinity College, Oxford. He became a priest at Douay in 1584 and went on the English mission in 1586. He was condemned for his priesthood with Fr John Hewitt and h.d.q. at York in 1588 aged *c.* 48. bd November 22, 1987. *November 29.*

EDWARD CAMPION, BD, MARTYR

Edward Campion (*vere* Edwards) was b. at Ludlow in 1552; he was h.d.q. for his priesthood at Canterbury in 1588. bd 1929. *Eduardus. October 1, iv, 7.*

EDWARD COLEMAN, BD, MARTYR

The first victim of the Titus Oates "plot" was a gentleman of Suffolk, Mr Edward Coleman. He was h.d.q. at Tyburn in 1678 on a false charge of conspiring with a foreign power to restore the Catholic Church in England. bd 1929. *December 3, ii, 596.*

EDWARD FULTHROP, BD, MARTYR

A layman, h.d.q. at York in 1597 for having been reconciled with the Church. bd 1929. *July 4, iii, 19.*

EDWARD JAMES, BD, MARTYR

A secular priest from Derbyshire, h.d.q. for

his priesthood at Chichester in 1588. bd. 1929. *October 1, iv, 8.*

EDWARD JONES, BD, MARTYR

A Welsh secular priest, h.d.q. in Fleet Street, London, for his priesthood in 1590. bd 1929. *May 6, ii, 243.*

EDWARD OLDCORNE, BD, MARTYR

Born at York, ordained in Rome, and admitted to the Society of Jesus. He worked as a priest in the English midlands for seventeen years and was h.d.q. at Worcester in 1606 for alleged complicity in the Gunpowder Plot. bd 1919. *April 7, ii, 51.*

EDWARD OSBALDESTON, BD, MARTYR

A secular priest b. at Osbaldeston, Lancaster. He studied at Rheims, was ordained in 1585 and sent on the English mission in 1589. He was betrayed by a former priest in 1594, imprisoned in York Castle and d. for high treason as a priest at York in 1594. bd November 22, 1987. *November 16.*

EDWARD POWELL, BD, MARTYR

A Welshman, fellow of Oriel, canon of Salisbury, and one of Catherine's counsels in Henry VIII's nullity suit. He was in prison for six years, condemned by attainder for denying the king's spiritual supremacy, and h.d.q. at Smithfield, London, in 1540. His feast is kept in Wales with Bd Richard Fetherston. bd 1886. *July 30, iii, 218.*

EDWARD ROSAZ, BD, BISHOP

Mgr Edoardo Giuseppe Rosaz, b. 1830, was bishop of Suso, Italy, until his death. He founded the Congregation of Franciscan Missionary Sisters of Suso. He inspired the Franciscan spirit and "alpine simplicity" in the charitable work of his nuns, and stressed the importance of direct care and concern for the poor and needy. d. 1903. bd July 14, 1991. *May 3.*

EDWARD SHELLEY, BD, MARTYR

One of the Sussex Shelleys, a layman who was hanged at Tyburn in 1588 for harbouring priests. bd 1929. *August 30, iii, 437.*

EDWARD STRANSHAM, BD, MARTYR

He was b. at Oxford and ordained priest in 1580; h.d.q. for his priesthood at Tyburn in 1586. bd 1929. *January 21, i, 140.*

EDWARD THWING, BD, MARTYR

Edward Thwing (or Thweng) was a secular priest b. at Heworth or Hurs near York. He studied at Rheims and at Rome and was ordained priest at Laon on December 20, 1590. He was sent on the English mission in 1597. He was imprisoned in Lancaster Castle, condemned for his priesthood and d. at Lancaster in 1600 at the age of thirty-five. bd November 22, 1987. *July 26.*

EDWARD WATERSON, BD, MARTYR

A Londoner who in his youth was offered a Turkish bride if he would turn Muslim; instead he turned Catholic at Rome, and was ordained at Rheims. He was h.d.q. for his priesthood in Newcastle, in 1593. bd 1929. *January 7, i, 49.*

*EDWARD THE CONFESSOR, ST

He was b. at Islip, near Oxford, in 1004, son of King Ethelred the Redeless, and succeeded Harthacanute on the throne of England in 1042. Edward was gentle, generous, without ambition, given to much prayer and to hunting, and his kingdom had peace and good government under his rule. He was the first king to touch for the "king's evil", and his ring is the subject of a well-known legend. In commutation of a vow to go on pilgrimage to Rome, he refounded the abbey of Westminster, and was buried in its church in 1066; his body still rests in its shrine beyond the sanctuary of the choir. Edward's holiness was widely recognized during his lifetime and he was cd in 1161; his feast is observed throughout the Western Church on October 13, the anniversary of the translation of his relics in 1163 (the day of his death was January 5). *October 13, iv, 100.*

*EDWARD THE MARTYR, ST

There was formerly considerable *cultus* of this English king, though there is little reason to regard him as a martyr. At the age of sixteen, in 979, he was murdered, to open the way to the throne for his half-brother Ethelred.

Edward's shrine was at Shaftesbury. His feast is kept in the diocese of Plymouth. *March 18, i, 627.*

EDWIN, ST, MARTYR
Edwin became effective king of Northumbria in 616, married as his second wife Ethelburga of Kent, and was himself baptized by her chaplain St Paulinus at York in 627. Bede records that there was perfect peace wherever the rule of King Edwin extended. The Mercians and Welsh marched against him in 633 and he was slain in the ensuing battle. Edwin was venerated as a martyr in England, but he seems to have had no liturgical *cultus*. *Edwinus.*
October 12, iv, 94.

*EGBERT, ST
Egbert was an English monk of Lindisfarne who, after studying in Ireland, went to Iona with the object of inducing the monks there to celebrate Easter according to the Roman reckoning. He was successful only on the day of his death in 729. St Egbert's feast is observed in the dioceses of Hexham and Argyll. *Egbertus. April 24, ii, 158.*

EGWIN, ST, BISHOP
Egwin became bishop of Worcester in 692 and by his severity against vice incurred the enmity of some of his flock. He made two pilgrimages to Rome, and after the first one founded, with King Ethelred of Mercia, the famous abbey of Evesham. d. 717. His feast is kept in the archdiocese of Birmingham. *Egwinus. December 30, iv, 643.*

EIGHTY-FIVE MARTYRS OF ENGLAND, SCOTLAND AND WALES, THE
The eighty-five English, Scottish and Welsh Martyrs suffered for their Catholic faith during the various Protestant persecutions of Catholics in the sixteenth and seventeenth centuries. They were arrested, tortured, tried and executed for treason because they offended against laws of Henry VIII and Elizabeth I, in force or ratified in later reigns and during the Commonwealth, generally in respect of the royal supremacy, against study abroad for the priesthood, and against pastoral work and saying Mass or assisting and harbouring priests in England and Wales. They range from a London printer executed at Tyburn in 1584 to an Irish Franciscan hanged in Wales in 1679. Sixty-three of the martyrs were priests—most of them were seminary priests trained in continental Europe—and twenty-two laypeople from all walks of life, from gentlefolk to servants. They were: Thomas Bullaker, Thomas Pilcher, Arthur Bell, Robert Dibdale, George Nichols, Robert Grissold, Stephen Rowsham, John Sugar, Robert Sutton, Roger Cadwallador, Humphrey Pritchard, Nicholas Woodfen, William Lampley, Richard Sargeant, Henry Webley, Henry Heath, Thomas Hunt, Montford Scott, Nicholas Garlick, Robert Ludlam, Edward Burden, George Errington, William Southerne, Hugh Taylor, Edward Bamber, George Beesley, George Haydock, Christopher Robinson, John Sandys, Thomas Sprott, John Bretton, Robert Bickerdike, Matthew Flathers, William Gibson, Ralph Grimston, Robert Hardesty, Nicholas Horner, Thurstan Hunt, Francis Ingleby, Peter Snow, William Spenser, Edmund Syke, Christopher Wharton, John Woodcock, Roger Wrenno, Thomas Atkinson, Marmaduke Bowes, Alexander Crow, John Fingley, Richard Hill, John Hogg, Richard Holiday, William Knight, Joseph Lambton, Robert Middleton, John Norton, Thomas Palaster, Nicholas Postgate, Richard Simpson, John Talbot, Robert Thorpe, Edward Thwing, Thomas Watkinson, Thomas Belson, Robert Drury, Thomas Pormont, Richard Yaxley, John Adams, John Hambley, William Pike, Robert Nutter, Edward Osbaldeston, William Thomson, John Thules, Thomas Whitaker, Edmund Duke, Roger Filcock, Alexander Blake, William Carter, Anthony Page, John Lowe, William Davies, Richard Flower, Charles Meehan, George Douglas (see separate entries for each of the foregoing). bd November 22, 1987. *November 22.*

EILUNED. See Aled

*ELESBAAN, ST
Elesbaan was the Aksumite Ethiopian king who recovered power in Himyar after the massacre of the martyrs of Najran. He seems

to have made amends for his cruel and re- vengeful spirit by later becoming an exem- plary monk at Jerusalem, but he is for several reasons an equivocal figure to find in the Roman Martyrology. *October 24, iv, 190.*

ELEUSIPPUS. *See under* Speusippus.

*ELEUTHERIUS, ST, ABBOT
An abbot near Spoleto at the end of the sixth century, of whose virtues and miracles St Gregory the Great writes in his *Dialogues*. *September 6, iii, 497.*

*ELHEUTHERIUS, ST, MARTYR
The story of the martyrdom of Eleutherius, his mother Anthia, and eleven others in Illyria during the second century, has been shown to be a pious romance of Greek origin. *April 18, ii, 120.*

*ELEUTHERIUS OF NICOMEDIA, ST, MARTYR
He was martyred at Nicomedia, *c.* 303; he had nothing to do with the burning of Diocletian's palace there. *October 2, iv, 9.*

*ELEUTHERIUS OF TOURNAI, ST,
BISHOP AND MARTYR
He is venerated as the first bishop of Tournai, who died from wounds inflicted by certain heretics in the year 532. The available infor- mation about him is not reliable. *February 20, ii, 381.*

ELEUTHERIUS. *See also under* Rusticus.

ELFLEDA, ST, VIRGIN
She was the daughter of King Oswy of North- umbria and St Eanfleda. She became a nun at Hartlepool and succeeded St Hilda as abbess of Whitby. She took a prominent part in the affairs of the time and appeared at synods on behalf of St Wilfrid of York. Bede gives an account of a meeting between St Elfleda and her friend St Cuthbert that took place at Coquet Island. d. 714. *February 8, ii, 278.*

ELFSTAN. *See* Elstan.

*ELIAS OF CAESAREA, ST, MARTYR
Five Egyptians, *viz.* Elias, Jeremy, Isaias, Samuel, and Daniel, on their return from

visiting the Christian confessors in the mines of Cilicia, were arrested at Caesarea in Pal- estine and brought before the governor with St Pamphilus and others. After torture they were all beheaded in 309. One Porphyry, who said that the bodies ought to be buried, was burned alive for so doing. There is an account of these martyrs by Eusebius who was living in Caesarea at the time. *February 16, i, 350.*

ELIAS. *See also under* Flavian.

*ELIGIUS, ST, BISHOP
Eligius, called in French *Eloi*, is the patron saint of metalworkers. He was himself a metalsmith of great skill, and was made master of the mint at Paris by King Clotaire II. He became a person of importance at the court, where he consorted with Audoenus, Desiderius of Cahors, and others who were afterwards venerated as saints. In 641 Clovis II appointed Eligius to the see of Noyon and Tournai, where he was as good a bishop as he had been a layman. He evangelized a considerable part of Flanders, founded a house of nuns under St Godeberta, and was the valued counsellor of the queen-regent St Bathildis, whose solicitude for slaves he shared. d. 660. *December 1, iv, 455.*

ELIJAH. *See* Elias.

*ELIZABETH, ST
Nothing is known about the mother of St John the Baptist except what can be gleaned from the Gospel of St Luke. Her feast is kept by the Maronites and Copts and by the Lat- ins of Palestine. *Elisabeth.* *November 5, iv, 267.*

ELIZABETH BAYLEY SETON, ST,
WIDOW
The first native-born American saint, she was born on August 28, 1774, in New York. Her father was a professor of anatomy. She married a merchant who died in 1803; she had five children. During her busband's lifetime she established a Protestant Society for the Relief of Poor Widows and Small Children. She was received into the Catho- lic Church on March 14, 1805. Estranged from her family, she founded a girls' school

in Baltimore in 1808. She had been known as the "Protestant Sister of Charity". In 1809 she founded a congregation of nuns, the Sisters of Charity of St Joseph. As their Superior, she became "Mother Seton". They moved to Maryland in 1809 and were known from 1812 as the Daughters of Charity of St Joseph. By the time of St Elizabeth's death in 1821, her congregation had twenty communities devoted to the care of orphans, the sick and above all the parochial schools. St Elizabeth was also a spiritual writer of note. cd 1975. *January 4.*

*ELIZABETH BICHIER DES AGES, ST, VIRGIN

Co-foundress of those Daughters of the Cross who are also known as the Sisters of St Andrew. She was b. near Poitiers in 1773, and in her youth, at the time of the French revolution, showed a marked business ability and enterprise. In 1796 she met St Andrew Fournet at Maillé, where after some years the beginnings of a new congregation took shape. It spread rapidly and unexpectedly, and Mother Elizabeth became associated with another priest who was to be canonized, Michael Garicoïts. She was a woman tenacious in purpose and straightforward in action; Louis Veuillot said she was "one of the finest-tempered characters ever seen: gentle resolute, strict, intelligent, industrious, above all, humble and contrite". d. 1838. cd 1947. *August 26, iii, 410.*

ELIZABETH RENZI, BD, VIRGIN

Sister Elisabetta Renzi, d. 1786, founded a sisterhood in Romagna, Italy, for the education of young girls from poor homes. She was undaunted by the problems she faced in her concern and care for the utterly poor and destitute. d. 1859. bd June 18, 1989. *August 14.*

ELIZABETH VENDRAMINI, BD, VIRGIN

Born April 9, 1790 at Bassano del Grappa, she became a Franciscan tertiary at thirty years of age and devoted herself to the care of orphaned girls. She opened a free school at Padua in 1829 and, in 1830, a religious Institute to help the orphaned poor, aged

women and the sick. She remained a Franciscan tertiary and d. in 1860. bd November 4, 1900. *April 2.*

*ELIZABETH OF HUNGARY, ST

Born at Bratislava in 1207, daughter of King Andreas II of Hungary and niece of St Hedwig. At the age of fourteen Elizabeth married Louis IV (Bd Ludwig), landgrave of Thuringia, and bore him three children, living happily until in 1227 he went crusading and d. at Otranto: "The world", cried Elizabeth, "is dead to me, and all that was joyous in the the world". Her subsequent life was full of suffering, a great deal of which was caused by the rigour and roughness of the director, Conrad of Marburg, to whom she had submitted herself; she abandoned all state, put on the dress of the Franciscan third order, and devoted herself to the poor, the sick and the aged, continuing the work she had already begun with the encouragement of Louis. St Elizabeth d. when still only twenty-four in 1231. cd 1235. *November 17, iv, 386.*

ELIZABETH OF MANTUA, BD, VIRGIN

Elizabeth Picenardi was a Servite tertiary at Mantua, and several young girls banded themselves together to live in community under her direction. d. 1468. bd 1804. *February 20, i, 383.*

*ELIZABETH OF PORTUGAL, ST

Born 1271, daughter of King Pedro III of Aragon, and was married to King Denis of Portugal, who was the source of considerable unhappiness to his wife, for he was selfish and dissolute. Elizabeth was particularly noted as a peacemaker—between her son Alfonso and his father, between Ferdinand IV of Castile and his cousin, and between Ferdinand and James II of Aragon. After the death of Denis she retired to a Poor Clare convent as a tertiary. In 1336 she set out on another errand of reconciliation; she was very ill at the time, and death overtook her. cd 1625. In her own country St Elizabeth is known by the Spanish form of her name, *Isabella. July 4, iii, 37.*

*ELIZABETH OF SCHÖNAU, ST, VIRGIN

Elizabeth was professed a nun at the Benedictine monastery of Schönau in 1147. From the age of twenty-three she was subject to extraordinary supernatural manifestations, accounts of which she wrote down; she was the blameless cause of a further fictitious elaboration of the legend of St Ursula. For the last seven years of her life she was abbess of the nuns at Schönau, while her brother Egbert, who wrote a memoir of her, governed the monks. d. 1164. *June 18, ii, 578.*

ELIZABETH THE GOOD, BD, VIRGIN

She was b. in 1386 at Waldsee in Württemberg and passed her life in a small community of Franciscan tertiaries nearby. She was one of the last of the medieval women mystics connected with the mendicant orders who were remarkable for their physical austerities, visions, and other abnormal phenomena. Bd Elizabeth received the *stigmata* and is reputed to have gone very long periods with hardly any natural food. d. 1420. c.c. 1766. *November 17, iv, 375.*

ELIZABETH OF THE TRINITY, BD, VIRGIN

St Elizabeth Catez of the Most Holy Trinity was b. 1880. She was a discalced Carmelite with a profound awareness of the presence of God and suffered ill health with great courage. d. 1906. bd November 25, 1984. *November 8.*

ELMO. *See* Erasmus *and* Peter Gonzalez.

ELOI. *See* Eligius.

ELPHEGE. *See* Alphege.

*ELZEAR, ST

He was b. in Provence in 1285 and inherited the barony of Ansouis and the county of Ariano; he married Bd Delphina of Glandèves. In the management of his territories in France and Italy and the conduct of his household Elzear was a most excellent example of the Christian nobleman, and he was chosen to be tutor to Prince Charles of Naples as well as for certain diplomatic missions. A tradition says that St Elzear was a Franciscan tertiary, and that for the last eight years of his life he lived in a brotherly relation with his wife. d. 1323. cd 1369. *Elzearius. September 27, iii, 661.*

*EMERENTIANA, ST, VIRGIN AND MARTYR

A Roman martyr of unknown date; she has come to be regarded as the foster-sister of St Agnes. *January 23, i, 152.*

*EMERIC, BD

In Magyar, *Imre.* The only son of St Stephen of Hungary; he predeceased his father in 1031. Though much venerated by the Magyars, little is known about Emeric. *November 4, iv, 266.*

*EMETERIUS AND CHELIDONIUS, SS, MARTYRS

Martyrs at Santander in Spain in 304, about whom little is now known. *Hemiterius. March 3, i, 467.*

*EMILIAN CUCULLATUS, ST

St Emilian-with-the-Hood, San Millán de la Cogolla, was a famous early saint of Spain, where he was a hermit and a monk in the mountains near Burgos and elsewhere. d. 574. *November 12, iv, 321.*

EMILIANA. *See under* Tharsilla.

*EMILY DE RODAT, ST, VIRGIN

Foundress of the Congregation of the Holy Family of Villefranche. She was b. near Rodez in France in 1787, and taught in a convent school for eleven years, during which she tried her vocation with three different congregations. Then in 1815 she started a school on her own for poor children in Villefranche, and from this the Congregation of the Holy Family gradually developed. St Emily had much to suffer, spiritually, in bodily health, and in her work, but she forged ahead and extended its scope. She had an almost dour wit, and was sometimes excessively careless of her personal appearance. One of her directors said of her that "she is a saint—but a headstrong saint". d. 1852. cd 1950. *Aemilia. September 19, iii, 603.*

*EMILY DE VIALAR, ST, VIRGIN

Foundress of the Sisters of St Joseph "of the Apparition" (*cf.* Matt. i, 18–21). This Emily was b. into a noble family at Gaillac in Languedoc in 1797, where for many years she was active in good works. Then, in 1832, she inherited money, and, with three companions, she started an organization for care of the needy and for children's education. This congregation was so successful, in spite of opposition and the misfortunes that befell it in Algeria, that it spread beyond France almost at once. Cardinal Granito di Belmonte characterized St Emily's spirit as "wise, understanding and most considerate", and her energy and achievements are the more remarkable in that, almost throughout her life, she suffered from a distressing physical disability. d. 1856. cd 1951.
June 17, ii, 571.

EMILY OF VERCELLI, BD, VIRGIN

Emily Bicchieri was b. at Vercelli in 1238 and, since she wished to be a nun, her father built a convent for her and some companions, which was put under the direction of the Friars Preachers; according to some, this was the first house of Dominican regular tertiaries. Emily was a tactful and enlightened prioress, and is said to have had the gift of miracles. d. 1314. c.c. 1769.
August 19, iii, 359.

EMMA, ST

Emma was the wife of William, landgrave of Friesach, with whom she lived in great content. But her two sons were murdered and her husband died on a journey, and for twenty-two years she lived a disconsolate widow. She founded a double monastery at Gurk in Carinthia. d. 1045. c.c. 1938. *Hemma.*
June 30, ii, 674.

EMMANUEL RUIZ, BD, MARTYR

The leader among the martyrs of Damascus (*q.v.*). He was a Spanish Franciscan, guardian of the friary at Damascus; when the mob broke in and called on him to apostatize he stood at the altar and refused, and was the first to be killed. d. 1860. bd 1926.
July 10, iii, 68.

EMMANUEL DOMINGO Y SOL, BD

Emmanuel Domingo y Sol was b. at Tortosa, Tarragon, Spain on April 1, 1836. He was ordained priest in 1860 and in 1883 he founded the Sacred Heart Fraternity of Diocesan Priests. d. January 25, 1909. bd March 29, 1987. *January 25.*

*EMMERAMUS, ST,
BISHOP AND MARTYR

He was a native of Poitiers who went to preach the gospel in Bavaria. He d. toward the end of the seventh century, from injuries received when attacked while on the way to Rome, and was venerated as a martyr; but the motive and circumstances of his murder are a mystery. *September 22, ii, 622.*

*EMYGDIUS, ST, BISHOP AND MARTYR

The legend of St Emygdius states that he was a German Christian who came to Rome and was sent as missionary bishop to evangelize the people of the Ancona Marches; there he was beheaded with three companions in 304. This saint is invoked in Italy against earthquakes, and his *cultus* in this form has spread to San Francisco and Los Angeles in U.S.A. *August 9, iii, 292.*

*ENCRATIS, ST, VIRGIN AND MARTYR

Otherwise *Engracia*. In some way unknown this Spanish girl bore such energetic witness to her faith that she was known as the "vehement maiden". She was mutilated at Saragossa, but seems to have survived the terrible torture. Date uncertain, but early. *April 16, ii, 100.*

ENDA, ST, ABBOT

Enda, or *Endeus*, is said to have been persuaded to become a monk by his sister St Fanchea. He established himself with his disciples on Aranmore, where they led a very penitential life. d. *c.* 530.
March 21, i, 656.

*ENECO, ST, ABBOT

Or Iñigo. An Aragonese hermit who was appointed abbot of Oña and filled the office with great distinction, his influence extending over the whole countryside. d. 1057. cd *c.* 1160. *June 1, ii, 442.*

*ENGELBERT, ST, BISHOP AND MARTYR

After being the rather unworthy holder of four valuable benefices he incurred excommunication, and when this was lifted he was made archbishop of Cologne at the age of thirty in 1216. From then on Engelbert's personal life appears to have been blameless, but it is doubtful if his *cultus* would either have arisen or been officially recognized had he not come to a violent end in 1225 on account of his defence of the rights of a nunnery. *Engelbertus.*
November 7, iv, 289.

ENGELMUND, ST

An English monk and the most successful of St Willibrord's missionaries in the Netherlands, where his centre was at Velsen, near Haarlem. d. c. 720. *Engelmundus.*
June 21, ii, 609.

ENGLAND AND WALES, THE MARTYRS OF

This term signifies those martyrs who suffered in consequence of the English Reformation, from 1535 till the end of the penal times. Of this great company Fisher and More were the first to be canonized; sixty-one others (fifty-two in 1886, nine in 1895) were recognized by Pope Leo XIII as having been equivalently canonized by Pope Gregory XIII in 1583; and 136 more were formally beatified in 1929; the Forty English Martyrs (*q.v.*) were canonized in 1970 (St Oliver Plunket, the Irish archbishop who suffered in London, was beatified separately in 1920 and canonized in 1975). Of these two hundred martyrs about a score were Welsh, and the rest mostly English. Two were bishops, eighty-four secular priests, sixty-six religious (including eight lay brothers), forty-four laymen and four laywomen. Another eighty-five English, Scottish and Welsh martyrs (*q.v.*) were beatified on November 22, 1987.

ENGRACIA. *See* Encratis.

*ENNODIUS, ST, BISHOP

Magnus Felix Ennodius, of a Gallo-Roman family, is chiefly remembered for his writings, hymns, letters, and an account of his own life and conversion; he was one of the last representatives of the ancient school of rhetoric. He was made bishop of Pavia c. 514, and was entrusted with two missions to the East by the Holy See. d. 521.
July 17, iii, 126.

*EPARCHIUS, ST, ABBOT

In French, *Cybard.* He became a monk against his parents' wishes, and was afterwards a solitary near Angoulême. d. 581.
July 1, iii, 4.

*EPHRAEM, ST, DOCTOR

Called "the Syrian", "the Deacon", and "the Harp of the Holy Ghost". Born at Nisibis in Mesopotamia c. 306, and became the greatest theologian, preacher and poet of the Syrian church. He was probably head of the episcopal school at Nisibis, but after that city was captured by the Persians he became a hermit or monk near Edessa. Ephraem was one of the first writers of hymns, which he undertook in the first place in opposition to local heretics who were spreading their doctrines by means of sung verses. He also wrote commentaries on the Scriptures and homilies, some of these also in metre, and his writings are extensively used in the various Syriac liturgies. Shortly before his death there was a terrible famine in Mesopotamia in which Ephraem was the leader in organizing relief and help for the sick, which included the provision of three hundred ambulances, *i.e.* litters. He seems to have d. in his hermit's cave a very short time afterwards, in 373, though some writers claim that he lived on till 378 or 379. St Ephraem was proclaimed a Doctor of the Church in 1920.
June 9, ii, 574.

*EPIMACHUS AND **ALEXANDER**, SS, MARTYRS

They suffered at Alexandria in 250; St Ammonaria and other virgin martyrs were put to death at the same time and place.
December 12, iv, 544.

EPIMACHUS. *See also* Gordian.

*EPIPHANIUS OF PAVIA, ST, BISHOP

A bishop of Pavia who rebuilt the city after it had been destroyed by Odoacer. The fever from which he d. was brought on by a journey into Burgundy to ransom some prisoners, in 496. *January 21, i, 139.*

*EPIPHANIUS OF SALAMIS, ST, BISHOP

Born in Palestine *c.* 310. As abbot of a monastery at Eleutheropolis he stood up to imperial persecution and wrote and preached against the errors of his age until he came to be regarded as the "oracle of Palestine". In 367 he became bishop of Salamis in Cyprus, but the later years of his life were clouded by the results of several headstrong actions on his part. The fame of St Epiphanius rests chiefly on his writings, which make him one of the Fathers of the Church. d. 403. *May 12, ii, 285.*

*EPIPODIUS AND ALEXANDER, SS, MARTYRS

Two young friends who were martyred at Lyons in 178 in the great persecution there. *April 22, ii, 144.*

EPISTEME. *See* Galation.

*EQUITIUS, ST, ABBOT

He founded a number of religious houses in Italy during the lifetime of St Benedict. d. March 7, *c.* 560. *August 11, iii, 303.*

*ERASMUS, ST, BISHOP AND MARTYR

Erasmus or Elmo was formerly widely venerated as the patron of sailors (*cf.* "St Elmo's Fire"). Nothing is actually known of his history but he is said to have been bishop at Formiae in the Campagna (where his relics were until 842), martyred in 303(?). *June 2, ii, 453.*

ERCONGOTA, ST, VIRGIN

She was the daughter of St Sexburga and went over to France to be a nun at Faremoutier. d. *c.* 660. *July 7, iii, 34.*

*ERCONWALD, ST, BISHOP

He founded the monastery of Chertsey and that of Barking, over which he put his sister, St Ethelburga, as abbess; in 675 he was appointed bishop of London. d. *c.* 686. His feast is kept in the dioceses of Westminster, Southwark and Brentwood. *Erconvaldus.*

May 13, ii, 299.

EREMBERT, ST, BISHOP

A monk of Fontenelle, who became bishop of Toulouse, and d. *c.* 672. *May 14, ii, 307.*

ERENTRUDE, ST, VIRGIN

She was a relative of St Rupert, and assisted him in his missionary work in Bavaria by conducting a religious house for women at Salzburg. d. *c.* 718. *Erentrudis. June 30, ii, 677.*

*ERHARD, ST, BISHOP

This saint had a *cultus* around Ratisbon, where what purport to be his crozier and part of his skull are still preserved. He is stated to have baptized St Odilia, and is sometimes described as an Irishman. He seems to have lived in the seventh century. *Erhardus. January 8, i, 53.*

*ERIC, ST, MARTYR

Eric was recognized king of Sweden in 1150. He was a man of much personal goodness, who spread Christianity in Sweden, and beat off the attacks of the heathen Finns. He was murdered by Danes, assisted by rebels against his just rule, in 1161. St Eric is the principal patron of Sweden. *Ericus. May 18, iii, 342.*

ERMENBURGA. *See under* Mildred.

ERMENGARD, BD, VIRGIN

She was b. *c.* 832, a great-granddaughter of Charlemagne, and became abbess of the royal convent of Chiemsee in Bavaria. d. 866. c.c. 1928. Another Bd Ermengard (Irmgard), d. *c.* 1100, is honoured in the diocese of Cologne. *Hermenegardis. July 16, iii, 119.*

ERMENGILD, ST

Or *Ermenilda*. Daughter of King Erconbert of Kent and St Sexburga, and wife of King Wulfhere of Mercia by whom she was the mother of St Werburga. On the death of her husband in 675 she became a nun and was abbess of Milton and Ely. d. 703. *Hermenegildis. February 13, i, 323.*

ERMINOLD, ST, ABBOT

He is venerated as a martyr, but his death in

1121 resulted from the conspiracy of a criminal faction among the monks of Prüfening, who resented his strict rule as abbot of that monastery. *January 6, i, 42.*

ESKIL, ST, BISHOP AND MARTYR

Eskil was an Englishman and a missionary bishop in Sweden with St Sigrid. He was stoned to death for protesting against a heathen festival at Strängnäs *c.* 1080. Eskilstuna is the place where his body was enshrined. *June 12, ii, 533.*

ESTERWINE, ST, ABBOT

He was appointed by his kinsman, St Benedict Biscop, to be abbot of Wearmouth, which he governed for four years. d. 686. *Esterwinus. March 7, i, 515.*

*ETHBIN, ST

He was a monk in Brittany; on being driven out by the Franks, it is said he took refuge in Ireland, and d. there *c.* 580. *Ethbinus. October 19, iv, 149.*

ETHELBERT, ST, MARTYR

He succeeded his father Ethelred as king of the East Angles and was treacherously murdered in 794, apparently for political reasons. Ethelbert was buried at Hereford and he had considerable *cultus* as a wonderworker and "martyr". His feast is still kept in the dioceses of Cardiff and Northampton. *Edilbertus. May 20, ii, 358.*

*ETHELBERT OF KENT, ST

Ethelbert, whose wife Bertha was a Christian, was ruling in Kent and far beyond when Pope St Gregory sent St Augustine to evangelize the English. Ethelbert received the missionaries well and was himself baptized on Whit Sunday in 597; unlike some other monarchs, he did not try to impose the new religion on his subjects by force. He helped to found Christchurch cathedral and the abbey of SS Peter and Paul at Canterbury, and established the see of Rochester and St Andrew's cathedral, and St Paul's cathedral in London. d. 616. St Ethelbert is commemorated liturgically in the dioceses of Westminster, Southwark, Nottingham and Northampton. *February 25, i, 414.*

*ETHELBURGA, ST, VIRGIN

She was a daughter of King Anna of the East Angles and became a nun at Faremoutiers in France, succeeding her half-sister, St Sethrida, as abbess. d. *c.* 664. Called *Aubierge* in France. *Edilburga. July 7, iii, 34.*

ETHELBURGA OF BARKING, ST, VIRGIN

When St Erconwald founded the double monastery of Barking in Essex he set his sister Ethelburga over it as abbess: she, in the words of St Bede, "behaved in all respects as became the sister of such a brother" and several marvels are recorded of her life and death. d. *c.* 678. St Ethelburga's feast is kept in the diocese of Brentwood. *October 12, iv, 95.*

ETHELBURGA OF LYMINGE, ST

This Ethelburga was the daughter of Ethelbert of Kent, and married the heathen King Edwin of Northumbria. She was accompanied to his court by St Paulinus as chaplain, and Edwin was in due course baptized, with many of his people. After his death, Ethelburga founded a convent at Lyminge in Kent, over which she presided as abbess. d. *c.* 647. *April 5, ii, 35.*

*ETHELDREDA, ST

Etheldreda (Audrey) was daughter of King Anna of the East Angles and married one Tonbert, who died three years later. She then retired to the isle of Ely, but after five years married again, young Prince Egfrid of Northumbria: however, she refused to consummate the marriage and, with the support of St Wilfrid, received the veil of a nun. About 672 she founded a double monastery at Ely (from which arose Ely cathedral) and governed it till her death in 679, setting a high example of asceticism and prayerfulness. A very large number of churches were dedicated in honour of this princess, whose feast is still observed in several English dioceses. *Ediltrudis. June 23, ii, 620.*

ETHELNOTH, ST, BISHOP

Ethelnoth the Good was archbishop of Canterbury in the days when the Danish Canute governed England; he translated the relics of his martyred predecessor, St Alphege, from London to Canterbury. d. 1038. There is no evidence of *cultus*. *Aedelnodus*. *October 30, iv, 222.*

ETHELWALD, ST

He followed St Cuthbert in the occupation of the hermitage on Farne Island where Cuthbert d., and St Bede relates a miracle he brought about to allay a storm of wind. d. 699. *Ethelwaldus. March 23, i, 664.*

ETHELWALD OF LINDISFARNE, ST, BISHOP

Ethelwald was a disciple of St Cuthbert, and from being abbot of Old Melrose was promoted to the bishopric of Lindisfarne in 721. He was living in the time of Bede, who speaks of his worthiness. d. *c*. 740. *February 12, i, 317.*

*ETHELWOLD, ST, BISHOP

A monk of Glastonbury, who became abbot of Abingdon *c*.955 and bishop of Winchester in 963. With St Dunstan and St Oswald of York he was one of the leaders of the religious revival in England at this period, and restored a number of monastic houses: among them were Newminster, Chertsey, Thorney and Peterborough. He is said to have translated the Rule of St Benedict into English, and was fittingly called "the father of monks". d. 984. *August 1, iii, 240.*

ETHIOPIA, MARTYRS OF. *See* Samuel
Marzorati and his two companions.

EUBULUS. *See* Adrian and Eubulus.

*EUCHERIUS OF ORLEANS, ST, BISHOP

A monk of Jumièges who was appointed bishop of Orleans in 721. Having opposed the confiscation of church revenues by Charles Martel, he was exiled in 737 first to Cologne and then to Liège. Eucherius was so well loved in the places of his banishment that he was allowed by those responsible for him to retire to a monastery, where he d. in 743. *February 20, i, 381.*

*EUGENDUS, ST, ABBOT

Otherwise *Oyend*. Abbot of Condat, near Geneva, later called after him Saint-Oyend, and then Saint-Claude. d. *c*. 510. *January 1, i, 5.*

EUGENE, ST, BISHOP

Eugen (Eoghan, Owen) is venerated as the first bishop at Ardstraw in Tyrone, predecessor of the see of Derry. He lived during the sixth century, and his feast is kept throughout Ireland. *Eugenius. August 23, iii, 390.*

*EUGENIA, ST, VIRGIN AND MARTYR

The legend of Eugenia is like that of St Marina and others, the tale of a woman disguised as a monk and accused of a crime she could not commit. It has been arbitrarily attached to the name of St Eugenia who was an early martyr in Rome, buried in the cemetery of Apronian on the Via Latina. *December 25, iv, 612.*

EUGENIA SMET, BD, VIRGIN

Eugenia Smet (Mother Mary of Providence) was b. at Lille in 1835. In 1856 she went to Paris and there founded the Helpers of Holy Souls, in which work she had the counsel and encouragement of St John Vianney; the congregation spread far during her lifetime and is now found all over the world. In carrying out her vocation Mother Mary had to contend with the suffering of merciless disease, as Pope Pius XII recalled at her beatification in 1957. d. 1871. *February 7.*

*EUGENIUS I, POPE

Eugenius was pope from 654 till his death in 657. He was generous and gentle, but firmly opposed the Monothelism of the Byzantine emperor, who threatened to roast the pope alive. It was probably this pope who received St Wilfrid on his first visit to Rome. *June 2, ii, 458.*

*EUGENIUS III, BD, POPE

St Antoninus called him "one of the greatest and one of the most afflicted of the popes". He was abbot of the Cistercian monastery of St Anastasius (Tre Fontane) at Rome and was elected pope in 1145. His election was at once challenged by the political Romans and he was in exile from the city, with a short break, for six years. Some of the minor troubles of his pontificate were concerned with England, *e.g.* the affair of St William of York. Eugenius at all times had the support and help of his master St Bernard, and it was said of him that he had "no arrogance, no domineering, no regality; justice, humility and reason claimed the whole man". d. 1152. c.c. 1872. *July 8, iii, 43.*

*EUGENIUS OF CARTHAGE, ST,
BISHOP

Eugenius was elected bishop of Carthage in 481 and the whole of his episcopate was one long struggle with the oppressions of the Arian Vandal kings. He was exiled for several years in the desert of Tripoli, where he shared the great hardships of his flock. He was recalled by Gontamund in 488 and allowed to reopen the Catholic churches, but was banished again eight years later. St Eugenius d. at Albi in 505. *July 13, iii, 89.*

*EUGENIUS OF TOLEDO, ST, BISHOP

He was a musician, poet, and archbishop of Toledo; d. 657. Another Eugenius, martyr, is miscalled "of Toledo" in the Roman Martyrology on November 15.
November 13, iv, 329.

*EULALIA OF MÉRIDA, ST, VIRGIN AND MARTYR

Eulalia was the most celebrated virgin martyr of Spain. She suffered at Mérida in 304 (?), and Prudentius wrote a hymn in her honour. Also known as Eulalia of Barcelona.
December 10, iv, 530.

*EULAMPUS AND EULAMPIA, SS,
MARTYRS

This brother and sister are said to have suffered martyrdom by the sword at Nicomedia, *c.* 310. *October 10, iv, 79.*

*EULOGIUS OF ALEXANDRIA, ST,
BISHOP

He was patriarch of Alexandria and a personal friend of St Gregory the Great, who wrote and told him about the beginnings of the conversion of the English. d. *c.* 607.
September 13, ii, 549.

*EULOGIUS OF CORDOVA, ST,
MARTYR

He was a prominent and distinguished priest of Cordova at the time of the Moorish persecution in the middle of the ninth century. He wrote *The Memorial of the Saints*, a record of the sufferings of Christians at that time, and was foremost in encouraging them to constancy. Eventually he was arrested for protecting a convert from Islam, St Leocritia, and was beheaded in 859. *March 11, i, 561.*

EUNAN. *See* Adamnan.

*EUPHEMIA, ST, VIRGIN AND MARTYR

Beyond the fact of her martyrdom nothing whatever is known of St Euphemia except that her *cultus* was widespread at an early date. Legends cluster round her name and she was greatly venerated in the East, especially at Chalcedon. She was named in the canon of the Ambrosian Mass.
September 16, iii, 567.

*EUPHRASIA, ST, VIRGIN

Euphrasia or Eupraxia refused to leave the convent in Egypt where she had been brought up to marry the senator to whom she had been betrothed, and spent the rest of her life there in great austerity and humility. There is more or less contemporary Greek record of her. d. *c.* 240. *March 13, i, 581.*

*EUPHRASIA PELLETIER, ST,
VIRGIN

She was b. in 1796, on an island off the coast of Brittany. Rose Pelletier joined the Institute of Our Lady of Charity of the Refuge in 1814, and became its superioress *c.* 1825. Later she was put at the head of a new foundation at Angers, from which, after many trials and troubles in which Mother Pelletier was distinguised by her humble but determined independence, arose the Institute of Our Lady of Charity of the Good Shepherd. At all times she showed heroic fortitude. cheerfulness and trust in God. d. 1868. cd 1940. *April 24, ii, 159.*

*EUPHROSYNE, ST, VIRGIN

There are no authentic accounts of the life of St Euphrosyne, who in the East is called

"Our Mother", and there is reason to doubt whether she ever existed. The "history" of her which we have is only a replica of the legend of St Pelagia (October 8). *January 1, i, 4.*

EUPHROSYNE OF POLOTSK, ST, VIRGIN

A dedicated woman who travelled in the East and brought the ikon of our Lady of Korsun from Constantinople to Russia. d. 1173 in Jerusalem, buried at Kiev. *May 23, ii, 377.*

*EUPLUS, ST MARTYR

He was a deacon at Catania in Sicily who was seized with a copy of the gospels on him; he refused under torture to sacrifice to the gods and was beheaded, in 304. *August 12, iii, 313.*

EUROSIA, ST, VIRGIN

She is venerated in Spain as a victim of the Moors in the eighth century and her *cultus* was introduced by Spanish soldiers and others into northern Italy. There is no mention of her before the fifteenth century and it is likely that she is a fictitious character. *June 25, iii, 313.*

EUSEBIA, ST, VIRGIN

Eldest daughter of St Adalbald and St Rictrudis, and succeeded her great-grandmother St Gertrude as abbess of Hamage at a very early age, not without objection from her mother. d. *c.* 680. *March 16, i, 607.*

*EUSEBIUS, ST, POPE

Eusebius, a Greek, was pope for a few months only, dying in exile in Sicily in 310. *August 17, iii, 340.*

EUSEBIUS OF CREMONA, ST, ABBOT

He went with St Jerome to Palestine and was sent by him to Europe to collect funds for the hostel for pilgrims. Eusebius was involved in a dispute about the teaching of Origen, which was carried on with considerable bitterness. He died, probably in Italy, *c.* 423. The tradition that he founded the monastery of Guadalupe in Spain is baseless. *March 5, i, 485.*

*EUSEBIUS OF GAZA, ST, MARTYR

Eusebius, Nestabus, Zeno and Nestor were slain by a mob at Gaza *c.* 362, they having been concerned in the destruction of a pagan temple there. *September 8, iii, 508.*

*EUSEBIUS OF ROME, ST

A priest of a patrician family in Rome who about the middle of the fourth century founded the "parish church" called after him *titulus Eusebii. August 14, iii, 328.*

EUSEBIUS OF SAINT GALL, ST, MARTYR

An Irish monk at St Gall in Switzerland, who became a hermit in the Vorarlberg. He was murdered by a peasant whose wicked life he had rebuked, in 884. *January 31, i, 215.*

*EUSEBIUS OF SAMOSATA, ST, BISHOP AND MARTYR

This Eusebius, bishop of Samosata, was a friend of St Basil and a vigorous opponent of the Arian heresy, on account of which he was exiled by the emperor Valens. He was killed by an Arian woman who threw a tile at his head, *c.* 379. *June 21, ii, 607.*

*EUSEBIUS OF VERCELLI, ST, BISHOP AND MARTYR

He was b. in Sardinia *c.* 283 and became the first known bishop of Vercelli. His life was chiefly spent in struggling with Arianism; for defying the emperor Constantius on this account he was banished with St Dionysius of Milan and Lucifer of Cagliari. He was taken to Palestine and other places in the East, where his sufferings were such that he is venerated as a martyr. He was eventually allowed to return to his see and d. there in 371. Eusebius was the first bishop who lived with his clergy under a rule and he is therefore specially honoured by canons regular. *August 2, iv, 569.*

EUSEO, ST

A hermit who lived near Serravalle in Piedmont during the fourteenth century. Nothing certain is known of him. *February 15.*

EUSTACE WHITE, ST, MARTYR

A seminary priest, b. at Louth, who after

grievous torture was h.d.q. for his priesthood
at Tyburn, in 1591. bd 1929. cd 1970.
December 10, iv, 533.

*EUSTATHIUS, ST, BISHOP
He was translated from Beroea to the see of
Antioch, and proved to be one of the dough-
tiest opponents of Arianism. In 331 he was
deposed by a heretical synod and banished.
He d., still in exile, *c.* 340. *July 16, iii, 117.*

*EUSTOCHIUM, ST, VIRGIN
Eustochium Julia was the daughter of St
Paula and she accompanied her mother to
Palestine, where she helped St Jerome in his
work on the Latin translation of the Bible.
On Paula's death Eustochium succeeded to
the direction of the community of women at
Bethlehem, where she d. *c.* 420.
September 28, iii, 665.

EUSTOCHIUM OF MESSINA, BD,
VIRGIN
Daughter of the Countess Matilda of Calafato.
She became a Poor Clare of the Conventual
observance near Messina in 1446, and desiring a more austere life she founded some
years later an Observant convent at a place
called the Maidens' Hill. Of this she became
abbess and attracted numerous subjects by
her virtues. d. 1468. c.c. 1782.
February 16, i, 354.

EUSTOCHIUM OF PADUA, BD,
VIRGIN
Eustochium was the daughter of an erring
nun at Padua in the fifteenth century. Her
own life was normal until she herself became a nun, when she became subject to
violent seizures, during the course of which
she displayed remarkable phenomena which
are witnessed to by contemporary evidence.
This lasted four years but she was eventually
admitted to vows, when she seems to have
recovered and to have earned the veneration
of her fellow nuns. Her last years were
bedridden and she d. at the age of twenty-six
in 1469. The *cultus* of this Eustochium at
Padua has never received formal approval.
February 13, i, 325.

*EUSTORGIUS II, ST, BISHOP
He became bishop of Milan in 512. He was
described as a man of great virtue, an excellent shepherd of his people, and his life and
episcopate were uneventful. d. 518.
Eustorgius I is also venerated as a saint.
June 6, ii, 488.

*EUSTRATIUS, ST, MARTYR
This martyr, with St Orestes, a soldier, and
others, is said to have suffered at Sebastea in
Armenis. Date unknown.
December 13, iv, 549.

EUTHYMIUS THE ENLIGHTENER,
ST, ABBOT
Son of St John the Iberian, whom he suc-
ceeded as abbot of Iviron on Mount Athos.
He translated many works from Greek into
Georgian, and also St Gregory's *Dialogues*,
and greatly benefited his monastery by his
firmness and virtues. d. 1028.
May 13, ii, 300.

*EUTHYMIUS THE GREAT, ST,
ABBOT
Born at Melitene in Armenia. He was ordained at home and went to be a monk near
Jerusalem, ever withdrawing further into the
wilderness towards Jericho. He was a stout
opponent of the Nestorian and Monophysite
heresies, and induced the Empress Eudoxia
to give up the latter. At different times he
founded two monasteries and a *laura* of
hermitages. He foretold the day of his death,
which happened in 473, and he was honoured as a saint immediately after.
January 20, i, 130.

EUTHYMIUS THE YOUNGER, ST,
ABBOT
Called also "the Thessalonian" or "the New".
While still under twenty he left his wife and
child and became a monk at Mount Olympus
in Bithynia. Later he went to Mount Athos to
learn the eremitical life and after being a
solitary in several places revived the monastery of St Andrew, near Salonika. He also
started a convent nearby and, when these
were both established, went to end his days
on Athos. d. 898. *October 15, iv, 122.*

*EUTROPIUS OF ORANGE, ST,
BISHOP
He was bishop of Orange at a time when the

diocese had been laid waste by the Visigoths, and was strongly tempted to give up his difficult task. d. *c. 476. May 27, ii, 405.*

*EUTROPIUS OF SAINTES, ST,
BISHOP AND MARTYR

He is honoured as the first bishop of Saintes, where he is supposed to have been martyred in the third century. *April 30, ii, 199.*

EUTROPIUS. *See also under* Tigrius.

*EUTYCHIAN, ST, POPE AND MARTYR

Eutychian became pope *c.* 275 and d. 283. Nothing is known of his life. He is called a martyr in the Roman Martyrology, but this is almost certainly an error. *Eutychianus. December 7, iv, 516.*

*EUTYCHIUS OF CARRHAE, ST,
MARTYR

This Eutychius (or Eustathius) was, with several companions, put to death by the Muslims in Mesopotamia for refusing to abjure Christ, in 741. *March 14, i, 591.*

EUTYCHIUS OF CONSTANTINOPLE, ST, BISHOP

Eutychius, patriarch of Constantinople from 552, is honoured in the East for his resistance to the emperor Justinian's interference in theological controversies. He was consequently banished from his see for twelve years. d. 582. *April 6, ii, 41.*

EVA OF LIÈGE, BD, VIRGIN

A recluse of Liège who on the death of Bd Juliana of Cornillon successfully took up her work in favour of a liturgical feast of the Blessed Sacrament. d. *c.* 1265. c.c. 1902. *May 26, ii, 400.*

EVANGELIST AND **PEREGRINE, BB.**

Schoolboy friends who together became Austin friars; they were both endowed with the same miraculous gifts and virtues, and d. within a few hours of one another, *c.* 1250. c.c. 1837. *Evangelista. March 20, i, 644.*

EVENTIUS. *See under* Alexander.

EVERARD HANSE, BD, MARTYR

A Northamptonshire man, a convert and a secular priest, who at his examination in London as a suspected person was tricked into denying the royal supremacy in religion. He was accordingly h.d.q. at Tyburn in 1581. bd 1886. His feast is kept in the diocese of Northampton. *Everardus. July 30, iii, 219.*

*EVERGISLUS, ST,
BISHOP AND MARTYR

He is venerated as bishop of Cologne and a martyr at the hands of heathen robbers during the fifth century, but it is likely that he lived a hundred or more years later and died in his bed. *October 24, iv, 194.*

EVERILD, ST, VIRGIN

She was the seventh-century foundress of a convent near York. *Everildis. July 9, iii, 55.*

EVERMOD, ST, BISHOP

A Premonstratensian canon, a personal disciple of St Norbert, who became abbot of Gottesgnaden, of Magdeburg, and first bishop of Ratzburg. He was an apostle of the Wends. d. 1178. *Evermodus. February 17, i, 358.*

*EVODIUS, ST, BISHOP

Evodius preceded St Ignatius in the see of Antioch, being ordained perhaps by St Peter himself; he is said to have been one of the seventy disciples appointed by our Lord. d. *c.* 64(?). *May 6, ii, 242.*

EVROULT. *See* Ebrulf.

*EWALDS, THE TWO, MARTYRS

Ewald (or Hewald) the Fair and Ewald the Dark were priests from Northumbria, missionaries in Westphalia. They were martyred, traditionally at Aplerbeke, near Dortmund, *c. Ewaldus. October 3, iv, 17.*

*EXPEDITUS, ST

There is good reason to doubt whether a martyr of his name ever existed; but the story which traces devotion to him to the receiving by a Paris convent of a package of relics marked *spedito* has been completedly disproved. *April 19, ii, 128.*

*EXSUPERANTIUS, ST, BISHOP

He had a peaceful and uneventful episcopate as bishop of Ravenna and d. in 418.
May 30, ii, 424.

*EXSUPERIUS, ST, BISHOP

In French, *Spire*. He became bishop of Toulouse *c.* 405 and was noted for his great generosity in alms-giving, sending gifts as far as Egypt and Palestine. d. *c.* 412.
September 28, iii, 664.

EXSUPERIUS. *See also under* Zoë.

EYSTEIN, ST, BISHOP

Eystein Erlandsson was the second archbishop of Nidaros in Norway, and he played an important part in the history of his country. Jocelyn of Brakelond refers to a visit he made to St Edmundsbury abbey in England. He defended ecclesiastical rights in the spirit of Thomas Becket. d. 1188. *Augustinus. January 26, i, 174.*

EZEKIEL MORENO DIAZ, BD, BISHOP

Ezequiel Moreno Diaz was born at Alfaro, Spain, on April 9, 1848. He became an Augustinian and a missionary in the Philippines, where he was ordained priest in 1871. He reorganized the order at Candelaria, Colombia, and became vicar apostolic of Casanare and later bishop of Pasto. He died in Madrid on August 19, 1906. bd November 1, 1975. *August 19.*

F

*FABIAN, ST, POPE AND MARTYR

He was martyred under Decius in 250 after being pope for fourteen years; St Cyprian wrote that the glory of his death corresponded with the purity and goodness of his life. *Fabianus. January 20, i, 128.*

FABIOLA, ST

She was a Roman patrician who divorced her dissolute husband and united herself with another man; after his death she did public penance for this and devoted her time and wealth to works of charity, establishing the first-known Christian public hospital in the West. She was associated in her good works with St Pammachius. In 395 she visited her friend St Jerome at Bethlehem, but he dissuaded her from trying to settle down there—she was too lively. St Fabiola d. in 399 and all Rome attended her funeral. *December 27, iv, 623.*

FACHANAN, ST, BISHOP

He was probably the first bishop in the district of Ross, and was the founder of the great monastic school at what is now Rosscarbery in County Cork. St Fachanan d. near the end of the sixth century, and his feast is kept throughout Ireland. *August 14, iii, 329.*

*FACUNDUS, ST, MARTYR

An early Spanish martyr at whose shrine the abbey bearing his name grew up, together with the town of Sahagún (Sant Facun). *November 27.*

FAINCHE. *See* Fanchea.

*FAITH, ST, VIRGIN AND MARTYR

The legend of St Faith and of the miracles at her shrine was very popular in the Middle Ages. She may have been martyred at Agen, but the date is problematical. *Fides. October 6, iv, 45.*

*FAITH, HOPE AND **CHARITY, SS,** MARTYRS

The maidens Faith, Hope and Charity, with their mother Wisdom are said to have been martyred at Rome under Hadrian. They, or a similar group, are venerated in both West and East (Pistis, Elpis, Agape, Sophia), but the story is probably a myth. *August 1, iii, 238.*

FANCHEA, ST, VIRGIN

Sister of St Enda. She is said to have founded a convent at Rossory in Fermanagh and to have been buried at Killaine. d. *c.* 530. *March 21, i, 656.*

*FANTINUS, ST

He was abbot of the Greek monastery of St Mercury in Calabria, which was destroyed by the Saracens. *c.* 980. Fantinus d. soon after, in exile in Greece. *August 30, iii, 448.*

*FARE, ST, VIRGIN

Fare was the sister of St Cagnoald and St Faro and in the face of bitter opposition she became a nun; the monastery she ruled for thirty-seven years afterwards became famous under the name of Faremoutiers. d. 657. *Burgundofara. April 3, ii, 21.*

*FARO, ST, BISHOP

From being chancellor at the court of King Dagobert I he became a priest of the diocese of Meaux, and c. 628 was made bishop of that see. He befriended St Fiacre when he arrived from Ireland, and founded a monastery for monks from Luxeuil. d. c. 672. *October 28, iv, 216.*

FASTRED, BD, ABBOT

He was a disciple of St Bernard, who made him first abbot of Cambron; afterwards he ruled Clairvaux and then Cîteaux itself. d. 1163. *April 21.*

FAUSTINUS. *See also under* Simplicius.

*FAUSTUS, JANUARIUS AND **MARTIAL, SS,** MARTYRS

They gave their lives for Christ in 304(?); Prudentius calls them the Three Crowns of Cordova, where they suffered. *October 13, iv, 103.*

FAUSTUS OF RIEZ, ST, BISHOP

From being abbot of Lérins he was promoted to the see of Riez, where he was as good a bishop as he had been an abbot. He was a strong opponent of Arianism and Pelagianism, but in certain of his writings himself propounded semi-pelagian error: for some years he was exiled from his see by the Arian king Euric. d. c. 493. *September 28, iii, 666.*

FEARGAL. *See* Virgil of Salzburg.

*FEBRONIA, ST, VIRGIN AND MARTYR

Legend states that St Febronia was a nun at Nisibis in Mesopotamia, learned in the Scriptures and beautiful of body, who was lopped limb by limb for refusing to renounce Christ and marry the nephew of the Roman magistrate. This story was widely diffused, especially in the East, but there is good reason to doubt whether Febronia ever existed. *June 25, ii, 637.*

FECHIN, ST, ABBOT

Said to have been a Connacht man. He founded a community of monks in Westmeath, probably at Fobhar (Fore), and d. during the great plague of 665. The name

"Ecclefechen" testifies to his *cultus* in Scotland. *January 20. i. 132.*

FELICIA OF MILAN, BD, VIRGIN

Felicia Meda was b. at Milan in 1378. After governing the Poor Clare convent of St Ursula for fourteen years she was sent to found a new house at Pesaro, where she was as successful and reverenced as she had been at Milan. d. 1444. c.c. 1812. *July 24, iii, 179.*

*FELICIAN, ST, BISHOP AND MARTYR

An early bishop of Foligno and the traditional apostle of Umbria. After being bishop for more than fifty years he d. from ill treatment while being taken to Rome for martyrdom, c. 254. *Felicianus.* *January 24, i, 160.*

FELICIAN. *See also* under Primus.

*FELICISSIMUS AND **AGAPITUS, SS,** MARTYRS

They were deacons of Pope St Sixtus II and were martyred in 258 on the same day as that pope and four other Roman deacons. *August 7, iii, 269.*

*FELICITY, ST, MARTYR

She was martyred in Rome and buried on the Salarian Way. It was said later that she was the mother of the Seven Brothers (*q.v.*). *See also* Perpetua and Felicity. *March 6, iii, 62.*

*FELICULA, ST, MARTYR

She is said to have been the foster-sister of St Petronilla (May 31) and to have suffered death for Christ a few days after her. *June 13, ii, 537.*

FELIM. *See* **Nathy.**

*FELIX II (III), ST, POPE

This Felix was pope from 483 till his death in 492. His pontificate was mostly taken up with disturbances concerning the Monophysite heresy, and little is known about the man himself. *March 1, i, 451.*

*FELIX "II", ST

This Felix was not a martyr nor was he a pope, though he was wrongly intruded into the see of Rome in the year 355. His name got into the Roman Martyrology through errors in the *Liber Pontificalis*. He is now listed in the *Annuario Pontificio* as an antipope. d. 365. *July 29, iii, 206.*

*FELIX III (IV), ST, POPE

During his pontificate of four years he was revered as a man of great simplicity, humility and kindness to the poor; he built the basilica of SS Cosmas and Damian. d. 530. *September 22, iii, 621.*

*FELIX AND ADAUCTUS, SS, MARTYRS

Felix was a Roman priest who was beheaded for his faith in 304 (?). A man who suffered with him is said to have been called Adauctus (*i.e.* the one added) because his name was not known, he being a stranger in Rome. *August 30, iii. 446.*

*FELIX AND CYPRIAN, SS, BISHOPS AND MARTYRS

These two bishops and hundreds of other clergy and lay people of Africa were driven into the desert and there left to perish by the Vandals under the Arian king Huneric, *c.* 484. *October 12, iv, 93.*

*FELIX AND FORTUNATUS, SS, MARTYRS

Brothers from Vicenza who suffered martyrdom at Aquileia. Date is uncertain. *June 11, ii, 524.*

*FELIX, FORTUNATUS AND ACHILLEUS, SS, MARTYRS

The priest Felix with his deacons Fortunatus and Achilleus were martyred at Valence in France, *c.* 212. *April 23, ii, 150.*

FELIX OF BOURGES, ST, BISHOP

Bishop of Bourges, where he d. *c.* 580. Little is now known of him. *January 1, i, 9.*

*FELIX OF CANTALICE, ST

Born in 1513 at Cantalice in Apulia, the child of peasant farmers. After a narrow escape from death, from bolting bullocks when he was ploughing, Felix became a Capuchin lay-brother. He lived for forty years in Rome, and was held in great regard

by St Philip Neri. Many miracles are recorded at his shrine. d. 1587. cd 1709. *May 18, ii, 344.*

*FELIX OF DUNWICH, ST, BISHOP

Felix, a Burgundian, preached the gospel with great success in Suffolk, Norfolk and Cambridgeshire, establishing a school on the Kentish model. Felix (whose name is found in Felixstowe) settled his episcopal see at Dunwich, a place now washed away by the sea. d. 648. His feast is kept in the diocese of Northampton. *March 8, i, 524.*

FELIX OF NANTES, ST, BISHOP

Felix was a man of learning and one of the most eminent of the bishops of Nantes, but little is now known of his life. d. 582. *July 7, iii, 33.*

FELIX OF NICOSIA, BD

Felix was b. at Nicosia in Sicily and was apprenticed to a shoemaker. After several fruitless attempts he was admitted as a Capuchin lay-brother: he reclaimed numerous sinners and was a devoted friend of the poor and sick, and had the gift of healing both bodies and souls. d. 1787. bd 1888. *June 1, ii, 452.*

FELIX OF NOLA, ST

Priest of Nola, near Naples, where his father, a Romano-Syrian soldier, was a landowner. Felix suffered persecution under Decius, but himself escaped from prison and rescued his bishop in miraculous circumstances. He was known far and wide for his generosity to the poor, and refused to go to law to recover an impounded estate. d. *c.* 260. Over a century later St Paulinus of Nola wrote of the crowds that came from all over Italy to the shrine of St Felix, of the miracles that took place there, and of the assistance he had himself received from Felix's intercession. *January 14, i, 80.*

*FELIX OF THIBIUCA, ST, BISHOP AND MARTYR

Felix, bishop of Thibiuca in Africa, was beheaded in 303, one of the first of Diocletian's victims, for refusing to deliver up the sacred books. He probably suffered at

Carthage; certainly not in Italy, as a later version of his *passio* has it.
October 24, iv, 188.

*FELIX OF TRIER, ST, BISHOP

A most holy man and extremely generous to the poor; he resigned his see of Trier because the circumstances of his election were looked on with suspicion by the Holy See and St Ambrose. Sulpicius Severus speaks of him with much respect. d. c. 400.
March 26, i, 684.

FELIX. *See also under* Nabor.

*FERDINAND OF CASTILE, ST

Ferdinand became king of Castile in 1217, when he was eighteen, and of León in 1230. For twenty-seven years he was engaged in almost uninterrupted warfare against the Muslims in Spain, campaigns which culminated in the capture of Seville in 1249. This successful crusading was the basis of the veneration of Ferdinand III in Spain, but he was as well an admirable ruler and virtuous man. By his second wife, Jane of Ponthieu, he was the father of Eleanor, wife of Edward I of England. d. 1252. cd 1671.
May 30, ii, 426.

FERDINAND OF PORTUGAL, BD

Prince Ferdinand the Trusty was b. at Sanarem in 1402, son of King John I of Portugal and Philippa, daughter of John of Gaunt. With his brother Henry the Navigator he led an expedition against the Moors in Africa; they were defeated at Tangier, and Ferdinand and others were given as hostages. At Arzilla he was imprisoned with a great deal of cruelty, but all his concern was for his companions and he was never heard to speak a hard word against his captors. He d. in a dungeon in 1443, after over five years of confinement. c.c. 1470. *June 5, ii, 483.*

FERGUS, ST, BISHOP

The feast of this eighth-century (?) bishop is kept by the dioceses of Dunkeld and Aberdeen; he was apparently an Irish missionary in Perthshire, Caithness, Buchan and Forfarshire. *Fergustus.*
November 27, iv, 436.

FERREOLUS, BD, BISHOP AND MARTYR

A seventh-century bishop, supposedly of Grenoble, whose ancient *cultus* was confirmed in 1907. *January 16, i, 103.*

*FERREOLUS AND FERRUTIO, SS, MARTYRS

A priest and a deacon who laboured as missionaries around Besançon and were martyred c. 212 (?). *June 16, ii, 552.*

*FIACRE, ST

He was a hermit at Kilfiachra in Ireland who went over to France, where he was given land for a hermitage by St Faro of Meaux; here he lived, greatly revered by the people, for the rest of his life and d. c. 670 (?). St Fiacre's shrine, at the place in Seine-et-Marne that bears his own name, is still resorted to and he is invoked against all sorts of physical ills. His feast is kept throughout Ireland. *Fiacrius. September 1, ii, 460.*

*FIDELIS OF COMO, ST, MARTYR

Fidelis was a martyr at Como (in 303?), where his tomb was known in the sixth century. *October 28, iv, 215.*

*FIDELIS OF SIGMARINGEN, ST, MARTYR

Mark Rey was born of a middle-class family at Sigmaringen in south Germany in 1577 and for some time practised as an advocate, especially on behalf of poor people. Then he joined the Capuchins, receiving the name of Fidelis, and for ten years wrote and preached against Calvinism, notably among the Swiss of the Grison Alps. His opponents raised the peasants against him by putting about the story that he was a political agent of the Austrian emperor, and he was set upon and killed between Sewis and Grüsch in 1622. cd 1745. *April 24, ii, 156.*

FILLAN, ST, ABBOT

Or *Foela*. He was the son of St Kentigern. After being abbot of a monastery near Saint Andrews, he went to live as a solitary in Perthshire. He was buried in Strathfillan. But these particulars are very doubtful. The *Aberdeen Breviary* relates some extravagant miracles of him. Eighth century. The diocese of Dunkeld has kept his feast. *Foelanus. January 19, i, 120.*

FINA. *See* Seraphina.

FINAN, ST, BISHOP

Finan, an Irish monk from Iona, succeeded St Aidan as bishop at Lindisfarne and for ten years efficiently and peacefully governed his huge diocese. He baptized Peada, king of the Middle Angles, and Sigebert, king of the East Angles, and sent missionaries into their territories. d. 661. His feast has been kept in the dioceses of Lancaster and Argyll and the Isles. *Fionanus. January 19, i, 120.*

FINBAR, ST, BISHOP

Fionnbharr (= White Head) is venerated as the founder of the city and see of Cork, he having established a monastery at the mouth of the river Lee which exerted a strong influence all over the south of Ireland; he founded other churches as well, and seems also have preached in Scotland. Accounts of St Finbar are full of conflicting statements and decorated with surprising wonders. He is said to have d. at Cloyne, *c.* 633. His feast is kept throughout Ireland. *Finnbarrus. September 25, iii, 634.*

FINNIAN LOBHAR, ST, ABBOT

The records of this saint are conflicting and untrustworthy: even the century of his birth is uncertain. His name is associated with the monastery of Clonmore and he is said to have been made abbot of Swords by St Columba. d. *c.* 560 (?). *Finianus. March 16, i, 606.*

FINNIAN OF CLONARD, ST, BISHOP

This Finnian was the outstanding figure among the holy men of Ireland in the period following the death of St Patrick. He founded a number of churches, monasteries and schools, the greatest of which was Clonard, and became known as the "teacher of the saints of Ireland". Clonard was famous for its biblical studies for several centuries. At the same time Finnian continued his missionary work. d. *c.* 549. The feast of St Finnian of Clonard is kept throughout Ireland. *December 12, iv, 544.*

FINNIAN OF MOVILLE, ST, BISHOP

It is said that he was b. near Strangford Lough, was a monk in Scotland, and ordained in Rome, and that when he returned to Ireland he brought with him biblical manuscripts that led to the incident of the psalter of St Columba, when the two quarrelled over an unauthorized translation. He established the monastery of Moville in county Down, which was one of the great schools of Ireland for several centuries. d. *c.* 579. In Ireland and elsewhere St Finnian is wrongly identified with St Frigidian of Lucca. *September 10, iii, 531.*

*FINTAN OF CLONEENAGH, ST, ABBOT

He was trained by Columba of Tir da Glas and settled at Cloneenagh in Leix as an anchorite, but he soon had many disciples, with whom he lived a life of very great rigour, so that the monks of neighbouring monasteries protested. The memory of Fintan is preserved in several stories of his austerity and marvels. d. 603. His feast is kept throughout Ireland. *Fintanus. February 17, i, 356.*

FINTAN OF RHEINAU, ST

He is said to have been carried off from Leinster by Norse raiders. He escaped, and became a monk at Rheinau in the Black Forest. d. 879. *November 15, iv, 350.*

FINTAN OF TAGHMON, ST, ABBOT

This Fintan, or Mannu, was one of the most austere of the early Irish monks. He founded the monastery of Taghmon in county Wexford about the beginning of the seventh century. Acccording to Scottish tradition he lived on Iona for a time. d. *c.* 635. *October 21, iv, 170.*

*FIRMINUS I, ST, BISHOP AND MARTYR

He was probably simply a missionary bishop in Gaul, martyred during the fourth (?) century, but he is venerated as the first bishop of Amiens. Another St Firminus is honoured as third bishop of Amiens, but he may be the same person. *September 25, iii, 632.*

FLANNAN, ST, BISHOP

Flannan is venerated as the first bishop at

Killaloe, during the seventh (?) century, and his feast is kept throughout Ireland. *Flannanus. December 18, iv, 582.*

*FLAVIAN, ST, BISHOP AND MARTYR
Flavian began his career as patriarch of Constantinople by refusing to acknowledge his promotion in 447 by making a present to the Emperor Theodosius II. He condemned the Monophysite teachings of Eutyches and received from Pope St Leo the famous "Dogmatic Letter" confirming the condemnation. At the "Robber Synod" of Ephesus in 449 the Monophysite Dioscorus and his followers assaulted Flavian so violently that he died of his injuries three days later. There is, however, some conflict of evidence as to the occasion and manner of his death. *Flavianus. February 18, i, 367.*

*FLAVIAN AND ELIAS, SS, BISHOPS
Flavian, patriarch of Antioch, and Elias, patriarch of Jerusalem, are named together in the Roman Martyrology, they having been driven into exile by the emperor Anastasius for upholding the Council of Chalcedon. They d. in 512 and 518 respectively. *July 20, iii, 154.*

*FLORA AND MARY, SS,
VIRGINS AND MARTYRS
Flora and Mary were Christian maidens of Cordova who gave themselves up to the Moors during the persecution; they were beheaded in 851. *November 24, iv, 419.*

FLORA OF BEAULIEU, ST, VIRGIN
A hospitaller nun of the order of St John of Jerusalem at the convent of Beaulieu, near Rocamadour. A number of spiritual trials and surprising physical phenomena are narrated of her by a biography whose value is uncertain. d. 1347. *October 5, iv, 38.*

*FLORENTIUS OF STRASBURG, ST,
BISHOP
He was made bishop of Strasburg after being a missionary in Alsace. He is said to have been an Irishman. Seventh century. *November 7, iv, 286.*

*FLORIAN, ST, MARTYR
He was a Roman military official who suf-

fered death for Christ in 304, at Lorch in Austria. *Florianus. May 4, ii, 230.*

FLORIBERT, ST, BISHOP
A bishop of Liège who was, among more amiable characteristics, "vehement in correcting". d. 746. *April 27, ii, 172.*

*FLORUS AND LORUS, SS, MARTYRS
According to a very unreliable Greek tradition these martyrs were brothers and both stonemasons: they handed over a temple on which they had been working to Christian worship and were accordingly put to death by the heathen. Their veneration had nothing to do with the worship of Castor and Pollux. *August 18, iii, 345.*

FOELAN. *See* Fillan.

FOILLAN, ST, BISHOP AND MARTYR
He was a brother of St Fursey and when Burghcastle was destroyed by the Mercians he crossed over to France with his other brother, St Ultan, and founded the abbey of Fosse. Foillan exercised considerable influence at the convent of Nivelles, and going from thence to Bavai one night in 655 he and his companions were murdered by robbers. St Foillan is venerated as "bishop and martyr" but nothing is known of his alleged episcopate and the circumstances of his death hardly constitute martyrdom. *Foelanus. October 31, iv, 230.*

FORANNAN, ST, ABBOT
He was one of the several Irish abbots of Waulsort in Belgium, where he introduced the Rule of St Benedict. d. 982. *April 30, ii, 200.*

FORTUNATUS. *See under* Felix (two), *and* Hermagoras.

FORTY MARTYRS OF ENGLAND AND WALES, THE
The Forty English and Welsh Martyrs suffered under the various Protestant persecutions of Catholics between 1535 and 1671. They were arrested, tortured, tried and executed for treason because they offended against laws of Henry VIII and Elizabeth I, in force or ratified in later reigns, generally

in respect of the royal supremacy, against study abroad for the priesthood, and against pastoral work and saying Mass in England and Wales. They were: SS John Houghton, Cuthbert Mayne, Margaret Clitherow, Swithin Wells, Richard Gwyn, John Almond, Edmund Arrowsmith, Ambrose Barlow, John Boste, Alexander Brian, Edmund Campion, Philip Evans, Thomas Garnet, Edmund Genings, Philip Howard, John Jones, John Kemble, Luke Kirby, Robert Lawrence, David Lewis, Anne Line, John Lloyd, Henry Morse, Nicholas Owen, John Payne, Polydore Plasden, John Plesington, Richard Reynolds, John Rigby, John Roberts, Alban Roe, Ralph Sherwin, Robert Southwell, John Southworth, John Stone, John Wall, Henry Walpole, Margaret Ward, Augustine Webster, Eustace White (see separate entries for each of the foregoing). cd October 25, 1970. *October 25. See also* Eighty-five Martyrs of England, Scotland and Wales.

*FOUR CROWNED MARTYRS, THE

There is confusion and uncertainty about the martyrs called the Four Holy Crowned Ones. They may have been four who suffered at Albano *c.* 305 (SS Severus and companions) or others in Pannonia about the same time (SS Claudius and companions): or they may have been neither. A basilica was dedicated in their honour in Rome in the fifth century. The Pannonian martyrs were said to be stone-masons who refused to carve an image of the heathen deity Aesculapius.
November 8, iv, 293.

FOURTEEN HOLY HELPERS, THE

A feast in honour of this group is celebrated in various parts of Germany on August 8 and other dates. The usual fourteen names are Achatius, Barbara, Blaise, Catherine, Christopher, Cyriascus, Denis, Erasmus, Eustace, George, Margaret, Panteleon, Vitus (all martyrs), and Giles. In France the Holy Helpers are fifteen, the extra one being our Lady. *August 8, iii, 280.*

FRA ANGELICO, BD

Giovanni da Fiesole, Dominican and Florentine painter of the early Renaissance,

b. 1378 at Vecchio and baptized as Guido or Guidolino. He was a novice at Cortona in 1408 and professed at Fiesole. Vasari said his paintings were the work of a saint or an angel. d. 1455. On account of the superlative integrity of his life and the almost divine beauty of his images, he was beatified by John-Paul II in an exceptional procedure on his own initiative: by Motu Proprio of October 3, 1982. *February 18.*

FRANCA OF PIACENZA, ST, VIRGIN

As abbess of St Syrus at Piacenza St Franca Visalta was persecuted on account of her strict discipline, and eventually was transferred to take charge of a new Cistercian community at Pittoli. d. 1218. c.c. by Pope Gregory X. *April 26, ii, 166.*

FRANCES D'AMBOISE, BD

Frances was the wife of Duke Peter of Brittany, after whose death in 1457 she increased the charitable works for which she was already known. She helped Bd John Soreth to introduce the Carmelite nuns into France, and herself joined the order at Vannes in 1468. d. 1485. bd 1863. *Francisca.*
November 4, iv, 266.

FRANCES ANNE CIRER CARBONNEL, BD, VIRGIN

Francisca-Ana Cirer Carbonnel, b. 1781, was the Spanish foundress of the Sisters of Charity. She led a life of poverty, consecration to prayer and obedience to the will of God, giving her possessions to the poor and to the parish. d. 1855. bd October 1, 1989. *February 27.*

FRANCES SCHERVIER, BD, VIRGIN

Sr Maria Franziska Schervier was b. at Aachen, Germany, in 1819, the daughter of a needle manufacturer. She became a Franciscan tertiary in 1844 and founded the Franciscan Sisters of the Poor in 1845, dividing the order into contemplative and active branches. Eventually there were two congregations, one German, one American. She was known as the "mother of the poor" and d. in December 1876. bd April 28, 1974. *December 14.*

*FRANCES XAVIER CABRINI, ST, VIRGIN

The first citizen of the United States to be canonized, but b. in Italy, in 1850. In 1880 she founded the Missionary Sisters of the Sacred Heart at Codogno in Lombardy, and in 1889, at the direction of Pope Leo XIII, extended her activities to North America; here she began her work among Italian immigrants by founding an orphanage and settling it at West Park, on the Hudson river. Among her other great foundations were the Columbus hospitals in New York and Chicago. Mother Cabrini carried her work to Latin America, visiting Nicaragua, Costa Rica, Chile, Brazil and the Argentine, often under most arduous conditions, and she had to overcome no little opposition. Mother Cabrini was a woman of quite extraordinary ability and tenacity, very strict and firm, but always just and loving, "a woman of fine understanding and great holiness", as Leo XIII said. d. at Chicago, 1917. cd 1946. *November 13, iv, 593.*

*FRANCES THE ROMAN, ST

She was b. in Rome in 1384 and married at an early age to Lorenzo Ponziano. She led a life of great devotion and penance, but without singularity or excess; she patiently bore terrible distresses in the death of her children, Lorenzo's banishment, and the confiscation of their estates: and contrived in forty years never to annoy her husband. On his death Frances joined the community of Benedictine oblates of the Tor de' Specchi, which she had founded in 1433 for retirement and charitable works (this community still exists). d. 1440. cd 1608. *March 9, i, 529.*

*FRANCIS BORGIA, ST

Born at Gandia in Aragon into the noble family of Borja in 1510. For nearly twenty years Francis led the life appropriate to a great nobleman, holding office at the court of the emperor and administering his Spanish estates. On the death of his wife in 1546 he relinquished these estates (he was the duke of Gandia) and joined the Society of Jesus. First as a preacher and then as father general of his order he became one of the chief instruments of the "Counter-Reformation"; he established the Jesuits throughout western Europe, sent missionaries to the Americas, and more than counterbalanced the evil justly associated with the name of Borgia. St Francis was the typical patrician saint, humble, determined, mortified, attracting all ranks by his kindness and courtesy. d. 1572. cd 1671. *Franciscus. October 10, iv, 74.*

FRANCIS DE CAPILLAS, BD, MARTYR

He was a Spanish Dominican missionary in the Philippines, who in 1642 was sent to the Chinese province of Fokien. Here he was martyred by beheading in 1648. bd 1909. Francis de Capillas is the earliest martyr of China to be beatified. *January 15, i, 98.*

FRANCIS DI BRUNO, BD

Franceso Faa' di Bruno was b. at Alessandria, Italy, on March 9, 1825. He enrolled at Turin military Academy, became an officer in 1846 but decided to read physics at the University where he eventually became a teacher. He was ordained in 1851 and started many initiatives to help under-privileged women. He founded the Little Sisters of Our Lady of Intercession. d. 1888. bd September 25, 1988. *March 27.*

*FRANCIS CARACCIOLO, ST

Born in the Abruzzi in 1563 of the noble Neapolitan family of the Caraccioli. He became a priest in gratitude for being cured of a disease akin to leprosy, and in 1588 founded with John Augustine Adorno the order of Minor Clerks Regular. The life of St Francis was one of prayer and penance combined with the establishment of the new congregation in Italy and Spain, where its members worked as missioners and in prisons and hospitals. They met with a good deal of opposition, and overwork led Francis to resign the government of the society. He refused several bishoprics and passed his last years in preaching and contemplation. d. 1608. cd 1807. *June 4, ii, 470.*

FRANCIS CHIEN, BD. *See* Dominic Henarez

FRANCIS CLET, BD, MARTYR

Francis Regis Clet was b. at Grenoble in

1748. He joined the Vincentians, and went as a missionary to China in 1791. He worked under the greatest difficulties, and for three years was entirely alone. In 1818 persecution became violent, and Father Clet was betrayed. At the age of seventy-two he was tortured and strangled, near Hankow, in 1820. bd 1900. *February 17, i, 362.*

FRANCIS COLL, BD

A Spanish Dominican priest, Bd Francisco Coll, O.P., b. 1812, founded the Congregation of the Annunciation, a community of nuns. d. 1869. bd April 29, 1979 at the first beatification ceremony presided over by John Paul II. *December 2.*

FRANCIS DICKENSON, BD, MARTYR

He was a secular priest, b. in Yorkshire, who was h.d.q. for his priesthood at Rochester in 1590. bd 1919. *April 30, ii, 201.*

FRANCIS GAGELIN, ST, MARTYR

Francis Isidore Gagelin was a priest of the Paris Foreign Missions, martyred by strangling at Bongson in Annam in 1833. bd 1900. cd June 19, 1988. *October 17.*

FRANCIS GALVEZ, BD, MARTYR

A Castilian Friar Minor of the Observance who was martyred by burning at Tokyo in 1623. bd 1867. *December 4, ii, 448.*

FRANCIS GARATE, BD

Br Francisco Garate, b. 1857, was a Spanish Jesuit and a university doorkeeper in Bilbao for forty years and noted for the "evangelizing power" of his humble service. d. 1919. bd October 6, 1985. *September 9.*

FRANCIS DI GIROLAMO, ST

Born in 1642 near Taranto, ordained priest in 1666, and became a Jesuit in 1670. Francis spent his life as a missioner in the kingdom of Naples, where from the outset his preaching attracted huge congregations and produced remarkable conversions: he once brought twenty Turkish prisoners to the faith. Many miracles were attributed to him. d. 1716. cd 1839. *May 11, ii, 280.*

FRANCIS GODOY, BD, MARTYR

A young kinsman of St Teresa of Avila and fellow martyr with Bd Ignatius Azevedo. d. 1570. bd 1854. *July 15, iii, 112.*

FRANCIS INGLEBY, BD, MARTYR

Francis Ingleby (or Ingolby) was a secular priest b. Ripley, Yorkshire. He studied at Rheims and was ordained priest on March 21, 1581 and sent on the English mission in April. He was imprisoned in York gaol and h.d.q. for high treason in 1586. bd November 22, 1987. *August 8.*

FRANCIS JACCARD, BD, MARTYR

A Savoyard priest, of the Paris Foreign Missions, martyred in Annam in 1838. bd 1900. cd June 19, 1988. *September 21.*

FRANCIS LAVAL, BD, BISHOP

François de Montmorency-Laval, the "Founder of the Church in Canada", was b. April 30, 1623 at Montigny-sur-Avre, France. He was ordained priest in 1647 and was appointed vicar apostolic of Canada and consecrated bishop in 1658. He went to Canada in 1659 and was bishop of Quebec from 1674. d. 1708. bd June 22, 1980. *May 6.*

FRANCIS PACHECO, BD, MARTYR

This Portuguese Jesuit was martyred at Nagasaki in Japan in 1626 together with two other Jesuits from Europe, two Japanese Jesuits, three Japanese laymen and a Korean. They were all burned alive. bd 1867. *June 20, ii, 450.*

FRANCIS PAGE, BD, MARTYR

He belonged to a Protestant family at Harrow-on-the-Hill, was reconciled with the Church, and ordained at Douay; h.d.q. for his priesthood at Tyburn in 1606. bd 1919. *April 20, ii, 137.*

FRANCIS PALAU Y QUER, BD

Francisco Palau y Quer was b. at Aytona, Catalonia, on December 29, 1811. He became a discalced Carmelite and was ordained priest in 1836. He spent many years in France. He founded two religious institutes and was a preacher, journalist and hermit. d. at Tarragon in 1872. bd April 24, 1988. *March 20.*

FRANCIS PATRIZZI, BD

He was received into the Servite Order by St Philip Benizi, and soon became famous as a missioner and preacher. d. 1328. c.c. 1743. *May 12, ii, 290.*

FRANCIS DE POSADAS, BD

A confessor of the Order of Preachers who was well known all over the south-west of Spain during the second half of the seventeenth century. d. 1713. bd 1818. *September 20, iii, 608.*

*FRANCIS DE SALES, ST, BISHOP AND DOCTOR

Born in Savoy in 1567, eldest son of a noble family. He was a student of law at Paris and Padua, but decided to become a priest and was ordained in 1593. He was sent as a missioner to the Protestants of Chablais where, after a poor start, he was notably successful. In 1599 he was nominated coadjutor of the bishop of Geneva, and in 1602 succeeded to the see. St Francis established a seminary at Annecy, organized conferences and synods of his clergy, and insisted on simple preaching and religious instruction. He met St Jane Frances de Chantal in 1604 and with her founded the order of Visitation nuns. He was one of the finest bishops and most attractive men that Christianity has ever produced, and his effect on the indifferent and on Protestants was most marked: "The man who preaches with love", he said, "preaches adequately against the heretics, even though he never utters a controversial word"; Cardinal du Perron said that he (the cardinal) could confute Protestants, but that Mgr de Sales could convert them. Of St Francis's written works the most famous are his *Treatise on the Love of God* and the *Introduction to the Devout Life.* St Francis was only fifty-six when he d. in 1622. cd 1665; declared Doctor of the Church in 1877, and patron saint of journalists and other writers in 1923. *January 24, i, 195.*

*FRANCIS SOLANO, ST

He was b. in 1549, joined the Observant Franciscans, and for years exercised his ministry in southern Spain. In 1589 he was sent as a missionary to South America and for twenty years he was a power among the Indians and the Spanish colonists: his denunciations of the corruptions of Lima brought panic to the citizens. St Francis had the gift of tongues, it is said, and many other miracles were related of him. d. 1610. cd 1726. *July 13, iii, 93.*

*FRANCIS XAVIER, ST

Francis Xavier was b. in Navarre in 1506 of noble parents and was by nature aristocratic, refined and ambitious. In 1534 he became the second of St Ignatius Loyola's original seven followers and proved to be perhaps the greatest individual missionary to the heathen since St Paul. He set out on his first journey, to the East Indies, in 1540, and within ten years he had made most successful visits to India, Ceylon, and other East Indian islands, Malaya and Japan; like many missionaries before and since he found that a very great difficulty in the way of his apostolate was presented by the trading and political Europeans, and he did not hesitate to tell the king of Portugal so. Francis Xavier d. on the island of Sancian in 1552, when about to enter China. He was bd in 1622, and Pope Pius X named him patron of foreign missions and of all works for the spreading of Christianity. *December 3, iv, 474.*

*FRANCIS-XAVIER BIANCHI, ST

Born in 1743 at Arpino and became a Barnabite clerk regular, in spite of great opposition from his family. He over-worked himself in his ministry, added severe austerities to already bad health, and at last lost the use of his legs. He inspired boundless veneration in Naples and miracles were attributed to him. d. 1815. cd 1951. *January 31, i, 217.*

*FRANCIS OF ASSISI, ST

It has been said of St Francis that he entered into glory in his lifetime, and that he is the one saint whom all succeeding generations have agreed in canonizing: but often this is rather on account of the listening birds, the hunted leveret, the falcon, and the nightingale in an ilex-grove (nothing extraordinary in his day, when Nature was still natural) than for those qualities that earned him canonization. He was b. at Assisi in 1181 or 1182, the son of a merchant. After a pleasure-seeking youth he left his home, and in 1209 founded the order of Friars Minor, capturing the imagination of his time by presenting poverty, chastity and obedience in terms of the troubadours and courts of love: numerous followers were soon forthcoming. In 1219 he went to the East to try to evangelize the Muslims, but without success, either among the crusaders or their infidel opponents. There were considerable internal difficulties in the new order, but in 1224 Francis's labours were supernaturally recognized by the imprinting of the *stigmata* of the Passion on his body—the first certainly recorded and most famous example of this phenomenon. The Franciscan nuns were established in concert with St Clare in 1212. St Francis d., still in deacon's orders, in 1226. cd 1228. *October 4, iv, 22; iii, 575.*

FRANCIS OF CALDEROLA, BD

A confessor of the Franciscan order who had a special gift for reconciling enemies; d. 1507. c.c. by Pope Gregory XVI. *September 28, iii, 676.*

FRANCIS OF CAMPOROSSO, ST

He was a Capuchin lay brother, who for many years begged alms for his brethren in the city of Genoa where he was greatly loved and respected by the people. He d. while nursing cholera victims in 1866. bd 1919. cd 1962. *September 17, iii, 586*

FRANCIS OF FABRIANO, BD

Born in 1251 and became a Friar Minor; he wrote a treatise in defence of the Portiuncula indulgence and is said to have been the first Franciscan to form a library. d. *c.* 1322. c.c. 1775. *April 22, ii, 147.*

FRANCIS OF LUCERA, BD

Francis Antony Fasani was b. in Apulia in 1681, and was admitted to the order of Conventual Friars Minor. He spent nearly all his life in his home town of Lucera, where he was revered and loved as another Francis of Assisi. d. 1742. bd 1951. cd April 13, 1986. *November 29, iv, 449.*

*FRANCIS OF NAGASAKI, ST, MARTYR

A representative figure among the seventeen Japanese laymen (three of whom were young boys) crucified with other martyrs at Nagasaki in 1597. He was a physician, a tertiary of St Francis, and a catechist. cd 1862. *February 5, i, 259.*

*FRANCIS OF PAOLA, ST

Born at Paola in Calabria in 1416. He was founder of the order of Minim friars, so called because they wished to be the least of all friars, which took its rise with the hermits that Francis attracted to his solitude in 1436. The order spread quickly with the fame of its founder, who was gifted with powers of miracle and prophecy, but it did not lack setbacks, St Francis being at one time threatened with imprisonment by the king of Naples. He was specially sent for by the dying Louis XI of France and was honoured by his two successors, who would not let him return to Italy. d. at Plessis-les-Tours in 1507. cd 1519. *April 2, ii, 10.*

FRANCIS OF PESARO, BD

This Francis ("Bd Cecco") was an early Franciscan tertiary who lived with others in community. A number of very remarkable occurrences are associated with his name. d. *c.* 1350. c.c. by Pope Pius IX. *October 1, iv, 6.*

FRANCO OF GROTTI, BD

While a fugitive from justice Franco Lippi joined a band of *condottieri* and until middle-age led a most evil life. He was brought to penitence by a temporary blindness, and when he was over sixty-five was admitted to the Carmelite Order as a lay-brother, in which capacity he edified Siena as much as he had formerly scandalized it. d. 1291. c.c. 1670. *Francus. December 11, iv, 542.*

FREDERICK ALBERT, BD

Federico Albert, b. 1820, was an Italian priest who founded the Vincentian Sisters of Mary Immaculate and served the young and poor with special zeal. d. 1876. bd September 30, 1984. *September 30.*

FREDERICK JANSSOONE, BD

Frédéric Janssoone was b. on November 19, 1838 at Ghyvelde, France. He entered the Franciscan novitiate in 1864 and was ordained priest in 1870. He went to the Holy Land in 1876 and worked incessantly to obtain funds for poor Palestinian Christians and for Christian interests. In 1881 he went to Canada and d. 1916 at Montreal. bd September 25, 1988. *August 4.*

FREDERICK OF LIÈGE, BD, BISHOP

He was appointed bishop of Liège in 1119 in place of the simoniacal Alexander, but d. in 1121, it is said poisoned by Alexander's supporter the count of Louvain. *Fridericus. May 27.*

FREDERICK OF REGENSBURG, BD

He is a confessor of the Augustinian friars, a lay-brother of their order at Ratisbon (Regensburg). d. 1329. c.c. 1909. *November 29, iv, 446.*

*FREDERICK OF UTRECHT, ST,
BISHOP AND MARTYR

He became bishop of Utrecht in 825 and was murdered in church at Maastricht in 838, it is said by men from Walcheren where Frederick had worked hard to extirpate the custom of incestuous marriage. *July 18, iii, 139.*

FREDIANO. *See* Frigidian.

*FRIDESWIDE, ST, VIRGIN

The legend of St Frideswide is late and untrustworthy, but she probably founded a nunnery at Oxford and d. there *c.* 735. Early in the twelfth century the monastery was refounded for the Austin canons, and the saint's shrine there was an important place of pilgrimage. St Frideswide's feast is observed in the archdiocese of Birmingham and she had a *cultus* at Bomy in Artois, under the corrupt name *Frévisse. Fredeswinda. October 19, iv, 150.*

FRIDOLIN, ST

Fridolin was a wandering Irish priest who founded the abbey of Säckingen on the Rhine, at an unknown date during the Merovingian period. Other particulars of his life are considered unreliable. He may have d. *c.* 538. *Fridolinus. October 3, iv, 18.*

*FRIGIDIAN, ST, BISHOP

Called in Italy *Frediano.* An Irishman who went on pilgrimage to Italy and became a hermit there on Monte Pisano. He was elected bishop of Lucca, where he formed the clergy of the city into a community of canons regular, which centuries later became part of the Canons Regular of the Lateran. St Gregory in his *Dialogues* narrates the miracle of Frediano diverting the course of the river Serchio, which threatened Lucca. St Frigidian's story is not devoid of uncertainty; he d. in 588(?). His feast has been observed throughout Ireland and by the Lateran canons regular. *Frigidianus. March 18, i, 626.*

*FROILAN, ST, BISHOP

He was bishop of León and one of the principal restorers of monasticism in Spain. d. 905 (?). *Froilanus. October 3, iv, 18.*

*FRONTO AND GEORGE, SS, BISHOPS

These saints were early apostles of Périgord, but their story has been completely overlaid with worthless legend. *October 25, iv, 198.*

*FRUCTUOSUS OF BRAGA, ST,
BISHOP

Fructuosus was a Visigoth of high rank. He devoted his estates to the poor, to freed slaves, and to endowing religious houses, some of which sheltered whole families. He himself was abbot of Complutum and in 656 was made archbishop of Braga, in the direction of which diocese he met with opposition that amounted to persecution. d. 665. *April 16, ii, 102.*

*FRUCTUOSUS OF TARRAGONA,
ST, BISHOP AND MARTYR

Fructuosus, bishop of Tarragona in Spain, with his deacons Augurius and Eulogius, was arrested in 259 during the persecution of Valerian, and all three were burned alive. There is an authentic account extant of the bishop's examination by the Roman governor and of the subsequent martyrdom. *January 21, i, 137.*

*FRUMENTIUS, ST, BISHOP

A youth from Tyre who was wrecked on the Ethiopian coast and, with another young man, St Aedesius, was taken to the royal court at Aksum, where both in time became officials. Frumentius was, *c*. 350, consecrated bishop at Alexandria by St Athanasius, and sent back to preach the gospel in Ethiopia. He is venerated as the apostle of that country. d. *c*. 380. *October 27, iv, 208.*

FULBERT, ST, BISHOP

Fulbert was a pupil of Gerbert at Rheims and a very distinguished scholar; under his care the cathedral school at Chartres became the chief one in France, and in due course he was promoted to the bishopric of that city. He was author of the hymn "Chorus novae Hierusalem". d. 1029. *April 10, ii, 63.*

FULCO OF NEUILLY, BD

He was parish priest at Neuilly-sur-Marne and a famous preacher throughout northwestern France. He was regarded with suspicion by some because he lived in a quite ordinary way, with no unusual ascetic practices. He was ordered by Pope Innocent III to preach the Fourth Crusade, but was saved by death from participating in that disastrous expedition. d. 1201. *March 2, i, 461.*

*FULGENTIUS, ST, BISHOP

Born in Africa in 468 of a senatorial family. Became a monk and abbot, and suffered under Arian Vandal persecution. Bishop of Ruspe in 508, but was banished by the Vandals with other bishops to Sardinia, where Fulgentius wrote a number of treatises, especially against Arianism. He finally returned to his diocese on the death of King Thrasimund in 523, and retired to a remote monastery a year before his death in 533. The theological and controversial writings of St Fulgentius are of considerable importance. *January 1, i, 6.*

FULRAD, ST, ABBOT

He was abbot of Saint-Denis, near Paris, and held several responsible offices under the Frankish kings. Fulrad was the delegate of King Pepin for the handing over to the Holy See of the exarchate of Ravenna and the duchy of the Pentapolis in 756. d. 784. *July 16, iii, 118.*

*FULSEY, ST, ABBOT

Born near Lough Corrib (on Inisquin ?) and established a monastery at Rathmat (Killursa ?) which soon became popular. Then he returned home and began to experience the remarkable ecstasies of which Bede and Aelfric write. St Fulsey came to England, where land was given him for a monastery at Burgh Castle, near Yarmouth, and then went on to Gaul, where he founded another monastery, at Lagny. He d. *c*. 648, and was buried at Péronne. His feast is observed in the diocese of Northampton and throughout Ireland. *Furseus. January 16, i, 101.*

*FUSCIAN, VICTORICUS AND **GENTIAN, SS,** MARTYRS

Fuscian and Victoricus are said to have been early missionaries in Gaul who were martyred near Amiens. Gentian, an old man, was killed while defending them from arrest. Date unknown. *Fuscianus. December 11, iv, 538.*

G

GABRA MICHAEL, BD, MARTYR

He was a dissident Ethiopian monk who in 1844 was reconciled with the Catholic Church and became a valuable helper of Bd Justin de Jacobis. When Theodore II became *negus*, Aba Michael was sentenced to death for refusing to apostatize. He was reprieved at the instance of the British consul, Walter Chichele Plowden, but was kept in chains and d. from ill-treatment in 1855. bd 1926. *September 1, iii, 465.*

*GABRIEL THE ARCHANGEL, ST

The Angel of the Annunciation (Luke i, 26; *see also* Daniel ix, 21 and Luke i, 10, 19). His feast was added to the general calendar of the Western Church in 1921.
September 29, i, 667.

*GABRIEL LALEMANT, ST, MARTYR

This Jesuit priest was put to death with St John de Brébeuf by North American Indians, after being tortured with appalling ferocity, on March 16, 1649. cd 1930.
September 26, iii, 645.

GABRIEL MARY, BD

Gilbert Nicholas was b. near Clermont in 1463, joined the Friars Minor, and became the confessor and helper of St Joan of Valois in founding the Annonciade nuns. The nickname of "Gabriel ab Ave Maria" was given to him by Pope Leo X. d. 1532.
August 27, iii, 423.

*GABRIEL POSSENTI, ST

Francis Possenti was b. of a middle-class family at Spoleto in 1838, and went to the Jesuit school in that town. There were apparently no clear indications of religious vocation in his youth, but after two serious illnesses and the death of his sister he entered the novitiate of the Passionists, taking the name of Gabriel-of-our-Lady-of-Sorrows. He was then eighteen and the remaining six years of his life are simply a record of an extraordinary effort to attain perfection in and by small things. An outstanding characteristic was his continual cheerfulness. In 1860 Brother Gabriel developed tuberculosis, and he d. two years later. cd 1920.
February 27, i, 429.

GABRIEL TAURIN DUFRESSES, BD, BISHOP AND MARTYR

One of the most effective missionaries of the Paris Society of Foreign Missions. He laboured in China for nearly forty years, and was consecrated bishop in 1801. He was martyred by beheading at Chintai in 1815. bd 1900. *September 14, i, 362.*

GABRIEL OF ANCONA, BD

Gabriel Ferretti was a confessor of the Franciscan Order at Ancona; d. 1456. c.c. by Pope Benedict XIV. *November 12, iv, 326.*

GAETANO. *See* Cajetan.

*GAIANA, ST, VIRGIN AND MARTYR

One of the traditional protomartyrs of the Armenian church, with St Rhipsime and other maidens. The romantic story of their fleeing to Armenia to escape the matrimonial intentions of the Emperor Diocletian is of no historical value. Fourth century (?).
September 29, iii, 680.

*GALATION AND EPISTEME, SS, MARTYRS

They are the hero and heroine of what is nothing more than a Christian continuation of the romance of Clitophon and Leucippe. Misled, possibly, by the example of some Eastern menologies, Cardinal Baronius unfortunately inserted their names in the Roman Martyrology. *November 5, iv, 268.*

*GALDINUS, ST, BISHOP

He was archdeacon of Milan, was created cardinal in 1165, then archbishop in the following year. The career of Galdinus was cast in extremely disturbed days and their hardships damaged his health, but such was his determination in discharging his office that he is reckoned one of the best Milanese archbishops. d. 1176. *April 18, ii, 122.*

GALFRIDO. *See* Walfrid.

*GALL, ST

Gall is the best known of the twelve monks who left Ireland with St Columban; he shared his master's exile from Luxeuil, but stayed on in Switzerland when Columban went into Italy. Gall was a missionary hermit in several places, especially at a place on the Steinach where the abbey and town of Saint-Gall subsequently sprang up. d. *c.* 635. His feast is observed throughout Switzerland and Ireland. *Gallus. October 16, iv, 126.*

*GALL OF CLERMONT, ST, BISHOP

He was bishop of Clermont in Auvergne, but very little is known of his life. d. 551. There was another St Gall bishop of Clermont a century later. *July 1, iii, 3.*

*GALLA, ST

She was the widow of a citizen of Rome (and sister-in-law of Boethius), whose life and death is briefly referred to by St Gregory in his *Dialogues.* d. *c.* 550. *October 5, iv, 36.*

*GALLICANUS, ST

It is not certain who this Gallicanus was, of whom it is said that he was a man of consular rank and of large charities, but probably he was the Roman consul with Symmachus in 330. He was not a martyr. *June 25, ii, 638.*

GALMIER. *See* Baldomerus.

GANDULF OF BINASCO, BD

He became a Friar Minor during the lifetime of St Francis and went to preach and pray on the island of Sicily, where he is greatly venerated. d. 1260. *Gandulphus. April 3, ii, 25.*

*GATIAN, ST, BISHOP

He is venerated as founder and first bishop of the see of Tours. Date uncertain. *Gatianus. December 18, iv, 581.*

GAUCHERIUS, ST, ABBOT

He founded the abbey of St John at Aureil for canons regular of St Augustine, and was the benefactor of St Stephen of Grandmont at Muret. d. 1140. cd 1194. *April 9, ii, 59.*

*GAUDENTIUS, ST, BISHOP

He was consecrated bishop of Brescia by St Ambrose *c.* 387, and was called by Rufinus "the glory of the teachers of the age wherein he lived". He was one of the bishops sent to the East by Pope St Innocent I to defend the cause of St John Chrysostom. d. *c.* 410. The Canons Regular of the Lateran keep the feast of another Gaudentius, bishop of Rimini, on October 14. *October 25, iv, 199.*

*GAUGERICUS, ST, BISHOP

Gaugericus (Géry) was for thirty-nine years bishop of Cambrai; the beginning of the city of Brussels is attributed to him. d. *c. August 11, iii, 305.*

*GELASIUS I, ST, POPE

During his pontificate of less than five years Gelasius, of African descent, showed himself one of the most capable and vigorous popes of the fifth century. The so-called Gelasian Sacramentary is of later date than him. He insisted on communion in both kinds, against the Manicheans. d. 496. *November 21, iv, 339.*

GEMMA, BD, VIRGIN

A recluse who lived and d. at Solmona in the Abruzzi, where she is still venerated. d. 1429. c.c. 1890. *May 12, ii, 291.*

*GEMMA GALGANI, ST, VIRGIN

This young girl was b. at Camigliano in Tuscany in 1878 and d. at Lucca in 1903. Her short life was a story of earnest religion and continuous suffering, both physical and spiritual, but spiritually her normal state was one of peace. She had some very strange experiences, and periodically recurring stigmata, and was often in a state of ecstasy. cd 1940. *April 11, ii, 75.*

*GENESIUS OF ARLES, ST MARTYR

The Genesius (Genès) is patron saint of Arles, near which city he gave his life for Christ. He was, says his legend, an official shorthand-writer, who protested against taking down a decree against Christians. Date unknown. *August 25, iii, 400.*

GENESIUS OF CLERMONT, ST, BISHOP

Bishop of Clermont in Auvergne. He was learned, benevolent and surpassingly good, beloved by old and young, rich and poor. d. *c.* 660. *June 3, ii, 465.*

*GENESIUS THE COMEDIAN, ST, MARTYR

He is said to have been converted, and subsequently martyred, while taking part in a burlesque of Christian rites in Rome in the days of Diocletian. Substantially the same story is told of others, *e.g.* Gelasius of Heliopolis, and the tale may be wholly fictitious. *August 25, iii, 398.*

*GENEVIEVE, ST, VIRGIN

Principal patroness of Paris. She was b. *c.* 422 at the village of Nanterre near Paris, and at an early age attracted the notice of St Germanus of Auxerre when he preached there. When she was fifteen she was consecrated a virgin by the bishop of Paris, after which she led a very austere life and undertook long journeys for charitable purposes. She was persecuted for a time, but vindicated by St Germanus. When Paris was captured by the Franks and threatened by the Huns, Genevieve stirred up the inhabitants to defence both by word and example, and Clovis himself is said to have consulted her. St Genevieve d. *c.* 500; her body was solemnly enshrined, and in later centuries many miracles in favour of the city of Paris were attributed to her intercession. *Genovefa. January 3, i, 28.*

GENGULF, ST

In French *Gengoul*. He was a Burgundian nobleman who is said to have been murdered by his wife's paramour in 760; the wonders credited to his relics led to a considerable *cultus*, and Hroswitha of Gandersheim wrote a verse account of his "martyrdom". *May 11, ii, 272.*

GENNADIUS, ST, BISHOP

He was abbot of San Pedro de Montes and bishop of Astorga in Spain. d. *c.* 936, *May 25, ii, 391.*

GENTIAN. *See* Fuscian.

GENTILIS, BD, MARTYR

He was an Italian Friar Minor who went as a missionary among the Mohammedans, and was eventually martyred in Persia in 1340. c.c. by Pope St Pius V. *September 5, iii, 496.*

GENULF, ST, BISHOP

In French *Genou*. He is honoured in Cahors as its first bishop, but there is no evidence for this attribution. He was probably a solitary, of unknown date. *Gengulphus. January 17, i, 110.*

*GEORGE, ST, MARTYR

There is reason to believe that St George was a martyr who suffered at Diospolis (Lydda, Ludd) in Palestine, probably before the time of Constantine; beyond this there seems nothing that can be affirmed with confidence. He is the subject of numerous legends, of which the dragon story is comparatively a late one. The East revered him in early times as a patron of soldiers and he was known in England long before he was adopted as its patron in the later Middle Ages; he was declared to be Protector of the Kingdom of England by Pope Benedict XIV. *Georgius. April 23, ii, 148.*

GEORGE BEESLEY, BD, MARTYR

A secular priest d. at Goosnargh (Goosenoor), Lancashire, who studied at the English College, Rheims. He was ordained priest in 1587 and sent on the English mission in 1588. He was arrested and tortured unavailingly under Topcliffe. He was h.d.q. in Fleet Street, London, in 1591 aged twenty-eight. bd November 22, 1987. *July 2.*

GEORGE DOUGLAS, BD, MARTYR

A secular priest, b. Edinburgh. He was ordained in Paris and was h.d.q. at York in 1587 for persuading the Queen's subjects to accept the Catholic faith. bd November 22, 1987. *September 9.*

GEORGE ERRINGTON, BD, MARTYR

A gentleman b. at Hirst (or Herst), Northumberland, who was imprisoned in York Castle for recusancy and there tricked by a Protestant minister into "persuading" him to be reconciled to Catholicism. He was executed at York in 1596 aged forty-two. bd November 22, 1987. *November 29.*

GEORGE GERVASE, BD, MARTYR

George Gervase (Jervis) was b. in 1569 at Bosham, and served with Drake's last expedition to the West Indies. He was ordained at Cambrai in 1603, and later was clothed with the Benedictine habit at Douay. In 1608 he was h.d.q. at Tyburn for his priesthood, the protomartyr of St Gregory's, Douay (now Downside). bd 1929. *April 11, ii, 74.*

GEORGE HAYDOCK, BD, MARTYR

A secular priest b. at Cottam Hall, Preston, Lancashire. He followed his father and brother to Douai and also studied at Rome and at Rheims, where he was ordained priest. He returned to England but was soon arrested in St Paul's Churchyard on February 6, 1582, and imprisoned in the Tower for over a year. He was examined in January 1584 and h.d.q. for high treason at Tyburn on February 12, 1584 aged twenty-seven. bd November 22, 1987. *February 12.*

GEORGE MATULAITIS, BD, BISHOP

Jurgis Matulaitis was b. on April 13, 1871 at Lugin on the borders of the then Russian Lithuania and Poland. He studied for the priesthood and changed his name to the Polish Matulewicz. He was ordained priest in St Petersburg in 1898 and became profes-

sor at Kielce seminary. From 1909 he restored the Marianite order. In 1918 he founded the Sisters of the Poor of the Immaculate Conception, and in 1923 the Servants of Jesus in the Eucharist. He became bishop of Vilnius on October 23, 1918 and was appointed apostolic visitor for Lithuania in 1925. He prepared the 1927 Concordat between the Holy See and his country. d. 1927. bd June 28,1987. *January 27.*

GEORGE MTASMINDELI, ST

George of the Black Mountain, a doctor of the Georgian (Iberian) church, b. 1014; he was a monk or hermit in Georgia, Syria, Mount Athos and Armenia. He revised some of the translations of St Euthymius the Enlightener and wrote original works. d. 1066. *June 27, ii, 653.*

GEORGE NAPPER, BD, MARTYR

George Napper (Napier) was a secular priest, b. at Holywell manor, Oxford, in 1550, h.d.q. for his priesthood at Oxford in 1610. bd 1929. *November 9, iv, 304.*

GEORGE NICHOLAS, BD, MARTYR

A secular priest b. at Oxford. He studied at Rheims from 1581 and was sent on the English mission in 1583. He was responsible for many conversions, including that of a celebrated highwayman, during his six years of activity. After arrest by the university officers he proved a stout controversialist. He was foully tortured in London but h.d.q. at Oxford in 1589 aged *c.* thirty-nine years. bd November 22, 1987. *July 5.*

GEORGE SWALLOWELL, BD, MARTYR

A former Protestant minister, h.d.q. at Darlington in 1594 for being reconciled with the Catholic Church. bd 1929. *July 26, iii, 181.*

GEORGE OF AMASTRIS, ST, BISHOP

He was first a hermit on Mount Sirik, then a monk of Bonyssa, and finally bishop of Amastris on the Black Sea. He was a true father of his people, and on one occasion the successful defence of the city against the Saracens was due to his influence over the inhabitants. d. *c.* 825. *February 21, i, 386.*

GEORGE THE YOUNGER, ST, BISHOP

Three eighth/ninth century bishops of Mitylene, the capital of Lesbos, were named George and were venerated as saints. The best known of them, "the Younger", was exiled for opposing Iconoclasm, his tomb becoming illustrious for miracles. d. c. 816. *April 7, ii, 46.*

GEORGE. *See also* Fronto.

GERALD OF AURILLAC, ST

Gerald, count of Aurillac, b. in 855, lived a holy life "in the world" at a time of considerable degeneracy and disorder. He was very generous to the poor, lived according to a daily rule, and founded a monastery for Benedictines on his estate. For the last seven years of his life he was blind. d. 909. *Gerardus, Giraldus. October 13, iv, 104.*

GERALD OF MAYO, ST, ABBOT

One of the Lindisfarne monks who accompanied St Colman to Ireland after the Synod of Whitby. He became abbot of the house for English monks that Colman founded, "Mayo of the Saxons". d. 732. *March 13, i, 584.*

GERALD OF SAUVE-MAJEURE, ST, ABBOT

He was appointed abbot of Saint Vincent's at Laon, but as the monks were unwilling to submit to proper discipline he resigned. With three companions he founded the abbey of Sauve-Majeure, near Bordeaux, and governed it till his death in 1095. He instituted the practice of celebrating Mass and Office for the deceased for thirty days after the death of a member of the community. cd 1197. *April 5, ii, 35.*

GERARD CAGNOLI, BD

A lay-brother of the Order of Friars Minor, to whose intercession numerous miracles were attributed; until he was forty he led a wandering life in Sicily. d. 1345. c.c. 1908. *Gerardus. December 1, iv, 460.*

*GERARD MAJELLA, ST

He was apprenticed to a tailor, entered the service of a bad-tempered bishop, followed his trade for some years and then, at the age of twenty-three, was received by the Redemptorists as a lay-brother, "a perfect model for those in that office", said Pope Pius IX. He soon attracted the notice of St Alphonsus Liguori, who deliberately shortened his novitiate. Brother Gerard was attached to various houses of the congregation in the neighbourhood of Naples, and his simple but shining goodness was recognized even to the extent of allowing him to be in effect spiritual director of several convents of nuns. There are many examples of his having brought secret sinners to repentance by reading their consciences, and numerous supernatural physical phenomena are related of him, especially "bilocation". He was also the agent of several miracles of healing, multiplying of food, etc., but like other saints, the biggest miracle of all was his own character. d. 1755. cd 1904. *October 16, iv, 131.*

*GERARD OF BROGNE, ST, ABBOT

He founded a monastery on his estate at Brogne near Namur and became its abbot. He was so successful as a superior that he was called upon to reform the life and rule of a score of monasteries, and he introduced the Rule of St Benedict into several houses. d. 959. *October 3, iv, 17.*

GERARD OF CLAIRVAUX, BD

This Gerard was the elder brother of St Bernard, whom he joined at Clairvaux, and became his right-hand man. d. 1138. One of St Bernard's sermons is in praise of his dead brother. *June 13, ii, 538.*

*GERARD OF CSANAD, ST, BISHOP AND MARTYR

He was a monk of San Giorgio Maggiore at Venice and later became apostle of a large part of Hungary, where he was made first bishop of Csanad by the prince St Stephen. During a resurgence of paganism St Gerard was killed by rebel soldiers and his body thrown into the Danube at Buda, in 1046. He is sometimes called Gerard Sagredo. *September 24, iii, 629.*

GERARD OF GALLINARO, ST

Gerard, Arduin, Bernard and Fulk are venerated in certain places in Italy as English pilgrims to the shrine of St Michael at Monte Gargano who were famed for their goodness. Nothing is known about them and their names are variously given; they came perhaps from Auvergne in the twelfth century. *August 11, iii, 306.*

*GERARD OF MONZA, BD

Gerard Tintorio was a young bourgeois of Monza in Lombardy who expended his fortune on building a hospital, to the service of which he devoted his whole life. d. 1207. c.c. 1582. *June 6, ii, 491.*

*GERARD OF TOUL, ST, BISHOP

As bishop of Toul he was famed for the charity shown during the famine of 982, and for his establishments of Greek and Irish monks who did much for religion and learning in the diocese. d. 994. *April 23, ii, 151.*

GERARD OF VILLAMAGNA, BD

A Tuscan solitary who is venerated as a tertiary of the Order of St Francis. d. 1245. c.c. 1833. *May 23, ii, 378.*

*GERASIMUS, ST, ABBOT

He was a disciple of some of the great fifth-century monks in Egypt and Palestine, and himself established a large settlement of hermits near Jericho. As a monastic leader in Palestine he was second only to St Sabas. d. 475. *March 5, i, 486.*

GEREBERNUS, ST, MARTYR

According to the legend, he was the chaplain of St Dympna, and murdered with her at Gheel, *c.* 650 (?). *May 15, ii, 320.*

*GEREMARUS, ST, ABBOT

In French *Germer*. He was the husband of the Lady Domana, also venerated as a saint, and after the death of their two children they both went "into religion". Geremarus became abbot of Pentale on the Seine. d. *c.* 658. *September 24, iii, 628.*

*GEREON, ST, MARTYR

Gereon and his companions probably represent a band of martyrs of unknown date venerated at Cologne, where their tomb was known in the fifth century; but their association with the Theban Legion is fictitious. *October 10, iv, 78.*

GERIUS, BD

In Italian *Girio*. Nothing can be asserted positively about Bd Gerius, except that he is the age-long patron of Monte Santo, near Loreto. d. 1298 (?). c.c. 1742. *May 24.*

GERLAC, ST

A Dutch soldier of disorderly life who was recalled to decent behaviour by the sudden death of his wife. He did seven years' penance in Rome and then returned to his native place, Valkenburg, where he lived for seven more years in a hollow tree. Neighbouring monks were so scandalized by this way of life that they are said to have refused him the sacraments when he was dying, *c.* 1170. *Gerlacus. January 5, i, 38.*

GERLAND OF CALTAGIRONE, BD

A member during the thirteenth century of one of the military orders, probably the Templars; he is venerated at Caltagirone in Sicily. *June 18.*

GERLAND OF GIRGENTI, ST, BISHOP

Nothing definite can be stated about this saint, except that he was a Norman who became bishop of Girgenti in Sicily. d. 1100. *February 25, i, 418.*

GERMAIN. *See* Germanus *and* Jermyn.

*GERMAINE OF PIBRAC, ST, VIRGIN

Germaine Counsin was b. *c.* 1579 at Pibrac, near Toulouse, daughter of a farm-labourer. She had ill health and a paralysed hand; she was ignored by her father and badly treated by her stepmother. As soon as she was old enough she was set to mind sheep and was thus employed for the rest of her short life. She was known throughout the neighbourhood for her efficiency in her work, her religious devotion, her patience under unkindness, her care for young children and for those even poorer than herself, and several miraculous happenings were associated with her name. Germaine was found dead on her pallet beneath the stairs on June 15, 1601. cd. 1867. *Germana. June 15, ii, 550.*

*GERMANICUS, ST, MARTYR

A young martyr at Smyrna who when thrown to the beasts encouraged them to attack him.

This was in the persecution during which St Polycarp suffered. *January 19, i, 118.*

*GERMANUS OF AUXERRE, ST,
BISHOP

By his mission against the Pelagian heresy St Germanus strengthened and consolidated the Church in Britain after the withdrawal of the Roman army. He became bishop of Auxerre after a secular career in Gaul, and was sent into Britain in 429 and again *c.* 445; thereafter the Church in Britain remained practically free from heresy for a space of eleven hundred years. It is recorded that by a ruse of St Germanus the Britons gained a great victory over marauding Picts and Saxons—the "Alleluia Victory". d. 448. His feast is kept on various dates in several English dioceses and in Wales.
August 3, iii, 251.

*GERMANUS OF CAPUA, ST, BISHOP

This Germanus was bishop of Capua and a friend of St Benedict. He was probably the legate sent by Pope St Hormisdas to heal the Acacian schism at Constantinople. d. *c.* 540.
October 30, iv, 222.

*GERMANUS OF CONSTANTINOPLE, ST, BISHOP

He became patriarch of Constantinople in 715 and as an energetic defender of the veneration of images came into collision with the emperor, Leo III the Isaurian; he was compelled to resign in 730, and d. in 732. *May 12, ii, 288.*

GERMANUS OF GRANFEL, ST,
MARTYR

With his young brother Numerian he entered the abbey of Romberg (later Remiremont) in the Vosges, and later went on to Luxeuil, whence he was made abbot of the new foundation at Granfel in the Val Moutier. Among his works here was to remake the road through the valley. He with, his prior St Randoald, was murdered by the followers of a local magnate whose oppression of the people Germanus had rebuked, *c.* 677.
February 21, i, 385.

*GERMANUS OF PARIS, ST, BISHOP

Born 496 near Autun. As bishop of Paris he was one of the most venerated churchmen of his age and the church afterwards known as Saint-Germain-des-Prés was named in his honour. He worked hard to check the licentiousness of the nobles and is said miraculously to have healed King Childebert I. d. 576. *May 28, ii, 410.*

GERMANUS OF VALAAM, ST, ABBOT

This Germanus (Herman) is venerated with St Sergius as the founder of the monastery on the Finnish island of Valaam (Valamo) in Lake Ladoga. It is not even certain when he lived: possibly *c.* 990. but more likely *c.* 1330. *June 28, ii, 662.*

GERMERIUS, ST, BISHOP

Germerius (Germier) was bishop of Toulouse in the sixth century according to his legend, which is untrustworthy.
May 16, ii, 327.

GEROLDUS, ST

The tomb of St Geroldus and his two sons is still a place of pilgrimage near Mitternach. In middle age he became a hermit there, and after his death in 978 his hermitage was occupied by his two sons Cuno and Ulric, monks from Einsiedeln. *April 19, ii, 129.*

*GERONTIUS, ST,
BISHOP AND MARTYR

A bishop of Cervia in the province of Ravenna, murdered on the highway by "ungodly men" in 501 (?). *May 9, ii, 262.*

GERTRUDE COMENSOLI, BD,
VIRGIN

Mother Gertrude Caterina Comensoli, b. 1857, founded the Sacramentine Sisters of Bergamo, Italy, and had a special devotion to the example of the poverty and humility of Christ and to the spirituality of the eucharist. d. 1903. bd October 1, 1989. *February 18.*

GERTRUDE OF ALTENBERG, BD,
VIRGIN

She was the third daughter of St Elizabeth of Hungary and became abbess of Altenberg, where she was one of the first in Germany to get permission for the feast of Corpus Christi. d. 1297. *Gertrudis. August 13, iii, 323.*

GERTRUDE OF DELFT, BD, VIRGIN

A *béguine* at Delft in Holland who, in 1340,

received the stigmata of our Lord's passion. She led a life of suffering for eighteen years, was much sought after, and had a strange knowledge of people's thoughts and distant events. Her name, "van Oosten", is said to be a nickname from her frequent repetition of the hymn "Het dag het in den Oosten", "The day breaks in the East". d. 1358. *January 6, i, 43.*

*GERTRUDE OF HELFTA, ST, VIRGIN

From her childhood Gertrude lived at the nunnery of Helfta in Saxony, and her life was without exterior incident. It was her supernatural revelations that made her name famous; these began at the age of twenty-six. Gertrude (who is called "the Great") was of considerable intellectual ability, as her writings show, but only the second book of the work commonly called the *Revelations of St Gertrude* is hers. She was the pupil of St Mechtildis, and with both the love of the heart of Jesus was a recurring theme. For the last ten years of her life Gertrude suffered greatly from physical ill health. d. 1302. The monastery of Helfta has been claimed for both the Benedictines and the Cistercians. *November 16, iv, 351.*

*GERTRUDE OF NIVELLES, ST,
VIRGIN

Younger daughter of Bd Pepin of Landen and Bd Itta, b. at Landen in 626. She was made abbess of her mother's foundation at Nivelles, and both abbey and abbess became famous; the Irish saints Foillan and Ultan settled nearby on land given by St Gertrude. d. 659. A good deal of folklore grew up around this Gertrude, who is honoured as a patroness of travellers and gardeners and invoked against the ravages of rats and mice. *March 17, i, 620.*

*GERVASE AND PROTASE, SS,
MARTYRS

The alleged relics of these martyrs were discovered by St Ambrose at Milan in 386, but even then nothing was remembered of them except their names and a vague tradition of their martyrdom. Their *acta* are fictitious, but it is believed that they were genuine martyrs who suffered during the second century. *Gervasius, Protasius. June 19, ii, 583.*

GERVINUS, ST, ABBOT

Canon of Rheims, monk of Verdun, and abbot of Saint-Riquier; he visited England several times, where he enjoyed the confidence of St Edward the Confessor. d. 1075. *March 3, i, 472.*

GÉRY. *See* Gaugericus.

*GETULIUS, ST, MARTYR

Getulius is said to have been the husband of St Symphorosa and to have been martyred at Tivoli with his brother and an official whom he had converted. *June 10, ii, 517.*

GHISLAIN. *See* Gislenus.

GIBRIAN, ST

He was the eldest of an Irish family alleged to have migrated from Ireland to Brittany and then to have settled as solitaries in the forest around the Marne. d. *c.* 515(?). *Gibrianus. May 8, ii, 251.*

GILBERT OF CAITHNESS, ST,
BISHOP

He was formerly honoured in Scotland as a zealous upholder of Scottish ecclesiastical independence of the archbishop of York. He was bishop of Caithness and d. 1245. *Gilbertus. April 1, ii, 5.*

*GILBERT OF SEMPRINGHAM, ST,
ABBOT

Founder of the only medieval religious order of English origin. He was b. at Sempringham in Lincolnshire, where he became a parson in 1123. He drew up a rule for seven women who wanted to live in community, and this developed into the Gilbertine Order of both canons and nuns. The order was governed by a master or prior general, an office which St Gilbert himself held till he lost his sight. He d. in 1189, at the age of 106. cd 1202. No attempt has ever been made to re-establish the order since its dissolution. St Gilbert's feast is observed in the dioceses of Nottingham and Northampton, and by the Canons Regular of the Lateran. *February 16, i, 351.*

GILDAS, ST

Called "the Wise". This sixth-century saint is chiefly known as the author of an "epistle" in which he violently attacks his contemporaries in the Isle of Britain, clerical and lay. He was a pupil of St Illtud, and he may have written his *De excidio Britanniae* while living solitary on Flatholm in the Bristol Channel. It is said that the last years of his life were spent at the monastery of Rhuys in Brittany, where he d. *c.* 570, but the Breton saint is more probably another man. The influence of Gildas extended also to Ireland. *January 29, i, 201.*

*GILES, ST, ABBOT

The legend of St Giles, with the incident of the wounded hind, was one of the most popular of the Middle Ages, but it derives chiefly from a tenth-century biography that is utterly untrustworthy. Giles was perhaps a Provençal hermit or monk in the sixth or eighth century. Over 160 churches were dedicated to his honour in England alone before the Reformation, and he was involved as the patron of cripples, beggars and blacksmiths. *Aegidius. September 1, iii, 457.*

GILES MARY, BD

Giles was a rope-maker who joined the Alcantarine Friars Minor at Naples when he was twenty-five, and spent the rest of his life as porter of the friary. d. 1812. bd 1888. *February 7, i, 275.*

GILES OF ASSISI, BD

One of the two most famous of the early followers of St Francis of Assisi. At first he accompanied Francis on his preaching journeys, but afterwards made several long pilgrimages and went to preach (unsuccessfully) to the Muslims in Tunis; the latter part of his life was spent in Italy again. Giles was exceedingly simple and single-minded, but endowed with a supernatural wisdom that caused him to be consulted by people of all kinds. d. 1262. c.c. by Pope Pius VI. *April 23, ii, 154.*

GILES OF LORENZANA, BD

Born *c.* 1443 in the kingdom of Naples, where he was a farmhand. He became a Franciscan lay-brother, and d. 1518. c.c. 1880. *January 14, i, 89.*

GILES OF PORTUGAL, BD

According to tradition this Giles was a medi-

cal student who became enmeshed in the practice of black magic. In consequence of a dream he gave this up, and became an exemplary Dominican friar at Valencia. d. 1265. c.c. 1748. *May 14, ii, 308.*

GIOVANNA BONOMO, BD, VIRGIN

A Benedictine nun, b. near Vicenza in 1606; she was a mystic and stigmatic whose writings had considerable influence. d. at Bassano, 1670. bd 1783. *March 1, iv, 672.*

GISLENUS, ST, ABBOT

In French *Ghislain*. He was abbot of a monastery near Mons, but there is no satisfactory account of his life. He is said to have had great influence on the family of St Vincent Madelgarius. d. *c.* 680. *October 9, iv, 71.*

GLADYS. *See under* Gundleus.

*GLYCERIA, ST, VIRGIN AND MARTYR

A Christian maiden who suffered martyrdom at Heraclea in the Propontis, *c.* 177. *May 13, ii, 296.*

*GOAR, ST

He was said to be a priest of Aquitaine who took to the solitary life near Oberwesel on the Rhine, but the extant particulars of his life are unhistorical. d. *c.* 575 (?). *July 6, iii, 24.*

GOBAN, ST, MARTYR

He was an Irish disciple of St Fursey in East Anglia and followed him to France; he was murdered by barbarians at the place now called Saint-Gobain, *c.* 670. *June 20, ii, 589.*

GODEBERTA, ST, VIRGIN

She was abbess of a convent at Noyon, which was directed by St Eligius. d. *c.* 700. *April 11, ii, 71.*

GODELEVA, ST

Godeleva was married at the age of eighteen to Bertulf of Ghistelles, and throughout the two years of her wedded life was treated by her husband with great neglect and cruelty, for which the reasons are unexplained. In 1070 (?) he had her strangled and drowned; fourteen years later the bishop of Tournai enshrined Godeleva's body in the church of

Ghistelles, and she has been venerated as a "martyr" in the neighbourhood ever since. *July 6, iii, 26.*

GODREY JONES. *See* John Jones.

*GODREY OF AMIENS, ST, BISHOP
From the abbacy of Nogent he was raised to the see of Amiens in 1104. He was noted for the severity of his discipline, which indeed seems to have been excessive, but he was as inflexible with himself as he was with others. d. 1115. *Godefridus.*
November 8, iv, 298.

GODFREY OF KAPPENBERG, BD
He was count of Kappenberg and a big landowner in Westphalia. Coming under the influence of St Norbert he, in the face of violent opposition from his relatives, turned his castle into a Premonstratensian monastery, built a convent for his wife and his two sisters, and himself became a Premonstratensian canon. He d. 1127, at the age of thirty and while still in minor orders. *January 13, i, 75.*

GODRIC, ST
He was first a trader and seafarer and then house-steward to a landowner in his native Norfolk. After several pilgrimages he became a hermit at Finchale in County Durham, where he lived for sixty years and d. in 1170. St Godric was endowed with extraordinary powers, especially of pre-vision and over animals. *Godericus. May 21, ii, 361.*

GOERICUS, ST, BISHOP
Also called *Abbo.* In thanksgiving for the restoration of his sight he became a priest, and succeeded St Arnulf as bishop of Metz. d. 647. *September 19, iii, 597.*

GOHARD, ST, BISHOP AND MARTYR
A bishop of Nantes who, in 843, was slain by raiding Northmen while celebrating Mass; many monks and priests were killed with him. *June 25, ii, 643.*

GOMIDAS, BD, MARTYR
Gomidas Keumurgian was b. in Constantinople *c.* 1656, married at the age of twenty, and was ordained priest in the dissident

Armenian Church. With his family he came into Catholic communion *c.* 1696, at a time when the number of Armenian reconciliations was causing alarm among the dissidents. In 1707 Gomidas was denounced to the Turkish authorities as a European agent, and the judge, somewhat unwillingly, condemned him to death. He was beheaded at Parmak-Kapu on the outskirts of Constantinople. bd 1929. A son of Bd Gomidas took the surname of "Carbognano", by which his father is sometimes called. *Cosmas.*
November 5, iv, 270.

GOMMAIRE. *See* Gummarus.

*GONSALO GARCIA, ST, MARTYR
A martyr of Japan, a Friar Minor, who was b. near Bombay, perhaps of Indian parents, in which case he would be the only Indian yet formally canonized. He was crucified at Nagasaki in 1597. cd 1862. *Gundisalvus.*
February 5, i, 259.

GONSALO OF AMARANTE, BD
A Portuguese priest who became a Dominican, but was allowed to live as a hermit. Some rather fanciful stories are told about this holy man. d. 1259 (?). c.c. 1560.
January 16, i, 103.

GONTRAN. *See* Guntramnus.

*GOOD THIEF, THE
A number of legends have grown up around the repentant thief who died beside our Lord on the cross, to whom the name of Dismas has been given. Nothing is known about him. *March 25, i, 676.*

*GORDIAN AND **EPIMACHUS, SS,**
MARTYRS
Epimachus is said to have been martyred at Alexandria in 250 and his body taken to Rome, while Gordian was later beheaded at Rome and buried in the same tomb at Epimachus. These martyrs certainly existed, but their extant *acta* are spurious. *Gordianus. May 10, ii, 265.*

*GORGONIA, ST
She was the eldest child of St Gregory Nazianzen senior and St Nonna and was married to one Vitalian, by whom she had

three children. She was noted for her love for the Church's public worship and for her generosity to the needy. d. *c.* 373.
December 9, iv, 524:

GORGONIUS, DOROTHEUS AND PETER, SS, MARTYRS
Roman martyrs buried on the Via Lavicana, of whom nothing is known except their fairly early *cultus.* Said to have been tortured and martyred during the Diocletian persecution. *September 9, iii, 512.*

*GORKUM, THE MARTYRS OF
Nineteen priests and religious who were captured by Calvinist forces at Gorkum in the Netherlands, and hanged on account of their religion, 1572. They were the Franciscan Nicholas Pieck (*q.v.*), with ten of his community, four secular clergy, one Augustinian canon and two Norbertine, and a Dominican. One Franciscan, Antony van Willehad, was ninety years old. cd 1867. *July 9, iii, 56.*

*GOTHARD, ST, BISHOP
Gothard (Godehard) while abbot of Niederaltaich in Bavaria was commissioned by the emperor St Henry to reform the monasteries in several German dioceses. He became bishop of Hildesheim in 1022 and was one of the outstanding prelates of that see. d. 1038. cd 1131. The Pass of St Gothard takes its name from a chapel built thereon and dedicated in honour of this saint. *May 4, ii, 231.*

GOTTSCHALK, ST
He was a Wendish prince who was slain at Lenzen in 1066 during a rising fomented by his heathen brother-in-law. There seems to be no solid reason for regarding him as either a saint or martyr. *June 7, ii, 496.*

GRATIA OF CATTARO, BD
For thirty years he was a fisherman in the Adriatic and then joined the Augustinian friars as a lay-brother, in which capacity miracles were recorded of him. d. 1508. c.c. 1889. *November 16, iv, 360.*

GREGORY THE GREAT, ST,
POPE AND DOCTOR
Gregory, the first monk to become pope, was

b. in Rome in the middle of the sixth century, son of a patrician and of a saint, Sylvia. After being papal legate at Constantinople he was elected to the supreme pontificate in 590 and proved to be the outstanding pope of the first thousand years of Christianity: some of his activities have their effect in the Church and the world today. Gregory sent St Augustine with other monks to convert the English, he encouraged monasticism, maintained the primacy of the Roman see in East and West, enforced the discipline of the clergy, left his mark on the Roman liturgy, defended central Italy against the Lombards, was a fine administrator—and with it all was a student and writer. Six of his written works, including the famous *Dialogues* and a book of homilies on the Gospels much used in the Divine Office, have come down to us; he was the fourth of the Doctors of the Western Church. "It is impossible to conceive what would have been the confusion, the lawlessness, the chaotic state of the Middle Ages without the medieval papacy: and of the medieval papacy the real father is Gregory the Great" (Milman). d. 604. *Gregorius. September 3, i, 566.*

*GREGORY II, ST, POPE
He became pope in 715. He encouraged the monks of St Benedict and re-established their abbey of Monte Cassino, and consecrated St Corbinian and St Boniface for Germany. Gregory had dealings with England over the East dispute, firmly opposed the Iconoclasm of the emperor Leo III, and checked the Lombard advance in Italy. d. 731. *February 11, i, 308.*

*GREGORY III, ST, POPE
The pontificate of Gregory III, a Syrian, was troubled at the beginning by the Iconoclasm of Leo the Isauran and at its end by incursions of the Lombards. He sent St Willibald to help St Boniface in Germany. d. 741. *December 10, iv, 531.*

*GREGORY VII, ST, POPE
He was b. in Tuscany *c.* 1020 and was baptized Hildebrand. His story belongs to the general history of the Church. After discharging various responsible offices at Rome he was elected pope by acclamation in

1073. Few men have been so admired by their friends and so bitterly attacked by their foes, both during life and after death. But his was an ungrateful and huge task, to reform the Church, enforce celibacy among the Western clergy, resist the encroachments of the temporal power, eliminate simony and abolish lay investiture. All admit that Gregory proved himself a stern Christian and a very great man. He d. in exile at Salerno in 1085. cd 1728. *May 25, ii, 386.*

*GREGORY X, BD, POPE

While archdeacon of Liège, Theobald Visconti preached the crusade and himself visited the Holy Land, where he was when elected Pope in 1271 (he was not even a priest at the time). He at once summoned the fourteenth ecumenical council, which met at Lyons in 1274, and brought about reunion, though this proved shortlived, of the Eastern Orthodox with the Catholic Church. d. 1276. His name was added to the Roman Martyrology by Pope Benedict XIV. *January 10, i, 66.*

GREGORY BARBARIGO, ST, BISHOP

Born at Venice in 1625. He was bishop first of Bergamo and then of Padua and was created cardinal in 1660, being looked on as another St Charles Borromeo. His charities were enormous; he founded a college and a seminary, which he equipped with a printing-press and a fine library, and was an earnest worker for the reconciliation of the Byzantines. d. 1697. bd 1761. cd 1960. *June 18, ii, 580.*

GREGORY GRASSI, BD,
BISHOP AND MARTYR

The leader of the first group of martyrs under the Chinese Boxers to be beatified. He was a Friar Minor from Piedmont, and vicar apostolic of Northern Shansi. He was sixty-seven years old when he was killed at Taiyuanfu on July 9, 1900, together with his coadjutor bishop, Francis Fogolla, and three other Franciscans, Bd Hermina Grivot (*q.v.*) and six other Franciscan Missionaries of Mary, and fourteen Chinese students and laymen. They were all beatified in 1946, with another bishop, Antony Fantosati, and

two priests, Franciscans, martyred at Hunan. *July 9, iii, 59.*

GREGORY LOPEZ, BD

He left his native Spain *c.* 1563 and became a hermit among the Indians of Mexico, where the Spanish colonists were very censorious of his way of life. He was vindicated by the archbishop of Mexico City, and at his death in 1596 he was widely respected and loved. His *cultus* spread all over Mexico, but it has never been officially confirmed. *July 20, iii, 155.*

GREGORY MAKAR, ST, BISHOP

He is said to have been an Armenian monk and bishop of Nicopolis, who fled from his see and wandered across Europe into France. At Pithiviers in the diocese of Orleans he settled down as a hermit, and received great respect for his austerities and miracles. d. *c.* 1010. *March 16, i, 608.*

*GREGORY NAZIANZEN, ST,
BISHOP AND DOCTOR

He was b. at Arianzus in Cappadocia *c.* 329, son of St Gregory the Elder and St Nonna, and read law for ten years at Athens. Instead of taking up his profession he joined St Basil in his retreat in Pontus, and later was ordained by his father, who was bishop of Nazianzus. He was consecrated bishop, but refused a diocese until in 380 he reluctantly accepted the see of Constantinople, which was then greatly troubled by the Arian heresy. A few months later Gregory resigned and retired to Nazianzus. He d. at his birthplace in 390. Gregory was gentle, retiring and peace-loving, and was most effective when writing. His works were particularly directed against Arianism; he also wrote homilies, poems and letters in large numbers. He was one of the greatest of theologians, called, in fact, "the Divine" (*Theologos*), one of the four great Greek Doctors of the Universal Church, and the third of the Three Holy Hierarchs of the Byzantines. *January 2, ii, 255.*

GREGORY OF EINSIEDELN, BD,
ABBOT

An Englishman who received the monastic habit at the monastery on the Caelian Hill in

Rome, and became abbot of Einsiedeln, *c.* 947. He brought this Swiss house to a high pitch of observance and influence. d. 996. *November 8.*

*GREGORY OF GIRGENTI, ST, BISHOP

He was Byzantine bishop of Girgenti in Sicily, now best remembered for his commentary on the book of *Ecclesiastes.* d. *c.* 603. *November 23, iv, 409.*

*GREGORY OF LANGRES, ST, BISHOP

Great-grandfather of St Gregory of Tours. He was *comes* of the district round Autun, and after the death of his wife was, late in life, made bishop of Langres. As a civil governor he was known for his severity, as a bishop for his mildness and charity. d. 539. *January 4, i, 30.*

*GREGORY OF NYSSA, ST, BISHOP

One of the great Christian family at Caesarea in Cappadocia of which his brother St Basil the great is the most famous. Gregory was at first a professor of rhetoric and married a lady named Theosebia; then he was ordained priest, and in 372 was appointed bishop of Hyssa on the edge of Lower Armenia. The diocese was a hot-bed of Arianism, but Gregory was wanting in tact and inexperienced in handling affairs, and for some time was (unjustly) excluded from his see. After Basil's death he came to the fore as a mainstay of orthodoxy and exerted great influence at the second ecumenical council (Constantinople I). Of Gregory's voluminous writings the chief is an instruction on the Christian faith called his *Catechetical Discourse.* d. *c.* 395. *March 9, i, 533.*

*GREGORY OF SPOLETO, ST, MARTYR

A priest at Spoleto said to have been beheaded in 304 for refusing to sacrifice to Jove, Minerva and Aesculapius. A fanciful passage in his *acta* states that he was saved from being roasted alive by an earthquake. His existence is more than doubtful. *December 24, iv, 604.*

*GREGORY OF TOURS, ST, BISHOP

Gerogius Florentius took the name of Gregory when he became bishop of Tours in 573. He was one of the most effective bishops of his day, but he is now best remembered as an historian and hagiographer. St Odo of Cluny spoke highly of his personal virtues. d. 594. *November 17, iv, 367.*

*GREGORY OF UTRECHT, ST, ABBOT

He was a monk under St Boniface, who made him abbot of St Martin's at Utrecht. After the death of Boniface in 754, Gregory administered the diocese as well for twenty-two years, but was apparently never consecrated bishop. Under his rule St Martin's abbey became a great missionary centre and a nursery of saints. d. *c.* 775 (?). *August 25, iii, 402.*

GREGORY OF VERUCCHIO, BD

He was dismissed for some improper reason from the Augustinian friary which his mother had founded at Verucchio, and was given shelter by the Franciscans at Monte Carnerio, near Reati. Here he d. at a great age in 1343. c.c. 1769. *May 4, ii, 232.*

*GREGORY THE ENLIGHTENER, ST, BISHOP

He is venerated as the apostle of the Armenians, but the particulars of his life are somewhat uncertain. He seems to have converted King Tiridates, to have been consecrated bishop by the archbishop of Caesarea, and to have set up his see at Ashtishat, where, with the aid of Greek and Syrian missionaries, he set himself to organize his church, strengthen the converts, and win over waverers. He consecrated his son Aristakes to succeed him, and d. *c.* 330. Armenian legends about St Gregory are full of very astonishing incidents, patently fictitious. *September 30, iii, 693.*

*GREGORY THE WONDERWORKER, ST, BISHOP

He was b. in Pontus and studied under Origen. At the age of forty he became bishop of his native Neocaesarea; it is said that when he was elected his diocese contained seventeen

Christians, and when he died there were seventeen pagans: his missionary methods included the association of games and merry-making with great feast days—a proceeding not so common then as later. Gregory's name, "the Wonderworker", explains itself, though but few reliable particulars of his miracles have survived. d. *c.* 268. *November 17, iv, 362.*

GREGORY. *See also under* Dominic.

GRIMBALD, ST, ABBOT
Grimbald was a monk of Saint-Bertin, from where he was invited to England by Alfred the Great. He was made abbot of the secular canons at Newminster in Winchester, and d. 903. *July 8, iii, 42.*

GRIMONIA, ST, VIRGIN AND MARTYR
She is venerated in Picardy, but the facts about her are hard to come by: she is said to have been a solitary from Ireland who at some unknown date was killed by her father for refusing marriage. *September 7, iii, 501.*

GUALA OF BRESCIA, BD, BISHOP
Guala Romanoni was an early disciple of St Dominic in Italy and first prior of the Preaching Friars at Brescia, a charge he afterwards resigned on account of civil strife. He saw the death of St Dominic in a dream. d. 1244. c.c. 1868. *September 3, iii, 482.*

GUARLFARDUS. *See* Wolfhard.

GUARDIAN ANGELS, THE
The oldest known Roman Sacramentary (the Leonine) refers to individual guardian angels. A votive Mass has been in use from the ninth century. Devotion to the Guardian Angels was particularly strong in England. Pope Paul V authorized a special Mass and office for them. In 1670 Clement X made it obligatory and determined the present date of commemoration. *October 2.*

*GUARINUS OF PALESTRINA, ST,
BISHOP
An Augustinian canon of Bologna who for his ability and virtue was appointed cardinal bishop of Palestrina. d. 1159. *February 6, i, 264.*

GUARINUS OF SION, ST, BISHOP
In French *Guérin*. Abbot of Aulps, near Geneva, who affiliated his monastery to Clairvaux but was taken away from it to be bishop of Sion in the Valais. St Bernard had a great esteem for St Guarinus. d. 1150. *January 6, i, 42.*

GUDULA, ST, VIRGIN
Daughter of St Amelberga and brought up at Nivelles under the care of her cousin St Gertrude. She led an austere life of prayer and good works in the house of her father, Count Witger. Seventh century. The relics of St Gudula were eventually translated in 1047 to the collegiate church in Brussels which now bears her name. *January 8, i, 54.*

GUDWAL, ST, ABBOT
Otherwise *Gurval*. He seems to have been an early missionary in Brittany; he founded the monasery of Plecit, near the island called after him, Locoal, and several other churches, but there is no trustworthy account of his life. Sixth century (?). *June 6, ii, 489.*

GUIBERT, ST, ABBOT
Guibert gave his estates to found a monastery at what is now Gembloux, himself becoming a monk at Gorze. He had to defend his establishment against his brother-in-law and also against the emperor Otto I, and he was a missionary among the local pagan settlers. d. 962. *Guibertus. May 23, ii, 375.*

GUIDO. *See* Guy.

*GUMMARUS, ST
In French *Gommaire*. He served in the court of Pepin, where he married the lady Guinimaria. She was of an extravagant and perverse disposition and Gummarus was an example of heroic virtue particularly in respect of his troublesome wife; but at length she became too much for him, a separation was arranged, and he d. as a solitary, *c.* 774. *October 11, iv, 88.*

GUNDLEUS, ST
Gwynllyw, anglicized as Woollo and latinized as Gundleus, is said to have been the husband of St Gwladys and father of St Cadoc. The couple ended their days as her-

mits at the places now called Newport and Bassaleg. Sixth century. Gladys or Gwladys is conventionally latinized as *Claudia*. *March 29, i, 699.*

GUNTHER, BD

Until he was fifty this Gunther, who was a cousin of St Stephen of Hungary, led the life of a worldly and ambitious nobleman. He then became a monk at Niederaltaich, but his conversion was incomplete and he continued to give free play to his ambitions. In 1009 he entered on an eremitical life, and from thenceforward made amends for his former excesses. d. 1045. *October 9, iv, 71.*

*GUNTRAMNUS, ST

Guntramnus, or Gontran, king of Burgundy, was honoured as a saint by his subjects after his death and his name found its way into the Roman Martyrology; but it is more than doubtful if his claims to holiness would obtain formal canonization for him today. d. 592. *March 28, i, 695.*

*GURIAS AND SAMONAS, SS, MARTYRS

Gurias and Samonas were martyrs at Edessa in Syria in the fourth century. The deacon Abibus (Habib) is venerated with them. *November 15, iv, 348.*

GUTHLAC, ST

Guthlac left the abbey of Repton to become a hermit in the middle of the Lincolnshire fens; he lived thus for over fifteen years, following as far as possible the examples of the Fathers of the eastern deserts. He had remarkable influence over wild nature. Guthlac was honoured in his life and still more after his death in 714; a monastery grew up around his tomb and dwelling-place which became the abbey of Croyland. *Guthlacus. April 11, ii, 72.*

GUY MARAMALDI, BD

A confessor of the Order of Preachers, well known as a theologian and preacher around Naples and Ragusa. d. 1391. c.c. 1612. *Guido. June 25, ii, 645.*

*GUY OF ANDERLECHT, ST

Guy, commonly called the Poor Man of Anderlecht, was lay sacristan of a church at Laeken, in Belgium, lost all his money in an investment, became a pilgrim, and ended his days *c.* 1012 in the public hospital at Anderlecht, near Brussels. He led a hidden life of much simplicity and mortification, and was credited with many miracles. *September 12, iii, 546.*

GUY OF CORTONA, BD

Guido Vignotelli sold all that he had and gave the proceeds in alms at the word of St Francis of Assisi; he became a hermit near his native town. d. *c.* 1245. *June 17, ii, 556.*

GUY OF POMPOSA, ST, ABBOT

Guy was abbot of Pomposa, near Ferrara. For some reason he was persecuted by Archbishop Heribert of Ravenna, but both St Peter Damian and the emperor Henry III had a more just opinion of St Guy. d. 1046. *March 31, i, 709.*

GWENFREWI. *See* Winifred.

H

HADRIAN. *See* Adrian.

HALLVARD, ST, MARTYR
The true history of St Hallvard, patron of Oslo in Norway, is obscure. According to tradition, he was murdered early in the eleventh century for refusing to give up to her pursuers a woman who asked his protection. *May 15, ii, 322.*

HARTMAN, BD, BISHOP
While canon of Salzburg cathedral he introduced life under a rule among the chapter, and later was called to be provost of the canons regular at Klosterneuburg: in 1140 he was elected bishop of Brixen and continued to do much for the canonical life in Germany. d. 1164. c.c. 1784. *Hartmannus. December 23, iv, 601.*

HARVEY, ST, ABBOT
Hervé is the most popular saint's name in Brittany after that of St Ives (Ivo). According to the late medieval biography, St Harvey was b. blind, but became abbot of Plouvien; later he transferred his community to Lanhourneau, where he spent the rest of his days and was famous for miracles. Sixth century. *Hervaeus. June 17, ii, 566.*

HAYMO OF SAVIGLIANO, BD
Haymo Taparelli, a Dominican, was appointed inquisitor general for Lombardy at the age of seventy. It was said that his whole life was a commentary on the text "To serve God is to rule". d. 1495. c.c. 1856. *Aimo. August 18, iii, 351.*

*HEDDA, ST, BISHOP
He was a monk who was made bishop of the divided diocese of Wessex in 676 and removed its see from Dorchester to Winchester. He was one of the first benefactors of the abbey of Malmesbury, and assisted King Ine in the drawing-up of his laws. d. 705. The feast of St Hedda is kept by the archdiocese of Birmingham. *July 7, iii, 34.*

*HEDWIG, ST
Hedwig (*Jadwiga*), of Moravian descent and aunt of St Elizabeth of Hungary, was b. in Bavaria c. 1174. She married Henry, duke of Silesia, by whom she had seven children, who were from time to time the occasions of a good deal of trouble for their parents. Hedwig was the devoted assistant of her husband, and together they founded several religious houses. After Henry's death in 1238 she passed most of her time with the Cistercian nuns at Trebnitz, near Breslau, following their exercises and caring for the sick and needy. d. 1243. cd 1267. *Hedwigis. October 16, iv, 124.*

HEDWIG OF POLAND, BD
Born in 1371, and was accepted as queen of Poland at the age of thirteen. For political reasons she married Jagiello, duke of Lithuania. She seems to have been a very saintly woman, and she is commonly called Blessed in Poland. d. 1399. *February 28, i, 445.*

*HEGESIPPUS, ST
He is chiefly remembered as the father of ecclesiastical history, on the strength of a work of which only a few chapters survive.

St Jerome testifies to his humble and apostolic spirit, "which he expressed by the simplicity of his writing". Hegesippus was a Jew of Jerusalem, but spent twenty years of his life in Rome. d. *c.* 180. *April 7, ii, 45.*

HEIMRAD, ST

Heimrad was a Swabian priest who wandered about Europe, mostly in Germany; his strange behaviour caused him to be regarded by some as a saint and by others as a lunatic. d. 1019. Many miracles were reported at his tomb at Wolfhagen in Hesse-Nassau. His *cultus* is purely a popular one. *June 28, ii, 660.*

HELDRAD, ST, ABBOT

A Provençal nobleman who provided a church, hospice and smallholdings for the people of Lambesc, near Aix. He afterwards was a monk and then abbot of Novalese at the foot of the Alps, where he seems to have anticipated the work of the canons of the Great St Bernard on the Mount Cenis pass. d. *c.* 842. *March 13, i, 587.*

*HELEN, ST

She was b. probably in Bithynia (certainly not in Britain). She married Constantius Chlorus, by whom she was the mother of the emperor Constantine the Great, and became a Christian in 313. St Helen was most liberal in alms and was responsible for the building of many churches, especially in Palestine, and her name is traditionally associated with the finding of the True Cross in a rock-cistern near Mount Calvary. d. *c.* 330. Her feast has been kept in the dioceses of Liverpool, Brentwood and Salford. *Helena. August 18, iii, 346.*

HELEN GUERRA, BD, VIRGIN

Hélène Guerra was the founder of the Congregation of Sisters of Saint Rita which now has houses in Italy, Brazil, Canada, the Philippines, Lebanon, and Iran. bd by Pope John XXIII on April 26, 1959 in the presence of some 5,000 sisters from these establishments. *April 26.*

HELEN OF ARCELLA, BD, VIRGIN

Helen Enselmini received the Poor Clare habit from St Francis himself at Arcella, near Padua; she was bedridden, blind and dumb before her death at the age of thirty-four in 1242. c.c. 1695. *November 7, iv, 290.*

HELEN OF BOLOGNA, BD

The devotion to Helen Duglioli at Bologna is a typical example of spontaneous popular *cultus*. She lived an uneventful life, married happily for thirty years to a citizen of that place, and d. in 1520. c.c. 1828. *September 23, iii, 627.*

HELEN OF SKÖVDE, ST

She was the widow of a Swedish nobleman, who put her time and property at the service of the poor and of religion. She was unjustly put to death in a family feud. *c.* 1160. Her *cultus* was approved in 1164 on the strength of the miracles alleged at her tomb. *July 31, iii, 228.*

HELEN OF UDINE, BD

After she had led a very happy married life for twenty-five years, Helen Valentini's husband died, and she decided to withdraw from the world; she became a tertiary of the Augustinian friars and was noted for her benefactions to the needy and suffering and for the austerities she inflicted on herself. d. 1458. c.c. 1848. *April 23, ii, 155.*

HELEN. *See also* Jolenta.

HELIER, ST, MARTYR

A sixth-century hermit on the island of Jersey, said to have been murdered by a heathen whom he tried to convert. He is commemorated in the diocese of Portsmouth. *Helerius. July 16, iii, 118.*

*HELIODORUS, ST, BISHOP

He was a friend of St Jerome and accompanied him to the East. Later he returned to his home at Aquileia and was appointed bishop of Altino, from whence he continued to support Jerome's work with material aid. d. *c.* 400. *July 3, iii, 12.*

HELPERS. *See* Fourteen Holy Helpers.

*HENRY II, ST

Henry the Good, b. in Germany in 972, became Holy Roman emperor in 1002 and his career belongs to the general history of Europe. Common accounts of his ascetic practices do not entirely accord with what is certainly known of his character and life: he was a temporal sovereign and a layman and his ways were not those of the cloister, and he was far from being an upholder of ecclesiastical aggrandizement in temporal affairs. He identified himself with those ideas of church reform that radiated from the abbey of Cluny. d. 1024. cd 1146. Henry's wife Cunegund is also numbered among the saints. *Henricus. July 13, iii, 105.*

HENRY ABBOT, BD, MARTYR

A layman who was tricked into "persuading" a man to become a Catholic, and for this offence was h.d.q. at York in 1597. bd 1929. *July 4, iii, 19.*

HENRY DORIE, ST, MARTYR

Henri Dorie was born in the Vendée on September 23, 1839, entered the Paris Foreign Missions in 1862, was ordained priest in 1864 and was sent to Korea in 1865. He was arrested on February 27 and beheaded on March 8, 1866. bd 1968. bd by John Paul II at Seoul in 1984. *March 8.*

HENRY HEATH, BD, MARTYR

Henry Heath OFM was b. at Peterborough of Protestant parents. He was at Cambridge University and became a Catholic when he was twenty-four. He studied at Douai and became a Franciscan priest as Brother Paul of St Magdalen. He led a frugal and scholarly life and went on the English mission in 1643, travelling barefoot to London, where he was soon arrested and h.d.q. at Tyburn in 1643 aged forty-four years. bd November 22, 1987. *April 17.*

HENRY MORSE, ST, MARTYR

He was b. in 1595, and received into the Church at Douay in 1618. He was ordained priest, and passed his noviceship as a Jesuit while imprisoned at York with a priest of the Society. After banishment, Father Morse returned to England and was a successful missioner. He returned again after a second exile, and was h.d.q. for his priesthood at Tyburn in 1645. bd 1929. cd 1970. *February 1, i, 231.*

HENRY DE OSSO Y CERVELLO, BD

Bd Enrico de Osso y Cervello, b. 1840. founded the order of the Sisters of the Company of St Teresa of Jesus. He was noted for his pastoral work, especially in the catechesis of young people and children, and for his emphasis on prayer. d. 1896. bd October 14, 1979. *January 27.*

HENRY SUSO, BD

The most famous pupil of Meister Eckhart, b. at Bihlmeyer, near Constance. He became a Dominican at an early age and was one of the greatest mystics of that order. He was a preacher for thirty-six years, underwent many grievous trials and received great consolations: but how far his alleged autobiography is authentic is a subject of discussion. *The Book of Eternal Wisdom* is the best known of his writings. d. 1365. c.c. 1831. *March 2, i, 464.*

HENRY WALPOLE, ST, MARTYR

Born in Norfolk and educated at Cambridge and Gray's Inn; he was reconciled with the Church, and became a Jesuit in 1584. h.d.q. for his priesthood at York, 1595. bd 1919. cd 1970. *April 7, ii, 50.*

HENRY WEBLEY, BD, MARTYR

A layman b. at Gloucester. He was condemned for aiding and assisting William Dean, a seminary priest, and h.d.q. at Mile's End Green, London, in 1588 when aged *c.* thirty years. bd November 22, 1987. *August 28.*

HENRY OF COCKET, ST

A Dane who became a hermit on Cocket Island off the coast of Northumberland. He d. in 1127 and was buried in the abbey church of Tynemouth. *January 16, i, 103.*

HENRY OF OLOMUC, BD, BISHOP

Henry Zdik was appointed bishop of Olomuc (formerly Olmütz) in 1126, and received the Premonstratensian habit in Jerusalem; on his return he founded the abbey of Strahov at Prague for canons of his order, as an example for the relaxed clergy of his diocese. d. *c.* 1150. *June 25, ii, 643.*

HENRY OF TREVISO, BD

Henry of Treviso (often called "San Rigo") was a labourer in that town and when he could no longer work subsisted on alms. His death in 1315 was the sign for an enthusiastic popular *cultus*, and very many miracles are said to have been wrought through his relics. c.c. by Pope Benedict XIV.
June 10, ii, 520.

HENRY OF UPPSALA, ST,
BISHOP AND MARTYR

An Englishman who became bishop of Uppsala in 1152. He accompanined St Eric of Sweden in an expedition against the Finns and remained in their country to organize the Church there. He was murdered in 1156 (?) by a Finn whom he had penanced for murder, and was venerated as a martyr and patron saint of Finland. *January 19, i, 123.*

HENRY THE SHOEMAKER, BD

Henry Michael Buche was a shoemaker at Arlon in Luxembourg. In 1645 he migrated to Paris where, with the help of Baron de Renty, he formed an association among his fellow-tradesmen whose members undertook a strict way of life and much charitable work. d.1666. There is apparently no evidence of *cultus* except the common appellation Saint or Blessed. *June 9, ii, 513.*

HERBERT, ST

He was a priest, a friend of St Cuthbert, who lived as a solitary on St Herbert's Island in Derwentwater. He died on the same day as his friend in 687. *Herbertus.*
March 20, i, 642.

*HERCULANUS OF PERUGIA, ST,
BISHOP AND MARTYR

He was a bishop of Perugia who was killed by the invading Goths *c.* 547. Another St Herculanus of Perugia, alleged martyr under Domitian, is a duplication of this one.
November 7, iv, 285.

HERCULANUS OF PIEGARO, BD

One of the foremost preachers of the Franciscan Order in Italy during the fifteenth century. d. 1451. bd 1860. *June 2, ii, 444.*

HERIBALD, ST, BISHOP

Abbot of St Germanus at Auxerre and then bishop of the same city. d. *c.* 857. *Heribaldus.*
April 25, ii, 162.

*HERIBERT, ST, BISHOP

Heribert was elected archbishop of Cologne in 998 and was one of the most distinguished of the prelates of that city. He was imperial chancellor and therefore closely connected with the politics of his day, but this did not make him neglectful of his diocese. The *cultus* of St Heribert was greatly encouraged by the monks of Deutz, a monastery he founded in collaboration with Otto III and where he was buried. d. 1021. *Heribertus.*
March 16, i, 608.

HERLUIN, BD, ABBOT

He was founder and first abbot of Bec, which became one of the most influential monasteries of the Middle Ages and gave Lanfranc and St Anselm to England. But there has been no real *cultus* of Herluin. d. 1078.
August 26, iii, 406.

HERMAN JOSEPH, BD

From about his seventh year until his death at a great age Bd Herman was the recipient of numerous visions which made him famous beyond the borders of Germany. He became a Premonstratensian canon at Steinfeld and was a model religious—and a clever mechanic. Certain writings are attributed to him, but the "revelations" about St Ursula are probably not his. d. 1241. *Hermanus.*
April 7, ii, 48.

HERMAN THE CRIPPLE, BD

Though almost completely disabled physically, Herman lived twenty years as a monk at Reichenau. He was a craftsman, mathematician and poet; he almost certainly wrote the hymn "Alma Redemptoris mater", and probably "Salve regina" as well. d. 1054. *See also* Germanus of Valaam.
September 25, iii, 638.

*HERMENEGILD, ST, MARTYR

Hermenegild was son of the Visigothic king of Spain Leovigild, by his first wife, and was brought up an Arian but became a Catholic on his marriage to the daughter of Sigebert of Austrasia. When Leovigild called on his son to give up his dignities in consequence of his conversion, Hermenegild refused; moreover, he took up arms and marched against his father. He was captured and, upon refusing to revert to Arianism, was put to death by his father, at the instigation of the stepmother, in 585. The question of whether Hermenegild is entitled to be honoured as a martyr has been much discussed. *Hermenegildus. April 13, ii, 82.*

*HERMENLAND, ST, ABBOT
First abbot of Aindre when it was founded by St Pascharius; he had the gift of prophecy and could read men's minds. d. *c.* 720. *Hermenelandus. March 25, i, 677.*

*HERMES, ST, MARTYR
He was a martyr in Rome who was venerated there and elsewhere in early times. By what process he came to be the titular saint of three churches in Cornwall is not clear. *August 28, iii, 434.*

HERMES. *See also under* Philip of Heraclea.

HERMINA GRIVOT, BD,
VIRGIN AND MARTYR
The superioress of the seven Franciscan Missionaries of Mary martyred with Bd Gregory Grassi and others by the Boxers at Taiyuangu in 1900. She was b. in Burgundy in 1866 and had come to China only recently; but her strength and courage inspired all the rest. bd. 1946. *July 9, iii, 59.*

HERMOGENES. *See under* Romula.

HERVÉ. *See* Harvey.

HESPERUS. *See under* Zoë.

*HESYCHIUS, ST
He was a disciple of St Hilarion, whom he accompanied from Palestine into Egypt. When Hilarion fled to Sicily, Hesychius spent three years searching for him and after his master's death conveyed his body back to Majuma, near Gaza, where he himself d. at the end of the fourth century. *October 3, iv, 16.*

*HESYCHIUS OF DUROSTORUM, ST,
MARTYR
A companion of St Julius (May 27), martyred shortly after him at Durostorum. *June 15, ii, 546.*

HEWALD. *See* Ewald.

HIDULF, ST, BISHOP
He was a bishop (of what diocese is not known—perhaps an auxiliary) who retired to the Vosges mountains and there founded the abbey of Moyenmoutier *c.* 676. d. *c.* 707. *Hidulphus. July 11, iii, 72.*

HILARIA. *See under* Claudius.

*HILARION, ST, ABBOT
Hilarion is venerated as the first hermit of Palestine, where he was b. near Gaza *c.* 291. He became a Christian at Alexandria and went to live in the desert south of Gaza. His holiness attracted followers and his miracles trippers, who were such a nuisance that he had to travel about seeking real solitude. In his old age he went in turn to Egypt, Sicily, Dalmatia and Cyprus, where he d. *c.* 371. *October 21, iv, 163.*

*HILARUS, ST, POPE
Hilarus was a Sardinian and was papal legate at the "Robber Synod" of Ephesus, from which he escaped with difficulty. He was elected pope in 461 and d. seven years later. Nothing is now known of his personal life. *February 28, i, 439.*

*HILARY OF ARLES, ST, BISHOP
This Hilary became a monk of Lérins under his relative St Honoratus, whom he accompanied to Arles when Honoratus became bishop there. He succeeded to that see, which he administered with a zeal not always tempered with discretion, and was twice reproved by the Holy See for his hasty conduct; nevertheless he was regarded in his diocese after his death in 449 as "Hilary of sacred memory", and in these words Pope St Leo I referred to him. *Hilarius. May 5, ii, 236.*

HILARY OF GALEATA, ST, ABBOT
Disciples gathered round his hermitage on

the river Ronco in Italy and he formed them into a community, naming the monastery Galeata; it was afterwards known as Sant' Ilaro and passed into the hands of the Camaldolese monks. d. 558. *May 15, ii, 320.*

*HILARY OF POITIERS, ST,
BISHOP AND DOCTOR

He was b. of pagan and noble parents and was married some years before he became a Christian. In 350 he was chosen bishop of his native Poitiers, and he threw himself wholeheartedly into the campaign against Arianism, in consequence of which he was exiled in Phrygia by the Emperor Constantius in 356. He continued the controversy in the East, until at last in 360 he was allowed to return to Poitiers, the Arians hoping he would be less troublesome there. d. *c.* 368. Most of St Hilary's writings are concerned more or less directly with the Arian controversy; he was declared a Doctor of the Church in 1851. *January 13, i, 77.*

HILDA, ST, VIRGIN

Hilda, kinswoman of St Edwin of Northumbria, lived "in the world" till she was thirty-three and then became abbess, first at Hartlepool and afterwards of the double monastery of Whitby (Streaneshalch). The success of her rule and the love she inspired in her subjects may be clearly seen in the pages of St Bede's *Ecclesiastical History*: among her monks were St John of Beverley and the poet Caedmon. At the synod at Whitby in 664 St Hilda and her community supported her Celtic customs in dispute. d. 680. Her feast is observed in the diocese of Middlesbrough. *November 17, iv, 369.*

*HILDEGARD, ST, VIRGIN

She was b. in 1098, became a nun at an early age, and was made prioress of Bd Jutta's community at Diessenberg. She moved her nuns to a desolate place on the Rupertsberg, near Bingen, in circumstances of great difficulty, and from there founded a daughter house and made numerous journeys among the ecclesiastical centres of the Rhineland. Hildegard was the first of the great German mystics, a poetess and a prophetess, a physician and a political moralist, who rebuked popes and princes, bishops and lay folk, with complete fearlessness and unerring justice. Among her written works are books on medicine and natural history. Hildegard's mystical writings, her visions and revelations, have provoked comparison both with Dante and William Blake, and in her own day she was called the "Sibyl of the Rhine": she was one of the great figures of the twelfth century. d. 1179. *Hildegardis.* *September 17, iii, 580.*

HILDEGARD, BD

This Hildegard was one of the several successive queens of Charlemagne, by whom she had nine children; not much is known of her personal life. She was a close friend of St Lioba and was honoured as the second founder of the abbey of Kempten, where her tomb was a place of pilgrimage. d. 783. *April 30, ii, 199.*

HILDEGUND OF MEHRE, ST

Upon the death of her husband Count Lothair she, not without family difficulties, turned her castle of Mehre, near Cologne, into a convent of Premonstratensian nuns, of which she became prioress. d. 1183. *Hildegundis.* *February 6, i, 265.*

HILDEGUND OF SCHÖNAU, ST,
VIRGIN

Of the several women of whom it is related that they lived disguised in a monastery of men, Hildegund is the only one in whose story there seems to be a measure of truth. After extraordinary adventures, she is said to have died a novice in the Cistercian abbey of Schönau in 1188. Her *cultus* has never been formally approved. *April 20, ii, 135.*

HILDELITHA, ST, VIRGIN

She was an English nun at Chelles or Faremoutiers who came to England to train St Ethelburga as abbess at Barking; she succeeded her pupil in that office and d. *c.* 717. Her feast is kept in the diocese of Brentwood with St Cuthburga. *September 3, iii, 481.*

HIMELIN, ST

He was said to be an Irish priest who, returning from a pilgrimage to Rome, wrought a miracle of turning water into wine, just before death overtook at him at Vissenaeken, near Tirlemont in Belgium, where he is still venerated. d. *c.* 750. *March 10, iv, 548.*

HIPPARCHUS. *See* Samosata, Martyrs of.

HIPPOLYTUS GALANTINI, BD

A silk-weaver at Florence who founded an institute to teach the Christian religion to children and ignorant adults: it was imitated all over Italy. d. 1619. bd 1824. *March 20, i, 650.*

*HIPPOLYTUS OF ROME, ST,
MARTYR

The Hippolytus celebrated by the Western Church on August 13 is a Roman priest who lived during the early part of the third century, a man of great learning and the most important theological writer in the early days of the Roman Church. For a time he allowed himself to be put forward as an antipope, but he was reconciled with the Church, was exiled to Sardinia for the faith, and d. of ill treatment there *c.* 235. He has been confused with the Hippolytus mentioned in the unreliable *acta* of St Laurence. *August 13, iii, 315.*

*HOMOBONUS, ST

Homobonus was a merchant of Cremona, married, and successful in his commerce. His charity and justice in spiritual and temporal matters so impressed his fellow citizens that, two years after his death in 1197, they petitioned the Holy See for his canonization, which duly took place in 1199. *November 13, iv, 334.*

HONORATUS KOZMINSKI, BD

He was b. at Biala Podlaska, Poland, on October 16, 1829. He became a Capuchin in 1848 and was ordained priest in 1852. He became a preacher and spiritual director. He founded some twenty associations and congregations under the Russian persecution d. 1916. bd October 2, 1988. *December 16.*

*HONORATUS OF AMIENS, ST,
BISHOP

He gives their names to the Faubourg and

Rue Saint-Honoré in Paris, but little is known of him except that he was bishop of Amiens and d. *c.* 600. *May 16, ii, 330.*

*HONORATUS OF ARLES, ST, BISHOP

A Gallo-Roman of consular family who *c.* 410 founded the great abbey of Lérins, after having studied monasticism in Greece. St Hilary of Arles gives an attractive account of the monks and their abbot. Honoratus very unwillingly accepted the bishopric at Arles three years before his death in 429. *January 16, i, 100.*

*HONORIUS, ST, BISHOP

He was the fifth archbishop of Canterbury, who succeeded St Justus in 627. One of his most important known acts was the consecration of St Felix as bishop of the East Angles; he also consecrated the first English bishop, St Ithamar of Rochester. d. 653. St Honorius is commemorated in the dioceses of Southwark and Nottingham. *September 30, iii, 695.*

HOPE. *See under* Faith.

*HORMISDAS, ST, POPE

He became pope in 514 and is famous in ecclesiastical history as the author of the confession of faith called the Formula of Hormisdas, whose acceptance in 519 at Constantinople ended the Monophysite Acacian schism. d. 523. *August 6, iii, 271.*

*HORMISDAS, ST, MARTYR

He was a noble Persian youth who, because he was a Christian, was sentenced to be an army camel-driver, *c.* 420. It is not known when or how he suffered death. August 8, iii, 281.

HROZNATA, BD, MARTYR

After the sudden death of his wife and child he founded the abbey of Tepl in Bavaria for Premonstratensians and himself joined the community. His violent death in 1217 is attributed to his defence of ecclesiastical immunities. c.c. 1897. *July 14, iii, 102.*

*HUBERT, ST, BISHOP

He succeeded St Lambert as bishop of Tongres-Maastricht *c.* 705, and removed the seat of the bishopric to Liège, of which city Hubert is honoured as founder. He was a zealous missionary in the Ardennes. In later times there was attributed to him an initial conversion due to a vision, like St Eustace's, of a stag with a crucifix between its horns. d. 727. *Hubertus. November 3, iv, 247.*

HUGH, LITTLE ST

In 1255 one Koppin (or Jopin) and eighteen other Jews of Lincoln were put to death on a charge of murdering a nine-year-old boy, Hugh. It is impossible to say now who was guilty; but the widespread anti-Semitism of the Middle Ages encouraged the slanderous rumour that the child had been killed by Jews out of hatred of Christianity, and his *cultus* as a martyr grew and flourished. *Hugo. August 27, iii, 421.*

HUGH FARINGDON, BD,
ABBOT AND MARTYR

Hugh Faringdon (*vere* Cook) was elected abbot of Reading in 1520. For some time he was on terms of good friendship with King Henry VIII. He was condemned to death, probably for denying the royal supremacy, and was h.d.q. at Reading on November 15, 1539. With him suffered BB John Eynon and John Rugg. bd 1895. The feast of these martyrs is kept by the dioceses of Portsmouth and Westminster and by the English Benedictines. *December 1, iv, 462.*

*HUGH GREEN, BD, MARTYR

He was a young gentleman of Lincolnshire, brought up a Protestant and reconciled with the Catholic Church while a student at Gray's Inn. For this he was hanged at Tyburn, on August 28, 1588. bd 1919. As a native of Grantham his feast is kept in the diocese of Nottingham. *September 1, iii, 465.*

HUGH TAYLOR, BD, MARTYR

A secular priest b. at Durham, who studied at the English College at Rheims and was ordained priest in 1584. He was sent on the English mission and arrested in 1585. He was h.d.q. at York on November 26, 1585 aged *c.* 25. bd November 22, 1987. *November 26.*

*HUGH OF UGUCCIONE, ST

One of the Seven Founders of the Servite Order (*q.v.*). *February 12, i, 311.*

HUGH OF ANZY, BD

He had a great reputation for wisdom and miracles and was in much request to assist in the reorganization and reform of monastic houses. He d. prior of Anzy-le-Duc *c.* 930. *April 20, ii, 134.*

HUGH OF BONNEVAUX, ST

He was a nephew of St Hugh of Grenoble and abbot of the Cistercian house of Bonnevaux. He was a man of much spiritual perception, and acted as mediator between Pope Alexander III and Frederick Barbarossa. d. 1194. c.c. 1907. *April 1, ii, 5.*

*HUGH OF CLUNY, ST, ABBOT

During the sixty years that he was abbot of Cluny he raised its prestige to extraordinary heights: he was an adviser of nine popes, consulted and respected by the sovereigns of western Europe, and had the ultimate control over two hundred monasteries; in 1068 he fixed the usages for the whole Cluniac congregation and during his rule its first English house was founded, at Lewes. One of his monks said of him, "It is hard to say which was the greater, his prudence or his simplicity.... He was never angry, except against sin." d. 1109. cd 1120. *April 29, ii, 188.*

HUGH OF FOSSE, BD, ABBOT

This Hugh was the principal assistant of St Norbert in the establishment of the Canons Regular of Prémontré and had much of the responsibility of conducting that house. When St Norbert was appointed archbishop of Magdeburg, Bd Hugh became abbot general of the Premonstratensians and over one hundred houses of the order were begun during his thirty-five years of administration. A letter from St Bernard to Hugh suggests that he was a man of somewhat impetuous disposition. d. 1164. c.c. 1927. *February 10, i, 296.*

*HUGH OF GRENOBLE, ST, BISHOP

Born 1052. While canon of the chapter of Valence he earned so great a reputation that in 1080 he was appointed bishop of Grenoble in view of the disorders that required remedying in that diocese. He was very successful in the task, and pope after pope refused his application to be allowed to resign. It was this St Hugh who welcomed St Bruno and his monks and gave them the land of La Chartreuse. d. 1132. The holiness of his life was so patent that he was canonized only two years after his death. *April 1, ii, 3.*

*HUGH OF LINCOLN, ST, BISHOP

Hugh was b. at Avalon in Burgundy in 1140 and was professed as a canon regular, but afterwards joined the Carthusians at the Grande Chartreuse. In 1175 he was sent to England to found the first charterhouse there, at Witham in Somerset, which he did under great difficulties with King Henry II. He was elected bishop of Lincoln in 1186, and was a vigorous defender of the rights of the people; he gained the respect of Richard I by withstanding unjust exactions. Much of the present cathedral of Lincoln is due to St Hugh, who found the church almost in ruins. He was a notable defender of the Jews against official oppression and popular spite. d. 1200. cd 1220. Hugh's feast is observed in several English dioceses and by the Carthusians. *November 17, iv, 370.*

*HUGH OF ROUEN, ST, BISHOP

He lived in days when pluralism was common and he was at the same time bishop of Rouen, Paris and Bayeux, and abbot of Fontenelle and Jumièges: but in his hands neither power nor wealth was abused and he was venerated as a saint accordingly. d. 730. *April 9, ii, 59.*

HUGOLINO MAGALOTTI, BD

A secular tertiary of the Friars Minor who led a life of prayer and manual work in Italy. d. 1373. c.c. 1856. *Hugolinus. December 11, iv, 542.*

HUGOLINO OF CORTONA, BD

There is very little information to be had about this Augustinian friar, whose surname was Zefferini: it is not clear even whether he lived in the fourteenth or fifteenth century. c.c. 1804. *March 22, i, 660.*

HUGOLINO OF GUALDO, BD

An Augustinian friar at Gualdo in Umbria, of whom little is known. d. 1260. c.c. 1919. *January 1, i, 14.*

HUMBELINE, BD

She was the only sister of St Bernard of Clairvaux, and married a nobleman. Bernard dissuaded her from a very worldly life and after some years she became a nun; she d. in 1135, abbess of Jully, near Troyes. c.c. 1703. *Humbelina. August 21, iii, 376.*

HUMBERT OF ROMANS, BD

Fifth master general of the Dominicans. In this office he devoted himself to the encouragement of studies, to the final revision of his order's liturgy, and to the development of missions in the East. He resigned at a general chapter in London in 1263, and d. at Valence in 1277. Though commonly called Blessed, his *cultus* has never been confirmed. *Humbertus. July 14, iii, 104.*

HUMBERT OF SAVOY, BD

Humbert III, Count of Savoy, was an ancestor of the Italian royal house. He was b. 1136, and was a capable and just ruler. He was married three, or even four times, and in his old age retired to the abbey of Hautecombe. It was probably here that he d. in 1188. c.c. 1838. *March 4, i, 482.*

HUMBERT OF BISIGNANO, BD

An Observant Franciscan lay-brother, very celebrated for miracles and wisdom; he was consulted by Popes Gregory XV and Urban VIII. d. 1637. bd 1882. *November 27, iv, 438.*

HUMILITY, ST

Born at Faenza in 1226. Both she and her husband became religious, Humility living for twelve years as a recluse; she then left her cell to direct the first house of Vallombrosan nuns at Malta, near Faenza, founding a second, at Florence, before her death in 1310. *May 22, ii, 368.*

HUMPHREY, ST, BISHOP

A monk of Prüm, who became bishop of Thérouanne in 856. His diocese was overrun by the Northmen and Humphrey wanted to resign, but he persevered and lived to restore the diocese. In his later years he was as well abbot of St Bertin's at Saint-Omer. d. 871. Also called *Hunfrid, Hunfridus. March 8, i, 525.*

HUMPHREY MIDDLEMORE, BD,
MARTYR

One of the English Carthusian martyrs (*q.v.*), a monk of the London Charterhouse, h.d.q. at Tyburn on June 19, 1535. His feast, with Bd Sebastian Newdigate, is kept in the archdiocese of Birmingham. *May 11, ii, 277.*

HUMPHREY PRITCHARD, BD,
MARTYR

Humphrey Pritchard (or ap Richard) was a devout pot-boy at the St Catherine's Wheel inn in Oxford, b. in Wales, who helped persecuted Catholics for some twelve years. He was arrested and sentenced for aiding and assisting seminary priests. When told he did not know what it was to be a Catholic, he replied that he knew what he was to believe and that he willingly died for so good a cause. He was hanged at Oxford in 1589. bd November 22, 1987. *July 5.*

HUNNA, ST

She was the wife of an Alsatian nobleman and was known to her neighbours as "the holy washerwoman" because of her willingness to lend a hand with any job. d. *c.* 679. cd 1520. *April 15, ii, 100.*

*HYACINTH, ST

He was a Polish Dominican who preached with great success in northern and central Europe, being credited with numerous miracles. But the details of his history are confused and uncertain. d. 1257. cd 1594. *Hyacinthus. August 17, iii, 338.*

HYACINTH CASTAÑEDA, ST,
MARTYR

One of the earliest beatified martyrs of Indo-China. He was a Spanish Dominican, who suffered much as a missionary in China and Tongking. He was beheaded with Bd Vincent Liem in 1773, twenty-eight years after two other Spanish Dominicans, BB Francis Gil and Matthew Leziniana. bd 1906. *November 7, ii, 77.*

HYACINTH. *See also under* Protus.

*HYACINTHA MARISCOTTI, ST,
VIRGIN

St Hyacintha presents the unusual case of a religious who began by being scandalously unfaithful to rule, was converted to better ways, relapsed, and so far recovered as to attain to heroic virtue. She belonged to a noble family at Vignarello, and when her younger sister was married was so annoyed and troublesome that her family insisted on her becoming a nun in a convent of Franciscan regular tertiaries at Viterbo. d. 1640. cd 1807. *January 30, i, 206.*

*HYPATIUS, ST, ABBOT

He was abbot of a monastery at Chalcedon and an early opponent of the Nestorian heresy. d. 446 (?). *June 17, ii, 563.*

I

IA, ST, VIRGIN
This maiden gave her name to St Ives in Cornwall (but not to the St Ives in Huntingdonshire), whither she is said to have come from Ireland in the sixth century. *February 3, i, 240.*

*IA, ST, VIRGIN AND MARTYR
She was a Greek slave, put to death with other Christians in Persia during the persecution by King Sapor II, in 360. Her story is quite unreliable. *August 4, iii, 264.*

IBAR, ST, BISHOP
He was a missionary in Ireland with St Patrick, and he was probably consecrated bishop. Ibar established a monastery on Beg-Eire (Beggery). Fifth century. *April 23, ii, 151.*

IDA OF BOULOGNE, BD
Ida was descended from Charlemagne and married Eustace II, count of Boulogne; by him she was the mother of Godfrey and Baldwin de Bouillon. After the death of her husband she utilized much of her great property in helping the poor and founding monasteries. d. 1113. *April 13, ii, 85.*

IDA OF HERZFELD, ST
Ida was of royal birth and brought up at the court of Charlemagne; on the death of her husband she retired from the court, passing the rest of her days in good works. Her biography consists mostly of improbable miracles. d. 825. *September 4, iii, 486.*

IDA OF LOUVAIN, BD, VIRGIN
The extant biography of this Ida, who entered a Cistercian convent at Roosendael, is full of surprising marvels, but is not a document that can be regarded with much confidence as a record of fact. d. *c.* 1300 (?). *April 13, ii, 86.*

IDA OF TOGGENBURG, BD
Ida is said to have been the wife of a Count Henry of Toggenburg, from whom she suffered most malignant persecution, but her detailed legend is wholly fictitious. d. 1226 (?). c.c. 1724. *November 3, iv, 253.*

IDESBALD, ST, ABBOT
Abbot of the Cistercian monastery of our Lady of the Dunes between Dunkirk and Nieuport. d. 1167. *April 18, ii, 122*

IGNATIUS AZEVEDO, BD, MARTYR
He joined the Society of Jesus at Coïmbra in 1548, attained office therein, and was greatly reverenced. In 1570 he was sent to Brazil a second time in charge of a band of missionaries; on the way their ship was stopped by a French privateer, whose Huguenot skipper had all the forty Jesuits, save one, put to death out of hatred of their faith. bd 1854. *July 15, iii, 112.*

IGNATIUS DELGADO, ST, MARTYR
Ignatius Delgado y Cebrián was a Spanish Dominican, vicar apostolic of Eastern Tongking, who died in prison from exposure and ill treatment in Vietnam in 1838, after having worked in that country for nearly

fifty years. bd 1900. cd June 19, 1988.
July 11, iii, 77.

IGNATIUS MANGIN, BD, MARTYR

A French Jesuit martyred in China by the Boxers in 1900. bd 1955. *July 20, iv, 672.*

IGNATIUS OF ANTIOCH, ST,
BISHOP AND MARTYR

Ignatius, bishop of Antioch, called "the God-bearer", was probably a disciple of St John the Evangelist. He was sent to Rome in his old age to be put to death as a Christian, and on the way he wrote seven letters to various churches: these have survived and are among the most precious documents of Christian antiquity. Little is known of Ignatius except from his letters; in Rome he was thrown to the lions, *c.* 107. He is named in the Roman canon. *October 17, i, 219.*

*IGNATIUS OF CONSTANTINOPLE, ST, BISHOP

This Ignatius ruled the see of Constantinople and his story is part of general church history. His refusal of holy communion to Bardas Caesar, on account of open incest, was the occasion of his expulsion from the patriarchal throne and the intrusion of Photius. Ignatius was restored in 867, after receiving very harsh usage, and he spent the remaining years of his life in discharging his office with vigilance and energy, though not without a dispute with Pope John VIII. d. 877. *October 23, iv, 184.*

*IGNATIUS OF LACONI, ST

Francis Peis was b. in Sardinia in 1701 and became a lay-brother with the Capuchin Franciscans near Cagliari. For sixty years he carried out the duty of questing for alms and other humble tasks, becoming one of the best-known and beloved figures of the island; miracles were attributed to his prayers. d. 1781. cd 1951. *May 11, ii, 281.*

*IGNATIUS OF LOYOLA, ST

Ignatius was b. at the castle of Loyola in 1491, a nobleman of Spain, and was bred to arms. After being wounded in battle against the French he heard the call of God and, after pilgrimage to the Holy Land, studied for holy orders. The lessons Ignatius had learned as a soldier he employed in the service of the Church, and in 1534 he began the foundation of the company of spiritual soldiers whose characteristic virtue was to be obedience: they were to be ready to go wherever the good of the Church required (originally they had intended to be missionaries in Palestine), and for four hundred years its members have distinguished themselves in all fields, but especially in education and in foreign missions. The character of Ignatius was strong and determined, a prominent note being the simplicity of his aim—the greater glory of God. He and the Society of Jesus played a very conspicuous part in the "Counter-Reformation", and his *Spiritual Exercises* continues to be a religious work of vast influence. From 1541 St Ignatius directed his society from Rome, and before his death his missionaries were found in the East Indies, Ethiopia, South America and elsewhere. d. 1556. cd 1622. *July 31, iii, 221.*

IGNATIUS OF ROSTOV, ST, BISHOP

Ignatius was bishop of Rostov during the thirteenth century, and had to defend his flock against the Mongols, pacify quarrelsome Russian nobles, and contend with superstition and debauchery. Little is known of the details of his life. d. 1288. *May 28, ii, 413.*

IGNATIUS OF ST AGATHA, BD

Ignazio da Santhia was b. in 1686 and spent six years as a secular priest. He became a Capuchin and a noted spiritual director, preacher and novice-master influential throught Piedmont. d. 1770. bd by Paul VI in 1966. *April 17.*

*ILDEPHONSUS, ST, BISHOP

Nephew of St Eugenius of Toledo, whom he succeeded in that see about 657. The writings of St Ildephonsus are notable for the fervour of their language concerning our Lady, and they had a marked effect on Spanish piety. She is said to have appeared to him in vision and to have given him a chasuble. d. 667. *January 23, i, 155.*

ILLTYD, ST, ABBOT

St Illtyd (Illtud) was one of the greatest of the

Welsh saints, but the details of his life are uncertain. He is said to have married one Trynihid; but "the desert" called him and he eventually founded the great monastery of Llanilltyd Fawr (Llantwit Major) which became a nursery of saints. The life of St Samson calls Illtyd "of all the Britons the most learned in the Scriptures". Sixth century. His feast is kept in the archdiocese of Cardiff and on Caldey Island, with which his name is associated. *Iltutus*.
November 6, iv, 274.

IMELDA, BD, VIRGIN

She was the daughter of Count Egano Lambertini, of Bologna; she is stated to have received her first holy communion miraculously, at the age of eleven, and to have died immediately after, in 1333. c.c. 1826.
May 13, ii, 301.

INDO-CHINA, MARTYRS OF. *See* One Hundred and Seventeen Martyrs of Vietnam.

IDRACT. *See under* Dominica.

INÉS. *See* Josepha of Benigamin.

*INGENUINUS, ST, BISHOP

Bishop of Seben in Tirol, who transferred the see to Brixen. He appears to have d. in exile, *c.* 605. *February 5.*

*INNOCENT V, BD, POPE

In the age of St Thomas and St Albert the Great, Peter of Tarentaise was an eminent theologian. He was made archbishop of Lyons in 1272, and took a leading part in the ecumenical council in that city on behalf of the reunion of the East. In 1276 he was elected pope as Innocent V, the first Dominican to occupy the pontifical chair, and his short rule was chiefly marked by his efforts on behalf of peace, especially among the Italian states. d. 1277. c.c. 1898.
June 22, ii, 618.

INNOCENT XI, BD, POPE

Benedict Odescalchi was elected to the papacy at the age of sixty-five in 1676. He condemned Gallicanism in France and Louis XIV's persecution of the Huguenots: "people must be led to the temple, not dragged", he said. He also condemned the Quietism of Miguel de Molinos, and certain lax propositions in morals—whereupon his opponents accused him of Jansenism. Innocent was a man of simple habits and of generous nature, but firm in his dealings with error and with ecclesiastical ambition and extravagance. d. 1689. bd 1956; but for French opposition he would probably have been beatified two hundred years earlier. *August 11.*

INNOCENT DE LA INMACULADA, BD, MARTYR

A Passionist priest, b. March 10, 1887 at Santa Cecilia nella Valle de Oro (Lugo, Spain). Inocencio was spiritual director and confessor of the Turón community of Brothers of the Christian Schools. He was executed by firing-squad during the Spanish Civil War, together with Bd Cirilo Bertrán and his companions (*q.v.*), De La Salle Brothers killed during the Republican campaign to secularize the Catholic schools in Spain. d. October 5, 1934. bd April 29, 1990.
October 5.

INNOCENT OF BERZO, BD

Giovanni Scalvinoni was b. to illiterate peasants at Niardo, Brescia, Italy on March 19, 1844. He entered Brescia seminary at seventeen and was ordained priest at twenty-three. He eventually became vicar of Berzo and on April 16, 1874 a Capuchin monk as Fr Innocenzo da Berzo. He filled several posts as novice-master, retreat-director, etc., and was noted for his self-denial. d. Bergamo March 3, 1890. bd by John XXIII November 12, 1961. *March 3.*

*INNOCENT OF TORTONA, ST, BISHOP

He was bishop of Tortona in Italy, but very little is known for certain about him. d. *c.* 350. *April 17, ii, 113.*

*INNOCENTS, THE HOLY, MARTYRS

The children murdered by order of King Herod as recorded in St Matthew's Gospel, 2: 16–18. Their number is not known, but it cannot have been large, legends to the contrary notwithstanding. They are venerated as martyrs, *flores martyrum,* who died not only for Christ, but instead of him. *December 28, iv, 626.*

*IRENAEUS AND MUSTIOLA, SS, MARTYRS

Irenaeus was a deacon martyred during the third (?) century at Ciusi; the matron Mustiola is said to have ministered to him and others in prison. *July 4, iii, 11.*

*IRENAEUS OF LYONS, ST, BISHOP

He was b. in Asia Minor *c.* 125, being a pupil of St Polycarp. From his writings he is accounted a Father of the Church; he was "a curious explorer of all kinds of learning", says Tertullian, and he was a principal opponent of Gnosticism. He came as a missionary to Gaul and was made bishop of Lyons. d. *c.* 203. A late tradition says that he was martyred, but this is highly improbable. The feast of St Irenaeus was extended to the whole Western Church only in 1922, whereas it had been celebrated in the East from early times. *June 28, ii, 656.*

*IRENAEUS OF SIRMIUM, ST, BISHOP AND MARTYR

He was bishop of Sirmium, the capital of Pannonia, and was arrested during the persecution of Diocletian: his mother, his wife, his children and his friends begged him to sacrifice to the gods, but he remained firm and was beheaded in 304. *March 24, i, 668.*

*IRMINA, ST, VIRGIN

She was said to be the eldest daughter of St Dagobert II. According to tradition she became a nun after undergoing a tragic love-affair; she was a zealous supporter of the missionary, St Willibrord. d. *c.* 710. *December 24, iv, 605.*

ISAAC I, ST, BISHOP

This Isaac (Sahak, Sahag) was called to rule the Armenian church *c.* 390, he being son of the katholikos St Nerses the Great. During his rule he did away with the custom of married bishops, confirmed the autonomy of his church, founded monasteries, and with St Mesrop laid the foundations of Armenian vernacular literature. d. 439. He is named in the *anaphora* of the Armenian Liturgy. *September 9, iii, 512.*

*ISAAC JOGUES, ST, MARTYR

One of the principal of the martyrs of North America (*q.v.*). With other Jesuits he arrived in Canada in 1636, and was seized by the Mohawks while on his way to relieve distress in the Huron country. He was tortured but escaped, and later returned to work among the Indians. He was tomahawked in an Iroquois village on October 19, 1646. cd 1930. *September 26, iii, 645.*

ISAAC OF CONSTANTINOPLE, ST, ABBOT

He warned the Arian emperor Valens to his face for the oppression of Catholics, and narrowly escaped death; later he became abbot of a large community of monks which he founded at Constantinople. d. *c.* 410. *May 30, ii, 423.*

*ISAAC OF CORDOVA, ST, MARTYR

He was a Christian notary under the Moorish government in Spain, but gave up his post to be a monk. Having denounced Mohammed during a debate with the chief magistrate of Cordova, he was tortured and put to death in 852. *June 3, ii, 465.*

*ISAAC OF SPOLETO, ST

Isaac was a Syrian who fled from Monophysite persecution and took up his abode in a cave on Monte Luco at Spoleto; he was regarded as the superior of the other hermits there. d. *c.* 550. *April 11, ii, 71.*

ISAAC. *See also under* Sapor.

ISABEL FERNANDEZ, BD

A Spanish widow who was beheaded in the Great Martyrdom at Nagasaki in 1622, for sheltering Bd Charles Spinola. Her son, a young boy, suffered with her. bd 1867. *Isabella. September 10, iii, 534.*

ISABEL OF FRANCE, BD, VIRGIN

She was a sister to St Louis of France. She refused several marriages, gave away much in alms, financed knights to go on the crusades, and founded the Poor Clare monastery of Longchamps, where she lived in retirement as a secular. d. 1270. c.c. 1521. *February 26, i, 427.*

ISABEL. *See also* Elizabeth of Portugal.

ISAIAH. *See* Isaias.

ISAIAS OF CRACOW, BD

Isaias Boner was an Augustinian friar and doctor of divinity of the University of Cracow. He was famous for his enthusiasm in expounding the Bible and the devotion that he kindled in his hearers. d. 1471. *February 8, i, 282.*

ISAIAS OF ROSTOV, ST, BISHOP

A monk of Kiev, elected to the see of Rostov in 1077, where he converted many heathen and was renowned for miracles. d. 1090. *May 15, ii, 282.*

*ISIDORE OF ALEXANDRIA, ST

He passed most of his life as governor of the hospital at Alexandria, but having incurred the anger of St Jerome (who suspected him of Origenism) he went away to Constantinople, where he d. 404. *Isidorus.* *January 15, i, 95.*

*ISIDORE OF CHIOS, ST, MARTYR

Isidore was a martyr on Chios (in 251?), but the details of his passion appear to be fictitious. *May 15, ii, 319.*

ISIDORE DE LOOR, BD

Isidore de Saint-Joseph, known as "Brother of the will of God", was an exceptionally devout Belgian Passionist who suffered his final illness with great fortitude. b. 1881, d. 1916. bd September 30, 1984. *October 6.*

*ISIDORE OF PELUSIUM, ST, ABBOT

An abbot in Egypt, much admired by St Cyril of Alexandria; a number of his letters are still preserved. d. *c.* 450. *February 4, i, 249.*

*ISIDORE OF SEVILLE, ST,
BISHOP AND DOCTOR

St Isidore presided over the see of Seville in the sixth/seventh century, but no satisfactory early account of his life exists. It is known that he was a very learned man, an ardent educationist, and an encourager of monasticism. Among his writings are a sort of encyclopaedia and works of history, geography, astronomy, biography and theology. At the council of Toledo in 633, St Isidore was responsible for the decree that there should be a cathedral school in every diocese, where the liberal arts, medicine, law, Hebrew and Greek should be taught. The completion of the Mozarabic liturgical rite is also attributed to him, and he finally converted the Visigoths from the Arian heresy. d. 636. Declared a Doctor of the Church in 1722. *October 6.*

*ISIDORE THE HUSBANDMAN, ST

Also known as "Isidore the Farmer", the patron of Madrid spent his life as a farm-labourer on an estate just outside the city and exemplified Christian perfection in this simple calling. His wife is also popularly venerated, as Santa María de la Cabeza. d. 1130. The miracles attributed to St Isidore's intercession gave an impetus in his *cultus*, and he was cd in 1622. *May 15, ii, 323.*

ISNARDO, BD

Isnardo of Chiampo received the religious habit from St Dominic himself and founded the first house of the Friars Preachers in Pavia. In spite of his austere life he was excessively fat and people used to ridicule him about it when he was preaching. d. 1244. c.c. 1919. *Isnardus. March 22, i, 659.*

ISRAEL, BD

A canon regular, provost of the house of Dorat in the Limousin, who d. in 1014. Little is recorded of his life. *December 31, iv, 649.*

ITA, ST, VIRGIN

Otherwise *Ida, Mida,* etc. The most popular Irish woman saint after St Brigid. She is said to have been b. near Drum, Co. Waterford. Wishing to dedicate herself to God she migrated to Hy Conaill, south-west of Limerick, where she gathered round her a large community of maidens and appears to have had a school for small boys. Many anecdotes and miracles are related to St Ita, some of them edifying, some preposterous. d. *c.*

570. Her feast is observed throughout Ireland. *January 15, i, 96.*

ITHAMAR, ST, BISHOP

He was the third bishop of Rochester and the first Englishman to occupy an English see, but nothing much more is known about him. d. *c.* 656. *June 10, ii, 518.*

ITTA (IDUBERGA). *See under* Pepin.

IVO, ST, BISHOP

The town of Saint Ives in Huntingdonshire takes its name from a local hermit who, according to a medieval legend, was a Persian bishop who had fled from his own country to England. He had nothing to do with Saint Ives in Cornwall (*see* Ia), but he is now the patron of Saint Ive in the same county. *April 24, ii, 157.*

IVO OF CHARTRES, ST, BISHOP

Ivo was promoted from being provost of the Augustinian canons of Saint-Quentin to be bishop of Chartres in 1091, where he was one of the most venerated prelates of his age. He was involved in difficulties with his sovereign, King Philip I, who wanted to contract an adulterous union, and strongly opposed the rapacity and simony of certain legates and other papal ecclesiastics. St Ivo was a voluminous writer, and some of his works have survived. d. 1116. *May 23, ii, 376.*

*IVO OF KERMARTIN, ST

Yves Hélory was b. near Tréguier in Brittany and became an ecclesiastical and civil lawyer. As diocesan "official" of Rennes he protected orphans, defended the poor, and administered justice with an impartiality and kindliness that made him respected and loved. The last fifteen years of his life were spent in parish work in Brittany, and he built a hospital out of his legal fees. d. 1303. cd 1347. *May 19, ii, 351.*

J

JACOPINO OF CANEPACI, BD
A Carmelite lay-brother who d. at Vercelli in 1508. c.c. 1845. *Jacobinus.*
March 3, i, 476.

JACOPONE OF TODI, BD
Jacopone Benedetti is famous as the putative author of the hymn "Stabat Mater dolorosa", and he certainly wrote many religious *laude* in Italian. In his own day he was well known, first as a "fool for Christ's sake", half-crazed by the tragic death of his young wife, and then as an irrepressible Franciscan Spiritual, whose activities caused him to be imprisoned. d. 1306. *December 25, iv, 614.*

JAMES BERHIEU, BD, MARTYR
Jacques Berthieu SJ was b. into a peasant family at Polminhac, Cantal, France on November 27, 1838 and ordained priest in 1865. He became a Jesuit in October 1873 and went to Madagascar as a missionary in December 1875. He was shot on June 8, 1896 during an uprising to re-establish idolatry. bd. by Pope Paul VI on October 17, 1965. *June 8.*

*JAMES THE GREATER, ST,
APOSTLE
All that is known about St James, brother of St John the Apostle, is to be found in the Gospels. He was a fisherman from Bethsaida. Outside of Spain, almost all scholars of consideration and critical students of history agree that this apostle never preached the gospel in Spain; and there is a like agreement that his relics were not conveyed thither after his death and enshrined at Santiago de Compostela. *Jacobus. July 25, iii, 182.*

JAMES THE LESS, ST, APOSTLE
James the Less, *i.e.* the younger, was the apostle who became first bishop of Jerusalem. He was martyred by being stoned to death or, as some say, thrown from a pinnacle of the temple. St James was the writer of the epistle in the Bible that bears his name. *May 3, ii, 203.*

JAMES BELL, BD, MARTYR
A secular priest under Queen Mary who conformed to the state church under Elizabeth. He repented of so doing and on that account was h.d.q. at Lancaster in 1584. bd. 1929. *April 20, ii, 137*

JAMES BERTONI, BD
James Philip Bertoni was a confessor of the Order of Servants of Mary at Faenza. d. 1483. c.c. 1766. *May 30, ii, 431.*

JAMES BIRD, BD, MARTYR
A young layman, nineteen years old, h.d.q. at Winchester in 1593 for being reconciled with the Catholic Church. bd. 1929. *March 25, i, 682.*

JAMES CARVALHO, BD, MARTYR
In Portuguese, *Diogo.* Born at Coïmbra in 1578. He was a Jesuit missionary in the Far East, chiefly in Japan, for fifteen years and the first priest to celebrate Mass in Hokkaido, the northern island. When a crisis of persecution came in 1623, Father Carvalho and a number of his flock were arrested and

taken in the most barbarous manner to Sendai, three attempts were made to make him and nine Japanese laymen apostatize by leaving them naked in freezing water, and they all died from the effects of exposure, the Jesuit last of all. d. 1624. bd 1867. *February 22, ii, 448.*

JAMES CHASTAN, ST, MARTYR

Jacques Honoré Chastan was born on October 7, 1803 at Marcoux, France. He was ordained priest in 1826, joined the Paris Foreign Missions in 1827, became a missionary in Siam and Malaya and entered Korea on December 31, 1836. He was arrested on September 6 and beheaded on September 21, 1839. cd at Seoul by John Paul II in 1984. *September 21, iii, 61.*

JAMES CLAXTON, BD, MARTYR

A seminary priest from the north of England, hanged for his priesthood at Isleworth, 1588. bd 1929. *August 28, iii, 437.*

JAMES COSAN, BD, MARTYR

Jaime Hilario Barbal Cosan was a Brother of the Christian Schools, b. January 2, 1898 at Enviny (Urgel, Spain), who taught at several De la Salle Schools. Executed on January 18, 1937, during the Spanish Civil War. He showed exemplary courage in the face of death. bd April 29, 1990. *January 18.*

JAMES CUSMANO, BD

Glacomo Cusmano, b. 1834, was a Palermo physician who became a priest and founded congregations for the service of the poor. He was noted for his courage and humility, begging in the streets of Palermo for the impoverished and working among them in a cholera epidemic. d. 1888. bd October 30, 1983. *March 14.*

JAMES DUCKETT, BD, MARTYR

Duckett, a London bookseller, born near Kendal, was hanged at Tyburn in 1602 for dealing in books with which "he furnished Catholics as well for their own comfort and instructions as for the assistance of their neighbours' souls". He had previously served a total of nine years' imprisonment on similar charges. bd 1929. *April 19, ii, 132.*

JAMES FENN, BD, MARTYR

He was b. near Yeovil in 1540, and became a schoolmaster in Somerset. On the death of his wife he was ordained priest at Rheims in 1580, and four years later was h.d.q. at Tyburn on a false charge of conspiracy. His young daughter Frances was present at the scaffold. bd 1929. *February 12, i, 318.*

JAMES LAVAL, BD

A French Holy Ghost Father, Bd Jacques-Desiré Laval, S.S.Sp., b. 1803, was a missionary among the people of the island of Mauritius for twenty-three years. d. 1864. bd April 29, 1979 at the first beatification ceremony presided over by John Paul II. *September 9.*

JAMES SALÈS, BD, MARTYR

Born in Auvergne in 1556, the son of a manservant, and became a Jesuit. In 1592, in company with William Saultemouche, a temporal coadjutor of the Society, he went to preach a course at Aubenas, a town of the Cévennes, where the Calvanists were very active. One night a gang of Huguenots came to plunder the church; the two Jesuits were seized and brought before an assembly of ministers who disputed with Father Salès about the Holy Eucharist. He was shot by order of the Huguenot leader, and Saultemouche was stabbed to death in trying to defend him; 1593. Both were bd 1926. *February 7, i, 274.*

JAMES STREPAR, BD, BISHOP

He was a Polish Franciscan, a successful preacher among the Orthodox of western Russia, and in 1392 was appointed archbishop of Galich. d. *c.* 1410. c.c. 1791. *October 21, iv, 172.*

JAMES THOMPSON, BD, MARTYR

He was a secular priest (*alias* Hudson), hanged at York in 1582. bd 1895. *November 28, iv, 441.*

JAMES WALWORTH, BD, MARTYR

A monk of the London Charterhouse, hanged in chains at York, with Bd John Rochester, in 1537. Their feast is kept in the dioceses of Leeds and Middlesbrough. *May 14, ii, 279.*

JAMES OF BEVAGNA, BD

He was prior of the first Dominican friary in his native town of Mevania (Bevagna) in Umbria, where he was very active in combating a local antinomian sect. d. 1301. c.c. 1400. *August 23, iii, 390.*

JAMES OF BITTETO, BD

Or "of Illyricum" (Dalmatia), his native country. A lay-brother of the Observant Franciscans, who spent most of his life at the friary of Bitetti, near Bari. d. *c.* 1485. bd by Pope Innocent XII.
April 27, ii, 175.

JAMES OF CERQUETO, BD

A hermit friar of St Augustine who d. in 1367, and whose tomb was honoured with miracles. c.c. 1895. *April 17, ii, 117.*

JAMES OF CERTALDO, BD

He was a monk in the Camaldolese monastery at Volterra, where he acted as parish priest, d. 1292. *April 13, ii. 85.*

JAMES OF LODI, BD

James Oldi was a wayward and pleasure-loving man of Lodi whose life was changed in rather striking circumstances, consequent on making an irreverent remark. His wife and he then became Franciscan tertiaries, and James was eventually ordained priest. d. 1404. *April 18, ii, 123.*

JAMES OF MANTUA, BD, BISHOP

James Benefatti, a Dominican, was made bishop of his native Mantua in 1303. Immediately after his death in 1338 he was venerated as a saint, though from time to time his memory was almost forgotten. c.c. 1859. *November 26, iv, 427.*

*JAMES OF THE MARCH, ST

James Gangala ("della Marca") was b. in the March of Ancona in 1394. He abandoned the law to become a Franciscan, and he was a fellow-worker of St John of Capistrano in spreading the Observant reform and in apostolic work in central and northern Europe; his preaching brought both Bd Bernardino of Fossa and Bd Bernardino

of Feltre into the Franciscan order, and it is said that not a day passed in forty years without his preaching the word of God. He was a strong supporter of the establishment of charitable pawn-shops (*montes pietatis*). d. 1476. cd 1726. *November 28, iv, 440.*

JAMES OF NAPLES, BD, BISHOP

James Capocci was a learned Augustinian friar who was promoted to be archbishop of Naples. d. 1308. c.c. 1911. *March 14, i, 594.*

*JAMES OF NISIBIS, DT, BISHOP

James was a Syrian monk who became bishop of Nisibis in Mesopotamia, but much of the traditional story of his life has been shown to be untrue and the writings formerly attributed to him are not his, He is much venerated in the East, being named in the *anaphora* of the Syrian and Maronite Liturgies. d. 338. *July 19, iii, 106.*

JAMES OF ULM, BD

James Griesinger left the army of Naples and became a Dominican lay-brother at Bologna; he was a master in the art of painting on glass, and during his fifty years of religious life that was his principal employment. d. 1491, bd 1825. *October 11, iv, 89.*

JAMES VORAGINE, BD, BISHOP

Bd James was a Dominican friar and in 1292 he was appointed archbishop of Genoa, but his claim to fame is the authorship of the *Legenda Sanctorum*, now known everywhere as "The Golden Legend". Of this extraordinarily popular book Caxton issued the first printed English edition at Westminster in 1483, when it had already been translated into four other vernacular languages. Bd James d. 1298. c.c. 1816. *July 13, iii, 92.*

JAMES THE ALMSGIVER, BD

James was a young Lombard lawyer and priest who bought a decayed hospital and restored it for the use of the poor. Discovering that in the past its revenues had been improperly appropriated by the bishops of Chiusi, he applied to the then bishop for restitution. It was refused, and Bd James obtained judgments against the see in both ecclesiastical and civil courts. Thereupon the bishop had him waylaid and murdered in 1304. *January 28, i, 190.*

*JAMES INTERCISUS, ST, MARTYR

This James was martyred in Persia c. 421. He is called *Intercisus*, "the Cut-to-Pieces", because he was put to death by his body being dismembered. *November 27, iv, 433.*

JAMES THE VENETIAN, BD

James Salomonius was a confessor of the Order of Preachers; he was prior of several houses in Italy and ended his life in semi-solitude at Forli. d. 1314. c.c. 1526. *May 31, ii, 436.*

JAMES. *See also* Didacus *and under* Marian.

*JANE DE CHANTAL, ST

Jeanne Françoise Frémyot was b. at Dijon in 1572 and in 1592 married the Baron de Chantal, with whom she lived happily for eight years, having four children. After her husband's death St Jane Frances, under the direction of St Francis de Sales, founded and presided over the Visitation nuns, of whom sixty-six convents were established during her lifetime: it was a congregation on entirely new lines, and met with much opposition, for it welcomed especially widows and those whose poor health prevented them from entering the other religious orders. St Jane Frances was an uncompromising, sensitive, rather intense person, who suffered a great deal in body and mind during her last years; St Francis, who loved her dearly, said she was "the perfect woman, whom Solomon hardly found in Jerusalem". d. 1641. cd 1767. *Joanna. December 12, iii, 369.*

JANE. *See also under* Joan.

*JANUARIUS, ST,
BISHOP AND MARTYR

According to his legend, Januarius (Gennaro) was bishop of Benevento, put to death for Christ at Pozzuoli during the persecution of Diocletian; but nothing exact is known of him or of those who suffered with him. All the fame of Januarius rests on the phenomenon called the liquefaction of the alleged relic of his blood, which is preserved in the cathedral of Naples, a happening of which there are records for the past four hundred years. *September 19, iii, 594.*

JANUARIUS. *See also under* Faustus.

JAPAN, MARTYRS OF. *See* Laurence Ruiz and Fifteen Companions.

JARLATH, ST, BISHOP

St Jarlath is venerated as founder of the see of Tuam, where he probably ruled a community of monks as their abbot-bishop. Little is known of him, but his monastic school was far-famed. d. *c.* 550. St Jarlath's feast is kept throughout Ireland. *Jarlathus. June 6, ii, 489.*

*JASON, ST, BISHOP

St Paul's host at Salonika (Acts xvii, 5–9). He is said to have become bishop of Tarsus and to have died on the island of Corfu. *July 12, iii, 83.*

JEANNE. *See under* Jane *and* Joan.

JEREMY. *See* Elias of Caesarea.

JEREMY OF VALACHIA, BD

Ieremia Stoica was a Rumanian Capuchin, b. 1556, who went to Italy where he lived for 40 years, noted for his spirituality and fraternal love for the poor and sick. d. 1625. bd October 30, 1983. *October 30.*

JERMYN GARDINER, BD, MARTYR

A layman, secretary to Stephen Gardiner, bishop of Winchester, h.d.q. with Bd John Larke in 1544. bd 1886. *Germanus. March 7, i, 564.*

*JEROME, ST, DOCTOR

Eusebius Hieronymus Sophronius, the father of the Church most learned in the text of the Bible, was b. *c.* 342 at Stridon in Dalmatia. After a varied life of study, solitude, activity, and travel he retired to Bethlehem in 385, where he carried on his

great work of revising and retranslating the Latin Bible or Vulgate. He was helped in this by some of the famous circle of women whom he had directed at Rome, notably St Paula. From history and his extant letters St Jerome is seen to have been an outspoken man, who made enemies as well as great friends (he referred to emenders of biblical texts as "presumptuous blockheads"): he was no admirer of moderation, whether in virtue or against evil; and his breach with his old friend Rufinus over the teaching of Origen is an unhappy story. But if he was swift to anger he was also swift to remorse, even more severe on his own shortcomings than on those of others. d. 420. St Jerome is often represented in pictures as a cardinal, because of services he discharged for Pope St Damasus. *Hieronymus.*
September 30, iii, 686.

JEROME DE ANGELIS, BD, MARTYR

A Sicilian Jesuit who was martyred by burning at Tokio in 1623. bd 1867.
December 4, iv, 448.

*JEROME EMILIANI, ST,

Born at Venice in 1481, and became a soldier and a loose liver. He was brought to reason by a seemingly miraculous deliverance from captivity, received holy orders, and gave himself to all kinds of charitable works throughout the Venetian territory; at Bergamo he started one of the first institutions to shelter penitent prostitutes. In 1532 St Jerome founded a congregation of clerks regular, primarily to take care of orphans, the Somaschi, so called from the place of their first establishment, Somascha in Lombardy. d. 1537. cd 1767. St Jerome was named the patron saint of orphans and abandoned children in 1928.
February 8, iii, 150.

JEROME HERMOSILLA, ST,
BISHOP AND MARTYR

A Spanish Dominican who succeeded Bd Ignatius Delgado as vicar apostolic of Eastern Tongking. He was beheaded in 1861. bd 1908. cd June 19, 1988.
November 1, iv, 284.

JEROME LU, BD, MARTYR

A Chinese lay catechist, beheaded for his religion at Maokeu in 1858. bd 1909.
February 17, i, 365.

JEROME RANUZZI, BD

A confessor of the Servites, who was for a time personal adviser to Frederick of Montefeltro, duke of Urbino. d. 1455. c.c. 1775.
December 11, iv, 543.

*JOACHIM, ST

Joachim is the name traditionally given to the father of our Lady. Nothing certain is known about him. *July 26, iii, 336.*

JOACHIM WALL. See John Wall.

*JOACHIM OF SIENA, BD

He belonged to the great Piccolomini family and joined the Servite Order, being distinguished therein for his devotion and goodness. d. 1305. bd by Pope Paul V.
April 16, ii, 105.

JOACHIMA DE MAS, ST, WIDOW

Foundress of the Carmelites of Charity. Joaquina de Vedruna was b. in Barcelona in 1783; she married Theodore de Mas, and had eight children. She was widowed in 1816. Ten years later, her children provided for, she began a religious community at Vich, for nursing the sick and for teaching; it soon spread in Catalonia, in spite of serious setbacks from civil war and secularist opposition. St Joachima's achievement was the more remarkable in that she was forty-two before she began her religious foundation, and for her last four years she was dying by inches from paralysis: she lived at a high level of trust, selflessness and prayer. d. 1854. bd 1940. cd 1959.
May 22, ii, 371.

JOAN DELANOUE, ST, VIRGIN

Foundress of the Sisters of St Anne of Providence of Saumur, where she was b. in 1666. From being the worst type of money-grubbing small shopkeeper, Joan underwent sudden conversion in 1698, and devoted the rest of her life to the care of orphans and old people; she gradually formed a religious congregation for the purpose, which before her death had spread to other places in France. "That little shopkeeper did more for the poor than all the town-councillors put together. What a woman! What a saint!": so spoke her fellow citizens. d. 1736. bd 1947. cd 1982. *Joanna. August 17, iii, 342.*

JOAN JUGAN, BD, VIRGIN

Jeanne Jugan, in religion Sr Mary of the Cross, b. 1792, was the French foundress, in 1839, of the Little Sisters of the Poor and lived a life of exemplary and heroic evangelical charity identifying with and begging for the impoverished and abandoned, especially the aged. She said: "It is so wonderful to be poor, to have nothing, and to expect everything from God's bounty". Today there are some 4,400 Little Sisters in 30 countries. d. 1879. bd October 3, 1982. *October 3.*

*JOAN DE LESTONNAC, ST.

She was a niece of Montaigne and wife of Gaston de Montferrant, by whom she had four children. At the age of forty-seven, when her husband was dead and her children provided for, Mme de Lestonnac became a Cistercian nun. The life was too much for her health and she left, but in 1606 she founded an institute of Religious of Notre Dame whose object was the education of girls of all social classes, especially in view of the Calvinism rampant in Bordeaux at that time. The institute prospered, but Mother de Lestonnac was removed from its control by the intrigues of one of the sisters; this woman eventually repented, but only a few years before the death of St Joan in 1640. cd 1949. *February 2, i, 237.*

JOAN DE MAILLÉ, BD, VIRGIN

Jeanne Marie was the daughter of the Baron de Maillé; she is said to have lived in virginity with her husband until his death in 1362. She then became a Franciscan tertiary and lived a very mortified and charitable life, suffering much from ill health. The closing years of her life she passed as a solitary at Tours. Some people regarded

Bd Jeanne as mad, and she received much unkindness from her relatives. d. 1414. c.c. 1871. *November 6, iv, 279.*

JOAN SODERINI, BD

She was b. at Florence in 1301, and joined the Servite regular tertiaries there. She was the constant attendant on St Juliana Falconieri during her last illness, and succeeded to her office. d. 1367. c.c. 1828. *September 1, iii, 464.*

*JOAN THOURET, ST, VIRGIN

Jeanne Antide Thouret was b. near Besançon in 1765, daughter of a tanner. In 1787 she became a Sister of Charity of St Vincent de Paul; these were dispersed at the revolution and Joan, who had not made her profession, eventually started a school and other good works at Besançon. By 1807 her helpers numbered a hundred and formed the new institute of Daughters of Charity under St Vincent's Protection, which three years later Mother Joan established at Naples as well. For some time, owing to the action of the archbishop of Besançon, there was schism among the nuns, but Joan was faithful to the directions of the Holy See and her foundation grew and prospered. d. 1826. cd 1934. *August 25, iii, 403.*

*JOAN OF ARC, ST, VIRGIN

Born at Domrémy in 1412, daughter of a peasant farmer. When she was seventeen, as a result of supernatural "voices", she induced Charles VII of France to entrust her with the leadership of an army against the English invaders. Her military successes enabled Charles to be crowned at Rheims within a few months. In 1430 Joan was captured by the Burgundians and sold to the English, who conspired with the bishop of Beauvais, Cauchon, to bring her before an ecclesiastical court which had been carefully "packed". This court decided that her "voices" were diabolical and that Joan was a heretic; she was then handed over to the secular arm and was burnt alive at Rouen, May 30, 1431. A revision of her trial declared her innocent in 1456, and she was cd in 1920. It must be noted that Joan was canonized as a holy maiden, and not as a martyr (which she was not) as is often supposed. *May 30, ii, 427.*

JOAN OF AZA, BD

She was a Spanish lady, wife of Felix de Guzman, who became the mother of two sons and a daughter and finally of that St Dominic who founded the Order of Preachers. d. *c.* 1190. c.c. 1828. *August 8, iii, 283.*

*JOAN OF FRANCE, ST

Often called Joan of Valois. She was the daughter of King Louis XI, b. 1464, and was misshapen in body. Her father married her to Louis of Orleans, who afterwards obtained a declaration of the nullity of the union. Joan thereupon went to live in retirement at Bourges, where, with the help of Bd Gabriel Mary, she founded the order of nuns of the Annunciation of our Lady (Annonciades) in 1501. d. 1505. cd 1950. *February 4, i, 252.*

JOAN OF ORVIETO, BD, VIRGIN

Bd Joan, called "Vanna", was a Dominican tertiary who led a life of devotion to God and care of the poor at Orvieto. d. 1306. c.c. 1754. *July 23, iii, 171.*

JOAN OF PORTUGAL, BD, VIRGIN

Born 1452, daughter of Alfonso V of Portugal. At the age of nineteen she entered the Dominican convent at Aveiro, but her father would not let her be professed and she was continually subject to annoyance from her relations, who wanted her to make a political marriage. d. 1490. c.c. 1693. *May 12, ii, 291.*

JOAN OF REGGIO, BD, VIRGIN

Joan Scopelli founded a Carmelite convent at Reggio, insisting that it should be endowed with freely given alms and not with the property she had inherited. d. 1491. c.c. 1771. *July 9, iii, 55.*

JOAN OF SIGNA, BD, VIRGIN

A number of miracles are related of this Franciscan tertiary, but very little is known of her life. She was a peasant girl at Signa, near Florence. d. 1307. c.c. 1798. *November 17, iv, 374.*

JOAN OF TOULOUSE, BD, VIRGIN

She was affiliated to the Carmelites at Toulouse and is reckoned the foundress of the Carmelite third order. But there is much uncertainty about her life. Fourteenth century. c.c. 1895. *March 31, i, 710.*

JOAN. *See also under* Giovanna *and* Jane.

*JOANNICIUS, ST

After being a soldier in the imperial army, Joannicius, at the age of forty, received the monastic habit; he was a notable opponent of Iconoclasm, and one of the leading monks of his age, living in various monasteries in Bithynia. Among his associates was St Theodore Studites. d. 846. *November 4, iv, 265.*

JOASAPH. *See under* Barlaam.

*JOHN, ST, APOSTLE AND EVANGELIST

St John, "the disciple whom Jesus loved", is often distinguished in English as "the Divine", that is, "the Theologian". He was a Galilean fisherman and younger brother of St James the Greater; to him was committed the care of his Mother by our Lord on the cross. St John was the author of the gospel which bears his name, of three canonical epistles, and of the Apocalypse. He is the only one of the Twelve Apostles who is certainly known not to have been a martyr, dying at Ephesus *c.*100, at a great age. The feast called of "St John before the Latin Gate", kept in the Western church on May 6, probably commemorates the dedication of a church at the place by the Porta Latina at Rome where, according to an old but unreliable tradition, the apostle was thrown into a vat of boiling oil by order of the emperor Domitian and was delivered unharmed. *Joannes. December 27, iv, 620* and *ii, 240.*

*JOHN I, ST, POPE AND MARTYR

He became pope in 523, and three years later went as head of an embassy to the emperor Justin I at Constantinople from Theodoric the Goth. On his return to Ravenna the pope was thrown into prison by Theodoric, on suspicion of having conspired with Justin. John d. a few days later as a result of this treatment, but his claim to be venerated as a martyr has been contested. *May 18, ii, 406.*

JOHN ADAMS, BD, MARTYR

A secular priest b. Winterbourne or Martin's Town, Dorsetshire. He studied and was ordained priest at Rheims and was sent on the English mission in 1581, was banished in 1585, returned and was arrested for high treason as a priest and d. Tyburn 1586 when aged *c.* forty-three years. bd November 22, 1987. *October 8.*

JOHN ALMOND, ST, MARTYR

He was b. at Allerton, near Liverpool, and worked on the English mission as a secular priest for ten years. He was h.d.q. for his priesthood at Tyburn in 1612. bd 1929. cd. 1970. *December 3, iv, 502.*

JOHN AMIAS, BD, MARTYR

Amias, or Anne, was a clothmonger at Wakefield who, on the death of his wife, went to the college at Rheims and was ordained. He was h.d.q. for his priesthood with Bd Robert Dalby at York in 1589. bd 1929. *March 16, i, 612.*

JOHN BECHE, BD, ABBOT AND MARTYR

John Beche (or Thomas Marshall) was translated in 1533 from the abbacy of St Werburgh's, Chester, to St John's, Colchester. He was a friend of More and Fisher. He was condemned in the same way and for the same reason as BB Richard Whiting and Hugh Faringdon, and was h.d.q. at Colchester a fortnight after them in 1539. bd 1895. His feast has been observed in the dioceses of Westminster and Brentwood and by the English Benedictines. *December 1, iv, 463.*

*JOHN BERCHMANS, ST

He was b. in 1599, son of a master-shoemaker at Diest in Brabant. He joined the Society of Jesus at the age of seventeen and was sent to Rome for his novitiate; many testimonies to the perfection of his life still exist, and from them it appears that he closely anticipated "the little way" of St Teresa of Lisieux. Assiduous study during the heat of a Roman summer undermined his health and he died at the age of twenty-two in 1621. Numerous miracles were attributed to his intercession and his *cultus* quickly spread to his native Belgium. cd 1888. *November 26, iv, 427.*

JOHN BODEY, BD, MARTYR

He was a layman, a fellow of New College, Oxford, who was h.d.q. at Andover in 1583 for denying the royal supremacy in spiritual matters. bd 1929. *November 2, iv, 244.*

JOHN BONNARD, ST, MARTYR

John Louis Bonnard was a priest of the Paris Society of Foreign Missions who was martyred by beheading in Tongking in 1852. bd 1900. cd June 19, 1988. *May 1, iv, 283.*

*JOHN BOSCO, ST

Born in 1815, son of a Piedmontese peasant. He became a priest and started boys' club and school work in Turin which was soon in a very flourishing state. Don Bosco as well made his name as a preacher, showed himself a born leader of boys, and before long miracles of healing were reported of him. He built a church in honour of St Francis de Sales, and here in 1854 he laid the foundations of the Salesian Congregation. Don Bosco also founded the Daughters of Our Lady Help of Christians, with St Mary Mazzarello, to do for girls what the Salesians were doing for boys, and an association of lay people to help in these educational works. He also undertook the building of new churches, and when he went abroad to collect for these he was everywhere acclaimed as a saint and money poured in. Don Bosco wore himself out with work, and he died in 1888. cd 1934. *January 31, i, 208.*

JOHN BOSTE, ST, MARTYR

A seminary priest from Westmorland who ministered in the northern counties for twelve years. h.d.q. for his priesthood at Durham in 1594. bd 1929. cd 1970. *July 24, iii, 181.*

*JOHN DE BRÉBEUF, ST, MARTYR

One of the principal of the Martyrs of North America (*q.v.*). He landed at Quebec with two other Jesuits in 1615 and laboured among the Indians for thirty-four years. In 1649 he was put to death with the most atrocious tortures by the Iroquois, together with St Gabriel Lalemant. *March 16, iii, 645.*

JOHN BRETTON, BD, MARTYR

John Bretton (or Britton) was a gentleman b. at West Bretton, Yorkshire. He was constantly persecuted for his faith and often had to leave his wife and family. In later life was falsely accused of treasonable statements, refused to deny his beliefs and d. at York in 1598 when aged sixty-nine. bd November 22, 1987. *April 1.*

*JOHN DE BRITTO, ST, MARTYR

Born in Portugal in 1647 and went to India as a Jesuit missionary. He became superior of the Madura mission and followed the example of Father de Nobili, living the life of an Indian in all things lawful. In 1686 he was tortured in the Marava country for preaching against Siva, and his recovery thereafter was deemed miraculous. He was eventually denounced for teaching Christianity by a disgruntled woman, and in 1693 was put to death. cd 1947. *February 4, i, 254.*

*JOHN BUONI, BD

Until he was about forty years old, this John lived a depraved life, making his living as an entertainer in the houses of the Italian nobility. A dangerous illness changed his heart and he became a hermit near Cesena, where a number of other penitents joined him; these John formed into a congregation, the "Boniti", which later was one of the constituent elements of the Augustinian hermit friars. Their founder led a most austere life and received many supernatural enlightenments. d. 1249. bd 1672. *October 23, iv, 185.*

JOHN CALABRIA, BD

Giovanni Calabria, b. October 8, 1873 at Verona, Italy, founded the Poor Servants of Divine Providence, with two divisions for men and women, to care for poor children. The Congregation now has houses in Italy, Latin America and Africa. d. 1954. bd April 17, 1987. *December 4.*

*JOHN CALYBITES, ST

After being a monk at Gomon on the Bosphorus, he returned home and lived disguised as a beggar outside his parents' house in a little hut, whence his name (*kalybe*). The same idea of disguise occurs in other legends, *e.g.* of St Alexis. d. *c.* 450. *January 15, i, 95.*

JOHN CAREY, BD, MARTYR

An Irish manservant, hanged at Dorchester in Dorset in 1594 for aiding a priest, Bd John Cornelius. bd 1929. *July 4, iii, 18.*

JOHN CASSIAN, ST, ABBOT

He was probably b. in what is now Rumania, *c.* 360; he was a monk in Egypt and elsewhere, but eventually arrived at Marseilles, where he founded a house of monks and another of nuns. For the guidance of his communities Cassian wrote two books, his *Institutes* and his *Conferences*, which were influential far beyond anything within his intention, and through St Benedict Cassian left his mark on all Christendom. d. *c.* 433. *July 23, iii, 169.*

JOHN DE CASTILLO, BD, MARTYR

One of the three Jesuit martyrs of Paraguay, stoned to death two days after the martyrdom of Bd Roque Gonzalez in 1628. bd 1934. *November 17, iv, 376.*

*JOHN CHRYSOSTOM, ST,
BISHOP AND DOCTOR

Born at Antioch *c.* 347. After his ordination in 386 he soon developed that great gift of eloquence which obtained for him the name of Chrysostom, "Golden Mouth". He was called to be archbishop of Constantinople in 398. Here he preached untiringly, founded hospitals and homes for the sick and needy, adjusted the troubles of the church of Ephesus, and sent missionaries to the Goths. In 403, at the Synod of The Oak, a gathering of John's enemies got him banished from his see. He was soon recalled, but, having offended the empress Eudoxia by his plain speech, he was exiled again, being sent into the depths of Armenia. From thence it was ordered that he be removed to Pytius in Colchis, but he succumbed during the journey and d. at Comana in Pontus, in 407. Chrysostom was the most prolific preacher of the four great Greek Doctors of the Church, and the first of the three outstanding hierarchs of the Eastern Church. During his later years he seems to have been sometimes rather unnecessarily violent and provocative in his language; but the story of his banishment is one of flagrant injustice, which the Roman see tried in vain to remedy. *September 13, i, 178.*

*JOHN CLIMACUS, ST, ABBOT

He is sometimes called John the Scholastic but the more usual name comes from his book the *Ladder* (*Klimax*) *to Paradise*, a mystical work intensely popular in both East and West in the Middle Ages. He was a monk of the monastery of Mount Sinai and afterwards a solitary in the same neighbourhood. Some years before his death he was made abbot at Sinai, and his fame as a holy man spread throughout Palestine and Arabia. d. *c.* 649. *March 30, i, 703.*

*JOHN COLOMBINI, BD

He was a merchant of Siena who for two-thirds of his life was an eminent citizen of that town, and avaricious, ambitious and bad-tempered. About 1344 he underwent a sudden conversion; after some years he arranged to separate from his wife, and formed a small society of men who preached penance and specialized in composing business and other private disputes. They were nicknamed the "Gesuati", and in 1367 were approved by Pope Urban V; in 1668 they were dissolved. Bd John d. in 1367, and was bd by Pope Gregory XIII. *July 31, iii, 228.*

JOHN CORNAY, ST, MARTYR

John Charles Cornay was a priest of the Paris Foreign Missions in Indo-China, and when a brigand chief denounced the Christians of Ban-no, he was "framed" by the chief's wife. He was kept in a cage, often in irons and cruelly beaten, for three months: and when he was examined by the mandarins he was expected to sing to them, as the beauty of his voice was well known. He was beheaded in 1837. bd 1900. cd June 19, 1988. *September 20, iii, 79.*

JOHN CORNELIUS, BD, MARTYR

An Irishman b. at Bodmin in 1557, ordained at Rome, he served the Lanherne mission for ten years; in 1594 he was admitted to the Society of Jesus, and in the same year was h.d.q. at Dorchester, Dorset, for his priesthood. Three laymen, Thomas Bosgrave, John Carey and Patrick Salmon, were hanged for aiding him. bd 1929. A feast of these Dorchester martyrs, with Bd Hugh Green, has been kept in the diocese of Plymouth. *July 4, iii, 18.*

*JOHN DAMASCENE, ST, DOCTOR

He was b. in Damascus about 690, son of a Christian official at the court of the khalif, and after a good education succeeded to his father's post. John filled this for some years, and then became a monk in the monastery of St Sabas near Jerusalem. He defended the veneration of images against the emperor, Leo the Isaurian, wrote a classical work *On the True Faith*, summing up and expanding the theology of the first Christian centuries, and was the greatest hymn-writer of the Eastern Church (with the possible exception of St Romanus). St John Damascene was the last of the Greek fathers and the first of the Christian Aristotelians. He died at Mar Saba *c.* 749. He was proclaimed a Doctor of the Church in 1890. *December 4, i, 689.*

JOHN DAT, BD, MARTYR

An Indo-Chinese priest beheaded in Tongking in 1798 at the age of thirty-four. Unlike so many indigenous martyrs in distant lands, details of his passion are forthcoming, accounts that survive having been written by two of his fellow-countrymen. He was a man of great calmness, much beloved by the people. He had been ordained only a few months. bd 1900. *October 28.*

JOHN DAVY. *See* Carthusian Martyrs.

JOHN DOMINICI, BD, MARTYR
Born at Florence in 1376 and became one of the most distinguished Dominicans of his era. He was the leader in the restoration of discipline to his order in Italy and was keenly interested in the education of the young. He was appointed archbishop of Ragusa and cardinal in 1408, and was instrumental in ending the schism in the papacy by encouraging Gregory II to resign. Bd John wrote two educational treatises of importance. d. 1419. c.c. 1832.
June 10, ii, 521.

JOHN DUCKETT, BD, MARTYR
He was a kinsman of Bd James Duckett and became a secular priest in 1639. While ministering in County Durham he was arrested for his priesthood and h.d.q. at Tyburn in 1644. bd 1929. *September 7, iii, 505.*

*JOHN EUDES, ST,
He was the son of a yeoman farmer, b. at Ri in France in 1601. He was ordained priest and for twenty years was a member of the French Oratory, engaged on mission work and study, and he twice distinguished himself by his fearlessness in attending victims of the plague. St John Eudes was one of the greatest "home missioners" of the seventeenth century, and an apostle of devotion to the Sacred Heart. But the work of his life was the foundation of the Sisters of Our Lady of Charity of the Refuge, from whom sprang the Good Shepherd nuns, and of a congregation for the sanctification of the clergy and aspirants to the priesthood (Congregation of Jesus and Mary, "Eudists"), in connection with which he established seminaries. d. 1680. cd 1925. *August 19, iii, 351.*

JOHN EYNON, BD, MARTYR
A Welsh priest (possibly a Benedictine monk), vicar of St Giles's, Reading, h.d.q. at Reading in 1539, with Bd Hugh Faringdon. bd 1895. *December 1, iv, 463.*

JOHN FELTON, BD, MARTYR
Felton was a layman, living in Southwark, who was h.d.q. in St Paul's churchyard in 1570 for affixing to the door of the bishop of London's house a copy of the bull of Pope St Pius V whereby Queen Elizabeth was excommunicated. bd 1886.
August 8, iii, 284.

JOHN FENWICK, BD, MARTYR
A Jesuit from Durham, h.d.q. at Tyburn for the Oates "plot", 1679. bd 1929.
June 20, ii, 598.

JOHN FINCH, BD, MARTYR
A yeoman farmer of Eccleston in Lancashire, h.d.q. at Lancaster in 1584 for being reconciled to the Church and for sheltering priests. bd 1929. *April 20, ii, 137.*

JOHN FINGLEY, BD, MARTYR
John Fingley (or Finglow) was a secular priest b. at Barmby-in-the-Marsh (or Barneby), Yorkshire. He studied at the English College at Rheims, was ordained priest on March 25, 1581 and sent on the English mission in April 1582. He was condemned for high treason as a Roman priest and for reconciling the Queen's subjects to Rome, and h.d.q. at York in 1586. bd November 22, 1987. *August 8.*

*JOHN FISHER, ST,
BISHOP AND MARTYR
Born in 1469, son of a draper at Beverley in Yorkshire. He was educated at Cambridge and in later life became chancellor of that university, which owes much to him. In 1502 he was appointed chaplain to the king's mother, Lady Margaret Beaufort, and in 1504 bishop of Rochester. He was a most devoted bishop at a time when bishops often were not, and so keen a scholar that he began to learn Greek when he was forty-eight and collected one of the finest libraries in Europe. Fisher was a reformer, but he preferred prayer before controversy and martyrdom before violence. He opposed Henry VIII's nullity suit and ecclesiastical

supremacy, and was in consequence attainted of misprision of treason; he was committed to the Tower and in 1535 beheaded on Tower Hill: though only sixty-six years old he was almost too weak to walk. cd 1935. The feast of St John of Rochester is kept throughout England with St Thomas More on July 9. *June 22, iii, 45.*

JOHN FOREST, BD, MARTYR

John Forest was a Franciscan friar of the Observance at Greenwich and confessor to Catherine of Aragon. In common with his fellow Observants he opposed the queen's "divorce", and was consequently kept in a state of semi-captivity. In 1538 he was tried for denouncing the king's supremacy over the Church and was burnt at Smithfield. bd 1886. His feast is kept by the Friars Minor. *May 22, ii, 370.*

JOHN GAVAN, BD, MARTYR

A Jesuit h.d.q. at Tyburn for the Oates "plot", 1679. bd 1929. *June 20, ii, 598.*

JOHN GROVE, BD, MARTYR

A layman, servant to Bd William Ireland, hanged at Tyburn in 1679 for the Oates "plot". bd 1929. *January 24, ii, 597.*

*JOHN GUALBERT, ST, ABBOT

He was b. of noble parents at Florence towards the end of the tenth century and was bred to arms. Having for love of virtue relinquished his obligation in a blood-feud, his action was miraculously recognized by Almighty God, and he shortly after became a monk. Dissatisfied with the observance of his monastery, he started a house of stricter life at Vallis Umbrosa, near Fiesole, from which developed the Vallombrosan congregation of Benedictines, which he directed until his death in 1073. cd 1193. *July 12, iii, 81.*

JOHN HAILE, BD, MARTYR

He was a secular priest, vicar of Isleworth, Middlesex, who was h.d.q. at Tyburn in 1535, one of the first group of English martyrs of the Reformation. bd 1886. His feast is kept in the diocese of Brentwood. *May 4, ii, 277.*

JOHN HAMBLEY, BD, MARTYR

A secular priest b. St Mabyn, Bodmin, Cornwall. He studied at Rheims, was ordained priest at Laon on September 22, 1584 and was sent on the English mission in 1585. He was arrested on his way to a marriage, sentenced for high treason as a priest, conformed, was reprieved and imprisoned, escaped, was taken again and h.d.q. Salisbury 1587 when aged *c.* twenty-seven years. bd November 22, 1987. *July 20.*

JOHN HEWETT, BD, MARTYR

He was arrested in the Netherlands on a false charge and sent to England by the Earl of Leicester: he was then indicted as a priest who had come into the kingdom, and hanged at Mile End Green in 1588. bd 1929. *October 5, iii, 438.*

JOHN HOGG, BD, MARTYR

A secular priest b. at Cleveland, Yorkshire, he studied at the English College at Rheims, was ordained priest at Laon in 1589 and went on the English mission. He was arrested on his way through the North of England, sentenced for high treason as an unlawful priest, and d. at Durham in May 1590. bd November 22, 1987. *May 27.*

JOHN HOUGHTON, ST, MARTYR

The first martyr of the Reformation in England. He was an Essex man, and had been twenty years a Carthusian monk at the time of his death; he was prior of the London Charterhouse. h.d.q. on May 4, 1535, with two others of the Carthusian martyrs (*q.v.*) and St Richard Reynolds and Bd John Haile. cd 1970. *May 4, ii, 277.*

JOHN INGRAM, BD, MARTYR

A seminary priest who ministered in Scotland. h.d.q. at Gateshead for his priesthood, 1594. bd 1929. *July 26, iii, 181.*

JOHN IRELAND, BD, MARTYR

A secular priest, vicar of Eltham in Kent, who was h.d.q. with Bd John Larke in 1544. bd. 1929. *March 11, i, 564.*

JOHN JONES, ST, MARTYR

John Jones (*alias* Buckley) was b. at Clynog Fawr and became a Franciscan. In 1592 he was sent from Rome on the English mission and was arrested and tortured in 1596. h.d.q. for his priesthood at St Thomas Waterings in the Old Kent Road, London, in 1598. bd 1929. cd 1970. *July 12, iii, 87.*

*JOHN JOSEPH, ST,

Charles Gaetano was b. in the island of Ischia in 1654. He became a Franciscan of the Alcantarine reform, was master of novices at Naples, and held other offices. When the Spanish friars in Italy separated from the Italians, St John Joseph ("of the Cross") was mainly instrumental in forming the Italian Alcantarine province and successfully conducted it through its difficult beginnings. He had the gift of miracles and other supernatural endowments. d. 1734. cd 1839. *March 5, i, 490.*

JOHN KEMBLE, ST, MARTYR

For fifty-three years he worked as a secular priest in Monmouthshire and Herefordshire, from his headquarters at Pembridge Castle. In his eighty-first year he was convicted for his priesthood and h.d.q. at Hereford in 1679. bd 1929. cd 1970. *August 22, iii, 383.*

*JOHN LALANDE, ST, MARTYR

A *donné* ("oblate") of the Jesuit mission in North America, and one of its martyrs. He was the helper of St Isaac Jogues, and was murdered the day after him in 1646. cd 1930 *October 19, iii, 645.*

JOHN LARKE, BD, MARTYR

Rector of St Ethelburga's, Bishopsgate, then of Woodford, Essex, and then of Chelsea, to which he was nominated by St Thomas More. He was h.d.q. at Tyburn in 1544 for denying the royal supremacy. bd 1886. His feast is observed in the diocese of Brentwood. *March 11, i, 564.*

JOHN DU LAU, BD. *See* September, Martyrs of.

*JOHN LEONARDI, ST

He was apprenticed to a druggist at Lucca *c.* 1550, but became a secular priest and founded the small congregation of Clerks Regular of the Mother of God. For some reason this undertaking was unpopular in Lucca, and John had to carry on his work elsewhere. He was helped by St Philip Neri, St Joseph Calasanctius and Cardinal Baronius, and Pope Clement VIII commissioned him to superintend the reform of the monks of Vallombrosa and Monte Vergine. d. 1609. cd 1938. *October 9, iv, 65.*

JOHN LICCIO, BD

A confessor of the Order of Preachers in Sicily; d. 1511. c.c. 1753. *November 14, iv, 344.*

JOHN LLOYD, ST, MARTYR

A Breconshire man and a secular priest in South Wales. He was h.d.q. for his priesthood at Cardiff in 1679. bd 1929. cd 1970. *July 22, iii, 166.*

JOHN LOCKWOOD, BD, MARTYR

He was a secular priest on the English mission for forty-four years, and was h.d.q. for his priesthood at York in 1642, when eighty-one years old. bd 1929. *April 13, ii, 87.*

JOHN LOWE, BD, MARTYR

A secular priest b. London. He was a Protestant minister but was converted, studied at Douai and Rome, where he was ordained priest and went on the English mission. He was *c.* thirty-three when he d. Tyburn 1586. bd November 22, 1987. *October 8.*

JOHN MARINONI, BD

He was chaplain to a hospital at Venice, then a canon of St Mark's cathedral, and finally, in 1530, a Theatine clerk regular. Bd John was an associate of St Cajetan, with whom he went to Naples and helped in the establishment of *montes pietatis*. d. 1562. c.c. 1762. *December 13, iv, 553.*

JOHN MARO. *See under* Maro.

JOHN MASON, BD, MARTYR

A layman from Kendal, hanged at Tyburn in 1591 for helping priests. bd 1929. *December 10, iv, 533.*

JOHN MASSIAS, ST

He was b. in Spain in 1585 and emigrated to Peru where, after working on a cattle ranch, he became a Dominican lay-brother at Lima. His physical austerities had to be restrained by his superior, and miracles were attributed to him by the poor of the city. d. 1645. bd 1837. cd 1975. *September 18, iii, 593.*

JOHN MAZZUCCONI, BD, MARTYR

Fr Giovanni Mazzucconi was one of the first members of the Pontifical Institute for Foreign Missions. He went as a missionary to the present-day Papua-New Guinea, and opposed such local practices as infanticide. He was killed with an axe in 1855. bd February 19, 1984. *September 25.*

JOHN MOYË, BD

He was b. near Metz in 1730 and was the founder of the Sisters of Divine Providence. He afterwards went as a missionary to China, where he suffered imprisonment and organized a society of Chinese women helpers. He d. at Trier, an exile of the revolution in France, in 1793, from typhoid contracted while working in a hospital. bd 1954. *May 4, iv, 672.*

JOHN MUNDEN, BD, MARTYR

Fellow of New College, Oxford, school-master in Dorset, and seminary priest. h.d.q. at Tyburn in 1584. bd 1929. *February 12, i, 319.*

JOHN NÉEL, BD, MARTYR

John Peter Néel, priest of the Paris Foreign Missions, was martyred by beheading in China in 1862, together with his Chinese catechist, Bd Martin. bd 1909. *February 17, i, 365.*

JOHN NELSON, BD, MARTYR

A Nelson of Skelton, Yorkshire. Went to Douay at the age of forty and was ordained in 1576. He was arrested in London and sentenced for refusing the oath of supremacy. h.d.q. at Tyburn 1578. Bd John was received into the Society of Jesus shortly before his death. bd 1886. *February 3, i, 245.*

*JOHN NEPOMUCEN, ST, MARTYR

He was b. in Bohemia *c.* 1345 (his appellation is derived from the name of his native town, Nepomuk), and became vicar general to the archbishop of Prague. According to local tradition, King Wenceslaus IV of Bohemia, who unjustly suspected his wife of infidelity, had John drowned in the Vltava for refusing to disclose Sophia's confessions, in 1393. No mention of this is made in contemporary documents, whereas the archbishop gave Rome a quite different account of the undoubted murder of John by the king. There has been acrimonious controversy on the subject. John Nepomucen was cd in 1729. *May 16, ii, 332.*

JOHN NEPOMUCENE NEUMANN, ST, BISHOP

He was born at Prachitz, now Czechoslovakia, on March 28, 1811. He studied theology in Prague and was ordained in New York in 1836. He eventually became a Redemptorist. In 1852 he was consecrated Bishop of Philadelphia. He built up the parochial school system, and wrote religious journalism and two major US catechisms. d. 1860. cd 1977. *January 5.*

JOHN NORTON BD, MARTYR

A gentleman b. in Yorkshire and resident at Laymsley. He was arrested for harbouring and assisting a priest (Bd Thomas Palaster) and d. at Durham in 1600. bd November 22, 1987. *August 9.*

JOHN NUTTER, BD, MARTYR

A seminary priest from Rheims, formerly a Protestant. h.d.q. at Tyburn, 1584. bd 1929. *February 12, i, 319.*

JOHN OGILVIE, ST, MARTYR

He was son of the head of the younger branch of the Ogilvies and of a daughter of

Lady Douglas of Lochleven; he was brought up a Calvinist and sent abroad to be educated; received into the Church at the Scots College, Louvain, at the age of seventeen in 1596. Ogilvie joined the Society of Jesus and, after a dozen years in Austria and France, was allowed to return to Scotland in 1613. He worked zealously for some time and made a few converts, but was betrayed in Glasgow and arrested. In a vain attempt to make him betray his co-religionists he was forcibly kept from sleep for eight days and nights on end. He was eventually hanged at Glasgow for denial of the royal supremacy in religion, 1615. bd 1929. cd 1976. *March 10, i, 552.*

JOHN DELLA PACE, BD
A hermit who founded at Pisa a confraternity of Brothers of Penance. d. *c.* 1332. c.c. 1856. *November 12, iv, 326.*

JOHN PAYNE, ST, MARTYR
He was a priest from Douay who had his headquarters with the Petres at Ingatestone in Essex. After imprisonment and torture he was condemned at Chelmsford on a trumped-up charge of conspiracy, and h.d.q. in that town in 1582. bd 1886. cd 1970. *April 2, ii, 16.*

JOHN PELINGOTTO, BD
He was the son of a merchant of Urbino, who became a Franciscan tertiary and gave all his life to prayer and almsdeeds. d. 1304. c.c. 1918. *June 2, ii, 443.*

JOHN PERBOYRE, BD, MARTYR
John Gabriel Perboyre held responsible posts in the Vincentian congregation for ten years before he was sent as a missionary to China in 1835. Persecution was renewed four years later, and Bd John was strangled in 1840, after undergoing incredible tortures. He was the first missionary in China to be beatified, in 1889.
September 11, iii, 542.

JOHN PIBUSH, BD, MARTYR
A seminary priest, from Thirsk, whose twelve years on the English mission were mostly spent in prison. h.d.q. for his priesthood at Southwark, 1601. bd 1929. *February 18, i, 373.*

JOHN PLESINGTON, ST, MARTYR
Born near Garstang and worked on the mission in North Wales and Cheshire. h.d.q. for his priesthood at Chester after the Oates "plot" in 1679. bd 1929. cd 1970. *July 19, ii, 599.*

JOHN PORRO, BD
John Angelo Porro was a confessor of the Servite Order, who d. at Milan in 1506. c.c. 1737. *October 24, iv, 194.*

JOHN RAINUZZI, BD
He is called "the Almsgiver" and is supposed to have d. at Todi in 1330, but the evidence concerning him is scanty and unsatisfactory. *June 8, ii, 505.*

*JOHN REGIS, ST
John Francis Regis was b. in 1597 and when eighteen joined the Society of Jesus at Béziers. He early showed his influence for good over people, especially children, and after his ordination in 1631 he was sent out to give missions. He worked unwearyingly mainly among the poorer folk of Languedoc and Auvergne; no hardships, from weather, travelling or any cause, could deter him, and he changed the lives of many and brought many Huguenots back to the Church. At Le Puy he established a refuge for penitent women, which was the occasion of his being slandered and of other difficulties being put in his way; he also set up a granary for the poor, and miraculously increased its contents. d. 1640. cd 1737. *June 16, ii, 558.*

JOHN RI, BD, MARTYR
A Korean layman, martyred in 1839. A letter he wrote from prison is extant. bd 1925. *September 21, iii, 612.*

JOHN DE RIBERA, ST, BISHOP
Son of a grandee of Spain and promoted to the archbishopric of Valencia in 1568, an office of great difficulty and responsibility which he filled for forty-two years. His

diocese was full of Moriscos and Jews, whose activities caused him alarm, and he was one of those responsible for the deportation of Moriscos from Valencia in 1609. St John's public acts and political views were not all on the same level of enlightenment with the personal virtues which caused his beatification in 1796 and canonization in 1960. d. 1611. *January 6, i, 43.*

JOHN RIGBY, ST, MARTYR

A layman, b. at Harrock Hall, Wigan, who was h.d.q. at Southwark in 1600 for being reconciled with the Holy See. bd 1929. cd 1970. *June 21, ii, 611.*

JOHN ROBERTS, ST, MARTYR

Born at Trawsfynydd in Merioneth in 1577. He was received into the Church abroad and professed a Benedictine at Compostela in 1600. St John was a chief assistant of Dom Augustine Bradshaw in the founding of the monastery of St Gregory at Douay, now Downside Abbey. At the same time he was engaged on the mission in England and several times imprisoned and released; his efforts for the sick during the plague of 1603 made his name known throughout the land. h.d.q. for his priesthood at Tyburn in 1610. bd 1929. cd 1970.
December 10, iv, 534.

JOHN ROBINSON, BD, MARTYR

A widower, ordained at Rheims in 1585. h.d.q. for his priesthood at Ipswich, 1588. bd 1929. *October 1, iv, 8.*

JOHN ROCHE, BD, MARTYR

An Irish waterman in London, who changed clothes with a priest, and was hanged for thus helping him to escape from prison, at Tyburn in 1588. bd 1929.
August 30, iii, 437.

JOHN ROCHESTER, BD, MARTYR

A monk of the London Charterhouse. He was hanged in chains at York on May 11, 1537, with Bd James Walworth. Their feast is kept in the dioceses of Leeds and Middlesbrough. *May 14, ii, 279.*

JOHN RUGG, BD, MARTYR

A prebendary of Chichester cathedral, living in retirement at Reading Abbey; h.d.q. with Bd Hugh Faringdon in 1539. bd 1895. *December 1, iv, 463.*

JOHN RUYSBROECK, BD

John Ruysbroeck, b. near Brussels in 1293, is one of the most famous of mystical writers. After his ordination he lived with his uncle, a secular canon, and then with others they withdrew to Groenendael and formed a community of contemplative Augustinian canons regular. John was an exemplary religious and he exercised a great influence on his contemporaries: among his writings are the *Adornment of the Spiritual Marriage* and the *Book of the Spiritual Tabernacle.* d. 1381. c.c. 1908. *Rusbrochius. December 2, iv, 472.*

JOHN SANDYS, BD, MARTYR

A secular priest b. in Cheshire or Lancashire. He studied at the English College at Rheims, was ordained priest, and sent on the English mission in 1584. He was arrested after some time and h.d.q. at Gloucester in 1586. bd November 22, 1987. *August 11.*

JOHN SARKANDER, BD, MARTYR

Parish priest at Holleschau in Moravia. During the Thirty Years' War he was accused by the Hussites of conspiring to bring Polish troops into the country and ordered to disclose the confessions of his penitent, Baron von Lobkovitz. On his refusal he was thrice racked and otherwise tortured, and died as the result, after a month's lingering in agony. d. 1620. bd 1859. *March 17, i, 622.*

JOHN SHERT, BD, MARTYR

A seminary priest, formerly a Protestant. h.d.q. at Tyburn in 1582. bd 1929. *May 28, ii, 415.*

JOHN SLADE, BD, MARTYR

A schoolmaster who was h.d.q. at Winchester in 1583 for having denied the royal supremacy in spiritual matters. bd 1929. *October 30, iv, 224.*

JOHN SORETH, BD

John Soreth was prior general of the Carmelites from 1451 to 1471, and was a forerunner of St Teresa in his efforts for the reform of that order, establishing houses of strict observance in every province. He inaugurated the first convents of Carmelite nuns, in the Netherlands *c.* 1452. He was a learned as well as a very holy man. d. 1471. c.c. 1865. *July 30, iii, 215.*

JOHN SOUTHWORTH, ST, MARTYR

This John was b. in Lancashire, ordained at Douay, and in 1619 sent on the English mission. He worked in London and Lancashire and in 1627 was sentenced to death but reprieved; he was in prison again in 1632 and four years later was most active on behalf of the victims of an outbreak of plague. In 1654 he was h.d.q. at Tyburn for his priesthood. bd 1929. cd 1970. St John's relics were found at Douay in 1927, and in 1930 were enshrined in Westminster cathedral. *June 28, ii, 662.*

JOHN SPEED, BD, MARTYR

A layman who was hanged at Durham in 1594 for helping priests. bd 1929. *February 4, iii, 181.*

JOHN STONE, ST, MARTYR

An Austin friar and doctor of theology. h.d.q. at Canterbury probably in 1539, for denying the royal supremacy. cd 1970. *May 12, ii, 292.*

JOHN STOREY, BD, MARTYR

As "the most noted civilian and canonist of his time", Storey was appointed the first regius professor of civil law at Oxford. After 1537 he married, practised as a barrister, and entered Parliament. Under Edward VI he opposed the Act of Uniformity and under Elizabeth the Supremacy bill and was imprisoned. He escaped abroad but was kidnapped, brought back, and condemned on a false charge of treason. h.d.q. at Tyburn, 1571. bd 1886. *June 1, ii, 444.*

JOHN SUGAR, BD, MARTYR

A secular priest b. at Wombourne, Staffordshire. He was at Merton College, Oxford, refused the oath of supremacy but became a minister at Cank. He became a Catholic, went to Douai, was ordained priest and returned to the English mission in 1601. He was arrested and condemned as a seminary priest, and h.d.q. at Warwick in 1604 aged *c.* forty-six years. bd November 22, 1987. *July 16.*

JOHN TALBOT, BD, MARTYR

A gentleman b. at Thornton-le-Street, Yorkshire. He was arrested for being in the company of Bd Thomas Palaster and for assisting him. He refused to go to the state church and d. at Durham in 1600. bd November 22, 1987. *August 9.*

JOHN THORNE, BD, MARTYR

A monk of Glastonbury, h.d.q. there in 1539 for "sacrilege", in that he had hidden monastic valuables from requisition by King Henry VIII. bd 1895. *December 1, iv, 462.*

JOHN THULES, BD, MARTYR

John Thules (or Thulis) was a secular priest, b. Whalley, Upholland, Lancashire. He studied at Rheims and at Rome, where he was ordained priest. He was imprisoned in Wisbeach Castle for some years and escaped but was later arrested and imprisoned at Lancaster with Bd Roger Wrenno and other Catholics. He was h.d.q. for high treason as a priest at Lancaster in 1616 at the age of forty-eight years. bd November 22, 1987. *March 18.*

*JOHN VIANNEY, ST

John Mary Vianney was b. at Dardilly in 1786. While an ecclesiastical student he was conscripted for the army and for over a year was, more or less accidentally, a deserter in hiding. His studies were so unsatisfactory that there was considerable difficulty about his ordination, but it eventually took place in 1815. Three years later M. Vianney was appointed *curé* of Ars, an obscure village near Lyons: here the rest of his life was spent and from thence his name sounded throughout the world. He was absorbed in his parish, but people came from all parts

of Europe to his confessional; he had gifts of healing and hidden knowledge, and was tormented by evil spirits; to any but spiritual means to spiritual ends he was indifferent; his clothes were ragged, his food poor, sleep insufficient, he had no learning—and in the twelve months before his death in 1859 over a hundred thousand pilgrims came to Ars. cd 1925. Named principal patron saint of parochial clergy in 1929.
August 4, iii, 285.

JOHN WALL, ST, MARTYR

A Lancashire man who became a secular priest and then a Franciscan, with the name of Father Joachim-of-St-Anne. After working in Worcestershire for over twenty years he was h.d.q. for his priesthood at Worcester in 1679. bd 1929. cd 1970.
August 26, iii, 409.

JOHN WOODCOCK, BD, MARTYR

John Woodcock OFM (alias John Faringdon, and in religion Fr Martin of St Felix), was b. at Clayton-le-Woods, near Preston, Lancashire, in 1603. He studied at St Omer and at the English College in Rome. He joined the English Franciscans at Douai. He eventually became a zealous worker on the English mission for many years, retired to the convent, but returned to Lancashire and was gaoled for two years and h.d.q. for treason at Lancaster in August 1646 when forty-three years of age. bd November 22, 1987. *August 7.*

JOHN ZEDAZNELI, ST

He was the leader of that band of Syrian monks, evangelists in Georgia (Iberia), that included St Scio Mghvimeli, St David Garejeli, and St Antony of Martkofi. They were the fathers of a very flourishing monasticism in Georgia. Sixth century.
November 4, iv, 264.

JOHN OF ALVERNIA, BD

Born at Fermo in 1259, became a Friar Minor in 1272, and was sent to La Verna, where he lived a semi-eremitical existence, preaching throughout the neighbouring country and northern Italy. He had the gift of infused knowledge and of reading souls. d. 1322. c.c. 1880. *August 13, iii, 324.*

JOHN OF AVILA, ST.

This John, a secular priest, was one of the most powerful religious influences in sixteenth-century Spain as a preacher, writer, and adviser of saints and sinners. His unfulfilled ambition was to be a missionary in Mexico: instead he was appointed missioner in Andalusia, where his fiery zeal made him enemies among the rich, who at one time delated him to the Inquisition for rigorism: he was acquitted. St John's letters are among the classics of Spanish literature. d. 1569. bd 1594. cd 1970.
May 10, ii, 268.

*JOHN OF BERGAMO, ST, BISHOP

He was bishop of Bergamo and a man of great holiness and learning. He is erroneously venerated as a martyr at the hands of the Arians: d. in peace c. 690.
July 11, iii, 71.

*JOHN OF BEVERLEY, ST, BISHOP

Born at Harpham and educated at Canterbury under SS Theodore and Adrian. He became a monk of Whitby, and was made bishop of Hexham and subsequently of York. Bede, who was ordained by St John, testifies to his holiness, as does Alcuin. In 717 John retired to the monastery he had founded at Beverley and d. there in 721. His shrine was a favourite pilgrimage place before the Reformation, and his feast is now kept by the dioceses in the north of England.
May 7, ii, 247.

JOHN OF BRIDLINGTON, ST

Little is known of the life of John Thwing, who studied at Oxford University and joined the Augustinian canons at Bridlington. In due course he became prior and ruled the house for seventeen years, dying in 1379. Many miracles were recorded at his tomb, and he was cd in 1401, his shrine attracting many pilgrims. St John's feast is celebrated by the Canons Regular of the Lateran and in the diocese of Middlesbrough.
October 21, iv, 171.

*JOHN OF CAPISTRANO, ST

Born at Capistrano in the Abruzzi in 1386. John was a lawyer and became governor of Perugia, but at the death of his wife when he was thirty he joined the Franciscans. He was a disciple and companion of St Bernardino of Siena in his preaching and in the establishment of the Observant reform. In 1451 he was sent by Pope Nicholas V into Bohemia to reconcile the Hussites; his methods of fulfilling that mission have been severely criticized. John was an active leader of the Hungarian resistance under Hunyadi Janos against the Turks, and was in Belgrade during the siege. d. October 23, 1456. cd 1724. *October 23, i, 693.*

*JOHN OF CHINON, ST

He was a hermit at Chinon during the sixth century and had a wide reputation as healer and seer. *June 27, ii, 653.*

JOHN III OF CONSTANTINOPLE, ST, BISHOP

He was appointed patriarch of Constantinople in 565, and he laid the foundation for the collection of Eastern church law called the *Nomokanon.* d. 577.
August 28, iii, 434.

JOHN OF DUKLA, BD

He was a Polish confessor of the Observant branch of the Friars Minor, and a successful missioner in Galicia. d. 1484. c.c. 1739. *September 28, iii, 671.*

*JOHN OF EGYPT, ST

This John was the most famous of the desert hermits after St Antony: he was consulted by emperors and his praises were sung by St Jerome, St John Cassian, St Augustine, and many others. He was a carpenter, born near Asyut, and went into the desert when he was twenty-five. He was noted for miracles of healing and for remarkable prophecies. Palladius gives an account of a visit that he paid to St John. d. 394. *March 27, i, 691.*

JOHN OF FIESOLE. *See* Fra Angelico.

JOHN OF GORZE, ST, ABBOT

A landowner near Metz, who in 933 revived the almost extinct abbey of Gorze. After being elected abbot in 960 he introduced reforms which spread to many other Benedictine houses. On one occasion he was sent on an imperial mission to the court of the khalif Abdur-Rahman at Cordova. d. 974. *February 27, i, 434.*

JOHN OF THE GOTHS, ST, BISHOP

This John, bishop of the Goths on the north of the Black Sea, is honoured in the East because of his defence of the veneration of holy images against the iconoclasts, He was eventually driven from his diocese by the invading Khazars. d. at Amastris in Asia Minor *c.* 800. *June 26, ii, 648.*

*JOHN OF KANTI, ST

This priest, a Silesian by birth, was nearly all his life a professor of Sacred Scripture and other subjects in the University of Cracow. He imposed penitential conditions of life on himself, and his goods were always at the disposal of the poor, who often "cleared him right out". d. 1473. cd 1767. *December 23, iv, 154.*

JOHN OF MATERA, ST

This John was b. at Matera in the kingdom of Naples, and became a monk in a community wherein his austerity made him unpopular. After wandering about and suffering a good deal of persecution, he settled at Pulsano, near Monte Gargano, where he founded a monastery which prospered; it was at one time the motherhouse of a small Benedictine congregation. d. 1139. *June 20, ii, 590.*

*JOHN OF MATHA, ST

John of Matha came from Provence, founded the Trinitarian Order for the redemption of captives, and d. at Rome in 1213. This is practically all that is known for certain of St John of Matha, as it seems that his more extended biographies are based on spurious records. *February 8, i, 276.*

JOHN OF MEDA, ST

This John's name is associated with the early days of the religious movement known as that of the *Humiliati*, but little is known of him. d. 1159 (?).
September 26, iii, 656.

JOHN OF MONTMIRAIL, BD

After marrying and begetting six children, this lord of Montmirail in France became a Cistercian monk at Longpont, *c.* 1210. He was a true forerunner of St Francis of Assisi, and many reliable particulars of his life have survived. d. 1217. c.c. 1908.
September 29.

*JOHN OF NICOMEDIA, ST, MARTYR

"A man of secular dignity" who, when the edict of Diocletian against Christians was published in Nicomedia, tore it down and was punished with death, in 303.
September, 7, iii, 502.

*JOHN OF PANACA, ST

He is said to have been a Syrian refugee from Monophysite persecution during the sixth century, and to have founded a religious house at Spoleto where he ended his days. *March 19, i, 633.*

JOHN OF PARMA, BD

John Buralli was b. in 1209 and became seventh minister general of the Friars Minor, in which capacity he made a visitation in England. He governed his order with great firmness in very troubled times for ten years, and was sent as papal legate to Constantinople. For the last thirty years of his life he lived in retirement at the hermitage of Greccio. d. 1289. c.c. 1777.
March 20, i, 646.

JOHN OF PENNA, BD

The story of Bd John of Penna, who spent his life in France and Italy, fills chapter 45 of the *Little Flowers of St Francis*. d. 1271. c.c. by Pope Pius VII. *April 3, ii, 25.*

JOHN OF PERUGIA, BD, MARTYR

St Francis of Assisi sent John of Perugia and Peter of Sassoferrato into Spain to preach the Gospel to the Moors. They were seized at Valencia and, upon refusing to accept Islam, were beheaded, in 1231. bd 1783.
September 1, iii, 463.

*JOHN OF PRADO, BD, MARTYR

A Franciscan of the Observance who was sent as a missionary with special powers to the Mohammedans of the Barbary coast, where he was martyred with two other friars in 1631. bd 1728. *May 24, ii, 385.*

JOHN OF RIETI, BD

Brother of Bd Lucy of Amelia; he was a confessor of the order of Hermit Friars of St Augustine. d. *c.* 1350. c.c. 1832.
August 9, iii, 296.

*JOHN OF SAHAGUN, ST

This John was b. at Sahagun in Spain in 1419 and educated at the Benedictine abbey of San Fagondez. He was ordained priest and received several benefices, but he gave them up (his conscience being touched in the matter of pluralism), and in 1463 became an Augustinian friar. He was a very effective preacher in the city of Salamanca, which at that time was peculiarly in need of an apostle. d. 1479. cd 1690.
June 12, ii, 526.

JOHN OF SALERNO, BD

John Guarna was prior of the first Dominicans in Etruria and founded the famous friary of Santa Maria Novella at Florence in 1221. d. 1242. c.c. 1783.
August 9, iii, 295.

JOHN OF TOSSIGNANO, BD, BISHOP

John Tavelli, a member of the now extinct order of the *Gesuati*, was chosen bishop of Ferrara in 1431. He is chiefly remembered for his translations of books of the Bible, etc., into Italian. d. 1446. c.c. 1748.
July 24, iii, 180.

JOHN OF TRIORA, BD, MARTYR

John Lantrua, b. in Liguria, became a Friar Minor in 1777 and a missionary in China in 1799. It was a time of almost unremitting persecution in that country, but he worked there for fifteen years before he was arrested. He was strangled at Changsha in 1816. bd 1900. *February 13, i, 363.*

JOHN OF VALENCE, BD, BISHOP

A Cistercian monk, abbot of Bonnevaux, who was chosen to take the place of an excommunicated bishop of Valence in 1141. d. 1146. c.c. 1901. *April 26, ii, 165.*

JOHN OF VALLOMBROSA, BD

This John was a Vallombrosan monk who became a secret necromancer; on being discovered he was imprisoned in a foul cell, and on his release was a changed man. He was given permission to live as a solitary, and he then turned his considerable intellectual abilities to better use. He enjoyed the friendship of St Catherine of Siena. d. c. 1380. *March 10, i, 550.*

JOHN OF VERCELLI, BD

He became the sixth master general of the Order of Preachers in 1264 and discharged his office with much energy and enlightenment. He fulfilled various missions for the Holy See, including drawing up the *schema* for the second oecumenical council of Lyons, and was one of the early exponents of devotion to the holy name of Jesus. d. 1283. c.c. 1903. *December 1, iv, 459.*

JOHN OF VICENZA, BD,
BISHOP AND MARTYR

John Sordi, also known as Cacciafronte, after his stepfather, was Benedictine abbot of St Laurence's at Cremona and bishop of Mantua, but resigned the see. He was then made bishop of Vicenza, and was murdered in 1183 by a man whom he had rebuked for embezzling episcopal revenue. He was at once acclaimed a martyr by the people of his diocese. *March 16, i, 610.*

JOHN OF VILNA, ST, MARTYR

John, Antony and Eustace, Lithuanians of high rank, were cruelly put to death out of hatred of the faith by pagans at Vilna in 1342. *April 14, ii, 95.*

JOHN OF WARNETON, BD, BISHOP

He was a pupil of St Ivo of Chartres, a monk of Mont-Saint-Eloi, archdeacon of Arras, and finally bishop of Thérouanne; it required a papal order to make him accept this last dignity. He was a firm but gentle prelate and refused to take any action against some people who tried to murder him. d. 1130. *January 27, i, 184.*

*JOHN THE ALMSGIVER, ST,
BISHOP

Made patriarch of Alexandria c. 608, when one of his first deeds was to distribute 80,000 pieces of gold to hospitals and monasteries; charity on this scale was continued throughout his pontificate. The whole of St John's life was to match. He d. in 619 (?) at Amathus in Cyprus, his birthplace. *January 23, i, 153.*

*JOHN THE BAPTIST, ST

The forerunner of the Messiah, Christ himself saying of him that, "Among those that are born of women there is not a greater prophet" (Luke vii, 28). St Augustine and other doctors are of the opinion that John was sanctified from original sin in his mother's womb, and the Church, contrary to her usual custom, celebrates with a feast his birthday in the flesh, on June 24—one of the earliest of Christian festivals. The Baptist's (*i.e.* Baptizer) life is narrated in the gospels, especially by St Luke, his death on account of his protest against the wickedness of Herod constituting him a martyr: his beheading is commemorated on August 29. St John is the first in the second series of saints named in the canon of the Mass; before the Reformation over 500 English churches were dedicated in his honour. *June 24, ii, 631 and iii, 440.*

JOHN BAPTIST. *See* at the end of the Johns.

*JOHN OF THE CROSS, ST, DOCTOR

John de Yepes was b. in the province of Old Castile in 1542, the son of a weaver of good family. He became a Carmelite friar in 1563 and was selected by St Teresa to be the first member of the first friary of the reformed observance, at Duruelo. The more public side of his life was in establishing this reform among the men Carmelites, and he underwent much persecution, including imprisonment at Toledo. It is as a supreme mystic that the Church calls St John a "doctor", his teaching being contained in half a dozen treatises, some poems and a few letters (*The Ascent of Mount Carmel, The Dark Night of the Soul, The Spiritual Canticle*, etc.). He was a faithful follower of ancient tradition, but he writes of God from experience and with hardly any reference to the mystical writings of his predecessors. St John was treated with great inhumanity by his superiors during the last months of his life; he d. at Ubeda on December 14, 1591. cd 1726. Declared Doctor of the Church in 1926. *November 24, iv, 413.*

JOHN THE DWARF, ST

John Kolobos, "the Dwarf", was a disciple of St Poemen in the desert of Skete. He was famous among the Egyptian monks of the fifth century, and amusing stories are told of his absentmindedness. He was by nature quick-tempered and conceited, yet was known among his fellows for his equability and humility. *October 17, iv, 138.*

*JOHN OF GOD, ST

Born in Portugal in 1495 and for forty years led an adventurous and varied life as shepherd, soldier, pedlar, and looking after Christian slaves among the Moors. He then settled in Granada to tend the sick and dying, and laid the foundations of the order of Brothers Hospitallers. This was in 1540; St John d. in 1550, and the order still flourishes and bears his name. John was cd in 1690, and later named (with St Camillus of Lellis) patron of hospitals, nurses and the sick. *March 8, i, 517.*

*JOHN THE GOOD, ST, BISHOP

John Camillus Bonus was bishop of Milan during the seventh century and contended strenuously against the monothelite heresy. d. 660. *January 10, i, 63.*

JOHN OF THE GRATING, ST, BISHOP

He received this name, *de Craticula*, from the metal railings that surrounded his tomb. He was a Breton and a disciple of St Bernard at Clairvaux. He founded Cistercian houses in Brittany and became bishop of Aleth, which see he removed to Saint-Malo. d. 1170. *February 1, i, 229.*

JOHN THE IBERIAN, ST, ABBOT

John the Iberian (Georgian), also called "the Hagiorite", parted from his wife and family and became a monk in Bithynia, with his son St Euthymius. Thence they went to the monastery of St Athanasius on Mount Athos, and there, *c.* 980, founded the still-existing monastery of Iviron for men of the Iberian nation. d. *c.* 1002. *July 12, iii, 85.*

*JOHN THE SILENT, ST, BISHOP

Born in 454 at Nicopolis in Armenia, where he established a monastery which he directed till he was made bishop of Colonia. After nine years he resigned and became a monk under St Sabas near Jerusalem; here he passed the rest of his life, living for long periods as a solitary in the desert. d. 558. *May 13, ii, 298.*

JOHN THE SINNER, BD

John Grande gave up the linen trade in Seville, changed his surname to *Pecador*, "the Sinner", and occupied a hermitage near Marcena. Then it was revealed to him that he was called to serve God in other ways, and he went to Xeres and devoted himself to the care of the sick and afflicted in the prison. His services in the public hospital caused him to be put in charge of a new one that was founded, and he joined the Hospitallers of St John-of-God and gathered a band of young helpers round him. Bd John never lost his interest in prisoners; when the English stormed Cadiz he looked after three hundred fugitive Spanish soldiers, and he is said to have foretold the destruction of the Armada. d. 1600. bd 1853. *June 3, ii, 467.*

JOHN THE SPANIARD, BD

A confessor of the Carthusian Order. He was first a monk at Montrieu in France, then of the Grande Chartreuse under St Anthelm, and was the first prior of the charterhouse of the Reposoir, near the lake of Geneva. Bd John drew up constitutions for the Carthusian nuns. d. 1160. c.c. 1864.
June 25, ii, 644.

JOHN BAPTIST MACHADO, BD,
MARTYR

He was a Portuguese Jesuit and a missionary in Japan and was martyred near Nagasaki in 1617, together with the Franciscan Bd Peter of Cuerva and a Japanese youth, Bd Leo. bd 1867. *Joannes Baptista.*
May 22, ii, 447.

*JOHN BAPTIST ROSSI, ST

This secular priest was b. in the diocese of Genoa in 1698 and spent all his life in Rome, where he was first curate and then a canon at the collegiate church of Sta Maria in Cosmedin. St John was specially noted for his work among the sick in hospitals, among the labourers in the City, and among homeless women, for whom he established a hospice. So sought after was he as a confessor that he was dispensed from his obligation of choir office. d. 1764. cd 1881.
May 23, ii, 379.

JOHN BAPTIST ROUSSEAU, BD

Jean-Baptiste Rousseau (Brother Scubilion) was born at Bourgogne, France, in 1797. He became a De La Salle Brother and worked in the French island colony of Réunion in the Indian Ocean from 1833 until his death, devoting himself to the catechesis of children and to the slaves (who spoke of him as a saint) and their liberation. He is an example of profound concern for the essential dignity and fraternity of all human beings. The cause for his beatification was opened in 1902. d. 1867. bd by John Paul II during a visit to Réunion, May 2, 1989.
December 20.

*JOHN BAPTIST DE LA SALLE, ST

Born at Rheims in 1651, and ordained at the age of twenty-six when he was already a canon of the cathedral chapter. The whole of his life was devoted to education, especially of the poor, and the establishment of the congregation of the Brothers of the Christian Schools; but he was not simply an administrator and organizer, he was a thinker and initiator of importance in the history of the education of the young. He set out his revolutionary system in the *Manual for Christian Schools*, among whose innovations were class instead of individual teaching and the learning of reading in the vernacular instead of in Latin. Of course he experienced bitter opposition, and at one moment the very existence of his congregation was in danger. d. 1719. cd 1900. Declared patron saint of schoolteachers in 1950. *April 7, ii, 315.*

JOHN BAPTIST TURPIN, BD

The leading priest among the group of martyrs put to death at Laval in France in 1792 by the revolutionaries. bd 1955.
October 17, iv, 672.

JOHN BAPTIST OF ALMODOVAR, ST

John Baptist of the Conception of Almodovar, the reformer of the Trinitarian Order, b. in Spain in 1561. In 1597 he founded a community of reformed Trinitarians at Valdepenas, which was approved at Rome. This caused a rift within the order, and St John Baptist was subjected even to personal violence by followers of the old ways. But thirty-four Trinitarian houses accepted the reform before his death at Cordova in 1613. bd 1819. cd 1975.
February 14, i, 339.

JOHN BAPTIST OF FABRIANO, BD

John Baptist Righi was a Friar Minor of great natural ability who from humility refused to acquire more learning than was needful for ordination; he led a life of great physical rigour. d. at Massaccio in 1539. c.c. 1903. *March 11, i, 564.*

JOLENTA OF HUNGARY, BD

Niece of St Elizabeth of Hungary and sister of Bd Cunegund. She was happily married

to Duke Boleslaus of Halich, and in widow-hood became a Poor Clare at Gniezno. The Poles call her Bd Helena. d. 1299.
June 15, ii, 550.

JONAH. *See* Jonas

*JONAS AND BARACHISIUS, SS,
MARTYRS
During the persecution of King Sapor these two Persian monks were tortured in divers ways and put to most cruel deaths, in 327. There is an extant account of their passion which seems to have been written by an eye-witness. *March 29, i, 696.*

JORDAN OF PISA, BD
Jordan of Pisa was one of the makers of the modern Italian language, being among the first to use the Tuscan dialect instead of Latin in his sermons. He received the Dominican habit at Pisa in 1280; and when he was lector there, Santa Maria Novella at Florence attained great celebrity as a place of studies. Jordan was an enthusiastic preacher, often for two hours on end. d. 1311. c.c. 1833. *Jordanus.*
March 6, i, 505.

JORDAN OF SAXONY, BD
He joined St Dominic in 1220, and at the third general chapter of his order was elected second master general. His time of office saw a great extension of the order. Jordan was an eloquent preacher (a sermon of his attracted Albert the Great to the Dominicans) and his words were such that their effect did not wear off. He was drowned while on the way to Palestine in 1237. c.c. 1828. *February 15, i, 343.*

*JOSAPHAT, ST,
BISHOP AND MARTYR
Josaphat Kuntsevich was b. at Vladimir *c.* 1582. He became a monk of the Byzantine rite and abbot of Vilna, at the time when the Orthodox dioceses of the province of Kiev were newly reunited with the Holy See. Josaphat's life was devoted to maintaining and spreading this union in the face of acute difficulties from Catholics as well as dissidents. In 1617 he became archbishop of Polotsk, and he added very necessary diocesan reform to his work of unity. His

combination of gentleness and firmness, knowledge and goodness, gained him many followers; but secular interests were against him, a reaction set in, and in 1623 he was murdered by a mob at Vitebsk in White Russia. cd 1867. *November 12, iv, 337.*

JOSAPHAT. *See also under* Barlaam.

JOSEMARIA ESCRIVA DE BALAGUER. *See* Joseph Mary Escrivá de Balaguer.

*JOSEPH, ST
Husband and guardian of the Blessed Virgin Mary, and foster-father of our Lord Jesus Christ. All that is certainly known of this "just man" is contained in chapters i and ii of the gospels of St Matthew and St Luke; but he was doubtless a young man. Devotion to St Joseph is relatively recent, but the instinct for holiness of the Christian folk at large has in the past 400 years raised him to the highest rank of the Church's saints. He has two feasts, on March 19 and on May 1, the latter as patron saint of workmen. *Josephus. March 19, i, 631.*

JOSEPH BALDO, BD
Fr Giuseppe Baldo, b. 1843, was an Italian priest of the Verona diocese, a teacher then a parish priest, who founded the Congregation of Little Daughters of St Joseph, and was active in social work for the poor and marginalized. d. 1915. bd October 31, 1989. *October 24.*

*JOSEPH BARSABAS, ST
The disciple of our Lord who was put in competition with St Matthias to succeed Judas Iscariot in the apostleship; he was probably one of the seventy-two disciples. *Josephus. July 20, iii, 153.*

*JOSEPH CAFASSO, ST
Joseph Cafasso was b. in 1811 in the same town of Piedmont as St John Bosco, whose close friend he became; it was he who persuaded Don Bosco where his vocation really lay. The full and noble life of this secular priest was deficient in external incident, but very full of interest for its selfless devotion to others, notably young

priests, and to the special needs of criminals and convicts. Cafasso's first biography was written by Don Bosco. d. at Turin, 1860. cd 1947. *June 23, ii, 628.*

*JOSEPH CALASANCTIUS, ST

Joseph Calasanz was the son of an Aragonese nobleman, b. in 1556. The first years of his priestly life were spent in pastoral and administrative work in his own country, but in 1592 he went to Rome and remained there, working for the free schooling of poor and neglected children. In face of great difficulties he established a congregation for the purpose, the Clerks Regular of the Religious Schools, or "Piarists". In later life, two of his subordinates caused Joseph to be removed from control of the congregation, until he was restored by a papal commission. Joseph's patience under these trials caused Pope Benedict XIV to refer to him as "a second Job". d. 1648. cd 1767. *August 25, iii, 413.*

*JOSEPH COTTOLENGO, ST

In 1827 Canon Joseph Benedict Cottolengo founded at Turin, without a penny of capital, a small hospital for the poor. It grew, and during the cholera epidemic of 1831 was transferred to the suburb of Valdocco and called the Little House of Divine Providence. It then grew even more quickly and branched into schools, almshouses, refuges, orphanages, asylums, workshops, conducted by several religious institutes which Don Cottolengo inaugurated. It is significant that for this vast and complex organization he kept no books or accounts and invested no money—he spent it as it came in. Today the Cottolengo Charitable Institute, which seeks out the most abandoned and miserable, has branches in several parts of the world. Its founder d. in 1842 and was cd in 1934. *April 29, ii, 191.*

JOSEPH DUSMET, BD, BISHOP

Giuseppe Benedetto Dusmet was b. at Palermo, Sicily, became a Benedictine of San Martino delle Scale and was ordained priest in 1842. He became prior of several monasteries and in 1816 archbishop of Catania; he was consecrated on March 10.

He devoted his life to the poor and suffering and to Benedictine affairs. He was made cardinal in 1888 and d. 1894. bd September 25, 1988. *April 4.*

JOSEPH FREINADEMETZ, BD

He was born on April 15, 1852 at Ojes in the Upper Adige region of the Tyrol. He was ordained priest in 1875 and entered the Society of the Divine Word at Steyl, the Netherlands, in 1878. He was co-founder of a mission at Shantung, China and died at Taikia on January 28, 1908, of typhus caught while caring for the sick. bd October 19, 1975. *March 2.*

JOSEPH GERARD, BD

Joseph Gérard was b. into a peasant family at Bouxières-aux-Chênes, Nancy, France, on March 12, 1831. He took his final vows as an Oblate of Mary the Immaculate in 1852. In 1853 he left France for South Africa, where he was ordained priest in 1854. In 1862 he went to Basutoland (now Lesotho) where he founded several missions, a convent and a school and d. in 1914. bd by Pope John Paul II in Lesotho on September 15, 1988. *May 29.*

JOSEPH LAMBTON, BD, MARTYR

Joseph Lambton (or Lampton) was a secular priest b. at Malton, Yorkshire. He studied at the English College at Rheims, and at the English College at Rome in 1589. He was ordained priest, sent on the English mission and immediately arrested. He was h.d.q. as an unlawful priest at Newcastle-upon-Tyne in 1592 when twenty-four years of age. bd November 22, 1987. *July 27.*

JOSEPH MANYANET Y VIVES, BD

Fr José Manyanet y Vives, b. 1833 in Catalonia, was the Spanish founder of the Congregation of Sons of the Holy Family and of the Institute of Missionary Daughters of the Holy Family of Nazareth. He had a heroic concern for the family and for children. d. 1901. bd November 25, 1984. *December 17.*

JOSEPH MARCHAND, ST, MARTYR

A priest of the Paris Society of Foreign Missions. He was martyred in Indo-China in 1835, his flesh being torn from his body with red-hot tongs. bd 1900. cd June 19, 1988. *November 30, iii, 78.*

JOSEPH MARY ESCRIVA DE BALAGUER, BD

Josemaría Escrivá de Balaguer was a Spanish priest and founder in 1928 of the Opus Dei organization. b. 1902. He was a supporter of General Franco, dictator of Spain. During a very short period, Bd Joseph built up a still-expanding network of bodies and structures, amounting in 1989 to 76,000 members of eighty-seven nationalities, usually drawn from or entering an educational élite. The declared aims of the apostolic work and spirituality of the organization (known as "the Work") are the sanctification of work, self-sanctification in work, and sanctification through work, for Christians in all states of life. News of the forthcoming and actual beatification met with extraordinarily adverse criticism across the world, based mainly on allegations of secretive, power-seeking and extremely right-wing attitudes and methods on the part of Bd Joseph and his well-chosen and carefully nurtured cadres. Many critics have also found the austere self-discipline practised by adepts unpalatable and psychologically suspect. The size and influence of Opus Dei show that many Catholics think otherwise. d. 1975. bd May 1992. *June 26.*

JOSEPH MKASA, ST, MARTYR

The first of the martyrs of Uganda (q.v.). He was beheaded on November 15, 1885, after rebuking King Mwanga for his debauchery and for murdering Protestant missionaries. bd 1920. cd 1964. *June 3, ii, 469.*

JOSEPH MOSCATI, ST

Professor Giuseppe Moscati was born into an aristocratic family at Benevento, Italy, on July 25, 1880. He began his medical career at the hospital for incurables in Naples and in 1908 was appointed to a chair at the Institute of Physiological Chemistry. Alongside scientific research he continued to attend patients in local hospitals free of charge. He died in 1927. Bd Joseph is cited as an exemplary practitioner of both faith and science. bd November 16, 1975. cd October 25, 1987. *November 16.*

JOSEPH NASCIMBENI, BD

Giuseppe Nascimbeni was b. at Torri di Benaco, Italy, on March 22, 1851. He was an exemplary parish priest who founded the Institute of Little Sisters of the Holy Family for pastoral work. d. 1922. bd April 17, 1988. *January 21.*

*JOSEPH ORIOL, ST

This Joseph was the son of humble parents at Barcelona, and was enabled by his parish priest to be ordained. He lived throughout his adult life on bread and water, engaged in the cure of souls: he was especially successful with soldiers and children. At one time he was strongly moved to go on the foreign missions; but while on his way to Rome he fell ill, and had a vision in consequence of which he returned home. St Joseph had the gift of miracle in an eminent degree. d. 1702. cd 1909.
March 23, i, 666.

*JOSEPH PIGNATELLI, ST

In the twenty years that followed the suppression of the Society of Jesus by Pope Clement XIV in 1773, Father Joseph Pignatelli lived at Bologna and devoted himself to studying the history of the order and spiritually and materially aiding its former members. In 1799 he was allowed to organize a quasi-novitiate and continued to work unceasingly for the restoration of the Society; so far as the kingdom of Naples was concerned this took place in 1804, and Father Joseph was named provincial, first of Naples and then of Italy. This priest of "manly and vigorous holiness" d. 1811. cd 1954. *November 28, iv, 442.*

JOSEPH RUBIO Y PERALTO, BD

Fr José María Rubio y Peralto, the "apostle of Madrid", b. 1864, was a Spanish Jesuit who cared for the poor of Madrid. d. 1929. bd October 6, 1985. *May 2.*

JOSEPH SANJURJO, ST, BISHOP AND MARTYR

With another bishop, St Melchior Sampedro, St Joseph, a Spaniard, was the leader of the group of martyrs of Vietnam (Indo-China), of 1857–62, beatified in 1951, some of the 117 canonized in 1988. The other twenty-three martyrs of this group were Tonkingese, nineteen of them lay people. cd June 19, 1988. *November 6, iv, 285.*

JOSEPH TOMMASI, ST

Born 1649, son of the duke of Palermo, and became a Theatine clerk regular. In 1673 he was called to Rome, where he soon won the reputation of a saint and also of a very fine scholar. His liturgical writings show him to have been a man of profound learning, critical spirit and independence of judgement. He was the confessor of Cardinal Albani and required his penitent to accept the papacy under pain of sin, and Clement XI, in his turn, imposed the cardinalate on Joseph Tommasi (properly *Tomasi*). In his titular church of San Martino ai Monti he would allow no music but plainchant, and would himself conduct the catechism classes there. Miracles are said to have taken place even before his death in 1713. bd 1803. cd 1986. *January 1, i, 15*

JOSEPH OF ANCHIETA, BD

José de Anchieta, the "apostle of Brazil", was b. March 19, 1534 at San Cristobal de la Laguna, Tenerife, Canary Islands. He became a Jesuit in 1551 and in 1553 went to Brazil as a missionary to the "Indios", whom he tried to defend against the colonists. He was ordained priest in 1566, was a religious superior and wrote catechetical and other works. He d. in 1597. bd June 22, 1980. *June 9.*

*JOSEPH OF ARIMATHEA, ST

All that is known about Joseph of Arimathea is to be found in the gospels in connection with our Lord's passion and burial. But he has been the subject of numerous legends: that which makes him the founder of the church of Glastonbury is of special interest in Great Britain, but there is not a shred of truth in the story. *March 17, i, 617.*

*JOSEPH OF CUPERTINO, ST

Joseph Desa was b. in 1603, and after some difficulty (as a youth he was not "bright") was received by the Conventual Franciscans as a lay tertiary servant; in 1625 he was admitted to the novitiate, and in due course professed and ordained. From this time onward St Joseph's life was one long succession of ecstasies, miracles of healing, and supernatural happenings on a scale not paralleled in the reasonably authenticated biography of any other saint. For example, during the seventeen years he was at the friary of Grottella, in southern Italy, over seventy occasions of levitation are recorded, and he is the classical example of this class of phenomenon. These manifestations were troublesome to some members of his order and during the later years of his life St Joseph was subjected to very severe treatment. He bore it with patience, increased his remarkable physical mortifications, and d. peacefully in 1663. cd 1767. *September 18, iii, 587.*

*JOSEPH OF LEONESSA, ST

Born in 1556 and professed as a Capuchin at Leonessa in Italy in 1574. He was sent on the mission in Turkey, where he ministered to the galley slaves, reconciled apostates to Islam, and was imprisoned and tortured for preaching the Gospel to the Moslems. He d. after an operation for cancer, 1612. cd 1745. *February 4, i, 253.*

*JOSEPH OF PALESTINE, ST

He was a well-known Jew of the biblical school at Tiberias, who became a Christian. The emperor Constantine gave him the rank of *comes*, "count", with authority to build churches in Galilee; this Joseph did, in the face of much opposition. Eventually he retired to Scythopolis, where he sheltered St Eusebius of Vercelli and other refugees from the Arians. d. *c.* 356. *July 22, iii, 163.*

JOSEPHA GIRBES, BD, VIRGIN

Josefa Naval Girbes was b. December 11, 1820 at Algemesi, Spain. She took a personal vow of chastity when eighteen. To provide instruction for girls and young women she started an embroidery workroom in her home and was an enthusiastic

auxiliary among the women of her parish. d. 1893. bd September 25, 1988.
February 24.

*JOSEPHA ROSSELLO, ST, VIRGIN

Foundress of the Daughters of our Lady of Mercy. She was b. in Italy in 1811, and for a time was in the service of an invalid. In 1837 she began a religious congregation in Savona to undertake works of mercy, notably rescue-homes for young women. St Josepha was one of those saints whose grandeur of soul was combined with a complete simplicity of outlook, and she carried on the arduous work of her successful foundation very quietly and very efficiently. d. 1880. cd 1949.
December 7, iv, 516.

JOSEPHA OF BENIGANIM, BD, VIRGIN

Born near Valencia in 1625 and became an Augustinian hermitess at Beniganim. Her name in religion was Josepha Maria, but in Spain she is called Inés. d. 1696. bd 1888.
January 21, i, 142.

JOSEPHINE BAKHITA, BD, VIRGIN

Mother Josephine Bakhita, a Sudanese nun, was the first Sudanese to be beatified. She was a former slave. After years of repression and humiliation, she entered the service of the Italian consul, her fifth owner, and became a governess to his daughter. In Italy she came into contact with the Canossian Daughters of Charity, and later joined the order. She was beatified by John Paul II on May 17, 1992 as a witness to evangelical reconciliation and forgiveness. *May 17.*

JOSSE. *See* Judoc.

JOVITA. *See* Faustinus.

JUDAS QUIRIACUS. *See* Cyriacus.

JUDE. *See* Simon and Jude.

JUDICAËL, ST

Judicaël, ruler of Brittany, was venerated in that country as a national hero and a holy man. He harried the Franks, until St Eligius

brought about a treaty with him, and in his old age retired to the monastery of Gaël, near Vannes. d. c. 660.
December 17, iv, 550.

JUDITH. *See* Jutta *and under* Salome.

*JUDOC, ST

Judoc, or Josse, was the younger brother of St Judicaël. In his later years he became a hermit at what is now Saint-Josse-sur-Mer. d. 668. St Judoc is named in several English medieval calendars and his relics are said to have been translated to Hyde Abbey at Winchester. *Judocus.*
December 13, iv, 550.

*JULIA, ST, VIRGIN AND MARTYR

She was put to death in Corsica, probably by Saracen marauders in the sixth or seventh century. Her legend is highly embellished. *May 22, ii, 367.*

JULIA BILLIART, ST, VIRGIN

Marie Rose Julie Billiart was the daughter of a peasant farmer in Picardy. She showed signs of unusual virtue at an early age, particularly by the patience with which she bore a nervous malady. After the Revolution she went to Amiens, where she laid the foundations of the Institute of Notre Dame for the education of girls and the training of religious teachers (the Sisters of Notre Dame de Namur). In 1804 St Julia was suddenly cured of her illness and the establishment of her congregation went on apace, spreading to Ghent, Namur and Tournai; for a time it was set back by the bad behaviour of a young priest, but Mother Julia was vindicated, and she spent the last seven years of her life in still further extending her foundation. d. 1816. bd 1906. "Mother Julia", said the bishop of Namur, "is one of those people who can do more for the Church of God in a few years than others can do in a century." cd 1969.
April 8, ii, 56.

JULIA OF CERTALDO, BD, VIRGIN

Julia was a domestic servant who, at the age of eighteen in 1337, joined the Augustinian third order at Florence. Then she returned to her home at Certaldo and lived as an ankress in a cell adjoining a church. d. 1367. c.c. 1819. *February, 15, i, 345.*

*JULIAN, ST, MARTYR

With his wife Basilissa he converted his house into a hospital (so that he has been confused with Julian the Hospitaller) and was eventually a martyr with others (304?); Basilissa d. in peace. The historical existence of this couple is very doubtful. *Julianus. January 9, i, 56.*

*JULIAN, CRONION AND BESAS, SS, MARTYRS

Three martyrs at Alexandria in 250; Julian was so gouty that he could not walk and Cronion was one of his bearers; Besas, a sympathetic soldier, was killed by the mob. *February 27, i, 431.*

JULIAN MAUNOIR, BD

Julian Maunoir, born near Rennes in 1605, was outstanding among those missioners who brought new life to the Christianity of Brittany during the seventeenth century. His methods were striking and full of enterprise, and were not looked on with favour by everybody—but the bishops backed him (Brémond uses the English word "revival" when writing of these missions). Maunoir, who was a Jesuit, devoted his whole life to the Bretons, "working and weeping, suffering and dying" for them. d. at Plévin, 1683. bd 1951. *January 28, i, 193.*

*JULIAN SABAS, ST

A Mesopotamian solitary who went to Antioch to refute a false charge of Arianism, and preached with great effect in that city. d. 377. *January 17, i, 110.*

*JULIAN OF ANTIOCH, ST, MARTYR

The panegyric preached on him by St John Chrysostom suggests that this martyr was the most important of the many named Julian. He suffered at Anazarbus in Cilicia, and his body was afterwards enshrined in a basilica at Antioch. Date unknown. *March 16, i, 604.*

*JULIAN OF BRIOUDE, ST, MARTYR

Or "of Auvergne". Julian was one of the most famous martyrs of Gaul, but the existing account of him is of little value. Third century (?). *August 28, iii, 434.*

*JULIAN OF LE MANS, ST, BISHOP

Venerated as the first bishop of Le Mans, but nothing is now known of him. His feast was kept throughout the south of England in the Middle Ages, perhaps because King Henry II was born at Le Mans. *January 27, i, 183.*

JULIAN OF NORWICH, BD, VIRGIN

The title Blessed is sometimes given to Dame Julian, who was a recluse at Norwich and d. with a great reputation for holiness *c.* 1423. The book in which she narrates her visions, *Revelations of Divine Love*, is the tenderest and most beautiful exposition in the English language of God's loving dealings with man. *May 13, ii, 301.*

*JULIAN OF TOLEDO, ST, BISHOP

Julian, archbishop of Toledo, was a person of very great civil and ecclesiastical power in the Spain of his day, and was the first bishop to exercise a primacy over the whole country. He was a voluminous writer, and he revised the Mozarabic liturgy. It is said that Julian was a Jew by descent, and he encouraged the sovereigns to revive the laws against the Jews. d. 690. *March 8, i, 524.*

JULIAN OF VALLE, BD

Three feasts are held annually at Valle in Istria in honour of this Franciscan, but beyond the fact that he was a local man, and must have died early in the fourteenth century, nothing is known about him. c.c. 1910. *May 11.*

JULIAN OF ST AUGUSTINE, BD

A tailor's apprentice at Medinaceli, in Castile, who became a Franciscan lay-brother. His extraordinary devotions and strange austerities at first gave the impression that he was mad and he was twice turned away from the order. Eventually he became an eloquent and popular preacher. d. 1606. bd 1825. *May 14, ii, 55.*

JULIAN THE HOSPITALLER, ST

According to an old but fictitious legend, St Julian in error slew his own parents and as penance built a hospice by a river where he tended the poor and rowed travellers across. In consequence many hospitals were dedicated in his honour, and he was looked on as a patron of innkeepers, travellers and boatmen. There has been a good deal of confusion between this Julian and others of the same name. *February 12, i, 314.*

JULIAN. *See also under* Theodulus.

*JULIANA, ST, VIRGIN AND MARTYR

Apparently she was martyred in the neighbourhood of Naples, perhaps at Cumae in 305, but nothing certain is known. *February 16, i, 349.*

*JULIANA FALCONIERI, ST, VIRGIN

Juliana was b. in 1270 at Florence and followed her uncle, St Alexis Falconieri, into the Order of Servites, becoming a tertiary and still living at home. In 1304 she established a community, the sisters working in a hospital, and St Juliana is honoured as the foundress of all women religious of the Servite Order, of whom the tertiaries are known as "Mantellate". The collect of her feast refers to the miraculous holy communion said to have been granted to her on her death-bed. d. 1341. cd 1737. *June 19, ii, 581.*

JULIANA OF MOUNT CORNILLON, BD, VIRGIN

Juliana was a nun of Cornillon, near Liège, and to her more than anybody else the institution of the feast of Corpus Christi is due. Her suggestion met with opposition, but the feast was formally adopted in the diocese of Liège in 1246. But Juliana was driven from her convent on a false charge, and she finally became a recluse at Fosse. d. 1258. c.c. 1869. *April 5, ii, 37.*

*JULITTA, ST, MARTYR

She was a wealthy woman of Caesarea in Cappadocia, who was denounced as a Christian by a man who coveted her property. She was sentenced to be burnt, walked into the flames, and was choked by the smoke, *c.* 303. *July 30, iii, 213.*

JULITTA. *See also under* Quiricus

*JULIUS, I, ST, POPE

Julius I, a Roman, became pope in 337. Three years later he held a synod against the Arians, his subsequent letter to the opponents of St Athanasius being, in the word of Mgr Batiffol, "a model of weightiness, wisdom and charity". St Julius built several churches in Rome. d. 352. *April 12, ii, 76.*

*JULIUS AND AARON, SS, MARTYRS

According to Gildas they were martyrs for Christ in Britain, he conjectures during the persecution of Diocletian. The place was traditionally Caerleon-upon-Usk. Their feast is observed in the archdiocese of Cardiff. *July 3, iii, 11.*

JULIUS RÈCHE, BD

Jules Rèche, or Brother Arnold, was b. at Landroff, Lorraine, in 1838. He worked from the age of ten to help his family. In 1862 he joined the Brothers of the Christian Schools, taught at Rheims from 1863 to 1877, then became novice-master. He d. in 1890 when fifty-two. bd November 1, 1987. *October 23.*

*JULIUS OF DUROSTORUM, ST, MARTYR

He was a veteran soldier of the Roman army who was put to death for professing Christianity at Durostorum (Silistria in Bulgaria), *c.* 302 (?). Other members of his legion suffered about the same time. *May 27, ii, 405.*

JUNIPER SERRA, BD

Junipero Serra was b. on November 24, 1713 on Majorca, Spain. He became a Franciscan in 1730 and was ordained priest in 1737. After teaching for a time, in 1749 he went to America. He was a missionary to the Indians of Texas and Mexico, then worked on the Californian mission. d. 1784. bd September 25, 1988. *August 28.*

*JUSTA AND RUFINA, SS,
VIRGINS AND MARTYRS

Martyrs in 287 (?) at Seville in Spain, where they are greatly venerated. In the course of ages one of them seems to have undergone a change of sex, for Justa was originally called Justus. *July 19, iii, 144.*

*JUSTIN, ST, MARTYR

St Justin, called "the Philosopher", was b. at Nablus in Palestine of pagan parents. He became a Christian when about thirty years old as a result of reading the Scriptures and observing the fortitude of the martyrs. He had deeply studied the philosophies of Greece and became the first notable Christian apologist, both to the Jews and the heathen; certain of his writings are extant. He was martyred in Rome, by beheading, *c.* 165. *Justinus. June 1, ii, 88.*

JUSTIN DE JACOBIS, ST, BISHOP

St Justin was born in 1800, brought up in Naples, and joined the Congregation of the Mission (Vincentians), being sent to Ethiopia in 1839. He handled a difficult charge with sensitive tact, and in 1848 was consecrated bishop as vicar apostolic at Guala; he narrowly escaped the martyrdom that overtook his fellow worker, Bd Gabra Michael. Cardinal Massaia wrote of St Justin that "God chose him to be a teacher even more by example than by words . . . , a great example of human perfection grounded on humbleness". d. by the roadside near Halai, 1860. bd 1939. cd 1975. *July 31, iii, 230.*

JUSTIN RANFER, ST, MARTYR

Just Ranfer de Bretennières was born on February 118, 1838 at Chalon-sur-Saone. He entered the Paris Foreign Missions in 1861, was ordained priest in 1864, arrived in Korea on May 27, 1865, and after his arrest on February 26 was beheaded on March 8, 1866. bd 1968. cd by John Paul II at Seoul in 1984. *March 8.*

*JUSTINA, ST, VIRGIN AND MARTYR

She was martyred at Padua, perhaps during the persecution of Diocletian; a medieval forgery associates her with St Prosdocimus, "a disciple of the blessed Peter". *October 7, iv, 51.*

JUSTINA OF AREZZO, BD, VIRGIN

A Benedictine nun of Arezzo who became a recluse at Civitella. Miracles of healing were attributed to her. d. 1319. c.c. 1890. *March 12, i, 578.*

*JUSTUS AND PASTOR, SS, MARTYRS

Prudentius numbers these two among the most glorious martyrs of Spain: they suffered at Alcalà in 304. *August 6, iii, 270.*

*JUSTUS OF BEAUVAIS, ST, MARTYR

Justus is said to have been put to death for Christ at Beauvais when a boy; he was formerly famous all over north-western Europe, but the extension of his *cultus* was in some measure due to confusion with other saints of the same name. His legend as it has come down to us is fabulous. *October 18, iv, 143.*

*JUSTUS OF CANTERBURY, ST,
BISHOP

Justus was appointed by St Augustine to be the first bishop of Rochester, and in 624 he became archbishop of Canterbury. Pope Boniface V, in sending Justus the *pallium*, wrote commending his work. d. *c.* 627. His feast is observed in the diocese of Southwark. *November 10, iv, 309.*

*JUSTUS OF LYONS, ST, BISHOP

As bishop of Lyons he assisted at the Synod of Aquilcia against the Arians, where he gained the respect of St Ambrose. He did not return to his see, but retired to Egypt, where he d. *c.* 390. *October 14, iv, 108.*

*JUSTUS OF URGEL, ST, BISHOP

The first recorded bishop of Urgel in Spain; he wrote a treatise on the *Song of Songs*. d. *c.* 550. *May 28, ii, 409.*

JUTTA, ST

The life of St Jutta (Judith) bears a resemblance to that of St Elizabeth of Hungary. Jutta was a Thuringian of noble family whose husband d. while on a pilgrimage to the Holy Land; after all her children had been provided for she became a poor pilgrim and wandered into Prussia, where she settled as a solitary near Kulmsee. She lived here four years till her death in 1260; many miracles were recorded at her grave. *May 5, ii, 239.*

JUTTA OF DIESSENBERG, BD,
VIRGIN

Jutta was the recluse who brought up St Hildegard, who said of her that she "overflowed with the grace of God like a river fed by many streams". She formed her followers into a community under the Rule of St Benedict. d. 1136. *December 22, iv, 597.*

JUTTA OF HUY, BD

Jutta (Juetta) was left a widow when she was eighteen. For ten years she nursed the sick in the lazar-house of her native Huy, near Liège, and then became an ankress in a cell close by. Here she lived forty years till her death in 1228. She was an influential mystic, and by her prayers converted her father and son to better living. *January 13, i, 76.*

JUVENAL ANCINA, BD, BISHOP

Born at Fossano in 1545. He was professor of medicine at the University of Turin and went to Rome as the physician of the Savoyard ambassador in 1575. Three years later he joined the congregation of the Oratory, was ordained, and sent to Naples, where he was soon respected and loved by the whole city. Juvenal was torn between desire for cloistered life and for active work among the poor; he disappeared for five months for fear he would be made a bishop, and eventually, in 1602, he was, of Saluzzo in Piedmont. On returning from his first episcopal visitation, which was marked by miracles, Bd Juvenal was poisoned by a friar whose evil life he had rebuked, in 1604. bd 1869. *Juvenalis.* *August 31, iii, 453.*

*JUVENAL OF NARNI, ST, BISHOP

He is venerated as the first bishop of Narni, but he has been confused with other bishops of the same name and little reliable information is available about him. d. *c.* 376. *May 3, ii, 224.*

*JUVENTINUS, ST, MARTYR

With St Maximinus, he was an officer in the army of Julian the Apostate. For criticizing the laws against Christians and refusing to sacrifice to idols they were beheaded at Antioch in 363. *January 25, i, 164.*

K

KATERI TEKAKWITHA, BD, VIRGIN

The "Lily of the Mohawks" was b. the daughter of a Mohawk chief and a Christian mother at Ossernenon, N.Y. in 1656. She was baptized by a Jesuit in 1676 and moved to a Christian village. She cared for the sick and aged and took a vow of perpetual virginity. d. 1680. bd June 22, 1980. *March 25.*

KATHERINE *See* Catherine.

KENELM, ST, MARTYR

Kenelm was said to have succeeded to the crown of Mercia at the age of seven and to have been killed by order of his ambitious sister. He is an historical character, but little is known of him except that he lived to adulthood. d. *c.* 815 (?). There was considerable *cultus* of Kenelm in the past (his shrine was at Winchcombe) and he is still commemorated in the dioceses of Birmingham and Clifton. *Kenelmus. July 17, iii, 127.*

KENNETH. *See* Canice.

KENNOCH, ST, VIRGIN

The life of this Scottish maiden is wrapped in obscurity and there is some doubt if she ever existed. *March 13, iv, 583.*

KENTIGERN, ST, BISHOP

Otherwise *Mungo* = "darling". According to Scottish tradition he became the leader of a small community at Glasgow and was consecrated bishop there, the first. He had a very disturbed life, and on one occasion had to flee into Wales. Many extravagant miracles are related of Kentigern, one of which is perpetuated in the ring and fish on the arms of the city of Glasgow. d. 603. His feast is kept throughout Scotland and in the dioceses of Liverpool, Lancaster, Salford and Menevia. *Kentigernus.*
January 14, i, 83.

KENTIGERNA, ST

Mother of St Fillan. When her husband d. she went from Ireland to Scotland, and lived as a hermitess on an island in Loch Lomond, where a church bears her name. d. 734. *January 7, i, 120.*

KESSOG, ST, BISHOP

Kessog, or Mackessog, was an Irish missionary bishop in Scotland. There is great uncertainty about his life and death (according to one account he was martyred at Bandry), but he certainly was venerated in Scotland in earlier ages. Sixth century. *March 10, i, 546.*

KEVIN, ST, ABBOT

Kevin or Coemgen was one of the great sixth-century saints of Ireland and founder of the famous monastery of Glendalough. How much fact underlies the legends that compose his extant biographies is uncertain. He is said to have been a Leinster man; remarkable miracles are recorded of him, and his soul-friend was St Kieran of Clonmacnois. St Kevin's feast is observed throughout Ireland. *Coemgenus.*
June 3, ii, 463.

KEYNE, ST, VIRGIN

St Keyne's *cultus* was well known in parts of South Wales and the west of England (her holy well is near Liskeard in Cornwall), but it is difficult to find out anything authentic about her. She is said to have been a daughter of Brychan of Brecknock and to have occupied a hermitage at Keynsham in Somerset, during the sixth (?) century. She is commemorated in the diocese of Clifton. *Keyna. October 8, iv, 63.*

*KIERAN OF CLONMACNOIS, ST, ABBOT

This Kieran (*Ciaran*) sometimes called "the Younger", was b. in Connacht. He went to the monastic school at Clonard, and then lived for some time with St Enda on Inishmore. In consequence of a vision Kieran left the Arans, wandered across Ireland, and eventually founded the monastery of Clonmacnois. The biographies of St Kieran speak much of his virtues and the miracles to which they gave rise. He apparently ruled Clonmacnois for only a short time, and d. *c.* 556 (?). His feast is kept throughout Ireland. *Queranus. September 9, iii, 513.*

KIERAN OF OSSORY, ST, BISHOP

Also called "of Saighir". Very conflicting accounts of this Kieran appear in the various "lives". He was probably one of the twelve whom St Patrick consecrated to the episcopate, and he is venerated as the first bishop in Ossory and founder of the monastery of Saighir. He was probably not the same as the Cornish St Piran. d. *c.* 530 (?). His feast is kept throughout Ireland. *Kiaranus. March 5, i, 487.*

*KILIAN, ST, BISHOP AND MARTYR

Kilian, with Colman, Totnan and others, were Irish missionaries sent from Rome to preach the gospel in Franconia, where they were martyred *c.* 689. St Kilian's feast is kept throughout Ireland. *Chilianus. July 8, iii, 40.*

KILIAN OF AUBIGNY, ST

This Kilian, a relative of St Fiacre, was a missionary in Artois during the seventh century. *November 13, iv, 330.*

KIZITO, ST, MARTYR

A thirteen-year-old "page", the youngest of the Uganda martyrs (q.v.). He went to his death "laughing as merrily" at his bonds "as if it were a game". bd 1920. cd 1964. *June 3, ii, 468.*

KOREA, THE 103 MARTYRS OF

The first Christian community in Korea was established entirely by laymen after the Koreans sent a representative for baptism in Peking in 1784.

At the end of the eighteenth century the nascent Christianity in Korea came under persecution. The years 1791, 1801, 1827, 1839, 1846 and 1866 were especially marked by cruel persecutions.

In 1801 there were more than 300 martyrs and for twenty-four years from 1802 a decree confirmed in 1839 and 1866 subjected Catholics to the death sentence; it was withdrawn only in 1882. 2,000 Christians are thought to have died in September 1866 alone, and 8,000 in 1870. Twenty-four martyrs were beatified on October 6, 1968: Simeon (Siméon) Berneux, bishop and vicar apostolic of Korea, fifty-two years of age; Antony (Antoine) Daveluy, bishop and vicar apostolic of Korea, forty-eight; Justus (Just) de Bretenières, twenty-eight; Louis Beaulieu, twenty-seven; Peter (Pierre-Henri) Dorie, twenty-seven; Peter (Pierre) Aumaitre, twenty-nine); Martin Luke (Luc) Huin, thirty: all priests of the French foreign missions based in Paris. The lay-people were: Peter (Pierre) Ryou Cheng-Noui, *c.* fifty; John Baptist (Jean-Baptiste) Nam Chong-Sam, fifty-four; Peter (Pierre) Choi Chi-Cheng, fifty-seven; John Baptist (Jean-Baptiste) Cheng Tsiung-Yen, fifty-five; Mark (Marc) Cheng, seventy-three; Alexis Yu Syei-Hpil, nineteen; Luke (Luc) Hoang Chai-Ken, fifty-two; Joseph Chang Nak-Su, sixty-four; Thomas Son Cha-Syen, thirty; Peter (Pierre) Cho Hoa-Sye, forty; Joseph Cho Yung-o, seventeen; Peter (Pierre) Ni Myeng-Sye, *c.* fifty; Bartholomew (Barthélemy) Cheng Mung-ho, *c.* sixty-five); Peter (Pierre) Son Syeng-Chi, *c.* forty-seven; Joseph Han Wen-Ye, *c.* thirty-eight; Peter (Pierre) Chen Wen-Chi, *c.* twenty-one; John (Jean) Ni Yung-il, *c.* forty-five.

SS Andrew Kim Taegon, Paul Chong Hasang and their 101 martyr companions are illustrious examples from among the some 10,000 Christians martyred in the history of Korean Christianity. They included three bishops and seven priests of the French missions to Korea: Mgrs Laurence Imbert, Simeon Berneux and Antony Daveluy, and Frs Peter Maubant, James Chastan, Justin Ranfer, Peter Dorie, Louis Beaulieu, Martin Luke Huin and Peter Aumaitre.

The martyrs ranged from young Peter Yu, thirteen, to Mark Chong, seventy-two, and included men and women, clergy and laity, rich and poor, peasants and aristocrats. John Paul II canonized the 103 martyrs in Seoul Cathedral on May 6, 1984. *October 6.*

KURIAKOSE CHAVARA, BD
Fr Kuriakose Elias Chavara, b. 1805, was the first Indian *beatus*. He was ordained priest in 1829 and in 1831 founded the Carmelite Order of Mary Immaculate. The order is affiliated to the Discalced Carmelites as a third order and now has more than 1,500 members. In 1866 he founded the women's Congregation, which now comprises more than 4,700 members. d. 1871. bd February 8, 1986, in Kerala. *February 8.*

L

*LADISLAUS, ST

Ladislaus I, king of Hungary, extended the borders of his state, kept its enemies at bay, made it politically great, ushered in an era of peace, and fostered Christianity in his dominions—in fact, was the complete national hero. He became king in 1077, and allied himself by marriage with Rupert of Swabia against the emperor, Henry IV. He gave full liberty to Jews and Muslims, refused to recognize political suzerainty in the Holy See, and was chosen commander-in-chief of the First Crusade. But he d. before it set out, in 1095. In Magyar he is called *Laszlo*. *June 27, ii, 654.*

LADISLAUS OF GIELNIOW, BD

Born in 1440, became an Observant Franciscan at Warsaw, and as minister provincial sent friars to evangelize Lithuania. He himself preached with much effect in every part of Poland. The flooding of the Pruth and Dniester and the consequent overthrow of the Tartars and Turks in 1498 were attributed by the Poles to the prayers of Bd Ladislaus. d. 1505. bd 1586. *May 21, ii, 276.*

*LAETUS, ST, BISHOP AND MARTYR

Laetus, bishop of Leptis Minor, was burned alive *c.* 484, one of the first victims of the Vandal Huneric. There are commemorated with him St Donatian and other African bishops, who were driven into the desert and left there to die. *September 6, iii, 496.*

*LAMBERT OF LYONS, ST, BISHOP

Abbot of Fontenelle and then bishop of Lyons; d. 688. *Lambertus.* *April 14, ii, 91.*

*LAMBERT OF MAESTRICHT, ST, BISHOP AND MARTYR

Lambert (*Landebertus*) became bishop of Maestricht *c.* 668, but in 674 was exiled from his see for seven years by the tyrannical Ebroin. On his return he was active in evangelizing the heathen of the Low Countries. Lambert was murdered *c.* 705. There is some uncertainty about the circumstances leading to his death, but he has been ever since venerated as a martyr. *September 17, iii, 579.*

LAMBERT OF VENCE, ST, BISHOP

A monk of Lérins who became bishop of Vence in 1114. d. 1154. *May 26, ii, 400.*

*LANDELINUS, ST, ABBOT

Born *c.* 625 near Bapaume. As founder of the great abbeys of Lobbes and Crespin and of two lesser houses, St Landelinus was held in much honour, but very little is known of his life. d. *c.* 686. *June 15, ii, 547.*

LANDERICUS OF PARIS, ST, BISHOP

In French *Landry*. He became bishop of Paris in 650 and is said to have established the first real hospital in that city, later famous as the Hôtel-Dieu. d. *c.* 660. *June 10, ii, 518.*

*LANDOALD, ST

A Roman priest, missionary in the country of Maestricht, who founded the church at Wintershoven. His servant Adrian, who was murdered by robbers while carrying alms to his master, was venerated as a martyr. d. *c.* 668. *Landoaldus. March 19, i, 634.*

LANFRANC OF CANTERBURY, BD,
BISHOP

Archbishop of Canterbury from 1070 to 1089. This great ecclesiastical statesman is commonly called "Blessed", but there seems to have been no public *cultus.*
May 24, ii, 383.

LANFRANC OF PAVIA, BD, BISHOP

His fifteen years of episcopate at Pavia were troubled by the attempts of the civil authorities to lay hands on ecclesiastical property. At length he decided to resign and join the Vallombrosan monks, but he d. first, in 1194. *June 23, ii, 622.*

LANVINUS, BD

A Carthusian monk who accompanied St Bruno to Calabria and succeeded him in the rule of the two Italian charterhouses; he was appointed visitor apostolic of all monastic houses in Calabria. d. 1120. c.c. 1893. *April 14, ii, 92.*

LARGUS. *See under* Cyriacus.

LASERIAN, ST, BISHOP

Otherwise *Laisren, Molaisse* and (probably) *Lamliss.* He is said to have twice visited Rome and to have practically settled the dispute about the date of Easter in the south of Ireland, where he always upheld the Roman observance. d. 639. His feast is kept throughout Ireland as bishop at Leighlin. *Laserianus. April 18, ii, 121.*

LAURA VICUNA, BD

She was b. at Santiago de Chile on April 5, 1891. Her father d. and the family fled before the revolutionaries and went to the south. Her mother left for the Argentine. Laura told the Sisters of Mary the Helper, where she was at school, that she wanted to join the order founded by Don Bosco. She told her mother that she had offered her life for her conversion. She d. at the age of thirteen in 1904. bd September 3, 1988. *January 22.*

*LAURENCE, ST, MARTYR

There are few martyrs whose names are so famous as that of St Laurence, who was one of the seven deacons of Rome under Pope St Sixtus II. He was put to death, according to tradition, by being roasted on a gridiron, three days after that pope was executed in 258. He was buried on the Via Tiburtina, where is now the fifth patriarchal basilica, of St Laurence-outside-the-Walls, and he is named in the canon of the Mass. *Laurentius. August 10, iii, 297.*

*LAURENCE GIUSTINIANI, ST,
BISHOP

He was one of the Giustiniani of Venice, b. there in 1381. In 1433 he was appointed bishop of Castello, and in 1451 he was translated to the see of Grado, whose archbishop had the title of patriarch; its residence was at the same time transferred to Venice, whence St Laurence is sometimes reckoned the first patriarch of Venice. In public life he was a zealous and generous prelate, in private a mortified and humble priest, who wrote several books on mystical contemplation. d. 1455. cd 1690. *September 5, iii, 489.*

LAURENCE HUMPHREY, BD,
MARTYR

A young lay convert who was h.d.q. at Winchester in 1591 for having spoken disrespectfully of Queen Elizabeth I when ill and in delirium. bd 1929. *July 7, iii, 36.*

LAURENCE IMBERT, ST,
BISHOP AND MARTYR

Laurent Imbert was born at Marignane on May 23, 1796. After being a missionary in China for twelve years, this priest of the Paris Foreign Missions went to Korea as its first vicar apostolic in 1837. He was arrested on August 11, 1839 and martyred by beheading at Seoul on September 21. bd 1925. cd at Seoul by John Paul II in 1984. *September 21, iii, 611.*

LAURENCE LORICATUS, BD

A hermit near Subiaco; he was called Loricatus, "the mailed", because of the coat of mail studded with spikes which he wore next to his skin. d. 1243. c.c. 1778. *August 16, iii, 337.*

LAURENCE MARIA SALVI, BD

Lorenzo Maria Salvi, an Italian Passionist, b. 1782, was particularly concerned with preaching and hearing confessions during retreats and missions among the ordinary people. He had a special devotion to the Child Jesus. d. 1856.
bd October 1, 1989.

LAURENCE NERUCCI, BD, MARTYR

Together with three other Servite friars he was sent from Tuscany to Bohemia to help oppose the Hussites. The monastery in which they stayed at Prague was attacked, and they were burnt to death in the church, together with sixty of their brethren, in 1420, the Servite Martyrs of Prague. c.c. 1918. *August 31, iii, 452.*

*LAURENCE O'TOOLE, ST, BISHOP

Lorcan Ua Tuathail was b. in 1128, probably near Castledermot. He became abbot of Glendalough at the age of twenty-five and archbishop of Dublin eight years later. Laurence did much to spread the canonical life among his clergy, but his reforms were handicapped by the upheavals of the times, in which he had to play an active part as negotiator and peace-maker. In 1179 he went to Rome for the Lateran Council and was appointed papal legate in Ireland; but before he could return he d. at Eu in Normandy, 1180. cd 1225. St Laurence's feast is kept throughout Ireland and by the Canons Regular of the Lateran.
November 14, iv, 341.

LAURENCE RICHARDSON, BD, MARTYR

A secular priest who ministered in Lancashire, and was h.d.q. at Tyburn in 1582.

bd 1929. His real name was Johnson. *May 30, ii, 415.*

LAURENCE RUIZ AND FIFTEEN COMPANIONS, SS, MARTYRS OF JAPAN

Lorenzo Ruiz, the first Filipino saint, was martyred at Nagasaki between 1633 and 1637 with fifteen other Catholics: nine Japanese, one Italian, one Frenchman and four Spaniards. They were beatified at Manila in 1981 and canonized on Mission Sunday, 1987, joining the 231 other Catholics martyred in sixteenth/seventeenth-century Japan who had already been declared saints. St Laurence was b. at Manila to Christian parents, and fled to Japan on July 10, 1636 to escape an unjust charge. He was hanged and decapitated in September 1637. His companions were also executed. The new saints, in addition to St Laurence, are: Spanish Dominican Fr Dominic (Domingo) Ibañez de Erquicia, Japanese Dominican auxiliary Francis Shoyemon: d. August 14, 1633; Japanese Dominican Fr James Kyushei Gorubioye Tomanga, Japanese lay catechist Michael Kurobioye: d. August 17, 1633; Spanish Dominican Fr Luke (Lucas) del Espíritu Santo, Japanese Dominican auxiliary Matthew Kohioye: d. October 19, 1633; Japanese Augustinian tertiary Magdalene of Nagasaki: d. October 15, 1634; Italian Dominican Fr Giordano Ansalone, Japanese Dominican Fr Thomas Hioji Rokuzayemon Nishi, Japanese Dominican tertiary Marina of Omura: d. November 11–17, 1634; Spanish Dominicans Fr Antony (Antonio) González, Fr Michael (Miguel) de Aozoraza, French Dominican Fr William (Guillaume) Courtet, Japanese Dominican Fr Vincent Shiwozuka, Japanese layman Lazaro of Kyoto: d. September 24–29, 1637. cd October 18, 1987.
September 24.

*LAURENCE OF BRINDISI, ST, DOCTOR

He was b. in 1559, became a Capuchin Franciscan, and in his studies showed a marvellous aptitude for languages. With Bd Benedict of Urbino he established the Capuchins in Germany, he preached in several

countries of central Europe, and was for a term minister general of his order. St Laurence was chaplain general to the forces against the Turks, and during the later years of his life he was much in demand among princes as a diplomat; but his religious writings were a more lasting achievement. Named Doctor of the Church by John XXIII. d. 1619. cd 1881.
July 23, iii, 172.

*LAURENCE OF CANTERBURY, ST, BISHOP

One of the monks who accompanied St Augustine to England. After being sent back to Rome to get further instructions from Pope St Gregory he succeeded Augustine as second archbishop of Canterbury. Owing to the activity of King Eadbald in upholding paganism Laurence was tempted to retire to France, but he was rebuked by St Peter in a dream and was successful in winning Eadbald over. d. 619. Feast kept in the dioceses of Westminster and Southwark.
February 3, i, 241.

LAURENCE OF RIPPAFRATTA, BD

Bd Laurence was an able lieutenant of Bd John Dominic in his reforming activities among the Dominicans; he was novice-master at Cortona, where he trained St Antoninus, Bd Fra Angelico and Benedict of Mugello, and was himself an able biblical scholar. d. 1457. c.c. 1851.
September 28, iii, 671.

LAURENCE OF SPOLETO, ST, BISHOP

One of a band who fled from Syria in 514 to escape the persecution of the Monophysite Severus of Antioch. They came to Rome, where Laurence was ordained and sent to preach in Umbria. He was bishop of Spoleto for twenty years, when he founded the abbey of Farfa and retired thereto. He is called "the Enlightener" because of his gift for healing blindness, both physical and spiritual. d. 576. *February 3, i, 240.*

LAURENCE OF VILLAMAGNA, BD

He belonged to the family of Mascoli and was one of the best known Franciscan

preachers of his time. d. 1535. c.c. 1923.
June 9, ii, 491.

LAURENTINUS See Pergentinus.

LAURUS. See Lorus.

*LAZARUS, ST

Nothing at all is known of the life of Lazarus subsequent to his being raised from the dead as narrated in the Gospel of St John, cap. xi. The tradition of the East is that he d. bishop at Kition in Cyprus. His presence and martyrdom at Marseilles is first heard of in the eleventh century; this baseless story seems to have arisen from the existence of a fifth-century bishop of Aix called Lazarus, and the bringing to France from Milan of relics of St Nazarius.
December 17, iv, 576.

*LAZARUS OF MILAN, ST, BISHOP

He was bishop at Milan while the Goths were ravaging Italy; he had much to suffer at their hands, but he ruled his flock faithfully and well. d. *c.* 450.
February 11, i, 304.

*LEANDER, ST, BISHOP

He was brother to St Isidore and St Fulgentius, and preceded the first of these in the see of Seville. Leander was banished after the execution of St Hermenegild by his Arian father, King Leovigild; on his return he was instrumental in retrieving the Visigoths from Arianism, and was responsible for two great synods, at Toledo in 589 and the following year at Seville. He was a close friend of St Gregory the Great, whom he persuaded to write his *Moralia*, but very little of St Leander's own writing has come down to us. d. 596. *February 27, i, 432.*

LEBUIN, ST

Lebuin (*Liafwine*) was a monk of Ripon who went as missionary to Friesland. He founded the church at Deventer, from whence he preached the gospel among the Saxons as well as the Frisians. d. *c.* 773.
November 12, iv, 324.

*LEGER, ST, BISHOP AND MARTYR

He was called from his monastery in Poitou in 663 to be bishop of Autun. In the upheavals that followed the death of King Clotaire II, Leger incurred the enmity first of Childeric II and then of Ebroin; he gave himself up to the troops of the latter rather than bring disaster on his flock, his eyes were put out, and he was interned. In 679 a court of bishops, creatures of Ebroin, pronounced St Leger to be deposed and he was executed secretly. The struggle between St Leger and Ebroin is a famous incident of Merovingian history, but it is not obvious why the bishop should be venerated as a martyr. *Leodegarius. October 2, iv, 9.*

LELIA, ST, VIRGIN

St Lelia (Liadhain?) is specially venerated in Limerick, but nothing is known for certain about her life. Sixth century (?). *August 11, iii, 305.*

*LEO THE GREAT, ST,
POPE AND DOCTOR

The wisdom of Pope Leo I, his defence of the Catholic faith against heresy, and his intervention with Attila the Hun and Genseric the Vandal raised the prestige of the Holy See to great heights and earned him the title of "the Great", which is shared by only two other popes, Gregory I and Nicholas I. He was elected in 440. Theologically his greatest achievement was in respect of Monophysitism: in a letter to St Flavian of Constantinople, he clearly set out the true faith concerning the natures of our Lord, condemning Nestorianism on the one hand and Monophysitism on the other; this, the "Dogmatic Letter" or "Tomos" of St Leo, was acclaimed as the teaching of the Church at the oecumenical council of Chalcedon in 451. Leo's numerous sermons are utilized for lessons in the Divine Office. d. 461. He was declared a doctor of the Church in 1754. *November 10, ii, 67.*

*LEO II, ST, POPE

He was a Sicilian and succeeded to the papal chair in 681. During his short pontificate he confirmed the condemnation, by the third general council of Constantinople, of his predecessor Pope Honorius I for "hedging" when he ought to have denounced outright the monothelite heresy. d. 683. *July 3, iii, 10.*

*LEO III, ST, POPE

He was a Roman, elected to the Holy See in 795, and the story of his pontificate belongs to general ecclesiastical history. Among the acts of Leo III was the coronation of Charlemagne as Holy Roman emperor and a refusal to allow the liturgical innovation of the addition of the word "Filioque" to the Nicene Creed. d. 816. *June 12, ii, 531.*

*LEO IV, ST, POPE

Leo IV became pope in 847 and his relatively short pontificate was a full one. His benefactions to churches take up twenty-eight pages in the *Liber Pontificalis*, he brought the relics of many saints into the City, and enforced clerical discipline. From this pope the Leonine City—the part of Rome including St Peter's and the Vatican—gets its name, he having surrounded it with a wall. d. 855. *July 17, iii, 128.*

*LEO IX, ST, POPE

On the death of Damasus II in 1048 the Alsatian bishop of Toul, Bruno, was elected in his place and took the name of Leo IX. He was greatly concerned for the reform of morals, especially by the suppression of simony, and he condemned the heresy of Berengarius about the Holy Eucharist. Leo was a man of much energy and several times crossed the Alps on ecclesiastical and political missions, but in 1053 he was taken prisoner by the Normans for resisting their ravages in southern Italy. He was released on account of his health, but d. in the following year. He it was who first proposed that the election to the papacy should be entirely in the hands of the cardinals. *April 19, ii, 126.*

LEO AND **PAREGORIUS, SS,**
MARTYRS

After Paregorius had suffered martyrdom at Patara in Lycia, his friend Leo was emboldened publicly to destroy some of the illuminations in the Temple of Fortune. Whereupon he was brought before the governor, sentenced and executed. It is likely that this story is a romance in an historical setting. *February 18, i, 366.*

*LEO OF MANTENAY, ST, ABBOT

In French *Lyé*. Leo passed his whole life at Mantenay, near Troyes, where he was first a monk at the local monastery and then its abbot. d. *c.* 550. *May 25, ii, 390.*

LEO OF SAINT-BERTIN, BD, ABBOT

He was a monk of Anchin who was elected abbot first of Lobbes and then of Saint-Bertin. It was he who, on behalf of Count Thierry, brought back from Jerusalem the alleged relic of our Lord's blood which has ever since been kept in the chapel of St Blaise at Bruges. d. 1163. *February 26, i, 427.*

*LEO OF SENS, ST, BISHOP

He was bishop of Sens, and a vigorous prelate, for he reproved both King Childebert and St Remigius. *April 22.*

*LEOBINUS, ST, BISHOP

Otherwise *Lubin*. He was a peasant lad of Poitiers who became a hermit, priest, abbot of Brou, and finally bishop of Chartres. d. *c.* 558. *March 14, i, 591.*

*LEOCADIA, ST,
VIRGIN AND MARTYR

The *cultus* of St Leocadia at Toledo has a respectable antiquity, but there is little certain known about her. She is said to have died in prison in that city in the persecution of Diocletian. *December 9, iv, 524.*

*LEOCRITIA, ST,
VIRGIN AND MARTYR

A martyr at Cordova under the Moors in 859, at the same time as St Eulogius, who had sheltered her. They were both flogged and beheaded. Also called *Lucretia*. *March 15, i, 597.*

LEODEGARIUS. *See* Leger.

*LEONARD, ST

Little reliance can be put on the late Life of St Leonard, according to which he was a Frankish nobleman, a convert of St Remigius, who formed a religious community at Noblac (now Saint-Léonard), and d. there *c.* 550 (?). There was formerly a *cultus* of this St Leonard in England. *Leonardus*. *November 6, iv, 273.*

LEONARD KIMURA, BD, MARTYR

A Japanese Jesuit lay-brother, burned at Nagasaki in 1619. bd 1867. *November 18, ii, 447.*

LEONARD MURIALDO, ST

Fr Leonardo Murialdo was b. in Turin in 1828 and died in 1900. He founded several homes for orphans and impoverished young workers and established the Pious Society of St Joseph for vocational training and religious education of young people. Their schools and centres spread throughout Italy. For his exemplary work in the social apostolate, Fr Leonard was beatified in 1963 and canonized in 1970. *November 3.*

*LEONARD OF PORT MAURICE, ST

Leonard Casanova was b. at Porto Maurizio on the Italian Riviera in 1676 and joined the strict *Riformati* branch of the Friars Minor. He was both a great missionary preacher and an encourager of the quasi-eremitical element in Franciscan life; to him was due considerable increase in the popularity of certain devotions, notably that of the stations of the cross. St Leonard was sent in 1744 to restore religious and civil order in Corsica, but his success was only ephemeral and his reforms broke down when he left the island. Although he was an unremitting missioner for forty-three years his written works fill many volumes. d. 1751. cd 1867. *November 26, iv, 429.*

LEONARD OF VANDOEUVRE, ST,
ABBOT

He introduced the monastic life into the valley of the Sarthe, where he was abbot of Vandoeuvre (now Saint-Léonard-des-Bois). d. *c.* 570. *October 15, iv, 121.*

*LEONIDES, ST, MARTYR

Leonides was the father of Origen and himself a learned philosopher; he was beheaded for the faith at Alexandria in 202. *April 22, ii, 145.*

LEONTIUS OF ROSTOV, ST, BISHOP AND MARTYR

A Greek monk of Kiev, elected bishop of Rostov *c.* 1051. He d. through ill-treatment by the heathen, *c.* 1077. He is venerated as the first priest martyr of Russia. *May 23, ii, 376.*

*LEOPOLD OF AUSTRIA, ST

Leopold the Good was b. at Melk in 1073 and succeeded his father as margrave of Austria in 1096. He married the imperial princess Agnes, a widow, and they had eighteen children. Leopold reigned successfully for forty years; three of his monastic foundations still exist, Heiligenkreuz (Cistercian), Klosterneuburg (Augustinian canons), and Mariazell (Benedictine). d. 1136. *Leopoldus. November 15, iv, 350.*

LEOPOLD OF GAICHE, BD

A Franciscan of Gaiche in Perugia. From 1768 to 1778 he was papal missioner in the States of the Church, and founded a retreat-house for Friars Minor at Monte Luco, near Spoleto. At Napoleon's invasion he was turned out, although he was seventy-seven years old, but he carried on with his pastoral work. d. 1815. bd 1893. *April 2, ii, 17.*

LEOPOLD MANDIC, ST

Adeodato Mandic (Leopoldo da Castelnovo in religion) was born at Castelnovo on the Dalmatian coast of the Adriatic on May 12, 1866. He left his family to become a Capuchin in 1884, when sixteen. He eventually moved to Padua and led an outwardly uneventful life of heroic service in the confessional. He was a cheerful, modest and patient confessor. He died at Padua on July 30, 1942 and was beatified by Paul VI on May 2, 1976. cd October 16, 1983. *July 30.*

LÉSIN. *See* Licinius.

LESMES. *See* Adelelmus.

LEU. *See* Lupus of Sens.

*LEUTFRIDUS, ST, ABBOT

In French *Leufroy.* After living as a hermit in various places he founded the monastery of La Croix-Saint-Ouen (afterwards Saint-Leufroy), near Évreux, which he ruled for nearly fifty years. d. 738. *June 21, ii, 610.*

LEWINA, ST, VIRGIN AND MARTYR

Lewina is supposed to have suffered martyrdom at the hands of the Saxons in Britain some time before their conversion to Christianity. Nothing is heard of her till 1058, when her relics were translated from Seaford in Sussex to Bergues in Flanders. *July 24, iii, 174.*

LEWIS. *See* Louis.

LIAFWINE. *See* Lebuin.

LIBERATA. *See* Wilgefortis.

*LIBERATUS, ST, ABBOT AND MARTYR

He was abbot of a monastery in North Africa who in 484 was martyred, with six of his monks, for opposing the Arian king Huneric. *August 17, iii, 340.*

LIBERATUS WEISS, BD, MARTYR.
See Samuel Marzorati and his two companions.

LIBERATUS OF LORO, BD

A thirteenth-century confessor of the Friars Minor, whose history is involved in some obscurity: he is said to have been associated with Bd Humilis and Bd Pacificus in a project of stricter observance. c.c. 1868. *September 6, iii, 500.*

LIBERT. *See* Lietbertus.

*LIBORIUS, ST, BISHOP

He was bishop of Le Mans, but nothing is known about his life. Fourth century. *July 23, iii, 169.*

LIBORIUS WAGNER, BD, MARTYR

He was b. at Mülhausen, Germany, on December 5, 1593 into a Lutheran family. He studied at Strasbourg and became a Catholic in 1621–2. He was ordained priest in 1625 and placed in charge of Protestants and Catholics at Altenmünster in the diocese of Würzburg. He was imprisoned and tortured by the Swedish Lutheran army but refused to recant. He was murdered on December 9, 1631 by the son of a Lutheran preacher. When bd by Pope Paul VI on March 24, 1974, he was cited as a model in the cause of unity and ecumenism. *December 9.*

LICINIUS, ST, BISHOP

Or *Lésin.* He was bishop of Angers, and so much beloved that when he wished to resign the clergy and people would not allow it. d. c. 616. *February 13, i, 322.*

LIETBERTUS, ST, BISHOP

Libert or *Liébert.* He came to the see of Cambrai in 1051 and, having failed to reach Jerusalem on pilgrimage, he built a church in honour of the Holy Sepulchre. Lietbertus was once carried off—but rescued—for daring to excommunicate the castellan of Cambrai for some atrocious behaviour. He was a true father to his people. d. 1076. *June 23, ii, 621.*

LIFARD. *See* Liphardus.

LIMNAEUS. *See under* Thalassius.

*LINUS, ST, POPE AND MARTYR

He was the immediate successor of St Peter in the see of Rome and d. *c.* 79. Linus is named among the martyrs in Eucharistic Prayer I, but no persecution of Roman Christians is known to have taken place in his time. *September 23, iii, 623.*

*LIOBA, ST, VIRGIN

In 748 St Lioba, with a number of other nuns from Wimborne, was sent to help St Boniface in Germany. They established their convent at Bischofsheim, where Lioba insisted equally on manual work and studies for all her nuns. She was greatly beloved by St Boniface, and her fame was widespread. d. 780. *September 28, iii, 668.*

*LIPHARDUS, ST, ABBOT

Lifard or *Liéfard.* It is said that he was a man of law at Orleans, who became a monk. With St Urbicius he gradually formed a community, at the place where Meung-sur-Loire now stands. Sixth century. *June 3, ii, 463.*

LIUDHARD, ST, BISHOP

Liudhard came to England as the chaplain of the Frankish princess Bertha when she married King Ethelbert of Kent. He is said to have contributed much to the conversion of Ethelbert and to have d. at Canterbury, where he was buried in the abbey of SS Peter and Paul, *c.* 602. *May 7, ii, 246.*

*LIVINUS, ST, BISHOP AND MARTYR

He is said to have been a missionary bishop from Dublin, martyred near Alost in Brabant in 657, but he is most probably identical with St Lebuin. His feast is kept throughout Ireland. *November 12, iv, 323.*

LOMAN, ST, BISHOP

According to legend Loman was a nephew of St Patrick and went with him to Ireland, but he may belong to a later period. He is associated with the church of Trim. *February 17, i, 356.*

*LOMBARDS, MARTYRS UNDER THE

St Gregory in his *Dialogues* speaks of a number of Christians in Campania who were slain by the Lombards *c.* 579 for refusing idolatrous worship. They are mentioned in the Roman Martyrology. *March 2, i, 457.*

*LONGINUS, ST, MARTYR

This is the name given to the soldier who pierced the side of our Lord on the cross. There are several legends about him and his alleged martyrdom, but the truth about his life is not known. *March 15, i, 594.*

LORUS. *See under* Florus.

LOUIS ALLEMAND, BD, BISHOP

This Louis was made archbishop of Arles in 1423 and cardinal soon after, and played a prominent part in the troubled ecclesiastical affairs of his day. He was a leader of the "conciliarists", took part in the setting up of the antipope Felix "V" by the Council of Basle, and was excommunicated and deprived of the cardinalate by Eugenius IV; he was restored by Nicholas V and, deeply repenting of his schismatic activities, retired to Arles where he administered his diocese with the virtue that had always characterized his private life. d. 1450. c.c. 1527. Louis Allemand is an outstanding example of how the Church in practice and not simply in theory looks so far as possible at the hearts rather than the exterior actions of men. *Ludovicus. September 16, iii, 573.*

LOUIS BEAULIEU, ST, MARTYR

Louis Beaulieu was born at Langon on October 8, 1840. He joined the Paris Foreign Missions in 1863, was ordained priest in 1864, was sent to Korea in 1865, and was arrested on February 27 and beheaded on March 8, 1866. bd 1968. cd by John Paul II at Seoul in 1984. *March 8.*

*LOUIS BERTRAND, ST

He was b. at Valencia in 1526, joined the Dominicans, and was sent to preach the gospel in South America in 1562. He worked in what is now Colombia for seven years, making numerous converts among the Indians both there and in some of the West Indian islands. On his return to Spain St Louis achieved fame as a preacher. d. 1581. cd 1671. *October 9, iv, 72.*

*LOUIS GRIGNION DE MONTFORT, ST

He was b. in 1673 and, after undergoing great hardships, became a secular priest. While chaplain to a hospital at Nantes he laid the foundations of the congregation of Sisters of the Divine Wisdom, but was forced to resign his post. He then became a missionary preacher and again met with much opposition, but he received the approval of the Holy See and carried on with his forceful methods of combating sin.

Shortly before his death Bd Louis founded the first establishment of the Missionary Priests of Mary. He was a great admirer of the Order of Preachers, of which he was a tertiary, and wrote a well-known book on *True Devotion to the Blessed Virgin.* d. 1716. cd 1947. *April 28, ii, 184.*

LOUIS MORBIOLI, BD

He was a young married layman of Bologna who was converted from loose living and became an example to the city, begging on behalf of the poor and teaching Christian doctrine to the young and ignorant. d. 1485. c.c. 1843. *November 16, iv, 359.*

LOUIS MOREAU, BD, BISHOP

Louis-Zéphyrin Moreau was b. in 1824 at Bécancour, Quebec, Canada and was ordained priest in 1846. In 1876 he became the fourth bishop of St-Hyacinthe, where he remained for twenty-five years. d. 1901. bd May 10, 1987. *May 24.*

LOUIS SOTELO, BD, MARTYR

A very able Spanish Franciscan missionary in Japan in the seventeenth century. Burnt alive at Simabura in 1624. bd 1867. *August 31, ii, 450.*

LOUIS VERSIGLIA, BD, BISHOP AND MARTYR

Mgr Luigi Versiglia was born on June 5, 1873 at Oliva Gessi, Pavia, Italy. Don Bosco sent him to study in Turin when he was twelve. He became a Salesian at sixteen. He was ordained in 1895 and was a novice-master for nine years. On January 7, 1906 he joined the first Salesian missionary venture to China, and was based at Macao. He was consecrated in 1921 and went to the south as vicar apostolic of Shiu Chow. He founded schools and seminaries there. In 1930 he embarked on the river Pak-Kong to visit a flock at Lin-Chow but was shot by pirates. d. 1930. bd May 15, 1983. *February 25.*

*LOUIS OF ANJOU, ST, BISHOP

He was b. in 1274, son of Charles II, king of Naples. After being held seven years a hostage in Barcelona, he was ordained priest, made his profession as a Friar Minor, and was consecrated archbishop of Toulouse. He lived to rule his see for only six months, during which time he earned the very greatest respect. d. 1297. cd 1317. *August 19, iii, 357.*

*LOUIS OF FRANCE, ST,

He was b. at Poissy in 1214 and succeeded to the throne of France when he was eleven. King Louis IX was a characteristic example of the good and great medieval layman; indifferent to comfort, humbly devoted to the poor and to religion, the father of eleven children, and a fighting man who admirably governed and consolidated his own kingdom. He defeated King Henry III of England at Taillebourg in 1242 and concluded an honourable treaty with him seventeen years later. Twice St Louis went crusading to the East, intent only on the Holy Places, ignoring political combinations, and achieving nothing: during the first venture he was captured by the Saracens in Egypt, and at the second he met his death, at Tunis, from typhus, in 1270. cd 1297.
August 25, iii, 394.

LOUIS OF THURINGIA, BD

Louis (Ludwig), landgrave of Thuringia, was the beloved husband of St Elizabeth of Hungary. He d. at Otranto while going on the crusade in 1227. His popular *cultus* in Germany has never been officially confirmed, but it seems to be eminently well deserved. *September 11, iii, 541.*

LOUIS. *See also* Aloysius *and* Ludovic.

*LOUISA ALBERTONI, BD

She was b. in Rome in 1473, and was happily married, with three daughters. When her husband died in 1506 she became a Franciscan tertiary and spent all her money on the poor, so that at the last she had herself to be supported by her family. d. 1533. c.c. 1671.
Ludovica. February 28, i, 447.

*LOUISA DE MARILLAC, ST

She was b. in 1591 and married Antony Le Gras, with whom she lived happily till his

death in 1625. Louisa then became the right hand of St Vincent de Paul in the establishment of the Daughters of Charity (now known throughout the world as the Sisters of Charity of St Vincent de Paul), was, indeed, their co-founder with him. She was a woman of clear intelligence, boundless courage, marvellous endurance in spite of poor health, and was always ready to efface herself for the good of the work in hand. d. 1660. cd 1934. *March 15, i, 598.*

LOUISA DE MONTAIGNAC, BD

Louise-Therese de Montaignac de Chauvance, b. May 14, 1820 at Le Havre, France, founded an "association of Christian women" at Montlucon. This became the Pious Union of the Oblates of the Sacred Heart in 1874, Louisa-Teresa was Superior-general and held this elective office until her death in 1885. She also founded the "Samuels" for the formation of young Christians who believed they had a vocation. There are now almost 500 Oblates in community or in secular life in Europe, Africa and Central America. Bd Louisa had a special devotion to the Sacred Heart. bd November 4, 1990. *June 22.*

LOUISA OF SAVOY, BD

She was a daughter of Bd Amadeus IX of Savoy and wife of Hugh of Châlons, with whom she lived happily for nine years. Then Hugh d. and Louisa was admitted to a Poor Clare convent at Orbe, where her life was as gracious as it had been in the world. d. 1503. c.c. 1839. *September 9, iii, 518.*

LOUP. *See* Lupus of Troyes.

LUAN. *See* Moloc.

LUBIN. *See* Leobinus.

LUCHESIO, BD

Luchesio and his wife Bonadonna gave themselves up in middle-age to a life of alms-deeds and penitence, and they are venerated as the first Franciscan tertiaries; but in fact it seems likely that others before

them had received the habit of the third order. d. 1260. c.c. 1694.
April 28, ii, 183.

*LUCIAN AND MARCIAN, SS,
MARTYRS

There was a group of martyrs at Nicomedia in 250 (?) of whom Lucian was one; Marcian and Florus are other names connected with them. Later ages made a fictitious romance out of them.
October 26, iv, 204.

*LUCIAN OF ANTIOCH, ST, MARTYR

Lucian was a scriptural scholar at Edessa, who afterwards went to Antioch and then to Nicomedia, where he was in prison for the faith for nine years under Diocletian, and at length received the crown of martyrdom in 312. *Lucianus. January 7, i, 46.*

*LUCIAN OF BEAUVAIS, ST,
MARTYR

He is alleged to have been a Roman missionary martyred at Beauvais. Date unknown. *January 8, i, 51.*

*LUCILLIAN, ST, MARTYR

A convert in his old age who was crucified at Byzantium in 273, at the same time as four Christian youths were beheaded; Paula, a woman who had looked after them in prison, suffered the same fate. Their story is probably a work of fiction. *Lucillianus. June 3, ii, 461.*

*LUCIUS, ST

According to a story which is not heard of before the sixth century, Lucius was a British "king" who wrote to Pope St Eleutherius (d. *c.* 189) asking him to send missionaries into Britain. Later amplifications embroider the story very considerably and inconsistently. Scholars seem unanimous in the view that the whole story is a fable. A Swiss legend states that Lucius of Britain became an apostle of the Grisons and d. at Chur. *December 3, iv, 481.*

*LUCIUS OF ADRIANOPLE, ST,
BISHOP AND MARTYR

Lucius was twice driven from his see of Adrianople for opposing Arianism, and eventually he was arrested with others for refusing to be in communion with those condemned by the Council of Sardica in 347. St Lucius d. in prison and his lay companions were beheaded, in 350.
February 11, i, 304.

LUCIUS. *See also under* Montanus, Ptolemaeus.

LUCRETIA. *See* Leocritia.

*LUCY, ST, VIRGIN AND MARTYR

Lucy suffered at Syracuse *c.* 304, but all else is only conjecture. The story that a disappointed suitor denounced her as a Christian and that she was exposed in a brothel where she suffered no harm was set out by the English St Aldhelm in prose and verse at the end of the seventh century, but he was relying on spurious *acta.* St Lucy is named in the canon of the Mass. *Lucia. December 13, iv, 548.*

*LUCY FILIPPINI, ST, VIRGIN

Born 1672 in Tuscany. At the request of Cardinal Barbarigo she went to Montefiascone to join Bd Rose Venerini in her work of training schoolmistresses; though not the foundress, St Lucy was the most influential early promoter of the *Maestre Pie* in Italy. In 1707 she was called to Rome by Clement XI to establish the first school of the institute there and greatly endeared herself to the people. d. 1732. cd 1930.
March 25, i, 683.

LUCY DE FREITAS, BD, MARTYR

The Japanese widow of a Portuguese merchant. When over eighty years old she was burnt alive at Nagasaki for sheltering a priest. d. 1622. bd 1867.
September 10, iii, 534.

LUCY OF AMELIA, BD, VIRGIN

The *cultus* of Lucy Bufalari, an Augustinian nun who d. at Amelia in Italy in 1350, was confirmed in 1832. She was a sister of Bd John of Rieti. *July 27, iii, 198.*

LUCY OF CALTAGIRONE, BD, VIRGIN

A Franciscan regular tertiary venerated at Caltagirone in Sicily and at Salerno. d. 1304 (?). c.c. 1514. *September 26, iii, 657.*

LUCY OF NARNI, BD, VIRGIN

Born at Narni in Umbria in 1476. After being released from a nominal marriage, she entered a convent of Dominican regular tertiaries. At Viterbo she received the *stigmata*, and in 1499 went to Ferrara to found a convent there under the patronage of Duke Ercole I. She was an incapable superior, the external difficulties of her task were more than usual, and when her patron died she was deposed. Lucy was treated by the new superior with a severity that was not short of persecution: the "fashionable mystic" became a hidden saint, and the people of Ferrara did not even realize she was still alive. The announcement of her death in 1544 caused an outburst of popular veneration; this *cultus* continued, and was confirmed in 1710. *November 16, iv, 360.*

LUDAN, ST

According to tradition he was an Irish or Scots pilgrim who d. by the wayside in Alsace on his way back from Jerusalem, and was buried near Hispheim in 1202 (?). *February 12, i, 318.*

*LUDGER, ST, BISHOP

Ludger, Liudger, a Frisian, was trained in the abbey school of Utrecht, studied under Alcuin in England, and later at Monte Cassino. He was a missionary in Friesland (including Heligoland) and then in northwest Saxony or Westphalia. He founded a monastery under the regulations of St Chrodegang at Münster, and when consecrated bishop in 804 he settled his see there. Ludger's gentleness, persuasiveness and personal attraction were strikingly successful in reconciling the Saxons, especially when contrasted with the results of Charlemagne's repressive measures. d. 809. *Ludgerus. March 26, i, 686.*

LUDMILA, ST, MARTYR

She was the widow of Borivoy, duke of Bohemia, and was entrusted with the upbringing of the young prince Wenceslaus. It was feared that under her influence he would seize the government of Bohemia during his minority and finally establish Christianity there; Ludmila was accordingly strangled by two of the heathen party, at Tetin in 921. *September 16, iii, 570.*

LUDOLF, ST, BISHOP

A Premonstratensian canon and bishop of Ratzburg, who suffered persecution from Duke Albert of Sachsen-Lauenberg. d. 1250. *Ludolphus. March 30, i, 702.*

LUDOVIC PAVONI, BD

Founder of the Sons of Mary Immaculate of Brescia, where he was b. in 1784. He was ordained priest in 1807, and devoted his whole life to the care and training of boys in his native city; it was to carry on his work that he founded his congregation, only a few years before his death. Don Pavoni was a characteristic example of the remarkable flowering of holiness and humanity in northern Italy during the nineteenth century. d. 1849. bd 1947. *April 1, ii, 7.*

LUDWIG. *See* Louis of Thuringia.

LUFTHILDIS, ST, VIRGIN

She inspired considerable local devotion around Cologne, but nothing certain is known of her life. d. *c.* 850(?). *January 23, i, 157.*

LUGHAIDH. *See* Molua.

*LUKE, ST, EVANGELIST

He was a Greek of Antioch, a physician by profession, and the companion of St Paul during part of his missions and his captivity at Rome. He wrote the Acts of the Apostles and the gospel which bears his name. It does not seem that he was a martyr or a painter of pictures. It is not known where or when he died. *Lucas. October 18, iv, 142.*

LUKE BELLUDI, BD

Born in 1200 and received the habit of the Friars Minor from St Francis at Padua. He was a close friend of St Antony, after whose death Luke was instrumental in building the great basilica at Padua in his honour. d. 1285. c.c. 1927. *February 17, i, 359.*

LUKE KIRBY, ST, MARTYR

A secular priest h.d.q. at Tyburn in 1582. bd 1929. cd 1970. *May 30, ii, 415.*

LUKE THE YOUNGER, ST

Also called Thaumaturgus, "the Wonder-worker". He was a Greek, brought up in Thessaly, who after many difficulties succeeded in being a hermit near Corinth, where he was famed for his austerity and miracles. After his death *c.* 946 his cell on Mount Joannitsa was called Soterion, the Place of Healing. *February 7, i, 271.*

*LULL, ST, BISHOP

Lull was a monk of Malmesbury, who joined St Boniface in Germany and became his right-hand man. After a visit to Rome he was consecrated bishop as coadjutor, and succeeded Boniface in the see of Mainz, where he was a most energetic pastor for thirty years. St Lull had in his day a great reputation for learning. d. 786. *October 16, iv, 129.*

*LUPICINUS, ST, ABBOT

Brother of St Romanus and co-founder of monasteries with him. He was excessively austere and saw to it that all the monks tried to emulate him. d. 480. *February 28, i, 438.*

*LUPUS OF SENS, ST, BISHOP

In French *Leu.* He became archbishop of Sens in 609. In consequence of slander Lupus was banished from his see by King Clotaire, but was recalled at the request of St Winebald of Troyes and the people. d. 623. *September 1, iii, 459.*

*LUPUS OF TROYES, ST, BISHOP

In French *Loup.* He married a sister of St Hilary of Arles, but after a time they parted by mutual consent and Lupus became a monk at Lérins. He was chosen bishop of Troyes in 426, and accompanied St Germanus of Auxerre to Britain to combat the Pelagian heresy. d. 478. *July 29, iii, 207.*

*LUTGARDIS, ST, VIRGIN

Lutgardis was a Benedictine nun near Tongres who afterwards undertook the even more austere life of the Cistercians. An account of her inner life and mystical experiences was written by the contemporary Thomas of Cantimpré. She was blind for eleven years before her death in 1246. Lutgardis is one of the most sympathetic figures among the medieval women mystics. *June 16, ii, 557.*

*LUXORIUS, ST, MARTYR

Luxorius was a converted soldier who was put to death in 303 (?) at Forum Trajanum in Sardinia. The youths Cisellus and Camerinus are said to have suffered with him. *August 21, iii, 373.*

LYDWINA OF SCHIEDAM, BD, VIRGIN

Lydwina is described in her proper office as "a prodigy of human suffering and of heroic patience". Born 1380, the daughter of a labourer. An accident while skating in 1396 brought on disease and illness of the most agonizing kind, and she became completely bed-ridden; when she was nineteen the symptoms became more revolting and more painful. Lydwina bore it all with extraordinary patience, and about 1407 she began to receive visions, but then incurred the suspicion of her parish priest: one trial was spared her—she was never neglected or misunderstood by her family. d. 1433. c.c. 1890. *April 14, ii, 95.*

LYÉ. *See* Leo of Mantenay.

*LYONS, THE MARTYRS OF

The passion of the martyrs of Lyons and Vienne, probably in the year 177, is described at length in a letter written by eye-witnesses. Outstanding among the many victims were Pothinus, Blandina and Attalus (*qq.v.*); others were the deacon Sanctus, the neophyte Maturus, a physician named Alexander and the boy Ponticus. The precious narrative is preserved in the pages of the *Ecclesiastical History* of Eusebius.
June 2, ii, 454.

M

MACANISIUS, ST, BISHOP

St Macanisius (Aengus MacNisse) is said to have been consecrated bishop by St Patrick; he made a monastic foundation, probably at Kells, which developed into the see of Connor. His feast is kept throughout Ireland. *September 3, iii, 478.*

*MACARIUS OF ALEXANDRIA, ST

This Macarius must be distinguished from Macarius the Elder, mentioned below: there is probably confusion of long standing between stories told of the two saints. Macarius the Younger went into the Thebald as an anchorite about 335, and from thence years later went into the deserts of Lower Egypt. Palladius was his disciple for a time and writes of the miracles and austerities of Macarius, who is named in the *anaphora* of the Coptic Mass. d. *c.* 394. *January 2, i, 19.*

*MACARIUS OF GHENT, ST

A pilgrim who d. in the monastic hospice at Ghent in 1012. He is said to have wandered from Antioch in Pisidia; great veneration was shown to his memory and he is still invoked against epidemic diseases (he d. from the plague) in Flanders. *April 10, ii, 62.*

*MACARIUS OF JERUSALEM, ST, BISHOP

This Macarius became bishop of Jerusalem in 314, and according to the popular account he was the means of identifying the True Cross when it had been found by St Helen.

Certainly it was to him that the emperor Constantine entrusted the building of the first church of the Holy Sepulchre and the Resurrection, which the bishop saw completed before his death in 335. *March 10, i, 544.*

*MACARIUS THE ELDER, ST

Born in Upper Egypt *c.* 300. He lived for sixty years in the desert of Skete, and for twenty of these years he said he had "never once eaten, drunk or slept as much as nature required". When he learned that he had not attained the degree of perfection of certain married women, he visited them in their town to learn of them. Macarius was ordained priest to minister to his fellow hermits. He is named in the *anaphora* of the Coptic Mass. d. 390. *January 15, i, 93.*

*MACARIUS THE WONDERWORKER, ST

This Macarius, famed for miracles, was abbot of Pelekete, near Constantinople, where he was persecuted for his opposition to Iconoclasm. He d. in exile *c.* 830. *April 1, ii, 2.*

MACARTAN, ST, BISHOP

St Aedh MacCairthinn is believed to have been consecrated by St Patrick and his feast is kept throughout Ireland as the first bishop at Clogher. Very little is known about him. d. *c.* 505. *Macartinus. March 26, i, 684.*

MACCUL. *See* Maughold.

MACEDONIUS, ST

A Syrian solitary whose miracles of healing were recorded by Theodoret, his mother having been one of the beneficiaries. d. *c.* 430. *January 24, i, 161.*

*MACHABEES, THE HOLY, MARTYRS

The Holy Machabees are the only "Old Testament saints" who figure in the general calendar of the Western Church, with a commemoration on August 1. They were an aged scribe named Eleazar, seven brothers, and their mother, Jews, probably of Antioch, who were put to death *c.* 168 B.C. under Antiochus IV Epiphanes for refusing to apostatize from Judaism. *August 1, iii, 237.*

MACHAR, ST, BISHOP

Machar (Mochumma) came to Scotland with St Columba and is venerated as the first bishop of Aberdeen, in which diocese his feast is still observed. Sixth century. *November 12, iv, 322.*

MACHUTUS. *See* Malo.

*MACRINA THE ELDER, ST

St Macrina and her husband suffered much during the persecution of Galerius and Maximinus; she brought up St Basil the Great and his holy brothers, who were her grandchildren. d. *c.* 340. *January 14, i, 82.*

*MACRINA THE YOUNGER, ST,
VIRGIN

She was the eldest of the ten children of St Basil the Elder and St Emmelia, and helped to bring up Basil the Great, Gregory of Nyssa, and the rest. Macrina afterwards directed a community of women in Pontus, and was famed for miracles. d. 379. *July 19, iii, 145.*

MADELEINE FONTAINE, BD,
VIRGIN AND MARTYR

The superioress of the four Sisters of Charity of St Vincent de Paul martyred at Arras in 1794 during the French Revolution

(they were the superioress; Bd Frances Lanel; Bd Frances Fanton; and Bd Joan Gérard). She was seventy-one years old. These four martyrs were beatified in 1920. *June 27, ii, 655.*

*MADELEINE SOPHIE, ST, VIRGIN

Madeleine Sophie Barat was b. at Joigny in 1779. Her brother Louis while a deacon gave her a good grounding in the liberal arts and she grew to be a girl of great charm and intelligence. In 1800, under the direction of the Abbé Varin, she took the first step towards what was to be the foundation of the Society of the Sacred Heart for the education of girls. At first the undertaking met with much success, and then for eight years Mother Madeleine had to contend with grave difficulties within the institute; this was followed by a period of further expansion. She lived to see her religious established in nine European countries and the Americas, and herself established 105 houses with schools, travelling all over western Europe for the purpose. d. 1865. cd 1925. *Magdalena Sophia.* *May 25, ii, 392.*

MADELGAIRE. *See* Vincent Madelgarius.

MADELGISILUS, ST

In French *Mauguille*. A hermit at Monstrelet, who is said to have come to France with St Fursey from Ireland. d. *c.* 655. *May 30, ii, 424.*

MADRON, ST

Madron, or Madern, has given his name to a large parish near Land's End but he has not been certainly identified. He has been variously said to be the same as St Medran, disciple of St Kieran of Saighir, the Welsh St Padarn, or a local man who went with St Tudwal to Brittany. Sixth century. *May 17, ii, 337.*

MAEDOC. *See* Aidan of Ferns.

MAELRUBHA. *See* Malrubius.

MAFALDA, ST

Her marriage with King Henry I of Castile having been declared null on account of consanguinity, Princess Mafalda became a Benedictine nun at Arouca in her native Portugal. She gave all her wealth to charitable uses and lived a life of much self-abnegation. d. 1252. c.c. 1793. *May 2, ii, 219.*

MAGDALEN ALBRIZZI, BD, VIRGIN

Magdalen Albrizzi was the prioress of a convent at Brunate, near Como, which under her rule was affiliated to the order of Augustinian friars; she is said to have healed the sick miraculously and to have foretold the future. d. 1465. c.c. 1907. *Magdalena. May 15, ii, 324.*

MAGDALEN DI CANOSSA, BD, VIRGIN

Foundress of the Canossian Daughters of Charity. Magdalen Gabriela, Marchioness of Canossa, was b. at Verona in 1774. She learned in a dream that she was to found a congregation for the care of poor children, but she was thirty-four years old before she was able to do so, with some help from Napoleon Bonaparte. Mother Magdalen combined her active work with contemplative life of a high order. d. 1835. bd 1941. *May 14, ii, 309.*

MAGDALEN PANATTIERI, BD, VIRGIN

She was a Dominican tertiary who lived a life of usefulness and charity in her own home at Trino-Vercellese in north-western Italy. Her life was notably lacking in external eventfulness. d. 1503. c.c. 1827. *October 13, iv, 106.*

MAGDALEN. *See also* Madeleine *and* Mary Magdalen.

MAGENULF, ST

Magenulphus (Meinulf) was brought up at the court of Charlemagne, was ordained, and founded a monastery for women on his estate at Böddeken, Westphalia. An incident with a stag, similar to that of St Eustace, is told of him. d. *c.* 857. *October 5, iv, 37.*

MAGI, THE. *See* Three Wise Men.

*MAGLORIUS, ST, BISHOP

Maglorius (Maelor) was said to be a son of St Umbrafel, uncle of St Samson, and to have succeeded his cousin as abbot and bishop at Dol. Afterwards he retired to the Channel Islands, where he built a monastery on Sark. Sixth century. St Maglorius is commemorated in the diocese of Portsmouth. *October 24, iv, 192.*

*MAGNERICUS, ST, BISHOP

He was bishop of Trier, and a man of "shining piety and sound learning". d. 596. *July 25, iii, 188.*

MAGNUS, ST, MARTYR

Magnus, co-earl of the Orkneys, was captured by the king of Norway, Magnus Barefoot. He escaped to the protection of King Malcolm III of Scotland, at whose court he repented of his youthful excesses and began a life of prayer and penance. In 1116 St Magnus was killed by his cousin Haakon for political ends, but was nevertheless venerated as a martyr. The cathedral of Kirkwall, where he was buried, was dedicated in his honour, and his feast is still observed in the diocese of Aberdeen. *April 16, ii, 103.*

MAHARSAPOR, ST, MARTYR

After three years of cruel imprisonment he was put to death for confessing Christ, in Persia in 421. *October 10, iv, 79.*

MAIMBOD, ST, MARTYR

A wandering Irish missionary in the diocese of Besançon, killed by pagans while preaching near Kaltenbrunn in Alsace, *c.* 880 (?), according to his legend. *January 23, i, 157.*

*MAJOLUS, ST, ABBOT

In French *Mayeul*. He became head of the congregation of Cluny in 965 and was a worthy peer of the early Cluniac abbots. He had the confidence of the emperors and Otto II was anxious that he should be chosen pope, but by preference Majolus was a scholar and monk. d. 994. *May 11, ii, 272.*

MAJORICUS. *See under* Dionysia.

*MALACHY, ST, BISHOP

Malachy O'More (Mael Maedoc Ua Morgair) was b. at Armagh in 1095 and became a priest of the archbishop St Celsus. He distinguished himself by his zeal and vigour and was in turn abbot of Bangor, bishop of Connor, and primate of Armagh, where his right to the see was bitterly opposed. In 1139, when order had been restored and the Irish church reorganized, he resigned and made a pilgrimage to Rome, in the course of which he visited Clairvaux; here he became very friendly with St Bernard and arranged for the first Cistercian foundation in Ireland, Mellifont. On a second journey to Rome he d. in St Bernard's arms at Clairvaux in 1148. cd 1190, the first Irishman to be formally canonized. The "prophecies" found in Rome in 1595 and attributed to St Malachy are spurious and were not written by him. His feast is observed by the Cistercians and the Canons Regular of the Lateran, as well as throughout Ireland. *Malachias.* *November 3, iv, 249.*

*MALCHUS, ST

Malchus (Malek), a monk in the desert of Chalcis, was kidnapped by Bedouin and made to wander with them over their grounds beyond the Euphrates. He was given a woman to wife, but she was already married and they lived as brother and sister, and eventually escaped together. Malchus returned to his monastery and d. there towards the end of the fourth century. St Jerome relates this tale, which may be no more than an edificatory romance. *October 21, iv, 168.*

MALLONUS. *See* Mellon.

*MALO, ST, BISHOP

His medieval legend says he was a monk of Llancarfan who went to Brittany and was a missionary bishop, first where the town of Saint-Malo now stands and then near Saintes. Seventh century. *Maclovius, Machutus. November 15, iv, 349.*

MALRUBIUS, ST, ABBOT

An Irish monk of Bangor who went as a missionary among the Picts, establishing a monastery at Applecross in Ross. d. 722. His feast is kept in the diocese of Aberdeen. *April 21, ii, 143.*

*MAMAS, ST, MARTYR

He was a shepherd at Caesarea in Cappadocia and was martyred there *c.* 275. His feast is widely observed in the East, where strange tales are told of him. *August 17, iii, 339.*

*MAMERTUS, ST, BISHOP

St Mamertus, archbishop of Vienne, is chiefly remembered as the originator of the days of penance and supplication called rogation days, still observed before the feast of the Ascension. d. *c.* 475. *May 11, ii, 269.*

MAMILIAN. *See* Maximilian (martyr).

MANECHILDIS, ST, VIRGIN

She was one of seven sisters, all of whom are venerated as saints in different parts of Champagne. She is said to have become a solitary, and is called in France *Ménéhould.* Sixth century (?). *October 14, iv, 109.*

*MANETTUS, ST

One of the Seven Founders of the Servite Order (*q.v.*). *February 12, i, 311.*

MANNES, BD

He was an elder brother of St Dominic and one of the sixteen original members of the Order of Preachers. d. *c.* 1230. c.c. 1834. *July 30, iii, 214.*

*MAPPALICUS, ST, MARTYR

Mappalicus and others were martyred at Carthage for refusing to sacrifice to the gods during the persecution under Decius, *c.* 250. *April 17, ii, 112.*

*MAR SABA, THE MARTYRS OF

Twenty monks of the monastery of St Sabas in the Jordan valley were killed, and many more wounded, out of hatred of Christianity when the Arabs raided their house in 796. The story is told in detail by one of those who escaped, Stephen the Poet. *March 20, i, 643.*

*MARCELLA, ST

Called by St Jerome the "glory of the ladies of Rome". After the early death of her husband she lived a retired life of prayer and alms-deeds. When the Goths plundered Rome in 410 they beat St Marcella to make her disclose the whereabouts of her supposed wealth, but she induced them to spare her pupil Principia from outrage. Marcella d. in the same year. *January 31, i, 213.*

MARCELLIAN. *See under* Mark.

*MARCELLINA, ST, VIRGIN

She was the elder sister of St Ambrose and received the veil of a consecrated virgin *c.* 353. d. *c.* 398. *July 17, iii, 126.*

*MARCELLINUS AND PETER, SS, MARTYRS

These martyrs were distinguished by being named in the canon of the Roman Mass but little information about them has survived. Marcellinus was a priest and Peter perhaps an exorcist, and they suffered death for Christ at Rome in 304. *June 2, ii, 452.*

MARCELLINUS CHAMPAGNAT, BD

Founder of the Little Brothers of Mary, or Marist Brothers. He was ordained priest with St John Vianney and the Venerable John Claud Colin in 1822, and two years after was released from parish work to devote himself to organizing his teaching brothers. He was always closely associated with Father Colin, whom he predeceased, in 1840. bd 1955. *June 6, iv, 672.*

*MARCELLINUS OF CARTHAGE, ST, MARTYR

He, with his brother, the judge Apringius, attempted to enforce the decisions of a conference at Carthage against the Donatists, with a severity that drew rebuke from his friend St Augustine. The schismatics replied by making a false accusation of civil disaffection against the brothers, and they were executed without trial in 413. *April 6, ii, 40.*

*MARCELLINUS OF EMBRUN, ST, BISHOP

An African priest, missionary in Dauphiné who became first bishop of Embrun; he was driven from his see by Arian persecution. d. *c.* 374. *April 20, ii, 133.*

*MARCELLUS, I, ST, POPE AND MARTYR

He d. after a very brief pontificate in 309. It does not appear that he actually was put to death for the faith, but rather d. in exile. *January 156, i, 100.*

*MARCELLUS AND APULEIUS, SS, MARTYRS

These martyrs have been fictitiously associated with Simon Magus (Acts viii, 9–25). Nothing certain is known about them. *October 7, iv, 51.*

*MARCELLUS AND VALERIAN, SS, MARTYRS

Marcellus was a priest martyr, left to die of exposure on the banks of the Saône, *c.* 178. The convert Valerian was beheaded shortly after, near Autun. *September 4, iii, 483.*

MARCELLUS CALLO, BD, MARTYR

Marcel Callo was b. at Rennes, France, on December 1876 into a working-class family. As an apprentice typographer he joined the Young Christian Workers (the Jocistes). During the war he was sent to Germany as a forced labourer and organized the JOC in the camp. The Gestapo arrested him for excessive Catholic activity. He was sent to Flossenburg, then to Mauthausen concentration camp, where he d. in 1945. bd October 4, 1987. *March 19.*

MARCELLUS SPINOLA Y MAESTRE, BD

Cardinal Marcelo Spinola y Maestre was b. at San Fernando on January 14, 1835. He was a lawyer before taking up the priesthood. He was bishop of Coria, then Malaga and later archbishop of Seville in 1896 and a cardinal in 1905. He was noted for his devotion to duty and the defence of the Church's interests and especially for his concern for the poor. d. 1906. bd March 29, 1987. *January 19.*

*MARCELLUS OF APAMAEA, ST, BISHOP AND MARTYR

A bishop of Apamaea in Syria, who was slain by the heathen while supervising the demolition of one of their temples in accordance with an imperial edict, *c.* 389. *August 14, iii, 328.*

*MARCELLUS OF PARIS, ST, BISHOP

He is venerated as a bishop of Paris who d. at the beginning of the fifth century. *November 1, iv, 238.*

MARCELLUS OF TOMI, ST, MARTYR

Marcellus, a tribune, with his wife and two sons and others were beheaded for refusing to worship the gods, probably at Tomi in Moesia. *c.* 287 (?). *August 27, iii, 416.*

*MARCELLUS AKIMETES, ST, ABBOT

He was the most distinguished of the Eastern monks whose rule was that the Divine Office should be sung in relays throughout the day and night (his surname means "not-rester"). Marcellus was third abbot of their chief monastery at Constantinople and during his rule the monks greatly increased in number and spiritual influence. He was an outstanding figure in his day and assisted at the Council of Chalcedon. d. *c.* 485. *December 29, iv, 638.*

*MARCELLUS THE CENTURION, ST, MARTYR

He was a centurion of the Roman army who was beheaded at Tangier in 298 because he threw away his arms and insignia in protest against heathen observances in celebration of the emperor's birthday. A very reliable text of his *acta* is extant. *October 30, iv, 220.*

MARCHELM, ST

Marchelm, or Marculf, was one of several young Englishmen who followed St Willibrord into Holland to evangelize the Frisians. He worked with St Lebuin at Deventer. d. *c.* 762. *Marculfus. July 14, iii, 100.*

*MARCIAN OF CONSTANTINOPLE, ST

A priest of Constantinople, appointed oeconomus of the Great Church by the patriarch Gennadius, in which office he built a number of churches in the city and restored that of the Anastasis. He suffered under false suspicion of Novatianism, and was famed for miracles. d. *c.* 471. *January 10, i, 63.*

*MARCIAN OF CYRRHUS, ST

He was a hermit-monk in the desert between Antioch and the Euphrates and was much embarrassed by his own reputation as a wonderworker. d. *c.* 388. *November 2, iv, 242.*

MARCIAN. *See also* Marian of Auxerre *and under* Abundius, Lucian *and* Nicander.

*MARCIANA, ST, VIRGIN AND MARTYR

Marciana, who was a martyr in Mauritania, *c.* 303, was much honoured in Spain, though there may have been confusion with another martyr of the same name. *January 9, i, 56.*

MARCOLINO OF FORLI, BD

Marcolino Amanni was b. in 1317 and became a Dominican at a very early age. His brethren failed to appreciate his holiness during his lifetime. d. 1397. c.c. 1750. *January 24, i, 161.*

MARCOUL, ST

Marcoul (*Marculfus*) founded a monastery of hermit-monks at Nanteuil, and it was through him that the kings of France were popularly believed to derive the gift of "touching for the King's Evil" (scrofula). For this reason Marcoul's name was formerly celebrated throughout France, and also as a patron against skin diseases. d. *c.* 558. *May 1, ii, 210.*

MARGARET BOURGEOYS, ST,
VIRGIN

Foundress of the Congregation of Notre Dame of Montreal. Margaret was b. at Troyes in 1620, and in 1653 arrived in Ville-Marie (then simply a fort, now the city of Montreal) to teach the children there, the first schoolmistress of the place. What followed was in the full tradition of Canadian pioneering, complicated by official opposition to unenclosed religious. For nearly half a century Mother Bourgeoys was the leading citizeness of Montreal: "goodness radiated from her benign personality". d. 1700. bd 1956. cd 1982.
January 12, i, 125.

MARGARET CLITHEROW, ST,
MARTYR

Margaret, daughter of Thomas Middleton, of York, became a Catholic soon after her marriage to John Clitherow. She was imprisoned for two years for recusancy, and opened her house as a refuge for priests, for which she was eventually arrested and charged. Maintaining that she was charged with no offence, she refused to plead and was sentenced to the barbarous death in that case made and provided—to be pressed to death by weights. This was carried out at York in 1586, when she was thirty years old. St Margaret, good-looking, witty, and very merry, is one of the most attractive and moving figures among the English martyrs. bd 1929. cd 1970. *March 25, i, 679.*

MARGARET COLONNA, BD, VIRGIN

She was a daughter of Prince Odo Colonna and led a life of penance and prayer in a house above Palestrina. She gathered round her a community to whom her brother, Cardinal James Colonna, gave the Poor Clare rule. d. 1280. c.c. 1847.
November 7, iv, 290.

*MARGARET MARY, ST, VIRGIN

Margaret Mary Alacoque was b. in Burgundy in 1647 and joined the Visitation Order at the age of twenty-four. She was the recipient of a number of revelations and visions: these had reference particularly to the love of the heart of Jesus for man, and in 1675 it was made known to her that it was the divine will that a liturgical feast should be kept in honour of the Sacred Heart and in reparation for man's ingratitude. Margaret Mary's task in commending this devotion was a difficult one, and she underwent other considerable trials: she was tempted to despair, vainglory and self-indulgence, and suffered from bodily sickness and misunderstanding by her fellows. She d. at the convent of Paray-le-Monial in 1690. cd 1920. *October 16, iv, 134.*

MARGARET POLE, BD, MARTYR

Margaret Plantagenet, niece of Edward IV and Richard III, married Sir Reginald Pole; when she was left a widow, Henry VIII created her countess of Salisbury in her own right, and she was governess to Princess Mary. She retired from court when the king married Anne Boleyn, and the opposition of her fourth son (afterwards Cardinal Pole) to the royal supremacy further angered Henry against her. Bd Margaret was lodged in the Tower of London but never brought to trial; an act of attainder was passed against her and she was beheaded on Tower Green in 1541 at the age of seventy. bd 1886. Her feast is kept in several English dioceses.
May 28, ii, 413.

MARGARET WARD, ST, MARTYR

With St John Roche, this gentlewoman helped a priest to escape from Bridewell jail and in consequence was hanged at Tyburn in 1588. bd 1929. cd 1970.
August 30, iii, 437.

MARGARET D'YOUVILLE, ST

Marie-Marguerite Dufrost de Lajemmerais d'Youville, foundress of the Grey Nuns of

Montreal, b. at Varennes, Canada, on October 15, 1701, was the first native-born Canadian saint. Known as the "Mother of universal charity", she was mother of six children and a widow. The order she founded in 1737 was known officially as the Sisters of Charity of the General Hospital. She ran a hospice and hospital during epidemics and the Franco-British conflict, and made a firm commitment to "our masters the poor", showing mercy and justice to people of all races, classes and conditions, whether enemy prisoners, slaves, the mentally handicapped, prostitutes, Indians, blacks or epileptics. d. at Montreal in 1771. cd December 9, 1991. *December 23.*

MARGARET OF CITTÀ-DI-CASTELLO, BD, VIRGIN

Also called "of Metola". She was a foundling, brought up by various families in Città-di-Castello, who spent her life looking after children for their mothers. She d. at the age of thirty-three in 1320. c.c. 1609. *April 13, ii, 87.*

*MARGARET OF CORTONA, ST

"The Magdalen of the Seraphic Order" was a farmer's daughter from Laviano in Tuscany. For nine years she was the mistress of a young nobleman, and in his sudden and violent death Margaret saw the judgement of God. She went with her young son to Cortona, and there she became a tertiary of St Francis, devoted herself to the care of the sick, and started a hospital. Her life was now as austere as it had formerly been easy, and her confessor narrates some remarkable visions and supernatural communications. Slanderous tongues and other trials induced her to live a more retired life, but later she renewed her activities and made many conversions of hardened sinners; she was the instrument also of marvels of bodily healing. d. 1297. cd 1728. *February 22, i, 396.*

MARGARET "OF ENGLAND", ST, VIRGIN

A Cistercian nun of Seauve-Bénite who was greatly venerated in the diocese of Puy-en-Velay in the middle ages. There is reason to think that she may have been of Hungarian birth, though her mother, with whom she went on pilgrimage to the Holy Land, was perhaps of English extraction. d. 1192. *February 3, i, 243.*

*MARGARET OF HUNGARY, ST, VIRGIN

Daughter of Bela IV, king of Hungary. She made her profession as a Dominican nun into the hands of Bd Humbert of Romans. The details of her extraordinary life of self-crucifixion are set out in the depositions of the witnesses for her beatification, seven years after her death, which are still in existence. Some of them have been described as "horrifying" and verging on fanaticism, and there was apparently a certain element of wilfulness in her self-immolation. d. 1270. cd 1943. *January 26, i, 176.*

MARGARET OF LORRAINE, BD

She was left a widow with three small children at the death of René of Alençon and devoted herself to their upbringing, to the care of their estates, and to relief of the needy. She retired to a Poor Clare convent at Argentan in 1519 and d. in 1521. c.c. 1921. *November 6, iv, 281.*

MARGARET OF LOUVAIN, BD, VIRGIN AND MARTYR

She was a maidservant at an inn at Louvain who was murdered by robbers whom she had seen kill her employers. Marvels are said to have accompanied the finding of her body. d. 1225 (?). c.c. 1905. *September 2, iii, 470.*

MARGARET OF RAVENNA, BD, VIRGIN

A young woman of Russi, near Ravenna, almost or quite blind, who suffered much injustice at the hands of her neighbours, though later many of them gathered round her to form a religious confraternity. d. 1505. *January 23, i, 157.*

MARGARET OF SAVOY, BD

Bd Margaret was related to the principal royal houses of Europe and married Theodore Paleologus, marquis of Montferrat, in 1403. She was noted for her wide charity, and after her husband's death in 1418 she took the habit of the Dominican third order and established a house, at Alba in Liguria, first of tertiaries and then of nuns: Margaret directed it for over forty years. Many ecstasies and miracles were reported of her, and she suffered a good deal of persecution, especially from Philip Visconti, whom she had refused to marry in 1418. d. 1464. c.c. 1669. *December 23, iv, 603.*

*MARGARET OF SCOTLAND, ST

Born in exile *c.* 1046, granddaughter of King Edmund Ironside of England, and in 1070 married King Malcolm Canmore of Scotland. Both in her private life and public activity she worked for the advancement of religion by the spiritual and temporal care of her people. She had six sons and two daughters, one of whom was "Good Queen Maud", wife of Henry I. Margaret d. in 1093, and was buried at the abbey of Dunfermline which she had helped to found; while on her death-bed she heard of the treacherous murder of her husband and son by the English at Alnwick. A priest who knew her well wrote that, "So pleasant was she even in severity that all loved her, men as well as women, loved her while they feared her and in fearing loved her". St Margaret is the secondary patroness of Scotland. cd 1250. *November 16, ii, 515.*

*MARGARET THE BAREFOOTED, ST

A woman of San Severino in Italy who suffered patiently for years from ill treatment by her husband. d. 1395 (?). *August 27, iii, 423.*

MARGARET THE PENITENT. *See* Pelagia the Penitent.

MARI. *See under* Addai.

MARIA GORETTI. *See* Mary Goretti.

*MARIAN AND JAMES, SS, MARTYRS

A church reader and a deacon martyred by beheading at Lambesa in Numidia in 259. Their *passio* is an authentic document of great interest. *April 30, ii, 198.*

*MARIAN OF AUXERRE, ST

Also called *Marcian.* He was a monk who was cowman and shepherd for his monastery, and had remarkable power over all animals. d. *c.* 488. *Marianus.* *April 20, ii, 134.*

*MARIANA DE PAREDES, ST, VIRGIN

Mariana, known as "the Lily of Quito", lived as a solitary in the house of her brother-in-law; she was notable for her physical mortifications, which were not free from extravagance and morbidity. During the earthquakes at Quito in 1645 she offered herself as a victim for the people, and d. soon after. cd 1950. *May 26, ii, 401.*

MARIANUS SCOTUS, BD

He was b. in Donegal, his real name being Muiredach MacRobartaigh. On his way to Rome in 1067 he was induced to attach himself to the Benedictine monastery of Michelsburg and then to the Upper and Lower monasteries at Regensburg, where he worked as a scribe. The abbess Emma gave him the church of St Peter and some land, on which in 1078 a monastery was built which was the origin of all the Irish monasteries in south Germany. Here Marianus continued to copy books, and at least one in his hand is known still to exist; he was also a poet and theologian. d. 1088. *February 9, i, 290.*

MARINA, ST, VIRGIN

Marina is the heroine of a pious romance; she lived in a monastery dressed as a boy and was charged with seducing an innkeeper's daughter. It should be noted that Marina is the Latin form of the Greek name Pelagia (*q.v.*), and *cf.* also Margaret on July 20. *February 12, i, 313.*

*MARINUS, ST

He gives his name to the tiny republic of San Marino in Italy; but the local legend that he was a fourth-century deacon who followed the trade of a mason at Rimini until he had to flee, from a woman who claimed to be his wife, to the wilds of Monte Titano, is completely fabulous. *September 4, iii, 484.*

*MARINUS AND ASTYRIUS, SS, MARTYRS

Marinus was a soldier, at Caesarea in Palestine, who was denounced as a Christian by a jealous rival and was accordingly put to death c. 262. The senator Astyrius gave his body honourable burial, but his own martyrdom seems to have been assumed rather than recorded. *March 3, i, 466.*

*MARIUS, ST, ABBOT

There is no reliable information about this sixth-century French monk, who is called Maurus in the Roman Martyrology and May in France. *January 27, i, 183.*

*MARIUS AND MARTHA, SS, MARTYRS

While on a visit to Rome Marius, a Persian, with his wife Martha and their sons Audifax and Abachum, gathered up and buried the relics of the martyrs. For this reason they were put to death, c. 260. *January 19, i, 117.*

*MARK, ST, EVANGELIST

St Mark was perhaps the young man who ran away at the taking of Jesus (Mark xiv, 51–52); he was with St Paul on his first mission and at other times; and according to ancient tradition he was intimately associated with St Peter, from whom he got his knowledge of our Lord's life and preaching. It is likely that Mark ended his life as bishop of Alexandria and was martyred there, c. 74. The singing of the litanies on April 25 has nothing to do in origin with St Mark or his feast. *Marcus. April 25, ii, 160.*

*MARK, ST, POPE

The only pope of this name was a Roman: he succeeded St Silvester in 336 but d. within the year. *October 7, iv, 51.*

*MARK AND MARCELLIAN, SS., MARTYRS

Marcus and Marcellianus, deacons and brothers, gave their lives for Christ c. 287. Their tomb in the catacomb of St Balbina at Rome was discovered in modern times. *June 18, ii, 577.*

MARK BARKWORTH, BD, MARTYR

Barkworth first came to the English mission as a secular priest, but was later clothed as a Benedictine in Navarre. He was h.d.q. for his priesthood at Tyburn in 1601. bd 1929. *February 27, i, 435.*

MARK CRISIN, BD, MARTYR

The Croatian Canon Mark Crisin (Korosy) and the Hungarian Stephen Poncgraz and the Czech Melchior Grodech, both Jesuits, were put to death with great barbarity by Calvinist soldiers at Kosice in Slovakia in 1619. bd 1905. *September 7, iii, 504.*

MARK FANTUCCI, BD

Bd Mark succeeded St John of Capistrano as vicar general of the Friars Minor of the Observance and to him was mainly due their preservation as a separate body when they looked like being compulsorily merged with the Conventuals. He was one of the several Franciscans active in the establishment of *monti di pietà*. d. 1479. c.c. 1868. *April 19, ii, 65.*

MARK OF ARETHUSA, ST, BISHOP AND MARTYR

This Mark was bishop of Arethusa in the Lebanon, and was martyred under Julian the Apostate, c. 365. His name was excluded from the Roman Martyrology by Cardinal Baronius, who suspected his orthodoxy, but Mark has been vindicated by the Bollandists. *March 29, i, 697.*

MARK OF MODENA, BD

A confessor of the Order of Preachers, celebrated as a missioner in northern Italy. d. 1498. c.c. 1857.
September 23, iii, 627.

MARK OF MONTEGALLO, BD

After practising as a physician Bd Mark agreed with his wife that they should both "enter religion", he becoming a Franciscan at Fabriano. Mark was one of the most vigorous and successful promoters of the charitable pawnshops known in Italy as *monti di pietà*. d. 1497.
March 20, i, 648.

MARMADUKE BOWES, BD, MARTYR

A married gentleman b. at Ingram Grange, Welbury, Cleveland. He entertained Fr Hugh Taylor in his house and was hanged at York in 1585 for harbouring and relieving a priest. bd November 22, 1987.
November 26.

MARO, ST

A hermit who lived in an abandoned temple near Cyrrhus in Syria and was much reverenced by St John Chrysostom. d. 433. A monastery, Bait-Marun, was built around his shrine, and this is said to have given their name to that body of Eastern Catholics called Maronites. Another Maro, St John Maro, reputed bishop in the seventh century, probably never existed.
February 14, i, 334.

*MARTHA, ST, VIRGIN

Martha was the sister of Mary (identified in the West with the Magdalen) and of Lazarus, "careful and troubled about many things". The story that she d. in the south of France deserves no credence.
July 29, iii, 205.

MARTHA. *See also under* Marius.

MARTHA LE BOUTEILLER, BD, VIRGIN

Sister Marthe Le Bouteiller (Aimée Adèle le Bouteiller) was born on December 2, 1816 at La Henrière, near Percy, in the Manche district of France. She joined the Congregation of the Sisters of St Madeleine Postel in 1842. She worked all her life in such humble locations as the kitchen or in the fields, for the community of the abbey of Saint-Sauveur le Vicomte. She carried refreshments for the sisters and was known as "Sister Cider". She led a constantly cheerful and devout life of service, radiating the love of God through the very plainness of her daily life. She dedicated herself entirely to God and to other people. She died in 1883. bd November 4, 1990.
March 18.

*MARTIAL OF LIMOGES, ST, BISHOP

Though well known as the reputed apostle of Limousin and first bishop of Limoges there are no reliable particulars of the life of St Martial, his legend being an extravagant forgery. d. *c.* 250. *Martialis.*
June 30, ii, 675.

MARTIAL. *See also under* Faustus.

*MARTIN, ST

This Martin, a solitary in Campania, is spoken of by St Gregory in his *Dialogues*. In the Roman Martyrology he is called Mark. d. *c.* 580. *Martinus.*
October 24, iv, 192.

*MARTIN I, ST, POPE AND MARTYR

He was a Tuscan and became pope in 649. Immediately after his election he condemned the monothelite heresy in the teeth of the emperor, Constans II. Martin was therefore seized by the imperial exarch, taken to Constantinople, most cruelly treated and banished to the Chersonese where he d. of ill treatment and starvation in 656 (?). He was the last pope to date to die a martyr. *April 13, iv, 319.*

MARTIN DE PORRES, ST

He was b. in Lima in 1579, son of a Spanish knight and Panama Indian, and is the first child of a marriage between black and white parents whose heroic virtue was formally recognized by the Church. Martin was a lay-brother and infirmarian in the Dominican friary of the Rosary at Lima and was a friend to all the poor in the city, especially the African slaves and including the stray cats and dogs. d. 1639. bd 1837. cd 1962. *November 3, iv, 269.*

MARTIN HUIN, ST, MARTYR

Martin Luc Huin was born on October 20, 1836 at Guyonvelle and became a priest of Langres diocese in 1861. He joined the Paris Foreign Missions in 1863. He entered Korea on May 27, 1865, and was beheaded on March 12 after his arrest on March 11, 1866. bd 1968. cd by John Paul II at Seoul in 1984. *March 12.*

MARTIN OF BRAGA, ST, BISHOP

He was a zealous missionary in Spain and bishop first of Mondoñedo and then of Braga. Martin was a man of learning and was compared by Fortunatus with his name-sake of Tours; some of his works, including a description of peasant customs and super-stitions, are extant. d. 579. *March 20, i, 636.*

MARTIN OF ST NICHOLAS AND MELCHIOR OF ST AUGUSTINE, BB, MARTYRS

Fathers Martin of St Nicholas and Melchior of St Augustine were Spanish Augustinians, martyred in Japan in 1632. bd April 23, 1989.

*MARTIN OF TOURS, ST, BISHOP

He was b. in Upper Pannonia, son of a Roman officer. Martin was drafted into the army, but refused to fight against German invaders on the ground that a Christian should not engage in war. He became a disciple of St Hilary of Poitiers and for ten years lived as a recluse, founding a community of hermit-monks which later became the Benedictine Abbey of Ligugé. He became bishop of Tours much against his will *c.* 371 and continued his monastic life as much as possible, establishing the mon-astery of Marmoutier near his episcopal city. He strongly opposed Ithacius of Ossanova for invoking the civil power and the death penalty against heretics, and protected the Priscillianists against persecution. St Martin was the pioneer of monasticism in Gaul and as such had considerable influence on the Celtic churches. He was, very properly, one of the most venerated of saints in Europe during the Middle Ages. d. 397. *November 11, iv, 310.*

*MARTIN OF VERTOU, ST, ABBOT

This rather nebulous saint was a hermit and missionary in Poitou in the sixth century and is said to have founded several monastic communities. *October 24, iv, 193.*

MARTINIAN, ST

He is alleged to have been a hermit at the "Place of the Ark", near Caesarea in Pales-tine, and to have been fruitlessly tempted by a woman called Zoë to give up that life and come to live with her. Instead he converted her and sent her to St Paula's convent at Bethlehem. But there is reason to doubt whether Martinian is an historical person. *February 13, i, 320.*

*MARTINIAN AND MAXIMA, SS

Martinian, his fellow servant the maiden Maxima, and others were beaten and exiled for their loyalty to Christ by the Vandals in Africa. They were cruelly put to death in 458, except Maxima, who d. in peace. *October 16, iv, 126.*

MARTINIAN. *See also under* Processus.

MARTIUS, ST, ABBOT

St Martius, or Mars, was abbot of Clermont and is spoken of by St Gregory of Tours in his *Vitae Patrum.* d. *c.* 530. *April 13, ii, 84.*

MARTYRIUS. *See under* Sisinnius.

MARTYRS

The following groups of martyrs who are commonly referred to by a group name are indexed herein under the specifying word: Arras, Compiègne, Crete, Damascus, Danes, Ebsdorf, Forty, Gorkum, Lombards, Lyons, Mar Saba, Mount Sinai, Najran, Nero,

Nicomedia, North America, Orange, Persian, Plague of Alexandria, Samosata, Scillitan, September, Serapeum, Uganda, Utica, Ursuline. In Butler's "Lives" certain other martyrs as well are grouped together, more or less arbitrarily, under the country where they suffered: China (i, 361; iii, 59), Indo-China, Vietnam (iii, 77; iv, 282), Japan (i, 259; ii, 445; iii, 533), Korea (iii, 611). Representative individuals from among these very numerous *beati* and *beatae* are referred to herein under their own names. *English Martyrs*. Each beatified martyr of the penal times in Great Britain is entered herein under his or her name. In addition there are the following group entries: Carthusian, Douay, England and Wales (general), Oxford University. In Butler's "Lives" many of these English martyrs are grouped under the following headings: Canterbury (iv, 7), Carthusian (ii, 277), Dorchester (iii, 18), Durham (iii, 181), London 1582 (ii, 415), London 1588 (iii, 436), London 1591 (iv, 532), the Oates Plot (ii, 596).

*MARUTHAS, ST, BISHOP

Maruthas, a doctor of the Syrian church, was bishop of Maiferkat in Mesopotamia. He compiled the records of the martyrs under Sapor and wrote hymns in their honour, as well as other works. He worked hard for the organization of the Church in Persia (for which he was much valued by St John Chrysostom) and his organization lasted until the Mohammedan invasion. d. *c.* 415. *December 4, iv, 489.*

*MARY, THE BLESSED VIRGIN

Mary was a Jewish maiden of the house of David; at her conception she was redeemed by anticipation and preserved by God from all stain of original sin (the Immaculate Conception, December 8). Mary was betrothed to a carpenter, St Joseph; at the Annunciation (March 25) the Second Person of the Blessed Trinity took flesh in her womb by the power of the Holy Ghost, and in due course she gave birth at Bethlehem to Jesus, the God-man, and so is properly called the Mother of God. Both before and after her miraculous childbearing she was a

virgin and so remained all her days, and she was for her whole life absolutely sinless. For the thirty years before the public ministry of Jesus began, Mary lived the outward life of any other Jewish woman of the common people; she was present at her Son's crucifixion, when he confided her to the care of the apostle St John; on the day of Pentecost the Holy Spirit descended on her with the apostles and other disciples in the upper room at Jerusalem, and that is the last reference to her in the Bible. The rest of Mary's earthly life was probably passed mainly at Jerusalem. There, it is believed, she d.; her body was preserved from corruption, and soon after taken into Heaven and reunited to her soul by an anticipation of the general resurrection. The celebration of this event, commonly called in the West our Lady's Assumption, is her principal feast, on August 15 (other feasts are: her Birthday, September 8; her Motherhood, January 1; her Presentation, November 21; her Queenship, August 22; her Sorrows, September 15; her Visit to Elizabeth, May 31; Our Lady of Lourdes, February 11; Our Lady of Mount Carmel, July 16; Our Lady of Ransom, September 24; the Holy Rosary, October 7). *Maria. August 15, iii, 331; see also i, 673, iii, 6, etc.*

*MARY, ST, MARTYR

She was a slave-girl in the household of a Roman senator and was revered as a martyr on account of her sufferings during persecution. Date unknown.
November 1, iv, 237.

MARY ANGELA ASTORCH, BD, VIRGIN

Sr Maria Angela Astorch, b. 1592, was a Spanish Capuchin nun of the order of St Clare. Whether in charge of novices or as abbess, she practised an exemplary spirituality and respected the individuality of others. 1665. bd May 23, 1982. *December 2.*

MARY ANGELES, BD, VIRGIN AND MARTYR

Sr Maria Angeles of St Joseph was a Spanish Carmelite b. at Getaje, Madrid, on March 6, 1905, and professed in 1931. She was murdered by Republican militiamen on July 24, 1936. bd March 29, 1987. *July 24.*

MARY ANNA SALA, BD, VIRGIN

Sr Maria Anna Sala joined the Marcelline Sisters when aged twenty-one and dedicated her life to teaching young girls character, commitment and obedience. bd October 26, 1980. *November 24.*

MARY BAOUARDY, BD, VIRGIN

Sr Marie de Jésus Crucifié was born Mariam Baouardy into a family of Greek-Melkite rite Christian Arabs on January 5, 1846 at Abellin (Zabulon) between Nazareth and Mount Carmel in the Holy Land. Orphaned at two, an uncle took her to Egypt and she became a servant in Christian families, arriving eventually at Marseilles when seventeen. When twenty-one, still semi-literate, she became a Carmelite at Pau and three years later was sent as a missionary to Bangalore, India. In 1875 she founded the Carmelite house at Bethlehem, choosing the design and overseeing its construction. She wished to be a "little sister to everyone" and is an example of desire for unity and reconciliation. Strange mystical phenomena were apparent throughout her life. She had planned another house at Nazareth when she died in an accident at the age of thirty-three. d. 1878. cd November 13, 1983. *August 26.*

MARY DEI BAGNESI, BD, VIRGIN

Maria Bartolomea was an invalid, for years bedridden, during her whole life, which was a record of suffering heroically borne. She lived at Florence and is venerated as a tertiary of the Order of Preachers. d. 1577. c.c. 1802. *May 28, ii, 414.*

MARY BORGIA, BD, VIRGIN AND MARTYR

Sr Maria Pilar of St Francis Borgia was b. on December 30, 1877 at Tarazona, Saragossa, Spain and professed in 1899. She was murdered by Republican militiamen on July 24, 1936. bd March 29, 1987. *July 24.*

MARY CATHERINE, BD, VIRGIN

Sister Marie-Catherine of St Augustine was born at Saint-Sauveur-le-Vicomte, Bayeux, France on May 3, 1632. She had special devotions to the Sacred Heart of Jesus and the sacred heart of Mary. She led an intense spiritual life but also dedicated herself to the care of the sick in Canada. She died in Quebec on May 8, 1668. bd April 23, 1989. *May 8.*

MARY DELUIL-MARTINY, BD, VIRGIN AND MARTYR

Mother Marie Deluil-Martiny was born in Marseilles, France, on May 28, 1841. In 1873 she founded a contemplative order, the Daughters of the Heart of Jesus, in Belgium. She favoured a simple and austere religious life centred on the love of Christ. Louis Chave, the convent gardener and an anarchist and anti-religious fanatic, murdered her on February 27 1884. bd October 22, 1989. *February 27.*

MARY DROSTE ZU VISCHERING, BD, VIRGIN

Maria Droste zu Vischering was born into a pious aristocratic family at Münster, Germany, on September 8, 1863. She entered the order of the Sisters of the Good Shepherd in 1883 and became superior of the community at Porto in 1894. She was especially concerned with the apostolate among prostitutes and unfrocked clergy. She died in 1899. bd November 1, 1975. *June 9.*

MARY ENRICA DOMINICI, BD, VIRGIN

Caterina Dominici (Sr Maria-Enrichetta Dominici) was b. near Turin, Italy, on October 10, 1829. She entered the Institute of Sisters of St Anne and Providence at Turin in 1850, cared for cholera victims, and in 1861 was elected and remained superior general of the order until her death in 1894. She was a model of humility and of sensitivity to the grandeur of God. bd May 7, 1978. *February 21.*

MARY EUGENIA MILLERET, BD,
VIRGIN

Mother Anne-Eugénie Milleret de Bron was b. at Metz on August 25, 1817. Originally inspired by Lacordaire and a Fr Combalot, on April 30, 1839 she founded the first Community of the Assumption in Paris. By her death in 1898 the order comprised twenty-nine houses; there are now 186 communities in thirty countries. bd February 9, 1975.
March 10.

MARY FORTUNATA VITI, BD,
VIRGIN

Maria Fortunata Viti was an Italian lay Benedictine of Veroli noted for her humility. d. 1922. bd 1967. *October 8.*

*MARY FRANCES, ST, VIRGIN

Mary Frances Basinsin was b. of a middle-class family at Naples in 1715. Her father tried brutally to force her into marriage, but she received the Franciscan tertiary habit in 1731 and continued to live at home until she became housekeeper to a priest, a post which she filled for thirty-eight years. She suffered much from bodily ill health and from the unkindness of her family, but added to these trials severe bodily auster-ities. St Mary Frances is said to have had extremely remarkable spiritual experiences, including the mystical marriage. d. 1791. cd 1867. *October 6, iv, 46.*

MARY GERHARDINGER, BD, VIRGIN

Mother Maria Teresa, b. Carolina Ger-hardinger in 1796, founded the teaching Sisters of Notre Dame for the Christian education of young girls, especially the rural poor. d. 1879. Her order now comprises some 7,500 sisters all over the world. bd November 17, 1985. *May 9.*

*MARY GORETTI, ST,
VIRGIN AND MARTYR

Maria Goretti was a twelve-year-old girl at Corinaldo in Italy who was killed in resist-ing a young man who tried to ravish her. She was a child of much goodness of life, the affair was not forgotten, and a dream of her converted her assailant while he was serving his prison sentence. d. 1902. cd 1950. *July 6, iii, 28.*

MARY GUYARD, BD, WIDOW

Marie Guyard of the Incarnation, the "Mother of the Church in America" and "Teresa of the New World", was b. October 28, 1599 at Tours, France. She was married in 1617, had a son, and was widowed within three years. She became an Ursuline in 1632 and one of the first women missionaries to the Americas. She was a noted educator and mystic. d. 1672. June 22, 1980. *April 30.*

MARY HAZE, BD

Marie-Therese (Jeanne) Haze, a Belgian nun, was born at Liège on February 12, 1782. She founded the Order of Daughters of the Cross of Liège, and was noted for inspiring a spirit of service to the poor and suffering. She showed exemplary devotion to the Blessed Sacrament and the Sacred Heart. She was especially concerned with the religious education of the marginalized people of her time. d. 1876. bd April 21, 1991. *January 7.*

MARY KASPER, BD, VIRGIN

Mother Maria Katharina Kasper was b. at Dernbach, Germany, on May 26, 1820 into a peasant family. She became a farm-worker and servant on her father's death. In 1845 she founded the Poor Handmaidens of Jesus Christ and remained the superior until her death in 1898. bd April 16, 1978. *February 2.*

*MARY MAGDALEN, ST

According to the tradition of the Western Church, Mary Magdalen, who is mentioned in all four gospels, is also identical with "the woman who was a sinner" and with the sister of Lazarus, though this identification is by no means unchallenged, especially by the Eastern fathers. The story that Mary Magdalen, with Lazarus, Martha and others, preached the gospel in Provence, d., and was buried there has been shown to be devoid of any probability. *Maria Magda-lena. July 22, iii, 161.*

MARY MAGDALEN MARTINENGO, BD, VIRGIN

A Capuchin nun at Brescia who d. in 1737 and was bd in 1900; her life was distinguished by extreme self-mortification. *July 27, iii, 200.*

*MARY MAGDALEN DEI PAZZI, ST, VIRGIN

She was b. of an illustrious Florentine family in 1566 and entered Carmel at the age of sixteen. She was grievously tried both by bodily disease and spiritual dryness, and by the assaults of unseen powers, and her patience was recognized by extraordinary graces, especially after holy communion. She filled various conventual offices with notable success. d. 1607. cd 1669. *May 25, ii, 416.*

*MARY MAGDALEN POSTEL, ST, VIRGIN

Born at Barfleur in 1756. Five years after she had opened a school for girls the French revolution broke out, and Julie Postel was a tower of strength to the loyal Catholics of Barfleur: she received permission to minister *viaticum* to the dying. In 1805, with the Abbé Cabart, she established at Cherbourg the first school of what were to be the Sisters of the Christian Schools of Mercy. For over thirty years the new congregation experienced bitter trials and troubles, but Mother Mary Magdalen persevered, and during the last few years of her life saw great expansion and achievement. d. 1846. cd 1925. *July 16, iii, 120. See also* Magdalen *and* Madeleine.

MARY MARGARET CAIANI, BD, VIRGIN

Maria-Margherita Caiani was an Italian nun, b. 1863, who founded an order dedicated to the Sacred Heart. d. 1921. bd April 23, 1989. *August 8.*

MARY DE MATTIAS, BD, VIRGIN

Foundress of the Sisters Adorers of the Precious Blood. She was b. in Italy in 1805, and in 1834 accepted an invitation to take charge of a school at Acuto, near Anagni, from which her congregation developed.

Bd Mary was greatly gifted in the giving of biblical and catechetical conferences to women's and girls' societies. She was encouraged in her work by Mgr George Talbot and Mgr (later Cardinal) Edward Howard in Rome, where she d. in 1866. bd 1950. *August 20, iii, 368.*

*MARY MAZZARELLO, ST, VIRGIN

Co-foundress, with St John Bosco, of the Daughters of our Lady Help of Christians. She was b. of peasant parents in 1837, and helped to found and run a Marian sodality at her native Mornese; in 1872 Don Bosco chose her as superioress for the community he installed at that place. She had a hard task, but she tackled it with simplicity and determination, and thirteen other convents were opened in Italy and France during her lifetime. Mother Mary of Mornese was only forty-four at her death in 1881. cd 1951. *May 14, ii, 313.*

*MARY MICHAELA, ST, VIRGIN

This Spanish woman of high birth (called Desmaisières in the documents of her cause) gave herself to various works of mercy and eventually founded the congregation of Handmaids of the Blessed Sacrament and of Charity, of which she became the first superioress. While attending cholera victims in Valencia she was infected herself, and d. in 1865. cd 1934. *August 25, iii, 405.*

MARY PARADIS, BD

Mother Marie-Léonie Paradis was b. in 1840 into a poor family in St John diocese, Quebec, Canada. She became a Holy Cross sister in 1870 and in 1880 founded the Little Sisters of the Holy Family to care for colleges, seminaries and presbyteries. d. 1912. bd during a papal visit to Canada on October 31, 1982. *May 3.*

MARY PRAT, BD, MARTYR

Mary Mercedes Prat, a nun of the Order of St Teresa of Jesus, b. at Barcelona on March 7, 1880. A dedicated Christian teacher, arrested and shot on July 24, 1936, during the Spanish Civil War. bd April 29, 1990. *July 24.*

MARY REPETTO, BD, VIRGIN

Maria Repetto was b. 1807 and at the age of twenty-two became a member of the cloistered Sisters of our Lady of Refuge. d. 1890. She nursed the sick through several cholera epidemics. bd October 4, 1981. *January 5.*

MARY RIVIER, BD, VIRGIN

Sr Marie-Anne Rivier, whom Pope Pius IX called the "female apostle", b. 1768, founded the French Congregation of the Sisters of the Presentation of Mary for the care and instruction of young people and especially the poor and orphans. She showed exemplary faith, joy and courage. d. 1838. bd May 23, 1982. *February 3.*

MARY DI ROSA, ST, VIRGIN

Foundress of the Handmaids of Charity of Brescia, where she was b. in 1813. In consequence of her work during the cholera epidemic of 1836, the idea of her congregation began to take shape, its work being to care for the sick in hospitals (The Handmaids anticipated Florence Nightingale on the field of battle by several years). "The Life of Mary di Rosa is a marvel that astonishes all who see it", said her adviser, Mgr Pinzoni, and she wore herself out by the age of forty-two. d. at Brescia, 1855. cd 1954. *December 15, iv, 566.*

MARY ROSE DUROCHER, BD, VIRGIN

Sr Marie-Rose Durocher of Montreal, b. 1811, was the Canadian foundress of the Sisters of the Holy Names of Jesus and Mary, whose work now extends to six countries. For 13 years she helped her brother in his presbytery before she could devote her order to the religious instruction of young girls and especially the poor. d. 1849. bd May 23, 1982. *October 6.*

MARY ROSE MOLAS Y VALLVE, ST, VIRGIN

María Rosa Molas y Vallvé was born at Reus, Spain, on March 24, 1815. She took the name Sister María Rosa on entering the Reus hospital as a member of an association of pious women helpers. In 1849 she started a hospital at Tortosa and with eleven companions worked to found the religious Sisters of Our Lady of Consolation, formally constituted in 1868. She established seventeen hospitals, schools and refuges for the poor. The order now has eighty-four houses and 796 members. d. 1876. bd May 8, 1977. cd December 11, 1988. *June 11.*

MARY SAGHEDDU, BD, VIRGIN

Sr Maria Gabriella Sagheddu was an Italian nun from Sardinia, b. 1914. She went through a profound conversion after the death of her favourite sister, and became active in the catechesis of the young and the service of the aged, and developed an intense prayer life. She was scarcely twenty-one when she left Sardinia to pursue her vocation as a Trappist, and later dedicated her life to Christian unity in an attitude of what John Paul II called "spiritual ecumenism" when he beatified her at the end of the week of prayer for Christian unity in 1983. She was the first woman to be beatified from the ranks of the youth section of Catholic Action. d. 1939. bd January 25, 1983. *April 23.*

MARY SCHININA, BD

Maria Schinina was born at Padua on April 10, 1844. She founded the Sisters of the Sacred Heart of Jesus for the service of a wide variety of people: orphaned girls, the old and infirm, the sick and prisoners. She also helped other religious Institutes, such as the Ladies of Charity and the Carmelites. d. 1910. bd November 4, 1990. *June 11.*

MARY SIEDLISKA, BD, VIRGIN

Mother Mary of Jesus the Good Shepherd was born Franziska Siedliska in 1842 and founded the Polish order of the Holy Family of Nazareth. d. 1902. bd April 23, 1989. *April 23.*

MARY SOLEDAD, ST, VIRGIN

Emanuela Torres-Acosta was b. in Madrid in 1826. At the age of twenty-five she joined a group who looked after the sick in a

Madrid parish, and thus she gradually formed the congregation of Handmaids of Mary Serving the Sick, wherein she took the name of Maria Soledad (*desolata*). She guided and built up this foundation for thirty-five years, bringing it to a high pitch of religious fervour and technical efficiency, and seeing it spread far and wide in Spain. d. 1887. bd 1950. cd 1970. *October 11, iv, 91.*

MARY DE SOUBIRAN, BD, VIRGIN

Foundress of the Society of Mary Auxiliatrix. She was b. near Carcassone in 1835, and early heard a call to the religious life, beginning by being a béguine at Castelnaudary. In 1864 she migrated with some of the community to Toulouse, there to begin the congregation "de Marie Auxiliatrice", our Lady of Help. Henceforward the life of Mother Mary Teresa was one of the most remarkable in the history of religious foundresses. On the one hand, she led an intense inner life, and wrote extensively on spiritual things; on the other, through the activities of a member of the congregation, she came to be dismissed from the society she had founded: at the age of forty she had to begin life all over again, by being accepted into another congregation. "I love God's purposes", she said, "I am nothing, his will is all." It was not till after Mother Mary Teresa's death in 1889 that her true story came to light, and her weakened congregation was rehabilitated. bd 1946. *October 20, iv, 157.*

MARY TERESA LEDOCHOWSKA, BD, VIRGIN

Mother Marie-Thérèse Ledochowska was born at Loosdorf, Austria, on April 29, 1863. Her father was a Polish count and her mother was Swiss. She was the niece of Cardinal Ledochowski. She followed her family to Poland in 1882 and in 1885 she went to Salzburg. A meeting with Cardinal Lavigerie persuaded her to take up the religious life and in 1894 she founded the Institute of St Peter Claver. She died in Rome on July 6, 1922. bd October 19, 1975. *July 6.*

MARY OF THE APOSTLES, BD, VIRGIN

Maria Theresia von Wüllenweber was the daughter of Baron Joseph Theodor von Wüllenweber, b. at Gladbach, Germany, in 1833. Under the guidance of Fr Johannes Jordan she founded the Sisters of the Divine Saviour and was noted for her resolute pursuit of religious perfection. bd 1968. *October 13.*

*MARY OF CEREVELLON, BD, VIRGIN

Also called *Maria de Socós*, "of Help". She is venerated as the first nun of the order of our Lady of Ransom (Mercedarians). Very little is known about her. d. 1290. c.c. 1692. *September 19, iii, 601.*

*MARY OF CLEOPHAS, ST

All sorts of legends have grown up around the name of Mary of Cleophas, but nothing is known about her beyond the references found in the New Testament. *April 9, ii, 58.*

*MARY OF EGYPT, ST

According to the earliest reference Mary of Egypt was an actress and courtesan who fled into the desert beyond Jordan to expiate her sins; she was found dead by two disciples of St Cyriacus, a hermit of the fifth/sixth century. Round this narrative there grew up an elaborate legend which attained enormous popularity, especially in the East. *April 2, ii, 14.*

MARY OF JESUS LOPEZ DE RIVAS, BD, VIRGIN

María de Jesús López de Rivas was b. at Tartanedo, Aragon, Spain on August 18, 1560. Recommended by St Teresa she became a Toledo Carmelite in 1577 and spent sixty-three years there. d. 1640. bd November 14, 1976. *September 13.*

MARY OF OIGNIES, BD, VIRGIN

She was b. at Nivelles in Belgium. Having been persuaded against her inclination to marry, it is said she induced her husband not to consummate the marriage, and they turned their house into a leper hospital. Mary practised great austerities and was often visited by visions and ecstasies, and later her husband let her go to live in a cell adjoining a church at Oignies. This Mary and other Netherland mystics are important in the history of the evolution of Catholic devotion during the Middle Ages, and she is one of the first of whom solid evidence about certain strange phenomena (*e.g.*, knowledge of what was happening at a distance) is forthcoming. d. 1213. *June 23, ii, 623.*

MARY OF PISA, BD

Mary Catherine Mancini was twice widowed before she was twenty-five and had seven children, most of whom d. young. After her second husband's death she came under the influence of St Catherine of Siena, and eventually entered the relaxed Dominican convent of Santa Croce, where she effected a reform. Then, with Bd Clare Gambacorta, she founded a new community, which greatly flourished. d. 1431. c.c. 1855. *January 28, i, 192.*

MARY OF PROVIDENCE, BD, VIRGIN

Marie de la Providence was b. Eugénie Smet at Lille, France on May 25, 1825. In 1856, at Paris, she founded the Congregation of Helpers of the Souls in Purgatory which, since her death on February 7, 1871, has spread all over the world with missions in China, Japan, Mexico, Indonesia, Africa, etc., and now has some 1,500 sisters in fifteen countries. bd by Pope Pius XII on May 26, 1957. *February 7.*

MARY OF THE INCARNATION, BD

Barbe Avrillot, known as "the beautiful Acarie", was the devoted wife of Peter Acarie, whose political activities involved his wife and children in considerable misfortune. Barbe was the prime mover in bringing the Teresian Carmelite nuns to France in 1604, and even acted as a sort of unofficial novice-mistress for them; but she herself, when a widow, was a nun for only four years: it was "in the world" that she

achieved holiness, as wife and mystic. d. 1618. bd 1791. *April 18, ii, 124.*

MARY OF TURIN, BD, VIRGIN

Marianna Fontanella, called Mary-of-the-Angels, showed the mystical and ascetical bent of her spirit from an early age and when she was sixteen became a Carmelite at Turin. She was of a vehement disposition, so that her austerities had to be restrained, and she was the subject of some remarkable phenomena, including a physically perceptible fragrance of holiness about her person. Many people, high and low, in Turin used to go to her for advice. d. 1717. bd 1865. *December 16, iv, 574.*

MARY *See also under* Flora *and* Isidore.

MASABKI. *See under* Damascus Martyrs.

*MATERNUS, ST, BISHOP

He was the first bishop of Cologne of whom there is any certain knowledge, and is heard of in connection with the Donatist controversy. d. *c.* 325. St Maternus was given mythical associations with St Peter in a ninth-century biography. *September 14, iii, 552.*

*MATILDA, ST

She was the wife of Henry the Fowler, and mother of, among others, the emperor Otto I, St Bruno of Cologne, and Hedwig, who became mother of Hugh Capet. Matilda suffered much from the behaviour of her sons Otto and Henry ("the Quarrelsome"), who resented the amount of money she spent on religious and charitable works and were jealous of one another. Her widowhood lasted for thirty-two years, of which the latter part was spent in retirement at one or other of the convents she had established. d. 968. *Mathildis. March 14, i, 592.*

MATILDA. *See also* Mechtildis.

*MATRONA, ST, VIRGIN AND MARTYR

She is said to have been the serving-maid of a Jewess who caused her to be martyred for her Christianity, at Salonika in 350 (?). Two other Matronas are mentioned in the

Acta Sanctorum on March 15, one a girl of Barcelona martyred at Rome and the other a maiden of Capua. *March 15, i, 595.*

*MATTHEW, ST,
APOSTLE AND EVANGELIST

Beyond what is told in the Bible (*e.g.* that he was a tax-collector by profession) no more is known of St Matthew except that he wrote the gospel that bears his name. The scene of his preaching is not known, nor is it certain that he d. a martyr. *Matthaeus. September 21, iii, 609.*

MATTHEW FLATHERS, BD, MARTYR

A secular priest b. at Weston, Otley, Yorkshire. He studied at the English College at Douai, was ordained priest at Arras in 1606 and sent on the English mission in that year. He was soon arrested and banished but returned to Yorkshire and was arrested and condemned as a priest. h.d.q. at York in 1608, aged forty-eight. bd November 22, 1987. *March 21.*

MATTHEW OF GIRGENTI, BD,
BISHOP

He left the Conventual Franciscans to join the Observants and became a close friend of St Bernardino of Siena, whom he accompanied on his preaching journeys in Italy. He became a noted preacher himself, and when he returned to his native Sicily he was appointed bishop of Girgenti. He set about reforming his diocese, but his reforms stirred up so much strife that he offered the resignation of his see, which was accepted. Bd Matthew was then refused admittance to the friary he had himself founded, because they feared he was too much of a firebrand. d. 1450. c.c. 1767. *October 21, iv, 173.*

MATTHEW OF MANTUA, BD

Matthew Carreri was a confessor of the Friars Preachers. Once, while on a voyage from Genoa to Pisa, he offered himself to some pirates in exchange for a captured woman and her daughter. d. 1470. c.c. 1482. *October 7, iv, 53.*

MATTHIA OF MATELICA, BD,
VIRGIN

Matthia Nazzarei was an early nun and abbess of the famous convent at Matelica in the March of Ancona. d. 1300. (?) c.c. 1765. *November 7, iv, 291.*

*MATTHIAS, ST, APOSTLE

The apostle of Christ who took the place of Judas Iscariot. Apart from the reference in the Acts of the Apostles there is no reliable source of information concerning him. He is said to have been martyred in Colchis. *May 14, i, 407.*

MATTHIAS MURUMBA, ST, MARTYR

Properly Matthias Kalemba; he was the oldest of the Uganda martyrs (*q.v.*) of 1886 and a district judge. He was butchered on the way to Namugongo, and left lingering in agony in the bush for three days before he died. bd 1920. cd 1964. *June 3, ii, 468.*

*MATURINUS, ST

Nothing is known of the true life of St Maturinus (Mathurin), whose *cultus* still exists in the dioceses of Sens and Meaux. Fourth century (?). *November 1, iv, 238.*

MAUGHOLD, ST, BISHOP

Maughold, or Maccul, is said to have been a brigand, converted by St Patrick, who was sent to the Isle of Man as a penitent and became bishop there. d. *c.* 498. He is commemorated in the archdiocese of Liverpool. *Maccaldus. April 27, ii, 172.*

MAUGILLE. *See* Madelgisilus.

MAURA, ST, VIRGIN

She passed her life in prayer and good works, living in her own home at Troyes where she d. while still young, *c.* 850. *September 21, iii, 610.*

MAURA AND BRIGID, SS,
VIRGINS AND MARTYRS

There is an old *cultus* of these maidens in Picardy, who according to legend were British princesses murdered on their way home from a pilgrimage to Rome during the fifth century. It is impossible to give a satisfactory account of them from the sources available. *July 13, iii, 88.*

MAURA. *See also under* Timothy.

MAURICE OF CARNOËT, ST, ABBOT

A confessor of the Cistercian Order, monk of Langonnet in Brittany and then abbot of Carnoët. d. 1191. c.c. by Pope Clement XI. *Mauritius. October 13, iv, 105.*

MAURICE OF HUNGARY, BD

Maurice Csaky, of the royal house of Hungary, became a Dominican at the same time as his wife also entered religion; his reputation was such that he is still venerated by the Magyars. d. 1336. *March 20, i, 647.*

MAURICE. *See also under* Theban Legion.

*MAURILIUS, ST, BISHOP

He was a disciple of St Martin of Tours and a zealous missionary, who occupied the see of Angers for thirty years. d. 453. *September 13, iii, 548.*

MAURUNTIUS, ST, ABBOT

He was the son of St Adalbald and St Rictrudis and succeeded to his father's estates; but he left secular life and founded a monastery at Breuil of which he became abbot. d. 701. *May 5, ii, 238.*

MAWES, ST, ABBOT

Mawes is said to have been a sixth-century monk who founded a church near Falmouth when on his way to Brittany; in that country he is called Maudez, and many churches are dedicated in his honour. *Maudetus. November 18, iv, 383.*

MAXELLENDIS, ST,
VIRGIN AND MARTYR

She was, it is said, slain by one Harduin of Solesmes in a fit of rage, because she wanted to be a nun and refused to marry him, *c.* 670. *November 13, iv, 330.*

MAXENTIA, ST, VIRGIN AND MARTYR

She was venerated at Beauvais as an Irish maiden who fled to France from a suitor and perished in similar circumstances to the last-named, at a place called Pont-Sainte-Maxence. In fact, nothing is known about her, not even the century in which she lived. *November 20, iv, 394.*

*MAXENTIUS, ST, ABBOT

Born at Agde *c.* 448. He left his home and joined a monastery in Poitou, of which he became abbot: its site is now called Saint-Maixent. Like many another bishop and abbot he is said miraculously to have saved his flock from raiding barbarians. d. *c.* 515. *June 26, ii, 647.*

MAXIMA. *See under* Martinian.

MAXIMIAN. *See under* Bonosus.

*MAXIMILIAN, ST, MARTYR

Or *Mamilian*. He was a youth of Theveste in Numidia who in 295 refused to do military service in the Roman army. He gave his Christianity as the reason for his refusal, and was executed. His *passio* is authentic. *Maximilianus, Mamilianus. March 12, i, 571.*

MAXIMILIAN KOLBE, ST, MARTYR

He was born in Russian Poland in 1894, at Zdunska Wola, near Lodz. His parents were Franciscan tertiaries. In 1910, after junior seminary, he became a Franciscan. His parents entered religious orders. His father fought against the Russians, who hanged him in 1914. Maximilian developed tuberculosis, started a sodality with a strong Marian emphasis, and a magazine produced eventually with others at Niepokalonow, near Warsaw. He started another community in Japan but returned in 1936 as Superior of the 760+ friars at Niepokalonow. After the German invasion in 1939 the community sheltered Polish and Jewish refugees and published articles critical of the occupiers. Maximilian was arrested during the drive to destroy the Polish intelligentsia and imprisoned in the heavy labour section of the

German concentration and extermination camp at Auschwitz (Oswiecim), a place of unparalleled suffering and of mass murder, on an industrial scale, mainly of Jews but also of Poles, gypsies and other "inferior" groups. Maximilian ministered heroically to his fellow friars. After an escape, in reprisal a married man from Maximilian's bunker was chosen for execution by starvation. Kolbe volunteered to take his place. He suffered for two weeks in a squalid death-hole, encouraging his fellow-inmates. He died by phenol injection on August 14, 1941. St Maximilian is a figure of exemplary selflessness, charity and spirituality, and of a form of sanctity appropriate to the vast cruelties and terrible inhumanity of the modern age. In the presence of the man whose life he had saved, he was canonized in 1982 by John Paul II. *August 14.*

*MAXIMILIAN OF LORCH, ST,
BISHOP AND MARTYR

He founded the church of Lorch, near Passau, and was martyred *c.* 284, according to his legend. *October 12, iv, 93.*

*MAXIMINUS OF AIX, ST

Historical research has hitherto failed to yield any reliable information about this saint, who is venerated in southern France as the first bishop of Aix, and as having come with St Mary Magdalen and others from Palestine to Provence. *June 8, ii, 501.*

*MAXIMINUS OF TRIER, ST, BISHOP

A bishop of Trier who was prominent in his opposition to Arianism and gave hospitality for two years to the exiled St Athanasius. d. *c.* 347. *May 29, ii, 419.*

*MAXIMINUS. *See also under* Juventinus.

*MAXIMUS OF EPHESUS, ST,
MARTYR

Maximus, a trader, was stoned to death at Ephesus (or at Lampsacus) in 250, for refusing to sacrifice to the gods. *April 30, ii, 198.*

*MAXIMUS OF RIEZ, ST, BISHOP

He was chosen second abbot of Lérins in 426 and was translated thence to the see of Riez. d. *c.* 460. *November 27, iv, 435.*

*MAXIMUS OF TURIN, ST, BISHOP

This Maximus was for many years bishop of Turin, but is remembered rather for his writings, homilies and so forth, which have survived. d. *c.* 467. *June 25, ii, 640.*

*MAXIMUS THE CONFESSOR, ST,
ABBOT

This Maximus, abbot of Chrysopolis (Skutari), was one of the foremost divines of the seventh century, a pillar of orthodoxy against monothelism and an upholder of the teaching authority of the Roman see. He was banished by the heretical emperor Constans II, and was so maltreated that he d., in great suffering, and at the age of eighty-two, in Colchis in 622. Maximus is best remembered to-day as a mystical writer, and is accounted one of the fathers of Byzantine mysticism. *August 13, iii, 320.*

MAXIMUS. *See also under* Claudius *and* Tiburtius.

MAY. *See* Marius.

MAYEUL. *See* Majolus.

MECHTILDIS OF EDELSTETTEN,
ST, VIRGIN

She was the abbess first of Diessen in Bavaria and then of Edelstetten, where she had to expel some of the nuns before order could be restored. Mechtildis had miraculous gifts and was greatly respected by her contemporaries. d. 1160. *Mathildis.* *May 31, ii, 435.*

MECHTILDIS OF HELFTA, ST,
VIRGIN

Mechtildis von Hackeborn was the novice-mistress of St Gertrude the Great and followed the same mystical way as her pupil; her "revelations", the *Book of Special Grace*, were written down by Gertrude.

She has never been canonized, but her feast is observed in numerous Benedictine convents. d. 1278. *November 16, iv, 351.*

*MEDARD, ST, BISHOP

Born *c.* 470, was ordained at the age of thirty-three, and in 530 became bishop of Vermandois. He is a very popular saint among the peasants of northern France, but most of the details given of his life are unsupported by good evidence. d. *c.* 560. *Medardus. June 8, ii, 502.*

*MEDERICUS, ST, ABBOT

In French *Merry.* He was abbot of St Martin's at Autun, and twice resigned his office to be a hermit. d. *c.* 700. *August 29, iii, 443.*

MÉEN, ST, ABBOT

Méen (Mewan) was perhaps a Welsh monk who went to Brittany during the sixth century and there settled. With St Austol he formerly had some *cultus* in Cornwall. *Mevennus. June 21, ii, 609.*

MEINGOLD, ST, MARTYR

Meingold is said to have been a nobleman in what is now Belgium, who did seven years of penance and pilgrimage for all the blood he had shed. He was set on and killed by some of his old enemies at Stierke. But a great deal of doubt surrounds the life and death of St Meingold. *February 8, i, 279.*

*MEINRAD, ST, MARTYR

Meinrad (Maynard) is venerated as the patron and in some sense the founder of the Benedictine abbey of Einsiedeln in Switzerland, which has kept an unbroken continuity since Carolingian times. He settled as a hermit at Einsiedeln, where he was murdered by two ruffians to whom he had given hospitality, in 861. *Meinradus. January 21, i, 139.*

MEINULF. *See* Magenulf.

MEINWERK, BD, BISHOP

Meinwerk was raised to the see of Paderborn in 1009. He rebuilt the cathedral, founded religious houses at Abdinghof and Paderborn, fortified the city with walls, and established a school where the teaching was first-rate and the discipline severe. For these and other works he had to be so active borrowing money that at times he became a nuisance to his richer friends. For all that he was one of the most worthy churchmen of his time. d. 1036. *June 5, ii, 482.*

MEL AND MELCHU, SS, BISHOPS

SS Mel, Melchu, Muinis and Rioch are said to have been the sons of Darerca, sister of St Patrick, whom they accompanied to Ireland as missionaries. Mel is venerated as the first bishop of Ardagh, but the records are conflicting and largely legendary. Fifth century. *February 6, i, 262.*

*MELAINE, ST, BISHOP

A bishop of Rennes, for whom King Clovis, after his conversion, had great respect. d. *c.* 530. *Melanius. November 6, iv, 274.*

MELANGELL, ST, VIRGIN

A maiden formerly venerated in Montgomeryshire. The legend attached to her name is a version of a widely known folktale—a hunted hare took refuge under her skirt. Date unknown. *Monacella. May 27, ii, 406.*

*MELANIA THE YOUNGER, ST

She belonged to the Roman patrician family of the Valerii and was a grand-daughter of St Melania the Elder. She married her cousin Pinian, and after the death of their two children and the Visigothic invasion they lived abroad: eventually St Pinian became a monk at Jerusalem and Melania joined a community of women near by. They especially occupied themselves with the care of the poor and the copying of books. d. 439. The memory of this St Melania was revived in modern times by Cardinal Rampolla. *December 31, iv, 646.*

MELCHIADES. *See* Miltiades.

MELCHIOR GRODECH, BD, MARTYR

A Czech Jesuit barbarously put to death by Calvinist soldiers at Kosice in Slovakia, 1619. bd 1905. *September 7, iii, 504.*

MELCHIOR SAMPEDRO, ST.

See Joseph Sanjurjo.

MELCHIOR OF ST AUGUSTINE, BD.

See Martin of St Nicholas.

*MELETIUS, ST, BISHOP

When he became archbishop of Antioch in 361 his diocese was divided by the Arian heresy and the whole of his pontificate of twenty years was troubled by this and other difficulties. Meletius was several times banished by the imperial power, but he slowly gained the bulk of Eastern support and he presided at the second oecumenical council, held at Constantinople in 381. He d. while the council was still sitting.
February 12, i, 316.

MELEUSIPPUS. *See under* Speusippus.

MELITO, ST, BISHOP

A bishop of Sardis in Lydia whose writings were praised by Eusebius and others. d. *c.* 180 (?). *April 1, ii, 1.*

*MELLITUS, ST, BISHOP

Mellitus followed St Augustine to England in 601 and was made the first bishop of London. He was banished for refusing holy communion to the heathen sons of King Sabert of the East Saxons, but was recalled to be archbishop of Canterbury in 619. d. 624. His feast is kept in the dioceses of Westminster, Brentwood and Southwark. *April 24, ii, 157.*

MELLON, ST, BISHOP

He is venerated as the first bishop of Rouen, in the fourth (?) century. He seems to give his name to Saint Mellons, near Cardiff. *Mallonus. October 22, iv, 178.*

*MENNAS, ST, MARTYR

All that is probably certain about St Mennas is that he was an Egyptian, martyred and buried at Karm Abu-Mina, near Alexandria.

He was afterwards made into a "warrior-saint", put to death in Phrygia and buried in Egypt, and his *cultus* was widespread in the East. *November 11, iv, 313.*

*MENNAS AND HERMOGENES, SS, MARTYRS

Mennas, Hermogenes and Eugraphus were said to be put to death by beheading at Alexandria. No reliance can be put on their *passio*, which was falsely ascribed to St Athanasius. *December 10, iv, 529.*

*MENNAS OF CONSTANTINOPLE, ST, BISHOP

He became patriarch of Constantinople in 536, and was concerned in the affair of the Three Chapters in the Monophysite controversy. d. 552. *August 25, iii, 401.*

*MENODORA, ST, MARTYR

The sisters Menodora, Metrodora and Nymphodora are the subjects of a Greek legend which makes them martyrs in Bithynia under Diocletian. *September 10, iii, 528.*

MERCEDES OF JESUS, BD, VIRGIN

Mercedes Molina was b. near Guayaquil, Ecuador, in 1828. She devoted her life to the care of orphans and became a missionary among the Indios. In 1873 she founded a sisterhood at Riobamba for the care of the most impoverished children. d. 1883. bd January 30, 1985 in Ecuador. *June 12.*

*MERCURIUS, ST, MARTYR

He is said to have been a Scythian officer in the Roman army, beheaded for the faith at Caesarea in Cappadocia. He was afterwards revered in the East as a "warrior-saint". *November 25, iv, 421.*

MERIADOC, ST

This saint, probably a Welshman, is venerated in Brittany, but his history is only conjectural: it is not even certain in which century he lived (sixth?). The parish church of Camborne in Cornwall is dedicated in his honour and he is the subject of the Cornish miracle-play, *Beunans Meriasek.*
June 7, ii, 493.

MERRY. *See* Medericus.

MESROP, ST

He was a missionary in Armenia under St Isaac the Great; to him is attributed the invention of the Armenian alphabet, the translation of the New Testament into that language, and the organization of studies and schools throughout the country, so that he is called in the intercession of the Armenian Mass, "Mesrop the Teacher". d. 441. *February 19, i, 374.*

*METHODIUS OF CONSTANTINOPLE, ST, BISHOP

Called "the Confessor". He was a strong opponent of the iconoclast heresy and was sent to Rome to report on the persecution to the Holy See. On his return to Constantinople in 821, he was thrown into prison, and remained there for seven years. In 842 he was made patriarch, and among his acts was to institute the Feast of Orthodoxy, still observed by the Byzantines, to commemorate the vindication of the true doctrine concerning holy images by the second Council of Nicaea. d. 847. *June 14, ii, 543.*

*METHODIUS OF OLYMPUS, ST, BISHOP AND MARTYR

He was bishop of Olympus in Lycia. Particulars are wanting of his life and martyrdom (*c.* 311), and his fame rests on his writings, especially his treatise on the Resurrection and the *Banquet of the Ten Virgins. September 18, iii, 592.*

METHODIUS. *See also under* Cyril.

METRODORA. *See under* Menodora.

*METROPHANES, ST, BISHOP

He was bishop of Byzantium (Constantinople) in the days of Constantine and probably the first bishop of that see. He had a great reputation for holiness throughout the Christian East, but little is known about him. d. *c.* 325. *June 4, ii, 473.*

*MEURIS AND THEA, SS., MARTYRS

Two women of Gaza in Palestine who suffered martyrdom *c.* 308. The second is probably the St Thea of July 25. *December 19, iv, 584.*

MEWAN. *See* Méen.

*MICHAEL THE ARCHANGEL, ST

Michael is regarded traditionally as the chief of the archangels, a special protector against the attacks of Satan, and, in the East, patron of the sick. He has two feasts in the Western Church: that of May 8, commemorating his alleged appearance at Monte Gargano in Italy during the fifth century, and that of September 29, the anniversary of the dedication of a church of St Michael on the Salarian Way at Rome, during the sixth century. *Michaël.* *September 29, iii, 677; ii, 249.*

MICHAEL CARVALHO, BD, MARTYR

After teaching in the Jesuit college at Goa for fifteen years he was sent as a missionary to Japan, which he reached only with great difficulty. He was roasted to death in 1624, together with BB Peter Vasquez, Louis Sotelo and two other Franciscans, also called Louis. bd 1867. *August 25, ii, 449.*

MICHAEL FEBRES CORDERO, ST

Miguel Febres Cordero was b. at Cuenca, Ecuador, on November 7, 1854. He was the first Latin-American member of the Brothers of the Christian Schools. He was a poet, linguist and Academician, and a humble and eloquent religious educator. He left for Europe in 1907. d. at Premia de Mar, Spain, in 1910. bd by Pope Paul VI in 1977. c. by John Paul II on October 21, 1984. *February 9.*

*MICHAEL GARICOÏTS, ST

Born in 1797, the son of a Pyrenean peasant. He became a secular priest and rector of a seminary, and in 1838 founded at Bétharram the congregation of Priests of the Sacred Heart (Bétharram Fathers) for home mission work. Aspirants were numerous, but Michael met with much opposition, which did not deflect him from his object. d. 1863. cd 1947. *May 14, ii, 312.*

MICHAEL GIEDROYĆ, BD

He was a crippled dwarf of noble family who took up his abode in a cell adjoining the church of the Augustinian canons at

Cracow. Here he led a life of great austerity and was famed for prophecy and miracles. d. 1485. *May 4, ii, 233.*

MICHAEL GHÈBRÈ. *See* Gabra Michael.

MICHAEL KOZAL, BD,
BISHOP AND MARTYR

Michal Kozal was b. in 1893, ordained priest in 1918 and, on the outbreak of war in 1939, became first auxiliary then bishop of Wloclawek, Poland. He was arrested by the Nazis on November 7, 1939, during the German occupation, as part of their drive to eradicate the Polish intelligentsia and elite. He was sent to a convent, and in 1941 to Dachau concentration camp, where he was murdered by injection in 1943. bd June 14, 1987. *January 26.*

MICHAEL PIO FASOLI, BD. *See* Samuel Marzorati and his two companions.

MICHAEL PRO, BD, MARTYR

Miguel Pro was b. at Guadalupe, Mexico, on January 13, 1891. He became a Jesuit and joined the Society in political exile in California, Spain and Belgium. He was ordained priest in 1925, returned to Mexico and exercised a clandestine ministry. After an attempt to assassinate General Obregon, he was arrested on November 18, 1927, shown to be innocent yet sentenced without trial and shot. 20,000 people attended his burial. bd September 25, 1988. *November 23.*

MICHAEL RUA, BD

Michele Rua was b. at Turin on June 9, 1837. He was one of the founding members of the Salesian order. He was ordained priest on July 29, 1860 and in 1863 Don Bosco appointed him director of a minor seminary. He succeeded Don Bosco in January 1888 and died at Turin in April 1910. Pope Paul VI honoured him as an upholder of tradition. b. October 29, 1972. *April 6.*

*MICHAEL DE SANCTIS, ST

Born in Catalonia *c.* 1590 and became a Trinitarian friar of the bare-footed branch.

He was twice superior at Valladolid and his short life was made noteworthy by his "innocence, penitence and love of God". d. 1625. cd 1862. *April 10, ii, 66.*

MICHAEL OF CHERNIGOV, ST,
MARTYR

After once running away, Duke Michael refused an act of idolatrous worship, and was beheaded by the Tartars, in 1246. *September 21, iii, 611.*

MICHELINA OF PESARO, BD

Michelina Metelli married a Malatesta, but she was not much more than twenty when her husband and only son died. She then became a Franciscan tertiary and devoted herself to the care of the poor and sick. d. 1356. c.c. 1737. *September 9, ii, 591.*

*MILBURGA, ST, VIRGIN

Elder sister of St Mildred and first abbess of the convent of Wenlock in Salop. She had the gift of healing, especially blindness, and a mysterious power over birds. d. *c.* 700. Her feast is kept in the diocese of Shrewsbury. *February 23, i, 405.*

MILDGYTHA, ST, VIRGIN

Sister of the preceding. She was perhaps at one time a nun at Minster-in-Thanet, but d. and was buried in Northumbria *c.* 676. *January 17, i, 406.*

MILDRED OF THANET, ST, VIRGIN

Mildred was an extremely popular saint in earlier times in England, but only a few particulars of her life are preserved. She was a granddaughter of Penda of Mercia and sister of SS Milburga and Mildgytha, and went to be trained in the convent of Chelles in France. She returned to England and became a nun at Minster-in-Thanet, where she succeeded her mother, St Ermenburga, as abbess. "She was merciful to widows and orphans, a comforter to all the poor and afflicted, and in all respects of easy temper and tranquil." She d. *c.* 700, and her relics were carried away to St Augustine's abbey church at Canterbury. *Mildreda. July 13, iii, 91.*

MILES GERARD, BD, MARTYR

A secular priest, b. at Wigan, who was h.d.q. for his priesthood at Rochester in 1590. bd 1929. *April 30, ii, 201.*

MILO, BD, BISHOP

Milo of Sélincourt, after being abbot of the Premonstratensian house of Dommartin, was raised to the bishopric of Thérouanne in 1131. He assisted St Bernard in his controversy with Gilbert de la Porrée. d. 1158. *July 16, iii, 119.*

*MILTIADES, ST, POPE AND MARTYR

Sometimes written *Melchiades*. Miltiades is chiefly remembered because it was during his short pontificate that the emperor Constantine granted toleration to the Church. He was an African, and is venerated as a martyr because he had suffered many things during the persecution of Maximian. d. 314. *December 10, iv, 528.*

MIRIN, ST, BISHOP

A seventh-century (?) Irish missionary in Scotland, whose shrine at Paisley became a place of pilgrimage. His feast is kept in the diocese of Paisley. He is not the same as the Cornish St Merryn, who is unidentified. *September 15, iii, 557.*

MOCHOEMOC, ST, ABBOT

He was a nephew of St Ita and was first a monk of Bangor in County Down under St Comgall, and then abbot of Liathmor, which he founded. Nothing else is recorded of St Mochoemoc but fantastic legends. Seventh century. *March 13, iv, 583.*

MOCHTA, ST, BISHOP

He was a Briton by birth, a personal disciple of St Patrick, and is regarded as the first bishop at Louth in Ireland. *August 19, iii, 356.*

MOCHUDA. *See* Carthage.

MOCHUMMA. *See* Machar.

MODAN, ST, ABBOT

St Modan is traditionally associated with the abbey of Dryburgh, but it seems to have been first founded long after his time. He preached at Stirling, Falkirk and along the Forth. Sixth century. *February 4, i, 249.*

MODESTUS. *See under* Vitus.

*MODOALDUS, ST, BISHOP

He was an uncle of St Gertrude of Nivelles, and as bishop of Trier was noteworthy for the number of his religious foundations. d. c. 640. *May 12, ii, 287.*

MODOMNOC, ST

Modomnoc is said to have been of the Irish royal line of O'Neill and to have been a disciple of St David in Wales. He then returned to Tibraghny in County Kilkenny. Sixth century. Legend associates St Modomnoc with the introduction of bees to Ireland—they followed him from Pembrokeshire. *February 13, i, 322.*

MODWENNA, ST, VIRGIN

There appear to be more than one maiden saint of this name and it seems impossible to disentangle them. A St Modwenna, or Monenna, near Burton-on-Trent has been confused with the Irish St Moninne or Darerca. *July 6, iii, 26.*

MOLAISSE. *See* Laserian.

MOLING, ST, BISHOP

Or *Daircheall*. He is said to have been a monk of Glendalough, then abbot at Tech Moling (St Mullins), and bishop at Ferns. His *cultus* is very ancient. d. 697. *Molingus. June 17, ii, 568.*

MOLOC, ST, BISHOP

Lughaidh, Luan. He is said to have been a Scot, trained in Ireland, who evangelized various parts of his native land. d. c. 572 (?). His shrine was at Mortlach, *i.e.* Murlach. *Moluanus. June 25, ii, 641.*

MOLUA, ST, ABBOT

This Molua (Lughaidh) founded monasteries in Ireland, the chief of which was at

Kyle in the Slieveblooms. His identity with the Scottish St Moloc has not been established. d. 608. *August 4, iii, 264.*

MOMMOLINUS, ST, BISHOP
A monk of Luxeuil who became bishop of Noyon. d. *c.* 686. *October 16, iv, 128.*

MONACELLA. *See* Melangell.

MONEGUNDIS, ST
A woman of Chartres who, after the death of her two daughters, shut herself up in a cell; later she migrated to Tours and followed the same way of life: her cell there became the nunnery of Saint-Pierre-le-Puellier. d. 570. *July 2, iii, 8.*

MONICA, ST
St Monica was b. of Christian parents in North Africa in 332, and married a pagan husband. He was converted by her gentleness and prayers just before his death, and thenceforward her life was the story of the conversion of her elder son, Augustine, afterwards bishop of Hippo and doctor of the Church. She followed him to Rome and to Milan (where St Ambrose was her friend and helper), and there her prayers and sufferings were rewarded; it was not possible "that the son of such tears should perish". St Monica d. at Ostia on the way back to Africa with Augustine in 387. *August 27, ii, 226.*

MONINNE. *See* Darerca.

MONTANUS, ST, AND OTHER
MARTYRS
In 259 there was an insurrection at Carthage, which was unjustly blamed upon the Christians. Montanus, Lucius and six others, all disciples of St Cyprian, were arrested, and we have a reliable contemporary account of their sufferings and death. After being kept in prison with hardly any food or drink for several months they were beheaded. One of them, Flavian, was reprieved because of his popularity with the people, but he insisted that the plea made for him, that he was not a deacon and therefore not liable to the death penalty, was

false; and accordingly three days later he, too, was beheaded. *February 24, i, 408.*

MONTFORD SCOTT, BD, MARTYR
Montford Scott (or Monford Scot) was a secular priest b. at Hawkestead in the diocese of Norwich who entered Douai College in 1574. He was ordained priest in 1575 and went on the English mission in 1577. He was noted for his abstinence and devotion for which he was said to have been arrested. He was h.d.q. in Fleet Street, London, in 1591 aged *c.* forty-one years. bd November 1987. *July 2.*

MORAND, ST
He was b. near Worms and after his ordination became a Cluniac monk. While serving the church of Altkirch in Alsace he distinguished himself as a missioner all over the neighbouring countryside. d. *c.* 1115. *June 3, ii, 466.*

MOSES, ST, BISHOP
An Arabian missionary bishop among the nomadic tribes of the Syro-Arabian desert. d. *c.* 372. *Moyses. February 7, i, 270.*

MOSES OF ROME, ST, MARTYR
He was a priest at Rome and one of the first to be arrested in the Decian persecution; he d. after a year's imprisonment, 251. *November 25, iv, 422.*

MOSES THE BLACK, ST, MARTYR
Moses was an Ethiopian, first a slave and then a brigand in Egypt; he was converted, became a monk and priest in the desert of Skete, and in old age was murdered by robbers, against whom he refused to defend himself. He was one of the most remarkable figures among the Desert Fathers during the fourth century. *August 28, iii, 435.*

MOUNT SINAI, THE MARTYRS OF
During the fourth century several groups of solitaries on Mount Sinai and in the desert of Raithu were put to death by Bedouin Arabs. They are mentioned in the Roman Martyrology and commemorated in the Byzantine rite. *January 14, i, 83.*

*MUCIUS, ST, MARTYR

A priest who was put to death for the faith at Constantinople in 304; his extant "acts" are spurious. *May 13, ii, 296.*

MUNCHIN, ST, BISHOP

The traditional patron of the diocese of Limerick, of whom practically nothing is known. He lived in the sixth/seventh century, but it is doubtful if he ever was a bishop. His feast is kept throughout Ireland. *January 2, i, 21.*

MUNGO. *See* Kentigern.

MUNNU. *See* Fintan of Taghmon.

MURTAGH, ST, BISHOP

Murtagh (Muredach) is venerated liturgically throughout Ireland as the first bishop in Killala, probably in the sixth century. *Muredachus. August 12, iii, 314.*

MUTIEN MARY WIAUX, ST

Louis Joseph (or Brother Mutien-Marie) Wiaux was b. on March 20, 1841 near Gosselles, Belgium. He joined the Brothers of the Christian Schools in 1856 when he was fifteen. He taught with humble devotion at Malonne College for fifty-eight years. d. 1917. cd December 10, 1989. *January 30.*

MUSTIOLA. *See under* Irenaeus.

MYLOR, ST, MARTYR

The story of the martyred prince Melorus (Mélar in Brittany, Mylor in Cornwall) is a medieval fable worked up out of several Celtic elements; whether it has any foundation in fact is not known. Its events were localized both in Brittany and Cornwall, but Mylor may really be another Breton, St Méloir (Melorius). *October 1, iv, 4.*

N

*NABOR AND FELIX, SS, MARTYRS
Martyrs under Diocletian (?) at Milan, where they have an ancient *cultus* and are named in the canon of the Ambrosian MaSS *July 12, iii, 84.*

*NAJRAN, THE MARTYRS OF
Najran, in south-western Arabia, was the scene in 523 of a massacre of Ethiopian and other Christians by Jews and heathen Arabs, a leader among the victims being the chief of the Banu Harith (called in the Roman Martyrology St "Aretas"). This massacre made a deep and awful impression which lasted for many generations in the East: Mohammed condemns it in the Koran. *October 24, iv, 190.*

*NARCISSUS, ST, BISHOP
When he was already very old Narcissus was made bishop of Jerusalem at the end of the second century. He retired from his see for a time in consequence of an unspecified false accusation made against him. He was greatly venerated by his people, who narrated several miracles of him. d. *c.* 215. *October 29, iv, 217.*

NARSES. *See* Nerses.

NATALIA, *See under* Adrian *and* Aurelius.

NATHALAN, ST, BISHOP
According to the medieval Aberdeen Breviary, Nathalan, believing that "amongst the works of man's hands the cultivation of the earth approaches nearest to divine contemplation", gave himself up to that occupation. His rather extravagant legend states that while on a pilgrimage to Rome he was made bishop, and on his return founded churches in Scotland. Seventh century. His *cultus* was confirmed for the diocese of Aberdeen in 1898. *Nathalanus. January 19, i, 118.*

NATHANIEL, NATHANAEL. *See* Bartholomew (apostle).

NATHY AND FELIM, SS
St Nathy was a priest at Achonry and St Felim was probably a regionary bishop in the Breffney country. Though not associated with one another, so far as is known, these two sixth-century (?) saints are celebrated throughout Ireland by a common feast. *Natheus, Fedliminus. August 9, iii, 293.*

*NAZARIUS AND CELSUS, SS, MARTYRS
The only certain thing about these martyrs is that St Ambrose found their reputed relics at Milan, where they are supposed to have suffered. *July 28, iii, 200.*

NECTAN, ST
Nectan was venerated as a martyr at his shrine at Hartland and elsewhere in the west of England during the Middle Ages, but nothing at all is known about him. He may have been a missionary from Wales in the sixth century. *June 17, ii, 565.*

NECTARIUS, ST, BISHOP

He succeeded St Gregory Nazianzen as archbishop of Constantinople, when, it is said, he was not yet even baptized. d. 397. *October 11, iv, 86.*

*NEMESIAN, ST,
BISHOP AND MARTYR

The Roman Martyrology names Nemesian and eight other African bishops who, with numerous lower clergy and lay people, suffered under the persecution of Valerian in 257. *Nemesianus. September 10, iii, 527.*

*NEMESIUS, ST, MARTYR

He was an Alexandrian who in 250, upon being acquitted on a charge of theft, was condemned as a Christian and executed with a number of criminals. *December 19, iv, 584.*

NEON. *See under* Claudius.

NEOT, ST

Nothing is certainly known of St Neot: according to medieval legends he was a monk of Glastonbury in the ninth century who became a hermit at the place now called Saint Neot in Cornwall. The St Neot venerated in Huntingdonshire may be a different man. *July 31, iii, 227.*

*NEREUS AND ACHILLEUS, SS,
MARTYRS

We learn from an inscription of Pope St Damasus that these were Roman soldiers who, on becoming Christians, left the army and were martyred, at an unknown date. Their extant "acts" are legendary. *May 12, ii, 284.*

*NERO, MARTYRS UNDER

On June 24 the Roman Martyrology mentions "the first fruits with which Rome, so fruitful in that seed, peopled Heaven", namely, those Christians who in the year 64 were put to death with refinements of cruelty by order of Nero on a false charge of having set fire to the city. That Nero himself had fired it is by no means certain. *June 24, ii, 633.*

NERSES, ST, BISHOP AND MARTYR

He was bishop of Sahgerd in Persia and, with his disciple Joseph, was beheaded under Sapor II in 343 for refusing false worship. A number of other martyrs are referred to in the *passio* of St Nerses. *November 19, iv, 393.*

NERSES I, ST, BISHOP AND MARTYR

This Nerses was the father of St Isaac the Great. After the death of his wife he became, *c.* 363, katholikos or chief bishop of the Armenian church, and laboured to spread Christianity, but some of his reforms displeased King Arshak, who banished him. The succeeding monarch, Pap, was atrociously wicked and would neither behave himself nor submit to the religious discipline that Nerses imposed on him; in the end, Pap poisoned the bishop, *c.* 373. *November 19, iv, 391.*

NERSES KLAIËTSI, ST, BISHOP

Nerses Klaiëtsi was the most famous writer of the twelfth-century Armenian renaissance and a vigorous strengthener of Christian unity. He became chief bishop of his people, as Nerses IV, in 1166. d. 1173. *August 13, iii, 322.*

NERSES LAMPRONATSI, ST, BISHOP

He was Armenian archbishop of Tarsus and played a chief part in the events which led to the reunion of Little Armenia with the Holy See in 1198. St Nerses d. in the same year. Among other literary works he translated the Rule of St Benedict into Armenian. *July 17, iii, 131.*

*NESTOR, ST, BISHOP AND MARTYR

A bishop in Pamphylia, put to death for the faith by crucifixion in 251. *February 26, i, 422.*

*NESTOR OF GAZA, ST, MARTYR

A youth who d. as the result of torture under Julian the Apostate, at Gaza in 362. *September 8.*

*NICANDER AND MARCIAN, SS,
MARTYRS

These martyrs perhaps suffered at Durostorum (Silistria in Bulgaria) in the fourth century, but the facts have been overlaid by fictitious embellishments.
June 17, ii, 561.

*NICARETE, ST, VIRGIN

She came from Nicomedia and was a supporter of St John Chrysostom at Constantinople; like St Olympias she suffered persecution and exile in consequence. d. *c.* 410. *December 27, iv, 624.*

*NICASIUS, ST, BISHOP AND MARTYR

He was a bishop of Rheims who, with his sister St Eutropia and several members of his clergy, was killed by invading barbarians while defending his flock, in 451 (?).
December 14, iv, 558.

NICEPHORUS DIEZ TEJERINA AND HIS TWENTY-FIVE COMPANIONS, BB, MARTYRS

Father Nicéforo (Vicente) Diez Tejerina and his twenty-five companions were Spanish Passionists of the Daimiel community, teachers and their students (sixteen of them were twenty-one years old and less) preparing for the priesthood and the Cuban, Mexican and Venezuelan missions, martyred during the anti-religious troubles in Spain on October 23, 1936. bd October 1, 1989. *October 23.*

*NICEPHORUS OF ANTIOCH, ST,
MARTYR

It appears that Nicephorus, who was said to be a martyr at Antioch *c.* 260, was the hero of a pious romance whose object was to teach the lesson of forgiveness of injuries.
February 9, i, 286.

*NICEPHORUS OF CONSTANTINOPLE, ST BISHOP

He was an official at the imperial court and distinguished himself as an opponent of Iconoclasm; while still a layman he was elected patriarch of Constantinople in 806, and incurred the strong disapproval of St Theodore and his Studite monks. At the second outbreak of Iconoclasm, under Leo the Armenian, Nicephorus was exiled and spent the last fifteen years of his life in a monastery he had founded on the Bosphorus. d. 828. *March 13, i, 584.*

*NICETAS, ST, ABBOT

He was abbot of Medikion on Mount Olympus in Bithynia, who with his monks was much persecuted for his opposition to the iconoclastic emperor Leo. He spent many years in prison. d. 824.
April 3, ii, 21.

NICETAS OF CONSTANTINOPLE, ST

He was a young patrician of Constantinople who became a monk there and distinguished himself by his opposition to the Iconoclasts. He d. in exile in Paphlagonia *c.* 838. *October 6, iv, 45.*

NICETAS OF NOVOGOROD, ST,
BISHOP

A monk of Kiev, who overcame the dangers of misapplied study and was made bishop of Novgorod in 1095. d. 1107.
January 31, i, 216.

NICETAS OF PEREASLAV, ST,
MARTYR

A tax-collector who repented of his wicked ways and withdrew from the world as a hermit; he was murdered by robbers. The miracles of healing attributed to him caused him to be venerated as a saint in Russia. d. 1186. *May 24, ii, 384.*

*NICETAS OF REMESIANA, ST,
BISHOP

This Nicetas was a missionary in the country around the lower Danube. It is strongly held by some scholars that he was the author of the thanksgiving hymn, "Te Deum". d. *c.* 414. *June 22, ii, 614.*

*NICETAS THE GOTH, ST, MARTYR

One of the Christian Visigoths put to death by their king Athanaric. Nicetas was a priest, who suffered near the lower Danube in 375. *September 15, iii, 555.*

NICETIUS OF BESANÇON, ST,
BISHOP

In French *Nizier*. A bishop of Besançon, friend of St Gregory the Great and of St Columban, as is said. d. *c.* 611 (?). *February 8, i, 278.*

*NICETIUS OF LYONS, ST, BISHOP

This Nicetius was bishop of Lyons for twenty years and d. in 573. *April 2, ii, 16.*

*NICETIUS OF TRIER, ST, BISHOP

Nicetius was the last Gallo-Roman bishop of Trier. He fearlessly opposed the cruelty of the Frankish nobles and even excommunicated Clotaire I for his crimes, so that for a time the bishop was banished. Nicetius was tireless in restoring to discipline a diocese that had suffered much from civil disorder, and he founded a school for young clerics. d. *c.* 566. *December 5, iv, 499.*

*NICHOLAS, ST, BISHOP

Although St Nicholas was, and still is, one of the most popular of saints both in the East and the West no more is certainly known of him than that he was bishop of Myra in Lycia in the fourth century, and that his alleged relics, stolen by Italian merchants in 1087, now rest at Bari, whence in the West he is often called "of Bari". The varied and in parts fantastic legends of St Nicholas are first heard of some five hundred years after his death; his patronage of children seems to have arisen from his restoring to life three murdered boys who had been pickled in a brine-tub. (St Nicholas = Sint Klaes = Santa Klaus.) He is also a patron of sailors, of captives, of several countries and provinces (including Russia), of many cities and dioceses (including Galway), and of churches innumerable. *Nicolaus. December 6, iv, 503.*

*NICHOLAS, I, ST, POPE

Nicholas the Great came to the papal chair in 858 and ruled for nine years. The chief event of his pontificate was the dispute with Photius at Constantinople. In other struggles this pope stood up to the great ones of the earth in defence of the integrity of Christian marriage, the protection of the weak, and the equality of all before the divine law: he rebuked emperors and kings and archbishops impartially. Nicholas was "patient and temperate, humble and chaste, beautiful in face and graceful in body... the champion of the people". d. 867. *November 13, iv, 331.*

*NICHOLAS ALBERGATI, BD,
BISHOP

Bd Nicholas was a Carthusian monk. In 1417 he was appointed bishop of Bologna and in 1426 a cardinal, and had so great a reputation as a mediator that he was called "the angel of peace". He played a prominent part in the Council of Florence, dying at Siena in 1443. c.c. 1744. *May 9, ii, 262.*

NICHOLAS FACTOR, BD

A confessor of the Friars Minor of the Observance in Spain, with whose name many marvels are associated. d. 1583. bd 1786. *December 14, iv, 562.*

*NICHOLAS VON FLÜE, ST

He was the son of a farmer, b. in Unterwalden in 1417, and twice fought in the military forces of his canton, where he was appointed magistrate and deputy for Obwalden in public affairs. He married when a young man and had ten children, several of whom distinguished themselves. When he was fifty, Nicholas left his family with their consent, and spent nineteen years as a hermit at Ranft. When the Swiss Confederation was convulsed with dissensions in 1481 it consulted Nicholas, and it is possible that he helped to draw up the Edict of Stans. d. 1487. As "Bruder Klaus" Nicholas was and is honoured throughout Switzerland as patriot and saint: ecclesiastics, politicians, historians and poets of all beliefs have sung his praises. cd 1947. *March 22, i, 660.*

NICHOLAS GARLICK, BD, MARTYR

A secular priest b. at Dinting, Glossop, Derbyshire. He was a schoolmaster for seven years. He was ordained priest at Douai in 1582 and went on the English mission in 1582–3. He was arrested and banished in 1585 but returned later that year. He was arrested in 1588 and h.d.q. for his priesthood in July of that year at Derby, aged thirty-three years. bd November 22, 1987. *July 24.*

NICHOLAS HORNER, BD, MARTYR

Tailor b. Grantley, Yorkshire. He was arrested with another layman for assisting a priest. He was hanged at Smithfield, London, 1590. bd November 22, 1987. *March 4.*

NICHOLAS OWEN, ST, MARTYR

It has been said that probably no single person did more for the preservation of the Catholic religion in England during the penal times than this workman, who in the reign of James I saved the lives of uncounted priests by his skill in devising hiding-places for them. After he had worked in this way for years he was admitted to the Society of Jesus as a temporal coadjutor. Owen was twice imprisoned and tortured; after his third arrest the torments inflicted in a vain attempt to make him betray his fellows and admit complicity in the Gunpowder Plot were so barbarous that he d. under them—literally torn apart. This was in the Tower of London in 1606. bd 1929. cd 1970. *March 22, i, 579.*

NICHOLAS PAGLIA, BD

Having heard St Dominic preach at Bologna he joined the Friars Preachers, and founded priories at Perugia and Trani. He became prior provincial of the Roman province and was "a holy and prudent man well versed in sacred lore". d. 1255. c.c. 1828. *February 14, i, 338.*

*NICHOLAS PIECK, ST, MARTYR

The leader of the group known as the Martyrs of Gorkum (*q.v.*). He was the guardian of the friary of Franciscans of the Observance at that place. d. 1572. cd 1867. *July 9, iii, 56.*

NICHOLAS POSTGATE, BD, MARTYR

Nicholas Postgate (or Posket) was a secular priest b. at Egton (Eyton) Bridge, Yorkshire. He studied at the English College at Douai and was ordained priest in March 1628. He was sent on the English mission in 1630. He worked diligently in Yorkshire for some fifty years and was betrayed by an exciseman. He d. at York in 1679 in his eightieth year. bd November 22, 1987. *August 7.*

NICHOLAS STENO, BD, BISHOP

Niels Stensen was b. 1638 at Copenhagen. A Danish scientist and scholar of considerable reputation, especially in medicine and geology, and always intent on the search for truth, he became a Catholic at Florence in 1667. He was ordained priest in 1675 and eventually vicar apostolic of Hanover and suffragan bishop of Münster and bishop for the largely Lutheran countries of northern Europe. d. 1686. His remains were interred at the basilica of San Lorenzo in Florence. bd October 23, 1988. *December 5.*

NICHOLAS TAVELIC AND HIS THREE COMPANIONS, SS, MARTYRS

See under Nicholas of Sibenik, Deodatus of Aquitaine, Peter of Narbonne, Stephen of Cuneo.

NICHOLAS WOODFEN, BD, MARTYR

Nicholas Woodfen (alias Wheeler and arraigned as Devereux) was a secular priest b. at Leominster, Herefordshire. He studied and was ordained at Rheims in 1581 and went on the English mission in the same year. He ministered in London, especially among members of the Inns of Court. He was caught by pursuivants and executed at Tyburn in 1586 aged *c.* thirty-six years. bd November 22, 1987. *January 21.*

NICHOLAS OF FORCA-PALENA, BD

He founded a society of hermits under the patronage of St Jerome in Naples, Florence and Rome, which was later amalgamated with the Hieronymites. d. 1449. c.c. 1771. *October 1, iv, 7.*

NICHOLAS OF LINKÖPING, BD,
BISHOP

Nicholas Hermansson was bishop of Linköping in Sweden and a counsellor of St Bridget, a poet and liturgist, an upholder of clerical celibacy, and a father to the poor and oppressed. d. 1391. *July 24, iii, 178.*

NICHOLAS OF SIBENIK, ST,
MARTYR

Nicholas Tavelić was for twenty years a Franciscan missionary among the Paterine heretics of Bosnia; he then went to Palestine, where he was martyred for preaching to the Muslims, in 1391. c.c. 1888. He and his three companions, Deodatus of Aquitaine, Peter of Narbonne and Stephen of Cuneo, were canonized by Pope Paul VI on June 21, 1970. *December 5, iv, 501.*

*NICHOLAS OF TOLENTINO, ST

He was b. near Fermo in Italy in 1245 and became a friar of the Augustinian Order. He led an uneventful life, distinguished for his patience and humility and unwearying assiduity in preaching; he was stationed at Tolentino for thirty years, where he was known as much for his selfless work in the slums as for his many miracles. d. 1305. cd 1446. *September 10, iii, 524.*

*NICHOLAS THE PILGRIM, ST

Nicholas was a young Greek who wandered about southern Italy carrying a cross and crying out "Kyrie eleison". He was generally treated as a tramp or a lunatic, but after his death at Trani in 1094 miracles were alleged at his tomb and he was cd in 1098.
June 2, ii, 459.

NICHOLAS THE STUDITE, ST,
ABBOT

A native of Crete who became abbot at Constantinople of the monastery of Studius. Together with the patriarch Nicephorus and others he was banished for opposing Iconoclasm. He continued to be a leader of orthodoxy, and was again exiled, for supporting the patriarch St Ignatius against

Photius. He was at last restored to freedom and d. among his monks in 863.
February 4, i, 251.

*NICOMEDES, ST, MARTYR

Nicomedes was venerated as a martyr at Rome at an early date, but nothing is known of his passion.
September 15, iii, 555.

*NICOMEDIA, THE MARTYRS OF

According to a Greek tradition, accepted by the Roman Martyrology, many thousands of Christians were burned alive in their church at Nicomedia while celebrating the feast of Christmas in 303, by order of Diocletian. But there are difficulties in the way of accepting the story in the form in which it has been preserved; there was, for instance, no feast of Christmas kept at Rome at that early date. *December 25, iv, 613.*

*NICON "METANOEITE", ST

He was first a monk at Chrysopetro and then a missionary for twenty years in Crete and in Greece. He received the name "Metanoeite" from his frequent calls to penance. d. 998. *November 16, iv, 426.*

*NILUS OF ROSSANO, ST, ABBOT

After a careless youth he became a monk and then abbot of the Byzantine monastery at St Adrian, near San Demetrio Corone in Calabria. The community was driven out by the Saracens *c.* 981, and for fifteen years lived at Vellelucio on land given by the abbey of Monte Cassino. In 1004 St Nilus was taken ill in the Alban hills and had a vision that here was the final abiding-place of his monks; he d. very soon after, but the migration was carried out, and thus was established the still flourishing Greek monastery of Grottaferrata, near Rome. St Nilus is accounted its first abbot.
September 26, iii, 654.

*NILUS THE ELDER, ST

He was an imperial official at Constantinople, who in middle life, *c.* 410, retired with one of his sons to the monastery at Mount Sinai, where he achieved a reputation as a theological, biblical, and ascetical

writer. Such, with additions, is the story. But Nilus the writer seems in fact to have spent his whole life in a monastery at Ancyra (Ankara) in Galatia.
November 12, iv, 320.

*NINIAN, ST, BISHOP

The "first authentic personage that meets us in the succession of Scottish missionaries". He was a bishop from Britain who established his see at Whitern (*Candida Casa*, the White House) in Wigtownshire, and he and his monks preached the gospel among the northern Britons and the Picts. d. 432 (?). The feast of St Ninian (Ninnidh) is kept throughout Scotland and in the dioceses of Lancaster and Hexham. *Ninianus.*
September 16, iii, 568.

*NINO, ST, VIRGIN

Nino is said to have been a slave girl, brought as a captive into Georgia (Iberia), who by her goodness, teaching and miracles brought about the conversion of many people, and eventually of the king and queen, in the earlier part of the fourth century. She is venerated as the Apostle of Georgia and it is possible that the story had some basis in fact, but it has become overlaid by many and contradictory legends. The Roman Martyrology, not knowing the maiden's local name, calls her "St Christiana". The Armenians associate her with the legend of their SS Rhipsime and Gaiana.
December 15, iv, 563.

NIZIER. *See Nicetius.*

*NOEL CHABANEL, ST, MARTYR

One of the Jesuit martyrs of North America (*q.v.*). His fate was for long uncertain, but eventually an Indian confessed to having killed him out of hatred of his religion, in 1649. cd 1930. *Natalis.*
September 26, iii, 645.

NOEL PINOT, BD, MARTYR

Noel Pinot, b. at Angers in 1747, was parish priest at Louroux-Béconnais at the time of the Revolution, and refused the illegal oath. He continued to minister in his parish, and

was eventually arrested when vested for MaSS After again refusing the oath, he was guillotined, still in his vestments, twelve days later, in 1794. bd 1926.
February 21, i, 391.

NON, ST

Non, Nonna or Nonnita is stated to have been the mother of St David of Wales; she was also venerated in Altarnun in Cornwall and Dirinon in Brittany. The circumstances of David's birth are not at all well attested. Sixth century.
March 3, i, 468.

NONIUS, BD

Nuñes Alvares de Pereira is a national hero of Portugal, having with King John I overcome the armies of Castile and established a Portuguese sovereign state. After the death of his wife, in 1422 Nonius entered the Carmelite Order as a lay-brother at Lisbon. d. 1431. c.c. 1918.
November 6, iv, 281.

*NONNA, ST

She converted her pagan husband, who is now known as St Gregory Nazianzen the Elder, and they were the parents of the younger saint of that name, of St Gorgonia and of St Caesarius, the last two of whom predeceased her. d. 374.
August 5, iii, 268.

*NORBERT, ST, BISHOP

Norbert was b. of a princely family at Xanten in 1080, and received minor orders, though interested only in worldly advancement. In 1115 he was converted by a narrow escape from death: he left the court of the emperor, was ordained priest and became a wandering preacher. At Prémontré in Laon he founded in 1120 a community of canons regular of strict observance which, under the name of Premonstratensians or Norbertines, spread with great rapidity; Norbert himself, however, was obliged to accept the bishopric of Magdeburg, where he was a vigorous reformer and more than once was the object of physical violence. He took an important part in the politics of the time and persuaded

the emperor Lothair II to lead an army into Italy to reinstate the exiled Pope Innocent II. d. 1134. cd 1582. *Norbertus.*
June 6, ii, 484.

*NORTH AMERICA, MARTYRS OF

A group of Jesuits with two lay helpers who were martyred by the Indians at various dates between 1642 and 1649. They were SS John de Brébeuf, Isaac Jogues, René Goupil, John Lalande, Antony Daniel, Gabriel Lalemant, Charles Garnier and Noel Chabanel (*qq.v.*). Their ceaseless labours in an unknown land, the shocking tortures some of them suffered, and their noble deaths excited the admiration of the historian Francis Parkman, who devoted a volume to the Jesuits in North America. These martyrs were canonized in 1930. Their feast is kept on March 16 by the Society of Jesus and on October 19 by the Church in North America. *September 26, iv, 645.*

NOTBURGA, ST, VIRGIN

Notburga was a younger contemporary of St Zita, and led a similar life in Bavaria, where she was a servant first in a noble family and then to a farmer. In later life she returned to the service of Count Henry, by whose wife she had been dismissed for giving away food to the poor. d. *c.* 1313. c.c. 1862. *September 14, iii, 553.*

NOTHELM, ST, BISHOP

He was elected archbishop of Canterbury in 734 and was St Bede's source for the records and traditions of that church when he was writing his *Ecclesiastical History.* d. *c.* 740. *October 17, iv, 140.*

NOTKER BALBULUS, BD

This monk of Saint-Gall, famous in the history of liturgical hymnody, is still honoured as a saint in Switzerland, one who was, in the words of a contemporary, "weakly in body but not in mind, stammering of tongue but not of intellect, pressing forward boldly in things divine—a vessel filled with the Holy Ghost without equal in his time". d. 912. c.c. 1512.
April 6, ii, 42.

NOVELLONE, BD

A shoemaker of Faenza and Franciscan tertiary who made numerous pilgrimages and was greatly revered locally. After his wife's death he became a hermit. d. 1280. c.c. 1817. *August 13, iii, 323.*

NUÑES. *See* Nonius.

*NUNILO AND ALODIA, SS, VIRGINS AND MARTYRS

They were the daughters of a Christian mother at Huesca in Spain and suffered from the brutality of a Mohammedan stepfather. They were beheaded for their faith in 851. *October 22, iv, 178.*

NUNZIO SULPRIZIO, BD

Born April 13, 1817 at Sansonesco in the Abruzzi. Orphaned at an early age, he suffered cruelty from an uncle without complaint and was sent to two homes for incurables. He d. May 5, 1836, when nineteen, in the care of a Swiss colonel in the service of the King of Naples. bd November 17, 1963, an example of the importance of religion for the poor and suffering. *May 5.*

NYMPHODORA. *See under* Menodora.

O

ODDINO OF FOSSANO, BD

Oddino Barrotti was a parish priest and guild chaplain at Fossano in Piedmont, whose devoted life and activities have never been forgotten in that town. d. 1400. c.c. 1808. *July 21, iii, 159*.

ODHRAN. *See* Otteran.

*ODILIA, ST, VIRGIN

According to tradition Odilia was the daughter of a Frankish lord who insisted that she be brought up away from her family because she was blind from birth. She recovered her sight miraculously, was reconciled with her father, and founded a nunnery at his castle of Hohenburg (Odilienberg) which she ruled till the end of her days. d. *c.* 720. There seems little in Odilia's legend that can be relied on as history; but Odilia, who is the subject of several legends, is the patron saint of Alsace, and Odilienberg has again become a popular place of pilgrimage in modern times. *Othilia. December 13, iv, 551*.

*ODILO, ST, ABBOT

He succeeded St Majolus as abbot of Cluny in 994, and was one of its great early abbots; under his rule the number of Cluniac houses rose rapidly. He was active in promoting the "peace of God" and instituted an annual commemoration of all the faithful departed. d. 1049. *January 1, i, 12*.

ODO OF CAMBRAI, BD, BISHOP

This Odo was a distinguished scholar, director of the cathedral school at Tournai, where he attracted students from foreign lands. Becoming dissatisfied with this life, he founded a community of Benedictines, from which he was removed after thirteen years to be bishop of Cambrai. But he refused to receive secular investiture from the emperor, and was exiled. d. 1113. *June 19, ii, 586*.

ODO OF CANTERBURY, ST, BISHOP

Born in East Anglia, of Danish parents. While bishop of Ramsbury in Wessex he was present at the battle of Brunanburh, and in 942 was made archbishop of Canterbury. St Odo, who was called "the Good", is said to have been the agent of a miracle in vindication of the Real Presence. d. 959. *July 4, iii, 15*.

*ODO OF CLUNY, ST, ABBOT

Odo was the second and one of the greatest abbots of Cluny. He succeeded St Berno in 927 and dedicated his life to the reform of the monasteries of France. By his regulation of the life of St Paul's outside-the-Walls of Rome he carried the spirit of Cluny beyond the borders of France, and his influence was felt far and wide; but he had also to contend with opposition. d. 942. *November 18, iv, 384*.

ODO OF NOVARA, BD

A Carthusian monk and prior of Geyrach in Slavonia, whence he was driven by the malice of the local bishop. Odo became chaplain to a convent at Tagliacozzo in Italy, where he lived to be nearly a hundred and d. in 1200. There is an account by contemporaries of his manner of life and the miracles attributed to him. c.c. 1859. *January 14, i, 85.*

ODORIC OF PORDENONE, BD

This Franciscan friar made one of the most remarkable journeys of the middle ages. He left his friary at Udine about 1317 and went to northern China via Armenia, Baghdad, Malabar, Ceylon, Sumatra, and Java. He was in Peking for three years and came home via Lhasa. Odoric dictated an account of his adventures to one of his brethren but does not say much about his missionary activities while on his travels; later accounts state that they were considerable. d. 1331. c.c. 1755. *Odericus. January 14, i, 88.*

ODULF, ST

He was the foremost helper of St Frederick in the completion of the evangelization of the Frisians. He was a native of Brabant and d. at Utrecht *c.* 855. The relics of St Odulf are said to have been taken to Evesham abbey in 1034. *Odulphus. June 12, ii, 532.*

OENGUS. *See* Aengus.

*OLAF, ST, MARTYR

In 1013 he helped Ethelred of England against the Danes and two years later drove the Danes and Swedes from Norway, of which country he is venerated as the apostle. He fetched over a number of priests from England but his zeal for Christianity was mixed up with violence and politics, and he was driven from his kingdom. In an attempt to recover it he was killed at the battle of Stiklestad in 1030. St Olaf had formerly a considerable *cultus* in England. *Olavus. July 29, iii, 208.*

OLGA, ST

She was a Scandinavian who married Igor, grand-duke of Kiev; after his assassination she became a Christian, and her grandson St Vladimir began the conversion of the Russian people. d. 969. *July 11, iii, 72.*

OLIVE, BD, VIRGIN AND MARTYR

Olive of Palermo is probably an imaginary person, heroine of a romance of martyrdom among the Mohammedans, by whom, curiously enough, her name is held in veneration at Tunis. *Olivia. June 10, ii, 519.*

OLIVER PLUNKET, ST, BISHOP AND MARTYR

Born in 1629 at Loughcrew in Meath. After his ordination at Rome in 1654 he was appointed a professor in the College *de Propaganda Fide* and in 1669 was named archbishop of Armagh. Disorder, enforced neglect and clerical timidity characterized the Church in Ireland at this time, and Plunket set himself to remedy them with great zeal. St Oliver was on excellent terms with the Protestant bishops and others, but in 1673 renewed persecution drove him into hiding. After Oates's "plot" he was betrayed and shut up in Dublin Castle. His first trial for "conspiring against the state" collapsed for lack of evidence, so he was sent to London, where the grand jury returned "no true bill"; he was not released, but by a flagrantly unjust court was found guilty. h.d.q. in 1681, the last Catholic to die for his faith at Tyburn. bd 1929. cd 1975. His relics are enshrined at Downside abbey. *Oliverius. July 11, iii, 73.*

*OLLEGARIUS, ST, BISHOP

Or *Oldegar*. He was a canon regular and governed monasteries in France before he was appointed bishop of Barcelona in his native land. Thence he was promoted to the archiepiscopal see of Tarragona, and was very active against the Moors, who had devastated the diocese. d. 1137. *March 6, i, 503.*

*OLYMPIAS, ST

She married Nebridius, prefect of Constantinople, but he d. very soon after and his widow consecrated herself and her fortune to the service of religion. Olympias was a close personal friend of St John Chrysostom and when he was exiled she suffered cruel persecution for her loyalty to him; from his

place of exile he entrusted her with important commissions. She withdrew to Nicomedia, and there d. *c.* 408, being not much more than forty years old.
December 17, iv, 577.

*OMER, ST, BISHOP

In Latin *Audomarus.* After being twenty years a monk of Luxeuil he was appointed to the bishopric of Thérouanne. The diocese was full of vice and error, and Omer gathered round him a notable band of holy monks to deal with the situation. He joined with St Bertinus in the establishment of the abbey of Sithiu, round which grew up the town now called Saint-Omer. d. *c.* 670.
September 9, iii, 516.

ONE HUNDRED AND SEVENTEEN MARTYRS OF VIETNAM

Various martyrs during the persecutions of Catholics in Indo-China between 1745 and 1862 were beatified in 1900, 1906, 1909 and 1951. On June 19, 1988 Pope John Paul II canonized 117 of them, including ninety-six Vietnamese (St Vincent Liem *et al.*); eleven Spaniards (including SS Francis [Francisco] Gil de Federich, Peter [Pedro] Almató, Hyacinth [Jacinto] Castaneda, Ignatius [Clemente Ignacio] Delgado, Dominic [Domingo] Henárez [bishop], Jerome [Jerónimo] Hermosilla [bishop], Valentine [Valentín] Berrio-Ochoa [bishop]); and ten French priests (SS Francis [François-Isidore] Gagelin, Joseph Marchand, John [Jean-Charles] Cornay, Francis [François] Jaccard, Peter [Pierre-Rose-Ursule] Dumoulin-Borie, Augustus [Augustin] Schöffler, John [Jean-Louis] Bonnard, Peter [Pierre-François] Néron, Theophanes [Jean-Théophane] Vénard, Stephen [Etienne-Théodore] Cuénot [bishop]).
November 24.

*ONESIMUS, ST, MARTYR

The runaway slave who is the subject of St Paul's epistle to Philemon, said to have been martyred *c.* 90. The Roman Martyrology confuses him with another Onesimus, who was bishop at Ephesus after St Timothy.
February 16, i, 349.

*ONUPHRIUS, ST

According to a certain abbot who met him St Onuphrius was a solitary in the Egyptian desert for seventy years: he dressed only in his own abundant hair and a loin-cloth of leaves. d. *c.* 400 (?). *June 12, ii, 528.*

OPPORTUNA, ST, VIRGIN

She was a sister of St Chrodegang of Séez and was abbess of the Benedictine convent at Almenèches. d. *c.* 770.
April 22, ii, 147.

*OPTATUS, ST, MARTYR

St Optatus with seventeen others was put to death for the faith at Saragossa in 304.
April 16, ii, 100.

*OPTATUS OF MILEVIS, ST, BISHOP

Optatus, bishop of Milevis in North Africa, was illustrious for his refutation of the errors of the Donatist schismatics; he wrote six treatises against them, in vigorous and spirited but conciliatory terms. St Augustine couples him with St Hilary of Poitiers and St Cyprian (like them he was a convert from heathenry), and St Fulgentius puts him in the same rank as St Ambrose and St Augustine. d. *c.* 387. *June 4, ii, 474.*

ORANGE, THE MARTYRS OF

Thirty-two nuns, of whom sixteen were Ursulines, thirteen Sacramentines, two Bernardines and one Benedictine, guillotined at Orange during the French Revolution. d. 1794. bd 1925. *July 9, iii, 59.*

ORINGA, BD, VIRGIN

The leader of a band of devout women who lived under the Rule of St Augustine at Castello di Santa Croce in the valley of the Arno. d. 1310. *January 4, i, 32.*

ORSIESIUS, ST, ABBOT

A close disciple of St Pachomius, whom he followed as abbot of Tabennisi. He wrote an ascetic treatise which St Jerome translated into Latin. d. *c.* 380. *June 15, ii, 547.*

OSANNA OF CATTARO, BD, VIRGIN

Catherine Cosie was the daughter of dissident Orthodox parents in Montenegro. She was reconciled with the Catholic Church at Cattaro, and became a Dominican tertiary, living in seclusion, but much sought after for her gift of counsel. d. 1565. c.c. 1928. *April 27, ii, 176.*

OSANNA OF MANTUA, BD, VIRGIN

Osanna Andreasi was b. at Mantua in 1449. In consequence of a vision while a child she became a Dominican tertiary, very active in works of mercy and imbued with the spirit of Savonarola. She was allowed many remarkable mystical experiences, for which there is contemporary evidence, and her "spiritual conversations" were written down by a close friend; these still exist. Osanna was a force in Mantuan society, and when Duke Frederick went to the wars in 1478 he put her in charge of his family and practically of his office. d. 1505. c.c. 1694. *June 20, ii, 592.*

OSBURGA, ST, VIRGIN

Osburga was a famous abbess at Coventry but no details of her life are known; she d. *c.* 1016, or perhaps much earlier. Her feast is still kept in the diocese of Birmingham. *March 30, i, 705.*

*OSMUND, ST, BISHOP

Osmund came to England with the Normans and was nominated bishop of Salisbury (Old Sarum) in 1078. He finished building its cathedral and instituted a chapter of canons, but is best remembered because the ordinal of services for his diocese was the basis of that "Sarum use" which spread throughout England and beyond and was normal in Great Britain until after the reign Queen of Mary. St Osmund was of a quiet and conciliatory disposition, and liked to spend his leisure copying and binding books. d. 1099. cd 1457. His feast has been kept in the dioceses of Westminster, Clifton and Plymouth. *Osmundus. December 4, iv, 492.*

*OSWALD OF NORTHUMBRIA, ST, MARTYR

Oswald was formerly venerated as one of the great national heroes of England, and his *cultus* extended so far as Switzerland. He defeated and slew in battle the Welsh king Cadwallon near Hexham in 634, and rightfully ascended the throne of Northumbria. Oswald had been baptized at Iona and received from there the bishop St Aidan to evangelize his kingdom. So great was the power and influence of St Oswald that he had some sort of nominal overlordship of the other English kings. He was killed in 642, fighting at Maserfield against the pagan Penda of Mercia and his Welsh Christian allies. He at once received *cultus* as a martyr, and his feast has been kept in the northern English dioceses and elsewhere. *Oswaldus. August 9, iii, 293.*

OSWALD OF WORCESTER, ST, BISHOP

He was nephew of St Odo of Canterbury, and became a monk at Fleury in France. Under St Dunstan he was appointed to the see of Worcester, and continued to administer it after he was promoted in 972 to the archbishopric of York. He was a strong and active supporter of Dunstan's policies, founding monasteries at Westbury-on-Trym, Ramsey and Worcester. St Oswald was more tactful in his activities than some reformers, a humble man and lover of quiet. d. 992. His feast has been observed in the arch-diocese of Birmingham. *February 28, i, 439.*

OSWIN, ST, MARTYR

He became king of Deira in 642, and was murdered at Gilling in Yorkshire by order of his cousin Oswy in 651. A monastery was built at Gilling, where St Oswin's tomb was illustrious for miracles, until the incursions of the Danes caused the relics to be translated to Tynemouth. *Oswinus. August 20, iii, 366.*

OSYTH, ST, VIRGIN AND MARTYR

According to her legend St Osyth was a nun, at the place now called Saint Osyth at the mouth of the Colne in Essex, who was murdered by Danish marauders *c.* 675 (?). *October 7, iv, 52.*

OTGER, ST

An English deacon and missionary with St Wiro in the Netherlands. Eighth century. *May 8, ii, 253.*

*OTHMAR, ST, ABBOT

He was given charge of the monastic settlement at Saint-Gall in Switzerland in 720, and organized the great abbey there, introducing the Rule of St Benedict. He was persecuted by neighbouring nobles, and d. in prison in 759. *Othmarus. Audomarus. November 16.*

OTTERAN, ST, ABBOT

Otteran (Odhran) was an abbot from Meath who went to Iona with St Columba and was the first to die there, in 563. Although this is practically all that is known of the saint his feast is observed throughout Ireland. *Otteranus. October 27, iv, 209.*

OTTILIA. *See* Odilia.

*OTTO, ST, BISHOP

Otto was bishop of Bamberg under the emperor Henry IV and laboured to reconcile that sovereign and his successor with the Holy See. He is said to have conducted a very successful mission among the Pomeranians, and is venerated as their apostle. d. 1139. cd 1189. *Otho. July 2, iii, 8.*

OUDOCEUS, ST

In Welsh *Euddogwy.* He is reputed to have been the disciple and nephew of St Teilo and his successor as abbot of Llandeilo Fawr. He is one of the four name saints of Llandaff cathedral but was never "bishop of Llandaff". *July 2, i, 289.*

OUEN. *See* Audoenus.

OUTRIL. *See* Austregisilus.

OXFORD UNIVERSITY, THE MARTYRS OF

Over forty members of the University of Oxford have been beatified as martyrs during the English persecution. A feast in their honour has been kept in the archdiocese of Birmingham on December 1.

OYEND. *See* Eugendus.

P

*PACHOMIUS, ST, ABBOT

The founder of Christian communal (as opposed to eremitical) monasticism. He was b. in the Upper Thebaïd c. 292, and after being discharged from the army became a Christian and a hermit. In 318 he began his first monastery at Tabennisi, near the Nile, and subsequently established six others, organizing them on a communal basis and providing a written rule to be observed by all. This was the first example of a number of religious houses grouped together with a common rule and a general superior. Pachomius was never a priest and would not present his monks for ordination, though he welcomed priests to join them. Before his death at Pabau in 348 he had three thousand monks in his communities. Pachomius is one of the four outstanding figures in the early history of Christian monasticism, and St Benedict made considerable use of the Egyptian rule when drawing up his own. *May 9, ii, 259.*

*PACIAN, ST, BISHOP

He was bishop of Barcelona in the fourth century and a voluminous writer, but few of his works have come down to us. He was the author of the famous declaration, "My name is Christian, my surname Catholic . . . ." d. c. 390. *Pacianus. March 9, i, 533.*

*PACIFICO, ST

This Pacifico, called "of San Severino" after his birthplace, was a Friar Minor of the Observance. In 1688, at the age of thirty-five, he became deaf and blind and almost a cripple: he had perforce to give up his successful active work, and passed the rest of his days in prayer, penance and alms-deeds. On several occasions he displayed the gift of prophecy. d. 1721. cd 1839. *September 24, iii, 631.*

PACIFICO OF CERANO, BD

Pacifico Ramota was b. in Novara in 1424 and became a Franciscan friar. He laboured in Italy and Sardinia, and wrote a treatise on moral theology highly thought of by his contemporaries. d. 1482. c.c. 1745. *June 9, ii, 506.*

PADARN, ST, ABBOT

Padarn had his headquarters near Aberystwyth, at Llanbadarn Fawr, *i.e.* the Great Monastery of Padarn, whence he evangelized the country round about. Fifth/sixth century. *Paternus. April 15, ii, 98.*

PAIR. *See* Paternus of Avranches.

*PALAEMON, ST

The teacher of St Pachomius in the desert; when Pachomius went away to make his foundation at Tabennisi, Palaemon accompanied him, and d. soon after. *January 11.*

PALLADIUS, ST, BISHOP

Palladius was consecrated and sent as the first bishop to the Irish c. 430. He landed at Arklow and founded three churches, but his mission was a failure and he soon

crossed over into Scotland, where he d. at Fordun in 432. His feast has been observed in the diocese of Aberdeen.
July 7, iii, 33.

PAMBO, ST

Pambo was one of the founders of the Nitrian group of monasteries in Egypt. He followed the usual austere life of the desert fathers, but had a less narrow outlook than many early monks on other ways of life: "Seek never to offend your neighbour" was his first theme. Among those who visited his cell were Rufinus and St Melania the Elder. d. c. 390. *July 18, iii, 137.*

*PAMMACHIUS, ST

He was a learned and charitable Roman layman, a close friend of St Jerome, who married the second daughter of Jerome's other great friend, St Paula. When he was a widower he joined with St Fabiola in founding the first pilgrims' hostel in the West, at Porto. d. 410.
August 30, iii, 446.

*PAMPHILUS OF CAESAREA, ST,
MARTYR

He is described by Eusebius as "the most illustrious martyr of his day for philosophical learning and every virtue". He was b. at Beirut, studied at Alexandria, and was ordained at Caesarea in Palestine, where he lived. He was reputed the greatest biblical scholar of his age and was well known for his munificence and because he treated slaves and dependants as his brothers. He was tortured for refusing to sacrifice to the gods of Rome and after two years of imprisonment was beheaded at Caesarea in 309, with eleven other martyrs.
June 1, ii, 437.

*PAMPHILUS OF SULMONA, ST,
BISHOP

This bishop of Sulmona and Corfinium in the Abruzzi was denounced by his flock as an Arian—apparently because he sang Mass before daybreak on Sundays. d. c. 700.
April 28, ii, 182.

*PANCRAS, ST, MARTYR

There is no reliable information about this St Pancras, who gave his name to a church and so to a borough and railway station in London. The well-known story of the boy-martyr is a fabrication, but a martyr called Pancras was certainly buried in the cemetery of Calepodius in Rome. *Pancratius.*
May 12, ii, 285.

*PANCRAS OF TAORMINA, ST,
BISHOP AND MARTYR

According to the Sicilian legend he was a disciple of St Peter and became first bishop of Taormina, being at the last stoned to death by brigands. *April 3, ii, 18.*

*PANTAENUS, ST

Pantaenus was a converted Stoic philosopher who taught with success at Alexandria. Little is known of his life, though he is said to have been at one time a missionary, perhaps in the Yemen and Ethiopia. d. c. 200. *July 7, iii, 32.*

*PANTALEON, ST, MARTYR

Or *Panteleimon.* There is known to have been a martyr of this name, but the legends which have survived about him are late and valueless. He is a patron saint of physicians, as it is said he practised their art without taking payment. His early *cultus* is connected with Nicomedia in Bithynia.
July 27, iii, 192.

*PAPHNUTIUS, ST, BISHOP

Sometimes distinguished as "Paphnutius the Great". He was an Egyptian bishop in the Upper Thebaïd, and was deprived of an eye and lamed in the persecution under Maximinus. He was a notable opponent of Arianism, and is said to have defended the marriage of clergy at the Council of Nicaea (he was himself a monk). d. c. 350 (?).
September 11, iii, 538.

PAPYLUS. *See* Carpus.

PARASCEVE. *See under* Photina.

PAREGORIUS. *See under* Leo.

*PARISIO, ST

A Camaldolese monk near Treviso, venerated in that order; little information about him has survived. d. 1267.
June 11, ii, 525.

PARTHENIUS. *See under* Calocerus.

*PASCHAL I, ST, POPE

Paschal I occupied the papal chair from 817 till his death in 824 and is specially remembered for having removed from the catacombs to various Roman churches the relics of many martyrs; but the grounds on which his name is included in the Roman Martyrology are obscure. *Paschalis.*
February 11, i, 311.

*PASCHAL BAYLON, ST

He was b. in Aragon in 1540, the child of peasants, and was a shepherd until he became a lay-brother of the Alcantarine reform of the Friars Minor. He led an uneventful life of prayer and work. On account of his devotion to the Blessed Sacrament and his defence of true eucharistic doctrine before a Calvinist mob he has been declared by the Holy See to be the patron of eucharistic congresses. d. 1592. cd 1690. *May 17, ii, 333.*

PASCHASIUS RADBERTUS, ST, ABBOT

Paschasius is best known as a prolific writer and scholar. He was novice-master at New Corbie and, though not a priest, abbot of Old Corbie, an office which he found uncongenial. d. *c.* 860. *April 26, ii, 164.*

PASTOR. *See under* Justus.

PATERNUS OF ABDINGHOF, ST

Little is known of this Paternus except that he was an Irish anchorite at Paderborn who lost his life when the town was burnt down in 1058, a disaster he had foretold.
April 10, ii, 64.

*PATERNUS OF AVRANCHES, ST, BISHOP

In French *Pair*. After many years as a monk and hermit he was made bishop of Avranches at the age of seventy. d. *c.* 564.
April 16, ii, 101.

PATERNUS. *See also* Padarn.

*PATIENS OF LYONS, ST, BISHOP

An archbishop of Lyons, whom St Sidonius Apollinaris calls a "holy, active, ascetic and merciful man", famed for his generosity to the poor. d. *c.* 480.
September 11, iii, 539.

*PATRICIA, ST, VIRGIN

A maiden venerated as one of the patrons of Naples whither, according to her legend, she had fled from Constantinople in order to become a nun. Date unknown.
August 25, iii, 400.

*PATRICK, ST, BISHOP

The patron saint and apostle of Ireland was a Romano-Briton, but the place of his birth *c.* 389 is unknown. In *c.* 403 he was carried off as a slave to Ireland but escaped after six years. About 432, having been consecrated bishop by St Germanus at Auxerre, he returned to Ireland to take up the work of the missionary St Palladius. The data of Patrick's labours supplied by his biographers are confused, sometimes contradictory, and often legendary. He travelled about the land, converting chiefs and people by his example and teaching: to impress the heathen Irish it was needful that the word should be confirmed by the signs which followed, and miracles supported his preaching. In some accounts of his life the space allotted to these is somewhat excessive: only by reference to his own writings can the deep and lasting impression that he made be understood. Patrick established what was to be the primatial church of Ireland at Armagh about the year 444. d. *c.* 461 at Saul on Strangford Lough. *Patricius.*
March 17, i, 612.

PATRICK SALMON, BD, MARTYR

An Irish manservant, hanged at Dorchester, Dorset, in 1594 for aiding and abetting a priest, Bd John Cornelius. bd 1929. *July 4, iii, 18.*

*PATROCLUS, ST, MARTYR

He was a Christian of Troyes of exceptional charity and goodness, who was martyred either in 259 or 275 by beheading. *January 21, i, 138.*

*PAUL, ST, APOSTLE

The Apostle of the Gentiles, a tent-maker by trade from Tarsus in Cilicia, whose life is related in the Acts of the Apostles and his doctrine set forth in his Epistles. He was well educated and as Saul the Pharisee bitterly persecuted the Christian Jews, only to be touched by the hand of the Lord and converted on the road to Damascus. His mission to the Gentiles was accomplished in three famous journeys over western Asia Minor and Greece, "in perils of robbers, from my own nation, from the Gentiles, in the city, in the wilderness, in the sea, from false brethren; in labour and painfulness", beaten, stoned, shipwrecked, imprisoned. Having been imprisoned at Caesarea in consequence of a tumult raised by the Jews at Jerusalem, Paul, as a Roman citizen, appealed from the procurator Festus to the emperor; accordingly he was taken to Rome, where "he remained two whole years in his own hired lodging, and he received all that came in to him". He was probably acquitted, made a fourth missionary journey, to Macedonia, and then returned to Rome, where he was martyred about the same time as St Peter. There is an apparently reliable tradition that he was beheaded on the Ostian Way, where the basilica and abbey of St Paul-outside-the-Walls now stand. Apart from his personal missionary work, St Paul has had through his letters an influence on Christianity and Christians that only increases as the years and centuries go by. In every liturgical office of St Peter in the Roman rite a commemoration was made of St Paul, and *vice versa*, as in the mass for June 29. *Paulus. June 29, ii, 669*; and *i, 162.*

*PAUL I, ST, POPE

He succeeded his brother Stephen III in 757 and was pope for ten years. He rebuilt the church of San Silvestro in Capite (now the English church in Rome) and gave it to monks of the Greek rite. A contemporary speaks of his kindness and wide-spiritedness. d. 767. *June 28, ii, 659.*

PAUL AURELIAN, ST, BISHOP

Paul Aurelian was a Romano-Briton and a fellow of SS Samson and Gildas under Illtyd. After some years he went as a missionary, eventually to Brittany. With his companions he founded a monastery at Porz-Pol on the isle of Ushant, and later settled at the place now called Saint-Pol-de-Léon, where he was consecrated bishop. d. c. 573. *March 12, i, 574.*

PAUL CHONG, ST, MARTYR

Paul Chong, b. 1795, was a leading Korean Christian whose father and brother had been martyred in 1801. He wrote to the Pope requesting priests. In 1831 Korea was made an apostolic vicariate and Paul organized the clandestine entry of three missionaries in 1836–7. He was beheaded the day after their martyrdom, on September 22, 1839. cd September 16, 1984. *September 22.*

*PAUL MIKI, ST, MARTYR

One of the earliest of Japanese Jesuits. He entered the Society of Jesus in 1580 and became an accomplished preacher and teacher. He was crucified with the other martyrs at Nagasaki in 1597. cd 1862. *February 6, i, 259.*

PAUL NAVARRO, BD, MARTYR

An Italian Jesuit martyr who was put to death by burning at Shimabara in Japan in 1622. bd 1867. *November 1, iii, 535.*

*PAUL I OF CONSTANTINOPLE, ST, BISHOP AND MARTYR

This Paul was bishop of Constantinople from c. 336. He figures in church history, but is otherwise little known. About the year 350 he was deported from his see by the

Arians, and is said to have been strangled, at Cucusus in Armenia. *June 7, ii, 492.*

PAUL IV OF CONSTANTINOPLE, ST, BISHOP

He became patriarch of Constantinople in 780, and advocated the restoration of sacred images, against the Iconoclasts. d. 784. *August 28, iii, 434.*

*PAUL OF CYPRUS, ST, MARTYR

He was martyred in the island of Cyprus during the iconoclast persecution for refusing to trample on a crucifix, c. 760. *March 17, i, 621.*

PAUL OF LATROS, ST

He was for many years a hermit in a cave on Mount Latros in Bithynia, where he attracted a number of followers. For a time he was a monk of Karia and worked in the kitchen, where the sight of the fire reminded him so forcibly of Hell that he burst into tears every time he looked at it. d. 956. *December 15, iv, 565.*

*PAUL OF NARBONNE, ST

A Roman missionary in Gaul, who d. at Narbonne where he had worked, c. 290. *March 22, i, 657.*

*PAUL OF THE CROSS, ST

Paul was b. at Ovada in Piedmont in 1694 and after an exemplary youth set to work, in consequence of a series of visions, to establish the congregation of clerks regular whose rule he had framed before he himself was ordained. By 1737 the first house ("retreat") of the Barefooted Clerks of the Cross and Passion (Passionists) was in being and, with some setbacks, the congregation made steady progress. St Paul himself preached throughout the Papal States and Tuscany, and among his practices was to pray daily for the reconciliation of the English. He was endowed with gifts of prophecy and healing, and crowds flocked to his sermons and confessional. d. 1775. cd 1867. *October 19, ii, 178.*

*PAUL THE HERMIT, ST

This Paul is venerated as the first hermit. He went into the Theban desert at the age of twenty-two and lived alone in a cave for ninety years. Here he was found by St Antony, who on a second visit found Paul dead, c. 342. The account of his life edited by St Jerome is a classic of desert-father literature; numerous stories of varying value are told of St Paul. *January 15, i, 91.*

*PAUL THE SIMPLE, ST

Leaving his wife on account of her unfaithfulness he became, although already an old man, a disciple of St Antony in the Egyptian Thebaïd. He is mentioned in the *Lausiac History* of Palladius. d. c. 339. *March 7, i, 513.*

PAUL. *See also under* John *and* Thea.

*PAULA, ST

We learn about St Paula from the letters of St Jerome, whose disciple she was. She was of a noble Roman family, b. in 347, and married Toxotius, by whom she had five children, among them St Blesilla and St Eustochium. After the death of her husband when she was thirty-two, Paula lived for a time in retirement and then went to Palestine. She settled near St Jerome at Bethlehem, forming a community of religious women and helping Jerome in his biblical work. Paula lived thus for some twenty years and d. in 404. *January 26, i, 171.*

PAULA CERIOLI, BD

Bd Paula, b. in 1816, was a wealthy widow, who in 1857 founded the Institute of the Holy Family of Bergamo, to look after orphans of both sexes. She was particularly concerned with their preparation for rural life. When her bishop told her that people said she was "cracked", she replied, "So I am—with the lunacy of the Cross". d. 1865. bd 1950. *December 24, iv, 606.*

PAULA FRASSINETTI, ST, VIRGIN

Born at Genoa in 1809. While living with her brother, who was parish priest at Quinto, she found her vocation in the schooling of poor children; she founded a society for the work, which developed into the congregation of Sisters of St Dorothy. d. 1882. bd 1930. cd 1984. *June 11, ii, 525.*

PAULA GAMBARA-COSTA, BD

She was b. near Brescia in 1473. She was a Franciscan tertiary and there is extant the rule of life drawn up for her by Bd Angelo of Chiavasso when she married. Her husband was vexed by what seemed to him the excessive charities dispensed by his wife, and even put another woman in charge of his household; but in time Paula regained his affection. d. 1515. c.c. 1845. *January 31, i, 216.*

PAULA OF MONTALDO, BD, VIRGIN

A Poor Clare of Mantua for over half a century; she had numerous mystical experiences. d. 1514. c.c. 1906. *August 18, iii, 350.*

PAULINE VON MALLINCKRODT, BD, VIRGIN

Mother Paulina von Mallinckrodt was b. at Minden, Westphalia, Germany, on June 3, 1817. In 1849 she founded the Sisters of Christian Charity. She died at Paderborn in 1881. bd April 14, 1985. *April 30.*

PAULINUS OF AQUILEIA, ST, BISHOP

Born *c.* 726 near Friuli, and as he grew up acquired a reputation for learning. He was greatly respected by Charlemagne and about 776 was promoted to the important see of Aquileia. Paulinus was concerned in confuting the adoptionist heresy then being spread in Spain, and preached the gospel to the Avars and other heathen. He also wrote a work of religious direction for the use of Duke Henry of Friuli. d. 804. *January 28, i, 188.*

*PAULINUS OF NOLA, ST, BISHOP

He was b. into a patrician family at Bordeaux *c.* 354, was educated by Ausonius, and inherited great wealth. After his retirement from state service he was converted to Christianity by his Spanish wife and St Delphinus of Bordeaux, and the couple gave away much of their wealth in charity. At the age of forty Paulinus was ordained priest and retired to Nola in Italy, where he built churches, an aqueduct, and other public works and *c.* 409 was made bishop. A number of letters and poems written by him are preserved, and they amply explain the affection and veneration that Paulinus enjoyed even during his lifetime. d. 431. *June 22, ii, 615.*

*PAULINUS OF TRIER, ST, BISHOP

While bishop of Trier he was expelled from his see with other bishops for supporting St Athanasius against the emperor Constantine. He was banished to Phrygia, where he d. in 358; his relics were brought back to Trier in 396, and there they remain. *August 31, iii, 450.*

*PAULINUS OF YORK, ST, BISHOP

He was one of the monks sent from Rome in 601 to join St Augustine in England. After twenty-four years of missionary work in Kent he evangelized the southern parts of Northumbria, and baptized King Edwin at York on Easter day, 627. Paulinus was bishop of that city but he was driven out by the Mercians, who killed St Edwin, and for the last ten years of his life he administered the see of Rochester. d. 644. His *cultus* was formerly very widespread; his feast is still kept in a number of English dioceses. *October 10, iv, 80.*

PEGA, ST, VIRGIN

She was the sister of St Guthlac and lived as a hermitess in Northamptonshire. She is said to have d. in Rome *c.* 719. *January 8, i, 54.*

*PELAGIA OF ANTIOCH, ST, VIRGIN AND MARTYR

This is the historical Pelagia, with whose name a whole cycle of extravagant fables is connected. She was a young Christian girl of Antioch who, when soldiers were sent to arrest her, jumped from the top of the house to avoid dishonour and was killed, *c.* 311. She is named in the canon of the Milanese Mass. *June 9, ii, 510.*

*PELAGIA OF TARSUS, ST,
VIRGIN AND MARTYR

This Pelagia was probably no more than the heroine of a pious romance, according to which she was roasted to death for refusing to marry the emperor Diocletian. *May 4, ii, 230.*

*PELAGIA THE PENITENT, ST

This Pelagia (or Margaret) probably has some confused connection with the Pelagia of June 9. The fiction that she was a repentant courtesan of Antioch who lived disguised as a male solitary at Jerusalem seems to have been the starting-point of the similar romances that are associated with the names of Marina, Euphrosyne, Theodora, etc. *October 8, iv, 59.*

*PELAGIUS, ST, MARTYR

In Spanish, *Pelayo*. Pelagius was a young boy left as a hostage among the Moors at Cordova. He was offered liberty and other inducements if he would accept Islam, and on his stubborn and repeated refusals he was put to death in 925. *June 26, ii, 649.*

*PELEUS, ST, MARTYR

The Egyptians Peleus, Nilus and Elias, priests, and a layman had been sentenced to hard labour in the quarries and were burned *c.* 310, probably at Phunon, near Petra, for conducting divine worship in the place of their detention. *September 19, iii, 596.*

PEPIN OF LANDEN, BD

The life of Pepin of Landen, mayor of the palace to Clotaire II, Dagobert I and St Sigebert and practically ruler of their dominions, belongs to general history. He was married to Bd Itta, was father of St Gertrude of Nivelles and St Begga, and was "a lover of peace, the constant defender of truth and justice". d. 640. *February 21, i, 384.*

*PEREGRINE LAZIOSI, ST

Born at Forli in 1260. During a popular rising he struck St Philip Benizi across the face and, Philip turning his other cheek, was seized with remorse. Peregrine joined the Servites, and at the height of his success as a friar was stricken with cancer of the foot; but on the night before it was to be amputated he was completely cured in his sleep. d. 1345. cd 1726. *May 1, ii, 211.*

*PEREGRINE OF AMITERNUM, ST,
BISHOP AND MARTYR

Peregrine (properly Cetheus) was bishop of Amiternum (Aquila); he was put to death by the Lombards *c.* 600 for asking for mercy for a condemned captive. *June 13.*

*PEREGRINE OF AUXERRE, ST,
BISHOP AND MARTYR

He is venerated as the first bishop of Auxerre, who was beheaded for the faith *c.* 261 by the Roman governor. *May 16, ii, 326.*

PEREGRINE OF FALERONE, BD

A personal disciple of St Francis of Assisi and a confessor of the Friars Minor. d. 1240. *September 6, iii, 500.*

PEREGRINE. See also under Evangelist.

*PERGENTINUS AND
LAURENTINUS, SS, MARTYRS

They are said to have been brothers at Arezzo who were martyred there in 251. Their real existence is uncertain. *June 3, ii, 460.*

*PERPETUA AND FELICITY, SS,
MARTYRS

Vivia Perpetua was a young married woman of good family and Felicity was a slave girl, who with four men were imprisoned at Carthage in 203. Eventually they were thrown to the beasts and those not thus killed were slain by the sword. The "acts" of these martyrs are one of the greatest and most moving of hagiological treasures that have come down to us; in the fourth century they were read publicly in the churches of Africa. They were written by two of the martyrs themselves, and completed by an eye-witness. Perpetua, and perhaps this Felicity, are named in the canon of the Roman Mass; their companions were SS Saturus, Saturninus, Revocatus, and Secundulus. *March 6, i, 493.*

*PERPETUUS, ST, BISHOP

He ruled the diocese of Tours for thirty years during the fifth century. The document purporting to be his will is now known to be a forgery of the seventeenth century. d. c. 494. *April 8, ii, 53.*

*PERSIAN MARTYRS, THE CXX

The 120 martyrs in Persia mentioned in the Roman Martyrology on April 6 are believed to have suffered at Seleucia-Ctesiphon under King Sapor II in 345. *April 6, ii, 39.*

*PETER, ST, APOSTLE

Simon Peter, leader or "prince" of the Apostles, was a fisherman on the Sea of Galilee, where he lived with his wife at Bethsaida, and was called to be an apostle with his brother Andrew. The most important and striking of the events of his life in Palestine as narrated in the gospels in his confession of faith in our Lord and Christ's subsequent charge to him, "Thou art Peter and upon this rock I will build my Church . . ." (Matt. xvi, 15–19); in striking contrast is his thrice-repeated denial of his Master at the house of Caiaphas. Almost all that is known for certain about his later life is derived from the Acts of the Apostles and allusions in his own and St Paul's epistles. Peter may have been for a time bishop at Antioch but it was at Rome that he established his permanent see. He was martyred there in 67 (?), and buried on the Vatican hill. The joint feast of St Peter and St Paul has been kept at Rome on June 29 probably at least since the beginning of the fourth century. *Petrus. June 29, ii, 664;* see also *i, 113, 392* and *iii, 236.*

PETER ALMATÓ, ST, MARTYR

A Dominican missionary from Catalonia, martyred in Indo-China with Bd Jerome Mermosilla in 1861. bd 1906. cd June 19, 1988. *November 1, iv, 284.*

*PETER ARBUES, ST, MARTYR

Peter Arbues, a canon regular, was provincial inquisitor for the kingdom of Aragon, around whom an undeserved legend of cruelty has grown up. He discharged the office for only a few months, preaching against fictitious Christians and apostates among the Moors and the Jews. He was responsible for no sentence of death and only two arrests were made at his instance. He was murdered in 1485. cd 1867. *September 17, iii, 585.*

*PETER ARMENGOL, BD

In the form that has come down to us the story of Bd Peter, a Mercedarian who worked among the Moors, is of very doubtful authenticity. d. 1304. c.c. 1686. *April 27, ii, 174.*

PETER AUMAITRE, ST, MARTYR

Pierre Aumaitre was born on April 8, 1837 at Aizecq, Charentes, and joined the Paris Foreign Missions in 1859. He was ordained priest in 1862, entered Korea in 1863 and was arrested and beheaded on March 12, 1866. bd 1968. cd by John Paul II at Seoul in 1984. *March 12.*

*PETER BALSAM, ST, MARTYR

He is probably identical with the Peter Abselamus whom Eusebius describes as having been burnt to death for the faith at Caesarea, in the year 311. Another account says that he was crucified. *January 3, i, 26.*

*PETER BAPTIST, ST, MARTYR

In 1597 twenty-six persons (twenty of them Japanese) were crucified for their Christian faith at Nagasaki. St Peter Baptist was the commissary of the Franciscan missionaries in Japan, a Spaniard by birth, who had previously ministered in Mexico and the Philippines. Five others of the martyrs were Franciscans and seventeen of them lay tertiaries of that order; the remaining three were Jesuits. All were canonized in 1862. *February 5, i, 259.*

PETER BETANCUR, BD

Pedro de San José Betancur, the "St Francis of the Americas", was b. in 1626 at Chasna, Tenerife, Canary Islands. He was a shepherd but went to Guatemala in 1650. He became a lay Franciscan and cared for the poor and sick, and founded a school, a hospital, homes for the poor and a community. d. 1667. bd June 22, 1980. *April 25.*

PETER BONILLI, BD

Pietro Bonilli was b. at San Lorenzo di Trevi, Italy, on March 15, 1841. He was ordained priest in 1863 and in 1888 he founded the Congregation of Sisters of the Holy Family to care for orphans and the poor. d. 1935 aged ninety-four. bd April 24, 1988. *January 5.*

*PETER CANISIUS, ST, DOCTOR

Canisius (Kanis) was b. at Nijmegen, then in Germany, in 1521, and joined the Society of Jesus. His energies were devoted to rebuilding the Church in the Empire after the disasters of the Reformation; he went to and fro in Germany, Austria, Switzerland and Bohemia, preaching, instructing, arbitrating, writing catechisms and other works, and reforming and establishing colleges and schools. In an age of violence he stands out as a man of moderation, and he did more to restore the faith and purify lives in south and west Germany than any other. He was one of the originators of the "Catholic press", and was the first "literary" Jesuit. d. 1597. He was the first saint to be declared a Doctor of the Church at his canonization (in 1925). *December 21, ii, 168.*

*PETER CHANEL, ST, MARTYR

Peter Louis Marie Chanel was b. in France in 1803, the son of a peasant. After some years of pastoral and professorial work, he went at the head of the first band of Marist missionaries to the Pacific in 1836. He was put to death by a savage chief out of hatred of the faith on Futuna Island in 1841, the first martyr of Oceania. Within two years the whole island was Christian. cd 1954. *April 28, ii, 186.*

*PETER CHRYSOLOGUS, ST, BISHOP AND DOCTOR

He was b. at Imola and became deacon to the bishop of that town. He was made archbishop of Ravenna c. 433, but little is known of his life beyond his assiduity in expounding the Christian religion by writing and preaching. His gifts as an orator earned him his name, Golden Speech; a number of sermons attributed to him are still in existence. d. *c.* 450. St Peter was declared a Doctor of the Church in 1729. *July 30, iv, 485.*

*PETER CLAVER, ST

Peter Claver was a young Jesuit at Palma and was fired by St Alphonsus Rodríguez with the desire to work for souls in the New World. He went to Colombia in South America in 1610 and soon saw that the people who most needed his ministrations were the Negro slaves, who were shipped from West Africa in great numbers under the most ghastly conditions. Claver declared himself to be "the slave of the Negroes for ever", and that is just what he was. He cared both for souls and bodies, brought numerous Negroes to a knowledge of Christianity and love of Christ by his careful teaching, and followed them up after they had been dispersed to the mines and plantations. He nursed sick and diseased whom others could hardly bear even to look at; but for the last four years of his life he was himself a sick man, and was sometimes neglected by his brethren in amazing fashion: since his death in 1654 he has never been forgotten, and never will be. cd 1888. St Peter Claver was declared patron of all enterprises in favour of the Negroes in 1896. *September 9, iii, 519.*

*PETER DAMIAN, ST, BISHOP AND DOCTOR

He was b. at Ravenna in 1007, an unwanted child, ill-treated, set to herd pigs and similar jobs, until he was put to school by a brother. He joined the hermit monks of Fonte Avellana, was soon famous for his learning, and became abbot. In 1057 he was made cardinal-bishop of Ostia. Whether as hermit or cardinal his time was devoted to vehement writing, preaching and otherwise actively working against the clerical abuses of his time, simony, incontinence, luxury, slackness. d. 1072. Declared Doctor of the Church in 1828. *February 21, i, 399.*

PETER DONDERS, BD

Fr Petrus Donders, apostle of the poor, b. 1809, was a Dutch Redemptorist who worked as a missionary to slaves, blacks and Indians, and especially lepers in Surinam for more than forty years. d. 1887. bd May 23, 1982. *January 14.*

PETER DUMOULIN-BORIE, ST,
MARTYR

A priest of the Paris Society of Foreign Missions, martyred in Indo-China in 1838. He was appointed bishop and vicar apostolic of Tongking while in prison, where he was frequently flogged and tortured. bd 1900. cd June 19, 1988. *November 24, iii, 78.*

PETER EYMARD, ST

Peter Julian Eymard was b. in France in 1811 and ordained in 1834, being a member of the Society of Mary. After over twenty years of apostolic work he was dispensed from his vows, and in 1857 founded the congregation of Priests of the Blessed Sacrament, having the duty of maintaining "perpetual adoration". The new foundation was beset with many difficulties, in coping with which Father Eymard was encouraged by St John Vianney, who recognized the founder as a true saint. d. 1868. bd 1925. cd 1962. *August 1, iii, 256.*

PETER FAVRE, BD

Peter Favre (Faber), the senior of the first companions of St Ignatius Loyola, was the first among the Jesuits to come to grips with the Protestant Reformation. He was sent to the conferences at Worms and Ratisbon in 1540–41, and soon saw that what was needed was not "talk" but a reform among Catholics. Accordingly he worked with tremendous energy, ability, and no little success to purify and strengthen the faithful of the Rhineland, Spain and Portugal. d. 1546. c.c. 1872. *August 11, iii, 306.*

*PETER FOURIER, ST

Born in Lorraine in 1565. He became an Augustinian canon regular and was given cure of souls at Mattaincourt in the Vosges, where he did marvellous work in a very troublesome parish. Here, with Bd Alix Le Clercq, he founded the Augustinian Canonesses Regular of Our Lady, for the education of girls, and himself instructed the early aspirants in pedagogical method, in which he was a pioneer; he was very urgent for free schooling for the poor. In 1622 the Holy See appointed Fourier visitor apostolic of his order and he organized the Lorraine houses into a reformed congregation, of which he was made superior general. d. 1640. cd 1897. *December 9, iv, 526.*

PETER FRANCIS JAMET, BD

Pierre-François Jamet was b. in 1762 at Fresne, France, and was ordained priest in 1787. He was chaplain and confessor to the Good Saviour nuns but refused to take the state oath demanded by the revolutionaries; he ministered in secret. After the Revolution he devoted himself to the care of the handicapped and was rector of Caen University from 1822 to 1830. bd May 10, 1987. *May 7.*

PETER FRASSATI, BD

A young Italian layman and Dominican tertiary, Pier Giorgio Frassati, b. Turin April 6, 1901, into a rich middle-class family. He became an engineering student and joined Don Sturzi's Popular Party in 1920, the university students' organization Pax Romana in 1923, and the St Vincent de Paul Conference in 1923. He practised his faith openly in spite of the anti-clerical ethos of the university and took part in the Catholic Youth Congress. He was an exemplar of chastity and spirituality, and noted for his attention to biblical studies and his interest in social questions. d. of polio in 1925. cd May 20, 1990 by John Paul II. *July 4.*

PETER FRIEDHOFEN, BD

Peter Friedhofen was b. at Weitersburg, near Koblenz, Germany, on February 25, 1819. In 1849 he founded the Order of Brothers of Mercy of Mary the Helper. d. in 1860. bd June 23, 1985. *December 21.*

PETER GEREMIA, BD

He was a law-student at Bologna who in consequence of a vision gave up that profession and joined the Friars Preachers.

He soon had a considerable reputation as a preacher and theologian, and was summoned to the Council of Florence. Though always engaged in active duties, he was by nature a contemplative and ascetic. d. 1452. c.c. 1784. *March 10, i, 550.*

PETER GONZALEZ, BD

Bd Peter was Dominican chaplain at the court of King St Ferdinand III of Leon and Castile, where he was a zealous reformer, and afterwards a preacher among the Moors of Cordova and the peasants of Galicia. d. 1246. c.c. 1741. Portuguese sailors invoke him as "St Elmo", by confusion with St Erasmus. *April 14, ii, 94.*

*PETER IGNEUS, BD, BISHOP

To demonstrate that Peter of Pavia had become bishop of Florence by simony, this Peter, a monk of Vallombrosa, passed through fire unharmed, whence his second name. There is a remarkable contemporary account of this. Peter was later appointed cardinal-bishop of Albano, and sent on missions to foreign states. d. 1089. *February 8, i, 281.*

*PETER MARTYR, ST

Peter of Verona was b. in that town in 1205; he joined the Friars Preachers, and was appointed inquisitor of Lombardy. He preached far and wide in mid and northern Italy against evil-living Catholics and the heresies of Catharism (which his parents had professed). By Catharists he was murdered while travelling from Como to Milan in 1252, and was cd as a martyr in the following year. This Peter Martyr must not be confused with Peter Martyr Vermigli, who was a Protestant leader in the sixteenth century. *April 20, ii, 186.*

PETER MAUBANT, ST, MARTYR

Pierre Philibert Maubant was born at Vassy, Calvados, on September 20, 1803. He was a priest of Bayeux diocese in 1829 and entered the Paris Foreign Missions. He reached Korea on January 12, 1836. He was arrested in September 6 and beheaded on September 21, 1839. bd 1925. cd at Seoul by John Paul II in 1984. *September 21, iii, 611.*

PETER NÉRON, ST, MARTYR

Peter Francis Néron, a priest of the Paris Foreign Missions, was martyred in Indo-China in 1860. bd 1919. cd June 19, 1988. *November 3.*

*PETER NOLASCO, ST

Born in Languedoc *c.* 1189. The spectacle of the sufferings of Christian slaves among the Moors in Spain fired him with the resolve to work for the redemption of such captives, and he was associated with the beginnings of the Mercedarian Order which existed for that purpose. By the Mercedarians he is regarded as their principal founder. The details of his life, however, are obscure. d. 1256. cd 1628. *January 28, i, 185.*

*PETER ORSEOLO, ST

Born 928 in Venice, and at the age of twenty was admiral of the Venetian fleet. After the murder of the doge Peter Candiani IV in 976, Orseolo (Urseolus) was appointed to the office, and safely guided Venice through a political crisis. Then, when he had been doge for only two years, he suddenly disappeared, not even his wife and son knowing where he had gone. He was eventually found at the abbey of Cuxa, on the border of France and Spain. He continued to live here for a time in austere retirement; then he became a complete solitary and so d. in 987. *January 10, i, 64.*

*PETER PASCUAL, BD,
BISHOP AND MARTYR

Peter was b. at Valencia and became a priest. In 1296 he was appointed to the see of Jaén, which at that time was still under Moorish domination. His activity in ransoming captives and preaching to the infidels caused him to be imprisoned; here he wrote a treatise against Islam, and was left to die in jail, in 1300. c.c. 1673. *December 6, iv, 508.*

PETER PETRONI, BD

Bd Peter joined the Carthusians at Mag-
giano, near Siena, when he was seventeen.
He brought about the conversion to better
ways of Boccaccio. d. 1361.
May 29, ii, 421.

*PETER REGALADO, ST

A Franciscan friar of Valladolid who
became superior of some friaries noted for
the austerity of their régime; hence his
name, "rule-enforcer". d. 1456. cd 1746.
May 13, ii, 303.

PETER ROGUE, BD, MARTYR

Born at Vannes in 1758, where he was
ordained, and afterwards joined the Lazarists at Paris. He refused to take the
"constitutional" oath, and was martyred by
the guillotine in 1796. bd 1934.
March 1, i, 457.

PETER SANZ, BD, BISHOP AND
MARTYR

A Spanish Dominican, vicar apostolic of
Fu-kien, who was martyred at Foochow in
China in 1747; his four fellow Dominican
missionaries were put to death in the
following year. They were all beatified in
1893. *May 26, ii, 402.*

PETER SNOW, BD, MARTYR

A secular priest b. at Ripon, Yorkshire. He
studied at Rheims and was ordained priest
and sent on the English mission in 1591. He
was arrested with Bd Ralph Grimston in
1598 and d. at York for treason. bd November 22, 1987. *June 15.*

PETER THOMAS, ST, BISHOP

Born in France in 1305, became a Carmelite, and eventually was sent as procurator
of that order to the papal court at Avignon.
From that time most of his life was spent
in missions and negotiations for the Holy
See, and in the discharge of these duties he
was notable for the simplicity of his manner
of living and the confidence which his
goodness inspired. Surprisingly enough, he
was virtually in charge of the military
expedition against Alexandria in 1365. Here

he was wounded and d. three months later
at Cyprus, in 1366. St Peter Thomas was
titular Latin patriarch of Constantinople. His
feast was approved for the Carmelites in
1608. *January 28, i, 191.*

PETER WRIGHT, BD, MARTYR

He was a Northamptonshire Jesuit who was
a chaplain in the royalist army during the
Civil War; he was hanged for his priesthood
at Tyburn in 1651. bd 1929.
May 19, ii, 353.

*PETER OF ALCANTARA, ST

He was b. at Alcántara in Spain in 1499. He
became a Franciscan of a reformed branch
of the order and in 1554 began a yet more
severe reform, whose members were
referred to as Alcantarines and existed until
the union of the Observants in 1897. St
Peter was one of the great Spanish mystics
of that time: St Teresa, whom he encouraged
and defended in her reform of the Carmelites, said of him that his austerities and
penances were "incomprehensible to the
human mind"; his treatise on prayer was
very greatly valued. d. 1562. cd 1669.
October 19, iv, 144.

*PETER OF ALEXANDRIA, ST,
BISHOP AND MARTYR

The twelve years of this Peter's episcopate
were darkened by continual struggles with
schism, heresy and persecution, crowned by
his own death for Christ in 311. By the
Copts he is called the "Seal and Comple-
ment of the Persecution", because he was
the last martyr put to death by public
authority at Alexandria.
November 26, iv, 423.

PETER OF ATHOS, ST

He is reputed to have been the first Christian
solitary on Mount Athos, but his Greek
legend is a fiction. Eighth century (?).
June 12, ii, 530.

PETER OF ATROA, ST, ABBOT

He was abbot of a monastery on the
Bithynian Olympus, and was persecuted as
a defender of the veneration of sacred

images. Many miracles were attributed to him. d. 837. *January 1, i, 10.*

*PETER OF BRAGA, ST, BISHOP

Principal patron of Braga and bishop there, probably in the fourth century; nothing is known of his life. *April 26, ii, 164.*

PETER OF CASTELNAU, BD, MARTYR

A Cistercian monk who was appointed by Innocent III apostolic delegate and inquisitor for the Albigensians. He was slain by them in 1208. *January 15, i, 98.*

PETER OF CAVA, ST, BISHOP

Peter Pappacarbone left the abbey of Cava, which his uncle St Alferius had founded, to be a monk at Cluny. He was recalled to be made bishop of Policastro, but he was not cut out for this office and resigned, and was appointed third abbot of Cava. He had great difficulty in imposing the severe observance of Cluny, but was successful and his monastery became very famous. d. 1123. *March 4, i, 481.*

PETER OF CHAVANON, ST

He was a secular priest who founded a monastery of Augustinian canons regular at Pébrac in Auvergne; he ruled it with such success that he was entrusted with the reform of several collegiate chapters. d. 1080. *September 11, iii, 540.*

PETER OF CUERVA, BD, MARTYR

A Spanish Franciscan, one of the first three martyrs of the second great Japanese persecution. He was beheaded near Nagasaki in 1617. bd 1867. *May 22, ii, 447.*

PETER OF GUBBIO, BD

Peter Ghisengi, a Hermit of St Augustine, seems to have been venerated chiefly on account of the wonders reported at his tomb in Gubbio in Tuscany. d. *c.* 1250 (?). c.c. by Pope Pius IX. *March 23, i, 665.*

PETER OF JULLY, BD

He was an Englishman and a friend of St Stephen Harding, whom he afterwards joined at the abbey of Molesme. At their own request he was made chaplain to the nuns at Jully (Juilly), and there he d. in 1136. *June 23, ii, 622.*

*PETER OF LAMPSACUS, ST, MARTYR

This Peter was martyred at Lampsacus in 251 and is commemorated with other martyrs, who suffered at Troas. But the details of their story are not trustworthy. *May 15, ii, 319.*

PETER OF LUXEMBURG, BD, BISHOP

He was a son of Count Guy of Luxemburg, and before he was eighteen years old had been made canon of Notre-Dame-de-Paris, bishop of Metz and cardinal (he was a deacon). In spite of glaring pluralism (common in his day) he was a young man of great holiness of character, but was cut off in his youth in 1387. bd 1527. *July 2, iii, 9.*

PETER OF MOGLIANO, BD

He was an Observant Franciscan and a preaching companion of St James of the March; it was said of him that he would die laughing. d. 1490. c.c. 1760. *July 30, iii, 217.*

PETER OF NARBONNE, ST, MARTYR

Pierre de Narbonne, from Provence, a Franciscan companion of St Nicholas of Sibenik (Nicholas Tavelic), was martyred by the Muslims at Jerusalem in 1393 and canonized by Pope Paul VI on June 21, 1970. *December 5.*

*PETER OF NICOMEDIA, ST, MARTYR

A chamberlain in the household of Diocletian, martyred at Nicomedia with Dorotheus and others in 303. *March 12, i, 573.*

PETER OF PISA, BD

Peter Gambacorta was b. at Pisa in 1355, son of the ruler of the republic. In 1380 he founded a small community of hermit-monks, called Poor Brothers of St Jerome, and not even the assassination of his father and two brothers could draw him from his retreat: like his sister, Bd Clare Gambacorta, he freely forgave the murderers. d. 1435. *June 17, ii, 570.*

PETER OF POITIERS, BD, BISHOP

He was bishop of Poitiers and is venerated in that diocese, particularly for his merciless denouncement of wickedness in high places. d. 1115. *April 4, ii, 29.*

PETER OF RUFFIA, BD, MARTYR

He was a Dominican, murdered by some sectaries in 1365, while discharging the office of inquisitor general in Piedmont and Lombardy. c.c. 1856.
November 7, iv, 291.

PETER OF SASSOFERRATO, BD, MARTYR

This Peter was sent into Spain by St Francis of Assisi to preach the gospel to the Moors, and was martyred at Valencia with Bd John of Perugia. d. 1231. bd 1783.
September 1, iii, 463.

*PETER OF SEBASTEA, ST, BISHOP

Brother of St Basil the Great and St Gregory of Nyssa. He succeeded Basil as abbot of the monastery which their mother had founded, and was made bishop of Sebastea in 380, when he had to combat the Arian heresy. Gregory of Nyssa testifies to his brother's great holiness. d. *c.* 391.
January 9, i, 57.

PETER OF SIENA, BD

Peter Tecelano was a comb-maker of Siena. After the death of his wife he became a Franciscan tertiary, went to live near the friary, and there carried on his trade till the end of his long life. His days were simple and uneventful, and he attained a high degree of contemplative prayer. d. 1289. c.c. 1802. *December 11, iv, 541.*

*PETER OF TARENTAISE, ST, BISHOP

Peter, a Cistercian monk, was appointed archbishop of Tarentaise in 1142 and found his diocese in a deplorable state. After thirteen years of reorganization he disappeared, but was found living as a lay-brother in a Swiss monastery, whereupon he had to return to his see. He zealously opposed the antipope Victor, and was commissioned to try to bring about a reconciliation between King Louis VII of France and Henry II of England; he was unsuccessful in his efforts and d. in 1175 while on his way back to Tarentaise. St Peter is one of the great figures of the Cistercian Order. cd 1191. *May 8, ii, 253. See also* Innocent V.

PETER OF TIFERNO, BD

A confessor of the Dominican Order at Cortona. d. 1445. c.c. by Pope Pius VII. *October 21, iv, 172.*

PETER OF TREJA, BD

He was an early Franciscan in central Italy, who after a long life of labour, adorned by miracles and the gift of prophecy, d. in 1304. c.c. 1793. *February 17, i, 360.*

PETER THE VENERABLE, BD, ABBOT

At the age of thirty in 1122 Bd Peter was called to the abbacy of Cluny, and during his rule the great Cluniac congregation reached a high point of influence and prosperity. Peter was a generous friend of Abelard, and himself was involved in a controversy with St Bernard about monastic observance. d. 1156.
December 29, iv, 640.

PETER. *See also under* Gregorius.

PETROC, ST, ABBOT

Petroc (Pedrog) was one of the most active missionary saints in the south-west of Britain during the sixth century, but nothing much is known about him: he probably came to Cornwall from Wales. Many churches in that county and Devon were dedicated in his honour and he gave his name to Padstow (Petrocstow); the centre of his *cultus* was afterwards at Bodmin. *Petrocus. June 4, ii, 475.*

PETRONAX, ST, ABBOT
He re-established the abbey of Monte Cassino in 717 and ruled it till his death, some thirty years later. *May 6, ii, 242.*

*PETRONILLA, ST,
VIRGIN AND MARTYR
The date and history of her passion are unknown, but she was certainly not St Peter's daughter, as she is called in the Roman Martyrology. *May 31, ii, 434.*

PETRONILLA OF MONCEL, BD,
VIRGIN
She was the first abbess of the convent of Poor Clares at Moncel in Burgundy, founded by King Philip le Bel. d. 1355. *May 14, ii, 309.*

*PETRONIUS, ST, BISHOP
He is said to have become bishop of Bologna *c.* 430, and to have founded the monastery of St Stephen there, whose buildings reproduced the general lines of the Holy Places at Jerusalem, a monument which still exists in a modified form. d. *c.* 445 (?). *October 4, iv, 33.*

PHARAILDIS, ST, VIRGIN
Otherwise *Varelde, Verylde, Veerle.* The accounts of this popular Belgian saint are confusing and improbable. The main tradition is that she was married against her will and, having dedicated her maidenhood to God, refused to live with her husband, who treated her with great cruelty. d. *c.* 740. *January 4, i, 31.*

*PHILASTRIUS, ST, BISHOP
He was a bishop of Brescia whom St Gaudentius praises in a panegyric for his "modesty, quietness, and kindness towards all men". He wrote a book against Arianism and other heresies, and was notably generous not only to the poor, but to tradesmen and others who lacked capital. d. *c.* 387. *July 8, iii, 138.*

*PHILEAS, ST, BISHOP AND MARTYR
Phileas was arrested soon after being made bishop at Thmuis in Egypt. From his prison at Alexandria he wrote a letter to his flock describing the sufferings of the Christian prisoners. He was beheaded, together with a Roman official named Philoromus, in 304. *February 4, i, 248.*

*PHILEMON AND APOLLONIUS, SS,
MARTYRS
Philemon was an Egyptian musician and entertainer who was converted to Christianity by Apollonius, a deacon from Antinoë. They were both seized under Diocletian and put to death at Alexandria *c.* 305. *March 8, i, 521.*

*PHILEMON AND APPHIA, SS,
MARTYRS
Apphia is supposed to have been the wife of that Philemon to whom St Paul addressed a letter about a runaway slave. They are said to have been martyred at their home at Colossae in Phrygia, or at Ephesus. *November 22, iv, 405.*

*PHILIBERT, ST, ABBOT
He founded the abbey of Jumièges and other religious houses, and was one of the ecclesiastics who stood up to the notorious Ebroin, mayor of the palace to Thierry III, for which he was imprisoned and banished for some years. d. *c.* 685. *Philibertus. August 20, iii, 367.*

*PHILIP, ST, APOSTLE
The apostle Philip is mentioned several times in the gospel of St John. According to an old tradition he preached the gospel in Phrygia after Pentecost, and d. at Hierapolis. It is not known for certain whether he was martyred. *Philippus. May 3, ii, 203.*

*PHILIP BENIZI, ST
Born at Florence in 1233, and gave up the medical profession to become a lay-brother of the Servants of Mary. He was taken away from his gardening to receive holy orders, and was in due course promoted to the

headship of the order, to his great discomfort. Philip's reputation for holiness spread, and it is said that in 1268 the cardinals were for making him pope; he fled by night and hid till the suggestion was withdrawn. From year to year he travelled visiting the houses of his order and working for peace between Guelphs and Ghibellines, and he assisted at the second general Council of Lyons. St Philip was the chief promoter and the best-known saint of the Servite Order. d. 1285. cd 1671. *August 23, iii, 385.*

PHILIP EVANS, ST, MARTYR
Born at Monmouth in 1645, became a Jesuit and worked on the mission in South Wales. He was h.d.q. for his priesthood at Cardiff in 1679. bd 1929. cd 1970. *July 22, iii, 166.*

PHILIP HOWARD, ST, MARTYR
Philip Howard, earl of Arundel and Surrey, for some years was neglectful of his estates, his wife, and his religion, but he mended his ways and was reconciled to the Church with his wife, Anne Dacre. In 1585 he was committed to the Tower of London, and in 1589 sentenced to death; the sentence was not carried out and he d. in the Tower at the age of thirty-eight, after ten years' imprisonment, in 1595. bd 1929. cd 1970. *October 19, iv, 152.*

*PHILIP NERI, ST
Born at Florence in 1515. For eighteen years he was a layman in Rome, beginning that work for souls which was to earn him the title of apostle of the City. After ordination he gathered some companions around him who formed the nucleus of the Congregation of the Oratory, and continued to live very simply, at the service of all, from the pope to a pot-boy. He exercised his apostleship particularly through the confessional; in his later years he was habitually enraptured when offering Mass. St Philip was an unusually fine, almost fastidious, man, and converted renaissance Rome by influencing

individuals rather than by exterior legislation or public exhortation; religious controversy he avoided. d. 1595. cd 1622. *May 26, ii, 395.*

PHILIP POWELL, BD, MARTYR
Born at Trallwng in Breconshire, educated at Abergavenny grammar school, and became a Benedictine at St Gregory's, Douay, in 1619. He was a priest for twenty years in Devonshire, and was then arrested on shipboard while on his way to Wales. h.d.q. for his priesthood at Tyburn in 1646. bd 1929. *June 30, ii, 680.*

*PHILIP OF HERACLEA, ST,
BISHOP AND MARTYR
The martyrdom in 304 of Philip, bishop of Heraclea, with whom suffered the priest Severus and the deacon Hermes, who had been a magistrate, is one of the best attested episodes of the Diocletian persecution. Philip, an aged man, refused to give up the sacred books or to sacrifice to the gods, and Hermes followed his example; after persuasion and torture had failed they were burned to death. Severus, who had been in hiding and gave himself up, suffered on the following day. *October 22, iv, 175.*

PHILIP OF ZELL, ST
This Philip was an Englishman who lived as a hermit near Worms and is said to have had great influence over King Pepin the Short. After his death a monastery was built on the site of his cell and the town of Zell grew up around it. Eighth century. *May 3, ii, 224.*

PHILIP RINALDI, BD
A Salesian priest, b. at Lu Monferrato in 1856. The third successor of Don Bosco, he directed the Salesians with perspicacity in answer to Pius XI's appeal, with special reference to the Asian and Eastern missions. A dynamic director of the Order. d. 1931. bd April 29, 1990. *April 29.*

PHILIP SIPHONG AND HIS SIX COMPANIONS, BB. *See* Seven martyrs of Thailand.

*PHILIP THE DEACON, ST

He was one of the seven deacons chosen by the Apostles, and he baptized the eunuch of Queen Candace of Ethiopia (Acts vi, viii). *June 6, ii, 487.*

PHILIPPA MARERI, BD, VIRGIN

Fired by meeting St Francis of Assisi, she sought to emulate him in her home, near Rieti in Umbria, and perhaps ran away to a hermitage. Later she formed a community of Franciscan nuns, under the direction of Bd Roger of Todi. d. 1236. *February 16, i, 352.*

PHILIPPINE DUCHESNE, BD, VIRGIN

This Frenchwoman introduced the Society of the Sacred Heart into America. She was b. at Grenoble in 1769, and was clothed as a Visitandine nun. After the Revolution she made a fruitless attempt to re-establish her community, and was then accepted by Mother Barat. In 1818 she landed at New Orleans with four other religious, and started the first free school west of the Mississippi at Saint Charles, Missouri. Mother Duchesne was a real pioneer, and carried out her task amid frontier trials and hardships. When she was over seventy she started a school for Indian children in Kansas, and had to be restrained from pushing on to the Rockies. "She was the St Francis of Assisi of the Society. Everything in and about her was stamped with the seal of a crucified life." d. 1852. bd 1940. *November 17, iv, 378.*

*PHILOGONIUS, ST, BISHOP

Philogonius, a barrister, was elected bishop of Antioch in 319, and was imprisoned for the faith; he was highly spoken of by St John Chrysostom. d. 324. *December 20, iv, 587.*

*PHOCAS OF ANTIOCH, ST, MARTYR

He is said to have been martyred at Antioch, but seems actually to be a derivative of St Phocas the Gardener. *March 5, i, 485.*

PHOCAS THE GARDENER, ST, MARTYR

All that is certainly known of this Phocas is that he lived, was martyred, and is greatly venerated in the East. According to legend he was a market-gardener at Sinope in Pontus. *September 22, iii, 617.*

*PHOEBE, ST

She is mentioned by St Paul in the last chapter of his epistle to the Christians at Rome. There is no reason to suppose that she was his wife, as has been alleged. *September 3, iii, 478.*

*PHOTINA, ST, MARTYR

According to a fable popular in the East she was the Samaritan woman with whom our Lord talked at the well, being afterwards martyred with others at Rome. Her name is associated with that of the apocryphal St Parasceve, also very popular in the East. Cardinal Baronius would seem to have entered Photina's name in the Roman Martyrology by an oversight. *March 20, i, 636.*

PIERINA MOROSONI, BD, MARTYR

She was b. on January 7, 1931 at Fiobbio di Albino, Bergamo, Italy. She worked in the Albino cotton factory and, influenced by Catholic Action, for which she worked in the parish, she developed a devout prayer-life. The need for her income in the home prevented her from becoming a missionary nun. In 1957 she was murdered on her way from the factory. bd October 4, 1987. *April 6.*

*PIERIUS, ST

A priest of Alexandria, famed for his learning and goodness; he was the teacher of St Pamphilus. d. *c.* 310. *November 4, iv, 263.*

PINIAN. *See under* Melania the Younger.

*PIONIUS, ST, MARTYR

Pionius, a priest of Smyrna, was arrested while observing with friends the anniversary

of the martyrdom of St Polycarp. After a long cross-examination they refused with violence to sacrifice in the pagan temple and were condemned to die. St Pionius was burnt alive and we have an eye-witness's account of his death. d. 250 (?).
February 1, i, 224.

PIRAN, ST, ABBOT

The *cultus* of St Piran was once widespread in Cornwall, but there is very little certain about him. His medieval identification with St Ciaran (Kieran) of Ossory is probably literary rather than historical. Sixth century (?). *March 5, i, 489.*

*PIRMINUS, ST, BISHOP

First abbot of Reichenau, and a missionary bishop in Baden. Being driven out by the civil power, he founded monasteries elsewhere, and d. in 753. He wrote a popular work of religious instruction.
November 3, iv, 248.

*PIUS V, ST, POPE

Michael Ghislieri was b. in Piedmont in 1504; he joined the Dominicans, was made a bishop in 1556 and a cardinal in the following year, and in 1565 was elected to the Holy See as Pius V. He was an austere and severe man at a time when austerity and severity were particularly needed. He enforced the reforms of the Council of Trent, combated Protestantism in the Empire and France, organized resistance against the threatening Turks (battle of Lepanto), excommunicated Queen Elizabeth I of England, reformed the public worship of the Roman rite, and reproved by example prelatical luxury, insisting strongly that bishops and other beneficed clergy must reside in their cures. d. 1572. cd 1712.
April 30, ii, 234.

*PIUS X, ST, POPE

Joseph Sarto was b. of humble parents in Venetia in 1835. He was ordained priest in 1858; bishop of Mantua, 1884; patriarch of Venice and cardinal, 1892; pope, 1903. The motto of Pius X's pontificate was "the renewal of all things in Christ": he urged daily communion at a time when it was still unusual and looked on with some suspicion, he facilitated the communion of children and the sick, and strongly encouraged Bible-reading; he dealt with the tendency called Modernism and boldly tackled the difficulties of the Church in France. Pius X was a man of remarkable simplicity and sweetness of character, one who "knew the unhappiness of the world and the hardships of life, and in the greatness of his heart wanted to comfort everybody". His threefold crown was poverty, humbleness and gentleness. He d. a fortnight after the outbreak of European war in 1914—its first great victim. cd 1954.
August 26, iii, 474.

PIUS CAMPIDELLI, BD

Br Pio di San Luigi Campidelli was b. 1868 into a poor family. He was a Passionist student for the priesthood and noted for his devotion to prayer. d. 1889. bd November 17, 1985. *November 3.*

PLACID RICCARDI, BD

A Benedictine monk of the monastery of St Paul outside the walls of Rome. d. 1915. bd 1954. *March 14, iv, 672.*

PLACIDA VIEL, BD, VIRGIN

She was b. in Normandy, of a farming family, in 1815, and became second superior general of the Sisters of the Christian Schools, in succession to St Mary Magdalen Postel. Mother Placida directed the congregation for thirty years, during which it increased sevenfold in membership. She was a woman of charm, good humour and quiet confidence in God. d. 1877. bd 1951. *March 4, iv, 483.*

*PLAGUE OF ALEXANDRIA, MARTYRS IN THE

In the year 261 Alexandria suffered from a terrible plague which had already devastated other parts of the empire. The Christians of the city visited and looked after the sick and comforted the dying regardless of their personal safety. Many of them, clergy and lay folk, themselves succumbed, and the Roman Church recognizes their heroism by making a commemoration in her martyrology of those whom "the faith of religious persons acknowledges as martyrs". *February 28, i, 436.*

*PLATO, ST, ABBOT

Abbot of Symboleon on Mount Olympus in Bithynia and then of Sakkudion, near Constantinople. He suffered persecution and imprisonment for opposing the divorce and subsequent attempted marriage of the emperor Constantine Porphyrogenitus. d. 814. *April 4, ii, 28.*

PLECHELM, ST, BISHOP

He was a Northumbrian who went into the Low Countries with St Wiro and became an apostle of Guelderland. Eighth century. *May 8, ii, 253.*

*PLUTARCH, ST, MARTYR

A pupil of Origen who was martyred with other students from the catechetical school at Alexandria in *c.* 202. *Plutarchus. June 28, ii, 658.*

*POEMEN, ST, ABBOT

Poemen was one of the most celebrated of the Fathers of the Desert. He retired to Skete during the second half of the fourth century and became abbot of a group of hermits who lived in the ruins of a heathen temple at Terenuthis. He was present at the death of St Arsenius, and himself d. soon after. *August 27, iii, 417,*

*POLLIO, ST, MARTYR

He was a lector of the church of Cybalae in Pannonia, martyred in 304. *April 28, ii, 181.*

*POLYCARP, ST, BISHOP AND MARTYR

One of the most famous of the Apostolic Fathers and a disciple of St John the Evangelist; he was bishop of Smyrna. St Ignatius on the way to martyrdom recommended him to his own church of Antioch, and soon after Polycarp wrote a letter on Ignatius's behalf to the Philippians: in St Jerome's time this letter was still publicly read in the churches of Asia. Another extant letter, written in the name of the church of Smyrna, describes Polycarp's martyrdom. After St Germanicus and others had been put to death he was seized and brought before the proconsul, where he confessed himself a Christian and refused to give divine honours to the emperor. The games being over, the people clamoured for him to be burned alive, and this was done, the old man meeting his death with calmness and fortitude, in 155 (or 166). *Polycarpus. February 23, i, 167.*

POLYDORE PLASDEN, ST, MARTYR

This martyr was a secular priest who ministered in London at the end of the sixteenth century. He was h.d.q. at Tyburn for his priesthood in 1591. bd 1929. cd 1970. *December 10, iv, 533.*

*POLYEUCTUS, ST, MARTYR

Polyeuctus was martyred at Melitene in Armenia *c.* 259 and a church was dedicated in his honour there before 377. Corneille, in his tragedy *Polyeucte*, makes use of elements that are found in the martyr's *acta*, but are fictitious. *February 13, i, 320.*

*POMPILIO PIRROTTI, ST

Pompilio Maria Pirrotti was a confessor of the Piarist congregation who taught school and preached missions in the kingdom of Naples. d. 1756. cd 1934. *July 15, iii, 113.*

*PONTIAN, ST, POPE AND MARTYR

He was pope from *c.* 230 to *c.* 235. He was exiled to Sardinia by the emperor Maximinus, and is said to have d. there from ill treatment. *Pontianus. November 19, iv, 391.*

*PONTIUS, ST, MARTYR

He is said to have died for Christ at Cimiez, near Nice, in the third century. *May 14, ii, 305.*

*PONTIUS OF CARTHAGE, ST

He was the deacon of St Cyprian of Carthage and went with him into exile at

Curubis. Pontius was the author of a biography and *passio* of Cyprian that are still extant. d. *c.* 260. *March 8, i, 520.*

PONTIUS OF FAUCIGNY, BD, ABBOT

The memory of Pontius of Faucigny, abbot of the canons regular at Abondance in Chablais, was greatly revered by St Francis de Sales. Pontius was also for a time abbot of the monastery of Sixt, which he had founded. d. 1178. c.c. 1896. *November 26, iv, 426.*

*POPPO, ST, ABBOT

He was first soldier, then pilgrim, then monk, under Abbot Richard of Saint-Vanne, for whom he reformed several monasteries, including that of Saint-Vaast at Arras. Poppo himself became abbot of Stavelot and was a sort of general superior of a group of monasteries in Lotharingia. d. 1048. *January 25, i, 166.*

*PORCARIUS, ST, MARTYR

Abbot of Lérins who, with nearly all his monks, was massacred by Moors *c.* 732; but there are difficulties about the story. *August 12, iii, 314.*

*PORPHYRY, ST, BISHOP

After years as a hermit in the desert of Skete and the Jordan valley he was consecrated bishop of Gaza in 396, more or less by force. Porphyry was intent on uprooting paganism and was given leave by the emperor Arcadius to destroy the temples in Gaza. It is not surprising to learn that the worshippers lost no opportunity of harassing the bishop and his flock. On the site of the temple of Marnas a great church was built which Porphyry consecrated in 408. He d. in 420 and his biography, written by his deacon Mark, is a valuable historical document. *February 26, i, 423.*

*POSSIDIUS, ST, BISHOP

Possidius, bishop of Calama in Numidia, was closely associated with St Augustine in his struggles against heresy, and suffered personal violence. He was driven from his see by the Arian Genseric and d. in exile, *c.* 440. *May 16, ii, 327.*

*POTAMIAENA, ST,
VIRGIN AND MARTYR

She would not purchase her freedom at the price of her chastity and was lowered slowly into a cauldron of boiling pitch, at Alexandria in 202. Her mother, St Marcella, was martyred at the same time. *June 28, ii, 658.*

*POTAMON, ST, BISHOP AND MARTYR

He was bishop of Heraclea in Egypt and was savagely tortured during the persecution of Maximinus Daia in 310; he met his death through brutal treatment by the Arians, *c.* 340. *May 18, ii, 342.*

*POTHINUS, ST,
BISHOP AND MARTYR

St Pothinus was the first bishop of Lyons and the leader of those martyrs of that city (*q.v.*) whose sufferings are recorded in a contemporary letter. Pothinus had probably "listened to those who had seen the Apostles"; in his ninetieth year he was mishandled by a mob and d. in prison from his injuries. *June 2, ii, 454.*

*PRAEJECTUS, ST,
BISHOP AND MARTYR

Otherwise *Priest, Prest, Preils, Prix.* Bishop of Clermont *c.* 666. He was slain by one who had a grievance against him, in 676. There is a contemporary account of his life and achievements. *January 25, i, 166.*

*PRAETEXTATUS, ST,
BISHOP AND MARTYR

Praetextatus, called *Prix* in France, was chosen bishop of Rouen in 549; Chilperic, king at Soissons, charged him with acts calculated to encourage rebellion, and he was banished. After Chilperic's death he returned to his see, but was pursued by the enmity of the queen, Fredegund, with whom the bishop had often to remonstrate. She eventually caused him to be murdered in 586. St Gregory of Tours witnesses to the falseness of the charges made against Praetextatus by his enemies. *February 24, i, 411.*

*PRAXEDES, ST, VIRGIN

Legend has it that Praxedes was the sister of St Pudentiana, and that she helped and sheltered Christians during persecution; but her extant *acta* have been semi-officially declared to be spurious. *July 21, iii, 157.*

*PRIMUS AND **FELICIAN, SS,** MARTYRS

Brothers who were martyred and buried at Nomentum, near Rome. The details of their passion are legendary. *June 9, ii, 509.*

*PRISCA, ST, VIRGIN AND MARTYR

The St Prisca, virgin and martyr, mentioned in the Roman Martyrology on January 18 has not been satisfactorily identified. *January 18, i, 115.*

PRISCA. *See also under* Aquila.

*PRISCILLA, ST

It is likely that St Priscilla was the wife of Manius Acilius Glabrio and mother of the senator Pudens; she gives her name to the most ancient of the Roman catacombs, above which was her villa, which it is believed that St Peter made his head-quarters. *January 16, i, 100. See also* Prisca.

*PRISCUS, ST, MARTYR

Priscus and other citizens of Besançon were martyred at Auxerre at an early date. He also is called *Prix* in French. *May 26, ii, 400.*

PRIX. *See* Praejectus, Praetextatus, Priscus.

PROBUS. *See under* Tarachus.

*PROCESSUS AND **MARTINIAN, SS.,** MARTYRS

Roman martyrs of uncertain date. The story that they were the gaolers of St Peter and St Paul in the Mamertine prison is baseless. *July 2, iii, 7.*

*PROCLUS, ST, BISHOP

He became patriarch of Constantinople in 434 and was distinguished for the gentle way in which he dealt with Nestorians and other heretics, saving the Armenian church from the errors of its East Syrian and Persian neighbours. According to tradition he added the singing of the Trisagion to the Liturgy, in miraculous circumstances. St Cyril of Alexandria and others speak highly of the goodness of Proclus. d. 446. *October 24, iv, 188.*

*PROCOPIUS, ST, MARTYR

There is extant a contemporary account, written by Eusebius of Caesarea, of the passion of St Procopius, who was the first victim of the Diocletian persecution in Palestine. He was in reader's orders at Scythopolis and was beheaded in 303 at Caesarea Maritima for refusing to sacrifice to the emperors. The simple narrative of Eusebius was the seed of nonsensical later legends, in the course of whose evolution St Procopius was split up into three different people, none of whom remotely resembled him. *July 8, iii, 39.*

*PROCULUS, ST, MARTYR

He is said to have been an officer in the Roman army, martyred at Bologna *c.* 304. *June 1, ii, 439.*

PROCULUS, ST, BISHOP AND MARTYR

A bishop of Bologna who was martyred by the Goths in 542. *June 1, ii, 439.*

*PROSPER OF AQUITAINE, ST

A layman who wrote on grace and free will in defence of St Augustine's teaching; he also compiled a world chronicle. d. in Rome, *c.* 465. *June 25, ii, 639.*

*PROSPER OF REGGIO, ST, BISHOP

He was a bishop of Reggio in Emilia during the fifth century. The Roman Martyrology mistakenly identifies him with St Prosper of Aquitaine. *June 25, ii, 639.*

PROTASE. *See under* Gervase.

PROTERIUS, ST, BISHOP AND MARTYR

Proterius was elected patriarch of Alexandria when the Eutychian Dioscorus was deposed by the Council of Chalcedon. The schismatic party was so violent that Proterius was in danger throughout his pontificate, and eventually was killed by the mob in a church, in 457. *February 28, i, 437.*

*PROTUS AND **HYACINTH, SS.,** MARTYRS

By tradition they were brothers and servants in the house of St Eugenia, and were martyred with their convert St Basilla. The story is fictitious, but the indubitable relics of St Hyacinth were discovered in the cemetery of St Basilla at Rome in 1845. *September 11, iii, 537.*

PRUDENCE, BD, VIRGIN

Prudentia Casatori was a hermitess of St Augustine at Milan and Como, chiefly known for the miracles recorded at her tomb. d. 1492. *May 6, ii, 243.*

PRUDENTIUS, ST, BISHOP

Prudentius, bishop of Troyes, was one of the most learned prelates of the Gallican church in the ninth century; he played a part in the controversies about predestination. d. 861. *April 6, ii, 42.*

*PTOLEMAEUS, ST, MARTYR

He was put to death *c.* 161 for being a Christian and instructing a woman in the faith. One Lucius and an unnamed man, both of whom protested at the injustice of the sentence, were executed at the same time. *October 19, iv, 148.*

*PUBLIA, ST

She was a widow, the leader of a community of women at Antioch, who incurred the wrath of Julian the Apostate: he overhead them singing Psalm 115 (113) and interpreted certain passages therein as an insult to himself. *October 9, iv, 68.*

PUBLIUS, ST, ABBOT

He founded monasteries for Greeks and Syrians in Syria, being himself first a hermit and then a cenobite. d. *c.* 380. *January 25, i, 165.*

*PUDENTIANA AND **PUDENS, SS,** MARTYRS

The Roman Martyrology names as martyrs in Rome the maiden Pudentiana (Potentiana) and her father Pudens, a senator. Opinions are divided as to whether this is the Pudens mentioned in 2 Timothy iv, 21. Their "acts" are fabulous. *May 19, ii, 347.*

*PULCHERIA, ST, VIRGIN

The story of St Pulcheria, Eastern empress with her brother Theodosius II and then with Marcian, belongs to general secular and ecclesiastical history. She was a firm opponent of Monophysitism, and her feast is kept by some Eastern churches, as once in parts of the West. d. 453. *September 10, iii, 528.*

Q

*QUADRATUS, ST, BISHOP

Bishop of Athens, a disciple of the Apostles, and an apologist who wrote a treatise for the emperor Hadrian. But it is not certain that these were one and the same man. Also called *Codratus*. d. *c.* 129.
May 26, ii, 399.

*QUENTIN, ST, MARTYR

The story of the passion of St Quentin has come down to us in a variety of embellished forms, but he seems certainly to have been an authentic martyr at the town on the Somme which is now called by his name. He is said to have been a missionary from Rome. *Quintinus. October 31, iv, 229.*

QUIRIACUS. *See* Cyriacus.

*QUIRICUS AND JULITTA, SS, MARTYRS

According to their fictitious legend Julitta was a widow from Iconium who fled from persecution but was martyred at Tarsus. Her three-year-old son Quiricus (Cyricus) had previously had his brains dashed out by an infuriated magistrate whose face he had scratched. Nothing is known about them really: it is likely that Quiricus was a real martyr around whom the legend subsequently grew up. *June 16, ii, 552.*

*QUIRINUS, ST, BISHOP AND MARTYR

Quirinus was bishop of Siscia (Sisak in Croatia), and during the persecution under Diocletian in spite of cruel beating refused to sacrifice to the gods. He was sent to the governor at Sabaria (Szombathely in Hungary) and there, since he still refused to sacrifice, he was drowned in the river Raab, in 308. *June 4, ii, 472.*

*QUITERIA, ST, VIRGIN AND MARTYR

This saint is much venerated on the borders of France and Spain, but nothing is certain about her; she may have been martyred at Aire in Gascony. *May 22, ii, 366.*

R

RABANUS MAURUS, BD, BISHOP

This prolific writer was one of the most learned men of his age. He was b. c. 784 probably at Mainz and was educated at Fulda and Tours where he became deeply attached to Alcuin. He learned Greek, Hebrew and Syriac and was made master of the monastery school at Fulda. Rabanus became abbot there in 822, and it was probably then that he wrote his homilies and drew up his martyrology. He gave up the office, only to be made archbishop of Mainz. He was as energetic as he was learned, assisting at numerous synods and having 300 poor fed at his house every day. d. 856. *February 4, i, 249.*

RADBOD, ST, BISHOP

He was the great-grandson of the last pagan king of the Frisians (also called Radbod) and he became bishop of Utrecht in 900. Some hymns and other poems that he wrote are still in existence. d. 918. *November 29, iv, 446.*

*RADEGUND, ST

St Radegund is one of the best-known figures of the sixth century in France. She had the misfortune to be one of the numerous wives of King Clotaire I, and when he murdered her brother she separated herself from him and was consecrated a deaconess by St Medard. She played a considerable part in religious and secular affairs, especially on behalf of peace, and was the foundress of the great monastery of the Holy Cross at Poitiers. d. 587. There are several churches dedicated in this saint's honour in England, and she is one of the titulars of Jesus College, Cambridge. *Radegundis. August 13, iii, 318.*

RAFKA AL-RAYES, BD

She was b. in 1832 and was a member of the Lebanese Maronite Order of St Anthony. She cultivated a semi-mystical acceptance of suffering from ill health. d. 1914. bd November 17, 1985. *November 17.*

RAINERIUS OF AREZZO, BD

A confessor of the Friars Minor of whom little is known. d. 1304. c.c. 1802. There was also a Bd Rainerius among the Capuchins, of Todi, who d. c. 1586. *November 12, iv, 326.*

*RAINERIUS OF PISA, ST

In Italian *Raniero*. After a dissipated youth at Pisa he was converted, and a trading journey into Palestine confirmed him in his new and austere way of life. On his return he lived a retired existence, first in one monastery and then in another. Both before and after his death St Rainerius had a great reputation for miracles, healing the sick through the instrumentality of blessed water, whence he was called "de Aqua". d. 1160. *June 17, ii, 569.*

RAINERIUS INCLUSUS, BD

Rainerius *Inclusus* is so called because he spent twenty-two years shut up in a cell adjoining the cathedral of Osnabrück; to this self-imposed imprisonment he added other austerities. d. 1237. *April 11, ii, 74.*

RALPH, ST, BISHOP

In French *Raoul*. Though probably not a monk he received several abbacies, and in 840 was made bishop of Bourges; he was active in public affairs, a man of learning, and founder of several religious houses. He compiled a book of pastoral instructions for the use of his clergy. d. 866. *Radulphus. June 24, ii, 610.*

RALPH ASHLEY, BD, MARTYR

A Jesuit lay-brother h.d.q. at Worcester in 1606 for being found in attendance on Bd Edward Oldcorne. bd 1929.
April 7, ii, 51.

RALPH CORBY, BD, MARTYR

Vere Corbington. He was a Jesuit who ministered in the county of Durham; he was condemned for his priesthood and h.d.q. at Tyburn in 1644. bd 1929.
September 7, iii, 505.

RALPH CROCKETT, BD, MARTYR

A schoolmaster in East Anglia who became a priest at Rheims, and was h.d.q. for his priesthood at Chichester, 1588. bd 1929.
October 1, iv, 8.

RALPH GRIMSTON, BD, MARTYR

A gentleman b. at Nidd, Knaresborough, Yorkshire. He was arrested for felony, *i.e.* for defending Bd Peter Snow when arrested with him. He d. at York in 1598. bd November 22, 1987. *June 15.*

RALPH MILNER, BD, MARTYR

An old illiterate husbandman in Hampshire, who was hanged at Winchester in 1591 for helping a priest, Bd Roger Dickenson. Milner was a convert, and was jailed for it on the day of his first communion. bd 1929.
July 7, iii, 36.

RALPH SHERWIN, ST, MARTYR

After being ordained at Douay and studying at the English College in Rome Sherwin came on the English mission in 1580. Within a few months he was arrested and tortured, and in 1581 was h.d.q. at Tyburn for complicity in a fictitious plot. bd 1886. St Ralph was the protomartyr of the "Venerabile" and his feast is kept in the diocese of Nottingham, within whose borders he was born. cd 1970. *December 1, iv, 464.*

RAMBERT, ST, MARTYR

He was one of the many victims of Ebroin, mayor of the palace to Thierry III of Austrasia; Ebroin had him ambushed and killed in the Jura mountains *c.* 680. But this appears insufficient reason for venerating him as a martyr. *Ragnebertus. June 13.*

RAOUL. *See* Ralph of Bourges.

*RAPHAEL THE ARCHANGEL, ST

He is called the "Healer of God" (see the book of *Tobias*) and is identified with the angel of the healing sheep-pool (John v, 1–4). His feast was extended to the whole Western Church in 1922. *Raphaël. September 29, iv, 187.*

RAPHAEL KALINOWSKI, ST

Rafal Jozef Kalinowski, b. Vilnius (then Russian Poland), 1835, into an aristocratic family, became an officer and was sentenced to ten years of forced labour for his part in the 1865 anti-Tsarist rising. In 1877 he became a discalced Carmelite. He was a notable educator and spiritual director; he was also prior of Wadowice monastery (John Paul II was born at Wadowice). He combined the secular virtue of Polish patriotism with spiritual eminence. d. November 15, 1907. Bd by John Paul II during his Cracow visit of June 23, 1983. Cd November 17, 1991 by John Paul II.
November 15.

RAPHAELA MARY, ST, VIRGIN

Raphaela Porras was b. near Cordova in 1850. In 1877, in rather curious circumstances, she started a congregation, the

Handmaids of the Sacred Heart, for educational and retreat work. For the last thirty-two years of her life she lived in Rome, with great patience and humbleness, as a simple sister of the congregation she had founded. d. 1925. bd 1952. cd 1977. *January 6, i, 44.*

RAPHAELA DE VILLALONGO, BD,
WIDOW

Rafaela Ybarra, b. 1843, was the Spanish Basque foundress of the Institute of the Guardian Angels and noted for her social conscience and activity. d. 1900. bd September 30, 1984. *February 23.*

RATHO, BD

Ratho gives his name to the healing shrine of Grafrath in Bavaria. He was count of Andechs and, after fighting in several campaigns, founded a Benedictine abbey at Wörth where he himself became a monk. d. 953. *May 17, ii, 339.*

RAYMUND LULL, BD, MARTYR

Born in 1232 on Majorca. When he was about thirty he was converted from his irregular life and determined to devote himself to the conversion of the Moors. He provided for his family, and after years of preliminary study crossed to Africa, where he was ill-treated, imprisoned and deported; this happened again some years later. In spite of receiving no encouragement from the Holy See or anywhere else, he made a third attempt, and d. in 1316 through being stoned in Algeria. Raymund (Ramón) realized that it was hopeless to try to convert Mohammedans knowing nothing of their religion and culture, and he spent many years travelling to the chief European centres of learning to encourage such studies and in a huge literary activity in Latin, Catalan and Arabic; he was responsible for the foundation of the first "missionary college". *Raymundus.*
September 5, iii, 494.

*RAYMUND NONNATUS, ST

He succeeded St Peter Nolasco as ransomer of the Mercedarians, and his career shares the obscurity of the early days of that order.

He is said at one time to have been a voluntary prisoner among the Moors to ransom other captives, and to have been made a cardinal just before his death in 1240. c.c. 1657. *August 31, iii, 449.*

RAYMUND OF CAPUA, BD

Bd Raymund is famous as the spiritual guide and right-hand man of St Catherine of Siena, to the leadership of whose "family" he succeeded after her death. He was elected master general of the Dominicans, and his reforms within the order earned him the title of its second founder. d. 1399. bd 1899. *October 5, iv, 39.*

RAYMUND OF FITERO, BD, ABBOT

When in 1157 the Moors threatened an attack on Calatrava, Abbot Raymund got King Sancho of Castile to give the town to the Cistercian abbey of Fitero if he could hold it against the Mohammedans. From among his recruits Raymund formed a military order for its defence, known as the Military Order of the Knights of Calatrava. d. 1163. c.c. 1719. *February 6, i, 265.*

*RAYMUND OF PEÑAFORT, ST

From being a dignitary of the church of Barcelona he became a Dominican in 1222, and preached among the Jews and Moors. He was summoned to Rome by Pope Gregory IX, for the study of canon law: his five books of decretals were the best-arranged part of it until its codification in our own day. In 1238 he was elected master general of his order, and encouraged St Thomas Aquinas to write the *Contra Gentiles.* He was taken by King James of Aragon to the island of Majorca, where he undertook the reformation of his sovereign's morals; failing in this, he returned to Barcelona in striking fashion—sailing on his cloak. St Raymund's part in the foundation of the Mercedarian Order is a matter of dispute. He d. at the age of a hundred in 1275. cd 1601. *January 7, i, 149.*

RAYMUND OF TOULOUSE, ST

He was a singer in the church of St Sernin at Toulouse, noted for his benefactions, especially towards the Jews. After the death

of his wife he received a canonry at St Sernin and restored the common life to the chapter. d. 1118. c.c. 1652.
July 8, iii, 43.

REDEMPTA. *See under* Romula.

REDEMPTUS. *See under* Dionysius.

REGINA. *See* Reine.

REGINALD OF ORLEANS, BD
Born in 1183 in Languedoc. He met St Dominic at Rome in 1218, when he immediately joined his new order of friars. Reginald organized the priory in connection with the University of Bologna, but his career was early cut short as he d. in 1220. c.c. 1875. *Reginaldus.*
February 17, i, 359.

*REGULUS OF SENLIS, ST, BISHOP
In French *Rieul*. He is venerated as the first bishop of Senlis, legendarily in the first century, probably in the third.
March 30, iv, 702.

*REINE, ST, VIRGIN AND MARTYR
Reine (Regina) was venerated as a maiden martyr at Alise, near Autun, at an early date, but nothing is known of her history.
September 7, iii, 500.

*REINELDIS, ST,
VIRGIN AND MARTYR
A daughter of St Amelberga, said to have been murdered by raiders at Saintes, near Hal, in Brabant, *c.* 680. *July 16, iii, 118.*

REINOLD, ST, MARTYR
According to tradition he was a monk of St Pantaleon's at Cologne. Being in charge of some building operations there he incurred the hostility of the masons by trying to make them work harder; so they killed him with their hammers and flung his body into the Rhine—but this hardly constitutes martyrdom. It is not even clear in what century he lived (tenth?). *January 7, i, 48.*

REMACLUS, ST, BISHOP
He was abbot of two monasteries in Austrasia before he was called on by King St Sigebert III to direct the establishment of the abbey of Stavelot-Malmedy. He was perhaps a missionary bishop. d. *c.* 675.
September 3, iii, 480.

*REMBERT, ST, BISHOP
A disciple of St Anskar and his successor as archbishop of Hamburg and Bremen. He preached among the Slavs, sold sacred vessels to ransom prisoners among the Northmen, and wrote a biography of St Anskar. d. 888. *Rembertus.*
February 4, i, 251.

*REMIGIUS, ST, BISHOP
In French *Remi*. Remigius, a great apostle of the Franks, was illustrious for his learning, eloquence and miracles during an episcopate of seventy years in the see of Rheims, but his biographical sources are rather unsatisfactory. The great event of his life was the baptism at Rheims of the Frankish king Clovis in 496. d. *c.* 530.
October 1, iv, 1.

*RENÉ GOUPIL, ST, MARTYR
One of the most remarkable among the Martyrs of North America (*q.v.*). His health had caused him to fail in his efforts to be a Jesuit, so he became a surgeon and went to America as a lay assistant to the missionaries. He was assistant to St Isaac Jogues and was the first of the group of martyrs to suffer, being tomahawked on September 29, 1642, for having traced the sign of the cross on the brow of some children. *Renatus.*
September 26, iii, 649.

*REPARATA, ST,
VIRGIN AND MARTYR
She was perhaps put to death at Caesarea in Palestine *c.* 250, but the extant account of her passion is spurious.
October 8, iv, 62.

*RESTITUTA, ST, VIRGIN AND MARTYR

An African girl who d. for Christ during the persecution of Valerian or Diocletian, at Carthage or elsewhere. Her relics are said to be at Naples. *May 27.*

*RESTITUTA OF SORA, ST, VIRGIN AND MARTYR

Nothing is known of the passion of this Roman maiden at Sora in *c.* 271 (?). *May 27, ii, 404.*

*RHIPSIME, ST, VIRGIN AND MARTYR

SS Rhipsime, Gaiana, and their maiden companions have been from early times venerated as the protomartyrs of the Armenian church, *c.* 312 (?), but nothing at all is now known of their history or the circumstances of their passion. They are referred to in the legend of St Gregory the Enlightener. *Ripsimis. September 29, iii, 680.*

*RICHARD, ST, "KING"

He was father of SS Willibald, Winebald and Walburga, and d. at Lucca while on a pilgrimage to Rome with his sons, in 720. His name is not known and he was not a king, but he is revered as "King Richard" at Lucca. *Richardus, Reccaredus. February 7, i, 270.*

RICHARD BERE. *See* Carthusian Martyrs.

RICHARD FETHERSTON, BD, MARTYR

He was archdeacon of Brecon and Latin tutor to the Princess Mary, daughter of Henry VIII. After speaking in convocation in favour of the validity of Queen Catherine's marriage he was imprisoned for six years, attainted for high treason, and h.d.q. at Smithfield, in 1540. bd 1886. His feast is kept in Wales with Bd Edward Powell. *July 30, iii, 218.*

RICHARD FLOWER, BD, MARTYR

A gentleman b. at Anglesey, North Wales. Together with Fr Richard Leigh and four other laypeople, he d. at Tyburn in 1588 for entertaining and relieving missionary priests. bd November 22, 1987. *August 30.*

RICHARD GWYN, ST, MARTYR

He was b. at Llanidloes in 1537, went to St John's College, Cambridge, repudiated Protestantism, married, and became a schoolmaster. He was imprisoned as a recusant and during four years in jail wrote many religious poems in Welsh that are still extant. St Richard was h.d.q. at Wrexham in 1584, the protomartyr of Wales among the penal-times martyrs. bd 1929. cd 1970. *October 25, iv, 202.*

RICHARD HERST, BD, MARTYR

Richard Herst was a farmer near Preston who was hanged at Lancaster in 1628, ostensibly for murder; his real offence was being a Catholic recusant. bd 1929. *August 29, iii, 443.*

RICHARD HILL, BD, MARTYR

A secular priest b. in Yorkshire. He studied at the English College at Rheims, was ordained priest in September 1589 and sent on the English mission. Arrested on his way through the North of England, he was sentenced for high treason as an unlawful priest. He d. at Durham in May 1590. bd November 22, 1987. *May 27.*

RICHARD HOLIDAY, BD, MARTYR

A secular priest b. in Yorkshire, he studied at the English College at Rheims, was ordained priest at Laon in 1589 and went on the English mission. He was arrested on his way through the North of England, sentenced for high treason as an unlawful priest, and d. at Durham in May 1590. bd November 22, 1987. *May 27.*

RICHARD KIRKMAN, BD, MARTYR

A secular priest, tutor in the household of Dymoke of Scrivelsby, who was h.d.q. at York in 1582 for denying the Queen's supremacy in spiritual matters. bd 1886. *August 22, iii, 383.*

RICHARD LANGHORNE, BD,
MARTYR

A barrister of the Inner Temple, h.d.q. at Tyburn in 1679 for the Oates "plot". bd 1929. *July 14, ii, 599.*

RICHARD LANGLEY, BD, MARTYR

A Yorkshire gentleman who was hanged at York in 1586 for sheltering priests in his houses. bd 1929. *December 1, iv, 470.*

RICHARD LEIGH, BD, MARTYR

A Londoner, hanged for his priesthood at Tyburn in 1588. He betrayed himself by offering to answer questions put to a Catholic under examination. bd 1929. *August 30, iii, 437.*

RICHARD MARTIN, BD, MARTYR

A gentleman of Shropshire, hanged at Tyburn in 1588 for "relieving" a priest—he had paid sixpence for Bd Robert Morton's supper. bd 1929.
August 30, iii, 437.

RICHARD NEWPORT, BD, MARTYR

A secular priest from Northamptonshire, h.d.q. for his priesthood at Tyburn in 1612. bd 1929. *May 30, ii, 431.*

RICHARD PAMPURI, ST

Riccardo Pampuri, b. 1897, a lay brother of St John of God who cared for the wounded at the front in WWI. d. 1930. cd November 1, 1989. *May 1.*

RICHARD REYNOLDS, ST, MARTYR

Bridgettine monk of Syon Abbey, Middlesex, who was h.d.q. at Tyburn for denying the royal supremacy, one of the first group of English martyrs, on May 4, 1535. bd 1886. His feast is kept in the archdiocese of Westminster and by the Bridgettine nuns. bd 1886. cd 1970. *May 11, ii, 277.*

RICHARD ROLLE, BD

Richard Rolle had a considerable popular *cultus* in the past, not yet confirmed by ecclesiastical authority though preparations for his canonization were begun soon after his death. He was b. at Thornton in Yorkshire *c.* 1300 and spent most of his life as a hermit, at Hampole and elsewhere in that county. More interest has been taken in Rolle than in any other English uncanonized saint, on account of the unique position which he holds among English mystical writers. His best-known work is the *Fire of Love*, and he seems as a man to have been as personally attractive as his writings. d. 1349. *September 29, iii, 682.*

RICHARD SERGEANT, BD, MARTYR

Richard Sergeant (alias Lee or Long) was a secular priest b. in Gloucestershire. He studied at Rheims and was ordained priest at Lyons. He was h.d.q. as a seminary priest at Tyburn in 1586. bd November 22, 1987. *April 20.*

RICHARD SIMPSON, BD, MARTYR

Richard Simpson (or Sympson) was a secular priest b. at Well, Ripon, Yorkshire. He was a Protestant minister, became a Catholic, was imprisoned at York, studied at Douai from 1577, was ordained priest and sent on the English mission. He was arrested, banished, returned and was caught passing from Lancashire to Derbyshire. He was reprieved at the Lent assizes of 1588, almost conformed, repented and was h.d.q. for high treason with Bd Nicholas Garlick and Bd Robert Ludlam at Derby in 1588 when *c.* thirty-five years of age. bd November 22, 1987. *July 24.*

RICHARD THIRKELD, BD, MARTYR

Born in County Durham and ordained abroad in 1579 when he was already an old man. h.d.q. at York in 1583, for "reconciling". bd 1886. *May 29, ii, 422.*

RICHARD WHITING, BD,
ABBOT AND MARTYR

The last abbot of Glastonbury came to that office in 1525. At the dissolution he refused to surrender his monastery to the Crown and he was sentenced to death for high treason, his offence apparently being that he recanted the oath recognizing the King's supremacy over the Church in England. Abbot Richard was h.d.q. at Glastonbury in 1539. With him suffered BB John Thorne and

Roger James, monks of the same abbey. bd 1895. The feast of these martyrs is kept in the dioceses of Westminster and Clifton, and by the English Benedictines.
December 1, iv, 461.

RICHARD YAXLEY, BD, MARTYR

A secular priest b. Boston, Lincolnshire, who studied and was ordained priest at Rheims, was sent on the English mission in 1586, and was arrested with Bd George Nicols in Oxford. He was interrogated there and in London and h.d.q. at Oxford in 1589 when aged twenty-nine years. bd November 22, 1987. *July 5.*

*RICHARD OF ANDRIA, ST, BISHOP

It seems to be agreed that this St Richard was an Englishman and bishop of Andria in Italy, but his reputed "life" is spurious. This states that he lived in the middle of the fifth century, but the twelfth is much more likely. *June 9, ii, 511.*

*RICHARD OF CHICHESTER, ST,
BISHOP

Richard of Wyche (*i.e.* Droitwich), after coping with a decayed family estate, went to Oxford, Paris and Bologna to study. He became chancellor of Oxford University and diocesan chancellor to St Edmund of Canterbury, after whose exile Richard was ordained and became parish priest of Deal. In 1244 he was appointed bishop of Chichester by Bd Boniface of Canterbury ("of Savoy") in opposition to King Henry III's unworthy candidate. He was prevented by force from taking possession of his see and had to administer it from a country rectory for two years. St Richard was a stern reformer of his clergy, a great almsgiver and simple in his own habits. d. 1253. cd 1262. St Richard's feast is observed in the dioceses of Southwark, Westminster and Birmingham. *April 3, ii, 22.*

RICHARDIS, ST

Richardis was the wife of the emperor Charles the Fat. She was falsely accused of unfaithfulness to her husband and is said to have cleared herself by ordeal by fire. But the two separated, and Richardis retired to a convent, where she d. *c.* 895. Her *cultus* was approved by Pope St Leo IX in 1049. *September 18, iii, 592.*

*RICHARIUS, ST, ABBOT

In French *Riquier*. He was converted by two Irish priests and himself studied in England. Richarius was a very successful preacher and induced King Dagobert to found a monastery for him at Celles. He ended his life as a hermit, *c.* 645. *April 26, ii, 164.*

RICHARIUS. *See also* Rizzerio.

RICHIMIR, ST, ABBOT

He founded a monastery at Saint-Rigomer-des-Bois on the river Loire and was its abbot until his death in *c.* 715. His memory has practically died out. *January 17, i, 112.*

RICTRUDIS, ST

Rictrudis was the wife of the Frankish St Adalbald, to whom she bore four children, all of them venerated as saints. After the murder of her husband, King Clovis II tried to force her to marry again, but with the assistance of St Amand she was enabled to become a nun and d. abbess of Marchiennes in 688. *May 12, ii, 288.*

RIEUL. *See* Regulus of Senlis.

*RIGOBERT, ST, BISHOP

Little is known of this archbishop of Rheims except that he was banished from his see for a time by Charles Martel. d. *c.* 745. *Rigobertus. January 4, i, 32.*

RIQUIER. *See* Richarius.

*RITA OF CASCIA, ST

The current account of St Rita is based on a biography written nearly 150 years after her death. She was b. into a peasant home in 1381 and married a brutal and dissolute husband; after his violent death she was admitted to the convent of the Augustinian nuns at Cascia. She was a most mortified religious, and sometimes rapt in ecstasy by contemplation of the passion of our Lord. d. 1457. cd 1900. *May 22, ii, 369.*

RIZZERIO, BD

Rizzerio was one of the two young men who offered themselves to St Francis of Assisi after his famous sermon at Bologna (he is referred to in the *Fioretti* as "Rinieri"). He was one of the most loved followers of Francis and became minister provincial of the friars in the Marches. d. 1236. c.c. 1836. *Richarius. February 7, i, 272.*

ROBERT ANDERTON, BD, MARTYR

A secular priest, b. at Chorley, who was h.d.q. for his priesthood in the Isle of Wight in 1586. bd 1929. *Robertus. April 25, ii, 163.*

*ROBERT BELLARMINE, ST,
BISHOP AND DOCTOR

Born in 1542 at Montepulciano and entered the Society of Jesus in 1560. He had a career of the greatest distinction, teaching theology at Louvain, teaching and preaching in Rome, working on the Vulgate Bible, rector of the Roman College: in 1598 he was made a cardinal, "as he had no equal for learning". For three years he occupied the archbishopric of Capua and gave up all other activities to look after his flock; he then became head of the Vatican Library and took a prominent part in all the affairs of the Holy See. Among other controversialists, he answered the Magdeburg "centuriators", King James I of England and the Scottish jurist Barclay. St Robert was one of the greatest polemical theologians and the foremost teacher against the doctrines of the Protestant reformers; his best-known writings are the four volumes of *Disputations*, his catechism of Christian doctrine, and the devotional works of his later years. d. 1621. cd 1930. Declared Doctor of the Church 1931. *September 17, ii, 292.*

ROBERT BICKERDIKE, BD, MARTYR

A gentleman b. at Low Hall or near Knaresborough, Yorkshire. He was arrested for being reconciled and for treasonable opinions, found not guilty, but retried and h.d.q. at York in 1586. bd November 22, 1987. *October 8.*

ROBERT DALBY, BD, MARTYR

Dalby was a convert minister who went to the Rheims college and was ordained priest. He was h.d.q. for his priesthood with Bd John Amias at York in 1589. bd 1929. *March 16, i, 612.*

ROBERT DIBDALE, BD, MARTYR

Robert (or Richard) Dibdale was a secular priest b. at Shottery, Worcestershire. He studied and was ordained at Rheims and arrived in England in 1584. He was said to have been a noted exorcist. He was h.d.q. at Tyburn in 1586 aged twenty-eight years. bd November 22, 1987. *October 8.*

ROBERT DRURY, BD, MARTYR

A secular priest b. Buckinghamshire. He studied at Rheims and Valladolid, was ordained priest and sent on the English mission in 1593. He worked mainly in London. He refused to take an anti-papal oath and d. at Tyburn in 1607 when aged *c.* thirty-nine years. bd November 22, 1987. *February 26.*

ROBERT GRISSOLD, BD, MARTYR

Robert Grissold (Greswold) was a devout farm labourer b. at Rom(w)ington, Warwickshire. He was arrested and imprisoned for a year with Bd John Sugar. He was sentenced for refusing to go to church and for assisting a seminary priest. He was hanged at Warwick in 1604. bd November 22, 1987. *July 16.*

ROBERT HARDESTY, BD, MARTYR

Layman b. in Yorkshire. He was arrested with Bd William Spenser and accused of harbouring and assisting a priest. He was hanged at York 1589. bd November 22, 1987. *September 24.*

ROBERT JOHNSON, BD, MARTYR

A priest of Douay, h.d.q. at Tyburn in 1582. bd 1929. *May 28, ii, 415.*

ROBERT LAURENCE, ST, MARTYR

One of the first three Carthusian martyrs (*q.v.*), h.d.q. at Tyburn on May 4, 1535. He

was prior of the charterhouse at Beauvale in Nottinghamshire. cd 1970.
May 11, ii, 277.

ROBERT LUDLAM, BD, MARTYR

A secular priest b. at Radbourne near Sheffield. He studied and was ordained priest at Rheims and went on the English mission in 1582. He was arrested and tried as a priest and hanged at Derby in 1588 aged *c.* thirty-seven years. bd November 22, 1987. *July 24.*

ROBERT MIDDLETON, BD, MARTYR

A Jesuit and a secular priest of the College of Seville, Spain, b. at York. He was arrested with Bd Thurstan Hunt and d. as an unlawful priest at Lancaster in 1601 when thirty-one years of age. bd November 22, 1987. *February 12.*

ROBERT MORTON, BD, MARTYR

A seminary priest from Yorkshire, hanged for his priesthood in Lincoln's Inn Fields, 1588. bd 1929. *August 28, iii, 437.*

ROBERT NUTTER, BD, MARTYR

Robert Nutter, OP, was b. at Burnley, Lancashire, studied and was ordained priest on December 21, 1581 at Rheims, and went on the English mission in 1582. He was imprisoned in the Tower in 1583–4, banished in 1585, returned and d. at Lancaster in 1600. bd November 22, 1987. *July 26.*

ROBERT SALT. *See* Carthusian Martyrs.

ROBERT SOUTHWELL, ST, MARTYR

He was b. at Horsham St Faith in Norfolk in 1561 and became a Jesuit at Rome at the age of seventeen; he came on the English mission in 1586. Southwell was a poet and prose-writer (best known for "The Burning Babe" and *Triumphs over Death* respectively), who shares the literary laurels of the English Jesuit province with Gerard Manley Hopkins. He was betrayed in 1592 and imprisoned for three years before he was brought to trial, being tortured many times. h.d.q. for his priesthood at Tyburn in 1595. bd 1929. cd 1970. *February 21, i, 386.*

ROBERT SUTTON, BD, MARTYR

A schoolmaster who, having been brought up a Protestant, was reconciled with the Church. For this he was hanged at Clerkenwell in 1588. bd 1929.
October 5, iii, 438.

ROBERT SUTTON, BD, MARTYR

He was b. at Burton-on-Trent, educated at Oxford and went to Douai where he was ordained priest and went on the English mission 1577–8. He worked chiefly in Staffordshire and was banished in 1585. On returning he was arrested, sentenced for high treason as a seminary priest and executed at Stafford in March or July 1588 aged *c.* forty-three years. bd November 22, 1987. *July 27.*

ROBERT THORPE, BD, MARTYR

Robert Thorp(e) was a secular priest b. in Yorkshire who studied at Rheims. He was sent on the English mission on May 9, 1585 and worked in Yorkshire where he was noted for his devotion and constancy. He was betrayed and arrested on Palm Sunday and d. at York in 1591. bd November 22, 1987. *May 31.*

ROBERT WATKINSON, BD, MARTYR

A secular priest of Hemingborough in Yorkshire, h.d.q. for his priesthood at Tyburn in 1602. bd 1929.
April 20, ii, 137.

ROBERT WIDMERPOOL, BD, MARTYR

A layman hanged at Canterbury in 1588 for getting a priest shelter in the Countess of Northumberland's house. bd 1929.
October 1, iv, 7.

ROBERT WILCOX, BD, MARTYR

A seminary priest who was arrested while ministering in Kent, and h.d.q. for his priesthood at Canterbury in 1588. bd 1929.
October 1, iv, 7.

ROBERT OF ARBRISSEL, BD, ABBOT

In 1099 he established adjoining communities of men and women in the valley of

Fontevrault under the Rule of St Benedict; their life was extremely austere, and the abbess was the supreme superior. After a stormy and difficult career he d. in 1117. Robert is usually called Blessed, but the title is a courtesy one. *February 25, i, 418.*

*ROBERT OF CHAISE-DIEU, ST,
ABBOT

Robert de Turlande was founder and first abbot of Chaise-Dieu in the Auvergne, which at his death in 1067 had over 300 monks. *April 17, ii, 113.*

ROBERT OF KNARESBOROUGH, BD

Robert Flower was b. at York *c.* 1160. After being a postulant at Newminster he became a hermit, eventually making his home in a cave by the river Nidd, near Knaresborough; here he earned a great reputation for holiness, and after his death in 1218 (or 1235?) was the object of a considerable *cultus,* which was never officially confirmed. This Robert has been sometimes confused with St Robert, Abbot of Newminster, who d. many years before him.
September 24, iii, 630.

*ROBERT OF MOLESMES, ST,
ABBOT

While abbot of Molesmes he received permission, with two of his monks, St Stephen Harding and St Alberic, to leave the monastery and retire to the forest of Cîteaux; here in 1098 the foundations of the Cistercian congregation were laid. Only a year later St Robert had, under obedience, to return to Molesmes, and he ruled that abbey successfully till his death in 1110. cd 1222. *April 29, ii, 189.*

*ROBERT OF NEWMINSTER, ST,
ABBOT

Born at Gargrave in Yorkshire, where he was rector before joining the Benedictines at Whitby. He took part in the founding of Fountains abbey, which became Cistercian, and from thence was appointed first abbot of Newminster in Northumberland. It was said of St Robert that he was "modest in

his bearing, gentle in companionship, merciful in judgement", and he ruled his abbey successfully for many years, founding three daughter houses. d. 1159. His feast is observed by the Cistercians and in the diocese of Hexham. *June 7, ii, 496.*

*ROCK, ST

All that is known with certainty of the life of this much-venerated saint is that he was b. at Montpellier and nursed the sick during a plague in Italy in the fourteenth century. He is invoked against pestilence and skin diseases. *Rochus. August 17, iii, 338.*

*RODERIC AND SOLOMON, SS,
MARTYRS

Roderic, a priest of Cabra in Spain, was betrayed by his Muslim brother and put to death for the faith, together with one Solomon, at Cordova in 857. *Rudericus, Salomon. March 13, i, 588.*

ROGATIAN. *See under* Donatian.

ROGER CADWALLADOR, BD,
MARTYR

Known on the English mission as Rogers, he was a secular priest b. at Stretton Sugwas, Herefordshire. He studied at Rheims, was ordained at Valladolid, and returned to England *c.* 1594. He worked zealously among the poor for sixteen years, was arrested on Easter Day 1610 and h.d.q. at Leominster in that year when *c.* forty-four years of age. bd November 22, 1987. *August 27.*

ROGER DICKENSON, BD, MARTYR

A seminary priest from London, h.d.q. for his priesthood at Winchester in 1591. bd 1929. *Rogerus. July 7, iii, 36.*

ROGER FILCOCK, BD, MARTYR

A Jesuit and a secular priest, he was b. Sandwich, Kent, and studied at the English Colleges at Rheims and Valladolid, where he was ordained priest. He was sent on the English mission in 1598, laboured for two years, and was admitted to the Society by Fr Garnet. He was to become a novice in Flanders but was imprisoned at Newgate and h.d.q. for high treason at Tyburn in 1600 at the age of *c.* thirty years. bd November 22, 1987. *February 27.*

ROGER LE FORT, BD, BISHOP

Roger's election to the see of Orleans is said to have been made in error, but he was an excellent bishop and was translated first to Limoges and then to the metropolitan see of Bourges. He established the feast of our Lady's conception in his dioceses and by will left all his property for the education of poor boys. d. 1367. *March 1, i, 455.*

ROGER JAMES, BD, MARTYR

A monk of Glastonbury who was h.d.q. at the same time as BB Richard Whiting and John Thorne. bd 1895. *December 1, iv, 462.*

ROGER WRENNO, BD, MARTYR

Roger Wrenno (or Worren) was a devout weaver b. at Chorley, Lancashire. He was imprisoned with other Catholics in Lancaster Castle but escaped with Bd John Thulis before the Lent Assizes of 1616. He was recaptured, refused the oath of allegiance in exchange for his life, and was hanged at Lancaster in 1616 when forty years of age. bd November 22, 1987. *March 18.*

ROGER OF ELLANT, BD

An Englishman who became a Cistercian monk at Lorroy in France and from thence founded the new monastery of Ellant in the diocese of Rheims. d. 1160. *January 4, i, 32.*

ROGER OF TODI, BD

In Italian *Ruggiero.* He was a personal follower of St Francis of Assisi, who appointed him spiritual director of the Poor Clare convent at Rieti. d. 1237. c.c. by Pope Benedict XIV. *January 14, i, 88.*

ROMAEUS, BD

He was a Carmelite lay-brother and the companion of St Avertanus; he caught the plague while nursing him, and d. a week later, 1380. c.c. by Pope Gregory XVI. *March 4, i, 419.*

*ROMANUS, ST, MARTYR

He was a doorkeeper of the Roman church who was martyred, it is said, the day before St Laurence in 258. *August 9, iii, 292.*

*ROMANUS, ST

A monk who encouraged and helped St Benedict when he first fled from Rome to Subiaco. d. *c.* 550. *May 22, ii, 366.*

*ROMANUS AND BARULA, SS, MARTYRS

St Romanus was a Palestinian deacon martyred at Antioch in 304. Nothing certain is known of his companion Barula, "a young boy", but he seems to be identical with a Syrian martyr named Barlaam. *November 18, iv, 383.*

*ROMANUS OF CONDAT, ST, ABBOT

Romanus retired from his monastery to a solitude in the Jura mountains, where he was joined by his brother Lupicinus. Together they founded the monasteries of Condat and Leuconne for men and La Beaume (St Romain-de-la-Roche) for women. These religious strove to imitate the monks of the Eastern deserts, but the climate obliged them somewhat to mitigate their austerities. d. *c.* 460. *February 28, i, 438.*

*ROMANUS OF ROUEN, ST, BISHOP

He was bishop of Rouen for ten years and d. *c.* 640. The chapter of Rouen formerly had the privilege of releasing a prisoner condemned to death every year on the feast of the Ascension in honour of this saint. *October 23, iv, 183.*

ROMANUS THE MELODIST, ST

Romanus, a Syrian, was one of the clergy of the church of Constantinople, probably during the sixth century, and the greatest of the Greek hymn writers: his compositions are still sung in the Byzantine rite. *October 1, iv, 3.*

ROMANUS. *See also under* Boris and Gleb.

*ROMARIC, ST, ABBOT

He was a monk of Luxeuil, formerly a Merovingian nobleman, who with St Amatus founded the abbey of Remiremont (*Romarici mons*) in the Vosges. Romaric succeeded Amatus as its abbot. d. 653. *December 8, iv, 521.*

ROMBAUT. *See* Rumold.

*ROMUALD, ST, ABBOT

Born *c.* 950 of the Onesti, dukes of Ravenna. To expiate his part in a duel in which his father had killed his opponent, he became a monk and then a hermit. For thirty years he wandered about reforming monasteries and establishing hermitages in northern Italy, the best-known and most lasting of his foundations being that of the Camaldolese hermit monks. This took place at Camaldoli, near Arezzo, *c.* 1012, and the order still exists as an independent branch of the Benedictines. There seems to have been a tendency to both restlessness and harshness in Romuald's character, but he attracted many during his life. d. 1027. cd 1595. *Romualdus. June 19, i, 266.*

*ROMULA, ST, VIRGIN

Romula in her old age lived with SS Redempta and Herundo near the church of St Mary Major in Rome; they were all three much respected by St Gregory the Great. Sixth century. *July 23, iii, 170.*

*ROMULUS, ST, BISHOP AND MARTYR

According to a late tradition the first bishop of Fiesole was Romulus, a convert of St Peter and martyr under Domitian. Nothing is known of him historically, but there is evidence of an early *cultus* of a St Romulus at Fiesole. *July 6, iii, 22.*

RONAN. *See* Rumon.

ROQUE GONZALEZ, ST, MARTYR

He was a missionary slain by Indians at Caaro in 1628, with SS Alphonsus Rodriguez and John de Castillo. bd 1934. cd 1988. These three Jesuits in Paraguay were the earliest martyrs of the Americas to be beatified. *Rochus. November 17, iv, 376.*

*ROSALIA, ST, VIRGIN

According to local tradition Rosalia was a girl of good family who passed her life as a recluse in a cave in Sicily. d. 1160 (?). Her alleged relics were found in 1624 and she was acclaimed as the patron saint of Palermo, the cessation of a plague being attributed to her intercession. *September 4, iii, 486.*

ROSE VENERINI, BD, VIRGIN

A physician's daughter, b. at Viterbo in 1656. She spent her life in the cause of education, and was a friend and encourager of St Lucy Filippini. She organized schools in many parts of Italy, and recruited and trained teachers who, after Rose's death, were formed into a religious congregation. d. at Rome, 1728. bd. 1952. *Rosa. May 7, ii, 248.*

*ROSE OF LIMA, ST, VIRGIN

She was of Spanish birth, at Lima in Peru in 1586. She led a life of penitential mortification in the midst of her family and at first to their annoyance, but eventually it was her work that helped to support her parents. She joined the third order of St Dominic and for fourteen years lived practically as an ankress, suffering much from spiritual desolation and encouraged with corresponding light. d. 1617. cd 1671. St Rose was the first canonized saint of the New World. *August 23, iii, 444.*

*ROSE OF VITERBO, ST, VIRGIN

Reliable accounts of the life of this saint are wanting. She was a Franciscan tertiary of humble birth and preached in the streets of Viterbo against the emperor Frederick II and the Ghibelline garrison. Marvels were attributed to her and she was much revered by the people, but a local convent refused to admit her into its community. d. *c.* 1252 (?). cd 1457. *September 4, iii, 487.*

ROSELINE, BD, VIRGIN

Roseline de Villeneuve was a Carthusian nun who became prioress at Celle-Roubaud in Provence. She had frequent visions, and the gift of reading hearts. d. 1329. c.c. 1851. *January 17, i, 112.*

ROSENDO. *See* Rudesind.

RUADAN, ST, ABBOT
He was one of the chief disciples of St Finnian of Clonard and founded the monastery of Lothra. d. *c.* 584.
April 15, ii, 99.

RUAN. *See* Rumon.

RUDESIND, ST, BISHOP
He belonged to a noble family of Spanish Galicia, where he is known as "San Rosendo". He gave up the episcopal see of Dumium (Mondoñedo) to enter the monastery of Cella Nueva of which he became abbot, and carried out extensive monastic reforms. His biography consists principally of miracles attributed to his intercession. d. 977. cd 1195. *Rudesindus.*
March 1, i, 454.

RUDOLF AQUAVIVA, BD, MARTYR
Rudolf Aquaviva and four other members of the Society of Jesus were slain at the Hindu village of Cuncolim in the district of Salsette, north of Bombay, in 1583; they had gone there to choose the site of a mission church. bd 1893. *Rudolphus.*
July 27, iii, 199.

*RUFINA AND **SECUNDA, SS,**
VIRGINS AND MARTYRS
Except their existence, their martyrdom and their early *cultus* at Santa Rufina on the Aurelian Way, nothing certain is known of these maidens. *July 10, iii, 64.*

RUFINA. *See also under* Justa.

RUFINUS. *See under* Valerius.

*RUFUS AND **ZOSIMUS, SS,**
MARTYRS
They were laymen who shared in the sufferings of St Ignatius of Antioch and were martyred under Trajan *c.* 107.
December 18, iv, 581.

RULE. *See* Regulus.

*RUMOLD, ST, MARTYR
In French *Rombaut.* The story that Rumold was an Irish bishop who was slain by the heathen while a missionary in Brabant *c.* 775 has little historical value; his feast is nevertheless observed in Ireland. He was a martyr in whose honour the cathedral of Malines is dedicated. *July 3, iii, 13.*

RUMON, ST
This Rumon was a sixth-century (?) monk, said to have come from Ireland, whose name (in the form of Ruan, and others) is found in several places in Devon and Cornwall; he may have been a monk of Glastonbury. Some have identified Rumon with the Breton St Ronan.
August 30, iii, 447.

RUMWALD, ST
There was formerly a *cultus* of Rumwald at Brackley and Buckingham; the surprising legend about him was that he d. at King's Sutton in Northamptonshire at the age of three days after having pronounced a profession of faith in a loud voice. This prodigy was dated in the seventh century. *Rumwoldus. November 3, iv, 247.*

*RUPERT, ST, BISHOP
While bishop at Worms he went to preach the gospel in Bavaria, which he did with such fruit that he has been called the apostle of that country. He was the originator of the church in Salzburg. St Rupert seems to have been French, not Irish, but his feast is observed throughout Ireland. d. *c.* 710. *Rupertus. March 29, i, 700.*

RUPERT AND **BERTHA, SS**
Rupert is said to have been a hermit who lived with his mother Bertha on the Rupertsberg, near Bingen, during the ninth century. Their *cultus* was popularized by St Hildegard three hundred years later.
May 15, ii, 322.

RUPERT MAYER, BD
He was b. at Stuttgart in 1876 and ordained priest in 1899. He became a Jesuit in 1900.

As a WWI chaplain he lost a leg in Rumania. He became an effective and courageous preacher, spoke the truth publicly before spies and resolutely opposed Nazism; he was forbidden to preach. The Gestapo arrested him three times after 1937. He was sent to a Gestapo prison, to Sachsenhausen concentration camp, and was confined in Ettal monastery from 1940 to 1945. He accepted his suffering with pride. His health ruined, he d. in 1945. bd May 3, 1987 at Munich. *November 1.*

*RUSTICUS, ST, BISHOP

He was a bishop of Narbonne, d. *c.* 461, of whom there are interesting archaeological survivals. *October 26, iv, 205.*

*RUSTICUS AND **ELEUTHERIUS, SS,** MARTYRS

The priest and deacon who are said to have suffered martyrdom with the bishop St Dionysius at Paris, *c.* 258 (?). *October 9, iv, 67.*

S

*SABAS, ST, ABBOT

St Sabas, one of the greatest of the early monks, was b. in Cappadocia in 439. After being a monk and solitary in various places for years he founded a large *laura* or semi-eremitical monastery in a wild gorge between Jerusalem and the Dead Sea; in 493 he was appointed superior general over all the hermit monks of Palestine; and he played an active part in the public ecclesiastical history of his time in the Near East. d. 532. The monastery he founded still exists, called after him Mar Saba, and is one of the oldest occupied monasteries in the world; its monks belong to the Eastern Orthodox Church. *December 5, iv, 494.*

*SABAS THE GOTH, ST, MARTYR

Sabas was a Christian Goth in what is now Rumania and belonged to the order of readers. In 372 he was seized by Gothic soldiers and, upon his refusing to eat food that had been sacrificed to idols, was tortured and then drowned in the river Mussovo, near Targoviste. *April 12, ii, 78.*

SABAS. *See also* Sava.

*SABINA, ST, MARTYR

She is the titular of the ancient church of St Sabina on the Aventine at Rome, but nothing is certainly known about her. Sabina is named in the canon of the Ambrosian Mass. *August 29, iii, 442.*

*SABINIAN, ST, MARTYR

He is believed to have been a martyr at Troyes in the early centuries. *Sabinianus. January 29, i, 201.*

*SABINUS, ST, BISHOP AND MARTYR

This martyred bishop is claimed by several Italian cities, but except that there was a martyr of this name buried near Spoleto nothing is known of him. *December 30, iv, 641.*

*SABINUS OF CANOSA, ST, BISHOP

Bishop of Canosa in Apulia and a friend of St Benedict. d. *c.* 566. The body of St Sabinus was eventually translated to Bari, where his relics were lost for a time and found in 1901. *February 9, i, 288.*

*SABINUS OF PIACENZA, ST, BISHOP

Bishop of Piacenza and a close friend of St Ambrose. When deacon he was sent on a mission to Antioch by Pope St Damasus. d. 420. *January 17, i, 111.*

SADOC, BD, MARTYR

Sadoc was one of the first Dominicans in Hungary, where he preached the gospel, and then founded a house of his order at Sandomir in Poland. In 1260 the town was ravaged by the Tartars and Sadoc and all his friars were slain while singing *Salve Regina.* c.c. by Pope Pius VII. *June 2, ii, 459.*

*SADOTH, ST, BISHOP AND MARTYR

He became bishop of Seleucia-Ctesiphon, the primatial see of Persia, during the persecution of Sapor II. He cared for his flock from a place of hiding, and then was arrested with 128 others. All were put to death, Sadoth at Bait-Lapat, *c.* 342. *February 20, i, 380.*

SAHAK. *See* Isaac I.

SAIRE. *See* Salvius (hermit).

*SALABERGA, ST

She was the mother of St Bauduin and St Anstrudis, and sister of St Bodo; by agreement with her second husband, she became abbess of the monastery which she had founded at Laon. d. *c.* 665. *September 22, iii, 621.*

SALOME, BD

After the death of her husband, Coloman of Hungary, she joined the Poor Clares and d. in her native Poland in 1268. c.c. by Pope Clement X. *November 17, iv, 374.*

SALOME AND **JUDITH, SS**

These two women are said to have been English recluses of royal blood at the monastery of Ober Altaich in Bavaria during the ninth century. The tradition is a late one, but it has been suggested that Judith may have been Edburga, the rather shocking daughter of Offa of Mercia, who was driven out of England and may have repented in this fashion. *June 29, ii, 673.*

SALVATOR LILLI, AND SEVEN ARMENIAN COMPANIONS, BB, MARTYRS

Fr Salvatore Lilli, b. 1853, was a Franciscan of the Friars Minor in charge of the Armenian parish of Mujuk-Deresi, Turkey. He was an enthusiastic missionary and founded three new villages and created work schemes. He helped people of all faiths, and was especially heroic in a cholera epidemic. He refused to renounce his faith and was murdered together with seven of his parishioners, humble peasants and devout Christians. d. 1895. bd October 3, 1982. *November 19.*

*SALVATOR OF HORTA, ST

A Spanish Franciscan lay-brother of the Observance, who lived at Horta, Barcelona, and other friaries in the sixteenth century. d. 1567. cd 1938. *March 18, i, 630.*

SALVIUS, ST

This Salvius (in French *Saire*) seems to have been a sixth-century hermit at Saint-Saire in Normandy. *October 28, iv, 215.*

*SALVIUS AND **SUPERIUS, SS,** MARTYRS

Their legend states that they were a bishop and his disciple who were murdered near Valenciennes *c.* 768 for the sake of the bishop's valuable girdle. The story is not well attested—but there is a lesson in it. *June 26, ii, 648.*

*SALVIUS OF ALBI, ST, BISHOP

Salvius became bishop of Albi in 574; he showed special devotedness to his flock during an epidemic in the year of his death, 584. *September 10, iii, 532.*

*SALVIUS OF AMIENS, ST, BISHOP

In French *Sauve*. Bishop of Amiens in the seventh century, famous for miracles. d. *c.* 625. A relic of this saint was formerly treasured at Canterbury cathedral. *January 11, i, 70.*

SAMONAS. *See under* Gurias.

SAMOSATA, THE MARTYRS OF

Hipparchus and Philotheus, two magistrates of Samosata, and their converts James, Paragrus, Abibus, Romanus and Lollian were crucified in 297 (or *c.* 308) for refusing to sacrifice to the gods during a public festival. *December 9, iv, 522.*

*SAMSON, ST, BISHOP

St Samson was one of the most important of the British missionary bishops of the sixth century. He was a monk under St Illtyd, and for a time abbot, perhaps of the monastery on Caldey Island. He visited Ireland, and after a sojourn in Cornwall passed over into Brittany, having been consecrated bishop by St Dyfrig. His centre was at Dol, from whence he made missionary journeys in all directions: his name is found in the Scilly and Channel islands and elsewhere. d. *c.* 565. Samson's feast is kept in the diocese of Cardiff and on Caldey Island. *Sampson. July 28, iii, 202.*

*SAMSON THE HOSPITABLE, ST

He founded a great hospital for the sick poor in Constantinople, some time during the fifth century, being himself both physician and priest. *June 27, ii, 652.*

SAMUEL MARZORATI BB AND HIS TWO COMPANIONS, MARTYRS

Fr Samuele Marzorati was born near Varese, Italy, on September 1670. Together with his fellow-Franciscans, Fr Liberatus Weiss (b. Konnersreuth, Bavaria, Germany, on January 4, 1675) and Fr Michael (Michele) Pio Fasoli (b. near Pavia, Italy, on May 3, 1676), he went as a missionary to Ethiopia in 1712, under the protection of Emperor Justos. During an anti-imperial uprising they were imprisoned and sentenced to death for preaching an alien religion. They refused to renounce the Catholic faith and were stoned to death on March 3, 1716. bd November 20, 1988. *March 3.*

SANCHIA OF PORTUGAL, ST,
VIRGIN

Daughter of King Sancho I and sister of SS Teresa and Mafalda. She helped to establish the friars in Portugal, and herself became a Cistercian nun in a convent she had founded. d. 1229. c.c. 1705.
March 17, ii, 570.

*SANCHO, ST, MARTYR

Born at Albi in France and carried away to Cordova by the Moors. He was enrolled in the guards of Abdur Rahman II but he openly rejected Mohammed. He suffered death by impalement in 851. *Sanctius. June 5, ii, 482.*

SANTES OF MONTE FABRI, BD

Santes Brancasino was a Franciscan lay-brother, whose *cultus* was confirmed by Pope Clement XIV. d. 1392.
September 6, iii, 500.

SANTUCCIA, BD

Santuccia Terrebotti was a devout woman of Gubbio who, in agreement with her husband, became a Benedictine nun. She inaugurated a reformed convent at Rome. d. 1305. *March 21, i, 657.*

SAPOR AND ISAAC, SS,
BISHOPS AND MARTYRS

Sapor and Isaac were bishops martyred in Persia in 339, the one dying in prison and the other being stoned to death. There suffered at the same time SS Mahanes, Abraham and Simeon.
November 30, iv, 452.

*SATURNINUS, ST, MARTYR

He was a Roman priest, said to have been from Carthage, martyred in 309 (?) and buried in the cemetery of Thraso on the Salarian Way. *November 29, iv, 445.*

*SATURNINUS AND DATIVUS, SS,
MARTYRS

Saturninus, a priest of Abitina in Africa, his four children, the senator Dativus, and others, were arrested in 304 and sent to Carthage for examination. Several of them were tortured, and the child Hilarion, when threatened by the magistrate, replied, "Go on then, but anyhow I am a Christian". It appears that they all d. in prison.
February 11, i, 303.

*SATURNINUS OF TOULOUSE, ST,
BISHOP AND MARTYR

Saturninus (Sernin) was a missionary, venerated as the first bishop of Toulouse. It is said that, having refused to sacrifice to the gods, he was tied by the feet to a bull which was then chased through the streets till the bishop's brains were dashed out. Third century (?). *November 29, iv, 445.*

*SATYRUS, ST

He was a lawyer and undertook the administration of the temporal affairs of the diocese of Milan for his brother St Ambrose. The integrity and kindliness of Satyrus were eulogized by St Ambrose in a funeral sermon. d. *c.* 379. *September 17, iii, 578.*

SAUVE. *See* Salvius of Amiens.

SAVA, ST, BISHOP

Born 1174, youngest son of the first Serbian sovereign, Stephen I Nemanya. At the age of seventeen he became a monk at Mount Athos and with his father founded the monastery of Khilandari, which still exists. In 1207 he returned to Serbia to help his brother Stephen II. He organized the first Serbian hierarchy of bishops, being himself appointed its metropolitan by the patriarch of Constantinople, and gave new life to religion in his country by establishing small houses of missionary monks. From Pope Honorius III Sava obtained the recognition, or a renewed recognition, of Stephen II as king of the Serbs. d. 1237. *Sabas.* *January 14, i, 86.*

SAVIN, ST

He is venerated as the apostle of the Lavedan district of the Pyrenees and is said to have been a hermit, but even the century (fifth?) in which he lived is a matter of conjecture. *Savinus. October 9, iv, 70.*

SAVINA PETRILLI, BD

She was b. at Siena on August 29, 1851. In 1874 she started a small group to care for the poor which became the Sisters of the Poor of St Catherine of Siena. There are now a thousand sisters in Italy, India, the Philippines and Latin America. d. 1923. bd April 24, 1988. *April 18.*

*SCHOLASTICA, ST, VIRGIN

The sister of St Benedict, who ruled a convent at Plombariola, near Monte Cassino, under her brother's direction. St Gregory in his *Dialogues* gives a moving account of St Benedict's last meeting with St Scholastica, three days before her death in 543. *February 10, i, 292.*

SCILLITAN MARTYRS, THE. *See* Speratus.

*SEBALD, ST

Sebald is venerated as the patron saint of Nuremberg in Bavaria. He is said to have accompanied St Willibald into Germany from Rome as a missionary in the Reichswald. Eighth century. *Sebaldus. August 19, iii, 357.*

*SEBASTIAN, ST, MARTYR

All that can be safely asserted about this famous saint is that he was a Roman martyr, who had some connection with Milan and was venerated there even in the time of St Ambrose, and that he was buried on the Appian Way (in 288?). According to the popular story he was shot to death with arrows. *Sebastianus. January 20, i, 128.*

SEBASTIAN APARICIO, BD

He was a valet and farm worker in Spain, then emigrated to Mexico, where he did well as a carrier and road contractor. After marrying and being widowed twice after middle age, he gave his property to the Poor Clares and at the age of seventy became a Franciscan lay-brother at Puebla de los Angeles. He lived this new life for twenty-six years, chiefly engaged in begging for the community, and d. in 1600. bd 1787. *February 25, i, 420.*

SEBASTIAN KIMURA, BD, MARTYR

A Japanese priest of the Society of Jesus, one of the first, martyred at Nagasaki by being burnt and suffocated by slow fire, in 1622. bd 1867. *September 10, iii, 534.*

SEBASTIAN MAGGI, BD

He was a friar of the Order of Preachers, b. at Brescia in Lombardy, where he worked doggedly for improved discipline. He was for a time confessor of Savonarola, whom he appreciated and admired. d. 1496. c.c. 1760. *December 16, iv, 573.*

SEBASTIAN NEWDIGATE, BD,
MARTYR

A monk of the London Charterhouse to whom King Henry VIII made a personal appeal to recognize the royal ecclesiastical supremacy. He refused, and was h.d.q. at Tyburn on June 19, 1535. His feast is kept in the archdiocese of Birmingham.
May 11, ii, 279.

SEBASTIAN VALFRÈ, BD

Born in Piedmont in 1629, and was an Oratorian priest at Turin. As a prefect of the Little Oratory and director of souls he was much sought after and took endless trouble with all who came to him, while he sought out sinners and converted them in marvellous fashion. He was especially like St Philip Neri in his cheerfulness, though he suffered grievous spiritual trials. d. 1710. bd 1834. *January 30, i, 207.*

*SEBBE, ST

He became king of the East Saxons in 664 and reigned justly for thirty years. He d. in London in 694 and was buried in St Paul's. There seems to have been no *cultus* of St Sebbe in the past, but his feast is now kept in the diocese of Brentwood. *Sebbus. September 1, iii, 461.*

SECUNDA. *See under* Rufina.

SECUNDINUS, ST, BISHOP

In Irish, Sechnall. He was a disciple of St Patrick, coming with him from Gaul into Ireland as a missionary. He wrote the earliest known Latin hymn written in Ireland, *Audite, omnes amantes Deum.* d. 447. *November 27, iv, 434.*

SEINE. *See* Sequanus.

SENAN, ST, BISHOP

This Senan, the most famous of the Irish saints of that name, was trained as a monk at Kilmanagh in Ossory. He is said then to have travelled and to have stayed with St David in Wales (there are also possible traces of him in Cornwall). He made several religious foundations and finally established a monastery on what is now called Scattery

Island, in the Shannon estuary. d. *c.* 560. He is commemorated throughout Ireland. *Senanus. March 8, i, 522.*

*SENATOR, ST, BISHOP

A legate of Pope St Leo I to Constantinople, afterwards bishop of Milan. d. 475.
May 28, ii, 409.

SENNEN. *See under* Abdon.

SENOCH, ST, ABBOT

He was a hermit at what is now Saint-Senou in Touraine and d. in 576. His biography was written by St Gregory of Tours, who knew him personally.
October 24, iv, 191.

SEPTEMBER, THE MARTYRS OF

These are 191 of the many people massacred in Paris on September 2–3, 1792, as "suspected persons". Practically all of the beatified were clergy, killed for refusing the oath and constitution of the clergy which had been condemned by the Holy See. Among them were John du Lau, archbishop of Arles, Francis de La Rochefoucauld, bishop of Beauvais, and his brother Louis, bishop of Saintes. 120 of them perished at the Carmelite friary in the rue de Rennes. bd 1926. *September 2, iii, 472.*

*SEQUANUS, ST, ABBOT

Also *Seine, Sigon.* He was a monk of Réomé who founded a monastery at the place now called Saint-Seine near the source of the river of that name. d. *c.* 580. *September 19, iii, 597.*

*SERAPEUM, MARTYRS OF THE

The Roman Martyrology on March 17 mentions those Christians who were killed by a heathen mob at Alexandria when they refused to worship in the temple of Serapis, in 390. *March 17, iv, 619.*

SERAPHINA, ST, VIRGIN

St Seraphina is specially venerated, as "Santa Fina", at San Geminiano in Tuscany. She was a young girl who suffered from a complication of painful and repulsive diseases, which she bore with wonderful cheerfulness in God's name. After the death of her parents she had only one friend to look after her properly, and she d. in her youth in 1253. *March 12, i, 577.*

SERAPHINA SFORZA, BD

She received considerable persecution from her husband Alexander Sforza, lord of Pesaro, and eventually left him and became a Poor Clare. Her prayers brought her husband to repentance before his death. d. *c.* 1478. c.c. 1754. *September 9, iii, 517.*

*SERAPHINO, ST

His life was of that uneventfulness which one associates with the vocation of a lay-brother (in this case of the Capuchins); he reached spiritual heights and many miracles are recorded of him. He d. at Ascoli Piceno in Italy in 1604. cd 1767. *October 17, iv, 141.*

*SERAPION, BD, MARTYR

He is said to have been b. in England, to have joined the Mercedarians in Spain, and to have been crucified by the Moors for preaching the gospel while a hostage among them in 1240. c.c. 1728. Another Serapion, martyr at Alexandria, is mentioned in the Roman Martyrology on November 14. *November 14, iv, 344.*

*SERAPION OF ANTIOCH, ST, BISHOP

This bishop of Antioch was a learned man, but has left few traces in history. d. *c.* 212. *October 30, iv, 219.*

*SERAPION OF THMUIS, ST, BISHOP

Serapion was bishop of Thmuis in Lower Egypt and played a considerable part in the ecclesiastical affairs of his day. His writings are lost but the *Euchologion* which he edited was discovered and published in the nineteenth century. d. *c.* 370. *March 21, i, 655.*

SERENICUS, ST, ABBOT

After being a hermit with his brother St Serenus he formed and directed a community near Hyesmes on the Sarthe. d. *c.* 669. *May 7, ii, 247.*

SERENUS, ST, MARTYR

Called "the Gardener", because he lived as an anchorite in a garden which he tended at Mitrovica (Sirmium) in Yugoslavia. Having drawn attention by an alleged insult to the wife of a Roman officer, he was arrested and found to be a Christian; having refused to sacrifice to the gods he was beheaded. But it is not certain to what extent this story is genuine. *February 23, i, 401.*

SERENUS. *See also under* Serenicus.

SERF, ST, BISHOP

There are several legends about St Serf, connecting him with Scotland and the Orkneys, but they are extravagant and even the century (sixth?) of his life is uncertain. He apparently d. and was buried at Culross. *Servanus. July 1, iii, 5.*

*SERGIUS I, ST, POPE

Sergius I was pope from 687 till his death in 701 and his life is a part of general ecclesiastical history. His *cultus* began immediately after his death. He had a number of interesting contacts with England. *September 8, iii, 509.*

SERGIUS OF RADONEZH, ST, ABBOT

The best known of all Russian saints. He was b. near Rostov *c.* 1315, and in 1335 took up the life of a hermit in a forest, some way from Moscow. Disciples gathered round, and the famous monastery of the Holy Trinity (Troitsa-Sergievskaya Lavra) came into being. Sergius, who had now been ordained priest, became very well known, and was consulted by Prince Dmitry Donskoy before he defied and routed the Tartars at Kulikovo Polye in 1380. St Sergius is in some respects reminiscent of

St Francis of Assisi, and the attraction of his personality gives him a similar place in Russian hearts to that of Francis in the West. The vision of the Mother of God recounted in the biography of St Sergius is one of the earliest things of the kind in Russian hagiography. He lived to be nearly eighty, when he had the first illness of his life and d. among his monks, in 1392.
September 25, iii, 639.

SERGIUS OF VALAAM, ST, ABBOT

Co-founder with St Germanus of Valaam (*q.v.*) of the monastery of that name in Lake Ladoga. They are said both of them to have been Greeks; but even the era of their life is uncertain. *June 28, ii, 662.*

SERLO, BD, ABBOT

A monk of Mont-Saint-Michel to whom William the Conqueror confided the abbey of Gloucester, where Serlo raised the community from two monks to one hundred. He wrote a letter of warning and rebuke to William Rufus, which the king received a few hours before he was killed in the New Forest. d. 1104. Serlo's name is found in two Benedictine martyrologies.
March 3, i, 473.

SERNIN. *See* Saturninus of Toulouse.

*SERVATIUS, ST, BISHOP

In French *Servais*. An early bishop of Tongres who had a considerable *cultus* in the Low Countries during the Middle Ages. d. 384. *May 13, ii, 297.*

*SERVULUS, BD

Servulus was a cripple who lived by begging at the porch of the church of St Clement at Rome; he shared the alms he received with his fellows and was revered by the whole neighbourhood. d. *c.* 590.
December 23, iv, 600.

SETHRIDA, ST, VIRGIN

Stepdaughter of Anna, king of the East Angles; she followed St Fare as abbess of Faremoutiers. d. *c.* 660. *July 7, iii, 34.*

SEURIN. *See* Severinus of Bordeaux.

SEVEN APOSTLES OF BULGARIA, THE

SS Cyril and Methodius (*q.v.*) had a general oversight of the Bulgars and after the death of Methodius five of his followers were missionaries among them. The chief of them was St Clement of Okhrida (d. 916), and the others were St Gorazd, St Nahum, St Sabas and St Angelarius. They are venerated liturgically in Bulgaria both collectively and separately. *July 17, iii, 130.*

*SEVEN FOUNDERS OF THE SERVITE ORDER, THE

Between 1225 and 1227 seven young Florentines joined the Confraternity of our Lady: they were Bonfilius Monaldo, Alexis Falconieri, Benedict (Amadeus) dell' Antella, Bartholomew (Hugh) Amidei, Ricovero (Sostenes) Uguccione, Gerardino (Manettus) Sostegni and John Buonagiunta. Together they had a vision of our Lady, as the result of which they withdrew from secular life and formed a community on the deserted slopes of Monte Senario. This was the beginning of the order of Servants of Mary or Servite friars. St Bonfilius was the first superior, St Buonagiunta the second, and St Manettus the fourth. St Amadeus became prior of the monastery at Carfaggio, St Hugh and St Sostenes spread the order in France and Germany. St Alexis, a lay brother, outlived them all and was the only one to see the order fully recognized. He d. 1310. They were all cd in 1887.
February 12, i, 311.

SEVEN MARTYRS OF THAILAND

The seven Thai (Siamese) martyrs elevated by the Church were Philip Siphong, a lay catechist; Sister Agnes Phila and Sister Lucy Khambang of the Servants of the Cross; Agatha Phutta, wife and mother; and three girls in their teens: Cecilia Butsi, Viviane Khampai and Mary Phon. They refused to renounce the Catholic faith and were murdered at Songkhon, on the banks of the Mekong River, in 1940. bd October 22, 1989.

*SEVEN SLEEPERS, THE

The legend of the Seven Sleepers of Ephesus, who were walled up in a cave by the emperor Decius and awoke alive under Theodosius II 362 years later, is a Christian version of a well-known folk theme. The truth of the story was questioned by Cardinal Baronius, but he did not exclude their entry from the Roman Martyrology. *July 27, iii, 193.*

*SEVERIAN, ST, BISHOP AND MARTYR

A bishop of Scythopolis who was murdered for his opposition to Monophysite heretics in 453. *Severianus. February 21, i, 384.*

SEVERINUS BOETHIUS, ST, MARTYR

This famous scholar and philosopher, author of *De consolatione philosophiae*, whose works were very influential in the Middle Ages, was accused of plotting against the Ostrogothic king Theodoric, by whose orders Boethius was imprisoned and executed at Pavia in 524. He is venerated as a martyr in that city and his feast annually observed, as it is in the church of St Mary *in Portico* at Rome. c.c. 1883. *October 23, iv, 180.*

*SEVERINUS OF AGAUNUM, ST, ABBOT

This Severinus was said to have been abbot of Agaunum, but this and other details of his life are not trustworthy. d. 507 (?). *February 11, i, 305.*

*SEVERINUS OF BORDEAUX, ST, BISHOP

In French *Seurin*. He was bishop of Bordeaux and d. *c.* 420. He has been wrongly identified with St Severinus, bishop of Cologne, who is also commemorated on October 23. *October 23, iv, 180.*

*SEVERINUS OF NORICUM, ST, ABBOT

The place of origin of St Severinus is unknown but we first hear of him as a hermit in the East. He then went as a missionary to Noricum (Austria). His first success was in famine-stricken Faviana, where his preaching touched the heart of a wealthy food-hoarder. He founded monasteries, of which the chief was on the Danube near Vienna, and earned the respect of the leaders of the barbarians. d. *c.* 480. *January 8, i, 52.*

*SEVERINUS OF SEPTEMPEDA, ST, BISHOP

An early bishop of Septempeda, now called after him San Severino, in the March of Ancona. There has been confusion between him and St Severinus of Noricum. d. 550 (?). *June 8, i, 53.*

SEVERUS. *See under* Four Crowned Martyrs *and* Philip of Heraclea.

SEXBURGA, ST

She was one of the saintly children of King Anna of the East Angles, and after the death of her husband, King Erconbert of Kent, she joined the nuns she had established at Minster in Sheppey. Afterwards she was abbess of Ely in succession to her sister St Etheldreda. d. *c.* 699. *July 6, iii, 25.*

SHARBEL MAKHLOUF, ST

Sharbel Makhlouf was b. May 8, 1828 at Biqa-Kafra in northern Lebanon. He became a Maronite Antonine monk in 1853 and was ordained priest in 1859. He became a hermit in 1875. d. 1898. He was the first eastern rite Catholic to be beatified (December 5, 1965). cd October 9, 1977. *December 24.*

SHENUTE, ST, ABBOT

One of the formative influences in Egyptian monasticism, who became a monk at Dair al-Abiad. He is said to have ruled over 4,000 monks and nuns, and he instituted something in the nature of monastic vows as now understood. He was an extremely severe superior. d. *c.* 466. *Sinuthius. July 1, iii, 1.*

SIBYLLINA BISCOSSI, BD, VIRGIN

A blind orphan who was adopted by some Dominican tertiaries in her native city of Pavia; when she was convinced that it was the will of God that she should not recover her sight she became an ankress in a cell adjoining the friars' church and lived thus to the age of eighty. d. 1367. c.c. 1853. *March 23, i, 665.*

SIDNEY HODGSON, BD, MARTYR

A layman hanged at Tyburn in 1591 for succouring priests. bd 1929. *December 10, iv, 533.*

*SIDONIUS APOLLINARIS, ST,
BISHOP

He was in turn soldier, statesman, country gentleman and bishop of Clermont in Gaul, and poet and man of letters all the time. His character and abilities were such that he was selected for the see of Clermont while he was still a layman, living with his wife and family on his estate in Auvergne. Sidonius was the last considerable writer of the Gallo-Roman school, but his letters are much more valuable and interesting than his verse; as a bishop he was distinguished for the simplicity and sincerity of his daily life. d. 479 (?). *August 21, iii, 374.*

SIDWELL, ST, VIRGIN AND MARTYR

She has given her name to a church and district in Exeter but nothing at all is known about her. An attempt has been made to identify her with Sitofolla, sister of St Paul Aurelian. *Sativola. August 1, i, 574.*

SIGEBERT OF AUSTRASIA, ST

After the death of his father, Dagobert I, Sigebert III governed Austrasia, his brother Clovis ruling in the rest of France. The reign of Sigebert was notably peaceful, and the young man gave himself up to good government and charitable works. d. 656. *Sigisbertus. February 1, i, 229.*

SIGFRID, ST, BISHOP

Sigfrid is venerated as the apostle of Sweden, but his history is obscure. He may have been a priest of York or Glastonbury, who went as missionary bishop to Scandinavia. Sigfrid converted King Olaf of Sweden and established bishops in East and West Gothland. His own centre was at Växjö; when it was plundered and his three nephews murdered by the heathen, he is said to have

refused to let the culprits be executed or to accept compensation from Olaf. d. *c.* 1045. *Sigfridus. February 15, i, 342.*

SIGFRID OF WEARMOUTH, ST, ABBOT

He was appointed abbot at Wearmouth, as coadjutor to St Benedict Biscop, and d. in 690. There is no trace of any liturgical *cultus. August 22, iii, 381.*

SIGIRAMNUS, ST, ABBOT

Sigiramnus (Cyran) was archdeacon of Tours, of which see his father was bishop, but his desire was for the contemplative life. He accordingly founded and directed the abbeys of Méobecq and Longoretum. d. *c.* 655. *December 5, iv, 501.*

SIGISBERT, BD

Traditionally a disciple of St Columban. He was a missionary in Switzerland and founded the monastery of Disentis. d. *c.* 636. c.c. 1905. *Sigisbertus. July 11.*

*SIGISMUND, ST, MARTYR

Sigismund was a king of Burgundy, of Vandal extraction, and corresponding instincts: he had one of his sons strangled for rebuking his stepmother. In remorse he refounded the great monastery of St Maurice at Agaunum in Valais. After being defeated in battle by the sons of Clovis, he lived in hiding in a monk's habit near Agaunum, but was found and put to death by King Clodomir, in 524. Thereafter he was revered as a martyr. *Sigismundus. May 1, ii, 209.*

*SILAS, ST

Silas (Silvanus) was a principal companion of St Paul of whom mention is made in the New Testament. *July 13, iii, 88.*

*SILVERIUS, ST, POPE AND MARTYR

Silverius was the son of Pope St Hormisdas and was chosen pope in 536 while still a subdeacon. He refused to restore the heretical bishop Anthimus to Constantinople at the request of the Monophysite empress Theodora; accordingly a charge of treason was trumped up against him and he was carried away prisoner. He d. of ill-treatment, or was murdered, on an island off Naples *c.* 537. *June 20, ii, 588.*

*SILVESTER I, ST, POPE

Silvester, a Roman, became pope in 314, less than a year after the emperor Constantine had granted toleration to Christianity. He is remembered rather on account of the events which followed this, including the Council of Nicaea, than of his personal life and achievements, of which little is known; but doubtful and spurious legends are not lacking. It is not true, for example, that Constantine granted numerous rights to Silvester and his successors and endowed the Church with the provinces of Italy, or that Silvester baptized the emperor. d. 335. *December 31, iv, 644.*

*SILVESTER GOZZOLINI, ST, ABBOT

He was b. at Osimo in 1177 and forsook first the law and then a secular canonry to become a hermit. In 1231 he organized his followers into a congregation under the Rule of St Benedict at Monte Fano, near Fabriano. St Silvester governed his monks with great wisdom and holiness for thirty-six years, and d. 1267. Equivalently cd 1598. A few monasteries of Silvestrines ("Blue Benedictines") still exist. *November 26, iv, 422.*

SILVESTER OF VALDISEVE, BD

Silvester Ventura was a wool-carder who in middle-age became a Camaldolese lay-brother at Florence. He was quite illiterate but so endowed with wisdom that he was often consulted by educated men. d. 1348. *June 9, ii, 512.*

*SILVIN, ST, BISHOP

A regionary bishop who preached the gospel to the heathen in the region of Thérouanne. He is said to have lived for forty years on fruit and vegetables and to have owned nothing except his clothes and a horse. d. *c.* 720. *Silvinus. February 17, i, 358.*

*SIMEON, HOLY

Holy Simeon, the just and devout man who awaited the consolation of Israel (Luke ii, 25), is named in the Roman Martyrology and his feast is observed in certain places. *October 8, iv, 59.*

*SIMEON BARSABAE, ST, BISHOP
AND MARTYR

One of the longest individual entries in the Roman Martyrology is devoted to St Simeon Barsabae, bishop of Seleucia-Ctesiphon, and his companions, martyrs in Persia in 341 during the persecution of King Sapor II. *See also* Barsabas. *April 21, ii, 141.*

SIMEON BERNEUX, ST, BISHOP AND
MARTYR

He was born at Chateau-du-Loir on May 14, 1814 and became a priest in the Mans diocese in 1837. He was sent by the Paris Foreign Missions to Tonking and Manchuria, then made vicar apostolic of Korea and consecrated in 1854. He sent to Korea on March 23, 1856, was arrested on March 6 and beheaded on March 8 1866. bd 1968. cd by John Paul II at Seoul in 1984. *March 8.*

SIMEON METAPHRASTES, ST

The principal compiler of the legends of the saints found in the menologies of the Byzantine church. He seems to have been an official of the Emperor Constantine VIII and to have d. *c.* 1000. *November 28, iv, 439.*

*SIMEON SALUS, ST

He was an Egyptian who lived a solitary life for twenty-nine years in the desert of Sinai; he then went to Emesa in Syria, where out of humility he behaved in such a way that people thought him demented (*salos*). Sixth century. *July 1, iii, 4.*

*SIMEON STYLITES, ST

The best known of the pillar-saints, the son of a Cilician shepherd, who became a monk in a Syrian monastery while still a boy; later he was dismissed from another monastery for his imprudent austerities. After some years as a hermit people used to throng to him, and it was to avoid them that he first took up his residence on a platform at the top of a pillar (*stylos*) on Mount Telanissae. He lived thus for thirty-seven years, gradually increasing the height of the pillar from about ten feet to about sixty. This extraordinary way of life aroused admiration (and imitation) as well as curiosity, and emperors and bishops as well as crowds of simple folk came to consult him. St Simeon d. on his pillar in his sixty-ninth year, in 459. *January 5, i, 34.*

*SIMEON STYLITES THE YOUNGER, ST

Born at Antioch *c*. 517. He joined a community of hermits and while still a boy began to live on a pillar, leading this strange life for over sixty years. Simeon was ordained and celebrated the holy Mysteries on a platform built on the pillar, and people flocked to him from all parts to seek his advice and to benefit from his miraculous powers. d. 592. *September 3, iii, 479.*

*SIMEON OF JERUSALEM, ST,
BISHOP AND MARTYR

He is said to have been a relative of our Lord (Matt. xiii, 55). He succeeded St James as bishop at Jerusalem and was crucified at a great age, *c*. 107. *February 18, i, 365.*

SIMEON OF LA CAVA, BD, ABBOT

During the twelfth/thirteenth century the abbey and congregation of La Cava in Italy was governed by a remarkable series of abbots. This Simeon was the first of the eight *beati* among them whose *cultus* was confirmed in 1928. *Cf.* St Alferius. *November 16, ii, 80.*

*SIMEON OF SYRACUSE, ST

He was b. at Syracuse in Sicily and became a monk and hermit in Palestine. He was sent on a mission by the abbot of Sinai to Duke Richard II in Normandy. After many adventures he reached Rouen and eventually

settled down as a recluse at Trier, where he was venerated by all as a saint and a wonderworker. d. 1035. cd 1042. *June 1, ii, 441.*

*SIMEON THE ARMENIAN, ST

He was an Armenian who was a pilgrim in Europe, where he earned a reputation for miracles and for heroic charity. d. 1016, at Padilirone in Italy. *July 26, iii, 190.*

*SIMON AND JUDE, SS, APOSTLES

No mention is made of St Simon "the Zealous" in the Bible except that he was one of the twelve apostles. St Jude (Thaddeus) is usually regarded as brother of St James the Less and was the author of the epistle which bears his name. According to the tradition of the West, SS Simon and Jude were martyred together in Persia, but the matter is very uncertain. *October 28, iv, 213.*

SIMON DE ROJAS, BD

A confessor of the Trinitarian Order, who was a chaplain at the court of Philip III of Spain. d. 1624. bd 1766. *September 28, iii, 676.*

SIMON STOCK, ST

Simon Stock, one of the best-known of Carmelite saints, was b. in Kent. He was elected prior general of the order in 1247 and his rule was marked by notable developments: for example, he established Carmelite houses in the four university towns of Oxford, Cambridge, Paris and Bologna, and put into effect modifications of the rule enabling the religious to live as mendicant friars rather than as hermits. According to Carmelite tradition our Lady appeared in a vision to St Simon and declared the privilege of the brown Carmelite scapular, in consequence of which its wearing has become so widespread a devotion in the Church. d. 1265. St Simon's feast is kept by the Carmelites and in the dioceses of Birmingham, Northampton and Southwark. *May 16, ii, 330.*

SIMON YEMPO, BD, MARTYR
A Japanese lay catechist, formerly a Buddhist monk, who was martyred by burning in 1623. bd 1867. *December 4, ii, 448.*

SIMON OF CASCIA, BD
Simon Fidati was b. *c.* 1295 at Cascia, joined the Austin friars, when he distinguished himself as a preacher and writer, and was called on to take part in the public life of Perugia, Florence and Siena. It has been suggested that certain ascetical works hitherto attributed to the Dominican friar Dominic Cavalca were really written by Simon Fidati; and it has been alleged that Luther (also an Austin friar) derived some of his teachings from views incautiously expressed by Bd Simon in his *De gestis Domini Salvatòris.* d. 1348. c.c. 1833. *February 3, i, 244.*

SIMON OF CRÉPY, ST
He was brought up at the court of William the Conqueror, in Normandy, avoided two royal marriages, and received the monastic habit at Condat in the Jura. He was called to Rome as a counsellor of the Holy See, and d. there *c.* 1082. *September 30, iii, 695.*

SIMON OF LIPNICZA, BD
He was a great preacher of the Friars Minor in Poland. d. 1482. bd 1685. *July 30, iii, 216.*

SIMON OF RIMINI, BD
Simon Ballachi was a lay-brother confessor of the Friars Preachers at Rimini. d. 1319. c.c. 1821. *November 3, iv, 254.*

SIMON OF TODI, BD
Simon Rinalducci was a distinguished preacher of the Austin friars who preferred to keep silence under a false accusation rather than cause dissension and scandal among his brethren. d. 1322. c.c. 1833. *April 20, ii, 137.*

*SIMPLICIAN, ST, BISHOP
He was friend and adviser to St Ambrose and succeeded him in the see of Milan at an advanced age. St Simplician considerably influenced the conversion of St Augustine. d. 400. *Simplicianus. August 13, iii, 317.*

*SIMPLICIUS, ST, POPE
Simplicius was pope for sixteen years in very troubled times and he made his influence felt in secular as well as ecclesiastical affairs. He was an energetic opponent of Monophysitism, but of his personal life no details are known. d. 483. *March 10, i, 545.*

*SIMPLICIUS AND FAUSTINUS, SS, MARTYRS
Simplicius, Faustinus and Beatrice (properly Viatrix) were martyrs in Rome of whom no reliable particulars are known. *July 29, iii, 206.*

*SIMPLICIUS OF AUTUN, ST, BISHOP
He was bishop of Autun in the fourth or early fifth century; nothing is known of him except legends related by St Gregory of Tours. *June 24, ii, 634.*

SINDULF, ST. *See* Basolus.

*SIRICIUS, ST, POPE
The name of Pope Siricius was added to the Roman Martyrology by Benedict XIV on account of his "learning, piety and zeal for religion". He ruled for fifteen years and d. in 399. *November 26, iv, 424.*

*SISINNIUS, ST, MARTYR
Sisinnius, Martyrius and Alexander are alleged to have been Cappadocians who were commissioned by St Vigilius of Trent to preach the gospel in Tirol. Here they were murdered by pagans in 397. *May 29, ii, 420.*

SISOES, ST
One of the best-known of the hermits of the Egyptian desert after the death of St Antony. "His zeal against vice was without bitterness". d. *c.* 429. *July 6, iii, 23.*

SIXTEEN MARTYRS OF JAPAN. *See* Laurence Ruiz and Companions.

SIX

*SIXTUS I, ST, POPE AND MARTYR

Sixtus I was pope from *c.* 117 to *c.* 127; he was a Roman by birth, but we have no particulars of his life or alleged martyrdom. *Xystus. April 3, ii, 18.*

*SIXTUS II, ST, POPE AND MARTYR

He succeeded Pope St Stephen I in 257 and in the following year was seized and beheaded while preaching to the Christian assembly. Sixtus II was the most highly venerated among the popes martyred after St Peter, and he is named in the canon of the Mass. *August 6, iii, 269.*

*SIXTUS III, ST, POPE

Sixtus III was pope from 432 till his death in 440. He built or restored several basilicas, and dedicated a number of churches, but of his personal life nothing is now known. *August 19, iii, 355.*

SMARAGDUS. *See under* Cyriacus.

*SOCRATES AND STEPHEN, SS, MARTYRS

The Roman Martyrology commits itself to the statement that these martyrs suffered in Britain. Nothing is known of them, but Bithynia would seem to be the more likely scene of their passion. *September 17, iii, 578.*

SOLA, ST

Sola was an English disciple of St Boniface in Germany. He was a hermit, and on the land given to him there grew up the abbey of Solnhofen. d. 794. *December 4, iv, 485.*

SOLANGIA, ST, VIRGIN AND MARTYR

She is venerated, in the French province of Berry, as a shepherdess who was killed by a young nobleman when she resisted his attempts on her chastity, *c.* 880. *May 10, iii, 267.*

SOLOMON, ST, MARTYR

This Solomon was the ruler of Brittany who successfully defended his country against both Franks and Northmen; he did penance for the crimes of his earlier years, and after his assassination in 874 was venerated as a martyr. There are many Breton legends about this national hero, who is called Selyf in their speech. *Salomon. June 25.*

SOLOMON. *See also under* Roderic.

*SOPHIA, ST, MARTYR

The legendary mother of SS Faith, Hope and Charity (*q.v.*). The great church of Constantinople is not dedicated in honour of "St Sophia" but to the Holy Wisdom (*Hagia Sophia*), that is, to Jesus Christ as the Word of God. *August 1, iii, 238.*

*SOPHRONIUS, ST, BISHOP

He was the patriarch of Jerusalem who convened a synod to condemn Monothelism, and sent a legate to urge the Holy See to do the same, which happened at the Lateran in 649. But before that Sophronius had been driven from his see when the Saracens took Jerusalem in 638, and he is thought to have d. of grief very soon after. This saint is generally identified with Sophronius the Sophist, the companion of John Moschus, author of the *Spiritual Meadow. March 11, i, 557.*

*SOSTENES, ST

One of the Seven Founders of the Servite Order (*q.v.*). *February 12, ii, 311.*

*SOTERIS, ST, VIRGIN AND MARTYR

A martyr at Rome, under Diocletian in 304, of whom St Ambrose speaks; she was related to his family. *February 10, i, 293.*

*SOZON, ST, MARTYR

According to a Greek legend, Sozon was a young Cilician shepherd who smashed an idol with his crook and was accordingly burned, at Pompeiopolis. Date unknown. *September 7, iii, 501.*

*SPERATUS, ST, MARTYR

Speratus and six other men and five women are known as the Scillitan Martyrs from the

place of their passion, Scillium in Africa, in 180. Their *acta* are unusually free from later editorial "improvement".
July 17, iii, 124.

*SPEUSIPPUS, ST, MARTYR

According to a fictitious legend, Speusippus, Eleusippus and Meleusippus were three twin brothers who, with their grandmother Leonilla, suffered martyrdom at Langres under Marcus Aurelius.
January 17, i, 109.

SPIRE. *See* Exsuperius.

*SPIRIDION, ST, BISHOP

Spiridion (Spyridon), shepherd of sheep and pastor of souls, figures in numerous stories of marvels. He became bishop of Tremithus in Cyprus and was mutilated during the persecution of Galerius; that he was present at the Council of Nicaea is a mistake. Fourth century. *December 14, iv, 556.*

*STANISLAUS KOSTKA, ST

Born in 1550, son of a Polish senator. He made up his mind to be a Jesuit, and was received into the Society at the age of seventeen in the face of angry opposition from his family. Stanislaus was more than a model novice, but before the year was out he had d., on August 15, 1568. He was indeed "made perfect in a short while and fulfilled many times by the angelic innocence of his life". cd 1726.
November 13, iv, 335.

*STANISLAUS OF CRACOW, ST, BISHOP AND MARTYR

Stanislaus Szczepanowski was b. in 1030 and appointed bishop of Cracow in 1072. He proved to be an exemplary bishop, to the extent of excommunicating his prince, Boleslaus II, for his oppressive rule and evil life. In revenge Boleslaus with his own hand murdered the bishop, while he was celebrating Mass, in 1079. There is some uncertainty and obscurity about this story, but Stanislaus was cd in 1253.
April 11, ii, 244.

STEPHANA QUINZANI, BD, VIRGIN

Born in 1457 near Brescia, and was a secular Dominican tertiary until she was enabled to found a convent of that order. A contemporary account is extant, signed by twenty-one witnesses, describing in detail one of the ecstasies in which Stephana represented in her own person the different stages of the passion of Christ. d. 1530. c.c. 1740. *January 2, i, 24.*

*STEPHEN, ST, MARTYR

The martyrdom of Stephen, the first deacon and the first martyr for Christ, whom St Luke calls "a man full of faith and of the Holy Ghost", is narrated in the Acts of the Apostles, caps. vi and vii; he was stoned to death by order of the Jewish Sanhedrin at Jerusalem, and among those "consenting to his death" was one Saul, the future St Paul. *Stephanus. December 26, iv, 616;* and *iii, 250.*

*STEPHEN I, ST, POPE AND MARTYR

He became pope in 254 and his short reign was notable for the controversy about the "rebaptizing" of people christened by heretics: St Stephen declared the practice to be opposed to the apostolic tradition of the Church. He d. in 257, it is said put to death by the heathen; but this is doubtful, for the earliest relevant sources say nothing of his martyrdom. *August 2, iii, 249.*

STEPHEN BANDELLI, BD

A confessor of the Order of Preachers, who d. at Saluzzo, near Turin, in 1450. c.c. 1856. *June 12, ii, 534.*

STEPHEN BELLESINI, BD

Born at Trent 1774 and joined the Augustinians. When his community was dispersed by revolution he devoted himself to the instruction of children, and was made inspector of schools for the Trentino by the government. He rejoined his order at Bologna, became master of novices at Rome, and finally parish priest at the shrine of our Lady of Good Counsel at Genazzano. He caught cholera while attending the sick during an epidemic and d. 1840. bd 1904.
February 3, i, 245.

STEPHEN CUÉNOT, ST,
BISHOP AND MARTYR

Born 1802, joined the Paris Foreign Missions, and was sent to Annam. During the persecution of 1833 he was consecrated bishop at Singapore and returned to Annam, where he made many converts and in fifteen years organized three vicariates in Cochin-China. When persecution again broke out in 1861 Bd Stephen was imprisoned, and d. within a few days, just before the order for his execution arrived. bd 1909. cd June 19, 1988. *November 14, iv, 283.*

*STEPHEN HARDING, ST, ABBOT

Stephen Harding, an Englishman by birth and education, was one of the founders of the Cistercian Order and himself drew up the constitutions of Cîteaux. On his way back from a pilgrimage to Rome he became a monk of Molesmes and in 1098 migrated with St Robert and the others to Cîteaux, where in 1109 he became abbot. He appointed St Bernard abbot of the daughter house at Clairvaux and in 1119 drew up the Charter of Charity; these famous constitutions inspired several later monastic codes. d. 1134. cd 1623. His feast is kept in the Plymouth diocese (he was probably b. at Sherborne), on March 28, and in Westminster. *April 17, ii, 114.*

STEPHEN PONCGRAZ, BD, MARTYR

A Hungarian Jesuit, tortured and killed by Calvinist soldiers at Kosice in Slovakia, in 1619. bd 1905. *September 7, iii, 504.*

STEPHEN ROWSHAM, BD, MARTYR

Stephen Rowsham (or Rousham) was a secular priest b. in Oxfordshire. He was at Oriel College and became minister of St Mary's church. He became a Catholic and was ordained a priest at Rheims. He was sent on the English mission and arrested in 1582, banished in 1585, returned in 1586 and was h.d.q. at Gloucester in 1587 aged *c.* thirty-two years. bd November 22, 1987. *February 12.*

STEPHEN OF CUNEO, ST, MARTYR

Stefano da Cuneo, from Genoa, a Franciscan companion of St Nicholas of Sibenik (Nicholas Tavelić), was martyred by the Muslims at Jerusalem in 1393 and canonized by Pope Paul VI on June 21, 1970. *December 5.*

*STEPHEN OF HUNGARY, ST

In Magyar *Istvan.* He succeeded his father Geza as sovereign of the Magyars of Hungary in 997. Stephen established the diocesan organization of Hungary and received from the Holy See the title of king, together with special rights whose nature is a matter of dispute. His religious and political policies and his military successes welded the Magyars into a unity, but his last years, after the death of his heir, Bd Emeric, were darkened by violent intrigues for the succession to the throne. d. 1038. His relics were enshrined by order of Pope St Gregory VII in 1083. *August 16, iii, 466.*

*STEPHEN OF MURET, ST, ABBOT

This Stephen is sometimes called "of Grandmont" and there is some obscurity about his career; but certainly *c.* 1110 he founded at Muret, near Limoges, a community of hermit monks. After his death in 1124 the community had to move from Muret to Grandmont, where it developed into the Grandmontine "reform" of the Benedictine Order; it is now extinct. Stephen was cd in 1189, at the instance of King Henry II of England. *February 8, i, 282.*

STEPHEN OF OBAZINE, ST, ABBOT

He was a priest in Limousin who with another founded an establishment of hermit monks in the forest of Obazine, and afterwards a large convent nearby. The unwritten rule was very strict, and lest it should become relaxed Stephen aggregated his foundations to the Order of Cîteaux in 1147. d. 1159. *March 8, i, 527.*

STEPHEN OF PERM, ST, BISHOP

A monk of Rostov who was a missionary to the Permiaks beyond the Volga, and insisted that every people should worship God in church in its own tongue. He was made the first bishop of Perm in 1383. d. in Moscow, 1396. *April 26, ii, 167.*

*STEPHEN OF RIETI, ST, ABBOT

St Gregory the Great refers several times to this saint as one "whose speech was so rude but his life so cultured". He was abbot of a monastery near Rieti and d. *c.* 560. *February 13, i, 321.*

STEPHEN OF SUROSH, ST, BISHOP

A Greek from Asia Minor who became bishop of Surosh (Sudak) in the Crimea. He was exiled for his opposition to Iconoclasm, and was an early missionary on the southern Russian border. d. *c.* 760. *December 15, iv, 565.*

STEPHEN OF SWEDEN, ST,
BISHOP AND MARTYR

Very little is known of this Stephen, "the apostle of the Helsings". He is said to have been a monk of New Corbie in Saxony who went as a missionary to Sweden and was slain by the heathen, at Uppsala or Norrala, in *c.* 1075. *June 2, ii, 458.*

STEPHEN OF VLADIMIR, ST, BISHOP

This Stephen followed St Theodosius Pechersky as abbot of the caves at Kiev, but soon left to establish a monastery elsewhere. He became bishop of Vladimir in 1091. d. 1094. *April 27, ii, 173.*

*STEPHEN THE YOUNGER, ST,
MARTYR

He was b. at Constantinople in 715 and was first the abbot and then a solitary at Mount St Auxentius. He was a strong and influential opponent of Iconoclasm, and both cunning and violence were used to try and win him over. Stephen was immovable, so he was first banished and then, in 765, stoned to death at the instigation of the emperor, Constantine V. Many other monks suffered for the same cause about the same time. *November 28, iv, 438.*

STEPHEN. *See also under* Socrates.

STILLA, BD, VIRGIN

A laywoman, foundress of the church of St Peter at Abenberg, near Nuremberg, where she has always been venerated since her death *c.* 1140. c.c. 1927. *July 19, iii, 149.*

*STURMI, ST, ABBOT

He was a Bavarian disciple of St Boniface, who sent him to preach the gospel in Saxony. To this end Sturmi helped to found a monastery in 744 which became the great abbey of Fulda. Later the missionary labours of the monks were handicapped by the action of the bishop of Mainz, St Lull, who caused the removal of St Sturmi from the abbacy for a time, and by the wars waged against the Saxons by Pepin and Charlemagne. d. 779. cd 1139. *December 17, iv, 579.*

*SULPICIUS I, ST, BISHOP

He was elected bishop of Bourges in 584, and St Gregory of Tours speaks of him with much respect. The name Severus became attached to him, perhaps to distinguish him from the following Sulpicius (who was surnamed Pius); this has caused no little confusion of St Sulpicius I of Bourges with Sulpicius Severus the writer, who is not numbered among the saints. d. 591. *January 29, i, 202.*

*SULPICIUS II, ST, BISHOP

While bishop of Bourges he defended his flock against the tyranny of an official of King Dagobert, and his care for the poor and afflicted caused him to be so beloved that his death in 647 was followed by extraordinary scenes of popular mourning. He is the titular saint of the famous Paris seminary of Saint-Sulpice. *January 17, i, 111.*

SUNNIVA, ST, VIRGIN

According to Norse legend Sunniva was an Irish princess who fled from her country with others, and the whole company was cast up by the sea on the island of Selje off the coast of Norway; one version says that they were there slain by people from the mainland. This is supposed to have happened during the tenth century. King Olaf

Tryggvason found some bones on Selje and built a church over them in 995. *July 8, iii, 42.*

SUPERIUS. *See under* Salvius.

*SUSANNA, ST, VIRGIN AND MARTYR
This Susanna is commemorated together with St Tiburtius, but there is no known connection between them. It is said that she was put to death for refusing, on account of a vow of virginity, to marry the emperor Diocletian's son-in-law; but the details of her story are devoid of foundation, though there is evidence for the existence of a St Susanna at Rome. *August 11, iii, 301.*

SUSANNA. *See also* Anne.

*SWITHBERT, ST, BISHOP
He was one of the monks who accompanied St Willibrord to Friesland in 690 and worked with great success in what is now south Holland and north Belgium. He was consecrated bishop without fixed see by St Wilfrid of York in 693. His labours on the right bank of the Rhine were ended by Saxon invasion, and St Swithbert spent his last years in a monastery that he founded on the site of the present Kaiserswerth. d. *c.* 713. *Suitbertus. March 1, i, 452.*

*SWITHIN, ST, BISHOP
Or *Swithun*. He was chaplain and counsellor to King Egbert of the West Saxons and was appointed to the see of Winchester in 852. He was a very worthy bishop and after his death in 862 an unusually large number of miracles was reported at his tomb. The origin of the popular superstition attached to his feast-day is not known. That feast is observed in the dioceses of Southwark and Portsmouth. *Swithunus. July 15, iii, 108.*

SWITHIN WELLS, ST, MARTYR
A gentleman from Brambridge in Hampshire, hanged near his own house in Gray's Inn Fields in 1591, for harbouring St Edmund Genings. "He was a witty man, skilled in diverse languages . . . , something given to honest and innocent diversions, yet always devout in prayer". bd 1929. cd 1970. *December 10, iv, 532.*

*SYAGRIUS, ST, BISHOP
He became bishop of Autun *c.* 560, and among the events of his episcopate entertained St Augustine and his monks on their journey from Rome to convert the English. d. 600. *August 2, iii, 4421.*

SYLVESTER. *See* Silvester.

*SYMMACHUS, ST, POPE
He became pope in 498 and the personal aspect of his pontificate is a record of persecution and slander which he suffered, especially from the supporters of the anti-pope Laurence. d. 514. *July 19, iii, 148.*

*SYMPHORIAN, ST, MARTYR
He was beheaded at Autun, in the second or third century, for spurning an image of the goddess Berecynthia. He is commemorated liturgically with St Timothy and St Hippolytus, but the three are otherwise unconnected. *Symphorianus. August 22, iii, 380.*

*SYNCLETICA, ST, VIRGIN
A wealthy Macedonian lady of Alexandria who distributed her fortune and lived for the rest of her life as a hermitess in a disused tomb. She suffered many inward spiritual torments but triumphed over them, only to be afflicted for four years with cancer, from which she eventually d. at the age of eighty-four *c.* 400. There is also commemorated on this day an Apollinaris Syncletica who is simply the heroine of a religious romance. *January 5, i, 33.*

T

TANCO, ST, BISHOP AND MARTYR

Or *Tatto*. According to the legend he was an Irishman who became abbot of Amalbarich in Saxony in succession to one suspiciously named Patto, and followed the same man as bishop of Verden. He was killed by the heathen while exhorting them to behave themselves, *c*. 808. *February 15, i, 342.*

*TARACHUS, ST, MARTYR

Tarachus, Probus and Andronicus were martyred at Tarsus in Cilicia in 304. Their *passio* has been very considerably embellished. *October 11, iv, 83.*

*TARASIUS, ST, BISHOP

Tarasius was a patriarch of Constantinople distinguished for his opposition to Iconoclasm. With the empress Irene he brought about the seventh oecumenical council (Nicaea II), at which images were ordered to be restored to the churches. He was persecuted by the emperor Constantine VI because he would not countenance his bigamous marriage, and at the same time was opposed by St Theodore and the Studite monks, who thought his attitude to the emperor too mild. d. 806. *February 25, i, 416.*

*TARSICIUS, ST, MARTYR

It is learned from a fourth-century poem by Pope St Damasus that one Tarsicius suffered a violent death at the hands of a Roman mob rather than give up to profanation the Blessed Sacrament which he was carrying. It is not known for certain that Tarsicius was a boy or an acolyte: Damasus does not say what he was. *August 15, iii, 335.*

TASSACH. *See* Asicus.

TATIAN DULAS, ST, MARTYR

A martyr tortured to death for deriding the gods of heathendom at Zephyrium in Cilicia, *c*. 310 (?). *Tatianus. June 15, ii, 546.*

*TATIANA, ST, VIRGIN AND MARTYR

Nothing whatever is known about this martyr, whose apocryphal "acts" are almost word for word the same as those of St Martina. *January 12, i, 203.*

TATTO. *See* Tanco.

TEILO, ST, BISHOP

Teilo, b. at Penally, near Tenby, was a great monastic leader in South Wales, his principal monastery being at Llandeilo Fawr in Carmarthenshire. He was a pupil of St Dyfrig and was venerated as his episcopal successor in the neighbourhood of Llandaff, whence his feast is now kept in the archdiocese of Cardiff. Sixth century. *Teilus. February 9, i, 288.*

TELEMACHUS. *See* Almachius.

*TERESA, ST, VIRGIN

Teresa-of-Jesus, or "of Avila", was one of the greatest, most attractive, and widely appreciated women whom the world has ever known, and the only one to whom the title Doctor of the Church is popularly, though not officially, given. She was b. at Avila in Spain in 1515 and, after a period of uncertainty, joined the Carmelites. There was another period of lukewarmness and distraction, for the discipline of the order was much relaxed, but this presented itself as a challenge to Teresa and in 1562 she founded the first convent of nuns of the restored primitive observance. This she followed up with sixteen further foundations all over Spain, as well as, with St John-of-the-Cross, establishing her reform among the friars: all this was in the teeth of violent opposition, labouring under ill health, and with no material resources. Teresa was, moreover, one of the greatest of mystical writers (*The Interior Castle, The Way of Perfection*, etc., with numerous letters), and received supernatural gifts as lofty as her doctrine. The character displayed in her autobiography and letters, forthright, realist, humorous, kindly, has endeared her to all succeeding generations: "she is great from head to foot, but the influence that radiates from her is immeasurably greater still", wrote the Dominican Bañez. d. 1582. cd 1622. *Teresia. October 15, iv, 111.*

TERESA COUDERC, ST, VIRGIN

Co-foundress with Father J. P. E. Terme, of the Congregation of our Lady of the Retreat in the Cenacle. She was b. in 1805, and was one of the first members of Father Terme's community at Aps. In 1828 she was made superioress at La Louvesc, where retreat-work came to be undertaken. But from 1838 Mother Teresa, who "had a power of spiritual discrimination rare in a woman", dropped more and more into the background, and for over forty years she led a life of holiness in obscurity. d. at Fourvière, 1885. bd 1951. cd 1970.
September 26, iii, 658.

TERESA JORNET E IBARS. *See* Teresa of Jesus.

TERESA MANETTI, BD, VIRGIN

Sr Teresa Maria of the Cross was b. on March 2, 1846 at San Martino near Florence. She was noted for her fervent devotion. She spent her entire life in her village

and d. there on *April 23, 1910.* bd October 19, 1986 at Florence. *April 23.*

*TERESA REDI, ST, VIRGIN

Teresa Margaret Redi was b. in 1747 and became a Carmelite at Florence in 1765. As infirmarian she was always cheerful and imperturbable, when most of the time she was more fit herself to be a patient than a nurse. d. 1770. cd 1934.
March 11, i, 565.

TERESA VERZERI, BD, VIRGIN

Foundress of the Daughters of the Sacred Heart. She was b. at Bergamo in 1801 and, after thrice trying her vocation as a Benedictine, formed a small community for teaching and other charitable works. As it grew, so did its trials and uncertainties, but Mother Teresa had the interest and help of Bd Ludovic Pavoni. She d. at Brescia during a cholera epidemic in 1852. bd 1946.
March 3, i, 476.

TERESA OF THE ANDES, BD,
VIRGIN

Sr Teresa of the Andes was the first Chilean *beata*. She was b. at Santiago de Chile on July 16, 1900. She was devoted to the service of the poor and became a Carmelite in 1919. d. April 2, 1920, having taken final vows on her death-bed. bd March 29, 1987 in Chile. *April 2.*

TERESA OF THE INFANT JESUS,
BD, VIRGIN AND MARTYR

A Spanish Carmelite b. at Mochales, Guadalajara, on March 5, 1909, professed in 1929. She was murdered by Republican militiamen on July 24, 1936. bd March 29, 1987.
July 24.

TERESA OF JESUS, ST, VIRGIN

Teresa de Jesús Jornet e Ibars was born at Aytona, Catalonia, Spain, on May 9, 1843. In 1872 she founded the Little Sisters of the Abandoned Aged. She d. at Liria on August 26, 1897. She was bd in 1958. There are now some 3,000 nuns of her order in 214 houses still caring for the old of many countries. cd January 27, 1974.
August 26.

*TERESA OF LISIEUX, ST, VIRGIN

The spread and enthusiasm of the *cultus* of the young Carmelite nun, Teresa-of-the-Child-Jesus, not exteriorly distinguished from hundreds of others, is one of the most remarkable religious phenomena of modern times. She was b. of lower-middle-class parents at Alençon in 1873 and, after a certain amount of opposition, became a Carmelite at Lisieux when she was only fifteen. During the remaining nine years of her life she remained in the same convent, became in effect novice-mistress, and d., after distressing illness, in 1897. Within a few years she became known throughout the world; her "little way" of simplicity and perfection in the doing of small things and discharge of daily duties became a pattern to numberless "ordinary" folk; her autobiography, written at the command of her superiors (and, as is now known, rather heavily "edited" by them—not for the better), is a famous book; countless graces and miracles are attributed to her intercession. cd 1925. This St Teresa is the patron saint of foreign missions and of all works for Russia, being so named by Pope Pius XI. *October 3, iv, 12.*

TERESA OF PORTUGAL, ST

One of the three holy daughters of Sancho I of Portugal. She married Alfonso IX of León, but after they had had several children the union was pronounced invalid on account of consanguinity. Teresa, therefore, returned to Portugal and founded a convent of Cistercian nuns at Lorvão, where she d. in 1250. c.c. 1705. *June 17, ii, 570.*

TERNAN, ST, BISHOP

He was an early missionary bishop among the Picts, seemingly at Abernethy, but even the century in which he lived is unknown. *June 12, ii, 529.*

THADDEUS. *See* Jude, *under* Simon.

THADDEUS MACHAR, BD, BISHOP

Thaddeus (Tadhg) MacCarthy was appointed bishop of Ross in 1482, but he was victim of a conspiracy and in 1488 was driven from his see. He was then nominated by the Holy See to the united dioceses of Cork and Cloyne, but was prevented by certain powerful families from taking up office. So he again appealed to Rome, but d. at Ivrea in Italy while returning home in 1497. He was buried in the cathedral there and his shrine was renowned for miracles. c.c. 1895. His feast is kept in Ivrea, Ross, Cork and Cloyne. *October 25, iv, 201.*

THAÏS, ST

The well-known story of Thaïs, a wealthy and beautiful courtesan of Alexandria, who was converted by St Paphnutius (or by St Bessarion or St Serapion) and became a recluse in a convent, is most probably only a moral tale invented for edification. *October 8, iv, 61.*

THALASSIUS AND LIMNAEUS, SS

Two fifth-century hermits of whom Theodoret writes from personal knowledge in his *Philotheus.* They lived in Syria, and Limnaeus, who was a disciple of St Maro, was famous for his power of healing. *February 22, i, 395.*

*THALELAEUS, ST, MARTYR

He is said to have been a physician who suffered death for Christ at Aegae in Cilicia in 284 (?). *May 20, ii, 357.*

THALELAEUS, ST

A hermit in Cilicia who led a fakir-like life in a sort of open barrel and was nicknamed *Epiklautos,* "weeping much". d. *c.* 450. *February 27, i, 431.*

*THARSILLA AND EMILIANA, SS, VIRGINS

They were aunts of St Gregory the Great and lived a holy life in the house of their father, Gordian, at Rome. d. *c.* 550. *December 24, iv, 605.*

*THEA AND VALENTINA, SS, MARTYRS

Thea and Valentina were sisters who were burned to death for Christ at Gaza in 308. A certain Paul was beheaded at the same time for praying aloud for the victims. *July 25, iii, 188.*

*THEBAN LEGION, THE, MARTYRS

According to the legend the Theban Legion consisted of Christian soldiers recruited in Upper Egypt. While on service in Gaul they refused to sacrifice to the gods (alternatively, they refused to kill innocent Christians in the course of their duty) and, after being twice decimated, were massacred almost to a man. This story had many ramifying legends, in which the principal names are SS Maurice (*primicerius* of the legion), Exsuperius, Candidus, Vitalis, Ursus, two Victors, Alexander at Bergamo, Adventor and Salutor at Turin, Gereon at Cologne. That St Maurice and some companions were martyred *c.* 287 near Agaunum (Saint Maurice-en-Valais) seems to be a fact of history, but that a whole legion was involved is highly improbable.
September 22, iii, 619.

*THECLA OF KITZINGEN, ST, VIRGIN

This Thecla was one of the nuns sent by St Tetta of Wimborne to help in the mission of St Boniface in Germany. She became abbess of Kitzingen. d. *c.* 790.
October 15, iv, 122.

THECLA. *See also under* Timothy.

THECUSA. *See under* Theodotus.

THEOBALD OF ALBA, ST

Theobald Roggeri is said to have belonged to a good family at Vico, near Mondovi, and to have left his home to become a lowly shoemaker at Alba; after a pilgrimage to Compostela he took up still more humble occupations, and shared all he earned with the poor and suffering; d. 1150. But there is no really reliable evidence for all this.
Theobaldus. June 1, ii, 443.

THEOBALD OF MARLY, ST, ABBOT

In French *Thibaud*. He was abbot of the Cistercian house of Vaux-de-Cernay, and a friend of St Louis IX. d. 1247.
July 27, iii, 198.

*THEOBALD OF PROVINS, ST

A son of Count Arnoul, b. at Provins in Brie in 1017, who left his home with another young nobleman and became a pilgrim and hermit. He finally settled down near Vicenza, where he was ordained priest, and d. there in 1066. *June 30, ii, 678.*

*THEOCTISTA, ST, VIRGIN

The tale of the death of St Theoctista, a woman solitary on the Greek island of Paros in the ninth century, is a fiction imitated from the last days of St Mary of Egypt. *Theoctistes. November 10, iv, 307.*

*THEODARD OF MAESTRICHT, ST, BISHOP AND MARTYR

He succeeded St Remaclus in the see of Maestricht. As he was murdered by robbers, *c.* 670, while on a journey undertaken in defence of the rights of the Church he was venerated as a martyr. *Theodardus.*
September 10, iii, 532.

THEODARD OF NARBONNE, ST, BISHOP

An archbishop of Narbonne who is described in the Montauban breviary as "an eye to the blind, feet to the lame, a father of the poor, and a comfort to the afflicted". d. 893.
May 1, ii, 210.

*THEODORA AND DIDYMUS, SS, MARTYRS

The story of Theodora and her rescue from a brothel by Didymus, for which they were both executed at Alexandria under Diocletian, is probably a purely fictitious narrative. *April 28, ii, 181.*

*THEODORA OF ALEXANDRIA, ST

The story of St Theodora of Alexandria is a romance, belonging to the same class as that of St Marina, concerned with a penitent woman who masqueraded as a monk. The Roman Martyrology speaks of her in very restrained terms. *September 11, iii, 538.*

*THEODORE AND THEOPHANES, SS

Two monks of Mar Saba, brothers, who were sent to Constantinople to oppose

Iconoclasm. They were treated with barbarity by the emperor Theophilus, who had verses cut in the flesh of their faces, whence they are called *Graptoi*, "the Written-on". Theodore d. in consequence of his sufferings *c.* 841, and Theophanes, who was a poet, followed him *c.* 845. *Theodorus. December 27, iv, 625.*

*THEODORE TIRO, ST, MARTYR

He is venerated, with St George and St Demetrius, as one of the three chief great "warrior-saints" of the East, but it is not certain that he was ever a soldier. He was probably a martyr, however, and his shrine at Euchaïta was a great place of pilgrimage. It seems clear that the similar St Theodore Stratelates is only a duplicate of the Tiro, invented to clear up the complexities of his legend. *November 9, iv, 301.*

*THEODORE OF CANTERBURY, ST,
BISHOP

He was b. at Tarsus in Cilicia and was a member of a Greek monastery in Italy. In 668, at the age of sixty-six, he was consecrated bishop and appointed to the see of Canterbury. Theodore proved one of the greatest of its archbishops: religion and learning alike flourished under his rule. He made visitations in all parts of the country, dealt with the difficulties between St Wilfrid and St Chad, and held the first national council, at Hertford in 673. St Theodore was himself involved in trouble with St Wilfrid of York about the extent of the northern diocese; it was at last composed with the help of St Erconwald. St Theodore found the Church in England a rather disorganized missionary body: he left it a properly organized province of the Catholic Church, looking to Canterbury as its metropolitan see. d. 690. His feast is observed in six English dioceses and by the English Benedictines. *September 19, iii, 598.*

THEODORE OF CHERNIGOV, ST,
MARTYR

This Theodore was the companion in martyrdom of St Michael of Chernigov, in 1246. *September 21, iii, 611.*

*THEODORE OF HERACLEA, ST,
MARTYR

One of the "military martyrs" honoured as such in the East. He was said to have been a military governor in Bithynia who suffered at Heraclea. This is the Theodore Stratelates referred to under Theodore Tiro, above. *February 7, i, 269.*

*THEODORE OF SYKEON, ST,
BISHOP

He was the son of an innkeeper at Sykeon in Galatia and founded several monasteries before he was made bishop of Anastasiopolis. d. 613. His biography was written by a contemporary, and it gives a remarkable picture of Byzantine life in Asia Minor. *April 22, ii, 146.*

THEODORE OF YAROSLAVL, ST

Theodore was duke of Yaroslavl and Smolensk, and after his death in 1299 he was revered as a saint. So, too, were his sons, David and Constantine, b. of his second wife. The three have a common feast in Russia. *September 19, iii, 601.*

*THEODORE THE SANCTIFIED, ST,
ABBOT

He was a disciple of St Pachomius, and followed him as abbot of Tabennisi and general superior of the whole "congregation" during the difficulties that followed the founder's death. One of St Theodore's miracles provides an early example of the use of blessed water as a sacramental. d. 368. *December 28, iv, 627.*

*THEODORE THE STUDITE, ST,
ABBOT

This Theodore was one of the most famous monks of the Byzantine church. He was made abbot of the monastery of Studius at Constantinople when it was in an advanced state of decay and under his rule it became one of the greatest monasteries of the world; St Theodore ranks with St Pachomius and St Benedict as a monastic legislator, his regulations spreading to Mount Athos, Russia, Serbia and Bulgaria, where and elsewhere they still form the basis of Eastern monastic life. He was also a notable witness to the authority of the see of Rome and a spirited defender of and sufferer for the veneration of holy images during the second Iconoclast persecution. For his defence of orthodoxy in this matter he was imprisoned for seven years, though his position concerning images was a notably moderate one (his methods were less moderate), being based solely on theological principles. In his monastery he especially fostered learned studies and the practice of the fine arts, particularly calligraphy. d. 826. *November 11, iv, 314.*

*THEODORET, ST, MARTYR

He was a priest of Antioch, beheaded in the time of Julian the Apostate. He is called "Theodore" in the Roman Martyrology, and there is confusion with a young Antiochene confessor of that name. *October 23, iv, 179.*

*THEODORIC, ST, ABBOT

In French *Thierry*. He was abbot of Mont d'Or, near Rheims, famous for his influence with evildoers. d. 533. *Theodericus. July 1, iii, 2.*

THEODOSIA, ST,
VIRGIN AND MARTYR

She was a nun of Constantinople who was tortured and killed in 745 for leading a riot of women against the destroyers of sacred images in the course of which an official was killed. *May 29, ii, 420.*

THEODOSIA. *See also under* Apphian *and* Theodota.

THEODOSIUS PECHERSKY, ST,
ABBOT

He was the principal influence in the formation of the monastery of the Caves at Kiev, combining active good works with contemplation, and he was an originator of the Russian institution of *startsy*, "spiritual directors". Theodosius emphasized communal rather than solitary life, and to the end of his days he shared in the house and field work of the monastery he directed. He was

the second saint to be canonized in Russia and the first of the "very-like ones", *i.e.,* Christlike monks; "If God's grace does not help and nourish us through the poor", he said, "what should we do with all our good works?" d. 1074. *July 10, iii, 65.*

*THEODOSIUS THE CENOBIARCH, ST

Born in Cappadocia in 423. He learned the elements of the religious life in Jerusalem and was given charge of a church on the Bethlehem road. He began to attract numerous disciples of various nationalities, whom he organized into a community. Sallust, patriarch of Jerusalem, gave Theodosius oversight of all the monasteries (as distinct from hermitages) in Palestine—whence his title of "Cenobiarch". The emperor Anastasius tried to bribe St Theodosius to support the Monophysite heresy, and his refusal and public exhortations to orthodoxy led to his banishment until the emperor's death. Theodosius d. in 529 at the age of 105. *January 11, i, 68.*

*THEODOTA OF CONSTANTINOPLE, ST, MARTYR

She was tortured and beheaded by the Iconoclasts *c.* 735 for hiding three *eikons* from the government searchers. Her real name was Theodosia. *May 29.*

*THEODOTA OF NICAEA, ST,
MARTYR

St Theodota with her three sons was martyred at Nicaea, perhaps in 304. *August 2, iii, 249.*

THEODOTA OF PHILIPPOPOLIS, ST, MARTYR

She is said to have been a martyr at Philippopolis in Thrace *c.* 318, but her *acta* cannot be taken seriously. They state that she was a converted harlot, whom the most violent tortures were unable to kill. *September 29, iii, 681.*

*THEODOTUS, ST, MARTYR

The story of the passion of SS Theodotus, Thecusa and their companions at Ancyra under Diocletian is in all probability a pious romance; it is better-written than most of its kind. *May 18, ii, 341.*

*THEODULUS AND JULIAN, SS,
MARTYRS

These two suffered at Caesarea immediately after SS Elias and his companions in 309. Theodulus was an old man, formerly in the household of the governor Firmilian, who without trial sentenced him to be crucified. Julian, a young catechumen, was burnt alive for honouring the bodies of the other martyrs. *February 17, i, 355.*

THEODULUS. *See also under* Agathopus, Alexander *and* Crete, Martyrs of.

THEOPHANES VÉNARD, ST, MARTYR
This priest of the Missions Étrangères of Paris was sent in 1854 to Western Tongking, where almost at once he was confronted with persecution. He suffered a long and bitter imprisonment, and was executed most barbarously in 1861. bd 1909. cd June 19, 1988. *February 2, iv, 282.*

*THEOPHANES THE CHRONICLER, ST, ABBOT
Leaving his wife, who became a nun, he founded two monasteries and governed one of them, Mount Sigriana, near Cyzicus, as abbot. The emperor Leo the Armenian, recognizing his influence, tried to convert Theophanes to Iconoclasm and when he failed had him beaten and imprisoned. After two years of close confinement he was banished in 817 to the island of Samothrace, where he d. seventeen days after his arrival as the result of the cruelty with which he had been treated. Theophanes wrote a short history of the world that is of considerable importance as a Byzantine document. *March 12, i, 576.*

THEOPHANES. *See also under* Theodore.

*THEOPHILUS OF ANTIOCH, ST, BISHOP
A second-century apologist who was bishop of Antioch. He was converted from pagan

philosophy through studying Christianity with a view to refuting it. d. *c.* 183. *October 13.*

*THEOPHILUS OF CORTE, ST
He was a Capuchin friar who spent his life preaching and establishing friaries in his native Corsica and various parts of Italy. d. 1740. cd 1930. *May 21, ii, 364.*

THEOPHILUS THE PENITENT, ST
Whatever his true history may have been, this Theophilus has come down to us as the hero of a religious romance in which, having been treated unjustly by his bishop, he made a pact with the Devil. When he repented he had a vision of our Lady, who returned the pact to Theophilus after he had done penance. *February 4, i, 247.*

*THEOPHYLACT, ST, BISHOP
He was bishop of Nicomedia and opposed Iconoclasm, prophesying a violent end for the emperor Leo the Armenian. Theophylact was accordingly banished and he d., still in exile, thirty years later in Caria, 845. *Theophylactus. March 7, i, 516.*

THEOTONIUS, ST
He was priest of Viseu in Portugal, where he worked indefatigably for the good of the people, twice publicly rebuking the queen for setting them a bad example. He became a canon regular at Coïmbra, and as prior of the house insisted on the most reverent and unhurried singing of the Divine Office. d. 1166. *February 18, i, 372.*

THEUDERIUS, ST, ABBOT
A monk from Lérins who established a monastery near Vienne; here during the last twelve years of his life he lived in an ankerhold by the church. d. *c.* 575. Theuderius is the "Chef" of Saint-Chef-d'Arcisse. *October 29, iv, 217.*

THIBAUD. *See* Theobald.

THIERRY. *See* Theodoric.

*THOMAS, ST, APOSTLE

All that is known of St Thomas the Apostle, called *Didymus*, "the twin", is what is told in the gospels: his incredulity about our Lord's resurrection has passed into proverbial speech. An old but unverified tradition makes St Thomas the apostle of southern India (where there are Christians of early origin); it states further that he was martyred near Madras and buried at Mylapore, but this is less deserving of credence. *July 3, iv, 589.*

THOMAS ABEL, BD, MARTYR

He was chaplain to Queen Catherine and was so active in the matter of the validity of her marriage with Henry VIII that he was imprisoned in the Tower and left without trial for six years. Eventually he was attainted for denying the king's spiritual supremacy, and h.d.q. at Smithfield in 1540. bd 1886. *July 30, iii, 219.*

THOMAS ALFIELD, BD, MARTYR

An Eton and King's man, a convert to the Church, ordained at Rheims, relapsed to Protestantism in prison, was again reconciled, and finally martyred for circulating a book in defence of Catholics. Hanged at Tyburn, 1585. bd 1929. *July 6, iii, 27.*

*THOMAS AQUINAS, ST, DOCTOR

He was b. at Rocca Secca, near Aquino, *c.* 1225, was educated first by the Benedictines of Monte Cassino, and became a Dominican in 1244. Thomas spent his relatively short life in teaching in France and Italy, writing and praying, deriving more light and help from the crucifix than from books. His principal works were the *Summa contra Gentiles* and the *Summa Theologica*, the classical scientific exposition of theology, a work of such vast extent that it has caused the author to be called the Universal Teacher. St Thomas was also a poet and in the proper office for the feast of Corpus Christi he welded poetry, theology and worship into a glorious work of art. Thomas d. while on his way to take part in the fourteenth oecumenical council (Lyons II) in 1274. "His wonderful learning", said Brother Reginald, "was far less due to his genius than to the effectiveness of his prayer." cd 1323. He was declared a doctor of the Church in 1567 and patron saint of universities and schools in 1880. *January 28, i, 509.*

THOMAS ATKINSON, BD, MARTYR

A secular priest b. in the East Riding of Yorkshire. He studied and was ordained priest at Rheims in 1588 and sent on the English mission. For thirty years he ministered lovingly to the poor. He was arrested in 1616, refused the oath and was h.d.q. at York. bd November 22, 1987. *March 11.*

THOMAS BECKET. *See* Thomas of Canterbury.

THOMAS BELSON, BD, MARTYR

A gentleman b. at Brill, Aylesbury. He was in Oxford to see his confessor and was arrested with Bd George Nicols, interrogated in London and Oxford for some priests, and d. at Oxford in 1589 when *c.* twenty-four years of age. bd November 22, 1987. *February 12.*

THOMAS BOSGRAVE, BD, MARTYR

A Cornish gentleman, hanged at Dorchester, Dorset, in 1594 for "aiding and abetting" a priest, Bd John Cornelius (Bosgrave had given him a hat). bd 1929. *July 4, iii, 18.*

THOMAS BULLAKER, BD, MARTYR

John Baptist (Thomas) Bullaker, OFM was b. at Midhurst, Chichester, Sussex, in 1602–4. He studied at St Omer, then at the English College at Valladolid in Spain and became a Franciscan priest. He was betrayed by the captain of the vessel bringing him to England in 1630 but eventually released. He served the poor and sick until his conviction in 1642 when he was h.d.q. at Tyburn or Dorchester aged *c.* forty years. bd November 22, 1987. *October 12.*

THOMAS CANTELUPE. *See* Thomas of Hereford.

THOMAS CORSINI, BD

A confessor of the Servite Order, in which he was a lay-brother. d. 1345. bd 1768. *June 23, ii, 626.*

THOMAS COTTAM, BD, MARTYR
He was admitted to the Society of Jesus at Rome and ordained at Rheims. After torture, he was h.d.q. at Tyburn in 1582. bd 1929. *May 30, ii, 415.*

THOMAS FELTON, BD, MARTYR
Son of Bd John Felton. He was a Minim friar, aged twenty and never ordained. Apparently he was a Protestant for a time, for he seems to have been sentenced for being reconciled. Hanged at Isleworth, 1588. bd 1929. *August 28, iii, 437.*

THOMAS FORD, BD, MARTYR
After ministering in Oxon and Berkshire, this secular priest was h.d.q. at Tyburn in 1582. bd 1929. *May 28, ii, 415.*

THOMAS GARNET, ST, MARTYR
First a secular priest and then a Jesuit, h.d.q. for his priesthood at Tyburn in 1608. St Thomas, the first martyr from St Omer's College, was a nephew of the famous Father Henry Garnet, S.J. bd 1929. cd 1970. *June 23, ii, 627.*

THOMAS GREEN. *See* Carthusian Martyrs.

THOMAS HEMERFORD, BD, MARTYR
A Dorset man, ordained by Bishop Goldwell at Rheims in 1583, and h.d.q. at Tyburn in the following year. bd 1929. *February 12, i, 318.*

THOMAS HOLFORD, BD, MARTYR
A seminary priest who ministered in Cheshire and London, where he celebrated Mass in the house of Bd Swithin Wells. h.d.q. for his priesthood at Clerkenwell, 1588. bd 1929. *August 28, iii, 437.*

THOMAS HOLLAND, BD, MARTYR
A Jesuit from Lancashire who ministered in London. h.d.q. for his priesthood at Tyburn, 1642. bd 1929. *December 12, iv, 548.*

THOMAS HUNT, BD, MARTYR
Thomas Hunt (or Benstead) was a secular priest b. in Norfolk who entered the English College in Seville in 1592. He went on the English mission, was imprisoned, escaped, again arrested and h.d.q. at Lincoln in 1600 aged *c.* twenty-six years. bd November 22, 1987. *February 12*

THOMAS JOHNSON. *See* Carthusian Martyrs.

THOMAS MAXFIELD, BD, MARTYR
A seminary priest, of Enville in Staffordshire, h.d.q. for his priesthood at Tyburn, 1616. bd 1929. *July 1, iii, 5.*

*THOMAS MORE, ST, MARTYR
Born in Milk Street, Cheapside, London, in 1478. More went to Oxford and was called to the Bar in 1501. His first wife was Jane Colt, and their house was a meeting-place of all the religious and learned men of the day, both from England and abroad. On the death of Jane, More married Alice Middleton; soon after, in 1516, he published *Utopia* and in the same year his swift advancement by King Henry VIII and Cardinal Wolsey began. In 1529 he succeeded the disgraced Wolsey as lord chancellor. In this office he had to proceed against heretics, which he did with scrupulous fairness and moderation. Having to oppose the king over his "divorce" and other matters, More resigned the chancellorship in 1532. In 1534, with St John of Rochester, he refused the oath imposed by the Act of Succession, and was imprisoned in the Tower for fifteen months. He was tried and convicted for opposing the Act of Supremacy (which made the king the head of the Church in England), and was beheaded on Tower Hill in 1535. cd 1935. It has been justly remarked that, even had this remarkable man not met his death as he did, he would have been a proper candidate for canonization as a confessor—both in public and private life St Thomas More was an ideal Christian. His feast, with St John of Rochester, is observed throughout England and Wales. *June 22, iii, 49.*

THOMAS PALASTER, BD, MARTYR

Thomas Palaster (or Palasor or Pallicer) was a secular priest b. at Ellerton-upon-Swale, Boulton, in the North Riding of Yorkshire. He studied at Rheims, and at the College of Valladolid, Spain, where he was ordained and sent on the English mission. He was arrested at Bd John Norton's house and d. as an unlawful priest at Durham in 1600 when c. thirty years of age. bd November 22, 1987. *August 9.*

THOMAS PERCY, BD, MARTYR

Thomas Percy, Earl of Northumberland, was beheaded at York in 1572 at the age of forty-four for his part in the Rising of the North against the religious policy of Elizabeth I. He had some scruples about the insurrection, but during nearly three years of imprisonment he resolutely refused to purchase his life and freedom by apostasy. bd 1895. His feast is observed in the dioceses of Hexham, Leeds and Middlesbrough. *August 26, iii, 407.*

THOMAS PICKERING, BD, MARTYR

A Benedictine lay-brother, h.d.q. at Tyburn in 1679 on charges arising out of the Oates "plot". bd 1929. *May 9, iii, 597.*

THOMAS PILCHER, BD, MARTYR

Thomas Pilcher or Pilchard was a secular priest b. at Battle, Sussex and educated at Rheims. He was ordained, sent to England in 1583, banished in 1585 and returned. He was h.d.q. at Tyburn or Dorchester in 1587 aged c. thirty years. bd November 22, 1987. *March 21.*

THOMAS PLUMTREE, BD, MARTYR

Born in Lincolnshire, scholar of Corpus Christi, Oxford, and rector of Stubton. At the Rising of the North he celebrated Mass in Durham cathedral, and was specially singled out for punishment. h.d.q. at Durham in 1570. His feast is kept in the diocese of Hexham. *February 4, i, 253.*

THOMAS PORMONT, BD, MARTYR

Thomas Pormont (or Portmore) was a secular priest b. Little Limber, Lincolnshire. He studied at Rheims and at Rome, where he

was ordained priest and sent on the English mission. He was arrested in August 1591, was cruelly racked in the Tower, and d. for high treason in St Paul's churchyard, London, in 1592 when c. thirty-two years old. bd November 22, 1987. *February 20.*

THOMAS REDING. See Carthusian Martyrs.

THOMAS REYNOLDS, BD, MARTYR

Thomas Reynolds (*vere* Green) was a secular priest on the English mission for nearly fifty years. When over eighty he was h.d.q. for his priesthood at Tyburn, in 1642. bd 1929. *January 21, i, 140.*

THOMAS SCRYVEN. See Carthusian Martyrs.

THOMAS SHERWOOD, BD, MARTYR

Sherwood intended to go to Douay to study for the priesthood, but was denounced as a Catholic and arrested in London. He was racked in the Tower in a vain endeavour to make him disclose where he had assisted at Mass, was condemned for denying the Queen's ecclesiastical supremacy, and h.d.q. at Tyburn in 1578. bd 1895. *February 7, i, 273.*

THOMAS SOMERS, BD, MARTYR

A secular priest from Westmorland who worked in the London district and was h.d.q. for his priesthood at Tyburn in 1610. bd 1929. *December 10, iv, 535.*

THOMAS SPROTT, BD, MARTYR

A secular priest b. at Skelsmergh, near Kendal, Westmorland. He studied at Douai, was ordained priest and sent on the English mission in 1596. He was arrested with Bd Thomas Hunt at an inn at Lincoln during a hunt for robbers. He was executed at Lincoln in July 1600 aged twenty-nine. bd November 22, 1987. *July*

THOMAS THWING, BD, MARTYR

He ministered for fifteen years in his native Yorkshire, and was h.d.q. at York in 1680 on account of the Oates "plot". bd 1929. *October 23, ii, 600.*

THOMAS TUNSTAL, BD, MARTYR

Thomas Tunstal, secular priest and Bene-dictine, came on the English mission in 1610 and spent most of the rest of his life in various prisons. h.d.q. for his priesthood at Norwich in 1616. bd 1929.
July 13, iii, 95.

THOMAS TZUGI, BD, MARTYR

A Japanese Jesuit who was martyred by burning at Nagasaki in 1627, with Bd Lewis Maki, in whose house he had celebrated Mass. bd 1867. *September 6, ii, 450.*

THOMAS WARCOP, BD, MARTYR

A gentleman hanged at York in 1597 for harbouring Bd William Andleby. bd 1929.
July 4, iii, 19.

THOMAS WATKINSON, BD, MARTYR

A gentleman b. at Hemingborough or Men-thrope, Yorkshire. He was a devout Catholic who assisted the missioners. He was arres-ted with Bd Robert Thorpe, was offered his life if he would go to church, refused and d. at York in 1591, bd November 22, 1987.
May 31.

THOMAS WELBOURN, BD, MARTYR

A schoolmaster, h.d.q. at York in 1605 for encouraging his neighbours to be reconciled with the Church. bd 1929.
August 1, iii, 241.

THOMAS WHITAKER, BD, MARTYR

A secular priest b. Burnley, Lancashire. He studied at the English College at Valladolid, where he was ordained priest, and was sent on the English mission in 1638. He laboured for five years before imprisonment at Lan-caster, an escape, and final arrest in 1643. He was gaoled for three years, refused a pardon, and d. at Lancaster in 1646 when thirty-five years old. bd November 22, 1987.
August 7.

THOMAS WHITEBREAD, BD, MARTYR

Five Jesuits were h.d.q. at Tyburn in 1679 on a false charge of conspiring to murder King Charles II, part of the Oates "plot". They were Thomas Whitebread, William Harcourt, John Fenwick, John Gavan and Antony Turner. Father Whitebread, an Essex man, was the provincial superior of the Jesuits in England. bd 1929.
June 20, ii, 598.

THOMAS WOODHOUSE, BD, MARTYR

He was arrested in 1561 and passed twelve years in prison, during which he was admitted by letter into the Society of Jesus. h.d.q. at Tyburn in 1573. bd 1886.
June 19, ii, 587.

THOMAS OF BIVILLE, BD

When a young man at Biville in Normandy Thomas Hélye undertook to teach the chil-dren of his village; later he was ordained and spent some years as a sort of diocesan missionary, and was famous for miracles. d. 1257. c.c. 1859. Bd Thomas's relics were hidden at the Revolution and are now again in their shrine at Biville.
October 19, iv, 151.

*THOMAS OF CANTERBURY, ST, BISHOP AND MARTYR

Thomas Becket was b. in 1118 in London, of Norman stock. In 1154, after filling various posts, he was ordained deacon and nominated archdeacon of Canterbury; in the following year he was lord chancellor—an apparently worldly man, vigorous, hot-tem-pered, fond of field sports, popular, magnifi-cent, a bosom friend of King Henry II. But when he was advanced to the primatial see of Canterbury in 1162 Thomas abandoned his luxury, resigned his secular office, and opposed the encroachments of the king on the liberties of the clergy and the rights of the Church. From being, in his own words, "a proud vain man, a feeder of birds and follower of hounds", he had become "a shepherd of sheep". The disputes went on for seven years, getting ever more violent, and St Thomas spent some time in exile; he returned to England on December 1, 1170 and at the same time King Henry in a fit of rage let fall imprudent words in the presence of his knights. Four of them came to Canterbury and in the evening of December

29 murdered the archbishop in a side chapel of his cathedral. The people canonized him as a martyr at once and the Holy See did so formally three years later. St Thomas's shrine made Canterbury one of the most important and famous cities in Christendom. *December 29, iv, 629.*

THOMAS OF CORI, BD

He was a shepherd in the Roman Campagna before he became an Observant Franciscan. He spent most of his life in the friary of Civitella, hidden among the mountains around Subiaco. d. 1729. bd 1785. *January 19, i, 127.*

THOMAS OF DOVER, "ST", MARTYR

Thomas of Hales was a Benedictine of Dover Priory who in 1295 was murdered by French raiders for refusing to give up the monastery valuables. There was a considerable local *cultus*, but to call him Saint is an almost entirely modern practice. *August 3, iii, 250.*

THOMAS OF FLORENCE, BD

Though only a lay-brother Thomas Bellacci was made master of the novices of the Observant Friars Minor at Fiesole; afterwards he opposed the Fraticelli in Tuscany and, when over seventy, preached in Syria, and narrowly escaped martyrdom by the Mohammedans. d. 1447. c.c. 1771. *October 25, iv, 200.*

*THOMAS OF HEREFORD, ST,
BISHOP

Thomas Cantelupe was a Norman, b. at Hambledon, near Great Marlow, *c.* 1218. He studied at Oxford and in Paris, was chancellor of Oxford University, and then chancellor of the realm. He found neither of these two posts easy, but was glad to return to Oxford when deprived of the great seal by King Henry III. In 1275 Thomas was elected bishop of Hereford, and his episcopate was largely a struggle with the lords spiritual and temporal who had encroached on his diocese. He was fearless in rebuking sinners in high places, and was particularly solicitous that all children should be confirmed. His last years were troubled by dissensions with Archbishop Peckham of Canterbury, and he had to seek out Pope Martin IV at Orvieto. He d. while still in Italy, in 1282. cd 1320. St Thomas's feast is observed in several English dioceses and by the Lateran canons regular. *October 3, iv, 19.*

THOMAS OF TOLENTINO, BD,
MARTYR

During the fourteenth century he was a Franciscan missionary in Armenia and Persia. On his way to Ceylon for China in 1321 he was seized by Mohammedans and beheaded. c.c. 1894. *September 5, ii, 60.*

*THOMAS OF VILLANOVA, ST,
BISHOP

He was brought up at Villanueva in Spain, the son of a miller, graduated with distinction in the University of Alcalá, and joined the Augustinian friars at Salamanca in 1516. Thomas filled various offices in his order with great success, and in 1544 was elected to the archbishopric of Valencia. He is particularly remembered for his love and goodness for the poor. They were his constant care both spiritually and temporally, and he was not interested in whether they were "deserving" or not; he was also notably averse from using the coercive weapons of the Church, and he established a special work on behalf of the Moriscos in order to keep them out of the hands of the Spanish Inquisition. Many examples are recorded of St Thomas's supernatural gifts, such as his power of healing and of multiplying food, and he left a number of theological writings. d. 1555. cd 1658. *September 22, iii, 613.*

THOMAS OF WALDEN, BD

Thomas Netter was b. at Saffron Walden *c.* 1375 and became a Carmelite friar. He was a prominent opponent of the Lollards and took part in the Council of Constance. King Henry V, whose confessor he was, d. in his arms. Thomas, whose *cultus* has never been confirmed, d. at Rouen in 1430 and miracles are said to have taken place at his tomb there. *November 2, iv, 243.*

THOMASIUS, BD

A Camaldolese monk who went to live as a solitary, and was lost sight of altogether until he was accidentally found. d. 1337. *March 25, i, 679.*

THORFINN, ST, BISHOP

Bishop Thorfinn of Hamar in Norway was exiled for upholding the Church's rights against King Eric. He d. in a Cistercian monastery near Bruges in 1285. *January 8, i, 55.*

THORLAC, ST, BISHOP

This great reforming bishop of the Church in Iceland studied abroad, and became bishop of Skalholt in 1178. His episcopate was devoted to an uphill struggle against abuses, particularly simony and the disregard of the canons against clerical marriage. d. 1193. He was canonized locally in 1198, but the *cultus* has never been confirmed. *December 23, iv, 602.*

THREE MISSIONARY MARTYRS OF ETHIOPIA. *See* Samuel Marzorati and his Two Companions.

THREE WISE MEN, THE

The men from the East, traditionally three, who visited the new-born Christ are variously known as the Three Holy Kings, the Three Wise Men, the Magi, Caspar, Melchior and Balthazar, etc. Their feast is kept on July 23 at Cologne because their alleged relics rest in the cathedral there. *July 23, iii, 168.*

THURSTAN HUNT, BD, MARTYR

Secular priest, b. Carleton Hall, Leeds, Yorkshire. He studied at Rheims and was ordained priest there by Cardinal de Guise on April 20, 1584 and sent on the English mission in 1585. He worked mainly in Lancashire. When trying to rescue another priest on his way to prison he was seized and sent to London but returned to Lancaster for execution in March 1601. d. Lancaster 1601 when forty-six years of age. bd November 22, 1987. *February 12.*

TIBBA, ST

She was associated with SS Cyneburga and Cyneswide at the abbey of Castor, and venerated with them at Peterborough. Seventh century. *March 6, i, 500.*

*TIBURTIUS, ST, MARTYR

The existence of this Roman martyr is certified by an epitaph by Pope St Damasus; but nothing is known about him, except that he was buried at The Two Laurels on the Via Labicana. Date unknown. *August 11, iii, 301.*

*TIBURTIUS AND VALERIAN, SS, MARTYRS

The martyrs Tiburtius, Valerian and Maximus were honoured at Rome at an early date, but no trustworthy particulars of them have survived. Their names are found in the legend of St Cecilia, wherein Valerian is represented as Cecilia's husband. Date unknown. *April 14, ii, 91.*

TIGERNACH, ST, BISHOP

The account of St Tigernach (Tierney) written from tradition centuries after his death cannot be considered historically accurate. His memory is associated with the monastery of Clones, and he is said to have succeeded St Macartan as bishop at Clogher. d. 549. *April 4, ii, 28.*

*TIGRIUS, ST, MARTYR

In the year 404 Tigrius, a priest, was tortured and exiled, and Eutropius, a reader, was put to death, on a false charge of setting fire to the cathedral and senatehouse at Constantinople as a protest against the banishment of St John Chrysostom. *January 12, i, 71.*

TILBERT, ST, BISHOP

He was the eighth bishop of Hexham and d. in 789. No details are known of his life. *September 7, iii, 504.*

TILLO, ST

Otherwise *Theau, Tilloine*. A Saxon captive in the Low Countries who became apostle of the district round Courtrai. Having retired to a hermitage at Solignaç, he d. at a great age *c.* 702. *January 7, i, 47.*

*TIMOTHY, ST, BISHOP AND MARTYR

The "beloved son in faith" of St Paul and his companion on his missionary journeys. To him, on his appointment as bishop in Ephesus while yet young, Paul wrote two pastoral epistles now in the canon of Holy Scripture. St Timothy is said to have been beaten and stoned to death for opposing heathen worship in the year 97. *Timotheus. January 26, i, 158.*

*TIMOTHY, ST, MARTYR

A martyr in Rome under Diocletian, buried on the Ostian Way. He is commemorated liturgically together with St Hippolytus and St Symphorian. *August 22, iii, 380.*

*TIMOTHY AND **MAURA, SS,** MARTYRS

Timothy and Maura were martyred in Upper Egypt three weeks after they had been married, *c.* 286, according to their legend. *May 3, ii, 223.*

TIMOTHY GIACCARDO, BD

Father Timoteo Giaccardo, b. 1896, was the first priest of the Society of St Paul, founded by Don Alberione for the apostolate of the word through the media. He worked to ensure that the gospel was spread through the press and by all possible modern means of communication. d. 1948. bd October 22, 1989. *January 24.*

*TIMOTHY OF GAZA, ST, MARTYR

Timothy, bishop of Gaza, was burnt to death for the faith at that place in 304. With him are named St Thecla, who was thrown to the beasts at Caesarea, and St Agapius, who suffered by drowning two years later. *August 19, iii, 355.*

TIMOTHY OF MONTECCHIO, BD

He was a confessor of the Franciscan Order in Italy. d. 1504. c.c. 1870. *August 26, iii, 406.*

*TITUS, ST, BISHOP

The Gentile disciple of St Paul, who was twice sent on missions to the church of Corinth. He was ordained bishop for the island of Crete, recalled by St Paul, and eventually returned to Crete where he d. Paul addressed a canonical epistle to him. *January 26, i, 260.*

TITUS BRANDSMA, BD, MARTYR

Fr Brandsma was b. into a peasant family at Bolsfard, the Netherlands, on February 23, 1881. He became a Carmelite and was ordained priest when twenty-four. From 1923 to 1942 he taught philosophy at Nijmegen University. From 1938 he vigorously attacked Nazi crimes and philosophy. During the German occupation he was arrested by the Gestapo on January 19, 1942 and sent to Dachau concentration camp, where he was murdered with an injection on July 26, 1942. bd November 3, 1985. *July 26.*

TORELLO, BD

Being suddenly converted from a dissolute life, Torello became a hermit near his native town of Poppi in the Casentino and lived a life of solitude and austerity for over fifty years. d. 1282. c.c. by Pope Benedict XIV. *March 16, i, 611.*

TORIBIO. *See* Turibius of Lima.

*TORQUATUS, ST, BISHOP AND MARTYR

He was, with his six companions, the first evangelizer of Spain in the first century, according to a medieval legend, but nothing certain is known about them. *May 15, ii, 319.*

TOTNAN. *See under* Kilian (martyr).

*TRIPHYLLIUS, ST, BISHOP

He was the disciple and companion of St Spiridion and was made bishop of Nikosia in Cyprus. St Jerome speaks of him as a most eloquent preacher and writer. d. *c.* 370. *June 13, ii, 538.*

*TROND, ST

He was a missionary in Brabant and founded a monastery at the place now called Saint-Trond, near Louvain. d. *c.* 690. *Trudo. November 23, iv, 413.*

*TROPHIMUS, ST, BISHOP

He was the first bishop of Arles, in the third or fourth century; that he was identical with the Trophimus of 2 Tim. iv, 20 is a medieval invention. *December 29, iv, 638.*

TRUDO. *See* Trond.

TRUMWIN, ST, BISHOP

He was made bishop over the southern Picts in 681, but a few years later was driven by the heathen from his see at Abercorn. He retired to the abbey of Whitby, and d. there *c.* 690. *February 10, i, 293.*

TUDWAL, ST, BISHOP

Tudwal was a sixth-century British monk who is venerated in Brittany as the first bishop in the district of Tréguier. His name occurs at three places in the Lleyn peninsula in Caernarvonshire. *Tudgualus. December 1, iv, 455.*

*TURIBIUS OF ASTORGA, ST, BISHOP

While occupying the see of Astorga in Spain he distinguished himself by his efforts against the Priscillanist heresy. d. *c.* 450. He has been confused with other Spanish saints of the same name. *April 16, ii, 101.*

*TURIBIUS OF LIMA, ST, BISHOP

Toribio de Mogrobejo was b. in 1538 in Spain and attracted the notice of King Philip II. After being president of the Inquisition of Granada (while still a layman), he was in 1580 appointed archbishop of Lima in Peru, where a reforming prelate was badly needed. For years St Turibius had to contend with the rapacity, arrogance and general wickedness of many of the Spanish conquerors, who were the strongest argument of the Peruvians against becoming Christians, and the Spanish clergy themselves were the first people the archbishop had to deal with. He served his flock with unremitting care, making visitations that took years to complete, founding churches, seminaries and hospitals, and fearing no man. d. 1606. cd 1726. *March 23, ii, 176.*

TUTILO, ST

A monk of Saint Gall and the religious and musical associate of Bd Notker Balbulus. He was also poet, painter and stone-carver, and noted for his aversion from publicity. d. *c.* 915. *March 28, i, 696.*

*TYCHON, ST, BISHOP

An early (fifth century?) bishop of Amathus (Limassol) in Cyprus, venerated there as a wonderworker and patron of vine-growers. *June 16, ii, 554.*

*TYRANNIO, ST, BISHOP AND MARTYR

A bishop of Tyre, who with others was martyred in Phoenicia in 310. On the same day the Roman Martyrology mentions other martyrs who suffered in the same district some six years earlier, as related by Eusebius. *February 20, i, 379.*

TYSILIO, ST, ABBOT

Tysilio (Suliau) appears to have been abbot of the church of Meifod in Montgomeryshire, who migrated to Brittany and settled at Saint-Suliac. Seventh century (?). *November 8, iv, 296.*

U

UBALD OF FLORENCE, BD

Ubald Adimari was a young man who was converted from a dissolute and turbulent life by St Philip Benizi, who admitted him to the Servite Order, with the happiest results. d. 1315. c.c. 1821. *Ubaldus. April 9, ii, 60.*

*UBALD OF GUBBIO, ST, BISHOP

Ubald Baldassini was b. at Gubbio *c.* 1100, and as dean of the cathedral introduced community life under rule among the canons. In 1128 he was appointed bishop of Gubbio and in that office continued to be a type of the lovable Christian produced by regular observance. On one occasion he defied Frederick Barbarossa in defence of the town. In Umbria his name is a household word for courage and goodness to this day. d. 1160. cd 1192. *May 16, ii, 325.*

UBALD. *See also* Vivaldo.

UGANDA, THE MARTYRS OF

The central African mission of the White Fathers was begun in 1878, and in 1886 King Mwanga resolved to stamp out the beginnings of Christianity in Uganda, to a considerable extent because it interfered with his own vicious habits. Many Christians, both Catholic and Protestant, were killed with horrible cruelty, and twenty-two Catholics among them were beatified in 1920 and canonized in 1964. Among them were Charles Lwanga, Joseph Mkasa, Matthias Murumba, Andrew Kagwa, Denis (Dionysius) Sebugwawo and Kizito (*qq.v.*). The last-named, a boy of thirteen, is representative of Mwanga's "pages" who were burned alive at Namugongo on Ascension day, 1886. *June 3, ii, 468.*

ULPHIA, ST, VIRGIN

An ankress at Saint-Acheul in the diocese of Amiens. d. *c.* 750. *January 31, i, 215.*

*ULRIC OF AUGSBURG, ST, BISHOP

Ulric was nominated bishop of Augsburg in 923, when that diocese had been laid waste by the Magyars. He was a model bishop, but in his old age he had to meet an unjust charge of nepotism. d. 973. The canonization of St Ulric by Pope John XV in 993 is the first solemn canonization by a pope of which there is record. *Udalricus. July 4, iii, 16.*

ULRIC OF ZELL, ST, ABBOT

He received the monastic habit at Cluny in 1052, from St Hugh himself. He founded a new house of his order at Zell in the Black Forest, and wrote down the constitutions and customs of the abbey of Cluny. d. 1093. *July 14, iii, 101.*

ULRICA NISCH, BD, VIRGIN

Ulrika Franziska Nisch was b. on September 18, 1882 into a very poor family in the village of Oberdorf-Mittelbiberach, Germany. She worked as a domestic servant, was hospitalized and in 1904 joined the Sisters of the Holy Cross of Ingenbohl, a Swiss order caring for her. She became a cook, and had profound mystical experiences. d. of TB on May 8, 1913, at thirty-one. bd November 1, 1987. *May 8.*

ULTAN OF ARDBRACCAN, ST, BISHOP

There are several Irish saints named Ultan (Ultain); this one appears to have been bishop in Ardbraccan during the seventh century. He was noted for his fondness for children and is said to have collected the writings of St Brigid and done other literary work. *September 4, iii, 485.*

ULTAN OF FOSSE, ST, ABBOT

He was brother to St Fursey and St Foillan and a monk with them at Burghcastle. He went to France and Belgium with Foillan, and became abbot of Fosse and of Péronne. d. 686. *May 2, ii, 218.*

UNCUMBER. *See* Wilgefortis.

*URBAN II, BD, POPE

The pontificate of Bd Urban II (Eudes of Lagery) is part of the general history of Europe. He was prior of Cluny and, first as cardinal-bishop of Ostia and in 1088 as pope, did much to extend the uncompromising Christianity of that monastic reform to church and people in general. He had to contend with the antipope Guibert, and he inaugurated the First Crusade, in consequence of an appeal for help against the Seljuk Turks from the Eastern emperor, Alexius I. Urban may have owed much of his policy and tenacity to the counsel of St Bruno, the Carthusian founder, whom the pope at his accession summoned to his side. d. 1099. bd 1881. *July 29, iii, 209.*

*URBAN V, BD, POPE

William de Grimoard, a Frenchman, was a great canonist and abbot of St Germain d'Auxerre. He was elected pope at Avignon in 1362 and took the papacy back to Rome, but he was forced to retire to France again in 1370; he d. in the same year. Urban was a patron of learning and Oxford was among the universities that profited by his help. c.c. 1870. *December 19, iv, 585.*

URBICIUS, ST, ABBOT

Co-founder with St Liphardus of the monastery of Meung-sur-Loire, of which he was the second abbot. Sixth century. *June 3, ii, 463.*

URSICINUS, ST, ABBOT

The missionary monk, a disciple of St Columban, who gives his name to Saint-Ursanne in Switzerland, where he had a small monastery. d. *c.* 625. *December 20, iv, 588.*

*URSMAR, ST, BISHOP

Abbot and bishop at Lobbes and a zealous missionary in Flanders. d. 713. *Ursmarus. April 19, ii, 129.*

URSULA. *See* Angela of Merici.

URSULA LEDOCHOWSKA, BD, VIRGIN

Mother Urszula Ledochowska, a Polish nun, b. 1865 at Lipnica Murowana in the diocese of Tarnow, was the foundress of a congregation of Ursuline sisters with its motherhouse at Pniewy, near Poznan. They were known in Poland as "Grey Ursulines". Bd Ursula devoted her life to the care and education of young people. In 1907 she left Cracow to work in St Petersburg, Russia. She had to leave Russia in 1914 and went to Scandinavia. Benedict XV approved her new congregation after World War I. Its work spread to other parts of Poland and abroad. Bd Ursula was called to Rome by the Holy See, where she died in 1939. She was beatified by John Paul II in 1983 before more than a million people in the Poznan Park of Culture. d. 1939. bd June 20, 1983. *May 26.*

URSULINA, BD, VIRGIN

A young woman of Parma who in consequence, as she alleged, of supernatural enlightenment visited both the Clementine and Urbanist popes and urged them to come to an agreement for the healing of the schism in the papacy. She narrowly escaped being tried for sorcery. d. 1410. *April 7, ii, 49.*

URSULINE MARTYRS, THE

Eleven Ursuline nuns who were guillotined at Valenciennes in 1794 because, having left the town at the revolution, they had returned and unlawfully reopened their school. bd 1920. *October 17, iv, 141.*

*UTICA, THE MARTYRS OF

A number of martyrs of uncertain date who were put to death at Utica in Africa. The expression "White Mass" used in reference to them does not arise from their bodies being calcined with lime but from the place of their execution, Massa Candida. *August 24, iii, 392.*

V

VAAST. *See* Vedast.

VACLAV. *See* Wenceslaus.

VALENCIENNES, THE MARTYRS OF. *See* Ursuline Martyrs.

VALENTINA. *See under* Thea.

*VALENTINE, ST, MARTYR
A priest of Rome who probably suffered in the persecution of Claudius the Goth *c.* 269. He was buried on the Flaminian Way and a basilica was built over his tomb in 350. This is the Valentine after whom "valentines" are named, a custom said to originate in the popular belief that birds begin to pair on this day. *Valentinus.*
February 14, i, 332.

VALENTINE, ST, BISHOP
This Valentine was a monk and missionary bishop in Tirol. d. *c.* 440 (?).
January 7, i, 47.

VALENTINE BERRIO-OCHOA, ST, BISHOP AND MARTYR
A Basque Dominican, vicar apostolic of Central Tongking. He was betrayed by an apostate and martyred by beheading in Indo-China, 1861. bd 1909. cd June 19, 1988.
November 1, iv, 284.

VALERIA. *See under* Vitalis.

*VALERIAN, ST, BISHOP AND MARTYR
When over eighty years old he was forced to die from exposure, near his episcopal city in Africa, for refusing to give up the sacred vessels to the Arian king Genseric, in 457. *December 15, iv, 564.* There are several other martyrs or reputed martyrs named Valerianus and Valerius. *See also under* Marcellus *and* Tiburtius.

*VALERIUS AND **RUFINUS, SS,** MARTYRS
Martyrs at or near Soissons towards the end of the third century, but whether missionaries or otherwise is not known.
June 14, ii, 542.

VALERIUS OF SARAGOSSA, ST, BISHOP
He suffered under Diocletian and was exiled, but d. in peace at Saragossa where he was bishop. The martyr St Vincent was his deacon. d. 315. *January 22, i, 142.*

VALÉRY. *See* Walaricus.

VANENG. *See* Waningus.

VANNE. *See* Vitonus.

*VARUS, ST, MARTYR
Varus is said to have been a Roman soldier in Upper Egypt who was martyred early in the fourth century for ministering to imprisoned Christians. *October 19, iv, 149.*

*VEDAST, ST, BISHOP
Otherwise *Vaast.* He was a fellow worker with St Remigius of Rheims and was by him appointed first bishop of Arras, where he

laboured for forty years with much fruitfulness. The English version of "Vedast" seems to have been "Foster": *cf.* St Vedast's church in Foster Lane, London. d. 539. *Vedastus. February 6, i, 262.*

VENANTIUS FORTUNATUS, ST,
BISHOP
Though his feast is observed in several French and Italian dioceses, Venantius Fortunatus is better known as a poet than as a saint. He was b. near Treviso *c.* 535, and at the age of thirty settled down at Poitiers where he was ordained priest; here he enjoyed the close friendship of St Radegund and, among numerous other poems, many of them personal panegyrics not free from flattery, wrote the great hymn "Vexilla regis prodeunt". He also compiled biographies of St Martin, St Radegund and other saints. Shortly before his death, *c.* 605, Venantius was appointed bishop of Poitiers. His letters to the nuns of Holy Cross are of great interest. *December 14, iv, 558.*

*VENERIUS, ST, BISHOP
He became bishop of Milan in 400 and his *cultus* was revived by St Charles Borromeo. d. 409. *May 4, ii, 231.*

VENTURA OF SPELLO, BD, ABBOT
He built a hospice and monastery for monks of the now extinct order of Cruciferi at Spello, near Assisi, and himself directed them as abbot. Twelfth century. *May 3.*

*VERDIANA, BD, VIRGIN
Born in 1432 at Castelfiorentino, where she lived in a hermitage adjoining a chapel of St Antony. Miracles were ascribed to her. She seems to have been associated with the Vallombrosan Order, but the Franciscans claim her as a tertiary. d. *c.* 1240. c.c. 1533. *February 16, i, 353.*

VEREMUND, ST, ABBOT
Under the rule of this abbot the monastery of Hyrache became the principal one in Navarre during the eleventh century. During a time of famine he is said through his prayers to have nourished over three thousand foodless people. d. 1092. *March 8, i, 526.*

*VERENA, ST, VIRGIN
The *cultus* of this Swiss maiden has a reasonable antiquity but nothing is known about her: she has been drawn into the legend of the Theban Legion. *September 1, iii, 459.*

VERONICA, ST,
Veronica is the name traditionally given to the woman who is said to have wiped the face of Jesus when he fell beneath his cross on the road to Calvary, and a number of legends have grown up around her. She is not mentioned in the Roman Martyrology. *July 12, iii, 82.*

*VERONICA GIULIANI, ST, VIRGIN
Born in 1660 and joined the Capuchinesses at Citta di Castello in 1667. From the time of her profession she experienced numerous visions and other mystical phenomena, the evidence for which constitutes St Veronica's case as possibly the most remarkable known to hagiology. She was at the same time a very level-headed and practical religious, and was novice-mistress of her convent for thirty-four years. d. 1727. cd 1839. *July 9, iii, 57.*

*VERONICA OF BINASCO, BD, VIRGIN
She was a daughter of peasants at Binasco, near Milan, and became a lay sister in a convent of Augustinian nuns. She was the subject of many remarkable visions and ecstasies, some of which seem to have been greatly exaggerated in the course of time. d. 1497. c.c. 1517. *January 13, i, 76.*

VIANCE. *See* Vincentian.

*VIATOR, ST
The companion in his retirement of St Justus of Lyons. d. *c.* 390. He gives its name to a congregation of clerks regular founded near Lyons in 1831. *October 21, iv, 109.*

VICELIN, ST, BISHOP

Bishop of Staargard in Holstein, and the apostle of the Wends, b. *c.* 1086. Among the districts this great missionary evangelized was Lübeck. He founded a house of Austin canons at Neumünster, and d. there in 1154. *December 12, iv, 547.*

*VICTOR III, BD, POPE

As Desiderius he was one of the greatest of the abbots of Monte Cassino, and in 1086 was elected pope by acclamation, taking the name of Victor. But his pontificate was very like that of St Celestine V: Rome was occupied by the imperial anti-pope, Guibert of Ravenna, the gentle Victor fled, and soon after d. at Monte Cassino, in 1087. c.c. by Pope Leo XIII. *September 16, iii, 571.*

*VICTOR MAURUS, ST, MARTYR

According to his legend he was a Mauretanian soldier who was beheaded for confessing the faith of Christ at Milan in 303; he is associated with the martyrs Nabor and Felix as a patron of the city. *May 8, ii, 250.*

*VICTOR OF MARSEILLES, ST, MARTYR

At Marseilles his tomb was a place of pilgrimage at an early date, and he was one of the most celebrated martyrs of Gaul; no trustworthy account of him has survived. *July 21, iii, 157.*

*VICTOR THE HERMIT, ST

In French *Vittré*. He was a hermit at Arcis-sur-Aube in Champagne, of whom St Bernard speaks in two of his sermons and for whose feast at the Benedictine monastery of Montiéramey he composed a proper office. d. *c.* 610. *February 26, i, 426.*

VICTORIA, ST, VIRGIN AND MARTYR

She was a Christian maiden at Abitina in Africa, who ran away from home to escape marriage with a heathen. When she was arrested with SS Saturninus, Dativus and their companions, her brother tried to get her released on the ground that she was out of her mind; she showed clearly that she was not, and suffered with the rest. *February 11, i, 303.*

*VICTORIA AND **ANATOLIA, SS,** VIRGINS AND MARTYRS

These sisters were probably martyred in Italy, but the true circumstances and date of their passion are not known. *December 23, iv, 599.*

VICTORIA OF GENOA, BD

Mary Victoria Fornari was the wife of Angelo Strata, of Genoa, by whom she had six children. After she had become a widow in 1587 she devoted herself entirely to her children, and when they were all provided for, founded the congregation of nuns known, from the colour of their cloaks, as "Blue Nuns" of Genoa. d. 1617. bd 1828. *September 12, iii, 547.*

VICTORIA. *See also under* Acisclus.

VICTORIA RASOAMANARIVO, BD, WIDOW

Victoria Rasoamanarivo, b. 1848, was a pillar of the Church in Madagascar. She had an unhappy married life and baptized her husband herself in 1888 when he was dying after an accident. In 1883, after the first Franco-Malagasy war, the Catholic missionaries had to leave the country. She encouraged young lay Catholics for three years through the Catholic Union, supported minimal liturgical practice, defended imprisoned Catholics and cared for the poor and lepers. bd April 30, 1989 by John Paul II at Antanarivo. *August 21.*

*VICTORIAN, ST, MARTYR

With four others Victorian was tortured and executed by the Arian Vandals at Hadrumetum in 484. *Victorianus.* *March 23, i, 663.*

VICTORIAN OF ASAN, ST, ABBOT

Abbot of Asan in Aragon, whose epitaph by Venantius Fortunatus speaks of his miracles and virtues. d. 558. *January 12, i, 72.*

VICTORICUS. *See under* Fuscian.

*VICTORINUS OF CORINTH, ST,
MARTYR

Victorinus and six other citizens of Corinth, after being persecuted in 249, were exiled, or retired, to Egypt. Here in 284 they finished their confession, being put to death in various cruel ways at Diospolis in the Thebaïd. *February 25, i, 412.*

*VICTORINUS OF PETTAU, ST,
BISHOP AND MARTYR

Victorinus, bishop of Pettau in Upper Pannonia, was distinguished as a scriptural exegete. He was probably martyred *c.* 303. *November 2, iv, 242.*

*VICTRICIUS, ST, BISHOP

With Hilary and Martin he was one of the three very great bishops in Gaul during the fourth century. About 350 he was sentenced to death for resigning from the Roman army on the ground that a Christian should not bear arms, and when next heard of he was bishop of Rouen. He undertook missionary work far beyond the bounds of his diocese, and on one occasion visited Britain to settle some local dispute. d. *c.* 407. *August 7, iii, 275.*

VIETNAM, MARTYRS OF. *See* One Hundred and Seventeen Martyrs of Vietnam

*VIGILIUS, ST, BISHOP AND MARTYR

Vigilius, made bishop of Trent in 385, practically completed the conversion of the Trentino to Christianity. But not wholly, for he was stoned to death at Rendena in 405, for overturning a statue of Saturn, as is said. Pope Benedict XIV stated that St Vigilius was the first martyr to be canonized by the Holy See. *June 26, ii, 646.*

*VIGOR, ST, BISHOP

St Vigor was a bishop of Bayeux, and a very vigorous missionary. d. *c.* 537. *November 1, iv, 238.*

VILLANA OF FLORENCE, BD

Villana de' Botti was the daughter of a Florentine merchant; she was an abnormally pious child, but after marriage went just as far the other way, until she reformed and joined the Dominican tertiaries. Her reform was complete and she made great progress in spiritual life; but after her husband's death she suffered from the evil tongues of some of her fellows. d. 1360. c.c. 1824. *February 28, i, 444.*

*VINCENT FERRER, ST

The life of this great Dominican saint has been considerably overlaid with legend. He was b. at Valencia *c.* 1350 and in troublous times travelled through Spain, France, Switzerland and Italy preaching penance, working many wonders, and converting thousands. St Vincent's other great work was in the mending of the so-called Great Schism of the West (he was a supporter of the popes of the Clementine obedience): "But for you", wrote Gerson to him after the deposition of Peter de Luna, "this union could never have been achieved". d. 1419. cd 1455. *Vincentius. April 5, ii, 31.*

VINCENT GROSSI, BD

Vincenzo Grossi was born at Pizzighettone, Italy, on March 9, 1845. He was ordained priest in 1869 and was an especially gifted preacher and catechist. He founded the Institute of the Daughters of the Oratory, which now has 400 sisters in sixty-eight houses. He died in 1917. bd November 1, 1975. *November 7.*

VINCENT LIEM, ST MARTYR

A Vietnamese Dominican, the first to be martyred; he was beheaded in Tongking in 1773. bd 1906. cd June 19, 1988. *November, 7, iii, 77*

VINCENT MADELGARIUS, ST,
ABBOT

Before he became a monk in the abbey of Haumont and took the name of Vincent, Madelgarius was the husband of St Waldetrudis; their children, Landericus, Madelberta, Aldetrudis and Dentelinus, are all venerated as saints. He founded the abbey of Soignies and d. there *c.* 687. *September 20, iii, 607.*

VINCENT PALLOTTI, ST

The pioneer and forerunner of organized Catholic Action, and founder of the Society of Catholic Apostolate ("Pallottini", or Pallottine Fathers). He was b. in Rome in 1795, and ordained priest in 1818. In him Rome had another Philip Neri; it was said that Don Pallotti "did all he could; as for what he couldn't do—he did that too". His congregation grew from a group of clergy and lay people organized for works of religion and social justice, and the high ideal he set before others he lived to the utmost himself. d. 1850. bd 1950. cd 1963.
January 22, i, 148.

*VINCENT DE PAUL, ST

St Vincent seems to have been b. in 1580 and ordained priest at the age of twenty. He was at first rather "worldly", but a change came when he went to Paris, where he was "taken up" by the Oratorian father Bérulle and by Mme de Gondi. The sad state of the French peasantry led to the foundation of the Congregation of the Mission (Vincentians, Lazarists) in 1625, and afterwards, with St Louisa de Marillac, of the Sisters of Charity. Monsieur Vincent was a man of unbounded love for the poor and unfortunate, whether galley-slaves, victims of war, or crofters in the Hebrides, so that his name is for ever associated with relief of the destitute; he triumphed over his own natural temperament and became a wonderful example of gentleness and humbleness. d. 1660. cd 1737. St Vincent is the patron saint of all charitable societies, notably of that great society that bears his own name.
September 27, iii, 141.

VINCENT ROMANO, BD

Vincenzo Romano was b. into a peasant family at Torre del Greco near Naples on June 3, 1751. He was ordained priest in 1775 and became parish priest in 1799. He started the practice of engaging chaplains for fishermen working away and an arbitration body for their disputes with employers. After the 1794 eruption of Vesuvius he helped rebuild houses. d. December 20, 1831. bd November 17, 1963.
December 20.

*VINCENT STRAMBI, ST, BISHOP

Born at Civita Vecchia in 1745, the son of a druggist. He entered the Passionist congregation, and was a much sought-after missioner. He had in 1801 to accept the see of Macerata and Tolentino, from which he was expelled seven years later for refusing the oath of allegiance to Napoleon. He returned in 1813 to his diocese, only to see it threatened again, by the occupation of the troops of Murat. Vincent himself interviewed both Murat and the general of the pursuing Austrians, and so saved Macerata from being sacked. At the instance of Leo XII he resigned his see and went to the Quirinal as the pope's confidential adviser, where he continued to lead a very mortified life. Among his penitents in Rome was Bd Anna Maria Taigi. d. 1824. cd 1950.
September 25, iii, 644.

*VINCENT OF AGEN, ST, MARTYR

He is said to have been a Gascon deacon who was martyred at Agen c. 300 (?).
June 9, ii, 510.

VINCENT OF AQUILA, BD

A lay-brother of the Friars Minor, "a man of much humbleness, of prayer, moderation and patience, gifted with the spirit of prophecy". d. 1504. c.c. 1785.
August 13, iii, 325.

VINCENT OF CRACOW, BD, BISHOP

Vincent Kadlubek was b. c. 1150 and was made bishop of Cracow in 1208. He was a notable reformer, and the first chronicler of Polish history and legend. d. 1223. c.c. 1764. *March 8, i, 528.*

*VINCENT OF LÉRINS, ST

Vincent, a monk of Lérins, is famous as the author of an early treatise against heresies, called the *Commonitorium*, in which is enunciated for the first known time that for a dogma to be regarded as true it must have been held "always, everywhere, and by all the faithful". He has sometimes been credited with the authorship of the so-called Athanasian Creed. d. c. 445.
May 24, ii, 382.

*VINCENT OF SARAGOSSA, ST, MARTYR

A deacon of Saragossa who suffered death in the year 304 at Valencia. His *cultus* spread throughout the Church at a very early date, and the accounts of his martyrdom were soon embroidered.
January 22, i, 142.

*VINCENTIA GEROSA, ST, VIRGIN

Born 1784 and for forty years gave herself to domestic duties and works of charity. Then about 1823 she was brought into intimate contact with St Bartholomea Capitanio, whom she helped in the founding of the Sisters of Charity at Lovere in Italy. After Bartholomea's death in 1833, Vincentia carried on with the work until her own death in 1847. She was a first-rate organizer, yet an extremely humble woman, and the congregation progressed rapidly under her guidance. cd 1950. *June 4, ii, 476.*

VINCENTIA LOPEZ, BD, VIRGIN

Foundress of the Daughters of Mary Immaculate. She was b. in Navarre in 1847, and her congregation developed out of a home for orphans and domestic servants established by her aunt in Madrid. The whole of Mother Vincentia's short adult life was devoted to the welfare of working girls. d. 1890. bd 1950. *December 26, iv, 619.*

VINCENTIAN, ST

He is said to have been a seventh-century hermit in Aquitaine (where he is called *Viance*), but there is no reliable evidence that he ever existed. *Vincentianus.*
January 2, i, 22.

VINDICIAN, ST, BISHOP

This saint played an important part in the ecclesiastical history of Flanders during the seventh century. He was bishop of Cambrai and is said to have been the messenger of protest from his fellow bishops to King Thierry after the murder of St Leger. He had a special interest in the abbey of St Vaast at Arras. d. 712. *Vindicianus.*
March 11, i, 558.

VIRGIL OF ARLES, ST, BISHOP

He was called from his monastery to be archbishop of Arles, and it appears that he consecrated St Augustine of Canterbury at the request of Pope St Gregory. The same pope rebuked Virgil for trying to convert Jews by force. d. *c.* 610. *Virgilius.*
March 5, i, 489.

*VIRGIL OF SALZBURG, ST, BISHOP

He was an Irish monk *Feargal* who *c.* 745 was made abbot of St Peter's at Salzburg. Later he became bishop of that city, and among other good works sent missionaries into Carinthia. Virgil was twice criticized by St Boniface of Mainz, the second charge raising difficulties with Pope St Zachary because of Virgil's views about the physical universe; what they were exactly is not clear. d. 784. cd 1233. His feast is kept throughout Ireland. *November 27, iv, 436.*

VIRGINIA BRACELLI, BD, WIDOW

Mother Virginia Centurione Bracelli, b. 1587, was married when fifteen though she wished to be a nun. At twenty she became a widow with two daughters. After their marriage she cared for abandoned girls and founded the Order of Our Lady of Mount Calvary to help them. d. 1651. bd September 22, 1985. *December 15.*

*VITALIAN, ST, POPE

He had a troubled pontificate from 657 till his death in 672. St Vitalian sent Theodore of Tarsus to England as archbishop of Canterbury. *Vitalianus.*
January 27, i, 184.

*VITALIS AND AGRICOLA, SS, MARTYRS

Nothing whatever is known about these martyrs, the existence of whose relics at Bologna is supposed to have been supernaturally revealed in 393.
November 4, iv, 263.

*VITALIS AND VALERIA, SS, MARTYRS

SS Vitalis and Valeria are said to have been the parents of SS Gervase and Protase and to have been likewise martyred, the one at Ravenna, the other at Milan. Their extant story is spurious. This Vitalis is named in the canon of the Ambrosian Mass. He was perhaps a martyr in the second century. *April 28, ii, 181.*

VITALIS OF SAVIGNY, BD, ABBOT

He was at different times chaplain to Robert of Mortain, a hermit, and founder of the great abbey of Savigny. Vitalis visited England several times, where on one occasion his sermon is said to have been understood by the common people even though they could understand only English. d. 1122. *September 16, iii, 573.*

VITONUS, ST, BISHOP

In French *Vanne.* He was bishop of Verdun for over twenty-five years and d. *c.* 525. His name, in its French form, is particularly remembered as that of the eponymous patron of the Benedictine congregation which had its origin at the abbey of Saint-Vanne in 1600. *November 9, iv, 304.*

VITTRÉ. *See* Victor the Hermit.

*VITUS, MODESTUS AND CRESCENTIA, SS, MARTYRS

The *cultus* of these three saints goes back to early times and they were martyrs in southern Italy. But nothing is known of their true history and the second and third were probably unconnected with the first; their legends are late and worthless compilations. St Vitus was invoked against epilepsy and kindred complaints, whence the name St Vitus' Dance. *June 15, ii, 545.*

VIVALDO, BD

Or *Ubald.* A tertiary of St Francis who nursed the leprosy-stricken Bd Bartolo of San Gimignano for twenty years. d. 1300. c.c. 1908. *May 21, ii, 275.*

VIVIANA. *See* Bibiana.

VLADIMIR, ST

Vladimir, great-prince of Kiev during the later tenth century, married Anne, sister of the Greek emperor Basil II, and was baptized, and Greek clergy began to evangelize the Russians: the conversion of the country is dated to begin from 989. Vladimir's personal conversion is said to have been very thorough, though he tried to win over his people by force. d. 1015. *Vladimirus. July 15, iii, 110.*

VODALUS, ST

Or *Voel.* A Scot or Irishman who preached the gospel in Gaul and became a hermit at Soissons. d. *c.* 720. *February 5, i, 258.*

VOLKER, BD, MARTYR

A monk of Sigeburg, near Lübeck, "a brother of great simplicity", who was murdered by heathen raiders in 1132. *March 7.*

*VOLUSIAN, ST, BISHOP

Volusian was a fifth-century bishop of Tours who was afflicted with a very bad-tempered wife. He was driven from his see by the Goths and d. in exile *c.* 496. *Volusianus. January 18, i, 116.*

VULFLAGIUS, ST

Or *Wulphy.* First a parish priest at Rue, near Abbeville, and then a solitary, a life he is supposed to have taken up in reparation for returning to the wife from whom he had parted. d. *c.* 643. There is little serious evidence for his legend. *June 7, ii, 494.*

*VULMAR, ST, ABBOT

He founded and directed a monastery on his father's estate at a place in Picardy now called Samer, *i.e.* Saint-Vulmar. d. *c.* 700. *Vulmarus. July 20, iii, 154.*

W

*WALARICUS, ST, ABBOT

Walaricus (Valéry) was a monk under St Columban at Luxeuil and then a missionary in northern France, where he became abbot of Leuconaus at the mouth of the Somme, where two towns are named after him. d. c. 620. This saint was specially invoked for a favourable wind by William the Conqueror before setting out for England in 1066. *April 1, ii, 1.*

*WALBURGA, ST, VIRGIN

She was a nun at Wimborne. When St Boniface was evangelizing the Germans she was sent out with other nuns to help him. She became abbess of the double monastery of Heidenheim, founded by her brother St Winebald. d. 779. St Walburga is honoured in France, Germany and the Low Countries under various names, *e.g.* Vaubourg, Walpurgis (*cf.* Walpurgisnacht, May 1, the eve of one of her festivals), and some of the attributes of the earth goddess Walborg seem to have been transferred to her. St Walburga's so-called miraculous oil is a fluid that exudes from the rock on which her shrine rests at Heidenheim. Her feast is observed in the diocese of Plymouth as well as in Germany. *February 25, i, 415.*

WALDEBERT, ST, ABBOT

In French *Walbert, Gaubert.* He was the best-known of the successors of St Columban as abbot of Luxeuil, which under his direction reached the height of its fame; it was he who introduced the Rule of St Benedict there. He had formerly been a military nobleman. d. c. 665. *Waldebertus. May 2, ii, 217.*

*WALDETRUDIS, ST

St Waldetrudis (Waudru) came of a family of saints, married a saint, Vincent Madelgarius, and had four holy children. After her husband had entered the abbey of Haumont, she founded a convent round which the town of Mons grew up. d. c. 688. *April 9, ii, 58.*

WALFRID, ST, ABBOT

Or *Galfrido.* A citizen of Pisa who with his wife and two children withdrew from secular life and became religious. Walfrid and some friends established a monastery at Palazzuolo, of which he was appointed abbot. d. c. 765. c.c. 1861. *Gualfredus. February 15, i, 341.*

WALSTAN, ST

He was b. at Bawburgh in Norfolk and spent his days as a farm-labourer at Taverham, near Costessey. d. 1016. His *cultus* seems never to have spread beyond that neighbourhood. There is still a St Walstan's Well at Costessey. *Walstanus. May 30, ii, 424.*

WALTER PIERSON, BD, MARTYR

A lay-brother, representative of the nine Carthusian martyrs (*q.v.*), five of them lay-brothers, who were chained upright to posts in Newgate prison and left to die of starvation, in 1537. Until she was stopped, Margaret Clement, adopted daughter of

St Thomas More, fed and tended these monks in prison. *Gualterius.* *May 11, ii, 279.*

WALTER OF L'ESTERP, ST, ABBOT
He was an Augustinian canon and abbot of L'Esterp in Limousin. He had so great a reputation for the conversion of sinners that Pope Victor II gave him special faculties for dealing with penitents. d. 1070. *May 11, ii, 274.*

WALTER OF PONTOISE, ST, ABBOT
Against his will he was made abbot of a new Benedictine house at Pontoise and from time to time during his life he tried to resign the office, once fleeing to Cluny and once elsewhere. At length he resigned himself to a life of administration instead of contemplation, and directed his abbey till he d., in 1095. *April 8, ii, 53.*

WALTHEOF, ST, ABBOT
Waltheof was a kinsman of William the Conqueror and a friend of St Aelred at the court of St David I of Scotland. He joined a community of Austin canons in Yorkshire and then became a Cistercian at Wardon in Bedfordshire, later being elected abbot of Melrose. Here he was noted for his care of the poor and for his personal humbleness. d. *c.* 1160. *Walthevus. August 3, iii, 254.*

WALTMAN, BD, ABBOT
He accompanied St Norbert to Antwerp to preach against certain heretics there, and in gratitude for his success was appointed abbot of St Michael's in that city. d. 1138. *Gualtmannus. April 11, ii, 73.*

*WANDREGISILUS, ST, ABBOT
In French *Wandrille*. He was a distinguished official at the court of King Dagobert I. In 629 both he and his wife retired into religious houses. After many years of varied experience as a monk St Wandregisilus founded the abbey of Fontenelle, which soon became under his guidance well known among the monasteries of western Europe. d. 668. *July 22, iii, 164.*

WANINGUS, ST
In French *Vaneng*. A wealthy lord under Clotaire III, and governor of the Pays de Caux, who in consequence of a vision of St Eulalia of Barcelona reformed his life. He helped St Wandrille by contributing towards his monastic foundation and himself founded a large convent near Fécamp. d. *c.* 683. *January 9, i, 58.*

WAUDRU. *See* Waldetrudis.

*WENCESLAUS, ST, MARTYR
After the murder of his grandmother St Ludmila, Wenceslaus (Vaclav) succeeded to the government of Bohemia; he patiently and firmly opposed the heathen party among his nobles and continued the evangelization of his country, which he acknowledged to be a fief of the Holy Roman emperor. Wenceslaus was slain out of jealousy by his brother in 929, and was acclaimed a martyr by the people. He is the patron-saint of Czechoslovakia; the occurrence of his name in a modern English carol has no significance. *September 28, iii, 663.*

WERBURGA, ST, VIRGIN
Daughter of King Wulfhere of Mercia and St Ermengild. She became a nun of Ely and founded other convents at Hanbury, Weedon and Threckingham. She d. at the last named *c.* 699, and later her body was enshrined in Chester cathedral. St Werburga (Werburh) is the patron of that city and her feast is kept in the dioceses of Birmingham and Shrewsbury. *February 3, i, 241.*

WIBORADA, ST, VIRGIN AND MARTYR
In German *Weibrath*. For some years she worked for Saint-Gall and other monasteries, binding books and so on, and then became a recluse in a cell adjoining the church of St Magnus at Saint-Gall. Here she was murdered by the invading Hungarians in 926. cd 1047. *May 2, ii, 218.*

*WIGBERT, ST, ABBOT
He was one of seven missionaries of this name who worked with St Boniface among the Germans, and became abbot of the

monasteries of Fritzlar and Ohrdruf. d. *c.* 738. Another St Wigbert was a missionary in Friesland. d. *c.* 690. *Wigbertus.* *August 13, iii, 322.*

*WILFRID, ST, BISHOP

He was a Northumbrian, b. in 634, and after studying at Canterbury, Lyons and Rome was made abbot of Ripon. Wilfrid worked zealously to substitute Roman for Celtic discipline in various matters, with notable success at the Synod of Whitby, but his enthusiasm led to serious troubles. He was appointed to the see of York, but was so long in taking it over that St Chad was put there in his place; Wilfrid was put in possession in 669, but King Egfrid encouraged St Theodore of Canterbury to divide the huge northern diocese. St Wilfrid made an appeal to Rome (the first recorded in English history) and was successful, but was banished by Egfrid. He spent five years evangelizing the South Saxons from Selsey, till in 686 he was recalled to the north. But Wilfrid had again to go into exile and make a second appeal to Rome. It was not till 706 that he was restored to Ripon and Hexham, St John of Beverley remaining at York; but he was then seventy-two years old and he d. soon after, in 709. St Wilfrid stands out as a man of unusual force of character, respected by his many opponents, and a fruitful missionary. His feast is kept in many English dioceses. *Walfridus, Wilfridus.* *October 12, iv, 96.*

WILFRID THE YOUNGER, ST, BISHOP

He was a disciple of St John of Beverley and succeeded him in the see of York. d. *c.* 744. *April 29, ii, 187.*

*WILGEFORTIS, ST, VIRGIN AND MARTYR

Wilgefortis (or Uncumber, Kümmernis, Livrade, etc.) is an entirely mythical personage round whom centres one of the most obviously false and preposterous of pseudo-pious romances. She was represented as a girl who grew a beard and moustache so that she would not have to be married, and was then crucified by her angry father. *July 20, iii, 151.*

*WILLEHAD, ST, BISHOP

He was a Northumbrian who *c.* 765 went to preach the gospel to the Frisians. He worked hard, but with not much success, and in 780 Charlemagne sent him among the Saxons: he was the first missionary to cross the Weser. After the revolt of Widukind, when he had to fly, Willehad was consecrated bishop and fixed his see at Bremen. d. 789. *Willehadus. November 8, iv, 297.*

WILLIAM ANDLEBY, BD, MARTYR

A secular priest who ministered in Yorkshire and Lincolnshire for twenty years. h.d.q. for his priesthood at York, 1597. bd. 1929. *Gulielmus, Willhelmus.* *July 4, iii, 19.*

WILLIAM BROWN BD, MARTYR

A layman h.d.q. at Ripon in 1605 for urging his neighbours to be reconciled with the Church. bd. 1929. *August 1, iii, 241.*

WILLIAM CARTER, BD, MARTYR

A printer, b. London, h.d.q. Tyburn 1584 for printing a work against Catholics attending Protestant churches which was falsely held to incite Catholics to murder the Queen. bd November 22, 1987. *January 11.*

WILLIAM DAVIES, BD, MARTYR

A secular priest, b. Colwyn Bay, North Wales. He studied and was ordained priest at Rheims and was sent on the English mission in 1585. He laboured for some years, and reclaimed many Catholics, but was imprisoned in Beaumaris Castle, suffered many indignities, refused to conform and was h.d.q. Beaumaris, Anglesey, 1593. bd November 22, 1987. *July 27.*

WILLIAM DEAN, BD, MARTYR

A Protestant minister who was reconciled with the Church and ordained at Rheims. He was hanged for his priesthood at Mile End Green in 1588. bd 1929. *August 28, iii, 436.*

WILLIAM EXMEW, BD, MARTYR

One of the Carthusian martyrs (*q.v.*), a monk of the London Charterhouse, h.d.q. at Tyburn on 19 June 1535.
May 11, ii, 279.

WILLIAM FILBY, BD, MARTYR

A secular priest h.d.q. at Tyburn in 1582. bd 1929. *May 30, ii, 415.*

WILLIAM FIRMATUS, ST

In consequence of a dream warning him against avarice, this William became a hermit at Laval and elsewhere in France, and made two pilgrimages to Jerusalem. d. c. 1090. *April 24, ii, 158.*

WILLIAM FREEMAN, BD, MARTYR

A secular priest from Yorkshire who was h.d.q. for his priesthood at Warwick in 1595. bd 1929. *August 13, iii, 325.*

WILLIAM GIBSON, BD, MARTYR

A servant b. near Ripon. He was noted for his piety and imprisoned for many years in York Castle. He was deceived and falsely accused by a fellow-prisoner, a Protestant minister. He d. at York in 1596. bd November 22, 1987. *November 29.*

WILLIAM GREENWOOD. *See*
Carthusian Martyrs.

WILLIAM GUNTER, BD, MARTYR

A newly-ordained Welsh priest, from Raglan, h.d.q. for his priesthood at Shoreditch, 1588, bd 1929. *August 28, iii, 437.*

WILLIAM HARCOURT, BD, MARTYR

His real name was Barrow. He was a Jesuit on the English mission for thirty-five years, and was h.d.q. for the Oates "plot" at Tyburn in 1679; he was over seventy years old. bd 1929. *June 20, ii, 598.*

WILLIAM HARRINGTON, BD,
MARTYR

Inspired by the example of St Edmund Campion, he went abroad and was ordained

at Rheims. h.d.q. for his priesthood at Tyburn in 1594. bd 1929.
February 18, i, 373.

WILLIAM HART, BD, MARTYR

Born at Wells, educated at Lincoln College, Oxford, and ordained in Rome in 1581. He worked on the mission in Yorkshire till he was betrayed by an apostate in the house of Bd Margaret Clitherow. Hanged at York in 1583. bd 1886. *March 15, i, 597.*

WILLIAM HARTLEY, BD, MARTYR

A former Protestant minister, who worked for a time with Campion and Persons. He was in prison for over three years, and was eventually hanged for his priesthood at Shoreditch, in 1588. bd 1929.
October 5, iii, 438.

WILLIAM HORN, BD, MARTYR

The last in time of the Carthusian martyrs (*q.v.*). He was a lay-brother who survived starvation and was removed to the Tower. After three years there he was h.d.q. for denying the royal supremacy in the Church, at Tyburn on August 4, 1540.
May 11, ii, 279.

WILLIAM HOWARD, BD, MARTYR

William was the grandson of Bd Philip Howard and was made Viscount Stafford after his marriage to Mary, sister of the last Baron Stafford, in 1637. He was a trusty, if undistinguished, supporter of King Charles I, and somewhat given to litigation. When over sixty he was denounced for complicity in the "Popish Plot" invented by Oates and, after two years' imprisonment, was beheaded on Tower Hill in 1680. bd 1929.
December 29, ii, 601.

WILLIAM IRELAND, BD, MARTYR

A Jesuit, of an old Yorkshire family, h.d.q. at Tyburn in 1679 on charges arising out of the Oates "plot". bd 1929.
January 24, ii, 597.

WILLIAM KNIGHT, BD, MARTYR

A gentleman b. at South Duffield, Hemingbrough, Yorkshire. He was imprisoned in

York Castle and accused with others of trying to reconcile a Protestant minister to Rome. He d. at York in 1596 when *c.* twenty-four years of age. bd November 22, 1987. *November 29.*

WILLIAM LACEY, BD, MARTYR

Mr and Mrs Lacey, Yorkshire gentlefolk, suffered persecution as recusants for fourteen years. After his wife's death Mr Lacey became a secular priest, and was h.d.q. at York in 1582 for denying the queen's supremacy in ecclesiastical matters. bd 1886. *August 22, iii, 382.*

WILLIAM LAMPLEY, BD, MARTYR

A glover b. at Gloucester. He was arraigned for persuading some of his relatives to become Catholics and was offered a pardon if he conformed. He was executed at Gloucester in 1588. bd November 22, 1987. *February 12.*

WILLIAM MARSDEN, BD, MARTYR

A secular priest, b. in Lancashire, h.d.q. for his priesthood in the Isle of Wight in 1586. bd 1929. *April 25, ii, 163.*

WILLIAM PATENSON, BD, MARTYR

A native of Durham who ministered as a priest in the western counties. h.d.q. for his priesthood at Tyburn in 1592. bd 1929. *January 22, i, 147.*

WILLIAM PIKE, BD, MARTYR

William Pike(s) was a joiner b. in Dorset who lived at Moors, near Christchurch, Hampshire. For being reconciled to Rome and denying the Queen's spiritual supremacy, he was h.d.q. at Dorchester in 1591. bd November 22, 1987. *February 12.*

WILLIAM REPIN AND NINETY-EIGHT COMPANIONS, BB, MARTYRS

Guillaume Repin was b. at Thouarcé, France. He was parish priest of Martigné-Briand for more than fifty years, was arrested on December 24, 1793 and guillotined on January 2, 1794 at the age of eighty-four for refusing to compromise his religious faith to accord with the demands of the revolutionaries. He and ninety-eight other people, priests, religious and lay-people martyred in the diocese of Angers during the 1793–94 extreme anti-clerical phase of the French Revolution, were beatified on February 19, 1984. *January 2.*

WILLIAM RICHARDSON, BD, MARTYR

The last martyr under Queen Elizabeth I. He was h.d.q. for his priesthood at Tyburn in 1603. bd 1929. *February 17, i, 361.*

WILLIAM SAULTEMOUCHE. *See* James Salès.

WILLIAM SCOTT, BD, MARTYR

Maurus William Scott, b. at Chigwell, was a Benedictine from the abbey of St Facundus in Spain. He was h.d.q. for his priesthood at Tyburn in 1612. bd 1929. *May 30, ii, 431.*

WILLIAM SOUTHERNE, BD, MARTYR

A secular priest b. at Ketton. He worked among the poor of Staffordshire on the English mission and was arrested at the altar and sentenced in his vestments. He was strangled and d.q. at Newcastle-under-Lyme in 1618 when aged thirty-nine. His head was fixed on one of the gates of Stafford. bd November 22, 1987. *April 30.*

WILLIAM SPENSER, BD, MARTYR

A secular priest b. at Gisburn, Yorkshire. He studied at Rheims and was sent on the English mission in 1584. He was h.d.q. for treason at York in 1589 when *c.* thirty-four years of age. bd November 22, 1987. *September 24.*

WILLIAM TEMPIER, BD, BISHOP

This William was chosen bishop of Poitiers in 1184 and was persecuted for his determined upholding of discipline. His tomb became a place of pilgrimage because of the miracles reported there. d. 1197. *March 27, i, 692.*

WILLIAM THOMSON, BD, MARTYR

William Thom(p)son, also known as Black-burn, was a secular priest, b. Blackburn, Lancashire, who studied at the English College at Rheims and was sent on the English mission. He was h.d.q. as a priest, and for remaining in England, at Tyburn in 1586 when aged *c.* twenty-six years. bd November 22, 1987. *April 20.*

WILLIAM WARD, BD, MARTYR

William Ward (*vere* Webster) was a secular priest from Westmorland. He was a missionary in England for thirty-three years, of which twenty were spent in prison. h.d.q. for his priesthood at Tyburn in 1641. bd 1929. *July 26, iii, 190.*

WILLIAM WAY, BD, MARTYR

He was b. at Exeter in 1531, and ordained at Rheims. h.d.q. for his priesthood at Kingston-on-Thames in 1588. Bd 1929. *September 23, iii, 439.*

WILLIAM OF AVIGNONET, BD, MARTYR

William Arnaud and two other Dominicans, Stephen of Narbonne and another Franciscan, two Benedictines, four secular clerics, and a layman, all directly or indirectly connected with the Inquisition set up by the Synod of Toulouse in 1228, were treacherously murdered by Albigensians at Avignonet in 1242. c.c. 1856. *May 29, ii, 421.*

*WILLIAM OF BOURGES, ST.
BISHOP

William de Donjeon became a monk in the abbey of Pontigny and was abbot first of Fontaine-Jean and then of Châlis. The see of Bourges desiring a Cistercian for its archbishop, William was elected in 1200. He had difficulties with the king, with his chapter, and with Albigensian heretics, all of which he overcame by his patience and firmness. d. 1209. cd 1218. *January 10, i, 65.*

*WILLIAM OF ESKILL, ST, ABBOT

A canon regular in Paris who was invited to Denmark to help in the reform of the monastic clergy there. He was made abbot of Eskilsoe, and laboured at his difficult task for thirty years. d. 1203. cd 1224. *April 6, ii, 43.*

WILLIAM OF FENOLI, BD

A confessor of the Carthusian Order: he was a lay-brother in the charterhouse *Casualarum* in Lombardy. d. *c.* 1205. c.c. 1860. *December 19, iv, 585.*

WILLIAM OF GELLONE, ST

Duke William of Aquitaine fought against the Saracens and was regarded as the ideal Christian knight. He founded the abbey of Gellone, near Aniane, and in later life himself became a monk there. d. 812. *May 28, ii, 411.*

WILLIAM OF HIRSCHAU, BD, ABBOT

He was second abbot of the refounded monastery of Hirschau in Württemberg, and had to deal both with the depredations of the local landowner and with the building-up of a stable community; his personal reputation attracted many suitable aspirants. He was particularly concerned for the welfare of the serfs of the district. Bd William was a man of varied accomplishments: he invented a clock, wrote verse, and wrote a treatise on music. d. 1091. *July 4, iii, 17.*

*WILLIAM OF MALEVAL, ST, ABBOT

Having spent many years in penance and pilgrimages, this William was set to reform a monastery near Pisa, but failed, and he began a community of his own on Monte Pruno. He was no more able to maintain discipline here, and retired to the solitude of Maleval, near Siena, in 1155. Here he was joined by a few followers, who afterwards became the congregation of Hermits of St William of Gulielmites; they are long ago extinct d. 1157. *February 10, i, 295.*

WILLIAM OF NORWICH, ST, MARTYR

A twelve-year-old boy alleged to have been put to death by two Jews out of hatred of the faith at Norwich in 1144; the body was found hanging from a tree in Mousehold Wood. There is no proof whatsoever for the story. Anti-Semitic fabrication, as in so many cases of this kind, is the source of the legend. *March 24, i, 671.*

WILLIAM OF POLIZZI, BD

William Gnoffi was a member of a mendicant community in Sicily; he submitted himself to severe bodily austerities in protection against the temptations to sinful sensuality to which he was subject, d. *c.* 1317. *April 16, ii, 106.*

WILLIAM OF ROCHESTER, ST,
MARTYR

According to tradition, William was a pilgrim from Perth who was murdered at Rochester in 1201. Miracles were alleged to have followed, and William's body was enshrined in the cathedral. *May 23, ii, 378.*

WILLIAM OF ROSKILDE, ST,
BISHOP

He was an Englishman, chaplain to King Canute, by whom he was made bishop of Roskilde in Denmark. He boldly stood up for Christian life against the iniquities of King Sweyn Estridsen and was a zealous missionary among the Danes. d. *c.* 1070. *September 2, iii, 470.*

WILLIAM OF SAINT-BÉNIGNE, ST,
ABBOT

He was b. near Novara in 962. Having become a monk at Cluny, he was sent as abbot to revive the old monastery of Saint Benignus at Dijon which became the headquarters of a reform covering Burgundy, Lorraine and Italy. At different times St William had to oppose the emperor St Henry, King Robert of France, and the Holy See. He refounded the abbey of Fécamp, which had importance for the ecclesiastical life of England, and d. there in 1031. *January 1, i, 12.*

WILLIAM OF SAINT-BRIEUC, ST,
BISHOP

William Pinchon was bishop of Saint-Brieuc in Brittany and his virtues and miracles were remarkable, but few details are known. d. 1234. cd 1247. *July 29, iii, 212.*

WILLIAM OF SCICLI, BD

William Cufitella was a Franciscan tertiary, who lived in solitude for seventy years near Scicli in Sicily. d. 1411. c.c. 1537. *April 3, ii, 50.*

WILLIAM OF TOULOUSE, BD

A confessor of the order of Hermit Friars of St Augustine; he was a celebrated preacher and director of souls. d. 1369. c.c. 1893. *May 18, ii, 343.*

*WILLIAM OF VERCELLI, ST,
ABBOT

Also called "of Monte Vergine". He was b. at Vercelli in 1085 and, after living as a pilgrim and hermit, came to Monte Virgiliano, now Monte Vergine, in the Apennines. Here he organized his disciples into a community of hermit-monks under a severe rule, and established similar houses, for men and for women, elsewhere. d. 1142. St William's second successor adopted the Benedictine rule, and Monte Vergine still exists as an abbey. *June 25, ii, 635.*

*WILLIAM OF YORK, ST, BISHOP

William Fitzherbert, or "of Thwayt", was appointed to the see of York in 1140; the appointment was contested on alleged grounds of simony and unchastity, but eventually he was consecrated and enthroned with the permission of Pope Innocent II. But his enemies were active, he was negligent of his own interests, and in 1147 he was deposed by Pope Eugenius III. For some years he lived a mortified life in retirement and was then restored to York by Pope Anastasius IV, where he was joyfully received. d. 1154. cd 1227. Among those who brought about the deposition of St William was St Bernard of Clairvaux. *June 8, ii, 503.*

*WILLIBALD, ST, BISHOP

He was b. in Wessex, the brother of SS Winebald and Walburga. After travelling for six years in the East (he is the first recorded English pilgrim to the Holy Land), he became a monk at Monte Cassino and was then sent to join St Boniface in Germany. He was made the first bishop of Eichstätt, where he converted many of the heathen and founded a large monastery at Heidenheim. d. *c.* 786. His feast is kept in the Plymouth diocese. *Willebaldus. June 7, ii, 494.*

*WILLIBRORD, ST, BISHOP

Born in Northumbria in 658, he was educated at Ripon and in Ireland. He was set out in 690 with eleven other English monks to preach the gospel to the Frisians, and six years later was consecrated bishop in Rome; he set up his chair at Utrecht. Under the protection of Pepin of Herstal, but with setbacks from the heathen Radbod, Willibrord made converts in all parts of Frisia, but his efforts in Denmark were unsuccessful; he is venerated as the Apostle of the Frisians, though he was not the only prominent one (*e.g.* St Swithbert). In his old age he retired to the monastery he had founded at Echternach, where he d. in 739. *Willibrordus. November 7, iv. 286.*

WILLIGIS, ST, BISHOP

Willigis was one of the outstanding ecclesiastical statesmen of the tenth century. Though of humble birth he was made archbishop of Mainz by the emperor Otto II, and he played a leading part in the affairs of the empire, which owed much of its influence at this time to him. He spread Christianity in southern Scandinavia and built and restored many churches. Willigis had a serious dispute with the bishop of Hildesheim, St Bernward, in which he admitted that he was wrong and retired gracefully. "His countenance was always unruffled, and his inward peace was even more remarkable." d. 1011. *February 23, i, 406.*

WILTRUDIS, ST

The widow of Berthold, duke of Bavaria, who became a nun and founded the convent of Bergen bei Neuburg. d. *c.* 986. *January 6, i, 42.*

WINEBALD, ST, ABBOT

Winebald became a missionary under St Boniface and, with his sister St Walburga,

governed the double monastery of Heidenheim that their brother St Willibald had established. His missionary work was hampered by bad health and by the ill will of his heathen neighbours. d. 761. *Winebaldus. December 18, iv, 582.*

*WINIFRED, ST, VIRGIN AND MARTYR

The spring of St Winifred (in Welsh *Gwenfrewi*) at Holywell in North Wales has been a place of pilgrimage and healing for over a thousand years, but great uncertainty surrounds the saint. The core of her legend is that she was attacked by Caradog of Hawarden because she refused his amorous advances, that her wounds were healed (or she was restored to life) by St Beuno, that a spring gushed out where this happened, that she became a nun at Gwytherin, and d. *c.* 650. All the information about her is too late to enable any certainties to be established. Her feast has been kept in the dioceses of Menevia and Shrewsbury. *Wenefrida. November 3, iv, 245.*

*WINNOC, ST, ABBOT

Winnoc and three other monks (said to have been British) were sent by St Bertinus to establish a monastery among the Morini at Wormhout, from whence they evangelized the neighbourhood. d. 717 (?). In 1030 the abbot's relics were translated to a monastery at Bergues-Saint-Winnoc. *Winocus. November 6, iv, 276.*

WINWALOE, ST, ABBOT

In French *Guénolé*. He was a Breton, who founded the monastery of Landévennec by Brest, and is presumably the same Winwaloe whose name is found in varying forms in Cornwall. His *cultus* in Brittany was widespread, but not much is now known about him. Sixth century. *Guengualoeus. March 3, i, 469.*

*WIRO, ST, BISHOP

Wiro, b. somewhere in the British Isles, was the companion of the missionaries St Plechelm and St Otger, first in their native land and then in the Netherlands. A monastery was afterwards founded on the

site of their church on the Odilienberg, near Roermond. Eighth century.
May 8, ii, 253.

WISDOM. *See* Sophia.

WISTAN, ST

He is said to have been murdered at Wistanstow in Salop in 849; there was a popular local *cultus* in Shropshire and at Evesham, whither Wistan's body was taken from Repton. His first burying-place was the subject of a peculiarly extravagant legend. *June 1, ii, 440.*

WITE, ST

An unknown saint whose relics remain in a medieval shrine in the parish church of Whitchurch Canonicorum in Dorset. It is generally assumed that the saint was a West Saxon woman. *Candida. June 1, ii, 438.*

WITHBURGA, ST, VIRGIN

She was the youngest of the holy daughters of King Anna of the East Angles; she lived an austere life in solitude at Holkham and at Dereham in Norfolk. d. *c.* 743.
July 8, iii, 41.

*WIVINA, ST, VIRGIN

She was foundress and abbess of the convent of Grand-Bigard, near Brussels. d. 1170 (?). *December 17, iv, 580.*

*WOLFGANG, ST, BISHOP

In 956 St Wolfgang became a teacher in the cathedral school at Trier; later he was made head master of the abbey school at Einsiedeln; from thence he went as a missionary into Pannonia, with disappointing results, and in 972 was appointed bishop of Regensburg. He governed the see for twenty-two years, restored canonical life among his clergy, and was held in the greatest respect both by the people and at the imperial court: he educated the young prince who was afterwards the emperor St Henry. d. 994. cd 1052. *Wolfgangus. October 31, iv, 230.*

WOLFHARD, ST

He was a saddler from Augsburg who plied his trade in Verona, till the discovery that he was looked on as a saint made him hide away as a hermit in a remote place. Later he became a Camaldolese monk. d. 1127. *Gualfardus. April 30, ii, 200.*

WOLFHELM, BD, ABBOT

As abbot of Gladbach, Siegburg and then Brauweiler he was a considerable figure in the religious life of his time, but not many details of his career are known. d. 1091. *April 22, ii, 147.*

WOOLLO. *See* Gundleus.

*WULFRAM, ST, BISHOP

He was said to be an archbishop of Sens who resigned his see in order to be a missionary among the Frisians, many of whom he converted. d. 703 (?). *Wulfrannus. March 20, i, 642.*

WULFRIC, ST

Wulfric, b. near Bristol, was a "hunting parson" of the Middle Ages who was turned to better ways by a conversation with a beggar. He became a hermit at Haselbury and d. there 1154. His tomb at Haselbury in Somerset used to be a place of pilgrimage. *February 20, i, 382.*

*WULFSTAN, ST, BISHOP

Born at Long Itchington in Warwickshire, studied at Evesham and Peterborough, monk of Worcester, and bishop there in 1062. He was an unlearned man but strong: he refused to give up his see at the Norman conquest, and was allowed to keep it. The suppression of the slave-trade from Bristol was attributed to his opposition. He rebuilt Worcester cathedral and d. 1095 at the age of eighty-seven. cd 1203. His feast is kept in the dioceses of Birmingham, Clifton and Northampton. *Wulstanus. January 19, i, 121.*

WULPHY. *See* Vulflagius.

WULSIN, ST, BISHOP

He was the monk whom St Dunstan put in charge when he restored the abbey of Westminster; Wulsin was blessed as abbot in 980 and became bishop of Sherborne in 993. d. 1005. *Vulsinus. January 8, i, 55.*

X Y Z

XYSTUS. *See* Sixtus.

YVES. *See* Ivo.

ZACHAEUS. *See under* Alphaeus.

*ZACHARY, ST

The father of St John the Baptist. He and his wife Elizabeth are named in the Roman Martyrology, and their feast is observed in Palestine, on November 5. *Zacharias. November 5, iv, 267.*

*ZACHARY, ST, POPE

He was a Calabrian Greek, elected pope in 741. He induced the Lombards not to attack Ravenna, sanctioned the assumption of the Frankish crown by Pepin, and was in close touch with St Boniface in Germany, whom he greatly helped. In all his works he joined a conciliatory spirit with far-sighted wisdom. d. 752. *March 15, i, 596.*

ZDISLAVA BERKA, BD

She is venerated as a tertiary of the Order of Preachers: a noblewoman of Bohemia, whose husband was at first not properly appreciative of the virtues of his wife. She is alleged to have appeared to him in glory after her death in 1252. c.c. 1907. *January 1, i, 14.*

*ZENO OF VERONA, ST, BISHOP

Zeno was made bishop of Verona during the reign of Julian the Apostate and is still honoured in that diocese. There are interesting particulars of him and his flock in some of his homilies that have survived. d. 371. *April 12, ii, 77.*

ZENO. *See also under* Eusebius of Gaza.

*ZENOBIUS, ST, BISHOP

He was a friend of St Ambrose and bishop of Florence; stories told of his miraculous powers provided subjects for several Florentine painters. d. *c.* 390 (?). *May 25, ii, 390.*

*ZITA, ST, VIRGIN

Zita, the patroness of domestic workers, was a maidservant in the family of a merchant of Lucca. She was not content with being a good servant, but was a good neighbour too, giving away her own clothes and food (and sometimes her master's) to the needy; for a time she suffered from the ill will of her fellow servants, who made mischief about her, but eventually she became the friend and confidant of the whole household. Several miraculous happenings are related to St Zita. She d. in 1278, having served the same family for forty-eight years. cd. 1696. *April 27, ii, 173.*

*ZOË, ST, MARTYR

According to the Greek legend she was a Christian slave at Attalia in Asia Minor who, with her husband Hesperus and two children, was roasted to death for refusing to eat food sacrificed to the gods *c.* 135. The name of St Hesperus appears in the Roman Martyrology as Exsuperius. *May 2, ii, 217.*

*ZOILUS, ST, MARTYR

He suffered with other martyrs at Cordova during the persecution of Diocletian (?); he is said to have been still only a youth.
June 27, ii, 652.

*ZOSIMUS, ST, POPE

Nothing is known of the personal life of St Zosimus, a Greek. His two years' pontificate was chiefly notable for a condemnation of Pelagianism. d. 418.
December 26, iv, 618.

*ZOSIMUS OF SYRACUSE, ST, BISHOP

For thirty years he was an obscure monk at Santa Lucia, near Syracuse, and was then in a strange way chosen as abbot. Subsequently he became bishop of Syracuse, and d. at a great age there *c.* 660.
March 30, i, 704.

ZOSIMUS. *See also under* Rufus.

AND MANY OTHER
HOLY MARTYRS CONFESSORS AND MAIDENS
IN OTHER PLACES:
THANKS BE TO GOD